The Culture of Science

ESSAYS AND ISSUES FOR WRITERS

John Hatton
University of California, Berkeley

Paul B. Plouffe
University of California, Berkeley

MACMILLAN PUBLISHING COMPANY
New York

Editor: Barbara A. Heinssen
Production Supervisor: Jane O'Neill
Production Manager: Roger Vergnes
Text Designer: Angela Foote
Cover Designer: Cathleen Norz
Cover illustration: Marjory Dressler
This book was set in Leawood Book by Americomp
and was printed and bound by Book Press.
The cover was printed by New England Book Components, Inc.

Macmillan Publishing Company
866 Third Avenue, New York, New York 10022

Macmillan Publishing Company is part of
the Maxwell Communication Group of Companies.

Maxwell Macmillan Canada, Inc.
1200 Eglinton Avenue East
Suite 200
Don Mills, Ontario M3C 3N1

Library of Congress Cataloging-in-Publication Data

Hatton, John.
    The culture of science : essays and issues for writers / John
Hatton and Paul B. Plouffe.
        p. cm.
    ISBN 0-02-351705-0 (paper)
    1. Science. 2. Technology. I. Plouffe, Paul B. II. Title.
Q158.5.H38 1993
500—dc20   92-18685
                                                  CIP

Printing: 1 2 3 4 5 6 7   Year: 3 4 5 6 7 8 9

ACKNOWLEDGMENTS

Clive Agnew and Andrew Warren. "Sand Trap." This article is reprinted by permission of *The Sciences* and is from the March/April 1990 issue.

Marcia Angell. "Prisoners of Technology: The Case of Nancy Cruzan." From *The New England Journal of Medicine*, Vol. 322, No. 17 (1990), pp. 1226–1228. Reprinted by permission of *The New England Journal of Medicine*.

Isaac Asimov and Frederik Pohl. "The Pollution of Space." Copyright © 1992 by Isaac Asimov and Frederik Pohl. From the book *Our Angry Earth* and reprinted with permission from Tom Doherty Associates, Inc., New York, NY. A Tor Book.

Eric J. Barron. "Earth's Shrouded Future." This article is reprinted by permission of *The Sciences* and is from the September/October 1989 issue.

Richard Bergland. "Confiteor: Neurosurgical Malfeasances." From *The Fabric of Mind*. Penguin Books, Australia, 1985. Reprinted by permission of the author.

Ruth Bleier. "Feminist Science: Change, Complexity, Contextuality, Interaction." Reprinted by permission of the publisher from Bleier, Ruth, *Feminist Approaches to Science*. (New York: Pergamon Press, © 1986 by Pergamon Press. All rights reserved.) Excerpts from pp. 200–206.

Daniel J. Boorstin. "The Republic of Technology." From *The Republic of Technology* by Daniel J. Boorstin. Copyright © 1978 by Daniel J. Boorstin. Reprinted by permission of HarperCollins Publishers.

Jacob Bronowski. "Isaac Newton's Model." From *The Common Sense of Science*. Harvard University Press, 1953. Reprinted by permission of the publisher.

Jacob Bronowski. "The Reach of Imagination," "Toward a Philosophy of Biology," and "The Values of

For Karolyn, Ian, and Erin
and
For Margaret Plouffe

ACKNOWLEDGMENTS

We would like to thank a number of people for their advice and support. Early on, Frederick Crews and Jayne Walker gave wise counsel. As the project progressed, Rudy Klaver, Dan Neumann, and Gary Rexroat listened to our ideas and graciously shared their knowledge. Jo Mancuso and Carolyn Morris made valuable editorial suggestions and lent moral support. Tom Philippi, Ralph Rader, and Bob Westfall encouraged us throughout. To these friends and colleagues, our sincere thanks.

We would also like to thank our colleagues at Macmillan: Rachel Wolf, assistant editor; Jane O'Neill, production supervisor; and Jennifer Hornik-Evans, copyeditor. Our special thanks to Barbara Heinssen, senior editor, whose professionalism (and judicious use of both the carrot and the stick) brought this project to completion.

Finally, our thanks to the following reviewers for their many helpful suggestions: Victoria Aarons, Trinity University; Alan Crooks, George Mason University; M. Jimmie Killingsworth, Texas A&M University; William Lay, Kalamazoo Valley Community College; Alan Lightman, Massachusetts Institute of Technology; Jane F. Lumley, Cornell University; Barry Pegg, Michigan Technological University; and Marie Redmond, Trinity College (Dublin).

CONTENTS

RHETORICAL CONTENTS

DEFINITION

DESCRIPTION

CLASSIFICATION

COMPARISON AND CONTRAST

ANALOGY

EXAMPLE

NARRATION

HUMOR

EXPOSITION

ANALYSIS OF CAUSE AND EFFECT

ARGUMENT

General Introduction

This book reflects two beliefs. The first is that, since our culture is overwhelmingly scientific and technological, every "educated" person should have at least a basic familiarity with science—with its central concepts, its way of knowing, and the limits of that knowledge—as well as with its place in our history and culture. The second belief is that writing—the act of writing—is an important instrument of learning and should therefore be an integral part of the educative process.

Education in the United States has been under scrutiny for some years now. And virtually every critic has come to the same conclusion: students don't know enough science—nor enough about science—and they can't write. We hope that this collection of essays and the accompanying questions will contribute to the broad effort now under way to address these problems. It cannot, of course, supply the science. That's the job of the science teacher and the science textbook. But it can contribute in other ways. It can help science students to see their particular discipline (astronomy, botany, chemistry, etc.) in the broader context of scientific culture, and it can help all students—science and non-science alike—to better understand the nature of the scientific enterprise and to locate it in its human and social setting.

This, at any rate is our hope. For if science is a culture in and of itself—a "second culture," as C. P. Snow called it, with its particular concerns, special language, and specialized literature—it is also a dominant force in the larger culture of which we are all a part. Indeed, science has played a defining role (perhaps *the* defining role) in the development of that culture over the last century or so, changing our understanding of the world, as well as the way we think about ourselves and our place within it. Nor is science simply

1

a matter of our understanding, for it reaches into our daily lives, influencing the way we live (and, increasingly, the way we die) and shaping the society we live in, as well as the one our children will inherit.

Because science touches most of us in this more general way, as an element of culture rather than as a body of knowledge, we begin this book with the broad view. Thus, Part I examines science from four perspectives: as a force for change; as a challenge to our sense of community; as an expression of the human struggle to make spiritual and moral as well as intellectual sense of the world; and as technology. These are not the only ways in which science can be talked about as an element of culture, but they do represent major points at which science and culture interact.

Part II turns to the enterprise of science itself, emphasizing its two main branches—the physical and the biological—and a few fundamental concepts. Since classical Newtonian physics is discussed in Chapter 1 as the culmination of the scientific revolution that began with Copernicus, we focus here on relativity, quantum theory, and evolution. But science is more than a body of knowledge. It is also (and perhaps more importantly) a way of thinking. Modern science was born when rational thought and empirical fact were for the first time unified into a systematic method of enquiry, when to the logic of reason in thinking about the world was joined "a ruthless appeal, at each bold deductive step back to the hard empirical facts," as Jacob Bronowski reminds us in "Isaac Newton's Model."

This emphasis on the method by which science proceeds reminds us again that science is a human activity carried out by men and women in the world of human affairs. It is, in other words, subject to the same limitations and social pressures, and constrained by the same moral and ethical imperatives, that govern men and women everywhere. In addition to the chapters on the physical and the biological sciences, therefore, Part II includes chapters on science as a way of knowing and on the limits of science and concludes with an examination of the role of conscience in the practice of science.

Part III develops this idea of conscience and ethics, but this time by focusing on four specific social issues: the unborn, the environment, gender, and education. Though hardly the only ways in which science engages important social and ethical concerns (the right to die and animal rights are two other issues that come to mind), these four represent major areas in which science has an important bearing on our lives as we approach the twenty-first century.

Our intention has been to produce a text that is flexible but at the same time thematically unified. The essays can be read independently or as a part of the larger units to which they belong, and the larger units themselves can be read as single units or as parts of the whole. But because the focus of the book has been fairly sharply limited, given themes (or issues) can be examined in a variety of different contexts. So, for example, Darwin's theory of evolution can be explored in Chapter 1 as a revolutionary idea in the context of intellectual history; in Chapter 6 as the grand ordering principle of the biological sciences; in Chapter 11 as an idea that informs the debate over the environment; and in Chapter 13 (with Stephen Jay Gould's "Moon, Mann, and Otto") as an issue that still gives rise to fierce debate within the educational establishment and, indeed, in society as a whole.

A second theme that can be similarly traced is technology. Thus, in Chapter 1 Robert Sinsheimer discusses genetic engineering as a force for change in our moral and social lives; in Chapter 2 Daniel Boorstin sees technology as a way of creating "a community of shared experience"; in Chapter 10 Leon Kass explores the implications of technology for the unborn; and in Chapter 11 Isaac Asimov and Frederik Pohl warn us that modern technology has already led to the pollution of space. All of these essays, and others, can be read, of course, in the context of Chapter 4 on "Technology." Other themes that can be similarly explored include medical science, the ethics of science, and the limits of scientific knowledge.

Each essay is followed by questions for discussion and suggestions for writing. The questions are designed to help the reader to a fuller understanding of the essay, to a critical examination of its argument, and to an analysis of its style and structure. We believe that by attending to such issues, and by writing about them, our readers will become not only more active readers but more thoughtful writers. For writing at its best is not simply the reporting of what we know, but the discovery of what we know. By gaining expressive mastery of our material we gain control over it and make it our own; writing, then, becomes an act of learning. We hope that by reading these essays on the culture of science, and by writing about them, our readers will be challenged to their own acts of discovery.

PART I

SCIENCE AND THE BROADER CULTURE

OVERVIEW

Although only a part of the human enterprise, science has shaped that enterprise to a remarkable degree. We look around us and see new technology appearing with unsettling rapidity, and if we are sometimes filled with wonder, we are often left with questions. How have all these changes come about? Has the influence of science on our lives always been so immediate? What was the relationship between science and the larger community in the past? Has this relationship always been—and is it now—a comfortable one? What form will it take in the next century? Other questions might be asked and other issues raised. Although most cannot be answered, we continue to ask and to wonder.

The essays in Part I attempt to shed light on these issues through an exploration of four ways in which science relates to the broader culture. Chapter 1 begins by examining some of the momentous changes wrought by science over the last few centuries, changes that have brought about a revolution, not merely in the amount of information we have about the physical world, but in the very ways we perceive ourselves in relation to that world. Chapter 2 goes on to look at various aspects of the relationship between science (and scientists) and the nonscientific community. For many, this relationship seems to be characterized by separation and alienation. Chapter 3 places science in the context of art and religion and suggests that science, too, is an expression of the human need to make moral and intellectual sense of the world. Finally, through an examination of several important issues raised by contemporary technology, Chapter 4 suggests that our resolution of these issues will determine the relationship between science and society as we enter the twenty-first century.

CHAPTER-BY-CHAPTER SUMMARY

Chapter 1

Chapter 1 explores several revolutionary moments in the development of modern science. In the first essay, Timothy Ferris describes the human and intellectual drama that began in the early sixteenth century with Copernicus's substitution of a heliocentric model for the traditional geocentric one. This drama continued into the seventeenth century with Kepler's discovery of the motion of the planets, and, as Jacob Bronowski tells us in the next essay, was transformed into a scientific revolution by the development of the "scientific method" and by Isaac Newton's working out of the modern concept of cause, an idea fundamental to the practice of science ever since. But perhaps an even more profound intellectual revolution took place in the mid-nineteenth century with the work of Charles Darwin. Ernst Mayr traces the important stages in Darwin's developing formulation of the theory that would change forever the way we think about the natural world and our relation to it. Less than half a century after the Darwinian revolution came the birth of modern physics, the consequences of which, as Werner Heisenberg tells us, changed the direction not only of physics but of human thought itself. Relativity, quantum theory, the uncertainty principle—these ideas have given us a radically new perspective on the universe and on our ability to know it. In the final essay of the chapter, Robert Sinsheimer directs our attention to the science of genetics and the technology of genetic engineering and suggests that recent developments in these areas are forcing us to face moral and ethical issues previously unimaginable.

Chapter 2

Chapter 2 examines several vital issues arising from the relationship between modern science and the broader community.
J. Robert Oppenheimer, deeply conscious of the enormous human devastation made possible by modern physics, suggests that the fundamental postulates of this science, with all they have taught us about the falsity of absolute positions, can be extended to help us better understand the need for tolerance within the global community. In the second essay, Fred Hoyle notes that modern science has developed a preference for "bigness," a sign, he be-

lieves, that scientists have come to confuse the magnitude of the apparatus supporting a scientific undertaking with the importance of the undertaking itself. This confusion, he suggests, is likely to lead some scientists away from science and into the "corridors of power." In the next essay, René Dubos reflects on society's view of the scientist as it has developed since the nineteenth century. He argues that this view has reflected an increasing lack of understanding of what scientists do and why they do it. In the fourth essay, Daniel J. Boorstin looks at the technological advances made possible by modern science. In these advances he sees both an opportunity for the creation of a truly democratic republic based on equality of experience and the possibility that a substitution of material for spiritual values will destroy the moral fabric of that republic. In the final essay of the chapter, Gerald Weissmann discusses what he sees as a split between art and science and suggests that this split may be the result of the specialization necessary for the advancement of both art and science.

Chapter 3

The relationship of science to both art and religion is taken up in Chapter 3. In the opening essay, Jacob Bronowski focuses on what art and science have in common, namely, the driving force of the imagination. Without imagination, he tells us, there would be neither art nor science. Werner Heisenberg then turns to the notion of beauty and traces the meaning of the term from ancient to modern times. He argues that beauty is as important to science as it is to the arts. In both of these areas beauty consists in the proper conformity of the parts to the whole. In mathematics, for example, the properties (or parts) of whole numbers conform to the underlying (or whole) system of axioms to which mathematics belongs. Unity is also an important issue for Victor Weisskopf in the third essay. Here he asserts that, though different in many respects, both art and science are expressions of the human need for wholeness. In the fourth essay, Albert Einstein takes up the issue of the relationship between science and religion, or, as some put it, between knowledge and belief. Far from being in conflict, he tells us, science and religion have the same goal: "the rational unification of the manifold," the reconciliation of the apparent opposition between "the one and the many." This drive toward reconciliation, he argues, is what links science and religion. In the final essay, Max Planck examines the principle of causality in science as it relates to our understanding of our own behavior. He argues that our behavior is governed not by the scientific law of causation but by the dictate of duty. This dictate is rooted in that deepest part of ourselves to which religion alone can speak.

Chapter 4

Chapter 4 takes up the subject of technology and suggests something of its mixed blessings. In the opening essay Joseph Weizenbaum discusses artificial intelligence. Can computers be made to think? Can they be intelligent? As Weizenbaum points out, we have no clear notion of what human intelligence really is. Thus, even though machines can be designed to do amazing things, until we can build into them the bewildering complex of social and cultural influences that play a large role in determining intelligence, it is pointless to speak of intelligent machines. This notion of our inability to precisely define and comprehend those qualities that make us human is taken up by Robert Gilmore McKinnell's essay on human cloning. Which human qualities would we duplicate and which discard if we were to clone the perfect human being? Would we clone only Einsteins? How could we duplicate the environmental and cultural conditions that to a large extent make individuals who they are? Faced with the prospect of human cloning, McKinnell says, "I would far rather be a machinist than a human cloner." Implicit in McKinnell's argument is the idea that certain elements of human experience are simply beyond the reach of science. As Frederick Turner tells us in the third essay of the chapter, modern science and technology are not the dehumanizing agents they are commonly made out to be. Rather, he says, they offer the promise of a more integrated relationship between man and nature. They give us the chance to reaffirm "our solidarity with nature . . . not that we shall rise above nature . . . rather, [that] we shall *be* nature." Like Turner, Freeman Dyson sees technology as a liberating force, as "a gift of God." He looks forward to the twenty-first century and sees three areas of science dominating: molecular biology and genetics; neurophysiology and complex information-processing networks; and space physics. These areas of research, he argues, will lead to revolutions in the technologies of genetic engineering, artificial intelligence, and space colonization. These revolutions, in turn, will radically change the conditions of our existence in the coming century. Chapter 4 closes with Marcia Angell's examination of one area of medical technology and the issues it raises. To what lengths should we go, she asks, to sustain the life of someone who has ceased to live in all but a vegetative sense? Do physicians have the authority to insist upon the use of life-sustaining technology even when the patients and their families have asked that it be withheld? The tragic irony of our technological success, she argues, is that "some people now fear living more than dying because they dread becoming prisoners of technology."

CHAPTER 1

Science as a Force for Change

☐ THE SUN WORSHIPERS

Timothy Ferris
(b. 1944)

Timothy Ferris, a science writer specializing in astronomy, has worked as a professional journalist and taught journalism at the City University of New York and the University of Southern California. He is currently a professor of journalism at the University of California, Berkeley. Ferris has contributed to such national magazines as *Harper's, The New Republic,* and the *New York Times Magazine.* His books include *The Red Limit: The Search for the Edge of the Universe* (1977); *Galaxies* (1980), which was nominated for an American Book Award in science in 1981; and *The Mind's Sky* (1991). In the following selection from *Coming of Age in the Milky Way* (1988), Ferris describes the human and intellectual drama associated with the struggle to construct a new model of the universe—an undertaking that began in the early sixteenth century with Copernicus's substitution of a heliocentric model for Ptolemy's geocentric one and ended more than a hundred years later with Kepler's triumphant discovery of the motion of the planets.

> There is no new thing under the sun.
>
> —*Ecclesiastes*

> Amazed, and as if astonished and stupefied, I
> stood still, gazing for a certain length of time with
> my eyes fixed intently upon it. . . . When I had sat-
> isfied myself that no star of that kind had ever
> shone forth before, I was led into such perplexity
> by the unbelievability of the thing that I began to
> doubt the faith of my own eyes.
>
> —*Tycho, on the supernova of 1572*

Mikolai Kopernik, though rightly esteemed as a great astronomer, was never much of a stargazer. He did some observing in his student days, assisting his astronomy professor at Bologna, Dominico Maria Novera, in watching an occultation of the star Aldebaran by the moon, and he later took numerous sightings of the sun, using an instrument of his own devising that reflected the solar disk onto a series of graph lines etched into a wall outside his study. But these excursions served mainly to confirm what Kopernik and everybody else already knew, that the Ptolemaic system was inaccurate, making predictions that often proved to be wrong by hours or even days.

Kopernik drew inspiration less from stars than from books. In this he was very much a man of his time. The printing press—invented just thirty years before he was born—had touched off a communications revolution comparable in its impact to the changes wrought in the latter half of the twentieth century by the electronic computer. To be sure, Greek and Roman classics had been making their way from the Islamic world to Europe for centuries, and with enlightening effect—the first universities had been founded principally to house the books and study their contents—but the books themselves, each laboriously copied out by hand, were rare and expensive, and frequently were marred by transcription errors. All this changed with the advent of cheap, high-quality paper (a gift of Chinese technology) and the press. Now a single competent edition of Plato or Aristotle or Archimedes or Ptolemy could be reproduced in considerable quantities; every library could have one, and so could many individual scholars and more than a few farmers and housewives and tradespeople. As books spread so did literacy, and as the number of literate people increased, so did the market for books. By the time Kopernik was thirty years old (and printing itself but sixty years old), some six to nine million printed copies of more than thirty-five thousand titles had been published, and the print shops were working overtime trying to satisfy the demand for more.

Kopernik was as voracious a reader as any, at home in law, literature, and medicine as well as natural philosophy. Born in 1473 in northern Poland, he had come under the sponsorship of his powerful and calculating uncle Lucas Waczenrode, later bishop of Warmia, who gave him books and sent him to the best schools. He attended the University of Cracow, then ventured south into the Renaissance heartland to study at the universities of Bologna and Padua. He read Aristotle, Plato, Plutarch, Ovid, Virgil, Euclid, Archimedes, and Cicero, the restorer of Archimedes' grave. Steeped in the literature and science of the ancients, he returned home with a Latinized name, as Nicolaus Copernicus.

Like Aristotle, Copernicus collected books; unlike Aristotle, he did not have to be wealthy to do so. Thanks to the printing press, a scholar who was only moderately well off could afford to read widely, at home, without having to beg admission to distant institutions of learning where the books were kept chained to the reading desks. Copernicus was one of the first scholars to study printed books in his own library, and he studied none more closely than Ptolemy's *Almagest*. Great was his admiration for Ptolemy, whom he admired as a thoroughly professional astronomer, mathematically sophisticated and dedicated to fitting his cosmological model to the observed phenomena. Indeed, Copernicus's *De Revolutionibus* (*On the Revolutions*), the book that would set the earth into motion around the sun and bring about Ptolemy's downfall, otherwise reads like nothing so much as a sustained imitation of Ptolemy's *Almagest*.

It is widely assumed that Copernicus proposed his heliocentric theory in order to repair the inaccuracies of the Ptolemaic model. Certainly it must have become evident to him, in his adulthood if not in his student days, that the Ptolemaic system did not work very well: "The mathematicians are so unsure of the movements of the sun and moon," notes the preface to *De Revolutionibus*, "that they cannot even explain or observe the constant length of the seasonal year." Prior to the advent of the printing press, the failings of Ptolemy's *Almagest* could be attributed to errors in transcription or translation, but once reasonably accurate printed editions of the book had been published, this excuse began to evaporate. Copernicus owned at least two editions of *Almagest*, and had read others in libraries, and the more clearly he came to understand Ptolemy's model, the more readily he could see that its deficiencies were inherent, not incidental, to the theory. So considerations of accuracy may indeed have helped convince him that a new approach was required.

But by "new," Copernicus the Renaissance man most often meant the rediscovery of something old. *Renaissance*, after all, means "rebirth," and Renaissance art and science in general sprang more from classical tradition than from innovation. The young Michelangelo's first accomplished piece of sculpture—executed in the classical style— was made marketable by rubbing dirt into it and palming it off, in Paris, as a Greek relic. Petrarch, called the founder of the Renaissance, dreamed not of the future but of the day when "our grandsons will be able to walk *back* into the pure radiance *of the past*" (emphasis added); when Petrarch was found dead, at the age of seventy, slumped at his desk after an all-night study session, his head was resting not on a contemporary volume but on a Latin edition of his favorite poet, Virgil, who had lived fourteen centuries earlier.

Copernicus similarly worked in awe of the ancients, and his efforts, like so much of natural philosophy then and since, can be read as a continuation of the academic dialogues of Plato and Aristotle.

Aristotle, the first of the Greeks to have been rediscovered in the West, was so widely revered that he was routinely referred to as "the philosopher," much as lovers of Shakespeare were to call him "the poet." Much of his philosophy had been incorporated into the world view of the Roman Catholic Church. (Most notably by Thomas Aquinas—at least until the morning of December 6, 1273, when, while saying mass in Naples, Thomas became enlightened and declared that "I can do no more; such things have been revealed to me that all I have written seems as straw, and I now await the end of my life.") From Aristotle, Copernicus acquired an enthusiasm for the universe of crystalline spheres—although, like Aristotle, Copernicus never could decide whether the spheres actually existed or were but a useful abstraction.

Copernicus also read Plato, as well as many of the Neoplatonic philosophers whose work ornaments and obfuscates medieval thought, and from them absorbed the Platonic conviction that there must be a simple underlying structure to the universe. It was just this unitary beauty that the Ptolemaic cosmology lacked. "A system of this sort seemed neither sufficiently absolute nor sufficiently pleasing to the mind," Copernicus wrote. He was after a grasp of the more central truth. He called it "the principal thing—namely the shape of the universe and the unchangeable symmetry of its parts."

Rather early on, perhaps during his student days in sunny Italy, Copernicus decided that the "principal thing" was to place the sun at the center of the universe. He may have drawn encouragement from reading, in Plutarch's *Morals,* that Aristarchus of Samos "supposed that the heavens remained immobile and that the earth moved through an oblique circle, at the same time turning about its own axis." (He mentions Aristarchus in *De Revolutionibus,* though not in this context.) Possibly he encountered more recent speculations about the motion of the earth, as in Nicole Oresme, the fourteenth-century Parisian scholar who pointed out that

> if a man in the heavens, moved and carried along by their daily motion, could see the earth distinctly and its mountains, valleys, rivers, cities, and castles, it would appear to him that the earth was moving in daily motion, just as to us on earth it seems as though the heavens are moving. . . . One could then believe that the earth moves and not the heavens.

Copernicus was influenced by Neoplatonic sun worship as well. This was a popular view at the time—even Christ was being modeled by Renaissance painters on busts of Apollo the sun god—and decades later, back in the rainy north, Copernicus remained effusive on the subject of the sun. In *De Revolutionibus* he invokes the authority of none other than Hermes Trismegistus, "the thrice-great Hermes," a fantastical figure in astrology and alchemy who had become the patron saint of the new sun-worshipers: "Trismegistus calls [the sun] a 'visible god,' Sophocles' Electra, 'that which gazes upon all things.' " He quotes the Neoplatonist mystic Marsilio Ficino's declaration that "the sun can signify God himself to you, and who shall dare to say the sun is false?" Finally, Copernicus tries his hand at a solar paean of his own:

> In this most beautiful temple, who would place this lamp in another or better position than that from which it can light up everything at the same time? For the sun is not inappropriately called by some people the lantern of the universe, its mind by others, and its ruler by still others.

Trouble arose not in the incentive for the Copernican cosmology, but in its execution. (The devil, like God, is in the details.) When Copernicus, after considerable toil, managed to complete a fully realized model of the universe based upon the heliocentric hypothesis—the model set forth, eventually, in *De Revolutionibus*—he found that it worked little better than the Ptolemaic model. One difficulty was that Copernicus, like Aristotle and Eudoxus before him, was enthralled by the Platonic beauty of the sphere—"The sphere," he wrote, echoing Plato, "is the most perfect . . . the most capacious of figures . . . wherein neither beginning nor end can be found"—and he assumed, accordingly, that the planets move in circular orbits at constant velocities. Actually, as Kepler would establish, the orbits of the planets are elliptical, and planets move more rapidly when close to the sun than when distant from it. Nor was the Copernican universe less intricate than Ptolemy's: Copernicus found it necessary to introduce Ptolemaic epicycles into his model and to move the center of the universe to a point a little away from the sun. Nor did it make consistently more accurate predictions, even in its wretchedly compromised form; for many applications it was less useful.

This, in retrospect, was the tragedy of Copernicus's career—that while the beauty of the heliocentric hypothesis convinced him that the planets ought to move in perfect circles around the sun, the sky was to declare it false. Settled within the stone walls of Frauenburg Cathedral, in a three-story tower that afforded him a view of Frisches Haff and the Gulf of Danzig below and the wide (though frequently cloudy) sky above—"the most remote corner of the earth," he called it—Copernicus carried out his sporadic astronomical observations, and tried, in vain, to perfect the heliocentric theory he had outlined while still a young man. For decades he turned it over in his thoughts, a flawed jewel, luminous and obdurate. It would not yield.

As Darwin would do three centuries later, Copernicus wrote and privately circulated a longhand sketch of his theory. He called it the "ballet of the planets." It aroused interest among scholars, but Copernicus published none of it. He was an old man before he finally released the manuscript of *De Revolutionibus* to the printer, and was on his death bed by the time the final page proofs arrived.

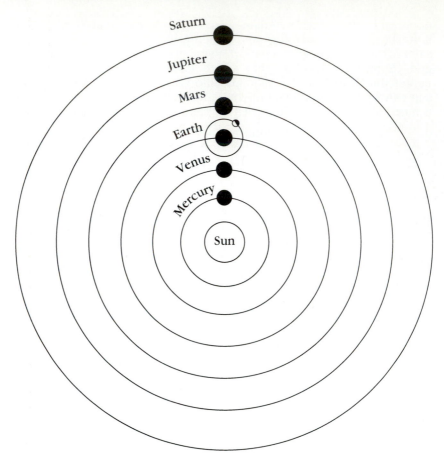

Copernicus's model of the solar system is generally portrayed in simplified form, as in this illustration based upon one in his *De Revolutionibus*. In its details, however, it was as complex as Ptolemy's geocentric model.

One reason for his reluctance to publish was that Copernicus, like Darwin, had reason to fear censure by the religious authorities. The threat of papal disapproval was real enough that the Lutheran theologian Andreas Osiander thought it prudent to oil the waters by writing an unsigned preface to Copernicus's book, as if composed by the dying Copernicus himself, reassuring its readers that divine revelation was the sole source of truth and that astronomical treatises like this one were intended merely to "save the phenomena." Nor were the Protestants any more apt to kiss the heliocentric hem. "Who will venture to place the authority of Copernicus above that of the Holy Spirit?" thundered Calvin, and Martin Luther complained, in his voluble way, that "this fool wishes to reverse the entire science of astronomy; but sacred Scripture tells us that Joshua commanded the sun to stand still, and not the earth.''

The book survived, however, and changed the world, for much the same reason that Darwin's *Origin of Species* did—because it was too technically competent for the professionals to ignore it. In addition to presenting astronomers with a comprehensive, original, and quantitatively defensible alternative to Ptolemy, *De Revolutionibus* was full of observational data, much of it fresh and some of it reliable. Consequently it was consulted regularly by astronomers—even by non-Copernicans like Erasmus Reinhold, who employed it in compiling the widely consulted *Prutenic Tables*—and thus remained in circulation for generations.

To those who gave it the benefit of the doubt, Copernicanism offered both a taste of the immensity of space and a way to begin measuring it. The minimum radius of the Copernican sphere of stars (given the unchanging brightnesses of the zodiacal stars) was estimated in the sixteenth century to be more than 1.5 million times the radius of the earth. This represented an increase in the volume of the universe of at least 400,000 times over al-Farghani's Ptolemaic cosmos. The maximum possible size of the Copernican universe was indefinite, and might, Copernicus allowed, be infinite: The stars, he wrote, ''are at an immense height away,'' and he expressed wonderment at ''how exceedingly vast is the godlike work of the Best and Greatest Artist!''

Interplanetary distances in Ptolemy were arbitrary; scholars who ventured to quantify them did so by assuming that the various orbits and epicycles fit snugly together, like nested Chinese boxes. The Copernican theory, however, precisely stipulated the relative dimensions of the planetary orbits: The maximum apparent separation of the inferior planets Mercury and Venus from the sun yields the relative diameters of their orbits, once we accept that both orbit the sun and not the earth. Since the relative sizes of all the orbits were known, if the actual distance of any one planet could be measured, the distances of all the others would follow. As we will see, this advantage, though purely theoretical in Copernicus's day, was to be put to splendid use in the eighteenth century, when astronomical technology reached the degree of sophistication required to measure directly the distances of nearby planets.

The immediate survival of Copernicanism was due less to any compelling evidence in its favor than to the waning fortunes of the Ptolemaic, Aristotelian model. And that, as it happened, was prompted in large measure by changes in the sky—by the apparition of comets, and, most of all, by the fortuitous appearance of two brilliant *novae*, or ''new stars,'' during the lifetimes of Tycho, Kepler, and Galileo.

Integral to Aristotle's physics was the hypothesis that the stars never change. Aristotle saw the earth as composed of four elements—earth, water, fire, and air—each of which naturally moves in a vertical direction: The tendency of earth and water is to fall, while that of fire and air is to rise. The stars and planets, however, move neither up nor down, but instead wheel across the sky. Aristotle concluded that since objects in the sky do not partake of the vertical motion characteristic of the four terrestrial elements, they must be made of another element altogether. He called this fifth element "aether," from the Greek word for "eternal," and invested it with all his considerable reverence for the heavens. Aether, he argued, never ages or changes: "In the whole range of time past," he writes, in his treatise *On the Heavens,* "so far as our inherited records reach, no change appears to have taken place either in the whole scheme of the outermost heaven or in any of its proper parts."

Aristotle's segregation of the universe into two realms—a mutable world below the moon and an eternal, unchanging world above— found a warm welcome among Christian theologians predisposed by Scriptures to think of heaven as incorruptible and the earth as decaying and doomed. The stars, however, having heard neither of Aristotle nor of the Church, persisted in changing, and the more they changed, the worse the cosmology of Aristotle and Ptolemy looked.

Comets were an old problem for the Aristotelians, since no one could anticipate when they would appear or where they would go once they showed up.* (It was owing to their unpredictability that comets acquired a reputation as heralds of disaster—from the Latin *dis-astra,* "against the stars.")† Aristotle swept comets under the rug—or under the moon—by dismissing them as atmospheric phenomena. (He did the same with meteors, which is why the study of the weather is known as "meteorology.")

But when Tycho Brahe, the greatest observational astronomer of the sixteenth century, studied the bright comet of 1577, he found evidence that Aristotle's explanation was wrong. He triangulated the comet, by charting its position from night to night and comparing his data with those recorded by astronomers elsewhere in Europe on the same dates. The shift in perspective produced by the differing locations of the observers would have been more than sufficient to show up as a difference in the comet's position against the background

---

* Comets are chunks of ice and dirt that fall in from the outer solar system, sprouting long, glowing "tails" of vapor and dust blown off by the sun's heat and by solar wind. The appearance of new comets cannot be predicted even today; they appear to originate in a cloud that lies near the outer reaches of the solar system, about which little is understood. Their orbits, altered by encounters with the planets and by the kick of their own vapor jets, remain difficult to predict as well.

† The cometary stigma persisted into the early twentieth century, when millions bought alms and patent medicines to protect themselves from the evil effects of comet Halley during its 1910 visitation. Several fatalities were reported, among them a man who died of pneumonia after jumping into a frozen creek to escape the ethereal vapors. A deputation of sheriffs intervened to prevent the sacrifice of a virgin, in Oklahoma, by a sect called the Sacred Followers who were out to appease the comet god.

stars, were the comet nearby. Tycho found no such difference. This meant that the comet was well beyond the moon. Yet Aristotle had held that nothing superlunar could change.

The other great empirical challenge to Aristotle's cosmological hegemony came with the opportune appearance, in the late sixteenth and early seventeenth centuries, of two violently exploding stars— what we today call *supernovae*. A star that undergoes such a catastrophic detonation can increase a hundred million times in brightness in a matter of days. Since only a tiny fraction of the stars in the sky are visible without a telescope, supernovae almost always seem to have appeared out of nowhere, in a region of the sky where no star had previously been charted; hence the name *nova*, for "new." Supernovae bright enough to be seen without a telescope are rare; the next one after the seventeenth century did not come until 1987, when a blue giant star exploded in the Large Magellanic Cloud, a neighboring galaxy to the Milky Way, to the delight of astronomers in Australia and the Chilean Andes. The two supernovae that graced the Renaissance caused quite a stir, inciting not only new sights but new ideas.

Tycho spotted the supernova of 1572 on the evening of November 11, while out taking a walk before dinner, and it literally stopped him in his tracks. As he recalled the moment:

> Amazed, and as if astonished and stupefied, I stood still, gazing for a certain length of time with my eyes fixed intently upon it and noticing that same star placed close to the stars which antiquity attributed to Cassiopeia.
> When I had satisfied myself that no star of that kind had ever shone forth before, I was led into such perplexity by the unbelievability of the thing that I began to doubt the faith of my own eyes.

The next supernova came only thirty-two years later, in 1604. Kepler observed it for nearly a year before it faded from view, and Galileo lectured on it to packed halls in Padua.

Scrutinized week by week through the pinholes and lensless sighting-tubes of the sixteenth- and seventeenth-century astronomers, the two supernovae stayed riveted in the same spot in the sky, and none revealed any shift in perspective when triangulated by observers at widely separated locations. Clearly the novae, too, belonged to the starry realm that Aristotle had depicted as inalterable. Wrote Tycho of the 1572 supernova:

> That it is neither in the orbit of Saturn . . . nor in that of Jupiter, nor in that of Mars, nor in that of any one of the other planets, is hence evident, since after the lapse of several months it has not advanced by its own motion a single minute from that place in which I first saw it; which it must have done if it were in some planetary orbit. . . . Hence this new star is located neither . . . below

the Moon, nor in the orbits of the seven wandering stars
but in the eighth sphere, among the other fixed stars.

The shock dealt to the Aristotelian world view could not have been
greater had the stars bent down and whispered in the astronomers'
ears. Clearly there was something new, not only under the sun but
beyond it.

Tycho was no Copernican. It was through Ptolemy that his passion
for astronomy had crystallized, when, on August 21, 1560, at the age
of thirteen, he watched a partial eclipse of the sun and was amazed
that it had been possible for scholars, consulting the Ptolemaic tables,
accurately to predict the day (though not the hour) of its occurrence.
It struck him, he recalled, as "something divine that men could know
the motions of the stars so accurately that they could long before
foretell their places and relative positions."

But when Tycho began making observations of his own, he soon
became impressed by the *in*accuracy of Ptolemy's predictions. He
watched a spectacular conjunction of Saturn and Jupiter on August
24, 1563, and found that the time of closest approach—which in this
case was so close that the two bright planets appeared almost to
merge—was days away from the predictions of the Ptolemaic tables.
He emerged from the experience with a lifelong passion for accuracy
and exactitude and a devotion to the verdict of the sky.

To compile more accurate records of the positions of the stars and
planets required state-of-the-art equipment, and that cost money.
Fortunately, Tycho *had* money. His foster father had saved King
Frederick II from drowning, dying of pneumonia as a result, and the
grateful king responded with a hefty grant to the young astronomer.
With it, Tycho built Uraniburg, a fabulous observatory on an island
in the Sund between Elsinor Castle (Hamlet's haunt) and Copen-
hagen. He ransacked Europe in search of the finest astronomical
instruments, complemented them with improved quadrants and
armillaries of his own design, and deployed them atop the turrets of
a magnificent castle that he equipped with a chemical laboratory, a
printing plant supplied by its own paper mill, an intercom system,
flush toilets, quarters for visiting researchers, and a private jail. The
grounds sported private game preserves, sixty artificial fishponds,
extensive gardens and herbariums, and an arboretum with three
hundred species of trees. The centerpiece of the observatory was a
gleaming brass celestial globe, five feet in diameter, on which a
thousand stars were inscribed, one by one, as Tycho and his colleagues remapped the visible sky.

No dilettante, Tycho drove himself and his assistants in a ceaseless
pursuit of the most accurate possible observations, charting the
positions of the stars and the courses of the planets night after night
for over twenty years. The resulting data were more than twice as
accurate as those of the preceding astronomers—precise enough, at
last, to unlock the secrets of the solar system.

Tycho, however, was an observer and not a theorist. His chief contribution to theoretical cosmology—a compromise geocentric model in which the planets orbit the sun, which in turn orbits the earth—created as many problems as it solved. Needed was someone with the ingenuity and perseverance to compose Tycho's tables into a single, accurate and simple theory.

Amazingly, just such a man turned up. He was Johannes Kepler, and on February 4, 1600, he arrived at Benatek Castle near Prague, where Tycho had moved his observatory and retinue after his benefactor King Frederick drank himself to death. Tycho and Kepler made for unlikely collaborators, with each other or anybody else. Tycho was an expansive, despotic giant of a man, who sported a belly of Jovian proportions and a gleaming, metal-alloy nose (the bridge of his original nose having been cut off in a youthful duel). Heroically passionate and wildly eccentric, he dressed like a prince and ruled his domain like a king, tossing scraps to a dwarf named Jepp who huddled beneath the dinner table. Kepler, for his part, was a prototypical outsider. Myopic, sickly, and "doglike" in appearance (his words) he came from the antipodes of nobility. His father was a mercenary soldier and a dipsomaniac wife-beater. His mother had

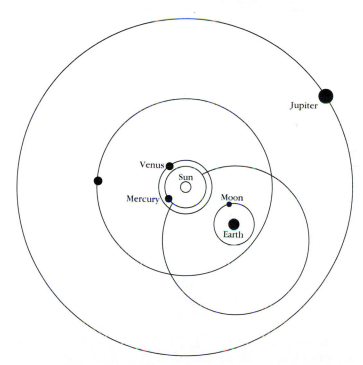

Tycho proposed a compromise between the Copernican and Ptolemaic models in which the sun orbited the earth, and was in turn orbited by the other planets. (Not to scale.)

been raised by an aunt who was burned alive as a witch, and she herself narrowly escaped the stake. (Among her other objectionable habits, she enjoyed spiking people's drinks with psychedelic drugs.)

Neurotic, self-loathing, arrogant, and vociferous, Kepler was drubbed with tiresome regularity by his classmates. He fared little better once out in the world, where he tried but failed to become a Lutheran minister. He sought solicitude in marriage, but his wife, he said with the bleak objectivity of a born observer, was "simple of mind and fat of body . . . stupid, sulking, lonely, melancholy." Kepler tried to make a living casting horoscopes, but was seldom paid; he spent much of his time trekking from one court to another to plead for his fee, drawing titters from the flunkies when he appeared, in his baggy, food-stained suit, tripping over himself with apologies and explanations, getting nowhere. His lifetime earnings could not have purchased the star-globe in Tycho's library.

Kepler's initial scientific endeavors amounted to a comedy of errors and absurdities. He tried to sight the stars using only a wooden staff suspended from a rope: "Hold your laughter, friends, who are admitted to this spectacle," he wrote of his makeshift observatory. His first great theoretical idea—which came to him with the force of revelation, halting him in mid-sentence while he was delivering a soporific lecture on mathematics in a high school in Graz, Austria— was that the intervals between the orbits of the planets describe a nest of concentric Platonic solids. They do not.

Yet this was the man who would discern the architecture of the solar system and discover the phenomenological laws that govern the motions of the planets, thus curing the Copernican cosmology of its pathologies and flinging open the door to the depths of cosmic space. An extraordinarily perspicacious theorist—no less exacting a critic than Immanuel Kant called him "the most acute thinker ever born"—Kepler was blessed with an ecstatic conviction that the world that had treated him so harshly was, nonetheless, fundamentally beautiful. He never lost either this faith or the clearheaded empiricism with which it was tempered, and the combination eventually rewarded him with some of the most splendid insights into the workings of the universe ever granted a mortal mind.

Kepler's chief source of inspiration was the Pythagorean doctrine of celestial harmony, which he had encountered in Plato. "As our eyes are framed for astronomy, so our ears are framed for the movements of harmony," Plato wrote, "and these two sciences are sisters, as the Pythagoreans say and we agree." In the final book of the *Republic,* Plato portrays with great beauty a voyage into space, where the motion of each planet is attended to by a Siren singing

> one sound, one note, and from all the eight there was a concord of a single harmony. And there were three others who sat round about at equal intervals, each one on her throne, the Fates, daughters of Necessity, clad in white vestments with garlands on their heads, Lachesis,

and Clotho, and Atropos, who sang in unison with the
music of the Sirens, Lachesis singing the things that
were, Clotho the things that are, and Atropos the things
that are to be.

Aristotle found all this a bit much. "The theory that the movement
of the stars produces a harmony, i.e., that the sounds they make are
concordant, in spite of the grace and originality with which it has
been stated, is nevertheless untrue," he wrote. Kepler sided with
Plato. The muddy tumult of the world, he felt, was built upon
harmonious and symmetrical law; if the motions of the planets seem
discordant, that is because we have not yet learned how to hear their
song. Kepler wanted to hear it before he died. At this he succeeded,
and the sunlight of his success banished the gloom of his many
failures.

The doctrine of celestial harmony was, literally, in the air, in the
new music and poetry of Kepler's generation and those that immediately followed it. Milton, who was always ransacking science for
promising themes, celebrated it in verses like this one:

> Ring out ye Crystall sphears,
> Once bless our human ears,
>   (If ye have power to touch our senses so)
> And let your silver chime
> Move in melodious time;
>   And let the Base of Heav'ns deep Organ blow,
> And with your ninefold harmony
> Make up full consort to th' Angelike symphony.

Even Shakespeare, who was rather unsympathetic toward astronomy, found room in the *Merchant of Venice* for a nod to Pythagoras:

> Sit, Jessica. Look how the floor of heaven
> Is thick inlaid with patens of bright gold.
> There's not the smallest orb which thou behold'st
> But in his motion like an angel sings,
> Still quiring to the young-eyed cherubims;
> Such harmony is in immortal souls,
> But whilest this muddy vesture of decay
> Doth grossly close it in, we cannot hear it.

The churches of the day rang with approximations of the music of the
spheres. The plainsongs and chants of the medieval cathedrals were
being supplanted by polyphony, the music of many voices that would
reach an epiphany in the fugues—the word *fugue* means "flight"—of
Johann Sebastian Bach. For Kepler, polyphony in music was a model
for the voices sung by the planets as they spun out their Pythagorean
harmonies: "The ratio of plainsong or monody . . . to polyphony," he
wrote,

> is the same as the ratio of the consonances which the
> single planets designate to the consonances of the plan-
> ets taken together. . . .
>
> . . . The movements of the heavens are nothing except
> a certain ever-lasting polyphony (intelligible, not audi-
> ble). . . . Hence it is no longer a surprise that man, the
> ape of his Creator, should finally have discovered the art
> of singing polyphonically, which was unknown to the an-
> cients, namely in order that he might play the everlast-
> ingness of all created time in some short part of an hour
> by means of an artistic concord of many voices and that
> he might to some extent taste the satisfaction of God the
> Workman with His own works, in that very sweet sense
> of delight elicited from this music which imitates God.

Kepler's interest in astronomy, like Tycho's, dated from his boyhood, when his mother took him out in the evening to see the great
comet of 1577 and, three years later, to behold the sanguine face of
the eclipsed moon. He was introduced to heliocentric cosmology at
the University of Tübingen, by Michael Mastlin, one of the few
Copernican academics of his day. Attracted to it partly out of mystical, Neoplatonic motives like those that had inspired Copernicus
himself, Kepler wrote of sunlight in terms that would have brought
a smile to the countenance of Marsilio Ficino:

> Light in itself is something akin to the soul. . . . And so it
> is consonant that the solar body, wherein the light is
> present as in its source, is endowed with a soul which is
> the originator, the preserver, and the continuator. And
> the function of the sun in the world seems to persuade
> us of nothing else except that just as it has to illuminate
> all things, so it is possessed of light in its body; and as
> it has to make all things warm, it is possessed of heat;
> as it has to make all things live, of a bodily life; and as
> it has to move all things, it itself is the beginning of the
> movement; and so it has a soul.

But Kepler's penchant for Platonic ecstasy was wedded to an acid
skepticism about the validity of all theories, his own included. He
mocked no thinker more than himself, tested no ideas more rigor-
ously than his own. If, as he avowed in 1608, he was to "interweave
Copernicus into the revised astronomy and physics, so that either
both will perish or both be kept alive," he would need more accurate
observational data than were available to Ptolemy or to Copernicus.
Tycho had those data. "Tycho possesses the best observations,"
Kepler mused. ". . . He only lacks the architect who would put all this
to use according to his own design." Tycho was "superlatively rich,
but he knows not how to make proper use of it as is the case with
most rich people. Therefore, one must try to wrest his riches from
him." Suiting action to intention, Kepler wrote adoring letters to

Tycho, who in reply praised his theories as "ingenious" if rather too a priori, and invited him to come and join the staff at Benatek Castle.

There the two quarreled constantly. Tycho, justly fearful that the younger and more incisive Kepler would eclipse him, played his cards close to his chest. "Tycho did not give me the chance to share his practical knowledge," Kepler recalled, "except in conversation during meals, today something about the apogee, tomorrow something about the nodes of another planet." Kepler threw fits and threatened to leave; at one point he had packed his bags and boarded a stage before Tycho finally summoned him back.

Realizing that he would have to give his young colleague something of substance to work on if he wanted to keep him on staff, Tycho devised a scheme redolent with the enmity that Kepler seemed to attract like lightning to a summit pine. "When he saw that I possess a daring mind," Kepler wrote, "he thought the best way to deal with me would be to give me my head, to let me choose the observations of one single planet, Mars." Mars, as Tycho knew and Kepler did not, presented an almost impossible challenge. As Mars lies near the earth, its position in the sky had been ascertained with great exactitude; for no planet were the inadequacies of both the Ptolemaic and Copernican models rendered more starkly. Kepler, who did not at first appreciate the difficulties involved, brashly prophesied that he would solve the problem of determining the orbit of Mars in eight days. Tycho must have been cheerful at dinner that night. Let the Platonist take on Mars. Kepler was still working on the problem eight years later.

Tycho, though, was out of time. He died on October 24, 1601, as the result of a burst bladder suffered while drinking too much beer at a royal dinner party from which he felt constrained by protocol from excusing himself. "Let me not seem to have died in vain," he cried repeatedly that night.

Kepler was to grant his dying wish. Named Tycho's successor as imperial mathematician (albeit, as befitting his lesser status, at a much reduced stipend), he pressed on in his search for a single, straightforward theory to account for the motion of Mars. If every great achievement calls for the sacrifice of something one loves, Kepler's sacrifice was the perfect circle. "My first mistake was in having assumed that the orbit on which planets move is a circle," he recalled. "This mistake showed itself to be all the more baneful in that it had been supported by the authority of all the philosophers, and especially as it was quite acceptable metaphysically." In all, Kepler tested *seventy* circular orbits against Tycho's Mars data, all to no avail. At one point, performing a leap of the imagination like Leonardo's to the moon, he imagined himself on Mars, and sought to reconstruct the path the *earth's* motion would trace out across the skies of a Martian observatory; this effort consumed nine hundred pages of calculations, but still failed to solve the major problem. He tried imagining what the motion of Mars would look like from the sun. At last, his calculations yielded up their result: "I have the answer," Kepler wrote to his friend the astronomer David Fabricius. ". . . The orbit of the planet is a perfect ellipse."

Now everything worked. Kepler had arrived at a fully realized Copernican system, focused on the sun and unencumbered by epicycles or crystalline spheres. (In retrospect one could see that Ptolemy's eccentrics had been but attempts to make circles behave like ellipses.)

Fabricius replied that he found Kepler's theory "absurd," in that it abandoned the circles whose symmetry alone seemed worthy of the heavens. Kepler was unperturbed; he had found a still deeper and subtler symmetry, in the *motions* of the planets. "I discovered among the celestial movements the full nature of harmony," he exclaimed, in his book *The Harmonies of the World,* published eighteen years after Tycho's death.

> I am free to give myself up to the sacred madness, I am free to taunt mortals with the frank confession that I am stealing the golden vessels of the Egyptians, in order to build of them a temple for my God, far from the territory of Egypt. If you pardon me, I shall rejoice; if you are enraged, I shall bear up. The die is cast.

And so on. The cause of his celebration was his discovery of what are known today as Kepler's laws. The first contained the news he had communicated to Fabricius—that each planet orbits the sun in an ellipse with the sun at one of its two foci. The second law revealed something even more astonishing, a Bach fugue in the sky. Kepler found that while a planet's velocity changes during its year, so that it moves more rapidly when close to the sun and more slowly when distant from the sun, its motion obeys a simple mathematical rule: Each planet sweeps out equal areas in equal times. The third law came ten years later. It stated that the cube of the mean distance of each planet from the sun is proportional to the square of the time it takes to complete one orbit. Archimedes would have liked that one. Newton was to employ it in formulating his law of universal gravitation.

Here at last was "the principal thing" of which Copernicus had dreamed, the naked kinematics of the sun and its planets. "I contemplate its beauty with incredible and ravishing delight," Kepler wrote. Scientists have been contemplating it ever since, and Kepler's laws today are utilized in studying everything from binary star systems to the orbits of galaxies across clusters of galaxies. The intricate etchings of Saturn's rings, photographed by the Twin Voyager spacecraft in 1980 and 1981, offer a gaudy display of Keplerian harmonies, and the Voyager phonograph record, carried aboard the spacecraft as an artifact of human civilization, includes a set of computer-generated tones representing the relative velocities of the planets—the music of the spheres made audible at last.

But the sun of learning is paired with a dark star, and Kepler's

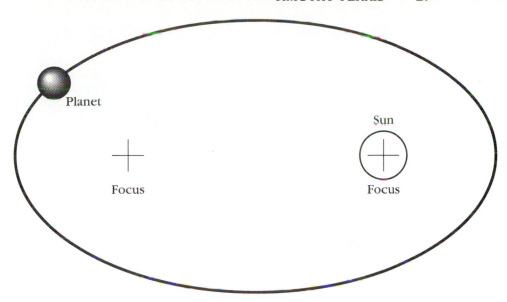

Kepler's first law: The orbit of each planet describes an ellipse, with the sun at one of its foci.

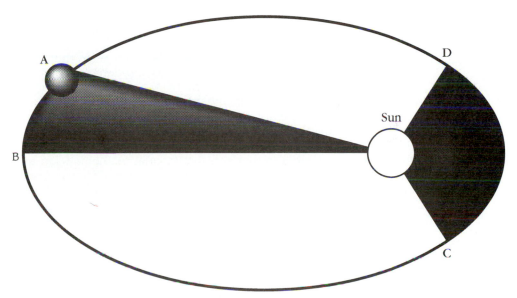

Kepler's second law: If time *AB* = time *CD,* area *ABSun* = area *CDSun.*

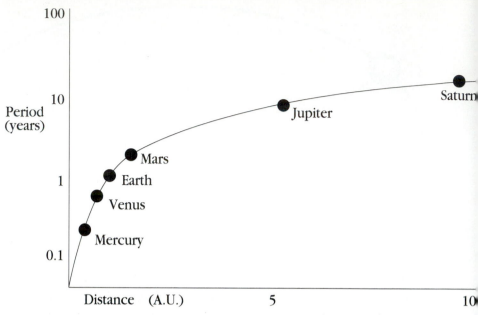

Kepler's third law: The cube of the distance of each planet from the sun is proportional to the square of its orbital period.

life remained as vexed with tumult as his thoughts were suffused with harmony. His friend David Fabricius was murdered. Smallpox carried by soldiers fighting the Thirty Years' War killed his favorite son, Friedrich, at age six. Kepler's wife grew despondent—"numbed," he said, "by the horrors committed by the soldiers"—and died soon thereafter, of typhus. His mother was threatened with torture and was barely acquitted of witchcraft (due, the court records noted, to the "unfortunate" intervention of her son the imperial mathematician as attorney for the defense) and died six months after her release from prison. "Let us despise the barbaric neighings which echo through these noble lands," Kepler wrote, "and awaken our understanding and longing for the harmonies."

He moved his dwindling family to Sagan, an outback. "I am a guest and a stranger here. . . . I feel confined by loneliness," he wrote. There he annotated his *Somnium,* a dream of a trip to the moon. In it he describes looking back from the moon to discern the continent of Africa, which, he thought, resembled a severed head, and Europe, which looked like a girl bending down to kiss that head. The moon itself was divided between bright days and cold dark nights, like Earth a world half darkness and half light.

Dismissed from his last official post, as astrologer to Duke Albrecht von Wallenstein, Kepler left Sagan, alone, on horseback, searching for funds to feed his children. The roads were full of wandering prophets declaring that the end of the world was at hand. Kepler arrived in Ratisbon, hoping to collect some fraction of the twelve thousand florins owed him by the emperor. There he fell ill with a fever and died, on November 15, 1630, at the age of forty-eight. On his deathbed, it was reported, he "did not talk, but pointed his index finger now at his head, now at the sky above him." His epitaph was of his own composition:

> Mensus eram coelos, nunc terrae metior umbras
> Mens coelestis erat, corporis umbra iacet.

> I measured the skies, now I measure the shadows
> Skybound was the mind, the body rests in the earth.

The grave has vanished, trampled under in the war.

Suggestions for Discussion and Writing

1. What does the author mean when he says that in drawing inspiration "less from stars than from books" Copernicus "was very much a man of his times"?

2. What were some of the important intellectual influences leading to Copernicus's new model of the universe? Was Copernicus in any sense a captive of those influences?

3. Why did Copernicus's heliocentric model work "little better" than Ptolemy's geocentric one? What does the author mean when he speaks of the tragedy of Copernicus's career?

4. Write a paragraph explaining why the heliocentric hypothesis was "a flawed jewel."

5. Why was the appearance of supernovae (violently exploding stars) important to the acceptance of Copernicanism? What important element of the Ptolemaic-Aristotelian model did their appearance undermine?

6. What was Tycho Brahe's great contribution to the changing view of the universe initiated by Copernicus?

7. What were Kepler's great strengths as a scientist? How did these strengths color his relationship with Tycho?

8. The author paints sharply contrasting portraits of Tycho and Kepler. How would you characterize his style in these descriptions? Does the style suit his purpose here?

9. Write a brief essay explaining why "the perfect circle" was Kepler's "sacrifice."

ISAAC NEWTON'S MODEL

Jacob Bronowski
(1908–1974)

The scientist and philosopher Jacob Bronowski was born in Poland, emigrated to England while still a boy, and later became a British citizen. He received his Ph.D. in mathematics from Cambridge University in 1933. In 1942, after several years of teaching, Bronowski turned his attention to the British war effort. As a researcher in the British Ministry of Home Security he conducted statistical analyses on the effects of bombing and in 1945 was sent to Japan to report on the effects of the atomic bombing of Hiroshima and Nagasaki. After the war Bronowski served in several governmental posts and was also a popular commentator for the British Broadcasting Corporation. His research at the Salk Institute for Biological Studies in San Diego, California, involved an attempt to define the biological and behavioral characteristics that are expressions of human uniqueness. This work formed the basis of the widely known television series (and subsequent book) *The Ascent of Man* (1974).

The range of Bronowski's intellectual interests was remarkable. He published work in the fields of literary criticism, the history and philosophy of science, and the role of science and the arts in the development of culture. Bronowski believed deeply that science was as much an act of the imagination as any art, and explored this view in such books as *Science and Human Values* (1956), *A Sense of the Future* (1977), and *The Visionary Eye: Essays on the Arts, Literature, and Science* (1978). In the following selection, taken from *The Common Sense of Science* (1951), Bronowski discusses Isaac Newton's major role in the scientific revolution of the sixteenth and seventeenth centuries. He focuses on two related aspects of Newton's achievement: his role in the development of what today we call "the scientific method" and his working out of the concept of cause, a fundamental notion in the practice of modern science.

(1)

The great revolutions in outlook are long in the making, and at last they change all our ways of thought. But the change strikes first in one field of knowledge, which has a special place in the social and intellectual life of the day. In the nineteenth century, the field of interest shared by laymen and specialists, in which the new biological sciences first took their stand, was the age of the earth and the descent of man. In the sixteenth and seventeenth centuries the central field of knowledge was astronomy. This was the field of greatest social importance to the trading countries and the trader classes. It was a practical, technical field; but it was not therefore despised as fit only for mariners and mathematicians. Astronomy was a gentleman's accomplishment like singing to the lute, as we see from the number of songs to the lute whose imagery is sprinkled with stars.

The steps by which there was prepared the great climax and transformation of astronomy in 1687 are now well known, and I will do no more than recall them briefly. Men have known for several thousand years that the sun and the planets move in regular ways against a background of stars which seem to be still. These regularities can be used to look forward as well as back: the Babylonians were able to use them to forecast eclipses of the sun. The sun, the moon and the planets can be pictured as being carried round the earth on these regular paths in great shells or spheres. Or the paths, which seen from the earth are curiously looped, can be thought of as the rolling of wheels upon wheels; it was in this way that Ptolemy and other Greeks in Alexandria patterned them on the night sky eighteen hundred years ago. Ptolemy's picture does not claim to explain the movement of the planets, if indeed we could make him understand this meaning of the word "explain" which has become natural for us. It gives an order to their movements by describing them, and so tells us where we may expect to see them next.

Two things happened in the sixteenth century to make astronomy ill at ease with this description; and they are both of interest, because they remind us that science is compounded of fact and logic. The Danish astronomer Tycho Brahe took better and more regular observations of the positions of the planets, and they showed that Ptolemy's paths, charming though they looked as mathematical curves, were really only rather crude guides to where the planets rolled. And even earlier, Copernicus showed that these paths were much simpler if they were looked at not from the earth but from the sun. Early in the seventeenth century, these two findings were combined by Kepler, who had worked for Brahe. Kepler used the measurements of Brahe and the speculations of Copernicus to frame general descriptions of the orbits of the planets; for example, he showed that, seen from the sun as focus, a planet sweeps out equal areas of its ellipse in each equal interval of time.

It was these empirical generalisations of Kepler which Newton and his contemporaries worked from when they began to look for a deeper order below the movements of the planets. They had also a new weapon of theory. For while Kepler had been at work in the north, Galileo in Italy had at last overthrown the physical conceptions in the works of Aristotle, which had long been attacked in Paris. By the time the Royal Society was founded, the complicated Greek ideas of motion with their conflict of earth and air, of impact and vacuum were out of the way. There were no clear new laws of motion yet; it was left to Newton to set these out; but there were fair descriptions of where and how masses in fact move, and no interest at all in where they ought to want to move.

(2)

What was the nature of Newton's insight? How did he exercise those great gifts, and seize the great opportunity which I have described?

If we put what he did most baldly, it is this: that he carried on the simplification which Kepler had begun, but carried it beyond geometry into physics. Ptolemy, Copernicus, Tycho Brahe and Kepler, at bottom all looked no further than to plot the paths of the planets. Kepler found likenesses between these paths deeper than anything in the traditional astronomy, for his were likenesses of motion as well as shape. Nevertheless his paths remained descriptions, more accurate and more concise than Ptolemy's, but no more universal. For even when Kepler speculated about an attraction of the planets to the sun he had no principle to link it to the movement of earthly masses. Galileo had the first glimpse of that; and there were others as the seventeenth century marched on, who knew what kind of principle they were looking for; but it was Newton who formulated it, sudden and entire. He said that change of motion is produced by force; that the motion between masses, whether apple, moon and earth, or planet and sun, is produced by gravitational forces which attract them to one another. And he alone of his contemporaries had the mathematical power to show that, if these forces are postulated in the right way, then they keep the planets spinning like a clockwork; they keep the moon on its orbit, and the tides moving under the moon; and they hold the universe together. These achievements are so great that they out-top astronomy; and they are only a part of Newton's whole achievement. But more than the achievement, it is the thought within which deserves our study. There is the searching conception of the universe as a machine; not a pattern but a clockwork. There is the conception of the moving forces within the machine: the single spring of action in gravitation. There is the brilliant compromise between the description of the astronomers and the First Cause of the theologians, in which Newton shaped once for all the notion of cause as it has remained ever since. Newton indeed has taken over just enough of the Aristotelean nature of things to make the world work by giving all matter a single nature—that it seeks to join with all other matter. And finally, there is his extraordinary solution of the ambivalence within all science, which is compounded mysteriously of fact and logic, in a way which still remains beyond analysis.

Of these massive achievements I shall single out two. One is Newton's working out of the concept of the cause, by making it over from its scholastic form in, say, St. Thomas Aquinas, to the modern form which now seems so obvious to us. This is one theme in this chapter. But I shall go to it by way of a related achievement, and to my mind one which is as remarkable: the marriage of the logical with the empirical method. What Newton did here has equally become a commonplace in scientific method, but one of which we are less aware.

(3)

In order to act in a scientific manner, in order to act in a human manner at all, two things are necessary: fact and thought. Science does not consist only of finding the facts; nor is it enough only to think, however rationally. The processes of science are characteristic of human action in that they move by the union of empirical fact and rational thought, in a way which cannot be disentangled. There is in science, as in all our lives, a continuous to and fro of factual discovery, then of thought about the implications of what we have discovered, and so back to the facts for testing and discovery—a step by step of experiment and theory, left, right, left, right, for ever.

This union of two methods is the very base of science. Whitehead, who in his philosophy laid stress on it, dated the Scientific Revolution from the moment when Galileo and his contemporaries understood that the two methods, the empirical and the logical, are each meaningless alone, and that they must be put together. In Whitehead's view, the Middle Ages were quite as logical in their speculations about nature as we are. It is not as rationalists that we have the advantage of them; our material successes stem from joining to their logic a ruthless appeal, at each bold deductive step, back to the hard empirical facts. The moment when this was begun, and the authority of the thought and the word was put to the challenge of fact, has long been dramatised in a scene at Pisa. Galileo is said to have dropped a large and a small mass from the Leaning Tower there; and they reached the ground more or less together, in flat contradiction of the pronouncements of Aristotle and Aquinas. But history is rarely so simple or so decisive. Galileo did not make this experiment at Pisa, an those who did could not make it work. And meanwhile logic was already thinking out the experiment. Independent spirits in the bolder school of Paris had for some time doubted Aristotle's dictum that larger masses fall faster. Their logical objection can be put in this way: that since three equal masses dropped together will all fall side by side, it is at least unlikely that two of them should suddenly begin to gain on the third merely because they happen to be tied or formed together into a larger mass.

We need not wonder too nicely whether we shall take this event or that thought as zero hour for the Scientific Revolution. No change of outlook is as direct as Whitehead implies, or as abrupt as I have sometimes dramatically pictured it. The beginnings of the Industrial

Revolution go back before 1760, and the beginnings of the Scientific Revolution go back long before 1660 or indeed that earlier day, real or fabled, on the Leaning Tower of Pisa about 1600. But our concern is not with beginnings; it is with the visible substantial change, from the outlook before to the outlook after. The outlook before the Scientific Revolution was content with scholastic logic applied to a nature of hierarchies. The Scientific Revolution ended that; it linked the rational and the empirical, thought and fact, theory and practical experiment. And this has remained the content of science ever since. From time to time great speculative scientists like Eddington have seemed to claim again that we can deduce all physical laws without any experiments. But when we study their work, we find that it is not at all a return to the Middle Ages; and that their real claim is that the physical laws can be deduced from far fewer critical experiments than we have been in the habit of thinking necessary.

(4)

Two great thinkers in the first half of the seventeenth century are usually coupled, the one with the rational and the other with the empirical approach in science. The method of logic is given to Descartes, and the method of experiment to Francis Bacon. And the two men do indeed form a nice contrast between what are usually held to be the French and the English habits of thought. Characteristically, Descartes did most of his scientific work in bed; and Bacon died of a cold which he may have caught when at the age of sixty-five he tried the experiment of stuffing a fowl with snow. Certainly the powerful influence of Descartes tended to run counter to the inquisitive English school, more perhaps because of its rigidity of form than its content. I have remarked that Huygens had been influenced by Descartes, whom he knew well as a boy; and this was one of the things which kept Huygens from understanding the full range of what Newton and the Royal Society were doing.

But the example of Descartes was as essential to Newton's frame of mind as was Bacon's. In some ways indeed it was more important. For the Royal Society was full of tireless experimenters in the grand and somewhat haphazard manner of Bacon. What it lacked was Descartes's search for system, his belief that nature is always and everywhere alike and a unity, which to him and Newton was symbolised by the universal power of mathematics. Descartes's whole life was shaped by a moment of insight in which suddenly, late one night, it was revealed to him with an immediacy which was almost physical, that the key to the universe is its mathematical order. To the end of his life, Descartes remembered the date of that revelation, November 10th, 1619—he was then twenty-three—and he always spoke of it with the awe of a mystic. By contrast, Bacon altogether underrated the importance of the mathematical method, and here his influence was bad.

I have said that the empirical and the logical methods in science must take alternate steps forward; a step in one makes ready for a step in the other. It is natural that the empirical method should stress the facts, and should ask the theoretically minded thinker to make his deductions from them. It is as natural that the thinker should construct a world and then look up to see how far in fact it is the world of fact. Most of us to day have a strong bias for the empirical. As laymen we feel that the facts are wonderful and the theory is always difficult; and we tend to think of all science as a logical process taking the facts and deducing from them some system which they determine. This is not what Newton did, nor indeed, surprising as it may seem, is it the usual method of science as we know it. On the contrary, what is surprising is that we should believe this deductive method to be practised or practicable.

What Newton did was something quite different. He took from the experiments of Galileo and other Italians some general notions about how masses behave: that they travel in straight lines and at a uniform pace, that they go on travelling so unless a force displaces them, and so on. So far, the method may be called deductive, because it rests fairly closely on experiment; although even here deduction does not give quite the right picture of the method, which calls for a great deal of mental experiment in building up possible worlds from different laws.

But it is at the next step that the break really comes. What Newton did now was to suppose that the general rules which fair-sized masses seem to obey are true of every piece of matter, whatever its kind or its size. And having decided to try this thought, he made himself a new world of his own, which he built up from minute pieces of matter each following the same laws or axioms. This world is just as much a construction as the abstract world of geometry which Euclid built up out of his axioms. Euclid defined a point, a line, a plane, and he laid down axioms which these are to obey in their mutual relations. He then constructed in a series of propositions a large number of consequences which flow from these. And what makes us honour Euclid is that this abstract world now turns out to be recognisably like that part of the real world which we can see and compare with our own eyes. We believe in his axioms, not because they are deduced from the real world, but because the consequences which he constructs from them fit the real world.

This was very much Newton's method too, but Newton almost for the first time applied it to the physical world. He supposed that everything in the world is assembled from small particles. He never defined these particles, and we have come to think of them as the atoms of Democritus and the poet Lucretius. Newton did not say this, and I am not sure that he believed it; I am not sure that he really wanted to get into arguments, whether these particles really could not be cut up into smaller ones. Although he wrote with great clarity, Newton was not good in argument and he tried to avoid it. This was not because Newton could not see his opponent's difficulty but because he had foreseen and resolved it in his own work so long ago that he despaired of helping anyone who could not work round it alone. As a result, Newton was a difficult and morose man in his relations with other scientists, and was not so much impatient as hopeless about persuading anyone who could not himself think through the natural but removable obstacles.

Newton then built up his world of unknown small particles assembled in such masses as the apple, the moon, the planets and the sun. Each of these assemblies is alike in his view in being made up of these minute pieces of matter. And in each of them the minute pieces obey the same laws: if they are at rest then they remain at rest, or if they are moving then they go on moving steadily in straight lines, until they are displaced by outside forces. And greatest among these forces is this, that each minute particle in Newton's world attracts every other equal particle with a force which depends only on their distance apart, falling off in such a way that when the distance is doubled, the force shrinks to a quarter.

Now this is naturally a fictitious world. It is a picture, and so far it has not even been shown to be a machine. That is, we do not even know at this stage whether it will go on doing whatever we started it doing. It might simply not work, either because all its particles would fly apart for ever, or because they would all collapse into the centre. So far in fact we have only the definitions and the axioms: the next step is, as in Euclid, to work out the propositions, that is the consequences of this shadow dance among the ghostly particles. And this is where Newton showed his power as a mathematician. Hooke and others who had already guessed at much the same picture got no further than general speculation because they lacked the mathematical skill to work out the exact consequences. First, it is necessary to show that under these laws an assembly of particles which form a compact sphere behaves towards anything outside the sphere simply like one heavy particle at its centre. The simplicity of the mathematics, which makes astronomy manageable, depends critically on this fact; and this fact in turn depends on a gravitation which falls as the square of distance and not in some other way. In a world with another law of gravitation, though it might differ only minutely from the law of inverse squares, round heavenly bodies would not act like single points of concentrated matter, and in general the planetary paths would be neither calculable nor stable.

And this is only the first step. Newton went on to show that as a result of this, the orbits of the planets can be calculated; that they are the ellipses which Kepler had measured; and that they remain stable paths turning like a divine clockwork. He went on to calculate the tides and the paths of comets; and so he slowly built up a picture of the world which is recognisably the world as the mariner sees it, and the astronomer, and the picnickers on Brighton beach. The world of speculation is suddenly seen to chime with the real world, with a triumphant note like a peal of bells.

It is this accord which makes us believe in Newton's picture, and underneath it in his laws. The laws are not a deduction from experiment in any obvious sense. Their success is not that they follow from the real world, but that they predict a world which is essentially like ours. And it is this success which gives us our faith in the substratum of tiny particles each obeying the laws on which Newton's picture is built. This assumption under the picture, this faith in a minute substratum has had important consequences in shaping our methods and our metaphysic ever since; and we shall have occasion to turn to it again.

(5)

In describing Newton's reconstruction of the starry world, I have likened it to Euclid's manner of building up something recognisably like the space round us from a set of hypothetical entities which are assumed to obey a few simple rules. Where Newton's achievement differs from Euclid's is in this: what is constructed is required to fit the observed facts more closely and in greater variety. I am tempted to say that the physical facts are also more immediate and more important than the facts of geometry. But I am not sure that this is not an illusion which we all have because Euclid's work has been part of civilised thinking for more than two thousand years, whereas Newton's, although now three hundred years old, still inspires in us something of the astonishing sense of destiny in simplicity which it had for his contemporaries. In fact, the fit of Euclid's geometrical construction to our space lies snugly under the physical fit of Newton's picture. But there is a difference. Newton's physics fits at more points, and had to be checked and enlarged to fit there in his time and throughout the eighteenth and nineteenth centuries. It has to meet more detailed and powerful experimental tests, because it is a construction which claims to fit from moment to moment a world in constant changing movement. This is what makes it more difficult and deeper than Euclid's reconstruction of the timeless, windless world of space.

And this is why I called Newton's method of the joining of the two strands in science, the rational and the empirical. Here the logical outlook of Descartes is joined with the experimental passion of Bacon; and it is right to recall again how able and how searching an experimenter Newton himself was. The *Principia* gives us a wonderful sense of his intellectual power, because the experimental work on which it rested at that stage had been done by others and was familiar. But the *Opticks* is as impressive a book with a more personal immediacy, because in it he takes us from one experiment to the next with such clarity and such insight that more than anything we are silenced by the roundness and coherence of his method. We have the sense here that nothing that matters has been left untested, and yet there is no random pottering about just to see if there might be anything in this or that as well. Newton had that insight which cannot be distracted, that gift for isolating and eliminating each logical alternative, which makes the profound experimental as well as the theoretical scientist: which makes of course simply the profound mind.

We do not see the young man of the *Opticks* in the measured pages of the *Principia,* though even when the *Principia* was printed, long after Newton had done the work in it, he was still in his forties. But the power is the same: to construct hypothetical parts and assemble them into a mechanism which shall fit at each stage the experimental checks and the real world; and at the same time to invent as in the *Opticks* or to identify as in the *Principia* the critical checks at the right points. That is why I underline the union of thought and fact, the rational and the empirical streams flowing together. The Scientific Revolution was the point of their confluence, and the power of the scientific method since then has derived, like the power of the Rhône, from two streams rolled into one.

(6)

The other great step which was taken at the Scientific Revolution was in giving a new and clear meaning to the concept of cause. There is a great deal of argument about causes in the scholastic writers of the Middle Ages. Aquinas has a formidable array of their categories—proximate causes, efficient causes, necessary causes and the First Cause. And under these concepts runs the medieval notion, that every part of nature is endowed with a human will and temper, and strives to a purpose of its own. These causes are all trappings of logic; but the notion of cause and effect as the sixteenth and seventeenth centuries slowly worked it out is not one of logical consequence. In the nineteenth century, philosophers tried with great pains to recover some logical, that is mental, necessity in the sequence of cause and effect: John Stuart Mill's is the outstanding effort. But this really is to try once again to inject into the physical world the workings of the human mind. It is a sort of pathetic fallacy of science, like that pathetic fallacy of poetry which makes nature weep with Milton for the death of Lycidas.

The notion of cause which since the Scientific Revolution is so natural and obvious to us is not the notion of a logical sequence. Like other great principles of science, such as the principles that nature is rational and is uniform, its sanction is metaphysical. In effect this means that it is a working rule based on our experience of the past and on the way that we organize our lives on that experience in order to meet the future. Our conception of cause and effect is this: that given a definite configuration of wholly material things, there will always follow upon it the same observable event. If we repeat the configuration, we shall always get the same event following it. As the sun sets, radio reception improves. As we press the switch, the light goes on. As the child grows, it becomes able to speak. And if the expected does not happen, if reception does not improve or the lamp does not light up, or the child persists in gurgling, then we are confident that the configuration from which we started was not the same. There has been something misplaced, we are sure, and this something is material and has injected a material difference into the assumed configuration, which has worked everywhere else and at all other times. The present influences the future and, more, it determines it.

This is the concept of cause which has been elevated to the rank of the central concept of science. And it did in fact play a major part in clarifying what was new at the Scientific Revolution, and made Newton's world different from that of Aristotle. When the world became a machine, this became the god within the machine.

Suggestions for Discussion and Writing

1. What was the importance of the experiment at the Leaning Tower of Pisa? What great challenge did it represent?

2. What distinctive habits of thought do Descartes and Bacon represent? Why, for Bronowski, are these two thinkers relevant to a discussion of Newton?

3. Newton himself said that "no great discovery was ever made without a bold guess." Write a paragraph explaining the nature of Newton's bold guess.

4. What does Bronowski mean when he says that Newton "made himself a world of his own," one that was "just as much a construction as the abstract world of geometry which Euclid built up out of his axioms"? Why was Newton's construction "more difficult and deeper" than Euclid's?

5. Ptolemy, Copernicus, Brahe, and Kepler were astronomers. In what sense was Newton much more than an astronomer?

6. Explain the concept of cause as Newton (and scientists ever since) understood it.

7. Speaking of Newton's laws, Bronowski says that "their success is not that they follow from the real world, but that they predict a world which is essentially like ours." Do you see a connection between the notion of prediction and the concept of cause as Newton understood it?

8. One philosopher of science has called Newton "the great unifier." Write an essay that examines this claim.

9. What, finally, are the principal characteristics of Newton's model?

☐ DARWIN, INTELLECTUAL REVOLUTIONARY

Ernst Mayr
(b. 1904)

Ernst Mayr, generally considered to be one of the greatest living commentators on biology, was born in Germany and received his Ph.D. in zoology from the University of Berlin in 1926. During the 1920s and '30s he was a member of several expeditions to the Southwest Pacific. His early work was largely in the field of ornithology; much of his more recent work has been more broadly focused on biology and the history and philosophy of evolution. Among his books are *Animal Species and Evolution* (1963), *Populations, Species, and Evolution* (1970), and *Evolution and the Diversity of Life* (1976). He was Alexander Agassiz Professor of Zoology at Harvard from 1953 to 1975. In the following selection from *Toward a New Philosophy of Biology* (1988), Mayr discusses some of the important intellectual landmarks in Darwin's developing formulation of a theory that laid the groundwork for perhaps the most fundamental revolution in the history of science.

W e live in a time of short memories. Only few papers nowadays cited in the scientific literature are more than three years old. And many of the younger generation are regrettably unaware of the revolutionary contributions made by the great men of the past. One can hardly find a better illustration for this than the work of Charles Darwin. Nearly all of his great innovations have become to such an extent an integral component of Western thinking that only the historians appreciate Darwin's pioneering role.

We speak rather glibly of the Darwinian revolution, but if one challenges the speaker to specify precisely just what he means by this term, one will invariably get an answer that is, at best, incomplete but more often partly wrong. I admit that it is almost impossible for a modern person to project himself back to the early half of the last century, to reconstruct the thinking of the pre-Darwinian period, that is, the framework of ideas that was so thoroughly destroyed by Darwin. What we must, therefore, do is to ask what were the widely or universally held views that were challenged by Darwin in 1859 in the *Origin*? I will endeavour to show that the intellectual revolution generated by Darwin produced a far more fundamental and far-reaching change in the thinking of the Western World than is usually appreciated. And I shall also make it clear that this was not merely an incidental by-product of some biological speculations, but that Darwin had a comprehensive programme, to review and, where necessary, to revolutionize traditional ideas. I shall show that Darwin was a bold and often quite radical revolutionary.

Let me preface my analysis by the comment that I shall try to avoid as much as possible analyzing by what pathway Darwin reached his novel ideas. Rather, I will begin by asking whether there was a prevailing world view in the West prior to 1859. The answer is no. Indeed, the prevailing thinking in England, France, or Germany was perhaps more different from that of the other two countries in the first half of the nineteenth century than in any period before or since. Natural theology was still dominant in England, but already obsolete in France and Germany. The conservative and rational France of Cuvier, as well as the romantic Germany of the *Naturphilosophen* were worlds apart from the England of Lyell, Sedgwick, and John Herschel. Darwin's intellectual milieu, of course, was that of England, and his arguments were directed against his peers and their thinking.

Let me now take up the major concepts or ideas which Darwin encountered and which he tried to modify or replace. By far the most comprehensive of these, in fact an all-pervading ideology, was that of creationism. By creationism is understood the belief that the world must be interpreted as reflecting the mind of the Creator. But physicists and naturalists interpreted the implementation of the mind of the Creator in different ways. The order and harmony of the universe made the physical scientists search for laws, for wise institutions in the running of the universe installed by the Creator. Everything in nature was caused, but the causes were secondary causes, regulated by the laws instituted by the primary cause, the Creator. To serve his Creator best, a physicist studied His laws and their working. Most naturalists, by contrast, concentrated on the wonderful adaptations of living creatures. These could not be explained readily as the result of general laws such as those of gravity, heat, light, or movements. Nearly all the marvellous adaptations of living creatures are so unique that it seemed vacuous to claim that they were due to "laws." It rather seemed that these aspects of nature were so special and unique that they could be interpreted only as caused by the direct intervention of the Creator, by His specific design. Consequently the functioning of organisms, their instincts, and their manifold interactions provided the naturalist with abundant evidence for design, and seemed to constitute irrefutable proof for the existence of a Creator. Darwin, even though a naturalist, tried valiantly to apply the thinking of the physicists, by looking for laws.

It was the task of natural theology to study the design of creation, and natural theology was thus as much science as it was theology. The two endeavours, theology and science, were indeed inseparable. Consequently, most of the greater scientific works of this period, as exemplified by Lyell's *Principles of Geology* (1830–33) or Louis Agassiz's *Essay on Classification* (1857), were simultaneously treatises of natural theology. Science and theology were fused into a single system and, as is obvious with hindsight, there could not be any truly objective and uncommitted science until science and theology had been cleanly and completely divorced from each other. The publication of Darwin's *Origin of Species* was to a greater extent responsible for this divorce than anything else. Although Darwin was not yet a complete agnostic in 1859, he argued throughout the *Origin* against creationism, the intrusion of theology into science. And when Darwin said "This whole volume is one long argument," he was clearly referring to his endeavour to "get theology out of science." In this effort Darwin was completely successful, and the historians accept the year 1859 as the end of creditable natural theology.

I used to believe that it was a loss of Christian faith that induced Darwin to seek a complete autonomy of science from theology. However, recent analyses have persuaded me that scientific findings had been primarily responsible for Darwin's change of mind. In particular it was Darwin's realization of the invalidity of three prominent doctrines among the numerous beliefs of creationism that was of crucial importance for Darwin's change of mind:

1. that of an unchanging world of short duration,
2. that of the constancy and sharp delimitation of created species, and
3. that of a perfect world explicable only by the postulate of an omnipotent and beneficent Creator.

As we shall presently discuss, Darwin's conclusions were reinforced by his conviction of the invalidity of several other tenets of creationism, such as the special creation of man, but the three stated dogmas were clearly of primary importance.

Even though Bishop Ussher's calculation that the world had been created as recently as 4004 years B.C. was still widely accepted among the pious, the men of science had long become aware of the great age of the earth. The researches of the geologists, in particular, left no doubt of the immense age of the earth, thus providing all the time needed for abundant organic evolution. Lamarck was the first to draw the necessary conclusions from this.

Among the various discoveries of geology the one that was most important and most disturbing for the creationist was the discovery of extinction. Already in the eighteenth century Blumenbach and others had accepted extinction of formerly existing types like ammonites, belemnites, and trilobites, and of entire faunas, but it was not until Cuvier had worked out the extinction of a whole sequence of mammalian faunas in the Tertiary of the Paris Basin that the acceptance of extinction became inevitable. The ultimate proof for it was the discovery of fossil mastodons and mammoths, animals so huge that any living survivors could not possibly have remained undiscovered in some remote part of the globe.

Three explanations for extinction were offered. According to Lamarck, no organism ever became extinct; there simply was such drastic transformation that the formerly existing types had changed beyond recognition. According to the progressionists, like Miller, Murchison, and Agassiz, each former fauna had become extinct as a whole and was replaced by a newly created, more progressive fauna. Such catastrophism was unpalatable to Charles Lyell, who produced a third theory consistent with his uniformitarianism. He believed that individual species became extinct one by one as conditions were changing and that the gaps thus created in nature were filled by the introduction of new species. Lyell's theory was an attempt at a reconciliation between those who recognized a changing world of long duration and those who supported the tenets of creationism.

The question of how these new species were "introduced" was left unanswered by Lyell. He bequeathed this problem to Darwin, who in due time made it his most important research program. Darwin thus approached the problem of evolution in an entirely different manner from Lamarck. For Lamarck, evolution was a strictly vertical phenomenon, more or less a temporalization of the *scala naturae,* proceeding in a single dimension, that of time. Evolution for him was a movement from less perfect to more perfect, an endeavour to establish a continuity among the major types of organisms, from the most primitive infusorians up to the mammals and Man. Lamarck's *Philosophie Zoologique* was the paradigm of what I designate as vertical evolutionism. Species played no role in Lamarck's thinking. New species originated all the time by spontaneous generation from inanimate matter, but this produced only the simplest infusorians. Each such newly established evolutionary line gradually moved up to ever greater perfection. Lamarck rightly called his work a "philosophy," because he did not present testable scientific theories.

Darwin was unable to build on this foundation but rather started from the fundamental question that Lyell had bequeathed to him. Although Lyell had appealed to "intermediate causes" as the source of the new species, his description of the process was that of special creation. "Species may have been created in succession at such times and at such places as to enable them to multiply and endure for an appointed period and occupy an appointed space on the globe." For Lyell, each creation was a carefully planned event. The reason why Lyell, like Henslow, Sedgwick, and all the others of Darwin's scientific friends and correspondents in the middle of the 1830s, accepted the unalterable constancy of species was ultimately a philosophical one. The constancy of species was the one piece of the old dogma of a created world that remained inviolate after the concepts of the recency and constancy of the physical world had been abandoned.

Another ideology which prevented Lyell from recognizing the change of species was *essentialism,* which had dominated Western thinking for more than two thousand years after Plato. According to the essentialist, the changing variety of things in nature is a reflection of a limited number of constant and sharply delimited underlying *eide,* or essences. Variation is merely the manifestation of imperfect reflections of the constant essences. For Lyell all nature consisted of constant types, each created at a definite time. "There are fixed limits beyond which the descendants from common parents can never deviate from a certain type." And he added emphatically: "It is idle . . . to dispute about the abstract possibility of the conversion of one species into another, when there are known causes, so much more active in their nature, which must always intervene and prevent the actual accomplishment of such conversions." For an essentialist there can be no evolution, there can only be a sudden origin of a new essence by a major mutation or saltation.

To the historian it is quite evident that no genuine and testable theory of evolution could develop until the possibility was accepted that species have the capacity to change, to become transformed into new species, and to multiply into several species. For Darwin to accept this possibility required a fundamental break with Lyell's thinking. The question which we must ask ourselves is how Darwin was able to emancipate himself from Lyell's thinking, and what observations or conceptual changes permitted Darwin to adopt the theory of a transforming capacity of species.

As Darwin tells us in his autobiography, he encountered many phenomena during his visit to South America on the *Beagle* which any modern biologist would unhesitatingly explain as clear evidence of evolution. Furthermore, when sorting his collections on the homeward voyage, his observations in the Galapagos Islands made him pen the memorable sentences (approximately July 1836): "When I see these islands in sight of each other and possessed of but a scanty stock of animals, tenanted by these birds but slightly differing in structure and filling the same place in nature, I must suspect they are varieties . . . if there is the slightest foundation for these remarks the zoology of the archipelagoes will be well worth examining: for such facts would undermine the stability of species." Yet, it is evident that Darwin at that date had not yet consciously abandoned the concept of constant species. This Darwin apparently did in two stages. The discovery of a second, smaller species of *Rhea* (South American ostrich) led him to the theory, consistent with essentialism, that an existing species could give rise to a new species, by a sudden leap. Such an origin of new species had been postulated scores of times before from the Greeks to Robinet and Maupertuis. Typological new origins, however, are not evolution. The diagnostic criterion of evolutionary transformation is gradualness. The concept of gradualism, the second step in Darwin's conversion, was apparently first adopted by Darwin when the ornithologist John Gould, who prepared the scientific report on Darwin's bird collections, pointed out to him that there were three different endemic species of mockingbirds on three different islands in the Galapagos. Darwin had thought they were only varieties.

The mockingbird episode was of particular importance to Darwin for two reasons. The Galapagos endemics were quite similar to a species of mockingbirds on the South American mainland and clearly derived from it. What was important was that the Galapagos birds were not the result of a single saltation, as Darwin had postulated for the new species of *Rhea* in Patagonia, but had gradually evolved into three different although very similar species on three different islands. This fact helped to convert Darwin to the concept of gradual evolution. Even more important was the fact that these three different species had branched off from a single parental species, the mainland mockingbird, an observation which gave Darwin the solution to the problem of the multiplication of species.

The problem of the introduction of new species posed by Lyell was thus solved by Darwin. New species can originate by what we now call geographical or allopatric speciation. This theory of speciation says that new species may originate by the gradual genetic transformation of isolated populations. By this thought Darwin founded a branch of evolutionism which, for short, we might designate as horizontal evolutionism, in contrast with the strictly vertical evolutionism of Lamarck. The two kinds of evolutionism deal with two entirely different aspects of evolution even though the processes responsible for these aspects proceed simultaneously. Vertical evolutionism deals with adaptive changes in the time dimension, while horizontal evolutionism deals with the origin of new diversity, that is, with the origin of new populations, incipient species, and new species, which enrich the diversity of the organic world and which are the potential founders of new evolutionary departures, of new higher taxa, of the occupants of new adaptive zones.

From 1837 on, when Darwin first recognized and solved the problem of the origin of diversity, this duality of the evolutionary process has been with us. Unfortunately, there were only few authors with the breadth of thought and experience of Darwin to deal simultaneously with both aspects of evolution. As it was, paleontologists and geneticists concentrated on or devoted themselves exclusively to vertical evolution, while the majority of the naturalists studied the origin of diversity as reflected in the process of speciation and the origin of higher taxa.

The first author to have proposed geographic speciation was the geologist L. von Buch (1825) in a short statement which he failed to develop any further. M. Wagner (1841) and Alfred Russel Wallace (1855) also proposed it independently of Darwin. The discovery of the divergence of contemporary, geographically isolated populations made it possible to incorporate the origin of organic diversity within the compass of evolution. For Darwin this was of crucial importance, because horizontal thinking permitted the solution of three important evolutionary problems:

1. The problem of the multiplication of species.
2. The resolution of the seeming conflict between the observed discontinuities in nature and the concept of gradual evolution.
3. The problem of the evolution of the higher taxa owing to common descent.

Perhaps the most decisive consequence of the discovery of geographic speciation was that it led Darwin automatically to a branching concept of evolution. This is why branching entered Darwin's notebooks at such an early stage.

HOW ARE RELATIVES CONNECTED?

For those who accepted the concept of the *scala naturae*—and in the eighteenth century this included most naturalists to a lesser or greater extent—all organisms were part of a single linear scale of ever-growing perfection. Lamarck still adhered, in principle, to this concept even though he allowed for some branching in his classification of the major phyla. Pallas and others had also published branching diagrams, but it required the categorical rejection of the *scala naturae* by Cuvier in the first and second decades of the nineteenth century before the need for a new way to represent organic diversity became crucial. The Quinarians experimented with indicating relationship by osculating circles, but their diagrams did not fit reality at all well. The archetypes of Owen and the Naturphilosophen strengthened the recognition of discrete groups in nature, but the use of the term *affinity* in relation to these groups remained meaningless prior to the acceptance of the theory of evolution.

Apparently very soon after Darwin had understood that a single species of South American mockingbird had given rise to three daughter species in the Galapagos Islands, he seemed to have realized that such a process of multiplication of species, combined with their continuing divergence, could give rise in due time to different genera and still higher categories. The members of a higher taxon then would be united by descent from a common ancestor. The best way to represent such common descent would be a branching diagram. Already in the summer of 1837 Darwin clearly stated that "organized beings represent an irregularly branched tree" (*Notebook B,* p. 21), and he drew several tree diagrams in which he even distinguished living and extinct species by different symbols. By the time he wrote the *Origin*, the theory of common descent had become the backbone of his evolutionary theory, not surprisingly so because it had extraordinary explanatory powers. Indeed, the manifestations of common descent as revealed by comparative anatomy, comparative embryology, systematics ("natural system"), and biogeography became the main evidence for the occurrence of evolution in the years after 1859. Reciprocally the stated biological disciplines, which up to 1859 had been primarily descriptive, now became causal sciences, with common descent providing explanation for nearly everything that had previously been puzzling.

In these studies the comparative method played an important role. To be sure, the practitioners of idealistic morphology and the Naturphilosophen had also practised comparison with excellent results. But the archetypes which they had reconstructed had no causal explanation until they were reinterpreted by Darwin as reflecting the putative common ancestors.

The theory of common descent, once proposed, is so simple and so obvious that it is hard to believe Darwin was the first to have adopted it consistently. Its importance was not only that it had such great explanatory powers but also that it provided for the living world a unity which had been previously missing. Up to 1859 people had been impressed primarily by the enormous diversity from the lowest plants to the highest vertebrates, but this diversity took on an entirely different complexion when it was realized that it all could be traced back to a common origin. The final proof of this, of course, was not supplied until our time, when it was demonstrated that even the prokaryotes have the same genetic code as animals and plants.

Perhaps the most important consequence of the theory of common descent was the change in the position of man. For theologians and philosophers alike man was a creature apart from all other living nature. Aristotle, Descartes, and Kant agreed in this, no matter how much they disagreed in other aspects of their philosophies. Darwin, in the *Origin,* confined himself to the cautiously cryptic remark, "Light will be thrown on the origin of Man and his history" (p. 488). But Ernst Haeckel, T. H. Huxley, and in 1871 Darwin himself demonstrated conclusively that humans must have evolved from an ape-like ancestor, thus putting him right into the phylogenetic tree of the animal kingdom. This was the end of the traditional anthropocentrism of the Bible and of the philosophers. To be sure, the claim that "man is nothing but an animal" was quite rightly rejected by all the more perceptive students of the human species, yet one cannot question that Darwin was responsible for a fundamental reevaluation of the nature of man and his role in the universe.

GRADUALISM

Darwin's solution for the problem of the multiplication of species and his discovery of the theory of common descent were accompanied by a number of other conceptual shifts. The most important one was his partial abandoning of essentialism in favour of gradualism and population thinking. The literature on the history of evolutionary biology lists numerous authors as forerunners of Darwin by having adopted evolutionism. When more closely examined, nearly all of these claims turn out to be invalid. Changes in the living world were ascribed to new origins by these earlier authors. But the sudden origin of a new species or still higher taxon is not evolution. Indeed, as has been rightly said by Reiser, if one is an essentialist, one cannot conceive of gradual evolution. Since an essence is constant and sharply delimited against other essences, it cannot possibly evolve. Change for an essentialist occurs only through the introduction of new essences. This was precisely Charles Lyell's interpretation of the introduction of new species throughout geological history, or Darwin's early explanation of the origin of the lesser ostrich of Patagonia.

The observation of nature seemed to give powerful support to the essentialist's claims. Wherever one looked one saw discontinuities, between species, between genera, between orders and even higher taxa. Quite naturally, the gaps between the higher taxa, like birds and mammals, or beetles and butterflies, were mentioned particularly often by Darwin's critics. And yet, as far back as Aristotle and his principle of plenitude, there had been an opposing trend. It was expressed in the *scala naturae,* and even such an arch-essentialist as Linnaeus stated that the orders of plants were touching each other like countries on a map.

Nevertheless Lamarck was the first person to apply the principle of gradualism to explain the changes in organic life that could be inferred from the geological record. But there is no evidence that Darwin derived his gradualistic thinking from Lamarck. References to gradual changes are scattered through Darwin's notebooks from an early time. Yet is it still somewhat uncertain what the exact sources of Darwin's gradualistic thinking were. One of the intellectual sources surely was Lyell's uniformitarianism, which Darwin had adopted quite early. There is also the fact that Darwin considered the changes of organisms either to be produced directly by the environment or to be at least an answer to the changes in the environment. Hence, "the changes in species must be very slow, owing to physical changes slow" (*Notebook C,* p. 17). Gradualness was also favored by Darwin's conclusion that changes in habit or behavior may precede changes in structure (*Notebook C,* pp. 57, 199). At that time Darwin still believed in a principle called Yarrell's Law, according to which it takes many generations of impact for the effects of the environment or of use and disuse to become strongly hereditary. As Darwin stated, "Variety when long in blood, gets stronger and stronger" (*Notebook C,* p. 136). Various other sources for Darwin's gradualistic thinking have been suggested in the recent literature, but to me it seems more likely that Darwin had arrived at his gradualism empirically.

At least three observations may have been influential. First, the slightness of the differences among the mockingbird populations on the three Galapagos islands and the South American mainland, as well as a similarly slight difference among many varieties and species of animals. Second, the barnacle researches, where Darwin complained constantly to what great extent species and varieties were intergrading. And third, Darwin's work with the races of domestic pigeons, where he convinced himself that even the most extreme races which, if found in nature, would be unhesitatingly placed by taxonomists in different genera were nevertheless the product of painstaking, long-continued, gradual, artificial selection. In his *Essay* of 1844, Darwin argues in favor of gradual evolution by analogy with what is found in domesticated animals and plants. And he postulates therefore that "there must have existed intermediate forms between all the species of the same group, not differing more than recognized varieties differ'' (p. 157). The abundant evidence which Darwin adduces in support of gradualism was to a considerable extent instrumental in the weakening and eventual refutation of essentialism. It was only by adopting a theory of gradual evolution that Darwin was able to escape from the constraints of essentialism. Yet evolutionary gradualism has remained a controversial subject to the present day.

NATURAL SELECTION

The concept for which Darwin is better known than for any other is that of natural selection. When we speak of Darwinism today, we mean evolution by natural selection. The meaning of natural selection, its limits, and the processes by which it achieves its effects are now the most active areas of evolutionary research.

The fundamental importance of the theory of natural selection when proposed in 1858/59 was that it challenged two of the most universally held ideologies of the period, that of cosmic teleology, and that of natural theology. According to the teleologists, the world either was established toward an end or was still moving toward an objective, either by the guiding hand of a Creator or by secondary causes, that is, by laws that were guiding the course of events toward an ultimate goal. All this was categorically denied by Darwin, for whom each evolutionary change was a singular event controlled by the temporary constellation of selection forces. Indeed, Darwin even stated that there would not be any change at all when there was no change in the environment. A nondeterministic process like natural selection was quite unintelligible for any philosopher thinking in terms of Newtonian laws.

Devastating as the denial of teleology was for many of Darwin's contemporaries such as Sedgwick and von Baer, the denial of design was even more sweeping. To explain all the beautiful adaptations of organisms, their adjustment to each other, their well-organized interdependence, and indeed the whole harmony of nature, as being the result of such a capricious process as natural selection was quite unacceptable to almost all of Darwin's contemporaries. The theory of natural selection amounted to the proposal to replace the hand of the Creator by a purely material and mechanical process, at that by one not deterministic and not predictive. As one critic put it, it dethroned God. Although an accommodation between religion and Darwinism was eventually reached, their mutual relation had first to go through a rather traumatic period. The current renaissance of the creationist movement shows that this relationship is still a precarious one.

CONCLUSION

Most students of the history of ideas believe that the Darwinian revolution was the most fundamental of all intellectual revolutions in the history of mankind. While such revolutions as those brought about by Copernicus, Newton, Lavoisier, or Einstein affected only one particular branch of science, or the methodology of science as such, the Darwinian revolution affected every thinking man. A world view developed by anyone after 1859 was by necessity quite different from any world view formed prior to 1859. It is therefore eminently proper that we pay tribute to the memory of this great man. But how can we explain Darwin's greatness?

That he was a genius is hardly any longer questioned, some of his earlier detractors notwithstanding. But there must have been a score of other biologists of equal intelligence who failed to match Darwin's achievement. What then is it that distinguishes Darwin from all the others?

Perhaps we can answer this question by investigating what kind of a scientist Darwin was. As he himself has said, he was first and foremost a naturalist. He was a splendid observer, and like all other naturalists he was interested in organic diversity and in adaptation. Naturalists are, on the whole, describers and particularists, but Darwin was also a great theoretician, something only very few naturalists have ever been. In that respect Darwin resembles much more some of the leading physical scientists. But Darwin differed from the run-of-the-mill naturalists also in another way. He was not only an observer but also a gifted and indefatigable experimenter whenever he dealt with a problem whose solution could be advanced by an experiment.

I think this suggests some of the sources of Darwin's greatness. The universality of his talents and interests had preadapted him to become a bridge builder between fields. It enabled him to use his background as a naturalist to theorize about some of the most challenging problems with which man's curiosity is faced. And contrary to widespread beliefs, Darwin was utterly bold in his theorizing.

Suggestions for Discussion and Writing

1. Where does Mayr state his thesis?

2. How does Mayr define creationism? What three prominent tenets of creationism were especially important in Darwin's rejection of this doctrine and his struggle to "get theology out of science"?

3. Select one of these tenets of creationism and, in a brief essay, explain how Darwin arrived at the conviction that it was invalid.

4. Discuss the role of geology in the development of Darwin's theory.

5. Why would the extinction of species disturb the creation-ists? Why would the multiplication of species disturb them?

6. Explain the ideology of essentialism. Why for the essentialist can there be no evolution?

7. What important problems did the "mockingbird episode" help Darwin solve?

8. Explain the difference between "vertical" and "horizontal" evolution. Why was "horizontal thinking" so important to the development of Darwin's ideas?

9. Why, according to Mayr, was the theory of "natural selection" such a revolutionary idea?

10. One philosopher of science calls Newton "the great unifier." Could the same be said of Darwin? Write an essay developing your view.

11. Mayr argues that Darwin was "completely successful" in removing theology from science. Could it be said that Eiseley, in "Science and the Sense of the Holy" (see Chapter 7), puts it back in? Write an essay defending your view.

THE ROLE OF MODERN PHYSICS IN THE PRESENT DEVELOPMENT OF HUMAN THINKING

Werner Heisenberg
(1901–1976)

Born in Duisburg, Germany, Werner Heisenberg received his Ph.D. in physics from the University of Munich at the age of 22. After working on unsolved problems in atomic structure with two renowned physicists, Max Born and Niels Bohr, Heisenberg published a paper in 1927 expressing the *uncertainty principle* (sometimes called the *principle of indeterminacy*), the idea with which he is most closely associated. That year he was appointed professor of theoretical physics at the University of Leipzig. In 1933 he was awarded the Nobel Prize for Physics.

Although not a political or philosophical supporter of the Nazi regime, Heisenberg headed the German atomic research project during World War II. After the war he was taken prisoner along with other leading German physicists and interned in England. He returned to Germany in 1946 and was appointed professor of physics at the University of Göttingen and director of the Max

Planck Institute. Heisenberg supported the development of nuclear power but spoke out forcefully on the catastrophic consequences of nuclear warfare.

Heisenberg's major contribution was in quantum mechanics, the area of physics having to do with events at the atomic and sub-atomic levels. His great insight was to regard quantum events as a different level of phenomena from those of classical physics, that is, from those governed by Newtonian mechanics. His uncertainty principle states that in the world of atoms and subatomic particles one cannot know the exact position and velocity of an object simultaneously. Specifying one of these quantities affects the value of the other; the act of observation disturbs and alters what is being observed. The uncertainty principle thus limits quantum-mechanical descriptions to a statement of probabilities rather than exact numerical predictions.

Heisenberg explored the broader philosophical and political implications of twentieth-century physics in several works, including the semiautobiographical *Physics and Beyond* (1971) and *Physics and Philosophy* (1958), from which the following essay is taken. Here, arguing that twentieth-century physics represents a fundamental shift from the rigid and materialistic framework of nineteenth-century scientific thought, Heisenberg suggests that the new scientific notions of openness and uncertainty can be extended to the geopolitical realm. Openness and uncertainty imply a need for tolerance and a willingness to accept multiple perspectives. In a geopolitical context, he suggests, such openness can make for the acceptance of widely dissimilar cultural traditions and may ultimately lead to global unification.

I t is probably true quite generally that in the history of human thinking the most fruitful developments frequently take place at those points where two different lines of thought meet. These lines may have their roots in quite different parts of human culture, in different times or different cultural environments or different religious traditions; hence if they actually meet, that is, if they are at least so much related to each other that a real interaction can take place, then one may hope that new and interesting developments will follow. Atomic physics as a part of modern science does actually penetrate in our time into very different cultural traditions. It is not only taught in Europe and the Western countries, where it belongs to the traditional activity in the natural sciences, but it is also studied in the Far East, in countries like Japan and China and India, with their quite different cultural background, and in Russia, where a new way of thinking has been established in our time; a new way related both to specific scientific developments of the Europe of the nineteenth century and to other entirely different traditions from Russia itself. It can certainly not be the purpose of the following discussion to make predictions about the probable result of the encounter between the ideas of modern physics and the older traditions. But it may be possible to define the points from which the interaction between the different ideas may begin.

In considering this process of expansion of modern physics it would certainly not be possible to separate it from the general expansion of natural science, of industry and engineering, of medicine, etc., that is, quite generally of modern civilization in all parts of the world. Modern physics is just one link in a long chain of events that started from the work of Bacon, Galileo and Kepler and from the practical application of natural science in the seventeenth and eighteenth centuries. The connection between natural science and technical science has from the beginning been that of mutual assistance: The progress in technical science, the improvement of the tools, the invention of new technical devices have provided the basis for more, and more accurate, empirical knowledge of nature; and the progress in the understanding of nature and finally the mathematical formulation of natural laws have opened the way to new applications of this knowledge in technical science. For instance, the invention of the telescope enabled the astronomers to measure the motion of the stars more accurately than before; thereby a considerable progress in astronomy and in mechanics was made possible. On the other hand, precise knowledge of the mechanical laws was of the greatest value for the improvement of mechanical tools, for the construction of engines, etc. The great expansion of this combination of natural and technical science started when one had succeeded in putting some of the forces of nature at the disposal of man. The energy stored up in coal, for instance, could then perform some of the work which formerly had to be done by man himself. The industries growing out of these new possibilities could first be considered as a natural continuation and expansion of the older trades; at many points the work of the machines still resembled the older handicraft and the work in the chemical factories could be considered as a continuation of the work in the dyehouses and the pharmacies of the older times. But later entirely new branches of industry developed which had no counterpart in the older trades; for instance, electrical engineering. The penetration of science into the more remote parts of nature enabled the engineers to use forces of nature which in former periods had scarcely been known; and the accurate knowledge of these forces in terms of a mathematical formulation of the laws governing them formed a solid basis for the construction of all kinds of machinery.

The enormous success of this combination of natural and technical science led to a strong preponderance of those nations or states or communities in which this kind of human activity flourished, and as a natural consequence this activity had to be taken up even by those nations which by tradition would not have been inclined toward natural and technical sciences. The modern means of communication and of traffic finally completed this process of expansion of technical civilization. Undoubtedly the process has fundamentally changed the conditions of life on our earth; and whether one approves of it or not, whether one calls it progress or danger, one must realize that it has gone far beyond any control through human forces. One may rather consider it as a biological process on the largest scale whereby the structures active in the human organism encroach on larger parts of matter and transform it into a state suited for the increasing human population.

Modern physics belongs to the most recent parts of this development, and its unfortunately most visible result, the invention of nuclear weapons, has shown the essence of this development in the sharpest possible light. On the one hand, it has demonstrated most clearly that the changes brought about by the combination of natural and technical sciences cannot be looked at only from the optimistic viewpoint; it has at least partly justified the views of those who had always warned against the dangers of such radical transmutation of our natural conditions of life. On the other hand, it has compelled even those nations or individuals who tried to keep apart from these dangers to pay the strongest attention to the new development, since obviously political power in the sense of military power rests upon the possession of atomic weapons.

It is obvious that the invention of the new weapons, especially of the thermonuclear weapons, has fundamentally changed the political structure of the world. Not only has the concept of independent nations or states undergone a decisive change, since any nation which is not in possession of such weapons must depend in some way on those very few nations that do produce these arms in large quantity; but also the attempt of warfare on a large scale by means of such weapons has become practically an absurd kind of suicide. Hence one frequently hears the optimistic view that therefore war has become obsolete, that it will not happen again. This view, unfortunately, is a much too optimistic oversimplification. On the contrary, the absurdity of warfare by means of thermonuclear weapons may, in a first approximation, act as an incentive for war on a small scale. Any nation or political group which is convinced of its historical or moral right to enforce some change of the present situation will feel that the use of conventional arms for this purpose will not involve any great risks; they will assume that the other side will certainly not have recourse to the nuclear weapons, since the other side being historically and morally wrong in this issue will not take the chance of war on a large scale. This situation would in turn induce the other nations to state that in case of small wars inflicted upon them by aggressors, they would actually have recourse to the nuclear weapons, and thus the danger obviously remains. It may quite well be that in about twenty or thirty years from now the world will have undergone so great changes that the danger of warfare on a large scale, of the application of all technical resources for the annihilation of the opponent, will have greatly diminished or disappeared. But the way to this new state will be full of the greatest dangers. We must, as in all former times, realize that what looks historically or morally right to the one side may look wrong to the other side. The continuation of the status quo may not always be the correct solution; it may, on the contrary, be most important to find peaceful means of adjustments to new situations, and it may in many cases be extremely difficult to find any just decision at all. Therefore, it is probably not too pessimistic to say that the great war can be avoided only if all the different political groups are ready to renounce some of their apparently most obvious rights—in view of the fact that the question of right or wrong may look essentially different from the other side. This is certainly not a new point of view; it is in fact only an application of that human attitude which has been taught through many centuries by some of the great religions.

It has frequently been discussed among the historians whether the rise of natural science after the sixteenth century was in any way a natural consequence of earlier trends in human thinking. It may be argued that certain trends in Christian philosophy led to a very abstract concept of God, that they put God so far above the world that one began to consider the world without at the same time also seeing God in the world. The Cartesian partition may be called a final step in this development. Or one may point out that all the theological controversies of the sixteenth century produced a general discontent about problems that could not really be settled by reason and were exposed to the political struggles of the time; that this discontent favored interest in problems which were entirely separated from the theological disputes. Or one may simply refer to the enormous activity, the new spirit that had come into the European societies through the Renaissance. In any case during this period a new authority appeared which was completely independent of Christian religion or philosophy or of the Church, the authority of experience, of the empirical fact. One may trace this authority back into older philosophical trends, for instance, into the philosophy of Occam and Duns Scotus, but it became a vital force of human activity only from the sixteenth century onward. Galileo did not only *think* about the mechanical motions, the pendulum and the falling stone; he tried out by experiments, quantitatively, how these motions took place. This new activity was in its beginning certainly not meant as a deviation from the traditional Christian religion. On the contrary, one spoke of two kinds of revelation of God. The one was written in the Bible and the other was to be found in the book of nature. The Holy Scripture had been written by man and was therefore subject to error, while nature was the immediate expression of God's intentions.

However, the emphasis on experience was connected with a slow and gradual change in the aspect of reality. While in the Middle Ages what we nowadays call the symbolic meaning of a thing was in some way its primary reality, the aspect of reality changed toward what we can perceive with our senses. What we can see and touch became primarily real. And this new concept of reality could be connected with a new activity: we can experiment and see how things really are. It was easily seen that this new attitude meant the departure of the human mind into an immense field of new possibilities, and it can be well understood that the Church saw in the new movement the dangers rather than the hopes. The famous trial of Galileo in connection with his views on the Copernican system marked the beginning of a struggle that went on for more than a century. In this controversy the representatives of natural science could argue that experience offers an undisputable truth, that it cannot be left to any human authority to decide about what really happens in nature, and that this decision is made by nature or in this sense by God. The representatives of the traditional religion, on the other hand, could argue that by paying too much attention to the material world, to what we perceive with our senses, we lose the connection with the essential values of human life, with just that part of reality which is beyond the material world. These two arguments do not meet, and therefore the problem could not be settled by any kind of agreement or decision.

In the meantime natural science proceeded to get a clearer and wider picture of the material world. In physics this picture was to be described by means of those concepts which we nowadays call the concepts of classical physics. The world consisted of things in space and time, the things consist of matter, and matter can produce and be acted upon by forces. The events follow from the interplay between matter and forces; every event is the result and the cause of other events. At the same time the human attitude toward nature changed from a contemplative one to the pragmatic one. One was not so much interested in nature as it is; one rather asked what one could do with it. Therefore, natural science turned into technical science; every advancement of knowledge was connected with the question as to what practical use could be derived from it. This was true not only in physics; in chemistry and biology the attitude was essentially the same, and the success of the new methods in medicine or in agriculture contributed essentially to the propagation of the new tendencies.

In this way, finally, the nineteenth century developed an extremely rigid frame for natural science which formed not only science but also the general outlook of great masses of people. This frame was supported by the fundamental concepts of classical physics, space, time, matter and causality; the concept of reality applied to the things or events that we could perceive by our senses or that could be observed by means of the refined tools that technical science had provided. Matter was the primary reality. The progress of science was pictured as a crusade of conquest into the material world. Utility was the watchword of the time.

On the other hand, this frame was so narrow and rigid that it was difficult to find a place in it for many concepts of our language that had always belonged to its very substance, for instance, the concepts of mind, of the human soul or of life. Mind could be introduced into the general picture only as a kind of mirror of the material world; and when one studied the properties of this mirror in the science of psychology, the scientists were always tempted—if I may carry the comparison further—to pay more attention to its mechanical than to its optical properties. Even there one tried to apply the concepts of classical physics, primarily that of causality. In the same way life was to be explained as a physical and chemical process, governed by natural laws, completely determined by causality. Darwin's concept of evolution provided ample evidence for this interpretation. It was especially difficult to find in this framework room for those parts of reality that had been the object of the traditional religion and seemed now more or less only imaginary. Therefore, in those European countries in which one was wont to follow the ideas up to their extreme consequences, an open hostility of science toward religion developed, and even in the other countries there was an increasing tendency toward indifference toward such questions; only the ethical values of the Christian religion were excepted from this trend, at least for the time being. Confidence in the scientific method and in rational thinking replaced all other safeguards of the human mind.

Coming back now to the contributions of modern physics, one may say that the most important change brought about by its results consists in the dissolution of this rigid frame of concepts of the nineteenth century. Of course many attempts had been made before to get away from this rigid frame which seemed obviously too narrow for an understanding of the essential parts of reality. But it had not been possible to see what could be wrong with the fundamental concepts like matter, space, time and causality that had been so extremely successful in the history of science. Only experimental research itself, carried out with all the refined equipment that technical science could offer, and its mathematical interpretation, provided the basis for a critical analysis—or, one may say, enforced the critical analysis—of these concepts, and finally resulted in the dissolution of the rigid frame.

This dissolution took place in two distinct stages. The first was the discovery, through the theory of relativity, that even such fundamental concepts as space and time could be changed and in fact must be changed on account of new experience. This change did not concern the somewhat vague concepts of space and time in natural language; but it did concern their precise formulation in the scientific language of Newtonian mechanics, which had erroneously been accepted as final. The second stage was the discussion of the concept of matter enforced by the experimental results concerning the atomic structure. The idea of the reality of matter had probably been the strongest part in that rigid frame of concepts of the nineteenth century, and this idea had at least to be modified in connection with the new experience. Again the concepts so far as they belonged to the natural language remained untouched. There was no difficulty in speaking about matter or about facts or about reality when one had to describe the atomic experiments and their results. But the scientific extrapolation of these concepts into the smallest parts of matter could not be done in the simple way suggested by classical physics, though it had erroneously determined the general outlook on the problem of matter.

These new results had first of all to be considered as a serious warning against the somewhat forced application of scientific concepts in domains where they did not belong. The application of the concepts of classical physics, e.g., in chemistry, had been a mistake. Therefore, one will nowadays be less inclined to assume that the concepts of physics, even those of quantum theory, can certainly be applied everywhere in biology or other sciences. We will, on the contrary, try to keep the doors open for the entrance of new concepts even in those parts of science where the older concepts have been very useful for the understanding of the phenomena. Especially at those points where the application of the older concepts seems somewhat forced or appears not quite adequate to the problem we will try to avoid any rash conclusions.

Furthermore, one of the most important features of the development and the analysis of modern physics is the experience that the concepts of natural language, vaguely defined as they are, seem to be more stable in the expansion of knowledge than the precise terms of scientific language, derived as an idealization from only limited groups of phenomena. This is in fact not surprising since the concepts of natural language are formed by the immediate connection with reality; they represent reality. It is true that they are not very well defined and many therefore also undergo changes in the course of the centuries, just as reality itself did, but they never lose the immediate connection with reality. On the other hand, the scientific concepts are idealizations; they are derived from experience obtained by refined experimental tools, and are precisely defined through axioms and definitions. Only through these precise definitions is it possible to connect the concepts with a mathematical scheme and to derive mathematically the infinite variety of possible phenomena in this field. But through this process of idealization and precise definition the immediate connection with reality is lost. The concepts still correspond very closely to reality in that part of nature which had been the object of the research. But the correspondence may be lost in other parts containing other groups of phenomena.

Keeping in mind the intrinsic stability of the concepts of natural language in the process of scientific development, one sees that—after the experience of modern physics—our attitude toward concepts like mind or the human soul or life or God will be different from that of the nineteenth century, because these concepts belong to the natural language and have therefore immediate connection with reality. It is true that we will also realize that these concepts are not well defined in the scientific sense and that their application may lead to various contradictions, for the time being we may have to take the concepts, unanalyzed as they are; but still we know that they touch reality. It may be useful in this connection to remember that even in the most precise part of science, in mathematics, we cannot avoid using concepts that involve contradictions. For instance, it is well known that the concept of infinity leads to contradictions that have been analyzed, but it would be practically impossible to construct the main parts of mathematics without this concept.

The general trend of human thinking in the nineteenth century had been toward an increasing confidence in the scientific method and in precise rational terms, and had led to a general skepticism with regard to those concepts of natural language which do not fit into the closed frame of scientific thought—for instance, those of religion. Modern physics has in many ways increased this skepticism; but it has at the same time turned it against the overestimation of precise scientific concepts, against a too-optimistic view on progress in general, and finally against skepticism itself. The skepticism against precise scientific concepts does not mean that there should be a definite limitation for the application of rational thinking. On the contrary, one may say that the human ability to understand may be in a certain sense unlimited. But the existing scientific concepts cover always only a very limited part of reality, and the other part that has not yet been understood is infinite. Whenever we proceed from the known into the unknown we may hope to understand, but we may have to learn at the same time a new meaning of the word "understanding." We know that any understanding must be based finally upon the natural language because it is only there that we can be certain to touch reality, and hence we must be skeptical about any skepticism with regard to this natural language and its essential concepts. Therefore, we may use these concepts as they have been used at all times. In this way modern physics has perhaps opened the door to a wider outlook on the relation between the human mind and reality.

This modern science, then, penetrates in our time into other parts of the world where the cultural tradition has been entirely different from the European civilization. There the impact of this new activity in natural and technical science must make itself felt even more strongly than in Europe, since changes in the conditions of life that have taken two or three centuries in Europe will take place there within a few decades. One should expect that in many places this new activity must appear as a decline of the older culture, as a ruthless and barbarian attitude, that upsets the sensitive balance on which all human happiness rests. Such consequences cannot be avoided; they must be taken as one aspect of our time. But even there the openness of modern physics may help to some extent to reconcile the older traditions with the new trends of thought. For instance, the great scientific contribution in theoretical physics that has come from Japan since the last war may be an indication for a certain relationship between philosophical ideas in the tradition of the Far East and the philosophical substance of quantum theory. It may be easier to adapt oneself to the quantum-theoretical concept of reality when one has not gone through the naïve materialistic way of thinking that still prevailed in Europe in the first decades of this century.

Of course such remarks should not be misunderstood as an underestimation of the damage that may be done or has been done to old cultural traditions by the impact of technical progress. But since this whole development has for a long time passed far beyond any control by human forces, we have to accept it as one of the most essential features of our time and must try to connect it as much as possible with the human values that have been the aim of the older cultural and religious traditions. It may be allowed at this point to quote a story from the Hasidic religion: There was an old rabbi, a priest famous for his wisdom, to whom all people came for advice. A man visited him in despair over all the changes that went on around him, deploring all the harm done by so-called technical progress. "Isn't all this technical nuisance completely worthless," he exclaimed, "if one considers the real values of life?" "This may be so," the rabbi replied, "but if one has the right attitude one can learn from everything." "No," the visitor rejoined, "from such foolish things as railway or telephone or telegraph one can learn nothing whatsoever." But the rabbi answered, "You are wrong. From the railway you can learn that you may by being one instant late miss everything. From the telegraph you can learn that every word counts. And from the telephone you can learn that what we say here can be heard there." The visitor understood what the rabbi meant and went away.

Finally, modern science penetrates into those large areas of our present world in which new doctrines were established only a few decades ago as foundations for new and powerful societies. There modern science is confronted both with the content of the doctrines, which go back to European philosophical ideas of the nineteenth century (Hegel and Marx), and with the phenomenon of uncompromising belief. Since modern physics must play a great role in these countries because of its practical applicability, it can scarcely be avoided that the narrowness of the doctrines is felt by those who have really understood modern physics and its philosophical meaning. Therefore, at this point an interaction between science and the general trend of thought may take place. Of course the influence of science should not be overrated; but it might be that the openness of modern science could make it easier even for larger groups of people to see that the doctrines are possibly not so important for the society as had been assumed before. In this way the influence of modern science may favor an attitude of tolerance and thereby may prove valuable.

On the other hand, the phenomenon of uncompromising belief carries much more weight than some special philosophical notions of the nineteenth century. We cannot close our eyes to the fact that the great majority of the people can scarcely have any well-founded judgment concerning the correctness of certain important general ideas or doctrines. Therefore, the word "belief" can for this majority not mean "perceiving the truth of something" but can only be understood as "taking this as the basis for life." One can easily understand that this second kind of belief is much firmer, is much more fixed than the first one, that it can persist even against immediate contradicting experience and can therefore not be shaken by added scientific knowledge. The history of the past two decades has shown by many examples that this second kind of belief can sometimes be upheld to a point where it seems completely absurd, and that it then ends only with the death of the believer. Science and history can teach us that this kind of belief may become a great danger for those who share it. But such knowledge is of no avail, since one cannot see how it could be avoided, and therefore such belief has always belonged to the great forces in human history. From the scientific tradition of the nineteenth century one would of course be inclined to hope that all belief should be based on a rational analysis of every argument, on careful deliberation; and that this other kind of belief, in which some real or apparent truth is simply taken as the basis for life, should not exist. It is true that cautious deliberation based on purely rational arguments can save us from many errors and dangers, since it allows readjustment to new situations, and this may be a necessary condition for life. But remembering our experience in modern physics it is easy to see that there must always be a fundamental complementarity between deliberation and decision. In the practical decisions of life it will scarcely ever be possible to go through all the arguments in favor of or against one possible decision, and one will therefore always have to act on insufficient evidence. The decision finally takes place by pushing away all the arguments—both those that have been understood and others that might come up through further deliberation—and by cutting off all further pondering. The decision may be the result of deliberation, but it is at the same time complementary to deliberation; it excludes deliberation. Even the most important decisions in life must always contain this inevitable element of irrationality. The decision itself is necessary, since there must be something to rely upon, some principle to guide our actions. Without such a firm stand our own actions would lose all force. Therefore, it cannot be avoided that some real or apparent truth forms the basis of life; and this fact should be acknowledged with regard to those groups of people whose basis is different from our own.

Coming now to a conclusion from all that has been said about modern science, one may perhaps state that modern physics is just one, but a very characteristic, part of a general historical process that tends toward a unification and a widening of our present world. This process would in itself lead to a diminution of those cultural and political tensions that create the great danger of our time. But it is accompanied by another process which acts in the opposite direction. The fact that great masses of people become conscious of this process of unification leads to an instigation of all forces in the existing cultural communities that try to ensure for their traditional values the largest possible role in the final state of unification. Thereby the tensions increase and the two competing processes are so closely linked with each other that every intensification of the unifying process—for instance, by means of new technical progress—intensifies also the struggle for influence in the final state, and thereby adds to the instability of the transient state. Modern physics plays perhaps only a small role in this dangerous process of unification. But it helps at two very decisive points to guide the development into a calmer kind of evolution. First, it shows that the use of arms in the process would be disastrous and, second, through its openness for all kinds of concepts it raises the hope that in the final state of unification many different cultural traditions may live together and may combine different human endeavors into a new kind of balance between thought and deed, between activity and meditation.

Suggestions for Discussion and Writing

1. In the first paragraph of his essay, Heisenberg claims that "in the history of human thinking the most fruitful developments frequently take place at those points where two different lines of thought meet." What "two lines of thought" is the author concerned with in this essay? What, for Heisenberg, are the broader social and political implications of their meeting?

2. In the opening pages of his essay, Heisenberg speaks of the relationship between science and technology. What is the nature of this relationship? What does Heisenberg mean when he says that "one must realize that [the expansion of technical civilization] has gone far beyond any control through human forces"?

3. In a brief essay, summarize Heisenberg's assessment of the significance of the development of nuclear weapons.

4. How, for Heisenberg, did the "aspect of reality" change in the sixteenth century? What was the "new authority"?

5. How does Heisenberg characterize the nineteenth-century view of science? Why, according to him, was this view inadequate?

6. Heisenberg argues that the nineteenth century's frame of concepts was dissolved in "two distinct stages." What were those two stages? In what way did the "experience of modern physics" allow the return of previously excluded "concepts like mind or the human soul or life or God"? Would you agree that, in some sense, Heisenberg overturns the traditional notion that the language of science cannot accommodate such concepts?

7. In what ways are the "doctrines" of "new and powerful societies" (derived from Hegel and Marx) confronted by the "philo-

sophical meaning" of modern physics? What is the nature of this confrontation?

8. Why might Japanese culture (and other cultures of the Far East) be more attuned to the "philosophical substance of quantum theory"?

9. In the final paragraph of his essay, Heisenberg gives his argument a more global dimension. He speaks of a general evolution toward world unification but is keenly aware of the forces competing against such a process. What are these forces? Why do they pose a danger? In light of recent geopolitical developments, can Heisenberg's essay (published in 1958) be considered prophetic? Write an essay developing your views.

GENETIC ENGINEERING: LIFE AS A PLAYTHING

Robert L. Sinsheimer
(b. 1920)

Robert Sinsheimer received his Ph.D. in biophysics from the Massachusetts Institute of Technology and has taught at several universities, including the California Institute of Technology, where he was a professor of physics, and the University of California, Santa Barbara, where he is currently a professor of biology. From 1977 to 1987 he served as Chancellor at the University of California, Santa Cruz. He is a member of both the National Academy of Science and the American Academy of Arts and Sciences. Sinsheimer's work has focused on the physical and chemical properties of nucleic acids, the replication of nucleic acids, and bacterial viruses. In the following essay, published in *Technology Review* (1983), he discusses some of the momentous moral and scientific issues raised by advances in genetic engineering.

In a process almost as old as the earth, a huge panoply of organisms has evolved. The process has been one of chance and selection, and the star player has been the gene. For 3 billion years, natural changes in the number, structure, and organization of genes have determined the course of evolution.

We have now come to the end of that familiar pathway. Genetics—the science of heredity—has unlocked the code book of life, and the long-hidden strategies of evolution are revealing themselves. We now possess the ability to manipulate genes, and we can direct the future course of evolution. We can reassemble old genes and devise new ones. We can plan, and with computer simulation ultimately anticipate, the future forms and paths of life. Mutation and natural selection will continue, of course. But henceforth, the old ways of evolution will be dwarfed by the role of purposeful human intelligence. In the hands of the genetic engineer, life forms could become extraordinary Tinkertoys and life itself just another design problem.

Genetic engineering is a whole new technology. To view it as merely another technological development may make sense for those who invest in its commercial exploitation. But such a view is myopic for anyone concerned with the future of humanity. I want to consider three major areas of concern that will surely arise from this new technology. The first is the transformation of the science of biology itself. The development of molecular genetics is a transition as profound for biology as the development of quantum theory was for physics and chemistry. Until recently, biology was essentially an analytical science, in which researchers undertook the dissection of nature as observed. Genetic engineering now furnishes us with the ability to design and invent living organisms as well as to observe and analyze their function. If we consider the significance of synthesis to the science of chemistry, we can perhaps envision the importance of this development for the science of biology.

A NEW BIOLOGY

The new techniques open the door to a detailed understanding of the form and organization of genetic structures in higher organisms, of the control of gene expression, and of the processes of cellular differentiation. Out of such knowledge will come a new biology that gives us the means to intervene in life processes at the most basic possible level.

The impact of this new biology on the practical and technical arts—the second area of development—will be profound. With this technology, human ingenuity could design agricultural crops that thrive in arid zones or brackish waters, that provide better human nutrition, that resist disease and pests. Human-designed crops, adapted to the needs of efficient agricultural technology, could leap ahead of their natural parasites and predators.

In chemistry, microorganisms could be programmed to carry out the complex organic synthesis of new pharmaceuticals, pesticides, and chemical catalysts. Other organisms could be programmed to degrade chemical compounds and reduce environmental pollution. In animal husbandry, the prospects seem equally bright for designing disease-resistant, fast-growing, nutritious animal forms. In medicine, we envision the synthesis of antibiotics, hormones, vaccines, and other complex pharmaceuticals. But these achievements, almost certainly feasible, will pale before the potential latent in the deeper understanding of biology.

Control over gene expression will provide a whole new array of therapies for genetic disorders. And that introduces the third domain of consequence and the most profound. With the decline of infectious diseases, genetic disorders are now increasingly the source of ill health. Diabetes, cystic fibrosis, sickle-cell anemia, and Tay-Sachs disease all stem from well-recognized genetic defects. The possibilities of human gene therapy—replacing the "bad" gene with the "good"—are extraordinary.

THE DARKER SIDE

It is not hard to sense the excitement, the challenge, the promise in all these ventures. But is there a catch? Is there a darker side to this vision as we have come to see in other new technologies? Some of us believe there may be—that life is not just another design problem, that life is different from nonlife. Just as nature stumbled upon life some three billion years ago and unwittingly began the whole pageant of evolution, so too the new creators may find that living organisms have a destiny of their own. They may find that genetic engineering has consequences far beyond those of conventional engineering.

As we become increasingly confident that this technology can, in fact, be achieved, there are a few major questions to be asked: Is it safe, is it wise, is it moral?

First, is it safe? If we can keep the developments open to public scrutiny, then I believe in the short term it probably is. We can monitor the hazards of any new product we introduce into the biosphere and can probably cope with any immediate, untoward consequence.

For the long term, however, I am considerably less sure. Life has evolved on this planet into a delicately balanced, intricate, self-sustaining network. Maintaining this network involves many interactions and equilibria that we understand only dimly. I would suggest that we must take great care, as we replace the creatures and vegetation of earth with human-designed forms, as we reshape the animate world to conform to human will, that we not forget our origins and inadvertently collapse the ecological system in which we have found our niche.

Through intensive study, we have learned of the different pathogens that prey on humans, animals, and major crops. But we have a very limited understanding of the evolutionary factors that led to their existence. We have limited knowledge about the reservoir of potential pathogens—organisms that could be converted by one or two or five mutations from harmless bugs into serious menaces. And thus we cannot really predict whether our genetic tinkering might unwittingly lead to novel and unexpected hazards.

More broadly, is it wise for us to assume responsibility for the structure and cohesion of the animate world? Do we want to engineer the planet so that its function requires the continuous input of human intelligence? Do we want to convert Earth into a giant Skylab? What happens to the reverence for life when life is our creation, our plaything? Will we have species with planned obsolescence? Will we have genetic olympics for homing pigeons or racing dogs? Will we have a zoo of reconstructed vanished species—dinosaurs or sabre-toothed tigers—or as-yet unimaginable species? Genetic engineering will inevitably change our sense of kinship with all our fellow creatures.

Will the extinction of species mean much when we can create new ones at will? Until now, we have all been the children of nature, the progeny of evolution. But from now on the flora and fauna of Earth will increasingly be our creations, our designs, and thus our responsibility. What will happen to our nature in such a world?

The most profound consequence of this technology is its application to humankind. The impetus to employ genetic engineering on the human race will come, I believe, out of our humanitarian tradition. Genetic engineering will be seen as just another branch of surgery, albeit at the most delicate level. Since we now know that many sources of human misery are genetic in origin, the urge to remedy these defects and even eliminate their transmission to succeeding generations will be irresistible. Thus, these changes will become part of the human genetic inheritance—for better or worse.

Having acquired the technology to provide genetic therapy, will we then be able to draw a line and restrict human genetic experimentation? How will we define a "defect"? And how will we argue against genetic "improvement"? Or should we? Will we even stop to consider the morality of what's being done?

The extent to which our more specifically human qualities—our emotions and intellects, our compassion and conscience—are genetically determined is not yet known. But geneticists cannot escape the dark suspicion that more is written in our genes than we like to think.

What will happen if we tamper with our physical or mental traits, given the complexity of human development and behavior? Such banal qualities as height or weight can surely affect one's identity, and good health has its own concomitants. How many of our greatest artistic works have been produced by the afflicted or the neurotic?

I suspect human genetic engineering is repugnant to many people because they think its purpose is to impose an identity upon a descendant, to replace the sport of Nature with models of human fancy.

In some sense, education is an attempt to impose an identity. An educational system demands adherence to values of attention, concentration, delayed gratification, and so on. Mere literacy, while enlarging freedom by opening new worlds of knowledge, destroys the freedom of innocence. Yet clearly we have long decided that the virtues of literacy outweigh any drawbacks. Universal literacy is regarded as good and mandated in most societies. Might there be similar genetic characteristics that we would come to regard as a universal good?

Cloning can be seen as an extreme effort to impose a particular identity—a particular character—upon a descendant. But all human genetic engineering will move us toward that extreme.

GENETIC LOTTERY

Genetic engineering is the ultimate technology, for it makes plastic the very user and creator of that technology. This new tool makes conceivable a vast number of alternative evolutionary paths. We may even be able to adapt humankind to varied technological regimes.

Will we try, for instance, to breed—or mutate—people fit to work in special environments? Miniature people to travel in space or live on our overpopulated Earth? Will we create people resistant to carcinogens, radiation, and pesticides to work in chemical factories, nuclear plants, and farms? Or, alternatively, will we breed people who are better able to tolerate cytotoxic drugs should they contract cancer? What intellectual abilities, psychological strengths and life-spans would we choose?

I hope it is clear that the whole character of human life is at issue. To use a simile: Life has been a game, like cards, where each of us seeks to make the best of the hands (or genes) dealt to us. Shall it become a game like football, a collective strategy in which people play assigned roles in a coordinated plan? Or might it become more like a card game with a rigged deck, with more aces and fewer treys? If so, who designates the aces?

How will people react when they realize that their very genes are the product of a social decision? Will they rebel against such pre-destination? Will they become sullen and passive? Or will our descendants be proud they were each "planned," not the product of a genetic lottery but the recipient of the best inheritance our culture could devise at the time? How will they then react should a better model become available during their teens?

To what extent should we consciously leave a place for the element of chance in human affairs?

I suspect there is no turning back from the use of this awesome knowledge. Given the nature of our society, which embraces and applies any new technology, it appears that there is no means, short of unwanted catastrophe, to prevent the development of genetic engineering. It will proceed. But this time, perhaps we can seek to anticipate and guide its consequences.

TAKING THE LARGER VIEW

I believe the university is the place to address and analyze the social consequences of technological innovation. Yet even in academia, pressures for immediate results distract researchers from the quest for deeper understanding. Indeed, a salient characteristic of our increasingly secular society is its emphasis on the short-term payoff. We must try to avoid this myopia in developing this new technology. We must seek to protect the larger view.

Among other things, we must insist that university research continue to be available for public scrutiny in the open scientific literature, that it not be secreted as proprietary information and industrial know-how. We must also insist that private funding directed toward patentable and profitable inventions does not grossly exceed public funding directed toward the general increase of knowledge, including an understanding of possible hazards.

I would suggest that what we sorely need now is a new group of trained professionals to mediate between scientists and engineers on the one hand and citizenry on the other. Such professionals should be practicing scientists more broadly educated in our humanistic traditions. They would be trained to understand the potential implicit in this new technology, able to balance the ethos of environmentalists with the concerns of those who cherish civil liberty, able to perceive the imperatives of a technological society and still bear in mind that technology exists to serve. They would remember that the human species is very diverse, that it encompasses both a Mahatma Gandhi and an Adolf Hitler.

Eccelesiastes tells us that "he that increaseth knowledge increaseth sorrow." The modern version might be "he that increaseth knowledge increaseth power." Western society has become, in a sense, an extraordinary machine for converting knowledge into power.

Human beings, of course, are sprung from the same DNA and built of the same molecules as all other living things. But if we begin to regard ourselves as just another crop to be engineered, just another breed to be perfected, we will lose our awe of humanity and undermine all sense of human dignity.

Suggestions for Discussion and Writing

1. What distinction is Sinsheimer making in the third paragraph when he says that genetic engineering is a "whole new technology" rather than "merely another technological development"?

2. How, according to the author, will the new biology differ from the old?

3. How would you characterize the author's attitude toward the new technology of genetic engineering? Cite specific examples of his language to support your view.

4. What rhetorical techniques (understatement, exaggeration, etc.) does the author use to make his case that the new technology has a "darker side"?

5. Why, according to Sinsheimer, will genetic engineering "inevitably change our sense of kinship with our fellow creatures"? Would you agree with his implicit claim that we indeed have a sense of kinship with "our fellow creatures"? Write an essay developing your views.

6. Sinsheimer suspects that "there is no turning back from the use of this awesome knowledge." In what sense is the new knowledge "awesome"? Do the physical sciences offer any parallels to recent developments in biology?

7. Does Sinsheimer support his view that "the old ways of evolution will be dwarfed by the role of purposeful human intelligence"?

8. What, according to the author, is "the larger view" that must be protected?

CHAPTER 2

Science and Community

THE SCIENCES AND MAN'S COMMUNITY

J. Robert Oppenheimer (1904–1967)

Following the publication of his first paper in 1926, J. Robert Oppenheimer quickly earned a reputation as one of the most gifted theoretical physicists of his generation. A native of New York City, he studied at Harvard, Cambridge, and Göttingen and went on to teach at the University of California, Berkeley, and the California Institute of Technology.

Despite his brilliant contributions to the analytical applications of quantum mechanics, Oppenheimer will always be best known as the leader of the Manhattan Project, an enterprise whose success was realized at Alamogordo, New Mexico, on July 16, 1945, with the detonation of the first atomic bomb. For Oppenheimer and many of his colleagues the success of Alamogordo raised profoundly troubling moral questions. Oppenheimer himself became an outspoken opponent of thermonuclear weapons on both moral and scientific grounds, and in the early 1950s came under attack by a federal government caught up in the hysteria of McCarthyism. In 1953, even though his loyalty as a citizen was acknowledged, the Atomic Energy Commission suspended him from his advisory position and revoked his security clearance. Ten years later, in an effort to make amends for its earlier action, the same commission bestowed on Oppenheimer the Enrico Fermi Award.

The following selection, originally delivered as a lecture in 1953, reflects Oppenheimer's deep concerns about the relation between science and society. He suggests that one of the fundamental postulates of modern physics, the notion of complementarity (that is, the recognition that a single event can be described in mutually exclusive but equally valid ways), can be extended to help us better understand the need for tolerance within the human community.

We have looked together into one of the rooms of the house called "science." This is a relatively quiet room that we know as quantum theory or atomic theory. The great girders which frame it, the lights and shadows and vast windows—these were the work of a generation our predecessor more than two decades ago. It is not wholly quiet. Young people visit it and study in it and pass on to other chambers; and from time to time someone rearranges a piece of the furniture to make the whole more harmonious; and many, as we have done, peer through its windows or walk through it as sight-seers. It is not so old but that one can hear the sound of the new wings being built nearby, where men walk high in the air to erect new scaffoldings, not unconscious of how far they may fall. All about there are busy workshops where the builders are active, and very near indeed are those of us who, learning more of the primordial structure of matter, hope some day for chambers as fair and lovely as that in which we have spent the years of our youth and our prime.

It is a vast house indeed. It does not appear to have been built upon any plan but to have grown as a great city grows. There is no central chamber, no one corridor from which all others debouch. All about the periphery men are at work studying the vast reaches of space and the state of affairs billions of years ago; studying the intricate and subtle but wonderfully meet mechanisms by which life proliferates, alters, and endures; studying the reach of the mind and its ways of learning; digging deep into the atoms and the atoms within atoms and their unfathomed order. It is a house so vast that none of us know it, and even the most fortunate have seen most rooms only from the outside or by a fleeting passage, as in a king's palace open to visitors. It is a house so vast that there is not and need not be complete concurrence on where its chambers stop and those of the neighboring mansions begin.

It is not arranged in a line nor a square nor a circle nor a pyramid, but with a wonderful randomness suggestive of unending growth and improvisation. Not many people live in the house, relatively speaking—perhaps if we count all its chambers and take residence requirements quite lightly, one tenth of one percent, of all the people in this world—probably, by any reasonable definition, far fewer. And even those who live here live elsewhere also, live in houses where the rooms are not labelled atomic theory or genetics or the internal constitution of the stars, but quite different names like power and production and evil and beauty and history and children and the word of God.

We go in and out; even the most assiduous of us is not bound to this vast structure. One thing we find throughout the house: there are no locks; there are no shut doors; wherever we go there are the signs and usually the words of welcome. It is an open house, open to all comers.

The discoveries of science, the new rooms in this great house, have changed the way men think of things outside its walls. We have some glimmering now of the depth in time and the vastness in space of the physical world we live in. An awareness of how long our history and how immense our cosmos touches us even in simple earthly deliberations. We have learned from the natural history of the earth and from the story of evolution to have a sense of history, of time and change. We learn to talk of ourselves, and of the nature of the world and its reality as not wholly fixed in a silent quiet moment, but as unfolding with novelty and alteration, decay and new growth. We have understood something of the inner harmony and beauty of strange primitive cultures, and through this see the qualities of our own life in an altered perspective, and recognize its accidents as well as its inherent necessities. We are, I should think, not patriots less but patriots very differently for loving what is ours and understanding a little of the love of others for their lands and ways. We have begun to understand that it is not only in his rational life that man's psyche is intelligible, that even in what may appear to be his least rational actions and sentiments we may discover a new order. We have the beginnings of an understanding of what it is in man, and more in simple organisms, that is truly heritable, and rudimentary clues as to how the inheritance occurs. We know, in surprising detail, what is the physical counterpart of the act of vision and of other modes of perception. Not one of these new ideas and new insights is so little, or has so short a reach in its bearing on the common understanding but that it alone could make a proper theme for "Science and the Common Understanding." Yet we have been, bearing in mind my limited area of experience, in that one room of the part of the house where physics is, in which I have for some years worked and taught.

In that one room—in that relatively quiet room where we have been together—we have found things quite strange for those who have not been there before, yet reminiscent of what we have seen in other houses and known in other days. We have seen that in the atomic world we have been led by experience to use descriptions and ideas that apply to the large-scale world of matter, to the familiar world of our schoolday physics; ideas like the position of a body and its acceleration and its impulse and the forces acting on it; ideas like wave and interference; ideas like cause and probability. But what is new, what was not anticipated a half-century ago, is that, though to an atomic system there is a potential applicability of one or another of these ideas, in any real situation only some of these ways of description can be actual. This is because we need to take into account not merely the atomic system we are studying, but the means we use in observing it, and the fitness of these experimental means for defining and measuring selected properties of the system. All such ways of observing are needed for the whole experience of the atomic world; all but one are excluded in any actual experience. In the specific instance, there is a proper and consistent way to describe what the experience is; what it implies; what it predicts and thus how to deal with its consequences. But any such specific instance excludes by its existence the application of other ideas, other modes of prediction, other consequences. They are, we say, complementary to one another; atomic theory is in part an account of these descriptions and in part an understanding of the circumstances to which one applies, or another or another.

And so it is with man's life. He may be any of a number of things; he will not be all of them. He may be well versed, he may be a poet, he may be a creator in one or more than one science; he will not be all kinds of man or all kinds of scientist; and he will be lucky if he has a bit of familiarity outside the room in which he works.

So it is with the great antinomies that through the ages have organized and yet disunited man's experience: the antinomy between the ceaseless change and wonderful novelty and the perishing of all earthly things, and the eternity which inheres in every happening; in the antinomy between growth and order, between the spontaneous and changing and irregular and the symmetrical and balanced; in the related antinomy between freedom and necessity; between action, the life of the will, and observation and analysis and the life of reason; between the question "how?" and the questions "why?" and "to what end?"; between the causes that derive from natural law, from unvarying regularities in the natural world, and those other causes that express purposes and define goals and ends.

So it is in the antinomy between the individual and the community; man who is an end in himself and man whose tradition, whose culture, whose works, whose words have meaning in terms of other men and his relations to them. All our experience has shown that we can neither think, nor in any true sense live, without reference to these antinomic modes. We cannot in any sense be both the observers and the actors in any specific instance, or we shall fail properly to be either one or the other; yet we know that our life is built of these two modes, is part free and part inevitable, is part creation and part discipline, is part acceptance and part effort. We have no written rules that assign us to these ways; but we know that only folly and death of the spirit results when we deny one or the other, when we erect one as total and absolute and make the others derivative and secondary. We recognize this when we live as men. We talk to one another; we philosophize; we admire great men and their moments of greatness; we read; we study; we recognize and love in a particular act that happy union of the generally incompatible. With all of this we learn to use some reasonable part of the full register of man's resources.

We are, of course, an ignorant lot; even the best of us knows how to do only a very few things well; and of what is available in knowledge of fact, whether of science or of history, only the smallest part is in any one man's knowing.

The greatest of changes that science has brought is the acuity of change; the greatest novelty the extent of novelty. Short of rare times of great disaster, civilizations have not known such rapid alteration in the conditions of their life, such rapid flowering of many varied sciences, such rapid changes in the ideas we have about the world and one another. What has been true in the days of a great disaster or great military defeat for one people at one time is true for all of us now, in the sense that our ends have little in common with our beginnings. Within a lifetime what we learned at school has been rendered inadequate by new discoveries and new inventions; the ways that we learn in childhood are only very meagerly adequate to the issues that we must meet in maturity.

In fact, of course, the notion of universal knowledge has always been an illusion; but it is an illusion fostered by the monistic view of the world in which a few great central truths determine in all its wonderful and amazing proliferation everything else that is true. We are not today tempted to search for these keys that unlock the whole of human knowledge and of man's experience. We know that we are ignorant; we are well taught it, and the more surely and deeply we know our own job the better able we are to appreciate the full measure of our pervasive ignorance. We know that these are inherent limits, compounded, no doubt, and exaggerated by that sloth and that complacency without which we would not be men at all.

But knowledge rests on knowledge; what is new is meaningful because it departs slightly from what was known before; this is a world of frontiers, where even the liveliest of actors or observers will be absent most of the time from most of them. Perhaps this sense was not so sharp in the village—that village which we have learned a little about but probably do not understand too well—the village of slow change and isolation and fixed culture which evokes our nostalgia even if not our full comprehension. Perhaps in the villages men were not so lonely; perhaps they found in each other a fixed community, a fixed and only slowly growing store of knowledge—a single world. Even that we may doubt, for there seem to be always in the culture of such times and places vast domains of mystery, if not unknowable, then imperfectly known, endless and open.

As for ourselves in these times of change, of ever-increasing knowledge, of collective power and individual impotence, of heroism and of drudgery, of progress and of tragedy, we too are brothers. And if we, who are the inheritors of two millennia of Christian tradition, understand that for us we have come to be brothers second by being children first, we know that in vast parts of the world where there has been no Christian tradition, and with men who never have been and never may be Christian in faith there is nevertheless a bond of brotherhood. We know this not only because of the almost universal ideal of human brotherhood and human community; we know it at first hand from the more modest, more diverse, more fleeting associations which are the substance of our life. The ideal of brotherhood, the ideal of fraternity in which all men, wicked and virtuous, wretched and fortunate, are banded together has its counterpart in the experience of communities, not ideal, not universal, imperfect, impermanent, as different from the ideal and as reminiscent of it as are the ramified branches of science from the ideal of a unitary, all-encompassing science of the eighteenth century.

Each of us knows from his own life how much even a casual and limited association of men goes beyond him in knowledge, in understanding, in humanity, and in power. Each of us, from a friend or a book or by concerting of the little we know with what others know, has broken the iron circle of his frustration. Each of us has asked help and been given it, and within our measure each of us has offered it. Each of us knows the great new freedom sensed almost as a miracle, that men banded together for some finite purpose experience from the power of their common effort. We are likely to remember the times of the last war, where the common danger brought forth in soldier, in worker, in scientist, and engineer a host of new experiences of the power and the comfort in even bleak undertakings, of common, concerted, co-operative life. Each of us knows how much he has been transcended by the group of which he has been or is a part; each of us has felt the solace of other men's knowledge to stay his own ignorance, of other men's wisdom to stay his folly, of other men's courage to answer his doubts or his weakness.

These are the fluid communities, some of long duration when circumstances favored—like the political party or many a trade union—some fleeting and vivid, encompassing in the time of their duration a moment only of the member's life; and in our world at least they are ramified and improvised, living and dying, growing and falling off almost as a form of life itself. This may be more true of the United States than of any other country. Certainly the bizarre and comical aspects impressed de Tocqueville more than a century ago when he visited our land and commented on the readiness with which men would band together: to improve the planting of a town, or for political reform, or for the pursuit or inter-exchange of knowledge, or just for the sake of banding together, because they liked one another or disliked someone else. Circumstances may have exaggerated the role of the societies, of the fluid and yet intense communities in the United States; yet these form a common pattern for our civilization. It brought men together in the Royal Society and in the French Academy and in the Philosophical Society that Franklin founded, in family, in platoon, on a ship, in the laboratory, in almost everything but a really proper club.

If we err today—and I think we do—it is in expecting too much of knowledge from the individual and too much of synthesis from the community. We tend to think of these communities, no less than of the larger brotherhood of man, as made up of individuals, as composed of them as an atom is of its ingredients. We think similarly of general laws and broad ideas as made up of the instances which illustrate them, and from an observation of which we may have learned them.

Yet this is not the whole. The individual event, the act, goes far beyond the general law. It is a sort of intersection of many generalities, harmonizing them in one instance as they cannot be harmonized in general. And we as men are not only the ingredients of our communities; we are their intersection, making a harmony which does not exist between the communities except as we, the individual men, may create it and reveal it. So much of what we think, our acts, our judgments of beauty and of right and wrong, come to us from our fellow men that what would be left were we to take all this away would be neither recognizable nor human. We are men because we are part of, but not because only part of, communities; and the attempt to understand man's brotherhood in terms only of the individual man is as little likely to describe our world as is the attempt to describe general laws as the summary of their instances. These are indeed two complementary views, neither reducible to the other, no more reducible than is the electron as wave to the electron as particle.

And this is the mitigant of our ignorance. It is true that none of us will know very much; and most of us will see the end of our days without understanding in all its detail and beauty the wonders uncovered even in a single branch of a single science. Most of us will not even know, as a member of any intimate circle, anyone who has such knowledge; but it is also true that, although we are sure not to know everything and rather likely not to know very much, we can know anything that is known to man, and may, with luck and sweat, even find out some things that have not before been known to him. This possibility, which, as a universal condition of man's life is new, represents today a high and determined hope, not yet a reality; it is for us in England and in the United States not wholly remote or unfamiliar. It is one of the manifestations of our belief in equality, that belief which could perhaps better be described as a commitment to unparalleled diversity and unevenness in the distribution of attainments, knowledge, talent, and power.

This open access to knowledge, these unlocked doors and signs of welcome, are a mark of a freedom as fundamental as any. They give a freedom to resolve difference by converse, and, where converse does not unite, to let tolerance compose diversity. This would appear to be a freedom barely compatible with modern political tyranny. The multitude of communities, the free association for converse or for common purpose, are acts of creation. It is not merely that without them the individual is the poorer; without them a part of human life, not more nor less fundamental than the individual, is foreclosed. It is a cruel and humorless sort of pun that so powerful a present form of modern tyranny should call itself by the very name of a belief in community, by a word "communism" which in other times evoked memories of villages and village inns and of artisans concerting their skills, and of men of learning content with anonymity. But perhaps only a malignant end can follow the systematic belief that all communities are one community; that all truth is one truth; that all experience is compatible with all other; that total knowledge is possible; that all that is potential can exist as actual. This is not man's fate; this is not his path; to force him on it makes him resemble not that divine image of the all-knowing and all-powerful but the helpless, iron-bound prisoner of a dying world. The open society, the unrestricted access to knowledge, the unplanned and uninhibited association of men for its furtherance—these are what may make a vast, complex, ever-growing, ever-changing, ever more specialized and expert technological world nevertheless a world of human community.

So it is with the unity of science—that unity that is far more a unity of comparable dedication than a unity of common total understanding. This heartening phrase, "the unity of science," often tends to evoke a wholly false picture, a picture of a few basic truths, a few critical techniques, methods, and ideas, from which all discoveries and understanding of science derive; a sort of central exchange, access to which will illuminate the atoms and the galaxies, the genes and the sense organs. The unity of science is based rather on just such a community as I have described. All parts of it are open to all of us, and this is no merely formal invitation. The history of science is rich in example of the fruitfulness of bringing two sets of techniques, two sets of ideas, developed in separate contexts for the pursuit of new truth, into touch with one another. The sciences fertilize each other; they grow by contact and by common enterprise. Once again, this means that the scientist may profit from learning about any other science; it does not mean that he must learn about them all. It means that the unity is a potential unity, the unity of the things that might be brought together and might throw light one on the other. It is not global or total or hierarchical.

Even in science, and even without visiting the room in its house called atomic theory, we are again and again reminded of the complementary traits in our own life, even in our own professional life. We are nothing without the work of others our predecessors, others our teachers, others our contemporaries. Even when, in the measure of our adequacy and our fullness, new insight and new order are created, we are still nothing without others. Yet we are more.

There is a similar duality in our relations to wider society. For society our work means many things: pleasure, we hope, for those who follow it; instruction for those who perhaps need it; but also and far more widely, it means a common power, a power to achieve that which could not be achieved without knowledge. It means the cure of illness and the alleviation of suffering; it means the easing of labor and the widening of the readily accessible frontiers of experience, of communication, and of instruction. It means, in an earthy way, the power of betterment—that riddled word. We are today anxiously aware that the power to change is not always necessarily good.

As new instruments of war, of newly massive terror, add to the ferocity and totality of warfare, we understand that it is a special mark and problem of our age that man's ever-present preoccupation with improving his lot, with alleviating hunger and poverty and exploitation, must be brought into harmony with the over-riding need to limit and largely to eliminate resort to organized violence between nation and nation. The increasingly expert destruction of man's spirit by the power of police, more wicked if not more awful than the ravages of nature's own hand, is another such power, good only if never to be used.

We regard it as proper and just that the patronage of science by society is in large measure based on the increased power which knowledge gives. If we are anxious that the power so given and so obtained be used with wisdom and with love of humanity, that is an anxiety we share with almost everyone. But we also know how little of the deep new knowledge which has altered the face of the world, which has changed—and increasingly and ever more profoundly must change—man's views of the world, resulted from a quest for practical ends or an interest in exercising the power that knowledge gives. For most of us, in most of those moments when we were most free of corruption, it has been the beauty of the world of nature and the strange and compelling harmony of its order, that has sustained, inspirited, and led us. That also is as it should be. And if the forms in which society provides and exercises its patronage leave these incentives strong and secure, new knowledge will never stop as long as there are men.

We know that our work is rightly both an instrument and an end. A great discovery is a thing of beauty; and our faith—our binding, quiet faith—is that knowledge is good and good in itself. It is also an instrument; it is an instrument for our successors, who will use it to probe elsewhere and more deeply; it is an instrument for technology, for the practical arts, and for man's affairs. So it is with us as scientists; so it is with us as men. We are at once instrument and end, discoverers and teachers, actors and observers. We understand, as we hope others understand, that in this there is a harmony between knowledge in the sense of science, that specialized and general knowledge which it is our purpose to uncover, and the community of man. We, like all men, are among those who bring a little light to the vast unending darkness of man's life and world. For us as for all men, change and eternity, specialization and unity, instrument and final purpose, community and individual man alone, complementary each to the other, both require and define our bonds and our freedom.

Suggestions for Discussion and Writing

1. Oppenheimer begins his essay by talking about the house called "science." What does he mean when he says that "from time to time someone rearranges a piece of the furniture to make the whole more harmonious"? A few lines later he speaks of the "new wings being built nearby, where men walk high in the air to erect new scaffoldings, not unconscious of how far they may fall." What does this imply about the scientific enterprise?

2. How does Oppenheimer characterize the house of science?

3. Paradox seems to be central to Oppenheimer's thought. Find some specific examples in this essay. Choose one example and write a brief essay in which you explain the paradox and discuss some of its implications.

4. Oppenheimer seems not to offer a clear statement of his thesis early in this essay. Do you see a connection between the absence of an explicit thesis statement and his extensive use of paradox?

5. In paragraph six, Oppenheimer argues that atomic systems can be described in various ways and that, although all these ways are necessary for a full understanding of the atomic world, only one way is "proper and consistent" in any specific instance. In other words, an understanding of atomic physics requires the scientist's acceptance of multiple perspectives. How does this need to accept multiple perspectives relate to the author's broader argument regarding community and "the larger brotherhood of man"?

6. Do you see any political implications in Oppenheimer's argument? Write an essay in which you explain your views.

7. The introduction to this essay gives a brief sketch of Oppenheimer's scientific career. Supplement this information with further reading and write an essay in which you relate Oppenheimer's arguments here to the events of his life.

☐ MOTIVES AND AIMS OF THE SCIENTIST

Fred Hoyle
(b. 1915)

Fred Hoyle, the British astronomer and novelist, is best known for his advocacy of the continuous creation or "steady-state" theory of cosmology. This theory, which sees the universe as existing in the same form today as it did in the past and will in the future, is now viewed by most astronomers as being less useful for describing the origin of the universe than the Big Bang theory. Nonetheless, Hoyle's contributions to astronomy have been recognized as among the most important of our time. He has had a distinguished academic career in both England and the United States and has received numerous honors, among them appointment as Fellow of the Royal Society and, in 1972, elevation to knighthood. Among Sir Fred's best-known works are *Galaxies, Nuclei, and Quasars* and *From Stonehenge to Modern Cosmology*. The following selection, taken from his *Of Men and Galaxies* (1964), addresses several important issues facing contemporary science and society, including the splitting of society into what C. P. Snow has called the "two cultures" and the negative effects that "bigness" has had on scientific research.

When I was recently in San Francisco I heard that an opinion poll had shown that a surprisingly large proportion of people were disturbed and suspicious about the scientist and his activities. What they undoubtedly had in mind was the nuclear bomb, the grisly horror that scientists are supposed to have unleashed on the world.

It is not usual for a really creative scientist to produce a weapon of war of his own volition. It is recorded that when the Greek colony of Syracuse was invaded by the Romans the great scientist Archimedes was persuaded to invent weapons the like of which had not been seen before—catapults, levers, cranes, all on an unprecedentedly big scale. Those Roman ships that were unwise enough to venture close inshore were seized by clawlike devices, bombarded by huge stones, overturned, and sunk. The defenders, greatly delighted with their victory, went on a three-day orgy. Meanwhile, the Romans landed down the coast, made their way overland, and finally entered the city from behind. In the ensuing sack, Archimedes was put to the sword because he was engaged on a geometrical problem, it is said, and refused to speak politely to the Romans when they arrived.

The essential point in this old story is that Archimedes was *persuaded* to make his cranes and levers, the patriotic motive being presumably the means of persuasion. It was the same with the nuclear bomb. Scientists were asked by their governments in time of war to produce the bomb. It is to be emphasized that work on the bomb was first started in Britain and was later carried to a conclusion here in the United States, both countries with democratic governments elected by the people. In short, the bomb was produced in our name. If we do not like it, we must blame ourselves, not the scientists who made it.

A word about the dictatorships, Russian and German. The dictatorships did not produce the bomb. There was no moral decision in this, however. The dictatorships did not produce the bomb because the people of a dictatorship are inherently less ingenious than the people of a democracy. Everything radically new is always produced in a democracy. In this connection the first sputnik was not conceptually new in any intricate way, not like the digital computer for example. The principle of the rocket was centuries old, and most of the development work necessary for the launching of satellites was done during the war and in military programs after the war. So I would not regard the Russian launching of the first sputnik in October, 1957, as an exception to my statement that dictatorships will always be behind in really new technological developments. The advantage of dictatorship is that coherent action is much easier to achieve—provided the dictator wants it. The disadvantage is that the natural inventiveness of the common people is suppressed. But this is by the way.

It is quite other matters that I wish to explore. I want to inquire how far the aims, motives, and pressures to which scientists are now exposed are affecting science itself. I was born in the year 1915, exactly in the middle of the first thirty years of the present century. These first thirty years may be said to have been the great age of science.

I am not attempting to argue that remarkable discoveries were not made before the twentieth century or that remarkable discoveries are not being made now. The achievements of Isaac Newton in the seventeenth century, of James Clerk Maxwell in the nineteenth, as well as the recent discovery of the Omega-minus particle, with all its current significance, spring immediately to mind. But let me remind you of some of the discoveries of the first part of our century. First, Max Planck's discovery of the quantum and Albert Einstein's special theory of relativity: then Ernest Rutherford's discovery of the atomic nucleus, Niels Bohr's atomic theory, the general theory of relativity, and, not to overextend the list, the tremendous discovery of wave mechanics.

It would, I think, be correct to say that everything that has happened in the second thirty years of this century, at any rate so far as the physical sciences are concerned, was already foreshadowed in the first thirty years. On the practical side, atomic energy was all there, in the pioneer work of Francis William Aston in the early 1920's. This was also the source of a great deal that has happened in recent years in my own subject, astronomy and astrophysics. Our understanding of the processes that take place within stars, and indeed of the history of matter itself, owes its origin and inspiration to those two or three remarkable decades. Modern field theory, the heart of physics, spans the period. It began with Maxwell; its development has continued through the 1950's up to the present moment; but I do not think it can be denied that the biggest ideas belong to the period between Planck and Werner Heisenberg, to the first quarter of the century, in fact.

I would like to begin my inquiry into the aims and motives of scientists by asking whether this was a matter of chance or whether something more was involved. We all know that the result of a baseball game, one particular game, may depend enormously on chance. The whole game can turn on whether a big hit goes fair or foul. Ten feet, depending perhaps on the way the ball curves in the wind, can make all the difference. Many games have to be played before it emerges which is the best club. The World Series is certainly not long enough to remove chance from the result, as any Yankee supporter with last year's Series in mind will tell you. In fact, a simple statistical analysis shows that about 150 games are necessary to get rid of chance effects, and this is exactly why the baseball season goes on for so long.

Chance effects also occur in science, and in all human activities. This, indeed, is one of the biggest problems the historian has to face up to, perhaps his biggest problem—to separate chance effects, *noise* as the physicist calls it, from systematic trends. I often suspect that some of my historical colleagues make the mistake of thinking it necessary to know everything about everything. Certainly teaching schedules and examination papers suggest all too often that history has become bogged down in fantastic and trivial detail, and that no serious attempt has been made to separate what is random from what is systematic. There are, of course, obvious dangers in making such a separation. It is all too easy to make a wrong separation and conveniently forget those details that point to the mistake. But exactly the same problem occurs in the sciences as well as in the humanities, and scientists have evolved methods for dealing with it.

Rather curiously, effectiveness in the separation of noise from systematic effects, the *signal* as we call it, seems to depend inversely on distance from the physical sciences. Serious arguments about signal and noise hardly ever arise in physics. As we move to the biological sciences the situation is often less clear. There have been famous arguments, such as the old question of whether acquired characteristics could be inherited. By and large these controversies have been satisfactorily and finally resolved, however. But passing from the biological sciences to the social sciences, and thence to the humanities, the picture gets less and less clear. This is why historical studies involve so much detail, and why the historian's examination papers look so horrible. He is not quite sure what is important and what is trivial, so everything has to go in.

The physical scientist cannot avoid sympathy with the historian when he comes to consider the problem of the first three decades of the present century. Were the achievements of these decades simply chance fluctuations, or was there a deeper reason for them? Evidently this question is of enormous importance, not only to the scientist himself, but to everybody. If something systematic has been involved, the inference is that science today is in decline, not disastrously or catastrophically, but sliding gently downhill.

One small indication that this might be so is that the question is never asked. In my experience most scientists take it for granted that all is well, that we are forging ahead as fast as it is possible to do, that, in Voltaire's words, "All is for the best in this best of all possible worlds." This, too, I would take as a small symptom of decline. Of course one can be too self-analytical. It does not pay to think too hard about the complicated mechanics of how to walk down a flight of steps; if you do you are likely to trip and break your neck. But the facts in this case are so striking that they should not be ignored.

Counsel for the defense would, I imagine, open its speech to the jury with the plea that today things are different and that they are different in a way that is no fault of the scientist in general or of the physicist in particular. The crucial facts on which the quantum theory was based came from a study of the spectrum lines emitted by excited atoms. All that was necessary to obtain these facts was to heat some gas to a few thousand degrees in the laboratory, to make it glow, and to analyze the light from the glow by passing it through a spectrograph. The basic facts could be acquired for an expenditure of a few hundred dollars. Now, from a purely scientific point of view, the problem of the modern high-energy physicist is closely analogous to that of the physicist at the beginning of the century. What is wanted nowadays is a spectroscopy, not of atoms, but of the very particles that physics used to consider as basic. For it appears that even these particles possess excited states, analogous to the excited states of atoms. When a particle changes its state it emits a kind of radiation, analogous to the glow of light from a hot gas. Thus, conceptually, the problem is very similar to old-fashioned spectroscopy, but economically it is completely different. To carry out any worthwhile experiment today in this field of physics costs millions of dollars, not hundreds. And easily within the foreseeable future the subject will reach the stage when experiments will cost hundreds of millions of dollars. Quite apart from the economics of the situation, a huge piece of equipment takes longer to construct than simple equipment, so progress is not only vastly more costly but also much slower. The validity of these arguments is beyond question; the issue is whether they represent the whole truth.

Everybody would admit that two of the best three or four discoveries in physics of the last ten years have come from very simple equipment, a little more expensive perhaps than the equipment used at the beginning of the century, but of negligible cost by modern standards. I refer to Rudolf Mössbauer's discovery, and to the discovery of the nonconservation of parity in weak interactions. It might be argued that these discoveries were exceptional, and that it would be unwise to read too much into them. I am not so sure about this. Certainly, I do not think that physics could have gone in any other way but that in which it has gone, namely building the huge contraptions of which the most outstanding are at Brookhaven and Berkeley in this country and at CERN in Geneva. These machines themselves can do us no harm. It is what we ourselves believe, what postulates we come to accept without question, that may be harmful. One very common postulate is that to be effective science, at any rate physics, must be big. It is this dinosaur mentality that may wreak the damage. The cases I have cited, of the Mössbauer effect and of the nonconservation of parity, show that up to the present the dinosaur postulate has not been correct. My prediction is that in the decade ahead it will also not be correct. It will not be correct, partly because remarkable new discoveries achieved by quite simple means will, I am sure, come along—man's ingenuity always seems capable of turning up the unexpected—and partly because it is in the nature of dinosaurs to reach an end, to become extinct.

A simple extrapolation of the trend of the last ten or fifteen years shows that the building of bigger and yet bigger machines must reach an end, if only because this activity cannot consume more than the total energy of the whole human species. At first sight this might seem like a sad confession of failure. It might seem as if the human species in its inquiry into the nature of things must of necessity come up against an ultimate barrier. I suspect that a way round the barrier will be found and that it will come not at all from dinosaur thinking. During the last year, astrophysicists have become interested in the properties of matter under conditions that can never be simulated in the laboratory. By this I mean conditions of density, of the spacing between particles, that not even the biggest machines we can contemplate would be able to approach. This is not very surprising. What would be surprising would be if the opposite were true. Think of the whole universe as a laboratory. Is it likely that within that laboratory conditions will not be found that cannot be produced in our own local laboratories?

Here I am suggesting a new type of thinking, of looking for our facts, not by setting up a deliberate experiment, but by using the information that reaches us from outside the Earth. I am suggesting that the sum total of that information greatly exceeds what can be achieved by all the experiments that can be performed in a local laboratory. The importance of laboratory experiments lies, not in their breadth or wideness, but in just the opposite, their narrowness. By setting up special conditions, by *designing* an experiment, it is possible to simplify and to separate into many pieces problems that would be too complicated if we were obliged to work with the full wealth of detail that exists in the universal laboratory. My point, however, is that the very need for local laboratory experimentation is an indication of a lack of sophistication. Of necessity one has to begin by following the simplest path. But this does not mean that the simplest path must always be followed. I foresee a day, perhaps not very far distant, when more and more use will be made of the universal laboratory. There will, of course, be no sudden transition from one method to the other. When difficulties arise in the interpretation of the things we see in the universal laboratory, then we must simplify things by making local experiments. But there will be a shifting balance between the two methods, and the shift will move steadily toward the wider laboratory. One of the dangers of dinosaur thinking is that it cannot remotely conceive this possibility.

I want now to come back to the question, is there a systematic difference between the physics of today and that of the first quarter of the present century? My belief is that the answer should be, yes. I believe that the cultural pattern in science today is vastly different. Dinosaur activities are an obvious cause of the difference. The old free and easy conditions have gone, the sort of conditions I remember when as a student in Cambridge, thirty years ago, I used to tiptoe past Rutherford's laboratory. We now have vast, slick, streamlined laboratories, more reminiscent of an industrial production plant than of a laboratory in the old sense. On the face of it, things look more efficient. But are they? I have a personal theory that in order to be efficient about the things that really matter it is necessary to be inefficient about the things that do not matter so much. If one is obliged to be efficient about everything the best that can be achieved is a moderate measure of competence. To produce high peaks of inspiration it is necessary that there should be low troughs, implying, I believe, some degree of muddle and inefficiency. Such variations are essential, just as they are in a great musical work where a moment of tenseness and excitement is built out of periods of quietness and calm.

I am not alone in deploring this change. Remarks very much along the lines of what I have been saying were made to me only a few months ago by the director of one of the largest of these superlaboratories. But it is not easy to see how things can be changed. Facilities costing upward of ten million dollars cannot be treated in quite the same happy-go-lucky fashion in which our forefathers treated their laboratory equipment. By this I mean that laboratories cannot be shut down for four or five days while one goes off on a fishing trip in the mountains. The trouble is that it is the fishing trips that lead to the big ideas. For better or for worse we seem to be stuck with a new cultural pattern in science. Big science involves a change in the behavior of scientists, and this I do not think we can avoid. What we *can* do is to stop the big science mentality from overwhelming all our science. We can recognize the unfortunate necessity of some dinosaur activity. We can avoid, above all, the mistake of thinking that unless one is big one is negligible. Maxwell, Planck, Einstein, Rutherford—none of these men depended on big science, they depended on big ideas.

The danger lies in imagining that things have changed irrevocably.

It is widely supposed, in my country and in universities in this country that do not command big facilities, that the situation is hopeless. Far from believing it hopeless, I would assert that there are probably as many as twenty really major discoveries in physics which are waiting around for somebody to pick up and which involve no major facility. I would suspect that to have a major facility would be an active handicap, since it is usually the case that the facility dictates the scientist's thoughts rather than the other way about. It is rather like making the mistake of having one's office in too perfect a building. People who work in marvelous buildings are dominated by those buildings, whereas it is the other way round for people who work in rabbit warrens. The builders of the great European medieval cathedrals knew this perfectly well. Walk into a big cathedral, and it wipes your brain clean of every thought. The same thing happens when you walk into these wonderful modern office blocks. The same thing happens all too easily in big science.

But it does not end here. Once you come to believe that bigness is everything, that the only way to get to the top of the heap is to be big, and since bigness costs a great deal of money, it is obvious that there will be an almighty scramble for money. It is also obvious that there will not be enough money going around to make every-body big. So a system of lobbying is bound to grow up. The lobbying will not be confined to ambitious, incompetent scientists. The best men will also be obliged to lobby, unless they are prepared to see those who are less able pass them in the race. It will be rare indeed that a considerable sum is voted to a man who has not invested a considerable amount of time and energy in pressing his own claims. It will be necessary for him to sit on numerous committees. In this country it will be necessary for him to employ a news bureau, or at any rate for his university to do so. The great men of the early part of this century did not give press conferences, nor did they spend 50 per cent or more of their time sitting on committees. Whether you agree with me or not about the present state of affairs, about its desirability or otherwise, I think you must agree that the cultural pattern is different from that which operated in the early years of the century.

So far, I have not blamed anyone for anything. And insofar as I am now going to blame someone, it will be the whole human species. There is not, and never has been, a human being who was capable of thinking straight, except by checking his thoughts against objective experience. I am not overlooking the mathematicians in making this statement. It is true that a mathematician may claim to have proved a result without appeal to objective experience and that all other mathematicians of his own day may agree with him. But experience shows that mathematicians of a succeeding generation will not agree. What constitutes proof in one generation is not the same thing as proof in another. In choosing mathematics I am concerned with the minimum of human emotion. In any thought process where emotions enter strongly it is enormously more difficult to avoid subjective rationalizations. For this reason it is well-nigh impossible for even the most responsible scientist to know exactly how far he should go in his requests for financial assistance, whether from state, government, or private sources.

By now I am building up a fairly considerable list of new cultural traits: dinosauric bigness, a submergence of inspiration in a humdrum kind of efficiency, endless committees, a tendency to grab every penny in sight. But more is still to come. There will be no disagreement that science has changed, and is changing, the world. In point of fact science has been changing the world since man discovered fire and made his first crude stone tools, only it was not called science then. The tempo has increased so rapidly in the last decade or two that everybody is now aware of the fact. In physics it never happens that one thing affects another without there being some sort of reverse action. The recoil of the rifle butt on your shoulder as the bullet is fired is a well-known example. Analogously, we cannot expect science to affect society without there being a reverse action. And once the connection becomes strong the reverse action will also be strong. This is one of the major ways, if not the major way, in which the cultural pattern in science has changed during the past thirty years, in which it is radically and completely different today from what it was in the early years of the century. Just as some degree of big science is unfortunately necessary, so some degree of connection between scientist and government is probably necessary. I would say that the future of science depends on how this relation turns out. What has happened to date is not particularly reassuring, as the opening remarks of this lecture already show.

A strong sign that all is not lost, however, comes from the remarkable fact that no outstanding scientist is to be found anywhere in any government of any country in the world. When you consider that almost every walk of life, scientists apart, is represented in the inner councils of government, this is indeed a remarkable fact. Some activities, economics and law particularly, breed politicians; science does not. I do not think the reason lies in political ineptness, in a lack of ability of scientists, some scientists, to fight an election successfully; the infighting that goes on in the scramble for funds would not disgrace the most adept politician. The reason lies elsewhere. Take an athlete out of training for six months, and he is no longer an athlete. It may be a little hard to say take a scientist, even a very good one, out of science for six months and he is no longer a scientist, but the statement is not a serious exaggeration. I think the absence of scientists from professional politics means that above all else scientists, essentially every one of them, want to remain what they are, scientists. This is the most heartening feature of the present state of affairs.

But it is inevitable that if scientists do not find their way into professional politics they will be formed into committees and asked to make recommendations to governments on a multitude of problems, where those problems are sensitively affected by scientific knowledge. Military defense is the obvious example, the example I began with at the outset. More and more in this century, political leaders have become constrained by weapons technology. Political decisions have turned on the availability or otherwise of technical devices. From both a moral and a political point of view it would have been better for Britain to declare war on Germany in 1938, at the time of the Munich debacle, than in 1939. I am convinced that the decision was delayed a year because of a lack of aircraft and of an adequate radar screen in 1938. In such circumstances it is quite inevitable that the scientist will find himself under heavy pressure to give a considerable amount of time to government problems.

There is a widespread belief that we all do our best work when we are young. But most of the evidence for this belief comes from modern times, because the expectation of life was much less in former generations than it is now, and people did not in general live very long anyway. So from the point of view of the present discussion the argument is circular and achieves nothing. We do know that in the arts, particularly music, the proposition is not true. In fact the reverse is true; the best work is frequently produced in later years. My belief is that the relation between age and quality of work is very largely cultural. Under modern conditions it is almost impossible for an outstanding scientist to continue effectively in his work beyond the age of about forty-five because of the inroads on his time that will be made by nonresearch activities. The insidious presumption is that a good man can afford some loss of time, in terms of our athletic analogy that he does not need to keep completely in training. It is, I believe, this presumption that does the damage. It is a handicap from which our forefathers did not suffer. I would claim that we simply cannot afford to lose half the working life of almost all of our best people, for it is precisely the best who are called on the most often.

As if all this were not enough, we now have the two cultures. Sir Charles Snow is perfectly right in asserting the existence of two cultures. Where he is wrong, in my opinion, is in suggesting that the second culture, the scientific culture, is desirable. Snow himself is fascinated by the concept of power, more I think than any other novelist, past or present. I do not mean that Snow is concerned with power for himself, but that he finds fascinating exactly the type of situation I have been describing. He likes the thought of committees meeting, of men flying to Washington, if need be across the Atlantic. It is exactly the things I have just been deploring that constitute the second culture. It is not by chance that our awareness of this second culture is quite new. In the early years of the century the second culture did not exist. There was then no sensible difference between the inspirations of the scientist and those of the musician, the writer, and the artist. It is only with the development of the concept of the "corridors of power," to quote Snow himself, that the second culture has emerged. My belief is that this second culture needs watching, not nearly so much from the point of view of the humanities as from the point of view of science itself. I believe it is potentially far more dangerous to science than it is to the humanities.

The future will depend much more on the environment in which the scientist is called on to operate than it will on the scientist himself. It is a mistake to imagine that potentially great men are rare. It is the conditions that permit the promise of greatness to be fulfilled that are rare. It is a mistake to imagine that men like Shakespeare, Michelangelo, Beethoven, Newton, or Einstein were unique specimens of the human species. Individuals with their inherent capabilities are being born all the time, everywhere, in all communities. What is so difficult to achieve is the cultural background that permits potential greatness to be converted into actual greatness. At birth we all possess the ability to grow up in any community, to speak any language, to accept any social convention, however absurd. We are even equipped to live in caves under the primitive conditions of the Stone Age, if need be. But it is quite a different story by the time we reach the age of twenty. As the years pass we become more and more highly specialized to the particular community in which we happen to have been born, eventually reaching such a high degree of specialization—geographical, cultural, technical—that we would be most unhappy to be obliged to change to any other conditions.

The abilities with which we are born for the most part do not survive this tremendous change. Occasionally, however, the improbable happens; an individual's great natural talent may be perfectly matched to the requirements of the society in which he is brought up. It is then that the promise of greatness is fulfilled. Examples immediately spring to mind: the poetry of the Elizabethan dramatists, Florentine painting, Viennese music, and I would say the science of the first years of the present century. We are still living with the memories of yesterday. The conditions that brought our forefathers to greatness have not wholly disappeared from present-day society. All is not yet lost. The traditions are there, and the ability is there. What happens in the future depends, I believe, on the way our civilization develops in the years ahead. It is probably a mistake to be too pessimistic. Equally it is a mistake to suppose that everything is bound to continue as it was in the past. The days of greatness did not continue for the Elizabethan poets, or the Florentine painters, or the Viennese musicians. Their days of greatness vanished, not suddenly and dramatically, but gently, with a gradual slide downhill. What I am questioning in this lecture is whether we today are sliding gently downhill. I do not suppose that anybody can say yea or nay for sure. It is well-nigh impossible when one is in the midst of a development to know exactly how things are going to turn out. But I think we can be certain, in general terms, of what is needed to halt the downward slide, if indeed the slide is taking place.

I say in general terms, because I do not know at all how the details would work out. The general principle of the matter is this: that which a community really wants, it gets. I place emphasis on the word "really." Obviously there is a sense in which every community throughout the world wants good science. Good science guarantees good technology; good technology guarantees freedom from hunger, and guarantees the military efficiency of the community in question. But this type of want is a selfish one and will not do. In a similar sense every community wants great achievements in the humanities; but I think most writers, musicians, and artists would agree that modern industrial societies do not *really* want good literature, music, or art. The essential point is to want the product, whatever it may be, for its own sake. Money is certainly not the answer. A hundred and forty years ago you could have bought a Schubert song for a few pence. Today you will not get one whatever you are willing to offer. It is as well to face the fact that the creative spirit cannot be bought. It cannot be engendered by five-year plans. My suspicion is that a community that claims to want creative activity in one field but not in others does not really want anything. This I believe to be the devastating answer to Snow's two cultures. I suspect that if there are two cultures, as I agree today there are, then tomorrow there will be no culture at all. It seems to me inevitable that if the creative person on the humanities side finds himself out of tune with society, then so will a creative man on the scientific side.

I said that I could say nothing about details, but I will end this lecture with one detail. Beware of efficiency. Remember that Einstein was generally regarded as a vague, impractical man. Many scientists still think this. Yet the truth is that Einstein's calculations were anything but vague; they had a level of precision and exactness of thought which those who accuse him of being impractical are themselves quite incapable of attaining. Remember, too, that the girl Mozart really wanted to marry said after his death that she had turned him down because she thought he was a scatterbrain, and that he would never make good. It seems to be characteristic of all great work, in every field, that it arises spontaneously and unpretentiously, and that its creators wear a cloak of imprecision. Wordsworth had matters right when he spoke of Newton: "The index of his mind, voyaging strange seas of thought, alone." The man who voyages strange seas must of necessity be a little unsure of himself. It is the man with the flashy air of knowing everything, who is always on the ball, always with it, that we should beware of. It will not be very long now before his behavior can be imitated quite perfectly by a computer.

Suggestions for Discussion and Writing

1. What points does Hoyle raise in the first four paragraphs? How do these points relate to the "other matters" to which he devotes the rest of the essay?

2. "The people of a dictatorship are inherently less ingenious than the people of a democracy." Would Oppenheimer agree (see the previous essay)?

3. In the fifth paragraph, Hoyle suggests that the first thirty years of the twentieth century "may be said to have been the great age of science." What factors, in Hoyle's view, made for this greatness?

4. Hoyle is suspicious of "bigness" in science. Why? What does bigness imply for him? Write an essay in which you discuss bigness as a value in contemporary culture.

5. What, for Hoyle, constitutes the second (i.e., scientific) culture? Why is this culture more dangerous to science than to the humanities?

6. "If there are two cultures, as I agree today there are, then tomorrow there will be no culture at all." Hoyle deplores the idea of "two cultures." In what way is the essay itself evidence of his commitment to the ideal of a single culture?

7. "Obviously there is sense in which every community throughout the world wants good science." What, for Hoyle, constitutes "good" science? What is the connection between good science and "good literature, music, or art"?

8. "Beware of efficiency." Why is efficiency suspect? What is the connection between this statement and the author's earlier assertion that "it is the fishing trips that lead to the big ideas"?

DEHUMANIZATION OF THE SCIENTIST

René Dubos
(1901–1982)

Bacteriologist, pioneering environmentalist, and professor of pathology and tropical medicine at Harvard University, René Dubos gained international recognition in the early 1940s for research that made possible the commercial production of antibiotics. French by birth, Dubos came to the United States in 1924 and received his doctorate from Rutgers University in 1927. Throughout a career distinguished by numerous awards, Dubos published prolifically, including more than twenty books on science and the environment. His *So Human an Animal* was awarded the 1969 Pulitzer Prize for nonfiction. In the following selection, excerpted from *Dreams of Reason* (1961), Dubos reflects upon the changing—and sometimes hostile—view of the scientist that has developed since the nineteenth century.

T hat "science will find a way out" is a dangerous illusion because it serves as an excuse for intellectual laziness and apathy. I shall try to show that this attitude, which corresponds in reality to a deterioration of public interest in the intellectual aspects of science, originates in part from a change of ideals among the scientists themselves.

Until Bacon's time the motivation of scientists was either plain curiosity or the philosophical urge to understand the world; the practical problems of life were hardly ever mentioned as a justification for their efforts. This does not mean that practical matters did not orient and influence somewhat the activities of scientists. It is obvious that in the past as today what scientists did was necessarily conditioned by the techniques at their disposal and by the preoccupations of their times. But the enormous gap that existed until 1800 between the large amount of theoretical knowledge and the paucity of applications derived from it bears witness to the fact that very few of the ancient scientists focused their efforts on practical issues. One example must suffice to illustrate how profoundly the Industrial Revolution changed in this regard the professional outlook of the scientific community.

William Thompson (Lord Kelvin) had proved himself a most gifted theoretical investigator during the early part of his life. Before the age of thirty-three he had published studies which constituted the foundation of thermodynamics, provided Maxwell with the mathematical clues to the electromagnetic theory of light and led Hertz to the discovery of radio oscillations. But instead of pursuing the large theoretical implications of his discoveries, Thompson soon shifted his efforts to technological developments and became the first great scientist to organize a laboratory devoted to industrial research. The change in scientific ideals that he symbolizes constitutes one of the most important characteristics of the nineteenth century. It has had such far-ranging consequences that we must consider in greater detail the forces involved in the conflict between the philosophy that "the true scientist has elected to know, not to do" and the other attitude, more common today, that the true role of science is to be, in I. Bernard Cohen's words, the "servant of man." . . .

Today, in our social structure, technological science is a commodity much in demand, and for this reason educational techniques are being developed for the assembly-line production of the human skills required to manufacture gadgets, products, and cures. Wherever this has been attempted with sufficient vigor, the results have been according to anticipation—most men can become effective technologists if adequately trained. Obviously, man finds it easy to behave as *homo faber* whether his function is to produce pineapples, antibiotics, automobiles, or guided missiles. But *homo sapiens* has never been produced on a large scale, and it is his genesis which is the real puzzle. . . .

It is often claimed that Pasteur's scientific activities originated from a concern with practical problems—for example, that his studies on fermentation had their basis in attempts to improve the quality of

French wines and beer, or that his interest in infectious processes developed from efforts to save the production of silkworms in France. Nothing could be further from the truth. In reality . . . Pasteur began his scientific life as a purely theoretical investigator and he was already a famous scientist when he began to work on practical problems. From 1847 to 1857 his dominating scientific interests were problems of no apparent practical significance but with large theoretical implications: the relation of molecular structure to optical activity, and the bearing of stereoisomerism on the origin of life; a few years later he became engrossed in other abstract thoughts concerning the biochemical unity of life. As time went on, however, he yielded more and more to the social pressures of his environment, and he spent the largest part of his productive life working on practical problems of fermentation and disease. He became increasingly involved in using science as an instrument of economic conquest rather than as a technique for understanding the universe. Repeatedly he expressed gratification at seeing that his labor would help man to gain mastery over the physical world and to improve human life. "To him who devotes his life to science," Pasteur wrote, "nothing can give more happiness than increasing the number of discoveries, but his cup of joy is full when the results of his studies immediately find practical applications."

There can be no doubt, in my opinion, that Pasteur was aware that his involvement in practical problems had interfered with the pursuit of his deeper scientific interests. He tried to justify his partial neglect of theoretical studies by the statement, "There are not two sciences. There is only science and the applications of science and these two activities are linked as the fruit is to the tree." Yet, despite these brave words and irrespective of his immense success and popular acclaim, it is certain that he often regretted the choice that had been imposed on him by the *Zeitgeist*. Time and time again he stated that he had been "enchained" by an inescapable forward-moving logic that had led him from the study of crystals to the problems of fermentation and then of contagious diseases. He came to believe that it was only through accidental circumstances that he had become involved in practical problems—important, of course, but not so deeply significant as those he had visualized early in life. Yet the desire of his early days to work on crystallography and on the nature of life apparently remained with him as a haunting dream. Pasteur's grandson, Professor L. Pasteur Vallery-Radot, has recently told a moving story which reveals the pathetic intensity of this inner conflict during Pasteur's later years.

> I see again that face, that appeared to be carved from a block of granite—that high and large forehead, those grayish-green eyes, with such a deep and kind look. . . .
> He seemed to me serious and sad. He was probably sad because of all the things he had dreamed of but not realized.

I remember one evening, at the Pasteur Institute. He was writing quietly at his desk, his head bent on his right hand, in a familiar pose. I was at the corner of the table, not moving or speaking. I had been taught to respect his silences. He stood up and, feeling the need to express his thoughts to the nearest person, even a child, he told me: "Ah! my boy, I wish I had a new life before me! With how much joy I should like to undertake again my studies on crystals!" To have given up his research on crystals was the eternal sorrow of his life.

Many modern scientists suffer from the schizophrenic attitude illustrated by . . . Pasteur. Fortunately, one particular aspect of science helps to minimize the inner conflicts generated by this attitude—namely, the fact, already mentioned and universally recognized, that it is often difficult to dissociate the theoretical from the practical aspects of science. Nevertheless, the conflicts are not entirely resolved by this interdependence of theory and practice. The uneasiness of scientists on this score is revealed by the fact that, whereas among themselves they claim that their primary interest is in the conceptual rather than the applied aspects of science, in public they justify basic research by asserting that it always leads to "useful" results, meaning by this the development of processes and products that can be converted into wealth or power. In a symposium on "basic research" recently held in New York, only one of the very distinguished participants dared take the position that the search for knowledge per se is an activity sufficient unto itself, one which does not need further justification.

Like Pasteur, other scientists seem to be afraid to admit in public—or do not really believe—that detached intellectual curiosity and desire to understand the universe are proper goals of scientific activity, whether or not "useful" results will ever follow. Yet, despite Francis Bacon's claim that "Knowledge, that tendeth but to satisfaction is but as a courtesan . . . ," the attempt to justify science only by its worldly products is fraught with dangers. Not only does it compromise the intellectual honesty of the scientific community for reasons that need not be discussed here; in my opinion, it also helps to foster among lay people a fundamental skepticism about and even contempt for science itself.

To be scornful of the ultimate intellectual and moral value of natural sciences is, of course, a very ancient attitude. Socrates' skepticism, as expressed in Plato's dialogues, has its counterpart in the talk about the bankruptcy of science that was widespread in literary and philosophical circles at the beginning of the present century. Until recently, however, the attitude of the skeptics was not one of hostility but rather one of impatience and disappointment at the fact that despite oft repeated promises, science had not yet solved for man the riddle of his nature and his destiny. Far more dangerous, it seems to me, are the expressions of contempt for science as an intellectual discipline, and for scientists as individuals, that have appeared repeatedly during the past few decades. Along with admiration for and awe at the power of science, there exists among the lay public, as pointed out by Margaret Mead, a curious mistrust of the scientist himself, as if he were something scarcely normal and human. This modern attitude toward the scientist is not far removed from that of primitives toward the shaman or medicine man, an individual regarded as essential to the group but one who is feared and often hated.

As typical of the hostile attitude toward science and scientists, I shall consider two books published respectively in 1913 and 1930: *The Tragic Sense of Life*, by Miguel de Unamuno, and *The Revolt of the Masses*, by José Ortega y Gasset. Both books have been translated into several languages and are still widely read and quoted; they have spread far and wide the doctrine of the bankruptcy of science. Although they deal with different themes, I shall consider them together since they have in common several aspects of the anti-science movement.

Unamuno and Ortega recognize, of course, the contributions made by science to human safety and comfort. But while they appreciate the merits of aspirin and motor cars, they are very little impressed by the kind of intellectual process involved in the technology that has produced these conveniences. Most scientific thinking, according to them, corresponds to a mechanical performance of a rather low order. Just as ancient societies used slaves for the affairs of everyday life, so modern societies produce and use scientific technicians for the same end. Consciously or unconsciously, Unamuno and Ortega have accepted to the letter Bacon's claim that the scientific method is so mechanical and foolproof as to be readily and effectively handled by small minds. They seem to have taken to heart his statement that "brutes by their natural instinct have produced many discoveries, whereas men by discussion and the conclusions of reason have given birth to few or none." As an extension of Bacon's aphorism, it seems worth while to quote at some length from the several pages in *The Revolt of the Masses* that Ortega devotes to the low intellectual caliber of scientists and their discoveries.

> The actual scientific man is the prototype of the mass-man. Not by chance, not through the individual failings of each particular man of science, but because science itself . . . automatically converts him into mass-man, makes of him a primitive, a modern barbarian. Experimental science has progressed thanks in great part to the work of men astoundingly mediocre, and even less than mediocre. That is to say, modern science . . . finds a place for the intellectually commonplace man and allows him to work therein with success. The reason of this lies in what is at the same time the great advantage and the gravest peril of the new science, and of the civilization

> directed and represented by it, namely, mechanisation. A fair amount of the things that have to be done in physics or in biology is mechanical work of the mind which can be done by anyone, or almost anyone. . . . The work is done . . . as with a machine, and in order to obtain quite abundant results it is not even necessary to have rigorous notions of their meaning and foundation. The specialist . . . is not learned, for he is formally ignorant of all that does not enter into his speciality; but neither is he ignorant, because he is "a scientist," and "knows" very well his own tiny portion of the universe. We shall have to say that he is a learned *ignoramus*. Anyone who wishes can observe the stupidity of thought, judgment, and action shown today in politics, art, religion, and the general problems of life and the world by the "men of science."

Scientists having become so mechanical and unconcerned with philosophical and truly intellectual problems, it is not surprising that, in Unamuno's words, "Science does not satisfy the needs of our heart and our will." Not only does it not deal with the problems of the real man "of flesh and bone," but it "turns against those who refuse to submit to its orthodoxy the weapons of ridicule and contempt."

Thus, according to Unamuno and Ortega, the modern scientist is thoroughly dehumanized, with no horizon beyond his specialized techniques, no awareness of distant human goals. Science fails to deal with the problems that are the real concerns of mankind; and, furthermore, it stultifies all higher aspirations by fostering and satisfying the mass aspects of human nature. Lest there be an illusion that the antiscience movement is peculiar to Latin countries, I shall conclude this discussion with remarks originating from the Anglo-Saxon world. In *The Human Situation,* W. Macneile Dixon asserted that "Science is the view of life where everything human is excluded from the prospect. It is of intention inhuman, supposing, strange as it may seem, that the further we travel from ourselves the nearer we approach the truth, the further from our deepest sympathies, from all we care for, the nearer are we to reality, the stony heart of the scientific universe." As pointed out by Kenneth E. Boulding in *The Image,* many are those all over the world who believe that: "Science might also be defined as the process of substituting unimportant questions which can be answered for important questions which cannot."

The contempt for science and the scientist illustrated by Unamuno's and Ortega's writings reflects an attitude now fairly widespread. To account for it, scientists are inclined to assume that the public does not have the training or the ability required to appreciate the intellectual beauty and the higher morality of science. But it might be worth while to consider the possibility that the antiscience movement has its origin in the behavior of the scientists themselves—in their own failure to convey to the public the nobler aspects of the scientific heritage, and in misleading assertions which create antagonism. It seems to me, for example, that some scientists have a tendency to derive a kind of unjustified intellectual haughtiness from their familiarity with experimental techniques of which the chief intellectual merit is that they happen to permit the solution of practical problems. These scientists exhibit pride of intellect in speaking of the scientific method as if it were something esoteric, superhuman in its power and precision, whereas it is in reality a very human activity supplemented by a few specialized techniques. Instead of bragging about the purely professional aspects of a "scientific method" that they really cannot define, should not scientists emphasize more than they do the spiritual, creative, and almost artistic aspects of all great scientific advances?

Scientists defend basic research in public by asserting that it cannot fail eventually to yield practical results, but they rarely advertise that knowledge per se is also a precious fruit of science. There is truth, of course, in Benjamin Farrington's statement that "man makes his mental history in the process of conquering the world," but only partial truth. Science, like philosophy, has long been pursued for its own sake, or rather, for the sake of intellectual satisfaction and increased understanding. Long before science could be justified by its industrial uses Ptolemy experienced the kind of intellectual intoxication that only knowledge can provide. "I know that I am mortal, a creature of a day; but when I search into the multitudinous revolving spirals of the stars, my feet no longer rest on the earth, but, standing by Zeus himself, I take my fill of ambrosia, the food of the gods." In a similar mood Kepler exclaimed, "Eighteen months ago the first dawn rose for me, three months ago the bright day, and a few days ago the full sun of a most wonderful vision." And at the end of his life Pasteur spoke lovingly of "the charms of our studies, the enchantment of science."

It would be interesting to know the reasons which have made such very great scientists as . . . Pasteur emphasize the practical worth of their studies and leave unexpressed their loftier intellectual goals. The most obvious interpretation of this attitude is that it was dictated by the wish to gain public approval. But there is no evidence that the public of their time would not have recognized and respected a purely intellectual scientific motivation. In fact, it seems to me that in all situations where the public has exhibited any interest in science, it has been just as eager to learn of the philosophical aspects as of the practical applications. . . .

Nothing could illustrate better the change that occurred in the focus of the scientific community during the Industrial Revolution than the sudden and complete disappearance of the term "natural philosophy." The schism between science and philosophy was the result of two forces which operated almost simultaneously. One was the recognition that knowledge could be used for creating wealth and power; the other was the rapid accumulation of new and unexpected facts which engendered a sense of humility before the complexity of nature and rendered scientists shy of extrapolating from factual knowledge into speculative thoughts. Then humility evolved into scorn for speculation, and today the statement "This is not science, this is philosophy" rules out of scientific discussion any statement that goes a step beyond established fact.

Yet it is apparent that today, as in the past, many scientists—among them some of the most brilliant and most effective—are eager to escape from the austere discipline of factual knowledge and to experience again the intoxication of philosophical thought. They may distrust Plato, but, like him, they seem to regard philosophy as the "dear delight." Witness the flurry of speculative books published by scientists as soon as some discovery enlarges the scope of their knowledge. The theory of evolution has been used by biologists as a platform to erect or justify religious, political, and economic philosophies. Familiarity with modern theoretical physics seems to warrant opinions not only on the structure of matter and its relation to energy, but also on the nature of life, the existence of free will, or the symbolism of language.

This return to scientific philosophy negates, it seems to me, the fears so commonly expressed that scientists are becoming a class apart from the rest of society by developing a culture without contact with the rest of human life. . . .

A while ago I used the names of Miguel de Unamuno and Ortega y Gasset to represent the movement which is often called antiscience. This was unfair to these authors because they are, in truth, the voice of humanity begging scientists to remember that man does not live by bread alone. They express also the fear of seeing science identified exclusively with power and technology at a time when it is beginning to reach populations which have never known it under any other guise. It should not be forgotten that in the Western World science was part of culture for several centuries before coming to be used extensively for practical ends. Even today this cultural heritage still conditions to a certain extent the manner in which science is pursued and employed in the countries of Western civilization. In contrast, science is being introduced in the underdeveloped parts of the world not as a cultural pursuit, but merely as a powerful and convenient tool—at best to be used for the production of material wealth, at worst for destructive purposes. For these reasons it seems to me that scientists and science writers betray a public trust when they neglect to emphasize the disinterested aspects of knowledge and are satisfied instead with claiming that all scientific discoveries eventually prove of practical use. On the one hand, there is no evidence that this is true. On the other hand, this attitude ignores the fact that today, as in the past, men starve for understanding almost as much as for food. In the long run the exclusive appeal to practical values may well endanger the future of science and its very existence.

It is obvious, of course, that during recent decades science has improved the lot of man on earth, even more successfully than Francis Bacon had anticipated. It is equally true, however, that for many centuries before the modern era, science had enriched mankind with a wealth of understanding at least as valuable as material riches. Scientists, like other men, win esteem and contribute to happiness more effectively by the exercise of wisdom than by the practice of power. And it is good for them to remember that, long before they had achieved technological mastery over nature and thus become servants of society, their functions as high priests of pure knowledge had given them ancient titles of nobility which they must continue to honor.

Suggestions for Discussion and Writing

1. What changes in "scientific ideals" took place in the nineteenth century? Explain the connection between these changes and the Industrial Revolution.

2. Early in his essay, Dubos identifies two common characterizations of scientists: those whose interests are essentially theoretical (i.e., those who have "elected to know, not to do"), and those whose interests are primarily practical (i.e., those who are, in some sense, the "servant[s] of man"). This distinction seems to imply that the theoretical scientist is somehow less interested in the common good. Would Pasteur agree? Do you agree? Write an essay developing your point of view.

3. "Along with admiration for and awe at the power of science, there exists among the lay public . . . a curious mistrust of the scientist himself, as if he were something scarcely normal and human." What evidence might be cited to support this view? Write an essay in which you explore the notion of the scientist as an "outsider." You might wish to consider images of the scientist in popular culture (Dr. Strangelove, Dr. Frankenstein, Mr. Spock, etc.).

4. Dubos quotes Miguel de Unamuno's view that "science does not satisfy the needs of our heart and our will." What do you understand Unamuno to mean by this? Would Heisenberg (Chapter 3) agree? Would Eiseley (Chapter 7) or Bronowski (Chapter 9)?

5. Dubos observes that some scientists tend to speak of "the scientific method as if it were something esoteric, superhuman in its power and precision." In reality, he argues, it is "a very human activity supplemented by a few specialized techniques." Does this view of the scientific method conform to those of Huxley and Pirsig in Chapter 7?

6. Hoyle emphasizes the need for "big ideas" rather than "big science." Do you see a connection between this emphasis on big ideas and Dubos's reference (in the last paragraph) to scientists as "high priests of pure knowledge"?

☐ THE REPUBLIC
OF TECHNOLOGY

Daniel J. Boorstin
(b. 1914)

Daniel J. Boorstin, historian, attorney, and educator, was born in Atlanta, raised in Tulsa, and educated at Harvard, Oxford, and Yale. In 1969, after twenty-five years on the history faculty at the University of Chicago, he became director of the National Museum of History and Technology at the Smithsonian Institution. From 1975 to 1987 he served as Librarian of Congress.

Boorstin's view of history emphasizes the role of individual initiative and pragmatism rather than that of class conflicts and ideology in the shaping of the American experience. Among his best-known works is *The Americans,* a trilogy that begins with the arrival of the Puritans in the New World and ends with the Apollo moon landing. Consistent with Boorstin's views, the trilogy attributes the dynamism and productivity of this country less to major political events than to a native instinct for expansion and the emergence of powerful entrepreneurs in business and industry. The development of new technologies is, for Boorstin, merely a manifestation of the quintessentially American compulsion to explore beyond the limits of the known.

The following selection, the title essay from *The Republic of Technology: Reflections on Our Future Community* (1978), addresses some of the issues that will face an increasingly technological America as it moves into the twenty-first century.

"**A** n athlete of steel and iron with not a superfluous ounce of metal on it!" exclaimed William Dean Howells before the centerpiece of Philadelphia's International Exhibition celebrating our nation's hundredth birthday. He was inspired to these words by the gigantic 700-ton Corliss steam engine that towered over Machinery Hall. When President Ulysses S. Grant and Emperor Dom Pedro of Brazil pulled the levers on May 10, 1876, a festive crowd cheered as the engine set in motion a wonderful assortment of machines—pumping water, combing wool, spinning cotton, tearing hemp, printing newspapers, lithographing wallpaper, sewing cloth, folding envelopes, sawing logs, shaping wood, making shoes—8,000 machines spread over 13 acres.

Others, especially visitors from abroad, were troubled by this American spectacle. "I cannot say that I am in the slightest degree impressed," announced the English biologist Thomas Henry Huxley, "by your bigness or your material resources, as such. Size is not grandeur, and territory does not make a nation. The great issue, about which hangs a true sublimity, and the terror of overhanging fate, is what are you going to do with all these things?''

The monster steam engine was an appropriate symbol of the American future, but not for the reason most of the spectators suspected. The special hopes, opportunities, and achievements, the fears and frustrations that marked the nation's grandeur in its second century—now to come—were to be even newer than visitors to the 1876 exposition could imagine. These came not from bigness but from a new kind of community. New ties would bind Americans together, would bind Americans to the larger world, and would bind the world to America. I call this community the Republic of Technology.

1

This community of our future was not created by any assemblage of statesmen. It had no written charter, and was not to be governed by any council of ambassadors. Yet it would reach into the daily lives of citizens on all continents. In creating and shaping this community the United States would play the leading role.

The word ''Republic'' I use as Thomas Paine, propagandist of the American Revolution, used it in his *Rights of Man,* to mean ''not any *particular form* of government'' but ''the matter or object for which government ought to be instituted . . . *respublica,* the public affairs, or the public good; or, literally translated, the public thing.'' This word describes the shared public concerns of people in different nations, the community of those who share these concerns.

In early modern times, learned men of the Western world considered themselves members of a Republic of Letters, the worldwide community of men who read one another's books and exchanged opinions. Long after Gutenberg's printing press had begun the process of multiplying books and encouraging the growth of literature in the languages of the marketplace, the community remained a limited one. Thomas Jefferson, for example, considered himself a citizen of that worldwide community because of what he shared with literary and scientific colleagues in France, Italy, Germany, Spain, the Netherlands, and elsewhere. When Jefferson offered the young nation his personal library (which was to be the foundation of the Library of Congress), it contained so many foreign-language books (including numerous ''atheistical'' works of Voltaire and other French revolutionaries) that some members of Congress opposed its purchase. The Republic of Letters was a select community of those who shared *knowledge.*

Our Republic of Technology is not only more democratic but also more in the American mode. Anyone can be a citizen. Largely a creation of American civilization in the last century, this republic offers a foretaste of American life in our next century. It is open to all, because it is a community of shared *experience.*

Behind this new kind of sharing was the Industrial Revolution, which developed in eighteenth-century England and spread over Europe and the New World. Power-driven technology and mass production meant large-scale imports and exports—goods carried everywhere in steam-driven freighters, in railroad freight cars, on transcontinental railway systems. The ways of daily life, the carriages in which people rode, the foods they ate, the pots and pans in their kitchens, the clothes they wore, the nails that held together their houses, the glass for their windows—all these and thousands of other daily trivia became more alike than they had ever been before. The weapons and tools—the rifles and pistols, the screws and wrenches, the shovels and picks—had a new uniformity, thanks to the so-called American System of Manufacturing (the system of interchangeable parts, sometimes called the Uniformity System). The telegraph and the power press and the mass-circulating newspaper brought the same information and the same images to people thousands of miles apart. Human experience for millions became more instantaneously similar than had ever been imagined possible.

This Republic of Technology has transformed our lives, adding a new relation to our fellow Americans, a new relation to the whole world. Two forces of the new era have proved especially potent.

The New Obsolescence

For most of human history, the norm had been continuity. Change was news. Daily lives were governed by tradition. The most valued works were the oldest. The great works of architecture were monuments that survived from the past. Furnishings became increasingly valuable by becoming antique. Great literature never went out of date. "Literature," Ezra Pound observed, "is news that *stays* news." The new enriched the old and was enriched by the old. Shakespeare enriched Chaucer. Shaw enriched Shakespeare. It was a world of the enduring and the durable.

The laws of our Republic of Technology are quite different. The importance of a scientific work, as the German mathematician David Hilbert once observed, can be measured by the number of previous publications it makes superfluous to read. Scientists and technologists dare not wait for their current journals. They must study "preprints" of articles and use the telephone to be sure that their work has not been made obsolete by what somebody else did this morning.

The Republic of Technology is a world of obsolescence. Our characteristic printed matter is not a deathless literary work but today's newspaper that makes yesterday's newspaper worthless. Old objects simply become second hand—to be ripe for the next season's recycling. In this world the great library is apt to seem not so much a treasure house as a cemetery. A Louis Sullivan building is torn down to make way for a parking garage. Progress seems to have become quick, sudden. and wholesale.

Most novel of all is our changed attitude toward change. Now nations seem to be distinguished not by their heritage or their stock of monuments (what was once called their civilization), but by their pace of change. Rapidly "developing" nations are those that are most speedily obsolescing their inheritance. While it took centuries or even millennia to build a civilization, the transformation of an "underdeveloped" nation can be accomplished in mere decades.

The New Convergence

The supreme law of the Republic of Technology is convergence, the tendency for everything to become more like everything else. Now the distinction is seldom made between nations that are "civilized" and those that are "uncivilized." Today, when we rely on the distinction between the "developed" and the "underdeveloped" or "developing" countries, we see the experience of all peoples converging. A common standard enables us to measure the rate of convergence statistically—by G.N.P., by per capita annual income and by rates of growth. Everyone, we assume, can participate in the newly shared experience.

A person need not be learned, or even literate, to share the fruits of technology. While the enjoyment of printed matter is restricted to those who can read, anybody can get the message from a television screen. The converging forces of everyday experience are both sublingual and translingual. People who never could have been persuaded to read Goethe will eagerly drive a Volkswagen.

The great literature that brings some people together also builds barriers. Literary classics may nourish chauvinism and create ideologies. Wars tend to reinforce national stereotypes and to harden ideologies. When the United States entered World War I, its schools ceased teaching German. Beethoven and Wagner were taboo. Still, at that very moment, American military research teams were studying German technology. Even while Indira Gandhi restricted American newsmen and American publications, she desperately tried to make the Indian technology more like the American. Technology dilutes and dissolves ideology.

In each successive world war, the competition in technology becomes more fierce—and more effective. The splitting of the atom and the exploring of space bear witness to the stimulus of competition, the convergence of efforts, the involuntary collaboration of wartime enemies. Technology is the natural foe of nationalism.

With crushing inevitability, the advance of technology brings nations together and narrows the differences between the experiences of their people. The destruction by modern warfare tends to reduce the balance of advantage between victor and vanquished. The spectacular industrial progress of Japan and Germany after World War II was actually facilitated by the wholesale destruction of their industrial plant.

Each forward step in modern technology tends to reduce the difference between the older categories of experience. Take, for example, the once elementary distinction between transportation and communication: between moving the person and moving the message. While communication once was an inferior substitute for transportation (you had to read the account because you couldn't get there), it is now often the preferred alternative. The television screen (by traditional categories a mode of communication) brings together people who still remain in their separate living rooms. With the increasing congestion of city traffic, with the parking problem, and with the lengthened holding patterns over airports, our television screen becomes a superior way of getting there. So, when it comes to public events, now you are often more there when you are here than when you are there!

Broadcasting is perhaps the most potent everyday witness to the converging powers of technology. The most democratic of all forms of public communication, broadcasting converges people, drawing them into the same experience in ways never before possible.

The democratizing impact of television has been strikingly similar to the historic impact of printing. Even in this, television's first half-century, we have seen its power to disband armies, to cashier presidents, to create a whole new democratic world—democratic in ways never before imagined, even in America. We cannot ignore the fact that the era when television became a universal engrossing American experience, the first era when Americans everywhere could witness in living color the sit-ins, the civil rights marches, was also the era of a civil rights revolution, of the popularization of protests on an unprecedented scale, of a new era for minority power, of a newly potent public intervention in foreign policy, of a new, more publicized meaning to the constitutional rights of petition, of the removal of an American President. The Vietnam War was the first American war which was a television experience. Watergate was the first national political scandal which was a television experience. The college-student protests of the sixties were the first nonsporting college events to become television experiences.

The great levelers, broadcast messages and images, go without discrimination into the homes of rich and poor, white and black, young and old. More than 96 percent of American households have at least one television set. If you own a set, no admission fee is required to enter TV land and to have a front seat at all its marvels. No questions are asked, no skill is needed. You need not even sit still or keep quiet. To enjoy what TV brings, the illiterate are just as well qualified as the educated—some would say even better qualified. Our Age of Broadcasting is a fitting climax, then, to the history of a nation whose birth certificate proclaimed that "all men are created equal" and which has aimed to bring everything to everybody.

2

We have reaped myriad benefits as citizens of the new Republic of Technology. Our American standard of living is a familiar name for these daily blessings. Our increased longevity, the decline of epidemics, the widening of literacy, the reduced hours of labor, the widening of political participation, our household conveniences, the reduction of the discomforts of winter and of summer, the growth of schools and colleges and universities, the flourishing of libraries and museums, unprecedented opportunities to explore the world—all are by-products of the New Obsolescence and the New Convergence. They have become so familiar that they are undervalued. But some strange fruit is apt to grow in the fertile orchards of our technological progress. If we remain aware of the special risks in the community of our future, we will run less risk of losing these unprecedented benefits that we have come to take for granted.

Here are a few of the forces at work in the Republic of Technology that will shape our American lives in the next century:

Technology invents needs and exports problems. We will be misled if we think that technology will be directed primarily to satisfying "demands" or "needs" or to solving recognized "problems." There was no "demand" for the telephone, the automobile, radio or television. It is no accident that our nation—the most advanced in technology—is also the most advanced in advertising. Technology is a way of multiplying the unnecessary. And advertising is a way of persuading us that we didn't know what we needed. Working together, technology and advertising create progress by developing the need for the unnecessary. The Republic of Technology where we will be living is a feedback world. There wants will be created not by "human nature" or by century-old yearnings, but by technology itself.

Technology creates momentum and is irreversible. Nothing can be uninvented. This tragicomic fact will dominate our lives as citizens of the Republic of Technology. While any device can be made obsolete, no device can be forgotten, or erased from the arsenal of technology. While the currents of politics and of culture can be stopped, deflected, or even reversed, technology is irreversible. In recent years, Germany, Greece, and some other countries have gone from democracy to dictatorship and back to democracy. But we cannot go back and forth between the kerosene lamp and the electric light. Our inability to uninvent will prove ever more troublesome as our technology proliferates and refines more and more unimagined, seemingly irrelevant wants. Driven by "needs" for the unnecessary, we remain impotent to conjure the needs away. Our Aladdin's lamp of technology makes myriad new genii appear, but cannot make them disappear. The automobile—despite all we have learned of its diabolism—cannot be magicked away. The most we seem able to do is to make futile efforts to appease the automobile—by building parking temples on choice urban real estate and by deferring to the automobile with pedestrian overpasses and tunnels. We drive miles—and when we are at the airport we walk miles—all for the convenience of the airplane. Our national politics is shaped more and more by the imperious demands of television. Our negotiations with the Genie of Television all seem to end in our unconditional surrender. We live, and will live, in a world of increasingly involuntary commitments.

Technology assimilates. The Republic of Technology, ruthlessly egalitarian, will accomplish what the prophets, political philosophers and revolutionaries could not. Already it assimilates times and places and peoples and things—a faithful color reproduction of the *Mona Lisa,* the voice and image of Franklin D. Roosevelt, of Winston Churchill, or of Gandhi. You too can have a ringside seat at the World Series, at Wimbledon—or anywhere else. Without a constitutional amendment or a decision of the Supreme Court, technology forces us to equalize our experience. More than ever before, the daily experience of Americans will be created equal—or at least ever more similar.

Technology insulates and isolates. While technology seems to bring us together, it does so only by making new ways of separating us from one another. The One World of Americans in the future will be a world of 250 million private compartments. The progression from the intimately jostling horse-drawn carriage to the railroad car to the encapsulated lone automobile rider and then to the seat-belted airplane passenger who cannot converse with his seatmate because they are both wearing earphones for the recorded music; the progression from the parent reading aloud to the children to the living theater with living audiences to the darkened motion-picture house to the home of private television sets, each twinkling in a different room for a different member of the family—these are the natural progressions of technology. Each of us will have his personal machine, adjusted, focused, and preselected for his private taste. CB radio now has begun to provide every citizen with his own broadcasting and receiving station. Each of us will be in danger of being suffocated by his own tastes. Moreover, these devices that enlarge our sight and vision in space seem somehow to imprison us in the present. The electronic technology that reaches out instantaneously over the continents does very little to help us cross the centuries.

Technology uproots. In this Republic of Technology the experience of the present actually uproots us and separates us from our own special time and place. For technology aims to insulate and immunize us against the peculiar chances, perils, and opportunities of our natural climate, our raw landscape. The snowmobile makes a steep mountain slope or the tongue of a glacier just another highway. Our America has been blessed by a myriad variety of landscapes. But whether we are on the mountaintop, in the desert, on shipboard, in our automobile, or on an airplane, we are protected from the climate, the soil, the sand, the snow, the water. Our roots, such as they are, grow in an antiseptic hydroponic solution. Instead of enjoying the weather given us "by Nature and by Nature's God" (in Jefferson's phrase), we worry about the humidifier and the air conditioner.

Many of these currents of change carry us further along the grand and peculiarly American course of our history. More than any other modern people we have been free of the curse of ideology, free to combine the nations, free to rise above chauvinism, free to take our clues from the delightful, unexplored, uncongested world around us. We have, for the most part, avoided the brutal homogeneities of the concentration camp and the instant orthodoxies that are revisable at the death of a Mao. During our first two centuries, a raw continent made us flexible and responsive. Our New World remains more raw and more unexplored than we will admit.

The Republic of Technology offers us the opportunity to make our nation's third century American in some novel ways. We remain the world's laboratory. We like to try the new as do few other peoples in the world. Our experiment of binding together peoples from everywhere by opportunities rather than by ideologies will continue. The Republic of Technology offers fantastic new opportunities for opportunity.

A world where experience will be created equal tempts us in new ways and offers new dilemmas. These are the New World dilemmas of our next century. Will we be able to continue to enrich our lives with the ancient and durable treasures, to enjoy our inheritance from our nation's founders, while the winds of obsolescence blow about us and while we enjoy the delights of ever-wider sharing? Will we be able to share the exploring spirit, reach for the unknown, enjoy the multiplication of our wants, live in a world whose rhetoric is advertising, whose standard of living has become its morality—yet avoid the delusions of utopia and live a life within satisfying limits? Can we be exhilarated by the momentum that carries us willy-nilly beyond our imaginings and yet have some sense of control over our own destiny?

Suggestions for Discussion and Writing

1. For Boorstin, the Republic of Technology "is open to all, because it is a community of shared *experience*." What, for him, constitutes this "shared experience"? Do you find any important elements of human experience missing from his formulation?

2. Toward the end of his essay, Boorstin asserts that Americans, more than any other modern people, "have been free of the curse of ideology." Do you agree? Is there such a thing as an American ideology? Write an essay in which you argue your position.

3. Boorstin says, "The great literature that brings some people together also builds barriers." Does he support this assertion? Do you agree with him?

4. What for Boorstin constitutes "community"? Write a brief essay in which you compare his view with that of Gerald Weissmann in the following selection.

5. Boorstin quotes Thomas Huxley, disturbed by what he observed at the Philadelphia Exhibition, as saying, "I cannot say that I am in the slightest impressed by your bigness or your material resources, as such. Size is not grandeur. . . ." Hoyle too is concerned about "bigness" and a preoccupation with material resources. What troubles these two scientists about "bigness"? Why is size not grandeur?

6. What traditional element of community is lost with the coming of "The New Obsolescence"?

☐ WORDSWORTH AT THE BARBICAN

Gerald Weissmann (b. 1930)

A native of Vienna, Gerald Weissmann emigrated to the United States in 1938 and became an American citizen in 1943. He received his M.D. from New York University in 1954 and went on to become a professor of medicine at that university's medical school. Widely recognized for his research in cell biology and the mechanisms of inflammation, Weissmann has throughout his career been associated with numerous national and international scientific institutes, including the Marine Biology Laboratory at Woods Hole, Massachusetts. His first collection of essays, *The Woods Hole Cantata* (1985), explores a wide range of medical and social concerns, all united by the author's insistence on placing science within its social context. In the following selection, taken from *The Doctor with Two Heads* (1990), Weissmann discusses the separation of art and science in contemporary culture.

The Barbican Arts and Conference Centre, a glum assembly of concrete high-rises and bunkered flats, overshadows the City of London. Oldest of London's districts, the City for several centuries presented a harmonious skyline in which no structure competed for attention with the splendid dome of St. Paul's Cathedral, designed by Christopher Wren. Pierced only by the occasional steeple of one of Wren's lesser masterpieces or by a Regency cupola, the townscape remained open to the English sky and its infrequent gift of sunshine. Seen at dawn from the distance of Westminster Bridge, the City prompted Wordsworth's claim that

Earth has not anything to show more fair:
Dull would be he of soul who could pass by
A sight so touching in its majesty:
This City now doth, like a garment, wear
The beauty of the morning; silent, bare,
Ships, towers, domes, theatres, and temples lie
Open unto the fields, and to the sky;
All bright and glittering in the smokeless air.

("Composed upon Westminster Bridge")

That description does not apply today. Although some of the majesty remains, the grime of the Industrial Revolution, the incendiary bombs of the Luftwaffe, and the towering cranes of modern planners have turned great parcels of the City of Wren and Wordsworth into a Houston-on-the-Thames. One might, of course, argue that the modern city isn't all bad news. Whereas Earth may not have had anything to show more fair than the London of 1802, it certainly may be said now to have places to show that are cleaner and healthier: the London of 1990, for one. By my reckoning, even the grim Barbican has at least two desirable features.

First, the planners have encased a rich cluster of cultural treasures within those concrete bunkers. The Arts Centre houses not only the London Symphony Orchestra but also the Royal Shakespeare Company. There are large and small concert halls, theaters, and cinemas, two exhibition salons, art galleries, the Museum of London, a botanical conservatory, and a variety of meeting and practice rooms. This mall of culture is flanked by associated shops, pubs, and restaurants that have been neatly apportioned among the concrete piazzas and dim loggias.

The second feature is probably unplanned. No doubt on the basis of the questionable experiments of Le Corbusier in sunnier climes, modern architectural canon decrees that its megaliths be hoisted on pylons, among which the pedestrian can amble in the shade. The Barbican, no rebel against canon, has pylons aplenty. Removed from cars and commerce by empty plazas and shop-free arcades, the pedestrian can pick his way among the pylons to avoid the rain but not—alas!—the wind of London in autumn. The avid jogger soon appreciates that the dreary acreage of traffic-free Barbican is perhaps the only spot in central London where he can plod for a few miles without becoming soaked or choked.

On a recent Saturday morning, I was taking a run through the Barbican and became lost among all those pillars. Dodging the drafts, I suddenly found myself in a semicircular corridor, carpeted in red and decorated with an excess of brushed chrome. Signs informed me that I was on level six of nine levels of the Barbican, and it struck me how appropriate it was that this place, so like the one described by Dante, was divided into levels or circles rather than old-fashioned floors or stories. The corridor along which I now loped was faced on one side by glass partitions, through which could be seen the administrative offices of the Barbican. They were brilliantly lit and empty, save for one large antechamber, in which a dozen or so overtly miserable people sat waiting before a Cerberus-like secretary.

Curious as to what the action was in this belly of the cultural beast, I stopped to read a small placard on the door: "AUDITIONS THIS SATURDAY 9:30 A.M. IN ROOM B." Through the glass, I could see that the sad young people were musicians—string players in their late teens or early twenties, with damp black cases containing violins, violas, or cellos lying at their feet or across their feet. The women's wet hair was very short, the men's very long, and all fidgeted with it a good deal. Puddles collected at their feet. They did not speak to each other and assumed the expected demeanor of poor relatives about to be read out of a rich uncle's will. It was nine forty-five, and the honcho or hiring committee was clearly not on board. As the group waited, they lapsed into positions that now resembled those of outpatients at an oral-surgery clinic. They leafed glumly through damp newspapers.

Their obvious discomfort, wet locks, and clearly precarious position aroused sympathy. I recalled Anthony Powell's comment: "Reverting to the University at forty, one was reminded of the unremitting squalor of the undergraduate existence." That squalor is a function not only of means but also of ways. The young—ambitious, feisty, and filled with single-minded delight in mastery of their métier—are forced to jump through so many mazes, to wait in so many anterooms. How few, if any, of these young talents here on the block will be making a living at the fiddle or cello a decade from now! How long a road to walk for the sake of art! And the career itself: How dependent on luck, on critics, on changing musical fashion! As I was in this avuncular vein, Wordsworth sprang again to mind:

> I think of thee with many fears
> For what may be thy lot in future years.
>
> ("To H. C.")

But these charitable sentiments were erased by details of the tableau behind the glass. I noticed that the newspapers in which many of the young instrumentalists were engrossed were of the sort that even the BBC calls the "tits-and-bum tabloids": the *Daily Mail,* the *Daily Express,* the dreadful *Star,* and Rupert Murdoch's *Sun.* Difficult as it may be for an American to abandon the notion that we lead the world in trashy journalism, it must be conceded that the Brits have us beat by a country mile. Pages of scandal and acres of milk-fed flesh are served up morning and evening by these pop tabloids to support the proposition that "*The Sun* never sets on the British rear." Hurricanes may have toppled the oaks of London, the stock markets of the world may have dribbled down the drain, missile treaties may have been signed or broken, but daily the tabloids of England display on page 1 the knees of Princess Di and on page 3 the breasts of a working-class model. This mass assault on modesty, taste, and women in general seems to arouse no great protest on the part of young Albion.

The irony at the Barbican was the sight of all those would-be virtuosos of high art—those future Heifetzes, Yo-Yo Mas, Jacqueline Du Prés—digging their noses into *The Star* with its glossy shot of Marvellous Mandy's bare *poitrine*. Mandy is alleged to have "sauce! But then the magnificent 19-year-old model does come from Worcester. And when she's not posing for the cameras, there's nothing Mandy likes more than reading romantic novels and tuning-in to her favorite telly shows." How unlike the view of women from gentle Wordsworth:

> A Being breathing thoughtful breath,
> A Traveller between life and death;
> The reason firm, the temperate will,
> Endurance, foresight, strength, and skill;
> A perfect Woman, nobly planned,
> To warn, to comfort, and command;
> And yet a Spirit still, and bright
> With something of angelic light.

("She Was a Phantom of Delight")

Those glorious vocables might seem more appropriate than *The Star* as morning reading for our young instrumentalists. They were, after all, about to make the most sublime noises of our civilization: Mozart rondos, Vivaldi concerti, the unaccompanied cello suites of Bach. Above their heads hung great posters announcing the masters: Rostropovich conducting Tchaikovsky, Jessye Norman singing Puccini, Itzhak Perlman playing Mozart. Oblivious to musical piety, the young paid more attention to Marvellous Mandy and her sisters of the tabloids. It struck me that only Wolfgang Amadeus Mozart might have shown the same preference.

With him in mind, the scene at the Barbican suggested other themes. Mozart, that foulmouthed angel, was the very model of an eighteenth-century Freemason. Skeptical, irreverent, without a trace of conventional piety, he anticipated not only the court manners of our John McEnroe but also the pop spirit of *The Star*. No guardian angel of Arts Centres he! How different in temperament from the CEO of English Romanticism:

> My heart leaps up when I behold
>   A rainbow in the sky:
> So was it when my life began;
> So is it now I am a man;
> So be it when I shall grow old,
>   Or let me die!
> The Child is father of the Man;
> And I could wish my days to be
> Bound each to each by natural piety.

Wordsworth, Coleridge, and Keats not only waged their Romantic revolution on behalf of "natural piety" but also presided over the expulsion of natural science from the temples of art, beginning with Isaac Newton. The English Enlightenment had been fueled by the science of Newton; the young Romantics seem to have decided that Newton himself must disappear with his Age. In verses that require no annotation by a psychohistorian, Wordsworth recalls his adolescent self peering from a college pillow to see by moonlight:

> The antechapel where the statue stood
> Of Newton with his prism and silent face.

> (*The Prelude,* Book III)

Once Newton the father was toppled from his Cambridge plinth, a young poet might dare to put the rainbow together again. *"O statua gentilissima, del Gran Commendatore,"* with that prism in the statue's hand! This somewhat Oedipal obsession with Newtonian optics on the part of the Romantics is well described by Marjorie Hope Nicolson in her *Newton Demands the Muse.* At a memorable dinner in 1817, Keats and Wordsworth agreed that Newton was the opposition. He had destroyed all the poetry of the rainbow by reducing it to its primary colors. "Wordsworth was in fine cue," and at the end of the evening, Keats and Wordsworth joined in the toast of Charles Lamb to "Newton's health, and confusion to mathematics!" Wordsworth's verse enlarged on the theme:

> Whatever be the cause, 'tis sure that they who pry and pore
> Seem to meet with little gain, seem less happy than before:
> One after One they take their turn, nor have I one espied
> That doth not slackly go away, as if dissatisfied.

> ("Star-Gazers")

Since natural science, the realm of those who "pry and pore," can yield no satisfaction and since it reduces Nature to mathematics, why not dispense with its study once and for all?

It could be argued that in England art and science parted company somewhere between 1805 and 1820, with the Two Cultures going their separate ways ever since. It cannot be coincidental that Wordsworth and company discovered Nature, or at least the rustic landscape of England, at that moment when the Industrial Revolution was about to change that landscape forever. I have a hunch that the poet's fear of Newton followed the peasant's fear of steam. It was not a prescient vision of future Barbicans but news of a railroad through his home turf at Windermere that provoked Wordsworth to cry: "Is there no nook of English ground secure from rash assault?"

Mad William Blake joined the anti-Newtonians. He was sure that the "Epicurean" philosophies of Bacon, Locke, and Newton were responsible for the dark satanic mills that were defacing England's green and pleasant land. With his characteristic precision of thought he managed to conflate all the enemies of the Romantic movement. A few samples offered by Nicolson suffice:

Item: "The End of Epicurean or Newtonian Philosophy . . . is Atheism."

Item: "God forbid that Truth should be confined to Mathematical Demonstration."

Item: "Nature says 'Miracle,' Newton says 'Doubt.' "

Item: "The House of the Intellect is leaping from the cliffs of Memory and Reasoning; it is a barren Rock; it is also called the barren Waste of Locke and Newton."

Item: "Art is the Tree of Life, Science is the Tree of Death."

Now these unkind aphorisms may be attributed to Blake's imperfect grasp of science, but I'm afraid that the prattle continues today. Cynthia Ozick, also a great fan of the Old Testament, has told readers of *The New York Times Book Review* that art deals with the world of men, science the world of God. O Newton! Thou shouldst be living at this hour.

When I emerged from the swank bowels of the Arts Centre, the rain had stopped. Since the western terraces of the Barbican are only a hundred or so yards from the medical school I was visiting, I headed toward Charterhouse Square. St. Bartholomew's Hospital Medical College is situated at its northern side and has together with the square maintained many of the older graces of the London townscape. Brick and limestone, arch and cupola, lawns and trees are disposed in easy lines; the visual grammar is traditional. In consequence, after crossing Aldersgate Street, the busy traffic artery that separates the Barbican from this oasis of amenity, I found myself on cobblestone beneath the falling leaves. It struck me as ironic that modern science, which is thriving, was housed in conventional structures, while classical music, which is not, is played mostly in temples of confused modern design.

On the steps of the residential hall sat a group of medical students. In age, dress, and demeanor they were indistinguishable from the string players across the road. Some were waiting for the results of an exam to be posted on the bulletin board in the pharmacology building. They cannot have been reassured by the warning that accompanied an earlier posting of grades on that board: "Those with Grade D are going to have to improve their performance if they are not going to sink." The dozen or so students sat under wet leaves, hard rock came from a car radio, and several were preoccupied with Marvellous Mandy in *The Star.* A second tableau!

On this Saturday morning in London, on either side of Aldersgate Street, sat the young of the Two Cultures waiting to have their performances judged. Poised between the safety of school and the hazards of a career, they seemed to be united only by the glitter of pop and the cramps of adolescence. Wordsworth might be called the first poet of modern adolescence; indeed, I've always considered the Romantics to be the laureates of freshman passion, the troubadours of testosterone. No one has gotten adolescent angst better than Wordsworth at Cambridge:

> Examinations, when the man was weighed
> As in a balance! of excessive hopes,
> Tremblings withal and commendable fears,
> Small jealousies, and triumphs good or bad . . .
> Wishing to hope without a hope, some fears
> About my future worldly maintenance,
> And, more than all, a strangeness in the mind.

> (*The Prelude,* Book III)

Wordsworth's turmoil at Trinity, his fear for his worldly maintenance, remind one that whatever else the Romantic rebellion accomplished, it was coincident with the gradual ascent of the middle classes. Only an aristocracy can afford a cult of the amateur; those who would busy themselves looking about for worldly maintenance, who would wish to rise from mine and mill and field, had better be very good at doing one thing. The middle class was asked to choose art or science, and the Romantics knew which side was theirs. By the 1840s the furrow between art and science had deepened: Wordsworth, Keats, Coleridge, Blake, and Lamb had succeeded in erasing the language of science from the blackboards of culture. And on the other side of the gap, the Royal Society began stripping its rolls of literati and amateurs. From 1847, the pattern was set that guaranteed that for over a century no British youth has been taught *both* art and science at the university level.

It may be a bit facile to trace the divorce in England between the Two Cultures to the Romantic revolution. But the unity of all cultural effort had been the unwritten rule of the Western world from Aristotle to Maimonides, from Avicenna to Spinoza, from the Florentine Accademia to the *philosophes.* And at the tables of the English Enlightenment, Wren supped with Boyle; Hooke drank with Hobbes. Nicolson's monograph has resurrected a whole school of poetry, the "scientific" poets of the eighteenth century, who spelled out the facts of science in the cadence of enlightened rhyme. The poet James Thomson saw the rainbow through the eyes of Newton:

> In fair proportion running from the red
> To where the violet fades into the sky
> Here, awful Newton, the dissolving clouds
> Form, fronting on the sun, thy showery prism,
> And to the sage-instructed eye unfold
> The various twine of light, by thee disclosed
> From the white mingled blaze.

> ("Spring")

The symbol of the prism posed no threat to the poets of the eighteenth century; it represented instead Enlightenment in all its radiant aspects. But Wordsworth saw the rainbow much as the ancients did and used that sign in the sky as a text for a sermon on natural piety.

I must admit that the cleavage of English science from its art in the nineteenth century has not served to diminish the vigor of either. We might in fact propose that without that sort of differentiation, we would still be back in the world of the eighteenth century. I'm clearly of two minds on this point. I wish there *were* areas of experience—other than pop culture or generational turmoil—on which the two groups of students I had seen that morning could agree. At the Barbican, in that tiresome failure of design, the theater directors were devoting their great skills to producing a cycle of Jean Genet's dramas. On the third floor of the pharmacology building at ancient Bart's, a sparkling team of scientists, led by Nobel laureate Sir John Vane, was solving the rebus of how sticky blood platelets cause heart attacks.

It is unlikely that modern drama would have differentiated to its absurdist phase, or that we could be influencing heart attacks by antiplatelet drugs, had we not first separated one art from another and one science from the next until no biologist has any idea as to what the astronomers are talking about. We have paid a heavy price for that differentiation. We have made junkyards of our cities, clowns of our rulers, gibberish of our journals, and boors of our chemists. We have made it almost impossible to hold general conversations on topics too complex for Marvellous Mandy and have reduced poetry to a hobby for professors. It is sometimes difficult to be sure what we have gained in the process—other than dramas of Genet and the discovery of how blood clots. I *am* sure that among the advantages we have gained has been a life span long enough for most of us to go expertly about any business we wish, including that of art or science. We have become not one culture, not two, but a thousand. We have become as differentiated as the tissues of our body and for the same purpose: perfection of the life *and* of the work.

Deep under the great trees of Charterhouse Square is the mass grave of 50,000 Londoners who died of the Black Death. High above the ancient grave, across Aldersgate Street, rise the towers of Barbican, where a healthy people of the thousand cultures breathe clean air and Stravinsky pulses among the pylons.

> I was the Dreamer, they the Dream; I roamed
> Delighted through the motley spectacle;
> Gowns grave, or gaudy, doctors, students, streets,
> Courts, cloisters, flocks of churches, gateways, towers.
>
> (*The Prelude*, Book III)

We owe to Wordsworth many towers, many walls.

Suggestions for Discussion and Writing

1. What is Weissmann's attitude toward the Barbican Arts and Conference Centre? What details of language, specific literary allusions, and other elements help establish this attitude?

2. Look up the meaning of the word "barbican." Does the name Barbican Arts and Conference Centre imply anything about the status of the arts in modern culture?

3. What is the effect of the reference to Sir Christopher Wren's Saint Paul's Cathedral and to Wordsworth's poem, "Composed upon Westminster Bridge"?

4. Why was Newton "the opposition" for Romantic poets in the early nineteenth century? Would Hoyle agree that, in England, "art and science parted company somewhere between 1805 and 1820, with the Two Cultures going their separate ways ever since"?

5. How is Weissmann's discussion of the British tabloid press relevant to his broader argument?

6. Toward the end of his essay, Weissmann suggests that "differentiation" *between* art and science as well as *within* the arts and sciences is a necessary condition for continued progress in both art and science. Do you agree? What, according to Weissmann, has been the cost of this differentiation?

7. What is the force of the final paragraph? What does Weissmann mean when he says, "We owe to Wordsworth many towers, many walls"?

8. What is the tone of this essay? How does it differ from that of Dubos's essay?

9. Write an essay on the idea of "community" in "Wordsworth at the Barbican."

CHAPTER 3

Science, Religion, and the Arts

THE REACH OF IMAGINATION

Jacob Bronowski
(1908–1974)

For a biographical sketch of the author, see page 30.
In the following essay, taken from *A Sense of the Future* (1974),
Bronowski argues that the creative imagination plays as important
a role in science as it does in the arts.

> Before me floats an image, man or shade,
> Shade more than man, more image than a shade.
>
> *W. B. Yeats,* Byzantium (*1930*)

For three thousand years, poets have been enchanted and moved
and perplexed by the power of their own imagination. In a short
and summary essay I can hope at most to lift one small corner of that
mystery; and yet it is a critical corner. I shall ask, What goes on in
the mind when we imagine? You will hear from me that one answer
to this question is fairly specific: which is to say, that we can describe
the working of the imagination. And when we describe it as I shall
do, it becomes plain that imagination is a specifically *human* gift. To
imagine is the characteristic act, not of the poet's mind, or the
painter's, or the scientist's, but of the mind of man.

My stress here on the word "human" implies that there is a clear
difference in this between the actions of men and those of other
animals. Let me then start with a classical experiment with animals

117

and children which Walter Hunter thought out in Chicago about 1910. That was the time when scientists were agog with the success of Ivan Pavlov in forming and changing the reflex actions of dogs, which Pavlov had first announced in 1903. Pavlov had been given a Nobel prize the next year, in 1904, although in fairness I should say that the award did not cite his work on the conditioned reflex, but on the digestive glands.

Hunter duly trained some dogs and other animals on Pavlov's lines. They were taught that when a light came on over one of the three tunnels out of their cage, that tunnel would be open; they could escape down it, and were rewarded with food if they did. But once he had fixed that conditioned reflex, Hunter added to it a deeper idea: he gave the mechanical experiment a new dimension, literally—the dimension of time. Now he no longer let the dog go to the lighted tunnel at once; instead, he put out the light, and then kept the dog waiting a little while before he let him go. In this way Hunter timed how long an animal can remember where it has last seen the signal light to its escape route.

The results were and are staggering. A dog or a rat forgets which one of three tunnels has been lit up within a matter of seconds—in Hunter's experiment, ten seconds at most. If you want such an animal to do much better than this, you must make the task much simpler: you must face it with only two tunnels to choose from. Even so, the best that Hunter could do was to have a dog remember for five minutes which one of two tunnels had been lit up.

I am not quoting these times as if they were exact and universal: they surely are not. Hunter's experiment, more than fifty years old now, had many faults of detail. For example, there were too few animals, they were oddly picked, and they did not all behave consistently. It may be unfair to test a dog for what it *saw*, when it commonly follows its nose rather than its eyes. It may be unfair to test any animal in the unnatural setting of a laboratory cage. And there are higher animals, such as chimpanzees and other primates, which certainly have longer memories than the animals that Hunter tried.

Yet when all these provisos have been made (and met, by more modern experiments), the facts are still startling and characteristic. An animal cannot recall a signal from the past for even a short fraction of the time that a man can—for even a short fraction of the time that a child can. Hunter made comparable tests with six-year-old children, and found, of course, that they were incomparably better than the best of his animals. There is a striking and basic difference between a man's ability to imagine something that he saw or experienced, and an animal's failure.

Animals make up for this by other and extraordinary gifts. The salmon and the carrier pigeon can find their way home as we cannot; they have, as it were, a practical memory that man cannot match. But their actions always depend on some form of habit: on instinct or on learning, which reproduce by rote a train of known responses. They do not depend, as human memory does, on the recollection of absent things.

Where is it that the animal falls short? We get a clue to the answer, I think, when Hunter tells us how the animals in his experiment tried to fix their recollection. They most often pointed themselves at the light before it went out, as some gundogs point rigidly at the game they scent—and get the name "pointer" from the posture. The animal makes ready to act by building the signal into its action. There is a primitive imagery in its stance, it seems to me; it is as if the animal were trying to fix the light in its mind by fixing it in its body. And indeed, how else can a dog mark and (as it were) name one of three tunnels, when it has no such words as "left" and "right" and no such numbers as "one," "two," "three"? The directed gesture of attention and readiness is perhaps the only symbolic device that the dog commands to hold on to the past, and thereby to guide itself into the future.

I used the verb "to imagine" a moment ago, and now I have some ground for giving it a meaning. "To imagine" means to make images and to move them about inside one's head in new arrangements. When you and I recall the past, we imagine it in this direct and homely sense. The tool that puts the human mind ahead of the animal is imagery. For us, memory does not demand the preoccupation that it demands in animals, and it lasts immensely longer, because we fix it in images or other substitute symbols. With the same symbolic vocabulary we spell out the future—not one but many futures, which we weigh one against another.

I am using the word "image" in a wide meaning, which does not restrict it to the mind's eye as a visual organ. An image in my usage is what Charles Peirce called a "sign," without regard for its sensory quality. Peirce distinguished between different forms of signs, but there is no reason to make his distinction here, for the imagination works equally with them all, and that is why I call them all images.

Indeed, the most important images for human beings are simply words, which are abstract symbols. Animals do not have words, in our sense: there is no specific center for language in the brain of any animal, as there is in the human brain. In this respect at least, we know that the human imagination depends on a configuration in the brain that has only evolved in the last one or two million years. In the same period, evolution has greatly enlarged the front lobes in the human brain, which govern the sense of the past and the future; and it is a fair guess that they are probably the seat of our other images. (Part of the evidence for this guess is that damage to the front lobes in primates reduces them to a state of Hunter's animals.) If the guess turns out to be right, we shall know why man has come to look like a highbrow or an egghead: because otherwise there would not be room in his head for his imagination.

The images play out for us events which are not present to our senses, and thereby guard the past and create the future—a future that does not yet exist, and may never come to exist in that form. By contrast, the lack of symbolic ideas, or their rudimentary poverty, cuts off an animal from the past and the future alike, and imprisons it in the present. Of all the distinctions between man and animal, the characteristic gift which makes us human is the power to work with symbolic images: the gift of imagination.

This is really a remarkable finding. When Philip Sidney in 1580 defended poets (and all unconventional thinkers) from the Puritan charge that they were liars, he said that a maker must imagine things that are not. Halfway between Sidney and us, William Blake said, "What is now proved was once only imagin'd." About the same time, in 1796, Samuel Taylor Coleridge for the first time distinguished between the passive fancy and the active imagination, "the living Power and prime Agent of all human Perception." Now we see that they were right, and precisely right: the human gift is the gift of imagination—and that is not just a literary phrase.

Nor is it just a literary gift; it is, I repeat, characteristically human. Almost everything that we do that is worth doing is done in the first place in the mind's eye. The richness of human life is that we have many lives; we live the events that do not happen (and some that cannot) as vividly as those that do; and if thereby we die a thousand deaths, that is the price we pay for living a thousand lives. (A cat, of course, has only nine.) Literature is alive to us because we live its images, but so is any play of mind—so is chess: the lines of play that we foresee and try in our heads and dismiss are as much a part of the game as the moves that we make. John Keats said that the unheard melodies are sweeter, and all chess players sadly recall that the combinations that they planned and which never came to be played were the best.

I make this point to remind you, insistently, that imagination is the manipulation of images in one's head; and that the rational manipulation belongs to that, as well as the literary and artistic manipulation. When a child begins to play games with things that stand for other things, with chairs or chessmen, he enters the gateway to reason and imagination together. For the human reason discovers new relations between things not by deduction, but by that unpredictable blend of speculation and insight that scientists call induction, which—like other forms of imagination—cannot be formalized. We see it at work when Walter Hunter inquires into a child's memory, as much as when Blake and Coleridge do. Only a restless and original mind would have asked Hunter's questions and could have conceived his experiments, in a science that was dominated by Pavlov's reflex arcs and was heading toward the behaviorism of John Watson.

Let me find a spectacular example for you from history. What is the most famous experiment that you had described to you as a child? I will hazard that it is the experiment that Galileo is said to have made in Sidney's age, in Pisa about 1590, by dropping two unequal balls from the Leaning Tower. There, we say, is a man in the modern mold, a man after our own hearts: he insisted on questioning the authority of Aristotle and St. Thomas Aquinas, and seeing with his own eyes whether (as they said) the heavy ball would reach the ground before the light one. Seeing is believing.

Yet seeing is also imagining. Galileo did challenge the authority of Aristotle, and he did look hard at his mechanics. But the eye that Galileo used was the mind's eye. He did not drop balls from the Leaning Tower of Pisa—and if he had, he would have got a very doubtful answer. Instead, Galileo made an imaginary experiment (or, as the Germans say, "thought experiment") in his head, which I will describe as he did years later in the book he wrote after the Holy Office silenced him, the *Discorsi . . . intorno a due nuove scienze,* which was smuggled out to be printed in The Netherlands in 1638.

Suppose, said Galileo, that you drop two unequal balls from the tower at the same time. And suppose that Aristotle is right—suppose that the heavy ball falls faster, so that it steadily gains on the light ball and hits the ground first. Very well. Now imagine the same experiment done again, with only one difference: this time the two unequal balls are joined by a string between them. The heavy ball will again move ahead, but now the light ball holds it back and acts as a drag or brake. So the light ball will be speeded up and the heavy ball will be slowed down; they must reach the ground together because they are tied together, but they cannot reach the ground as quickly as the heavy ball alone. Yet the string between them has turned the two balls into a single mass which is heavier than either ball—and surely (according to Aristotle) this mass should therefore move faster than either ball? Galileo's imaginary experiment has uncovered a contradiction; he says trenchantly, "You see how, from your assumption that a heavier body falls more rapidly than a lighter one, I infer that a (still) heavier body falls more slowly." There is only one way out of the contradiction: the heavy ball and the light ball must fall at the same rate, so that they go on falling at the same rate when they are tied together.

This argument is not conclusive, for nature might be more subtle (when the two balls are joined) than Galileo has allowed. And yet it is something more important: it is suggestive, it is stimulating, it opens a new view—in a word, it is imaginative. It cannot be settled without an actual experiment, because nothing that we imagine can become knowledge until we have translated it into, and backed it by, real experience. The test of imagination is experience. But then, that is as true of literature and the arts as it is of science. In science, the imaginary experiment is tested by confronting it with physical experience; and in literature, the imaginative conception is tested by confronting it with human experience. The superficial speculation in science is dismissed because it is found to falsify nature; and the shallow work of art is discarded because it is found to be untrue to our own nature. So when Ella Wheeler Wilcox died in 1919, more people were reading her verses than Shakespeare's; yet in a few years her work was dead. It had been buried by its poverty of emotion and its trivialness of thought: which is to say that it had been proved to be as false to the nature of man as, say, Jean Baptiste

Lamarck and Trofim Lysenko were false to the nature of inheritance. The strength of the imagination, its enriching power and excitement, lies in its interplay with reality—physical and emotional.

I doubt if there is much to choose here between science and the arts: the imagination is not much more free, and not much less free, in one than in the other. All great scientists have used their imagination freely, and let it ride them to outrageous conclusions without crying "Halt!" Albert Einstein fiddled with imaginary experiments from boyhood, and was wonderfully ignorant of the facts that they were supposed to bear on. When he wrote the first of his beautiful papers on the random movement of atoms, he did not know that the Brownian motion which it predicted could be seen in any laboratory. He was sixteen when he invented the paradox that he resolved ten years later, in 1905, in the theory of relativity, and it bulked much larger in his mind than the experiment of Albert Michelson and Edward Morley which had upset every other physicist since 1881. All his life Einstein loved to make up teasing puzzles like Galileo's, about falling lifts and the detection of gravity; and they carry the nub of the problems of general relativity on which he was working.

Indeed, it could not be otherwise. The power that man has over nature and himself, and that a dog lacks, lies in his command of imaginary experience. He alone has the symbols which fix the past and play with the future, possible and impossible. In the Renaissance, the symbolism of memory was thought to be mystical, and devices that were invented as mnemonics (by Giordano Bruno, for example, and by Robert Fludd) were interpreted as magic signs. The symbol is the tool which gives man his power, and it is the same tool whether the symbols are images or words, mathematical signs or mesons. And the symbols have a reach and a roundness that goes beyond their literal and practical meaning. They are the rich concepts under which the mind gathers many particulars into one name, and many instances into one general induction. When a man says "left" and "right," he is outdistancing the dog not only in looking for a light; he is setting in train all the shifts of meaning, the overtones and the ambiguities, between "gauche" and "adroit" and "dexterous," between "sinister" and the sense of right. When a man counts "one, two, three," he is not only doing mathematics; he is on the path to the mysticism of numbers in Pythagoras and Vitruvius and Kepler, to the Trinity and the signs of the zodiac.

I have described imagination as the ability to make images and to move them about inside one's head in new arrangements. This is the faculty that is specifically human, and it is the common root from which science and literature both spring and grow and flourish together. For they do flourish (and languish) together; the great ages of science are the great ages of all the arts, because in them powerful minds have take fire from one another, breathless and higgledy-piggledy, without asking too nicely whether they ought to tie their imagination to falling balls or a haunted island. Galileo and Shakespeare, who were born in the same year, grew into greatness in the same age; when Galileo was looking through his telescope at the moon, Shakespeare was writing *The Tempest;* and all Europe was in ferment, from Johannes Kepler to Peter Paul Rubens, and from the first table of logarithms by John Napier to the Authorized Version of the Bible.

Let me end with a last and spirited example of the common inspiration of literature and science, because it is as much alive today as it was three hundred years ago. What I have in mind is man's ageless fantasy, to fly to the moon. I do not display this to you as a high scientific enterprise; on the contrary, I think we have more important discoveries to make here on earth than wait for us, beckoning, at the horned surface of the moon. Yet I cannot belittle the fascination which that ice-blue journey has had for the imagination of men, long before it drew us to our television screens to watch the tumbling of astronauts. Plutarch and Lucian, Ariosto and Ben Jonson wrote about it, before the days of Jules Verne and H. G. Wells and science fiction. The seventeenth century was heady with new dreams and fables about voyages to the moon. Kepler wrote one full of deep scientific ideas, which (alas) simply got his mother accused of witchcraft. In England, Francis Godwin wrote a wild and splendid work, *The Man in the Moone,* and the astronomer John Wilkins wrote a wild and learned one, *The Discovery of a New World.* They did not draw a line between science and fancy; for example, they all tried to guess just where in the journey the earth's gravity would stop. Only Kepler understood that gravity has no boundary, and put a law to it—which happened to be the wrong law.

All this was a few years before Isaac Newton was born, and it was all in his head that day in 1666 when he sat in his mother's garden, a young man of twenty-three, and thought about the reach of gravity. This was how he came to conceive his brilliant image, that the moon is like a ball which has been thrown so hard that it falls exactly as fast as the horizon, all the way round the earth. The image will do for any satellite, and Newton modestly calculated how long therefore an astronaut would take to fall round the earth once. He made it ninety minutes, and we have all seen now that he was right; but Newton had no way to check that. Instead he went on to calculate how long in that case the distant moon would take to round the earth, if indeed it behaved like a thrown ball that falls in the earth's gravity, and if gravity obeyed a law of inverse squares. He found that the answer would be twenty-eight days.

In that telling figure, the imagination that day chimed with nature, and made a harmony. We shall hear an echo of that harmony on the day when we land on the moon, because it will be not a technical but an imaginative triumph, that reaches back to the beginning of modern science and literature both. All great acts of imagination are like this, in the arts and in science, and convince us because they fill out reality with a deeper sense of rightness. We start with the simplest vocabulary of images, with "left" and "right" and "one, two, three," and before we know how it happened the words and the numbers have conspired to make a match with nature: we catch in them the pattern of mind and matter as one.

Suggestions for Discussion and Writing

1. How does Bronowski define "imagination"? What elements does "imagining" involve? What does he mean by "image"?

2. In a brief paragraph summarize the significance of Hunter's findings.

3. Describe Galileo's reasoning in the experiment at Pisa. Do you agree that the imagination was involved here?

4. Does Bronowski distinguish between the literary/artistic imagination and the scientific imagination?

5. What does Bronowski mean when he says that "the test of imagination is experience"? Explain why this "is as true of literature and the arts as it is of science."

6. Toward the end of his essay, Bronowski speaks of Newton's "brilliant image." What was that image? Newton, says Bronowski, thought about "the reach of gravity." Do you see any particular significance in Bronowski's language here?

7. Bronowski uses personal pronouns (I, we, you) throughout. At one point he writes, "Suppose, said Galileo, that you drop . . ." and at another, "I make this point to remind you . . ." What tone does such language establish? How does this tone compare with that of Heisenberg in "Science and the Beautiful" (this chapter)? Cite specific examples to support your views.

8. When Bronowski says that the great ages of science and the arts "flourish (and languish) together," he implies a close connection between science and art. Do you see any such connection between science/technology and the arts in the late twentieth century? Write an essay in which you develop your views.

9. Bronowski says, "The richness of human life is that we have many lives; we live the events that do not happen (and some that cannot) as vividly as those that do; and if thereby we die a thousand deaths, that is the price we pay for living a thousand lives." What does Bronowski mean here? Write an essay in which you explore the significance of these ideas in your own life.

☐ SCIENCE AND THE BEAUTIFUL

Werner Heisenberg (1901–1976)

For a biographical sketch of the author, see page 51.

In the following essay, taken from *Physics and Beyond* (1971), Heisenberg explores two ancient concepts of the Beautiful: first, that beauty is to be found in the "proper conformity of the parts to one another, and to the whole," and second, that it consists in the reflection in the material world of the eternal "one"—that is, of the ultimate principle of all existence. Both of these concepts have informed the development of modern science, Heisenberg argues, and, indeed, make its practice possible.

Perhaps it will be best if, without any initial attempt at a philosophical analysis of the concept of "beauty," we simply ask where we can meet the beautiful in the sphere of exact science. Here I may perhaps be allowed to begin with a personal experience. When, as a small boy, I was attending the lowest classes of the Max-Gymnasium here in Munich, I became interested in numbers. It gave me pleasure to get to know their properties, to find out, for example, whether they were prime numbers or not, and to test whether they could perhaps be represented as sums of squares, or eventually to prove that there must be infinitely many primes. Now since my father thought my knowledge of Latin to be much more important than my numerical interests, he brought home to me one day from the National Library a treatise written in Latin by the mathematician Leopold Kronecker, in which the properties of whole numbers were set in relation to the geometrical problem of dividing a circle into a number of equal parts. How my father happened to light on this particular investigation from the middle of the last century I do not know. But the study of Kronecker's work made a deep impression on me. I sensed a quite immediate beauty in the fact that, from the problem of partitioning a circle, whose simplest cases were, of course, familiar to us in school, it was possible to learn something about the totally different sort of questions involved in elementary number theory. Far in the distance, no doubt, there already floated the question whether whole numbers and geometrical forms exist, i.e., whether they are there outside the human mind or whether they have merely been created by this mind as instruments for understanding the world. But at that time I was not yet able to think about such problems. The impression of something very beautiful was, however, perfectly direct; it required no justification or explanation.

But what was beautiful here? Even in antiquity there were two definitions of beauty that stood in a certain opposition to one another. The controversy between them played a great part, especially during the Renaissance. The one describes beauty as the proper conformity of the parts to one another, and to the whole. The other, stemming from Plotinus, describes it, without any reference to parts, as the translucence of the eternal splendor of the "one" through the material phenomenon. In our mathematical example, we shall have to stop short, initially, at the first definition. The parts here are the properties of whole numbers and laws of geometrical constructions, while the whole is obviously the underlying system of mathematical axioms to which arithmetic and Euclidean geometry belong—the great structure of interconnection guaranteed by the consistency of the axiom system. We perceive that the individual parts fit together, that, as parts, they do indeed belong to this whole, and, without any reflection, we feel the completeness and simplicity of this axiom system to be beautiful. Beauty is therefore involved with the age-old problem of the "one" and the "many" which occupied—in close connection with the problem of "being" and "becoming"—a central position in early Greek philosophy.

Since the roots of exact science are also to be found at this very point, it will be as well to retrace in broad outline the currents of thought in that early age. At the starting point of the Greek philosophy of nature there stands the question of a basic principle, from which the colorful variety of phenomena can be explained. However strangely it may strike us, the well-known answer of Thales—"Water is the material first principle of all things"—contains, according to Nietzsche, three basic philosophical demands which were to become important in the developments that followed: first, that one should seek for such a unitary basic principle; second, that the answer should be given only rationally, that is, not by reference to a myth; and third and finally, that in this context the material aspect of the world must play a deciding role. Behind these demands there stands, of course, the unspoken recognition that understanding can never mean anything more than the perception of connections, i.e., unitary features or marks of affinity in the manifold.

But if such a unitary principle of all things exists, then—and this was the next step along this line of thought—one is straightway brought up against the question how it can serve to account for the fact of change. The difficulty is particularly apparent in the celebrated paradox of Parmenides. Only being is; non-being is not. But if only being is, there cannot be anything outside this being that articulates it or could bring about changes. Hence being will have to be conceived as eternal, uniform, and unlimited in space and time. The changes we experience can thus be only an illusion.

Greek thought could not stay with this paradox for long. The eternal flux of appearances was immediately given, and the problem was to explain it. In attempting to overcome the difficulty, various philosophers struck out in different directions. One road led to the atomic theory of Democritus. In addition to being, non-being can still exist as a possibility, namely as the possibility for movement and form, or, in other words, as empty space. Being is repeatable, and thus we arrive at the picture of atoms in the void—the picture that has since become infinitely fruitful as a foundation for natural science. But of this road we shall say no more just now. Our purpose, rather, is to present in more detail the other road, which led to Plato's Ideas, and which carried us directly into the problem of beauty.

This road begins in the school of Pythagoras. It is there that the notion is said to have originated that mathematics, the mathematical order, was the basic principle whereby the multiplicity of phenomena could be accounted for. Of Pythagoras himself we know little. His disciples seem, in fact, to have been a religious sect, and only the doctrine of transmigration and the laying down of certain moral and religious rules and prohibitions can be traced with any certainty to Pythagoras. But among these disciples—and this was what mattered subsequently—a preoccupation with music and mathematics played an important role. Here it was that Pythagoras is said to have made the famous discovery that vibrating strings under equal tension sound together in harmony if their lengths are in a simple numerical ratio. The mathematical structure, namely the numerical ratio as a source of harmony, was certainly one of the most momentous discoveries in the history of mankind. The harmonious concord of two strings yields a beautiful sound. Owing to the discomfort caused by beat-effects, the human ear finds dissonance disturbing, but consonance, the peace of harmony, it finds beautiful. Thus the mathematical relation was also the source of beauty.

Beauty, so the first of our ancient definitions ran, is the proper conformity of the parts to one another and to the whole. The parts here are the individual notes, while the whole is the harmonious sound. The mathematical relation can, therefore, assemble two initially independent parts into a whole, and so produce beauty. This discovery effected a breakthrough, in Pythagorean doctrine, to entirely new forms of thought, and so brought it about that the ultimate basis of all being was no longer envisaged as a sensory material—such as water, in Thales—but as an ideal principle of form. This was to state a basic idea which later provided the foundation for all exact science. Aristotle, in his *Metaphysics,* reports that the Pythagoreans,

> who were the first to take up mathematics, not only advanced this study, but also having been brought up in it they thought its principles were the principles of all things. . . . Since, again, they saw that the modifications and the ratios of the musical scales were expressible in numbers; since, then, all other things seemed in their whole nature to be modelled on numbers; and numbers seemed to be the first things in the whole of nature, they supposed the elements of numbers to be the elements of all things, and the whole heaven to be a musical scale and a number.

Understanding of the colorful multiplicity of the phenomena was thus to come about by recognizing in them unitary principles of form, which can be expressed in the language of mathematics. By this, too, a close connection was established between the intelligible and the beautiful. For if the beautiful is conceived as a conformity of the parts to one another and to the whole, and if, on the other hand, all understanding is first made possible by means of this formal connection, the experience of the beautiful becomes virtually identical with the experience of connections either understood or, at least, guessed at.

The next step along this road was taken by Plato with the formulation of his theory of Ideas. Plato contrasts the imperfect shapes of the corporeal world of the senses with the perfect forms of mathematics; the imperfectly circular orbits of the stars, say, with the perfection of the mathematically defined circle. Material things are the copies, the shadow images, of ideal shapes in reality; moreover, as we should be tempted to continue nowadays, these ideal shapes are actual because and insofar as they become "act"-ive in material events. Plato thus distinguishes here with complete clarity a corporeal being accessible to the senses and a purely ideal being apprehensible not by the senses but only through acts of mind. Nor is this ideal being in any way in need of man's thought in order to be brought forth by him. On the contrary, it is the true being, of which the corporeal world and human thinking are mere reproductions. As their name already indicates, the apprehension of Ideas by the human mind is more an artistic intuiting, a half-conscious intimation, than a knowledge conveyed by the understanding. It is a reminiscence of forms that were already implanted in this soul before its existence on earth. The central Idea is that of the Beautiful and the Good, in which the divine becomes visible and at sight of which the wings of the soul begin to grow. A passage in the *Phaedrus* expresses the following thought: the soul is awe-stricken and shudders at the sight of the beautiful, for it feels that something is evoked in it that was not imparted to it from without by the senses but has always been already laid down there in a deeply unconscious region.

But let us come back once more to understanding and thus, to natural science. The colorful multiplicity of the phenomena can be understood, according to Pythagoras and Plato, because and insofar as it is underlain by unitary principles of form susceptible of mathematical representation. This postulate already constitutes an anticipation of the entire program of contemporary exact science. It could not, however, be carried through in antiquity, since an empirical knowledge of the details of natural processes was largely lacking.

The first attempt to penetrate into these details was undertaken, as we know, in the philosophy of Aristotle. But in view of the infinite wealth initially presented here to the observing student of nature and the total lack of any sort of viewpoint from which an order might have been discernible, the unitary principles of form sought by Pythagoras and Plato were obliged to give place to the description of details. Thus there arose the conflict that has continued to this day in the debates, for example, between experimental and theoretical physics; the conflict between the empiricist, who by careful and scrupulous detailed investigation first furnishes the presuppositions for an understanding of nature, and the theoretician, who creates mathematical pictures whereby he seeks to order and so to understand nature—mathematical pictures that prove themselves, not only by their correct depiction of experience, but also and more especially by their simplicity and beauty, to be the true Ideas underlying the course of nature.

Aristotle, as an empiricist, was critical of the Pythagoreans, who, he said, "are not seeking for theories and causes to account for observed facts, but rather forcing their observations and trying to accommodate them to certain theories and opinions of their own" and were thus setting up, one might say, as joint organizers of the universe. If we look back on the history of the exact sciences, it can perhaps be asserted that the correct representation of natural phenomena has evolved from this very tension between the two opposing views. Pure mathematical speculation becomes unfruitful because from playing with the wealth of possible forms it no longer finds its way back to the small number of forms according to which nature is actually constructed. And pure empiricism becomes unfruitful because it eventually bogs down in endless tabulation without inner connection. Only from the tension, the interplay between the wealth of facts and the mathematical forms that may possibly be appropriate to them, can decisive advances spring.

But in antiquity this tension was no longer acceptable and thus, the road to knowledge diverged for a long time from the road to the beautiful. The significance of the beautiful for the understanding of nature became clearly visible again only at the beginning of the modern period, once the way back had been found from Aristotle to Plato. And only through this change of course did the full fruitfulness become apparent of the mode of thought inaugurated by Pythagoras and Plato.

This is most clearly shown in the celebrated experiments on falling bodies that Galileo probably did not, in fact, conduct from the leaning tower of Pisa. Galileo begins with careful observations, paying no attention to the authority of Aristotle, but, following the teaching of Pythagoras and Plato, he does try to find mathematical forms corresponding to the facts obtained by experiment and thus, arrives at his laws of falling bodies. However, and this is a crucial point, he is obliged, in order to recognize the beauty of mathematical forms in the phenomena, to idealize the facts, or, as Aristotle disparagingly puts it, to force them. Aristotle had taught that all moving bodies not acted upon by external forces eventually come to rest, and this was the general experience. Galileo maintains, on the contrary, that, in the absence of external forces, bodies continue in a state of uniform motion. Galileo could venture to force the facts in this way because he could point out that moving bodies are, of course, always exposed to a frictional resistance and that motion, in fact, continues the longer, the more effectively the frictional forces can be cut off. In exchange for this forcing of the facts, this idealization, he obtained a simple mathematical law, and this was the beginning of modern exact science.

Some years later, Kepler succeeded in discovering new mathematical forms in the data of his very careful observations of the planetary orbits and in formulating the three famous laws that bear his name. How close Kepler felt himself in these discoveries to the ancient arguments of Pythagoras, and how much the beauty of the connections guided him in formulating them, can be seen from the fact that he compared the revolutions of the planets about the sun with the vibrations of a string and spoke of a harmonious concord of the different planetary orbits, of a harmony of the spheres. At the end of his work on the harmony of the universe, he broke out into this cry of joy: "I thank thee, Lord God our Creator, that thou allowest me to see the beauty in thy work of creation." Kepler was profoundly struck by the fact that here he had chanced upon a central connection which had not been conceived by man, which it had been reserved to him to recognize for the first time—a connection of the highest beauty. A few decades later, Isaac Newton in England set forth this connection in all its completeness and described it in detail in his great work *Principia Mathematica.* The road of exact science was thus pointed out in advance for almost two centuries.

But are we dealing here with knowledge merely, or also with the beautiful? And if the beautiful is also involved, what role did it play in the discovery of these connections? Let us again recall the first definition given in antiquity: "Beauty is the proper conformity of the parts to one another and to the whole." That this criterion applies in the highest degree to a structure like Newtonian mechanics is something that scarcely needs explaining. The parts are the individual mechanical processes—those which we carefully isolate by means of apparatus no less than those which occur inextricably before our eyes in the colorful play of phenomena. And the whole is the unitary principle of form which all these processes comply with and which was mathematically established by Newton in a simple system of axioms. Unity and simplicity are not, indeed, precisely the same. But the fact that in such a theory the many are confronted with the one, that in it the many are unified, itself has the undoubted consequence that we also feel it at the same time to be simple and beautiful. The significance of the beautiful for the discovery of the true has at all times been recognized and emphasized. The Latin motto *"Simplex sigillum veri"*—"The simple is the seal of the true"—is inscribed in large letters in the physics auditorium of the University of Göttingen as an admonition to those who would discover what is new; another Latin motto, *"Pulchritudo splendor veritatis"*—"Beauty is the splendor of truth"—can also be interpreted to mean that the researcher first recognizes the truth by this splendor, by the way it shines forth.

Twice more in the history of exact science, this shining forth of the great connection has been the crucial signal for a significant advance. I am thinking here of two events in the physics of our own century: the emergence of relativity theory and the quantum theory. In both cases, after years of vain effort at understanding, a bewildering plethora of details has been almost suddenly reduced to order by the appearance of a connection, largely unintuitable but still ultimately simple in its substance, that was immediately found convincing by virtue of its completeness and abstract beauty—convincing, that is, to all who could understand and speak such an abstract language.

But now, instead of pursuing the historical course of events any further, let us rather put the question quite directly: What is it that shines forth here? How comes it that with this shining forth of the beautiful into exact science the great connection becomes recognizable, even before it is understood in detail and before it can be rationally demonstrated? In what does the power of illumination consist, and what effect does it have on the onward progress of science?

Perhaps we should begin here by recalling a phenomenon that may be described as the unfolding of abstract structures. It can be illustrated by the example of number theory, which we referred to at the outset, but one may also point to comparable processes in the evolution of art. For the mathematical foundation of arithmetic, or the theory of numbers, a few simple axioms are sufficient, which, in fact, merely define exactly what counting is. But with these few axioms we have already posited that whole abundance of forms which has entered the minds of mathematicians only in the course of the long history of the subject—the theory of prime numbers, of quadratic residues, of numerical congruences, etc. One might say that the abstract structures posited in and with numbers have unfolded visibly only in the course of mathematical history, that they have generated the wealth of propositions and relationships that makes up the content of the complicated science of number theory. A similar position is also occupied—at the outset of an artistic style in architecture, say—by certain simple basic forms, such as the semicircle and rectangle in Romanesque architecture. From these basic forms there arise in the course of history new, more complicated, and also altered forms, which yet can still, in some way, be regarded as variations on the same theme; thus, from the basic structures there emerges a new manner, a new style of building. We have the feeling, nonetheless, that the possibilities of development were already perceivable in these original forms, even at the outset; otherwise, it would be scarcely comprehensible that many gifted artists should have so quickly resolved to pursue these new possibilities.

Such an unfolding of abstract basic structures has assuredly also occurred in the instances I have enumerated from the history of the exact sciences. This growth, this constant development of new branches, went on in Newtonian mechanics up to the middle of the last century. In relativity theory and the quantum theory we have experienced a similar development in the present century, and the growth has not yet come to an end.

Moreover, in science, as in art, this process also has an important social and ethical aspect; for many men can take an active part in it. When a great cathedral was to be built in the Middle Ages, many master masons and craftsmen were employed. They were imbued with the idea of beauty posited by the original forms and were compelled by their task to carry out exact and meticulous work in accordance with these forms. In similar fashion, during the two centuries following Newton's discovery, many mathematicians, physicists, and technicians were called upon to deal with specific mechancial problems according to the Newtonian methods, to carry out experiments, or to effect technical applications; here, too, extreme care was always required in order to attain what was possible within the framework of Newtonian mechanics. Perhaps it may be said in general that by means of the underlying structures, in this case Newtonian mechanics, guidelines were drawn or even standards of value set up whereby it could be objectively decided whether a given task had been well or ill discharged. It is the very fact that specific requirements have been laid down, that the individual can assist by small contributions in the attainment of large goals, and that the value of his contribution can be objectively determined, which gives rise to the satisfaction proceeding from such a development for the large number of people involved. Hence even the ethical significances of technology for our present age should not be underestimated.

The development of science and technology has also produced, for example, the Idea of the airplane. The individual technician who assembles some component for such a plane, the artisan who makes it, knows that his work calls for the utmost care and exactitude and that the lives of many may well depend upon its reliability. Hence he can take pride in a well-executed piece of work, and delights, as we do, in the beauty of the aircraft, when he feels that in it the technical goal has been realized by properly adequate means. Beauty, so runs the ancient definition we have already often cited, is the proper conformity of the parts to one another and to the whole, and this requirement must also be satisfied in a good aircraft.

But in pointing thus to the evolution of beauty's ground structure, to the ethical values and demands that subsequently emerge in the historical course of development, we have not yet answered the question we asked earlier, namely, what it is that shines forth in these structures, how the great connection is recognized even before it is rationally understood in detail. Here we ought to reckon in advance with the possibility that even such recognition may be founded upon illusions. But it cannot be doubted that there actually is this perfectly immediate recognition, this shuddering before the beautiful, of which Plato speaks in the *Phaedrus.*

Among all those who have pondered on this question, it seems to have been universally agreed that this immediate recognition is not a consequence of discursive (i.e., rational) thinking. I should like here to cite two statements, one from Johannes Kepler, who has already been referred to, and the other, in our own time, from the Zürich atomic physicist Wolfgang Pauli, who was a friend of the psychologist Carl Jung. The first passage is to be found in Kepler's *Harmony of the World:*

> That faculty which perceives and recognizes the noble proportions in what is given to the senses, and in other things situated outside itself, must be ascribed to the soul. It lies very close to the faculty which supplies formal schemata to the senses, or deeper still, and thus adjacent to the purely vital power of the soul, which does not think discursively, i.e., in conclusions, as the philosophers do, and employs no considered method, and is thus not peculiar only to man, but also dwells in wild animals and the dear beasts of the field. . . . Now it might be asked how this faculty of the soul, which does not engage in conceptual thinking, and can therefore have no proper knowledge of harmonic relations, should be capable of recognizing what is given in the outside world. For to recognize is to compare the sense perception outside with the original pictures inside, and to judge that it conforms to them. Proclus has expressed the matter very finely in his simile of awakening, as from a dream. For just as the sensorily presented things in the outer world recall to us those which we formerly perceived in the dream, so also the mathematical relations given in sensibility call forth those intelligible archetypes which were already given inwardly beforehand, so that they now shine forth truly and vividly in the soul, where before they were only obscurely present there. But how have they come to be within? To this I answer that all pure Ideas or archetypal patterns of harmony, such as we were speaking of, are inherently present in those who are capable of apprehending them. But they are not first received into the mind by a conceptual process, being the product, rather, of a sort of instinctive intuition of pure quantity, and are innate in these individuals, just as the number of petals in a plant, say, is innate in its form principle, or the number of its seed chambers is innate in the apple.

So far Kepler. He is, therefore, referring us here to possibilities already to be found in the animal and plant kingdoms, to innate archetypes that bring about the recognition of forms. In our own day, Adolf Portmann, in particular, has described such possibilities, pointing, for example, to specific color patterns seen in the plumage of birds, which can possess a biological meaning only if they are also perceived by other members of the same species. The perceptual capacity will therefore have to be just as innate as the pattern itself. We may also consider bird song at this point. At first, the biological requirement here may well have been simply for a specific acoustic signal, serving to seek out the partner and understood by the latter. But to the extent that this immediate biological function declines in importance, a playful enlargement of the stock of forms may ensue, an unfolding of the underlying melodic structure, which is then found enchanting as song by even so alien a species as man. The capacity to recognize this play of forms must, at all events, be innate to the species of bird in question for certainly it has no need of discursive, rational thought. In man, to cite another example, there is probably an inborn capacity for understanding certain basic forms of the language of gesture and thus, for deciding, say, whether the other has friendly or hostile intentions—a capacity of the utmost importance for man's communal life.

Ideas similar to those of Kepler have been put forward in an essay by Pauli. He writes:

> The process of understanding in nature, together with the joy that man feels in understanding, i.e., in becoming acquainted with new knowledge, seems therefore to rest upon a correspondence, a coming into congruence of preexistent internal images of the human psyche with external objects and their behavior. This view of natural knowledge goes back, of course, to Plato and was . . . also very plainly adopted by Kepler. The latter speaks, in fact, of Ideas, preexistent in the mind of God and imprinted accordingly upon the soul, as the image of God. These primal images, which the soul can perceive by means of an innate instinct, Kepler calls archetypes. There is a very wide-ranging agreement here with the primordial images or archetypes introduced into modern psychology by C. G. Jung, which function as instinctive patterns of ideation. At this stage, the place of clear concepts is taken by images of strongly emotional content, which are not thought but are seen pictorially, as it were, before the mind's eye. Insofar as these images are the expression of a suspected but still unknown state of affairs, they can also be called symbolic, according to the definition of a symbol proposed by Jung. As ordering operators and formatives in this world of symbolic images, the archetypes function, indeed, as the desired bridge between sense perceptions and Ideas, and are therefore also a necessary precondition for the emergence of a scientific theory. Yet one must beware of displacing this *a priori* of knowledge into consciousness, and relating it to specific, rationally formulable Ideas.

In the further course of his inquiries, Pauli then goes on to show that Kepler did not derive his conviction of the correctness of the Copernican system primarily from any particular data of astronomical observation, but rather from the agreement of the Copernican picture with an archetype which Jung calls a *mandala* and which was also used by Kepler as a symbol for the Trinity. God, as prime mover, is seen at the center of a sphere; the world, in which the Son works, is compared with the sphere's surface; the Holy Ghost corresponds to the beams that radiate from center to surface of the sphere. It is naturally characteristic of these primal images that they cannot really be rationally or even intuitively described.

Although Kepler may have acquired his conviction of the correctness of Copernicanism from primal images of this kind, it remains a crucial precondition for any usable scientific theory that it should subsequently stand up to empirical testing and rational analysis. In this respect, the sciences are in a happier position than the arts, since for science there is an inexorable and irrevocable criterion of value that no piece of work can evade. The Copernican system, the Keplerian laws, and the Newtonian mechanics have subsequently proved themselves—in the interpreting of phenomena, in observational findings, and in technology—over such a range and with such extreme accuracy that after Newton's *Principia* it was no longer possible to doubt that they were correct. Yet even here there was still an idealization involved, such as Plato had held necessary and Aristotle had disapproved.

This only came out in full clarity some fifty years ago when it was realized from the findings in atomic physics that the Newtonian scheme of concepts was no longer adequate to cope with the mechanical phenomena in the interior of the atom. Since Planck's discovery of the quantum of action, in 1900, a state of confusion had arisen in physics. The old rules, whereby nature had been successfully described for more than two centuries, would no longer fit the new findings. But even these findings were themselves inherently contradictory. A hypothesis that proved itself in one experiment failed in another. The beauty and completeness of the old physics seemed destroyed, without anyone having been able, from the often disparate experiments, to gain a real insight into new and different sorts of connection. I don't know if it is fitting to compare the state of physics in those twenty-five years after Planck's discovery (which I, too, encountered as a young student) to the circumstances of contemporary modern art. But I have to confess that this comparison repeatedly comes to my mind. The helplessness when faced with the question of what to do about the bewildering phenomena, the lamenting over lost connections, which still continue to look so very convincing—all these discontents have shaped the face of both disciplines and both periods, different as they are, in a similar manner. We are obviously concerned here with a necessary intervening stage, which cannot be bypassed and which is preparing for developments to come. For, as Pauli told us, all understanding is a protracted affair, inaugurated by processes in the unconscious long before the content of consciousness can be rationally formulated.

At that moment, however, when the true Ideas rise up, there occurs in the soul of him who sees them an altogether indescribable process of the highest intensity. It is the amazed awe that Plato speaks of in the *Phaedrus,* with which the soul remembers, as it were, something it had unconsciously possessed all along. Kepler says: *"Geometria est archetypus pulchritudinis mundi";* or, if we may translate in more general terms: "Mathematics is the archetype of the beauty of the world." In atomic physics this process took place not quite fifty years ago and has again restored exact science, under entirely new presuppositions, to that state of harmonious completeness which for a quarter of a century it had lost. I see no reason why the same thing should not also happen one day in art. But it must be added, by way of warning, that such a thing cannot be made to happen—it has to occur on its own.

I have set this aspect of exact science before you because in it the affinity with the fine arts becomes most plainly visible and because here one may counter the misapprehension that natural science and technology are concerned solely with precise observation and rational, discursive thought. To be sure, this rational thinking and careful measurement belong to the scientist's work, just as the hammer and chisel belong to the work of the sculptor. But in both cases they are merely the tools and not the content of the work.

Perhaps at the very end I may remind you once more of the second definition of the concept of beauty, which stems from Plotinus and in which no more is heard of the parts and the whole: "Beauty is the translucence, through the material phenomenon, of the eternal splendor of the 'one.' " There are important periods of art in which this definition is more appropriate than the first, and to such periods we often look longingly back. But in our own time it is hard to speak of beauty from this aspect, and perhaps it is a good rule to adhere to the custom of the age one has to live in, and to keep silent about that which it is difficult to say. In actual fact, the two definitions are not so very widely removed from one another. So let us be content with the first and more sober definition of beauty, which certainly is also realized in natural science, and let us declare that in exact science, no less than in the arts, it is the most important source of illumination and clarity.

Suggestions for Discussion and Writing

1. Heisenberg starts his essay by recounting an experience from his early boyhood. Reflecting on this experience, he says, "Far in the distance, no doubt, there already floated the question whether whole numbers and geometrical forms exist, i.e., whether they are there outside the human mind or whether they have

merely been created by this mind as instruments for understanding the world." In what way does this reflection prepare us for the larger thematic concerns of this essay?

2. What two definitions of beauty does Heisenberg identify? Which of these two does he examine during the course of his essay?

3. Heisenberg asserts that "the mathematical structure, namely the numerical ratio as a source of harmony, was certainly one of the most momentous discoveries in the history of mankind." Does Heisenberg support this assertion?

4. How, according to Heisenberg, did the Pythagoreans establish a close connection "between the intelligible and the beautiful"?

5. What, in Heisenberg's view, was Plato's contribution to an understanding of the "Beautiful"? Do Plato's ideas help explain why Heisenberg, as a small boy, was struck by the beauty of mathematics?

6. Explain the tension between the views of Pythagoras and Plato on the one hand and Aristotle on the other. Does this tension (or conflict) point to the way in which science gets done?

7. Heisenberg says that "Galileo begins with careful observations, paying no attention to the authority of Aristotle, but, following the teaching of Pythagoras and Plato, he does try to find mathematical forms corresponding to the facts obtained by experiment and thus arrives at his laws of falling bodies." Does this picture of Galileo's method correspond to that offered by Bronowski in "The Reach of Imagination"?

8. How, according to Heisenberg, does "the shining forth of the Beautiful" show itself in—and affect the progress of—exact science? How does he resolve the parts/whole (one/many) opposition? What examples does he offer? How does he give this "shining forth" a social and ethical component?

9. What connection does Heisenberg make between the state of physics in the early part of this century and "the circumstances of contemporary modern art"? Do you agree with his assessment? Does Heisenberg hold out any hope for the future of art?

10. "Rational thinking and careful measurement belong to the scientist's work, just as the hammer and chisel belong to the work of the sculptor. But in both cases they are merely the tools and not the content of the work." Write an essay in which you develop this statement.

11. Do you find it surprising that Heisenberg, one of the great physicists of the twentieth century, should be so interested in philosophy and the Beautiful? Does his essay itself offer an explanation? Write an essay developing your views.

☐ ART AND SCIENCE

Victor F. Weisskopf
(b. 1908)

The renowned physicist Victor Weisskopf was born in Vienna and received his Ph.D. in physics in 1931 from the University of Göttingen. He came to the United States in 1937 and became an American citizen in 1942. From 1943 to 1946 he worked as a group leader on the Manhattan Project (which developed the atomic bomb) in Los Alamos, New Mexico. Since 1946 he has taught at the Massachusetts Institute of Technology, where he is currently Institute Professor Emeritus and Professor of Physics Emeritus. Weisskopf has made major contributions to the fields of quantum mechanics, electron theory, and particle physics. Among his numerous national and international honors and awards are the Max Planck Medal (1956), the National Medal of Science (1980), and the Enrico Fermi Award (1988).

One of the most admired and popular physicists of our time, Weisskopf has been a leader in explaining science—and its role in society—to the public. He has written several books, among them *Knowledge and Wonder: The Natural World as Man Knows It* (1962) and *Physics in the Twentieth Century* (1974). In the following selection, taken from *The Privilege of Being a Physicist* (1989), Weisskopf argues that, like art, science is an expression of man's search for unity and meaning in the universe.

What could be more different than science and art? Science is considered a rational, objective, cool study of nature; art is often regarded as a subjective, irrational expression of feelings and emotions. But is that so? One can just as well consider scientific discoveries as the products of imagination, of sparks of sudden insight, whereas art could be viewed as the product of painstaking work, carefully adding one part to the other by rational thinking. Surely art and science have something in common: Both are ways to deal with experience and to lift our spirits from daily drudgery to universal values. But the roles of art and science in society certainly are very different. Science, unfortunately, is a closed book for most people outside the scientific community; its influence on society, however, is decisive in two ways. One is through science-based technologies that have fundamentally changed the social texture of society and our style of life. The other is by means of the philosophical implications of scientific insights, which, it is often asserted, support a materialistic, rationalistic view of the world around and within us. The role of art is not so easy to define. It does, or should, contribute to a deeper appreciation of our existence and should help us to endure and understand the human predicament. Unfortunately, much of contemporary art is also a closed book to many.

Let us start with the diversity of human experiences. There are outer and inner experiences, rational and irrational ones, social experiences between two or many human beings, and experiences with the nonhuman part of nature. Our reactions to these experiences are manifold and varied. We think and ponder about them. We are oppressed or elated by them. We feel sadness and joy, love and hate. We are urged to act, to communicate to others. We try to relate them to patterns of living. We make use of them to improve our lives and to avoid material and emotional hardships. We also use them to influence people by rational or emotional arguments and, unfortunately, also by the application of brutal force.

All these experiences and the way we deal with them are the raw material of human creativity. What are its manifestations? The creative spirit shapes it into various forms of most diverse character: myths, religions, philosophies, diverse arts and literatures, architecture, sciences, medicine and technology, and social structures. These manifestations are directed toward many aims, practical and spiritual. Their actual effects upon humankind are sometimes positive and constructive, sometimes negative and destructive, and often with little relation to what the creators intended.

SPACE IS BLUE

Most forms of human creativity have one aspect in common: the attempt to give some sense to the various impressions, emotions, experiences, and actions that fill our lives, and thereby to give some meaning and value to our existence. Meaning and sense are words difficult to define but easy to grasp. We cannot live without meaning—oh, yes, we can, but a meaningless life would seem empty and cold. The crisis of our time in the Western world is that the search for meaning has become meaningless for many of us.

Different forms of human creativity often seem to be incommensurable, mutually exclusive, or even contradictory. I believe, however, that a better word is *complementary,* a term that has acquired a more focused significance since its use by Niels Bohr. My main purpose here will be to point out the complementarity, in Bohr's sense, between the different avenues of human creativity—in particular between the arts and sciences. Even within physics itself, we deal with concepts and discourses that on the surface are contradictory and mutually exclusive but that on a deeper level are what Bohr aptly has called complementary. They represent different aspects of reality; one aspect excludes the other, yet each adds to our understanding of the phenomenon as a whole. The quantum state of an atom evanesces when it is observed by a sharp instrument designed to locate the electron. The state is restituted when the atom is left alone and given enough time to return to its original state. Both aspects—quantum state and location—are complementary to each other; they are necessary concepts to provide a full insight into atomic reality.

Similar complementarities appear in all fields of human cognition, as Bohr often pointed out. They have to do with the question of relevance. In the atom, the wave picture (quantum state) is relevant for certain aspects of its reality, the particle picture for others. There are different ways of perceiving a situation, ways that may seem unconnected or even contradictory but that are necessary for understanding the situation in its totality. A simple example may suffice for the moment. A waterfall may be an object of scientific study, in which case the velocity distribution and the size of the droplets and their electric charge are relevant; it may be something to be technologically exploited as a source of water power, in which case the quantity of water, its height and smoothness of flow are relevant; or it may be the object of a poem describing the beauty or the overwhelming force of the phenomenon; then very different properties become relevant. Consider that well-known conversation between Felix Bloch and Werner Heisenberg about the subject of space. Bloch was reporting to Heisenberg some new ideas about the relevance of certain mathematical structures in space when Heisenberg, his mind drifting into other avenues of experience, exclaimed, "Space is blue and birds are flying in it!"

THE HOLISTIC APPROACH

We face a world of many dimensions and infinitudes, of which the world of the natural sciences is only a subdivision. The separation of the natural world outside ourselves from the internal world of the mind is an ever-recurring problem of philosophy and subject to questions and doubts.

Natural science, of course, is built upon some kind of separation of the external from the internal world; it regards the objects of its study as distinct and independent from the emotions and psychologic reactions that they may evoke in the observer. Emotions and the inner self are not excluded as objects of scientific investigation. But such studies are performed in a detached way, either by studying what is going on in the human brain by the methods of neurophysiology or by systematically analyzing human emotions and reactions with the methods of psychology.

Science is a relatively new creation of the human intellect. Before its appearance, the approach to human experience was essentially holistic. Myths, religions, and philosophies try to derive the totality of human experience, external and internal, from one leading principle and thus to provide it with a well-defined meaning. Everything is connected and represents the will of one or many gods; every event, every phenomenon is an expression of a deeper meaning strongly felt but only partially revealed when the course of events is interpreted. That deeper meaning need be neither logical nor unidirectional; it was often regarded as the result of warring forces, such as good and evil.

Art has always played an essential part in this holistic approach. It was, to a large extent, a servant of myth, religion, and philosophy and was a most suitable instrument to transmit holistic thoughts and emotions, transforming them into concrete, visible, or audible entities. Think of Greek sculpture, Homer's poetry, the Gothic cathedrals, and Bach's Passions. There they stand, works of art, representing ideas and symbols immediately and directly, with all their spirit and power. They impose upon the beholder their meaning and their general validity, their grandeur, terror, or beauty—if the beholder is part of the human soil from which the myths or religions grew.

It is often said that another source of art exists: the immediate urge to embellish and decorate objects of special value and significance. There is not much difference between this and the intensification of symbols and ideas. The embellished objects are symbols that art renders significant; they acquire a meaning beyond their ordinary role through decoration and embellishment.

Whenever the mythological and religious fervor begins to weaken, art tends to separate from these realms and acquire an independent role, replacing myth and religion to an increasing extent. It continues to create realizations of ideas and emotions that are important and significant in the culture of the time, although they may no longer be derived from a myth or a religion. Art serves as a powerful synthesizer of human experiences of the day, presenting to us messages of joy or sadness, greatness or meanness, beauty or terror, salvation or torture that cannot be transmitted in any other way. Two periods of separation between art and religion are well-known: one is that of Hellenistic-Roman art; the other is our own period, which started in the Renaissance and has resulted in an almost complete separation in modern times.

Art, just like myth and religion, is a holistic approach to human experience. Every true work of art transforms and molds a complex of many varied impressions, ideas, or emotions into a unique entity; it compresses a great variety of internal or external perceptions into a single creation. It expresses a whole truth—if this word may be applied here—and not a partial one or an approximation of the truth. If it is a great work of art, it cannot be improved, changed, or redone in order to comply with new insights that were not taken into account in the first creation. It is an organic whole that says what it says in its own special way. At different epochs it may mean different things to the beholder or listener or reader; it will be interpreted in different ways: it may have more meaning at one period and less at another. It may mean different things to different groups of people, but it is valid and effective only in its original form. As R. M. Rilke said:

Der Dichter einzig hat die Welt geeinigt
Die weit in jedem auseinander fällt.
Das Schöne hat er unerhört bescheinigt
Und da er selbst noch feiert was ihn peinigt
Hat er unendlich den Ruin gereinigt
Und auch noch das Vernichtende wird Welt.

Here is a translation by Douglas Worth:

Only the poet gathers what keeps falling
Apart in each of us unformed and furled;
In one hand beauty past belief enthralling
The other full of darkness so appalling
Yet sanctioned by his holy touch. Then balling
The two together he remakes the world.

THE SCIENTIFIC WORLD VIEW

The holistic tradition, which stresses totality of human experience, suffered an important change with the birth of natural science. A new era began. Instead of reaching for the whole truth, people began to ask limited questions in regard to the natural world. They did not ask questions such as "What is matter?" "What is life?" "What is the nature of the universe?" Instead, they asked, "How does the water flow in a tube?" "How does a stone fall to earth?" "What makes the blood flow through the veins?" General questions were shunned in favor of investigating separable phenomena, where it was easier to get direct and unambiguous results.

Then the great miracle happened: from the systematic study of many detailed phenomena, whose relevance was not obvious at all at the start, some fundamental insights into the basic structure of nature emerged. The renunciation of immediate contact with absolute truth, the detour through the diversity of experience, paid off. The restraint was rewarded as the answers to limited questions became more and more general. The study of moving bodies led to celestial mechanics and an understanding of the universality of the gravitational law. The study of friction and of gases led to the general laws of thermodynamics. The study of the twists of frog muscles and of voltaic cells led to the laws of electricity that were found to be the basis of the structure of matter. Some sensible answers emerged to those holistic questions that were shunned at the beginning. The nonholistic approach led to holistic results.

The holistic character of scientific insights differs greatly in character from that of myth, religion, and art. First, it does not directly include what we commonly refer to as the human soul, our feelings of awe or desolation, our ambitions, our convictions of right or wrong. It includes only the physiological and psychological phenomena accompanying these realities. The holistic character refers to the unity of natural phenomena outside our "souls." Second, and equally characteristic, scientific insights are always tentative, open to improvement and change; they have a restricted validity, appearing as incomplete perceptions of parts of a greater truth hidden in the plenitude of phenomena, a truth that is slowly but steadily revealed to us. Every step toward more insight adds to the value of previous steps. Scientific creations do not stand, each by itself, as works of art; they cannot be regarded as separable entities. They are parts of a single edifice that is collectively assembled by scientists and whose significance and power are based upon the totality of contributions. In German this is referred to by the untranslatable term *"Das 'Weltbild' der Naturwissenschaften."* Newton said, "I stand on the shoulders of giants." His work, like that of Einstein and other great scientists, comprises only a few stones of this edifice—albeit rather large ones at pivotal locations.

It must be said, however, that there is something like a collective edifice of achievement in the arts. There is tradition which develops from one period to the next; Mozart could not have written his music without Haydn and the development of baroque music since Bach and Handel; Schubert and Brahms would not have been without Beethoven. Michelangelo's art builds upon Greek art and that of the early Renaissance. We understand a work of art much better when it is considered with the cultural framework of its time. Art grows from a cultural soil fertilized by previous creations. In this sense the artist also "stands on the shoulders of giants."

ART VERSUS SCIENCE

The scientific culture differs from the artistic one in several respects. Here are a few important examples. There exists something that may be called scientific progress. We definitely know and understand more today than we did before. Einstein's theory of gravity is nearer to the "truth" than Newton's. If Newton were alive today he would freely, and probably enthusiastically, admit that Einstein's theory is an advance, compared with his own (a statement that is hard to prove; nevertheless it is convincing to every scientist.) No such progress can be found in art. There is no reason why a Gothic sculpture should be considered better than a Romanesque one, or why Raphael represents an advance compared to early medieval art, or Mahler compared to Mozart. True enough, there is a tendency to increased sophistication in art as time proceeds. The means of expression become more manifold, varied, and intricate. Of course, a similar tendency exists in the sciences. In the latter case, however, it is connected with a genuine increase of insight into, and understanding of, nature. The increased sophistication of art may have led to a wider scope of subject matter and a greater variety of creative forms but hardly to a more powerful force of artistic expression.

Another characteristic difference between art and science concerns the role and significance of the original creation: the distinction between content and the form in which it is expressed. It is much harder to separate these two elements in art than in science. The way the content is expressed plays an essential role in art; indeed, it is what makes the difference between art and mere description or photography. Any change in the way of expression would change and weaken the content of a work of art. You cannot paraphrase or explain it without greatly diminishing its impact. I remember my literature teacher in high school who asked us to repeat a poem by Goethe "in our own words." What a ridiculous request! The same is true about translations. Evidently they are necessary to provide access to literature that would otherwise remain inaccessible. But a translated poem or novel cannot exert the same impact as the original does on somebody who is well-versed in the language. Nevertheless, commentaries or analyses are useful to deepen the impact of the original work, but they cannot replace it. The weakness of describing the content of a work of art is especially obvious in music, which seems so inappropriate to talk about in words but, after all, the theologians also talk about God.

In science, the situation is very different. The original creation of the scientist, his first publications of the idea, are read and appreciated by the bulk of scientists only for a few years. Later, they are of interest only to historians of science. The important part of the creation is its content, which in most cases is better brought to effect in later presentations, usually by other authors. In most instances, the original creator of a new insight was not fully aware of its significance and of its connection with other fields. It takes time to do so and it is done by scientists with different points of view. For example, any scientist who wants to become acquainted with and appreciate Einstein's work today would read books such as Steven Weinberg's *Gravitation and Cosmology,* instead of Einstein's original papers. Here, we face a major difference to the situation in the arts, where the original creation remains the most effective presentation of its content. It requires considerably higher standards from the artist. As Bertrand Russell said, "In art nothing worth doing can be done without a genius; in science even a moderate capacity can contribute to a supreme achievement." Perhaps we find a parallel with the situation in science when we consider dramatic arts and music, where the performance is an act of interpretation that may change the original significance of the work to the better or worse.

Another factor is the emotional impact of scientific and artistic creations. The work of art represents a personal entity which is transmitted to, and reexperienced by, other individuals as a personal experience. A scientific insight into the workings of nature is an impersonal entity, an abstraction from a multitude of specific direct or vicarious experiences and creative ideas of many individuals; it is understood by other individuals as an impersonal general intellectual entity. The work of art produces in the recipients very personal feelings of joy, sadness, spiritual elevation, or tragic dejection that are an essential part of the message. A scientific idea may also produce feelings and emotions, such as awe, joy of insight, satisfaction, and the like. But they are not an essential part of the message.

It is often said that the role of intuition is a common factor in art and science. Rarely is any advance made in science without an intuitive perception of some idea or of some hidden relations. In art, of course, intuition is the essential driving force of creativity. However, scientific and artistic intuition are not always of the same character. True enough, the first spark of an idea or the first glimpse of some grand unification may come to the scientist in a similar unexplainable flash of insight as an artistic revelation. But, more often than not, scientific intuition comes from an unconscious or half-conscious awareness of existing knowledge or of connections between concepts that have not yet been consciously realized. But any intuitive scientific insight must be rationally validated afterward before it can be incorporated into the scientific edifice. In contrast, artistic intuition is the main instrument of creation and does not require any additional validation; it reigns superior and is the highest instance of judgment over and above the mold of style and fashion.

THE COMPLEMENTARITY OF ART AND SCIENCE

Both art and science give us deeper insights into our environment. But this environment is not at all the same. For science (only natural sciences are considered here) it is the natural world in which we live, including our own body and brain. For art, it also contains the natural world, albeit in a different way (remember Heisenberg's space), but it mostly consists of the vast real of personal ideas, feelings, emotions, reactions, moods, attitudes, and relations between human beings. One might object to this and assert that all these elements are also subject to a scientific approach as phenomena within our brain. This certainly is true, but just as science approaches external natural events in a thoroughly different way than art, so does it approach the internal landscape of what we may call our souls.

This difference has very much in common with Niels Bohr's complementarity. There are several contradictory, mutually exclusive approaches to reality. The scientific approach to a phenomenon is complementary to the artistic approach. The artistic experience evanesces when the phenomena are scientifically explored, just as the quantum state is temporarily destroyed when the position of the particle is observed. We cannot at the same time experience the artistic content of a Beethoven sonata and also worry about the neurophysiological processes in our brains. But we can shift from one to the other.

Both aspects are necessary to get at the full reality of the phenomenon. We may admire the starry sky and the vastness of variety of star patterns, or we may contemplate the physical nature of the stars and star systems, their motions and their developments from the big bang to their present stage. We can be impressed by a clear sunset because of the beautiful blending of colors or because of some thoughts connected with this symbol of the end of a day in human life; however, we can also be impressed by the processes of refraction and scattering of light in the atmosphere by suspended particulate matter.

A similar complementarity characterizes science and religion or myth. Religious approaches to human experiences are contradictory to the scientific one only in a superficial way. The following anecdote may illustrate it. In a Jewish theological seminary, a discussion took place about the proofs of the existence of God. It lasted several hours. Finally, a rabbi got up and said: "God is so great, He doesn't even need to exist!" Existing is generally used as a scientific term; in this sense it obviously does not apply to religious concepts that have an "existence" in a complementary realm of human experience. Jean Hamburger expresses the complementary situation succinctly in his book, *La Raison et la Passion.* "We must accept the idea that man can acquire all kinds of truths. But let us not mix them up; we would risk that the mixture would dissolve them all."

The contrast between complementary approaches is not necessarily between rational thinking and emotional feeling; one can and does talk rationally about emotional impressions and about art, myths, and religion. Yet it is a very different type of discourse—lucid and concise within its own intrinsic scale of values, but fragile and indefinite when judged by the peculiar requirements of scientific intercourse. One view complements the other, and we must use all of them in order to get a full experience of life. Scientists in particular may become aware of this need because their professional life is one-sided: "In the morning I go from mystery to reality; in the evening from reality to mystery." But mystery is another form of reality. No wonder so many scientists are actively or passively interested in music, the most irrational of the arts.

Here again one may look at the situation in complementary ways. True enough, music is "irrational" in the sense that there is no "objective" way to prove what musical passage is right or wrong. But the structure of music is related to structure in science, especially in mathematics. I refer to symmetry, repetition of a passage in a different key, inversions of tunes, and many other topological features. No wonder scientists are attracted by the fugues of Bach.

The vast difference or complementarity of art and science ought to be so obvious that it should need no further comment. But there exists a subgroup of scientists who do not subscribe to this statement. Let us call them the "science chauvinists." They maintain that progress in neurophysiology and brain science will lead finally to an adequate scientific understanding of what is going on in our brain when we create or enjoy a work of art or when we are so spiritually elevated by art or religion that we sense a deeper meaning in it. Going one step further—now the subgroup becomes noticeably smaller—they maintain that we then may be able to create art or replace it scientifically by certain nerve stimulations, because we then would know its neurological function.

The notion of scientific insight into the essence of art is based on a number of fallacies. True, there is no imaginable limit to our understanding of brain action and of the identification of definite nerve processes with emotional, moral, or aesthetic thoughts or feelings. We may expect tremendous progress in this field of science within a few decades. But there are several reasons why there seems to be a definite limit to fundamental scientific understanding of such matters. One reason has to do with the fact that any scientific research is based upon reproducibility of results. Certain phenomena in our souls that are relevant to the arts are not reproducible. Every human being (except identical twins) not only has a different set of genes, but he or she has been subject to a different set of impressions. Some of these differences may be considered irrelevant in certain respects—for example, a medical doctor will treat a disease successfully by the same methods, whether the patient is an Einstein or a half-wit. But for the development of human cultures and traditions the differences become most relevant. Human culture is an amplifier for both the genetic differences and those acquired by experience. A nonrecurring unique combination of such differences makes the artist capable of creating a work of art. It also determines the unique way in which an individual experiences that work of art. How can such a process be scientifically analyzed when it occurs only once? Do we not face here a typical complementary situation between the structure of the nervous system on the one side and the creation and perception of art on the other? Indeed, does not the specific uniqueness of a work of art represent a fundamental obstacle to the application of scientific analysis to the creative and perceptive process?

The same problem also appears in the social sciences. Nonrecurring, unique events occur frequently in the minds of human beings; they have decisive influences on the social fabric of society because of the amplifier effect of human culture. This effect may turn out to be a serious impediment to reliable scientific predictions in the social sciences; it may also be a fundamental difficulty when animal sociobiology is applied to human societies.

I must confess that I may run into the same error that Niels Bohr committed when, some time ago, he argued that the processes of life are complementary to physics and chemistry. He based his conclusion on the fact that a strict chemical analysis of life processes requires the death of the investigated creature. Therefore, he considered it possible that living matter may represent a different state of matter, complementary to the nonliving state, an analogy to the atomic quantum state that is destroyed by an attempt to look at its detailed structure. He was wrong—as the discovery of DNA and all that followed have clearly shown. I do not think that I commit a similar error, but if I do I am in good company. I believe there are fundamental obstacles to a full scientific understanding of the creative processes in art that cannot be bridged over, just as no new physical theory will ever get rid of wave-particle complementarity.

SENSE, MEANING, AND HOPE

Art and science have this in common: they provide meaning and sense to human experience. But the sense of the meaning is thoroughly different. It has been observed that art transforms general experiences into a single and unique form, whereas science transforms detailed single experiences into a general form. Either of the two transformations results in a holistic product: the work of art and scientific insight. But there are vast differences between the two. We have already mentioned the tentative, unfinished character of our scientific perception of nature. It represents only part of a truth that is developed step by step, whereas a work of art is finished and transmits its full message at all times, although the message may not be always interpreted in the same way.

In what sense does the universe make sense? In the sense you sense a sense. Every true scientist feels a sense, consciously or unconsciously. If he did not, he would not go ahead, with that fervor so common among scientists, in his search for something that he calls the truth. Surely a large dose of ambition is mixed into the fervor—acclaim, tenure, a Nobel Prize—but there is no denying that it exists. It is based upon a conviction that what the scientist does is worthwhile and will lead to an increase of insight, something that is great and valuable beyond any doubt, even if the fallibility of humankind makes the wrong use of it. Great insight leads to great power; great power always leads to great abuse.

The decay of a sense of meaning and the increase of cynicism in our culture have also contaminated natural scientists. These trends have shaken the conviction of some members of that community, but there is still a good deal of belief in the purpose and meaning of their collective work. I cannot help feeling that they represent a "happy breed of men" among so many others who grapple with the problems of meaning, sense, and purpose.

The emerging scientific *Weltbild* contains much to support the enthusiasm and fervor of its propagators. The great unifying principles that underlie the plentitude of events become clearer with every decade. An outline of a history of the universe from the big bang to the human brain is taking shape, and it becomes ever more convincing with the discoveries and insights that emerge from year to year. What is more startling and uncanny than the recent observation of the optical reverberation of the origin of the universe in the form of a cold radiation that fills all space? What is more impressive than the steady growth of our insights into the structure of matter, from molecules and atoms to nuclei, electrons, nucleons, and quarks, and our growing understanding of nature's fundamental forces? What is more overwhelming than the recognition of the chemical basis of life, in which the stability of the molecular quantum state emerges as the true basis of the fact that the same flowers appear again every spring?

Do we find a similar fervor and sense of purpose among other groups? Surely we do. We find it among those who are devoted to creative, artistic activities among those who try to improve the social fabric of our times in many different ways. However, they face a much greater challenge. The problems of natural science are much less messy, much less interwoven with the complexity and fragility of the human mind. It is easier to perceive an underlying order in the flow of natural events if human behavior is excluded.

The decay of previously existing sources for meaning, sense, and purpose—such as myth and religion—has left a great void in our minds, a void that craves to be filled. Every human being craves meaning and sense to his existence. The answers to these cravings must, by necessity, be holistic. They must embrace the totality of human experience and endow it with luster and light. With the decay of myth and religion, all that was left was an autonomous art that has made itself independent of any prevalent religion, and a new, most vigorous intellectual development that is science. Can these two enterprises serve as providers of meaning and sense? Goethe said

> He who has Art and Science also has religion
> But those who do not have them better have religion.

Goethe's remark points out an important element common to both expressions of the human mind: their true significance is not easily accessible to a larger part of humankind. Of course, there are many expressions of art, and some of science, that are indeed appreciated by large groups of people—such as folk art, popular science, and science fiction. Pop art, jazz, and rock music play an important role, arousing enthusiasm in large parts of the population. However, these manifestations are not the most effective providers of sense and meaning. The grandest creations and achievements of art and science serve as inspirational sources only to a small minority of humans; their values seem to be unsuitable for a wider spread. The large majority cannot get meaning, sense, and purpose from these sources. They crave some sort of religion, as Goethe says. Perhaps the greatest problem of our day is that this craving is no longer fulfilled by the conventional religions and that there is nothing to replace them.

The kind of meaning that science provides to its perpetrators has not proved satisfactory for this craving, even though everybody is fully aware that we live in an age dominated by science and technology. On the contrary, to a large extent this awareness is tied to practical applications, among which the military ones and the destructive effects of technology on the environment play an important role. The scientific insights into the greatness and unity of the universe, in the large and in the small, have not penetrated much into the minds of the people. This is probably the fault of scientists who do not try hard enough to transmit the elation they feel at the peak moments of their work. They are too much immersed in their narrow specialties and do not seek to express sufficiently the deep connections their insights have provided. It also is partly the fault of the artists and writers of today who neglect this task. Is it not the duty of art to remold all that is great and awe-inspiring in our culture and to lend it a form that stirs the souls of people? Perhaps the great ideas of science are not suitable to inspire outsiders with any true elation.

What is it, then, that contemporary art expresses? It reflects a frantic search for some kind of meaning by trying to go in many hitherto untried directions. We observe an outburst of new ways and forms of expression. From time to time, indeed, something really great and beautiful is created but, more often than not, what we see are the results of wild experimentation for the sake of being different from what has been done before. Perhaps this frantic search is a symptom of a lack of sense and meaning. Perhaps it is a method to arrive at a meaning.

Many creations of contemporary art, especially literature, deal with the tragedy and depth of our lack of purpose and meaning. In this effort our art is powerful, heart-rending, and deeply depressing. It acts as an amplifier of what is meant by the void in the mind; it follows the great tradition of art by elevating this to grand tragedy. Even cynicism has been ennobled by contemporary art. But in it we do not often enough find those ingredients that permeated art in past centuries—beauty and hope. This is perhaps the reason why the classical works of art have retained their power and significance. They seem today even more powerful and significant because they contain many of the ingredients missing in much of contemporary art.

Our material and spiritual world is in disorder and in danger of destruction. The great insights and elations of science, as well as of art, have not much impact on most of the people because these values cannot produce a ground swell of meaning capable of per-meating the collective mind. Among the younger generation, how-ever, there are many signs and portents of a craving for sense and purpose and for the dignity of the individual. This ground swell appears in various forms; some are constructive, some destructive. There are promising efforts to improve the social and spiritual cli-mate; there are cults and semireligious sects. All too often some of these cults and sects have led to misconceived mysticism and to a concentration on the inner self, without the necessary relationship to society. There may come a day when scientific and artistic meaning will combine and help to bring forth that ground swell of meaning and value for which there is so great a need. The growing awareness of this need is in itself an important element that brings people together and creates common values and even elations. There is always hope—for hope.

Suggestions for Discussion and Writing

1. What points does Weisskopf make by recounting the conversation between Felix Bloch and Werner Heisenberg? Do you find it significant that Heisenberg rather than Bloch changes the direction of the conversation? (In connection with this essay, you might wish to read Heisenberg in Chapter 1 and Hazen and Trefil in Chapter 5.)

2. Compare the role of tradition in art and science.

3. What kind of reader does the author assume? Support your view with specific evidence from the text.

4. Why is it more difficult to separate content and form in art than in science?

5. What do you understand the author to mean by "complementarity"? How does it help us to understand the relationship between art and science?

6. In what sense is mystery "another form of reality"?

7. Write an essay in which you compare and contrast the ways in which art and science are "holistic."

8. The author says that our "craving" for "meaning, sense, and purpose" is "no longer fulfilled by the conventional religions and that there is nothing left to replace them." Do you agree? Write an essay defending your views.

▭ SCIENCE AND RELIGION

Albert Einstein
(1879–1955)

That his name has become synonymous with genius indicates the extent of Albert Einstein's contributions to human knowledge. His work changed not only the direction of twentieth-century science but also the course of modern history. Born in Ulm, Germany, Einstein was educated both in that country and in Switzerland. His work earned him the Nobel Prize in 1921 and the Coply Medal of the Royal Society in 1925. Countless other honors and awards were bestowed upon him throughout his career.

While working in Switzerland in 1905, Einstein published the series of papers that marked the beginning of his international fame. The first of these papers, "The Special Theory of Relativity," dealt with the attributes of motion, time, and space. Einstein postulated that these parameters are relative (not absolute) because they are measured in relation to the position of the observer. In another paper, "The Quantum Law of the Emission and Absorption of Light," he offered proof of Max Planck's theory that claimed that energy exists in the form of small packets, or quanta. The ensuing development of this concept of energy led to the creation of the atomic bomb. Einstein's third paper, "The Theory of Brownian Movement," presented an analysis of the irregular motion of minute particles of matter suspended in a fluid, as first observed in 1827 by the Scottish botanist Robert Brown. By developing a mathematical formula for measuring the path and relative speed of these particles, Einstein confirmed that this motion was atomic in nature—that is, it was caused by collisions between the particles and the fluid molecules, which are in constant thermal movement. This confirmation provided a major piece of corroborative evidence for the atomic theory. In 1916 Einstein published his "General Theory of Relativity" (an expansion of his Special Theory), which is principally concerned with the large-scale effects of gravitation in space.

Having already made enemies during World War I by his refusal to support German nationalism, Einstein found himself an early target of the Hitler regime and in 1933 was forced to flee to America, where he became a citizen in 1940. In the early days of World War II, Einstein communicated to President Roosevelt his fears of Nazi efforts to build an atomic bomb. His concerns prompted the government to establish the Manhattan Project, which, under the leadership of J. Robert Oppenheimer, ultimately created the bomb. Einstein's subsequent career in this country was distinguished by both the continuation of his remarkable scientific work and his advocacy of humanitarian causes. He was associated with Princeton's Institute for Advanced Study from the time of his arrival until his death.

The first part of the following selection, excerpted from his *Out of My Later Years*, was originally given as an address at the Princeton Theological Seminary in May 1939. The second part is taken from *Science, Philosophy and Religion*, published in 1941. Here, Einstein notes the differences between science and religion but argues that both are manifestations of the human need to achieve unity and wholeness.

I

During the last century, and part of the one before, it was widely held that there was an unreconcilable conflict between knowledge and belief. The opinion prevailed among advanced minds that it was time that belief should be replaced increasingly by knowledge; belief that did not itself rest on knowledge was superstition, and as such had to be opposed. According to this conception, the sole function of education was to open the way to thinking and knowing, and the school, as the outstanding organ for the people's education, must serve that end exclusively.

One will probably find but rarely, if at all, the rationalistic standpoint expressed in such crass form; for any sensible man would see at once how one-sided is such a statement of the position. But it is just as well to state a thesis starkly and nakedly, if one wants to clear up one's mind as to its nature.

It is true that convictions can best be supported with experience and clear thinking. On this point one must agree unreservedly with the extreme rationalist. The weak point of his conception is, however, this, that those convictions which are necessary and determinant for our conduct and judgments cannot be found solely along this solid scientific way.

For the scientific method can teach us nothing else beyond how facts are related to, and conditioned by, each other. The aspiration toward such objective knowledge belongs to the highest of which man is capable, and you will certainly not suspect me of wishing to belittle the achievements and the heroic efforts of man in this sphere. Yet it is equally clear that knowledge of what *is* does not open the door directly to what *should be*. One can have the clearest and most complete knowledge of what *is,* and yet not be able to deduct from that what should be the *goal* of our human aspirations. Objective knowledge provides us with powerful instruments for the achievements of certain ends, but the ultimate goal itself and the longing to reach it must come from another source. And it is hardly necessary to argue for the view that our existence and our activity acquire meaning only by the setting up of such a goal and of corresponding values. The knowledge of truth as such is wonderful, but it is so little capable of acting as a guide that it cannot prove even the justification and the value of the aspiration toward that very knowledge of truth. Here we face, therefore, the limits of the purely rational conception of our existence.

But it must not be assumed that intelligent thinking can play no part in the formation of the goal and of ethical judgments. When someone realizes that for the achievement of an end certain means would be useful, the means itself becomes thereby an end. Intelligence makes clear to us the interrelation of means and ends. But mere thinking cannot give us a sense of the ultimate and fundamental ends. To make clear these fundamental ends and valuations, and to set them fast in the emotional life of the individual, seems to me precisely the most important function which religion has to perform in the social life of man. And if one asks whence derives the authority of such fundamental ends, since they cannot be stated and justified merely by reason, one can only answer: they exist in a healthy society as powerful traditions, which act upon the conduct and aspirations and judgments of the individuals; they are there, that is, as something living, without its being necessary to find justification for their existence. They come into being not through demonstration but through revelation, through the medium of powerful personalities. One must not attempt to justify them, but rather to sense their nature simply and clearly.

The highest principles for our aspirations and judgments are given to us in the Jewish-Christian religious tradition. It is a very high goal which, with our weak powers, we can reach only very inadequately, but which gives a sure foundation to our aspirations and valuations. If one were to take that goal out of its religious form and look merely at its purely human side, one might state it perhaps thus: free and responsible development of the individual, so that he may place his powers freely and gladly in the service of all mankind.

There is no room in this for the divinization of a nation, of a class, let alone of an individual. Are we not all children of one father, as it is said in religious language? Indeed, even the divinization of humanity, as an abstract totality, would not be in the spirit of that ideal. It is only to the individual that a soul is given. And the high destiny of the individual is to serve rather than to rule, or to impose himself in any other way.

If one looks at the substance rather than at the form, then one can take these words as expressing also the fundamental democratic position. The true democrat can worship his nation as little as can the man who is religious, in our sense of the term.

What, then, in all this, is the function of education and of the school? They should help the young person to grow up in such a spirit that these fundamental principles should be to him as the air which he breathes. Teaching alone cannot do that.

If one holds these high principles clearly before one's eyes, and compares them with the life and spirit of our times, then it appears glaringly that civilized mankind finds itself at present in grave danger. In the totalitarian states it is the rulers themselves who strive actually to destroy that spirit of humanity. In less threatened parts it is nationalism and intolerance, as well as the oppression of the individuals by economic means, which threaten to choke these most precious traditions.

A realization of how great is the danger is spreading, however, among thinking people, and there is much search for means with which to meet the danger—means in the field of national and international politics, of legislation, or organization in general. Such efforts are, no doubt, greatly needed. Yet the ancients knew something which we seem to have forgotten. All means prove but a blunt instrument, if they have not behind them a living spirit. But if the longing for the achievement of the goal is powerfully alive within us, then shall we not lack the strength to find the means for reaching the goal and for translating it into deeds.

II

It would not be difficult to come to an agreement as to what we understand by science. Science is the century-old endeavor to bring together by means of systematic thought the perceptible phenomena of this world into as thoroughgoing an association as possible. To put it boldly, it is the attempt at the posterior reconstruction of existence by the process of conceptualization. But when asking myself what religion is I cannot think of the answer so easily. And even after finding an answer which may satisfy me at this particular moment, I still remain convinced that I can never under any circumstances bring together, even to a slight extent, the thoughts of all those who have given this question serious consideration.

At first, then, instead of asking what religion is I should prefer to ask what characterizes the aspirations of a person who gives me the impression of being religious: a person who is religiously enlightened appears to me to be one who has, to the best of his ability, liberated himself from the fetters of his selfish desires and is preoccupied with thoughts, feelings, and aspirations to which he clings because of their superpersonal value. It seems to me that what is important is the force of this superpersonal content and the depth of the conviction concerning its overpowering meaningfulness, regardless of whether any attempt is made to unite this content with a divine Being, for otherwise it would not be possible to count Buddha and Spinoza as religious personalities. Accordingly, a religious person is devout in the sense that he has no doubt of the significance and loftiness of those superpersonal objects and goals which neither require nor are capable of rational foundation. They exist with the same necessity and matter-of-factness as he himself. In this sense religion is the age-old endeavor of mankind to become clearly and completely conscious of these values and goals and constantly to strengthen and extend their effect. If one conceives of religion and science according to these definitions then a conflict between them appears impossible. For science can only ascertain what *is*, but not what *should be*, and outside of its domain value judgments of all kinds remain necessary. Religion, on the other hand, deals only with evaluations of human thought and action: it cannot justifiably speak of facts and relationships between facts. According to this interpretation the well-known conflicts between religion and science in the past must all be ascribed to a misapprehension of the situation which has been described.

For example, a conflict arises when a religious community insists on the absolute truthfulness of all statements recorded in the Bible. This means an intervention on the part of religion into the sphere of science; this is where the struggle of the Church against the doctrines of Galileo and Darwin belongs. On the other hand, representatives of science have often made an attempt to arrive at fundamental judgments with respect to values and ends on the basis of scientific method, and in this way have set themselves in opposition to religion. These conflicts have all sprung from fatal errors.

Now, even though the realms of religion and science in themselves are clearly marked off from each other, nevertheless there exists between the two strong reciprocal relationships and dependencies. Though religion may be that which determines the goal, it has, nevertheless, learned from science, in the broadest sense, what means will contribute to the attainment of the goals it has set up. But science can only be created by those who are thoroughly imbued with the aspiration toward truth and understanding. This source of feeling, however, springs from the sphere of religion. To this there also belongs the faith in the possibility that the regulations valid for the world of existence are rational, that is, comprehensible to reason. I cannot conceive of a genuine scientist without that profound faith. The situation may be expressed by an image: science without religion is lame, religion without science is blind.

Though I have asserted above that in truth a legitimate conflict between religion and science cannot exist, I must nevertheless qualify this assertion once again on an essential point, with reference to the actual content of historical religions. This qualification has to do with the concept of God. During the youthful period of mankind's spiritual evolution human fantasy created gods in man's own image, who, by the operations of their will were supposed to determine, or at any rate to influence, the phenomenal world. Man sought to alter the disposition of these gods in his own favor by means of magic and prayer. The idea of God in the religions taught at present is a sublimation of that old concept of the gods. Its anthropomorphic character is shown, for instance, by the fact that men appeal to the Divine Being in prayers and plead for the fulfillment of their wishes.

Nobody, certainly, will deny that the idea of the existence of an omnipotent, just, and omnibeneficent personal God is able to accord man solace, help, and guidance; also, by virtue of its simplicity it is accessible to the most undeveloped mind. But, on the other hand, there are decisive weaknesses attached to this idea in itself, which have been painfully felt since the beginning of history. That is, if this being is omnipotent, then every occurrence, including every human action, every human thought, and every human feeling and aspiration is also His work; how is it possible to think of holding men responsible for their deeds and thoughts before such an almighty Being? In giving out punishment and rewards He would to a certain extent be passing judgment on Himself. How can this be combined with the goodness and righteousness ascribed to Him?

The main source of the present-day conflicts between the spheres of religion and of science lies in this concept of a personal God. It is the aim of science to establish general rules which determine the reciprocal connection of objects and events in time and space. For these rules, or laws of nature, absolutely general validity is required— not proven. It is mainly a program, and faith in the possibility of its accomplishment in principle is only founded on partial successes. But hardly anyone could be found who would deny these partial successes and ascribe them to human self-deception. The fact that on the basis of such laws we are able to predict the temporal behavior of phenomena in certain domains with great precision and certainty is deeply embedded in the consciousness of the modern man, even though he may have grasped very little of the contents of those laws. He need only consider that planetary courses within the solar system may be calculated in advance with great exactitude on the basis of a limited number of simple laws. In a similar way, though not with the same precision, it is possible to calculate in advance the mode of operation of an electrical motor, a transmission system, or of a wireless apparatus, even when dealing with a novel development.

To be sure, when the number of factors coming into play in a phenomenological complex is too large, scientific method in most cases fails us. One need only think of the weather, in which case prediction even for a few days ahead is impossible. Nevertheless no one doubts that we are confronted with a causal connection whose causal components are in the main known to us. Occurrences in this domain are beyond the reach of exact prediction because of the variety of factors in operation, not because of any lack of order in nature.

We have penetrated far less deeply into the regularities obtaining within the realm of living things, but deeply enough nevertheless to sense at least the rule of fixed necessity. One need only think of the systematic order in heredity, and in the effect of poisons, as for instance alcohol, on the behavior of organic beings. What is still lacking here is a grasp of connections of profound generality, but not a knowledge of order in itself.

The more a man is imbued with the ordered regularity of all events the firmer becomes his conviction that there is no room left by the side of this ordered regularity for causes of a different nature. For him neither the rule of human nor the rule of divine will exists as an independent cause of natural events. To be sure, the doctrine of a personal God interfering with natural events could never be *refuted,* in the real sense, by science, for this doctrine can always take refuge in those domains in which scientific knowledge has not yet been able to set foot.

But I am persuaded that such behavior on the part of the representatives of religion would not only be unworthy but also fatal. For a doctrine which is able to maintain itself not in clear light but only in the dark, will of necessity lose its effect on mankind, with incalculable harm to human progress. In their struggle for the ethical good, teachers of religion must have the stature to give up the doctrine of a personal God, that is, give up that source of fear and hope which in the past placed such vast power in the hands of priests. In their labors they will have to avail themselves of those forces which are capable of cultivating the Good, the True, and the Beautiful in humanity itself. This is, to be sure, a more difficult but an incomparably more worthy task. After religious teachers accomplish the refining process indicated they will surely recognize with joy that true religion has been ennobled and made more profound by scientific knowledge.

If it is one of the goals of religion to liberate mankind as far as possible from the bondage of egocentric cravings, desires, and fears, scientific reasoning can aid religion in yet another sense. Although it is true that it is the goal of science to discover rules which permit the association and foretelling of facts, this is not its only aim. It also seeks to reduce the connections discovered to the smallest possible number of mutually independent conceptual elements. It is in this striving after the rational unification of the manifold that it encounters its greatest successes, even though it is precisely this attempt which causes it to run the greatest risk of falling a prey to illusions. But whoever has undergone the intense experience of successful advances made in this domain is moved by profound reverence for the rationality made manifest in existence. By way of the understanding he achieves a far-reaching emancipation from the shackles of personal hopes and desires, and thereby attains that humble attitude of mind toward the grandeur of reason incarnate in existence, and which, in its profoundest depths, is inaccessible to man. This attitude, however, appears to me to be religious, in the highest sense of the word. And so it seems to me that science not only purifies the religious impulse of the dross of its anthropomorphism but also contributes to a religious spiritualization of our understanding of life.

The further the spiritual evolution of mankind advances, the more certain it seems to me that the path to genuine religiosity does not lie through the fear of life, and the fear of death, and blind faith, but through striving after rational knowledge. In this sense I believe that the priest must become a teacher if he wishes to do justice to his lofty educational mission.

Suggestions for Discussion and Writing

1. Early in his essay Einstein articulates the rationalist thesis "starkly and nakedly." What is this thesis and what "weak point" does Einstein identify in it? Do you see any danger in stating an opponent's viewpoint in its "crass form"?

2. Explain Einstein's distinction between "knowledge" and "belief."

3. Why, for Einstein, is the "rationalistic standpoint" alone insufficient as a guide for our conduct?

4. Einstein says that the "fundamental ends" toward which the individual should strive gain their authority not from reason but from tradition. They are there, he says, "as something living, without its being necessary to find justification for their existence," and they "come into being not through demonstration but through revelation, through the medium of powerful personalities." Do you agree with Einstein's evident acceptance here of the authority of

tradition? Or with his implied view that such "powerful traditions" are necessary to a healthy society? Does Einstein appear to be undervaluing individual responsibility? Write an essay in which you explore some of the implications of his views.

5. Einstein speaks of "the highest principles . . . given to us in the Jewish-Christian religious tradition." Should a multicultural society like ours accept the authority of those principles and that tradition? How might Einstein have responded to contemporary arguments calling for either the deemphasis of the Judeo-Christian tradition or equal recognition of other traditions? Write an essay developing your views.

6. In the last two paragraphs of Part I the author's tone appears to change. How might this shift be explained?

7. Einstein is quite clear in his definition of "science." Why is a definition of "religion" so much more difficult? Why, for Einstein, can science and religion never be in legitimate conflict?

8. Why, for Einstein, does the concept of "a personal God" make for conflicts between the spheres of religion and science? Do you agree with Einstein that the concept of a personal God is based on "fear and hope"? Write an essay defending your views.

9. If Einstein were forced to give his definition of religion (as he does of science), what might it be? Does he himself give the impression of being a religious man?

10. At the end of his essay Einstein says that science "seeks to reduce the connections discovered [among facts] to the smallest possible number of mutually independent conceptual elements" and that "it is in this striving that [science] encounters its greatest successes." Would Heisenberg agree? (See "Science and the Beautiful" in this chapter.) Would Eisley? (See "Science and the Sense of the Holy, Chapter 7.)

☐ THE MYSTERY OF OUR BEING

Max Planck
(1858–1947)

Born in Kiel, Germany, Max Planck developed a lasting interest in thermodynamics (the area of science that deals with heat, mechanical energy, and energy transformations) while studying for his Ph.D. at the University of Berlin, where he later taught theoretical physics for nearly forty years. In keeping with an early interest in music, he also became an accomplished pianist.

Planck stands as a major figure in the development of modern physics. One of his early professors advised him that the fundamental questions of physics had all been solved, a view widely held at the time. Many questions remained, of course, but the established laws of Newtonian mechanics (that is, of "classical" physics) seemed to offer the key to a complete understanding of matter and energy. With his enunciation of the *quantum* theory in 1900, Planck changed this overly confident view and laid the ground for the momentous changes that were to take place in physics in the next twenty years.

Planck's quantum theory grew out of his work on black-body radiation. Unable to reconcile observed measurements with predictions based on classical assumptions, he proposed the revolutionary idea that a radiating body gives off energy not in a continuous stream but rather in discrete "packages," which he called "quanta." A beam of light, for example, "really" consists of tiny, separate packages of light energy. In developing his theory, Planck formulated a constant (Planck's Constant) that is fundamental to modern physics. Applying his notion of quanta to black-body radiation, Planck was now able to predict experimental results within an acceptable range of error. The scientific community was amazed by this notion of discreteness, but within a few years Einstein successfully applied the quantum theory to explain the photoelectric effect, an achievement that was soon followed by successful applications in other areas. Planck's work was a watershed in modern physics. The designation "classical," as opposed to "modern," physics is now generally taken to mean "before Planck."

Planck himself, though, was no revolutionary. Like his friend Einstein, he was unhappy with the new probabilistic interpretations of quantum mechanics put forward by Werner Heisenberg and others and tried unsuccessfully to reconcile predictions based on probabilities with classical ideas of causality. Also like Einstein, he was deeply interested in philosophical questions concerning causality and free will and, as the following essay taken from *Where Is Science Going?* (1932) suggests, saw no conflict between science and religion. Planck argues that the "mystery of our being" is beyond the reach of science and therefore ultimately unknowable.

Planck died in Göttingen at the age of 89. His gravestone bears only his name and the equation expressing Planck's Constant.

W e might naturally assume that one of the achievements of science would have been to restrict belief in miracle. But it does not seem to do so. The tendency to believe in the power of mysterious agencies is an outstanding characteristic of our own day. This is shown in the popularity of occultism and spiritualism and their innumerable variants. Though the extraordinary results of science are so obvious that they cannot escape the notice of even the most unobservant man in the street, yet educated as well as uneducated people often turn to the dim region of mystery for light on the ordinary problems of life. One would imagine that they would turn to science, and it is probably true that those who do so are more intensely interested in science and are perhaps greater in number than any corresponding group of people in former times; still the fact remains that the drawing power of systems which are based on the irrational is at least as strong and as widespread as ever before, if not more so.

How is this peculiar fact to be explained? Is there, in the last analysis, some basically sound foothold for this belief in miracle, no matter how bizarre and illogical may be the outer forms it takes? Is there something in the nature of man, some inner realm, that science cannot touch? Is it so that when we approach the inner springs of human action science cannot have the last word? Or, to speak more concretely, is there a point at which the causal line of thought ceases and beyond which science cannot go?

This brings us to the kernel of the problem in regard to free will. And I think that the answer will be found automatically suggested by the questions which I have just asked.

The fact is that there is a point, one single point in the immeasurable world of mind and matter, where science and therefore every causal method of research is inapplicable, not only on practical grounds but also on logical grounds, and will always remain inapplicable. This point is the individual ego. It is a small point in the universal realm of being, but, in itself, it is a whole world, embracing our emotional life, our will, and our thought. This realm of the ego is, at once, the source of our deepest suffering and, at the same time, of our highest happiness. Over this realm, no outer power of fate can ever have sway, and we lay aside our own control and responsibility over ourselves only with the laying aside of life itself.

Here is the place where the freedom of the will comes in and establishes itself, without usurping the right of any rival. Being emancipated thus, we are at liberty to construct any miraculous background that we like in the mysterious realm of our own inner being, even though we may be at the same time the strictest scientists in the world, and the strictest upholders of the principle of causal determinism. It is from this autarchy of the ego that the belief in miracles arises, and it is to this source that we are to attribute the widespread belief in irrational explanations of life. The existence of that belief in the face of scientific advance is a proof of the inviolability of the ego by the law of causation in the sense which I have mentioned. I might put the matter in another way and say that the freedom of the ego here and now, and its independence of the causal chain, is a truth that comes from the immediate dictate of the human consciousness.

And what holds good for the present moment of our being holds good also for our own future conduct in which the influences of our present ego play a part. The road to the future always starts in the present. It is, here and now, part and parcel of the ego. And for that reason, the individual can never consider his own future purely and exclusively from the causal standpoint. That is the reason why fancy plays such a part in the construction of the future. It is in actual recognition of this profound fact that people have recourse to the palmist and the clairvoyant to satisfy their individual curiosity about their own future. It is also on this fact that dreams and ideals are based, and here the human being finds one of the richest sources of inspiration.

Science thus brings us to the threshold of the ego and there leaves us to ourselves. Here it resigns us to the care of other hands. In the conduct of our own lives, the causal principle is of little help; for by the iron law of logical consistency, we are excluded from laying the causal foundations of our own future or foreseeing that future as definitely resulting from the present.

But mankind has need of fundamental postulates for the conduct of everyday existence, and this need is far more pressing than the hunger for scientific knowledge. A single deed often has far more significance for a human being than all the wisdom of the world put together. And, therefore, there must be another source of guidance than mere intellectual equipment. The law of causation is the guiding rule of science, but the Categorical Imperative—that is to say, the dictate of duty—is the guiding rule of life. Here intelligence has to give place to character, and scientific knowledge to religious belief. And when I say religious belief here I mean the word in its fundamental sense. And the mention of its brings us to that much discussed question of the relation between science and religion. It is not my place here nor within my competency to deal with that question. Religion belongs to that realm that is inviolable before the law of causation and, therefore, closed to science. The scientist as such must recognize the value of religion as such, no matter what may be its forms, so long as it does not make the mistake of opposing its own dogmas to the fundamental law upon which scientific research is based, namely, the sequence of cause and effect in all external phenomena. In conjunction with the question of the relations between religion and science, I might also say that those forms of religion which have a nihilist attitude to life are out of harmony with the scientific outlook and contradictory to its principles. All denial of life's value for itself and for its own sake is a denial of the world of human thought and, therefore, in the last analysis, a denial of the true foundation not only of science but also of religion. I think that most scientists would agree to this and would raise their hands against religious nihilism as destructive of science itself.

There can never be any real opposition between religion and science. Every serious and reflective person realizes, I think, that the religious element in his nature must be recognized and cultivated if all the powers of the human soul are to act together in perfect balance and harmony. And, indeed, it was not by any accident that the greatest thinkers of all ages were also deeply religious souls, even though they made no public show of their religious feeling. It is from the cooperation of the understanding with the will that the finest fruit of philosophy has arisen, namely, the ethical fruit. Science enhances the moral values of life because it furthers a love of truth and reverence—love of truth displaying itself in the constant endeavor to arrive at a more exact knowledge of the world of mind and matter around us, and reverence, because every advance in knowledge brings us face to face with the mystery of our own being.

Suggestions for Discussion and Writing

1. Planck seems to be surprised that the growth of science has not limited a belief in miracles. How might he define "miracle"? Why is science as a discipline at odds with the notion of miracles?

2. Writing in the early 1930s, Planck observes that "the drawing power of systems which are based on the irrational is at least as strong and as widespread as ever before, if not more so." Could the same be said of the last decade of the twentieth century? Write a brief essay supporting your views.

3. What does Planck mean by "the individual ego"? In what sense is it "a whole world"? Why is it "the source of our deepest suffering and, at the same time, of our highest happiness"? Write an essay in which you compare these ideas with Bronowski's assertion in "The Reach of Imagination" (this chapter) that "the richness of human life is that we have many lives; we live the events that do not happen (and some that cannot) as vividly as those that do; and if thereby we die a thousand deaths, that is the price we pay for living a thousand lives."

4. In what sense is the scientific notion of cause opposed to the idea of free will?

5. Why is science not an appropriate guide for human conduct?

6. Planck says that "religion belongs to that realm that is inviolable before the law of causation and, therefore, closed to science." Would Heisenberg ("Science and the Beautiful," this chapter) and Eiseley ("Science and the Sense of the Holy,"

Chapter 7) agree? Write an essay in which you compare Planck's views with those of one of these authors.

7. Planck ends his essay with the statement that "every advance in knowledge brings us face to face with the mystery of our own being." Write an essay in which you describe how some new knowledge you acquired affected your sense of self.

CHAPTER 4
Technology

ARTIFICIAL INTELLIGENCE

Joseph Weizenbaum
(b. 1923)

Joseph Weizenbaum, who emigrated from Germany to America as a child, has had a distinguished career as a computer scientist, educator, and author. After working for several years at General Electric, Weizenbaum joined the faculty at MIT in 1963 where he became a full professor of computer science in 1970. The following selection is taken from one of his best-known books, *Computer Power and Human Reason* (1976). Here he argues that because we have no clear notion of what human intelligence is, attempts to produce "intelligent" computers are misguided.

F ew "scientific" concepts have so thoroughly muddled the thinking of both scientists and the general public as that of the "intelligence quotient" or "I.Q." The idea that intelligence can be quantitatively measured along a simple linear scale has caused untold harm to our society in general, and to education in particular. It has spawned, for example, the huge educational-testing movement in the United States, which strongly influences the courses of the academic careers of millions of students and thus the degrees of certification they may attain. It virtually determines what "success" people may achieve in later life because, in the United States at least, opportunities to "succeed" are, by and large, open only to those who have the proper credentials, that is, university degrees, professional diplomas, and so on.

When modern educators argue that intelligence tests measure a subject's ability to do well in school, they mean little more than that these tests "predict" a subject's ability to pass academic-type tests. This latter ability leads, of course, to certification and then to "success." Consequently, any correlation between the results of such tests and people's "success," as that term is understood in the society at large, must necessarily be an artifact of the testing procedure. The test itself has become a criterion for that with which it is to be correlated! "Psychologists should be ashamed of themselves for promoting a view of general intelligence that has engendered such a testing program."

My concern here is that the mythology that surrounds I.Q. testing has led to the widely accepted and profoundly misleading conviction that intelligence is somehow a permanent, unalterable, and culturally independent attribute of individuals (somewhat like, say, the color of their eyes), and moreover that it may even be genetically transmittable from generation to generation.

The trouble with I.Q. testing is not that it is entirely spurious, but that it is incomplete. It measures certain intellectual abilities that large, politically dominant segments of western European societies have elevated to the very stuff of human worth and hence to the *sine qua non* of success. It is incomplete in two ways: first, in that it fails to take into account that human creativity depends not only on intellect but also crucially on an interplay between intellect and other modalities of thought, such as intuition and wisdom; second, in that it characterizes intelligence as a linearly measurable phenomenon that exists independent of any frame of reference.

Einstein taught us that the idea of motion is meaningless in and of itself, that we can sensibly speak only of an object's motion relative to some frame of reference, not of any *absolute* motion of an object. When, in speaking informally, we say that a train moved, we mean that it moved relative to some fixed point on the earth. We need not emphasize this in ordinary conversation, because the earth (or our body) is to us a kind of "default" frame of reference that is implicitly assumed and understood in most informal conversation. But a physicist speaking as a physicist cannot be so sloppy. His equations of motion must contain terms specifying the coordinate system with respect to which the motion they describe takes place.

So it is with intelligence too. Intelligence is a meaningless concept in and of itself. It requires a frame of reference, a specification of a domain of thought and action, in order to make it meaningful. The reason this necessity does not strike us when we speak of intelligence in ordinary conversation is that the required frame of reference—that is, our own cultural and social setting with its characteristic domains of thought and action—is so much with us that we implicitly assume it to be understood. But our culture and our social milieu are in fact neither universal nor absolute. It therefore behooves us, whenever we use the term "intelligence" as scientists or educators, to make explicit the domain of thought and action which renders the term intelligible.

Our own daily lives abundantly demonstrate that intelligence manifests itself only relative to specific social and cultural contexts. The most unschooled mother who cannot compose a single grammatically correct paragraph in her native language—as, indeed, many academics cannot do in theirs—constantly makes highly refined and intelligent judgments about her family. Eminent scholars confess that they don't have the kind of intelligence required to do high-school algebra. The acknowledged genius is sometimes stupid in managing his private life. Computers perform prodigious "intellectual feats," such as beating champion checker players at their own game and solving huge systems of equations, but cannot change a baby's diaper. How are these intelligences to be compared to one another? They cannot be compared.

Yet forms of the idea that intelligence is measurable along an absolute scale, hence that intelligences are comparable, have deeply penetrated current thought. This idea is responsible, at least in part, for many sterile debates about whether it is possible "in principle" to build computers more intelligent than man. Even as moderate and reasonable a psychologist as George A. Miller occasionally slips up, as when he says, "I am very optimistic about the eventual outcome of the work on machine solution of intellectual problems. Within our lifetime machines may surpass us in general intelligence."

The identification of intelligence with I.Q. has severely distorted the primarily mathematical question of what computers can and cannot do into the nonsensical question of "how much" intelligence one can, again "in principle," give to a computer. And, of course, the reckless anthropomorphization of the computer now so common, especially among the artificial intelligentsia, couples easily to such simpleminded views of intelligence. This joining of an illicit metaphor to an ill-thought-out idea then breeds, and is perceived to legitimate, such perverse propositions as that, for example, a computer can be programmed to become an effective psychotherapist. . . .

But, and this is the saving grace of which an insolent and arrogant scientism attempts to rob us, we come to know and understand not only by way of the mechanisms of the conscious. We are capable of listening with the third ear, of sensing living truth that is truth beyond any standards of provability. It is *that* kind of understanding, and the kind of intelligence that is derived from it, which I claim is beyond the abilities of computers to simulate.

We have the habit, and it is sometimes useful to us, of speaking of man, mind, intelligence, and other such universal concepts. But gradually, even slyly, our own minds become infected with what A. N. Whitehead called the fallacy of misplaced concreteness. We come to believe that these theoretical terms are ultimately interpretable as observations, that in the "visible future" we will have ingenious instruments capable of measuring the "objects" to which these terms refer.

There is, however, no such thing as mind; there are only individual minds, each belonging, not to "man," but to individual human beings. I have argued that intelligence cannot be measured by ingeniously constructed meter sticks placed along a one-dimensional continuum. Intelligence can be usefully discussed only in terms of domains of thought and action. From this I derive the conclusion that it cannot be useful, to say the least, to base serious work on notions of "how much" intelligence may be given to a computer. Debates based on such ideas—e.g., "Will computers ever exceed man in intelligence?"—are doomed to sterility.

I have argued that the individual human being, like any other organism, is defined by the problems he confronts. The human is unique by virtue of the fact that he must necessarily confront problems that arise from his unique biological and emotional needs. The human individual is in a constant state of becoming. The maintenance of that state, of his humanity, indeed, of his survival, depends crucially on his seeing himself, and on his being seen by other human beings, as a human being. No other organism, and certainly no computer, can be made to confront genuine human problems in human terms. And, since the domain of human intelligence is, except for a small set of formal problems, determined by man's humanity, every other intelligence, however great, must necessarily be alien to the human domain.

I have argued that there is an aspect to the human mind, the unconscious, that cannot be explained by the information-processing primitives, the elementary information processes, which we associate with formal thinking, calculation, and systematic rationality. Yet we are constrained to use them for scientific explanation, description, and interpretation. It behooves us, therefore, to remain aware of the poverty of our explanations and of their strictly limited scope. It is wrong to assert that any scientific account of the "whole man" is possible. There are some things beyond the power of science to fully comprehend.

The concept of an intelligence alien to certain domains of thought and action is crucial for understanding what are perhaps the most important limits on artificial intelligence. But that concept applies to the way humans relate to one another as well as to machines and their relation to man. For human socialization, though it is grounded in the biological constitution common to all humans, is strongly determined by culture. And human cultures differ radically among themselves. Countless studies confirm what must be obvious to all but the most parochial observers of the human scene: "The influence of culture is universal in that in some respects a man learns to become like all men; and it is particular in that a man who is reared in one society learns to become in some respects like all men of his society and not like those of others." . . .

Every human intelligence is thus alien to a great many domains of thought and action. There are vast areas of authentically human concern in every culture in which no member of another culture can possibly make responsible decisions. It is not that the outsider is unable to decide at all—he can always flip coins, for example—it is rather that the *basis* on which he would have to decide must be inappropriate to the context in which the decision is to be made.

What could be more obvious than the fact that, whatever intelligence a computer can muster, however it may be acquired, it must always and necessarily be absolutely alien to any and all authentic human concerns? The very asking of the question, "What does a judge (or a psychiatrist) know that we cannot tell a computer?" is a monstrous obscenity. That it has to be put into print at all, even for the purpose of exposing its morbidity, is a sign of the madness of our times.

Computers can make judicial decisions, computers can make psychiatric judgments. They can flip coins in much more sophisticated ways than can the most patient human being. The point is that they *ought* not be given such tasks. They may even be able to arrive at "correct" decisions in some cases—but always and necessarily on bases no human being should be willing to accept.

There have been many debates on "Computers and Mind." What I conclude here is that the relevant issues are neither technological nor even mathematical; they are ethical. They cannot be settled by asking questions beginning with "can." The limits of the applicability of computers are ultimately statable only in terms of oughts. What emerges as the most elementary insight is that, since we do not now have any ways of making computers wise, we ought not now to give computers tasks that demand wisdom.

Suggestions for Discussion and Writing

1. In what ways, according to Weizenbaum, is IQ testing incomplete? What does Weizenbaum mean when he says that IQ testing "characterizes intelligence as a linearly measurable phenomenon that exists independent of any frame of reference"?

2. Weizenbaum speaks of intuition and wisdom as "modalities of thought" involved in intelligence. Write a brief paragraph in which you define "wisdom." How does it differ from knowledge? What other "modalities of thought" might Weizenbaum have cited?

3. Do you agree with the author that we can speak about "intelligence" only within "specific social and cultural contexts"? Has your intelligence or that of someone you know ever been misjudged because it was not placed within a "frame of reference"?

4. What does the author mean when he says that "the human individual is in a constant state of becoming"? How is this notion relevant to his argument regarding artificial intelligence?

5. Weizenbaum says that a computer's "intelligence" must "always and necessarily be absolutely alien to any and all authentic human concerns" and that though computers may "be able to arrive at 'correct' [judicial and psychiatric] decisions in some cases," they do so "on bases no human being should be willing to accept." What does he mean by "authentic human concerns"? On what bases, according to Weizenbaum, do computers arrive at their decisions? Why shouldn't we be willing to accept those bases?

6. Near the end of his essay, Weizenbaum concludes that "the relevant issues [in the debate on "computer and mind"] are neither technological nor even mathematical; they are ethical." In what sense are the relevant issues here ethical? Write an essay explaining your views.

7. Weizenbaum argues that "Every human intelligence is . . . alien to a great many domains of thought and action" and that "there are vast areas of authentically human concern in every culture in which no member of another culture can possibly make responsible decisions." What are the implications of this statement for our multicultural society?

☐ A HUNDRED EINSTEINS?

Robert Gilmore McKinnell
(b. 1926)

Robert Gilmore McKinnell, born in Springfield, Missouri, received his Ph.D. from the University of Minnesota, where he is currently a professor of genetics and cell biology. His research has been in the transplantation of cell nuclei and in the use of mutant genes as nuclear markers. He has also worked extensively in the cell biology of cancer. In the following selection from his book, *Cloning: A Biologist Reports* (1979), McKinnell explores some of the less frequently acknowledged implications of human cloning.

An elephant has not yet been cloned. Neither has a shrew, a mouse, a rabbit, or a human (successfully). Although little has been inscribed about cloned shrews and other small mammals, much has been written about clonal humans. Most is the work of science-fiction writers, philosophers, theologians, and lawyers. As far as I know, biologists experienced in cloning technology have *not* written about any aspect of cloning other than their own experiments.

Perhaps I am an exception because I, as a teacher in a university classroom, respond to frequent questions about the implications of cloning humans. It seems appropriate that a nuclear transplanter contemplate the significance of his discipline and be willing to discuss the subject for the benefit of students and other interested individuals. Obviously, speculation is just that regardless of the qualifications of the speculator. I wish to assure the reader that much of what follows is speculation, that it represents my thoughts and does not necessarily represent the views of other cloners.

If cloning were available for the benefit of humans, how would it be used? Clonal astronauts, armies of genetic replicates, or spare parts? These concepts are not mine, but I consider them here because they have been written about so much and because they suggest some biological problems that can very properly be addressed by a biologist, especially one with experience in cloning.

COSMONAUT CLONATES—BRILLIANT BUT HOW BENEFICIAL?

Consider the possibilities. Why tolerate a hodgepodge of nearly middle-aged people of variable stature, intellectual capacity, and emotional stability on an expedition to the moon? Why not find *the* man or woman with psyche and soma that is the quintessence of all that is noble—and send clones of so splendid an individual to the moon. The idea is appealing. It weds late twentieth-century rocket engineering to late twentieth-century biological concepts in a conjugal fantasy of artificial humans and real but hard-to-believe rockets.

However appealing the idea, the postulated lunar clones are in some ways inadequate. The deficiencies of the group relate to its identicalness, including chronological age. If such a group were produced, it would take no less than 25 to 35 years for the clone to be of appropriate intellectual development and have the requisite manual skills to run a spaceship. A cloned human will mature no faster than an ordinary human, just as it takes no less time for a cloned frog to grow than it does for an ordinary frog. I suspect that the pace of scientific and technological development will increase, which will make prognostication of future needs exceedingly difficult—and delay will not be easily suffered. Selecting a genotype for a lunar or planetary mission 30 years in the future would be like having tapped John Glenn in 1931 for his 1962 global orbit in *Friendship 7*. Few can plan so far ahead.

There are other potential problems relating to chronology. All conventional clones of replicate astronauts would be the same age. Is this desirable? Many believe that intelligence does not decline as humans age. Contrary to what was previously supposed, intelligence as measured in at least some tests actually increases into the sixth and seventh decades. The genes do not change over the decades. What changes is the expression of the genes, and this is what intelligence tests measure. Judges, philosophers, and statesmen frequently blossom in their sixth or later decades. Ice skaters, molecular biologists, gymnasts, and military jet pilots flower younger. Would we really want a space capsule inhabited entirely by individuals of identical age? Space probes in the 1970s were populated by men of different ages.

Certainly, biocrats with the resources to produce clones of space explorers would also have the resources to produce a group of genetically identical but chronologically disparate, splendid space explorers. Genetic replicas need not be the same age. If we envision the consequences of cloning humans, we may envision another biotechnical achievement of the twentieth century—cryobiology. Human cells survive for at least 16 years at −78°C. Intact embryos of mice may be frozen, thawed, and transferred to foster mothers, with normal live births ensuing. Thus our procedure for producing genetically identical individuals of different ages would be as follows: identify individuals with appropriate genes and put their body cells in culture; freeze the culture; every several years thaw a sample of frozen cells and clone them. An alternative to this procedure would be to clone a number of individuals at one time, freeze the embryo clones at an early stage, and then at intervals of several years, thaw and transfer the cloned embryo to a receptive foster mother who would give birth to the future astronaut 9 months later. Thus we would obtain a group in which we exploit a superb genotype during the strength and vigor of its youth and simultaneous with the wisdom and judgment of its later years.

Feminists should resent an all-male clone group. There are intrinsic differences between males and females. An example: although females generally have less brute strength, they survive longer. Let the unisexuality of conventional clones not interfere with the desire to have a truly magnificent isogenic group.

The biologist who has muscle enough to manipulate genes and ages would also have the technical strength to manipulate the expression of sexual characteristics. For many years it has been possible to control sex among vertebrate embryos by adding the appropriate hormone. Why not manipulate the expression of sex-determining genes in astronaut clones? Deliberate sex reversal (in contrast to sex-surgery alteration) has not been accomplished in humans. However, human cloning has the prerequisite of egg enucleation and successful cell surgery. Given this as yet to be accomplished capability with human cells, it seems likely that the simpler technique of early administration of estrogenic hormones in vitro would provide anatomically appearing females from genetic males. Similarly, testosterone in a culture medium would result in females that were anatomically male. Thus a genetically male clone would be manipulated with hormones so that both male and female individuals would ensue. A clone of lunar explorers, *not* like those envisioned by science writers, but of various ages and both sexes, and all of a single glorious genetic constitution, could be engineered.

Two considerations become obvious at this point. One relates to the rather formidable biotechnology that has developed in recent years. The discussion of proposed and seemingly feasible variant clones witnesses to the impressive control over reproduction, growth, and differentiation that is possible in the late twentieth century. The other relates to the diversity in a microcosm (such as a space capsule) and diversity in this goodly frame, the earth. Most of us will agree that a diversity of kinds of people is desirable in communities such as universities, factories, armies, and nations. How do you run a university with only art historians? Or newspapers with editors but no reporters or printers? A spaceship lacking diversity among its personnel would probably be unsafe and dull. If diversity is required, why not obtain it in the conventional way, by finding qualified individuals produced, perhaps prosaically but nevertheless usefully, by sexual reproduction. This guarantees diversity far in excess of that which results from manipulating factors of isogenic groups.

So, the basic question is: Are clonal cosmonauts necessary—or even desirable?

THE MENACE OF AN ARMY OF GENETIC REPLICATES

Détente results in easing of fears about what occurs behind an iron, bamboo, or plastic curtain. Tension grows when détente falters—and fears return. It has been suggested in the nonscientific literature that some distant enemy may develop a nascent army of powerful, unfeeling human automatons—produced by cloning. They are a potential menace presumably because they are not the results of conventional sexual reproduction. They are pictured as unfeeling monsters. Surely such an army would move across a battlefield in a way so terrible that it almost defies the human imagination. Do we compete by producing our own cloned armies, or do we bow to extinction? Before this question causes the reader apprehensiveness and consternation, let us recall the previous discussion on cloned astronauts.

Lives there a dictator who would create an army to do battle 18 years hence? Military and political leaders thrive on power—not latent but highly visible and immediate power. Both Adolph Hitler and Franklin Roosevelt, men of enormous authority and command, assumed political control of their respective nations in the 1930s. Had cloning been available to each at the onset of his career as a national leader, no political consequence would have ensued because both were dead when their hypothetical cloned armies would be entering pubescence.

I suspect that a despot wants more from biotechnology than an isogenic army, with unproved characteristics, that will not be available for almost two decades.

100 MR. EINSTEINS AND RECONSTITUTING SLAIN LEADERS

Genetically identical Albert Einsteins and Adolph Hitlers have been illustrated in popular journals. Several years ago Nobel laureate Joshua Lederberg wondered what the characteristics of a cloned version of Nobel laureate Einstein would be. If one assumes that a cloned Einstein would have at least some attributes of Einstein, it is not unreasonable to assume that a cloned political chieftain would have some of the characteristics of that chieftain.

But *how much* would replicate Einsteins, Hitlers, or future dictators resemble their originals? I don't think the carbon copy would be a faithful replica of the prototype. Consider the social scene in the nineteenth century Europe of Einstein (born in 1879). Contrast that with our world. If someone had cultured body cells from Einstein before his death, had frozen them, and then transplanted his thawed, body-cell nuclei in the 1970s, no notion of the outcome of the cloning experiment would be available until the early 1990s—over a century after the original was born! The cloned Einstein would miss World War I and World War II. Wouldn't this make the clone in some ways different from its original?

I first crossed the Atlantic Ocean on a ship that took six days from Quebec City to Liverpool. I was in my twenties. My youngest child, with her siblings, crossed the Atlantic in six hours during her first year of life and crossed it twice again by age six. I am convinced that the ease of travel, the instant communication in our world, and other late 20th-century developments, will expand the intellectual horizons of my children. They cannot be the same children they would have been had they been born when I was. How could a 20th-century Einstein be the same as a 19th-century Einstein? The replicate would not even look the same as the original. Growth patterns have changed in the past half century. It is well known that soldiers in World War II could not fit into the uniforms their fathers wore in World War I. Although Einstein's genes might remain stable, the *expression* of his genes in replicate Einsteins certainly would not.

WHERE EXPECTATION EXCEEDS CAPABILITY

The capacity of biologists to fabricate genetic replicate frogs has led to an anticipation of carbon-copy humans. It is perhaps in this arena of biological endeavor that the capacity (or will) to produce and the popular expectation diverge the most. I believe it is rational to expect cancer control in the future; I believe it is sensible to anticipate new insights into the immune process; I believe that graceful aging is a reasonable hope for a greater proportion of our population in the future. I have faith that cloning will contribute to each of these areas. However, I never expect to witness the construction of carbon-copy humans. I do not believe that nuclear transplantation for the purpose of producing human beings will ever routinely occur.

There are two compelling reasons for my conviction. The first, which I discussed earlier, relates to the indispensable biological requirement for diversity—diversity that is most efficiently gained through conventional sexual reproduction. The second reason, discussed in the previous section, relates to the ability of the cloning procedure to produce carbon copies. Genetic replicates perhaps—carbon copies never. Epigenesis is a term biologists use to describe the unfolding of potentialities in a developmental system. A fertilized egg of a sea urchin or a frog is not a miniature sea creature or a tiny hopping amphibian. Rather, it is a single cell that has, under certain environmental conditions, the capacity to develop into an adult organism. The fulfillment of that capacity is absolutely wedded to the environment. If the reader does not believe that, try placing a marine egg in hot water or permit a frog-breeding pond to dry up. Expectation is not fulfilled in the modified environment. Development is contingent upon an environment. Epigenesis is plastic in that minor fluctuations in the physical environment result in minor fluctuations in the structure of an organism. A slight diminution of an essential growth factor in an experimental animal's diet results in somewhat less growth.

The social environment of the human organism is far more complex and subtle than the physical environment. Personality is as epigenetic as is the soma. The zygote of Hitler was not a despotic leader. Neither was the neonate Hitler a dictator. Circumstances—history—the environment—evoked the genes of young Adolph Hitler to be expressed as the oppressor we remember. Although it is true that biologists can induce the replication of a genetic apparatus in certain instances, they do not have now nor are they ever likely to have the power to clone the social environment. The feature of development known as epigenesis prevents the creation of carbon-copy people. Thus expectation exceeds capability—even in the late twentieth century.

A boy baby reared as a girl baby acts like a girl baby. A contemporary American acts like a contemporary American. Had Mr. Einstein been cloned 20 years ago, that clone might be more concerned with sports cars, the ERA, in vitro fertilized babies, and rock music than with mathematics and physics. I would speculate that he might be consumed with concern about polluted air, polluted water, and over-refined and artificially preserved food. He might well think that mathematics and physics are not relevant (he might even fail to consider relevant or not relevant to what?). And so the argument goes. A cloned dictator could be a clerk-typist and a cloned assassinated president might become a professor. I know of no competent psychologist or behavioral biologist who could or would predict anything about what the expression of an individual's genes as a new person would be 20 years hence.

CLONING AND COMPASSION
IN THE MEDICAL ARTS

It has been suggested that human cloning can serve a humanitarian function. Consider, if you will, a marriage in which one of the individuals has a genetic defect. The partner without the defect could be cloned, the union would be blessed with one or more children, and the genetic defect eliminated.

But there may be practical problems involved in a woman carrying to term her own clone. It is possible for fetal cells to break loose during gestation and find their way to the mother's tissue. Pregnant women carry not only a baby but membranes and tissues of fetal origin. Some of the tissues are concerned with nutrition of the fetus and are known as "trophoblast" cells. Ordinarily, the immune system of the mother rejects the "foreign" trophoblastic tissue after birth. What happens to the mother who has fetal trophoblast cells spread throughout her body that are genetically identical to herself? Presumably, she would not have the capacity to reject the cells and a fragment of the fetus would become as malignant as any other cancer. Instead of having the pleasure of seeing whether her clone outdoes herself, she might die of cancer related to the pregnancy.

If a man or a woman is physically vigorous enough to consider having himself or herself cloned, but has a genetic defect that prevents reproduction, the defect is probably recessive. The examination of cells and fluid from within the pregnant uterus, amniocentesis, has proved useful for detecting subtle genetic differences. Given these two facts, I wish to make a modest proposal: Instead of resorting to cloning which may be even less available in the future than heart transplants are now, why not let the couple who fear genetic disease in their offspring utilize antenatal diagnosis. Even if both partners carry recessive genes for the defect, only one of four embryos will manifest the condition or have the potentialities for the condition. That unfortunate fetus, at most a 25% risk, could be diagnosed early in pregnancy and terminated by legal abortion. One may quibble about appropriate antenatal tests being not yet available for all genetic disease. Permit me to remind the reader that human cloning and mouse cloning, for that matter, is still well in the future, but examination of amniotic fluid and amniotic cells already permits in utero diagnosis of certain human diseases.

It might be a character-building exercise to adopt a child and forget cloning under the conditions described. If one parent has the strength to forgo biological parenthood because of possible genetic effects, I would suggest that the other parent emulate the first, do a socially constructive thing, adopt and enjoy parenthood without adding to the biological burden of an overpopulated planet.

Additionally, there is the unresolved problem of whether a mother is a mother to the clone of her husband. Is the father the father or a brother to his infant clone? And will love or resentment emerge when the asexually created twig realizes that he or she was created on a bench with a micromanipulator instead of as a consequence of sexual love? Personally and subjectively, I find that in a chaotic world with an uncertain future, both a mother *and* a father are reassuring. Humans are notoriously resistant to advances in the technology of parturition. Perhaps my apprehensiveness about the lack of a conventional parent may be in the same category as the fear voiced by some of painless childbirth. I admit that my reaction is emotional, not scientific.

I freely admit to love of parents and love of family. I also recognize that I would love any young individual reared in my home. So, why not love the cloned offspring of my mate? Conversely, why shouldn't my spouse have concern and affection for my cloned self?

The relationship would be novel. Perhaps learning, because the genetic makeup is identical, would be enhanced. I suspect that whether or not a cloned individual communicated more readily with its genomic parent than it would with anyone else would depend upon individual circumstances. It seems to me just as likely that the clone would reject its single "parent" as it would be especially fond of that parent. I know of no way that one could predict whether rejection or acceptance would occur.

Even though an attempt has been made, I still think, as I said earlier, that I will not witness cloning of a human being. Although it might be compassionate to assist a childless couple to have a child through cloning, the relatively elaborate technology required for this procedure does not address any major medical problem. Is it moral to spend large sums of money for biomedical equipment and salaries for technical personnel to *reproduce* people when worldwide lack of people is no problem at all? When overpopulation is the problem?

Are there medical problems that could be addressed with the technique?

SPARE PARTS—A REASON FOR CLONING?

The acceptance of tissue transplants without rejection among members of an isogenic group is a possible benefit of the cloning technique. Rejection of grafted tissue among individuals within a clone does not occur, just as an identical twin does not reject surgically transplanted tissue obtained from its genetically identical sibling. Because of this, some writers have suggested that one or more clones be fabricated to serve as a source of spare parts for a nuclear donor. Mechanics refer to the dismantling of an intact engine for parts to repair another engine as "cannibalism"—it is my feeling that the term is particularly apt in the situation proposed. It seems to me that it might well be ego-shattering to find at age 21 that one was fabricated on the bench so that one's clonemate could have a spare kidney should it be needed. It could be proposed that if one wished to utilize human cloning for spare parts, one should not make intact whole people, but should manufacture specific spare parts and then only as they are needed.

Consider the situation of a president of the United States with an aging and infirm heart. Both Presidents Eisenhower and Johnson were afflicted with heart trouble. I suggest that it would be feasible to obtain a microscopic biopsy from an ailing chief executive, and, either directly or after in vitro culture, insert a nucleus from a cell of the biopsy into an enucleated egg from an appropriate ovulated woman. If the cell-biology theory relating to the genetic equivalence of adult nuclei is correct, it would not matter from what type of tissue the biopsy was obtained. Thus, as the theory permits, skin, bone marrow, or liver would be equally acceptable as a source of diploid nuclei for transplantation.

But how is a heart obtained from the proposed cloning operation? Let me postulate that a heart could be produced in the following manner. The cloned president would be placed in the uterus of an appropriate surrogate mother, who would not be expected to carry the clone to term. Within the first month of embryonic development, only weeks after uterine implantation, and many months before "quickening," the heart is differentiated embryonically and autonomous beating begins. Appropriate organ culture techniques are not yet available, but may be in the not distant future. The organ rudiment, in this case a heart, would be removed from the cloned embryo and put in culture. The remainder of the embryo, not yet "alive" by some people's standards, would be discarded. Growth is rapid in organ culture and there is no need to predict that an inordinate growth period would be needed. A fertilized egg grows from a speck to 6 to 10 pounds in nine months. A heart of appropriate size for an adult might be grown in half that time. The chief executive who provided the biopsy would then become the recipient of the cloned heart.

The proposed transplant system stands in stark contrast to the macabre wait for the sudden demise of a suitable donor. After the dead donor's heart is transplanted, the recipient must evermore be monitored for possible rejection of the organ that sustains his or her life. How much better it would be to implant a new heart, genetically identical to the first, but more youthful by a half dozen decades. Critics will say, and accurately, that the isogenic implanted heart, *because* of its very identicalness to the former heart, would become prey to the same disease that afflicted the first. True. However, if it took six decades for the first heart to succumb, even if the second lasted only half that time, it would serve a life-prolonging function. Further, it could be that the second heart would benefit from increased knowledge of those insults that make American hearts so vulnerable to disease. Perhaps the chief executive with his or her new heart could be coaxed into not smoking or cajoled into consuming fewer fatty steaks. It seems to me that if one wants to prognosticate a suitable use that is potentially scientifically feasible for the cloning procedure, one may very well wish to consider the tailor-making of organs for the maintenance of already existing life.

The proposal for spare parts, like any other activity that requires immense technical skill and money, would never be available for all. Who would decide who gets a cloned heart? Who would be the recipient? There are, of course, many precedents for the inequitable distribution of medical care. Recently, the late Duke of Windsor became the recipient of a piece of artificial aorta in Houston. Surely his life was extended. Would we deny the duke his extra years because others were unable to seek competent medical diagnosis and superb surgical assistance to be equally served?

Spare parts—how simple. Not resolved, however, is the problem of risk to the surrogate mother, the risk that accompanies any pregnancy. Also not solved is how to dispose of the fragment of embryo "not alive" by some people's standards. I am not a lawyer and so I have personal difficulties with legal definitions that attempt to define when life begins. As a biologist, I think of the continuity of life—and I believe that the "lifeless" fragment that provided a heart rudiment is, in fact, a part of the continuity of life—and the surgeon who would dissect from it a heart would be terminating the life of an unborn human. I would not do that.

Whole books have been written about the ethics of abortion. It is not my purpose to consider the morality of such a sensitive issue here. Rather, it is my purpose to illustrate how human cloning might be medically useful. If human cloning becomes a reality, then society through elected representatives must pass enabling legislation (to protect the physician) or enact laws that proscribe the procedure (to prevent abortion for cloning or other surgical acts considered undesirable). I suggest that these legislative acts will be promulgated only when the surgical skills become available.

I also suggest that the issues are far more complex than is apparent at first sight. If we had the resources to clone a human to save a significant life, would abortion of the clone (to provide an embryonic heart) in fact be abortion? I ask this question because is not the significant act of a conventional abortion the termination of a life? The clone would be a cellular extension of an already existing life and termination of the embryonic clone does not terminate the individual who donated the diploid nucleus. Further, termination of the cloned embryonic life in the hypothetical situation would have the potentiality of *extending* the life of the donor of the diploid nucleus. Thus, would an abortion be an abortion in the special sense when its only significant feature would be life extension? I do not know the answers to these questions, and I doubt if many of the writers who suggest that cloning be used to provide spare parts do either.

There are other ethical considerations regarding cloning.

MORE ON ETHICS AND MORALS

If human cloning does happen, there is a real potential for developmental abnormalities. There is no reason to believe that manipulation of human eggs and nuclei would be any more free of technical error and mishap than manipulation of amphibian eggs and nuclei. Is this a reason *not* to clone? I believe not. Abnormal offspring are a real hazard of conventional sexual reproduction. There is no guarantee that a fetus will be entirely normal. Although the statistical chance of birth defects may be calculated at about 7%, parents never know in advance what problems may occur during any particular pregnancy. Nature is imperfect and so is the potential synthetic human produced by cloning. Should risk of imperfection be a deterrent in cloning any more than it is a deterrent in sexual reproduction? My answer to this is "No," provided there is good reason to clone in the first place. I have already suggested that I believe *reproduction* by cloning is not desirable—not all agree with me.

There are other questions. Since cloning will allow for close inspection of the operated egg, who will have the responsibility of terminating the life of a transplant egg that appears to be developing abnormally? I suspect that an abnormally cleaving egg will die before it becomes an abnormal baby—this is generally true (with exceptions) of amphibian eggs. Since abortion of a conventionally conceived fetus is legal, I see no reason why a grossly abnormal egg should not be aborted in vitro. But is loss of an embryo before implantation in the uterus truly abortion? Again, I profess ignorance.

There are, of course, other problems. Who will be the surrogate mother, that is, who will provide a foster uterine environment for a nuclear transplant human? One way of dealing with that question is to avert it and propose that an artificial placenta be used for the nine months of fetal development. It is my judgment that we are far more advanced in the technology of ovulation and micromanipulation of nuclei than we are in the technology of devising an artificial placenta. Thus it may well be that the decision to clone humans will be made long before extracorporeal gestation is possible, which would liberate women from the burden of pregnancy.

Liberation from the burden (and joy?) of pregnancy calls to mind how, until very recently, artificial formulas were thought to provide new freedom to young mothers. Although it is true that bottles provide nourishment to the baby during the mother's absence, some thoughtful individuals now question if laboratory-devised food is as good for the newborn as is mother's milk, and they point out that both baby and mother seem to do better with the warm human contact of baby's lips to mother's breast. These comments concerning the technology of baby feeding may reveal some of my skepticism about the technology of extracorporeal pregnancy.

If human cloning is resorted to for whatever reason, some women will probably volunteer to be surrogate mothers and be chosen as such. Is this morally undesirable? I do not know. One reason that it may be unacceptable is that it involves a risk to the life of a mother who is not even carrying her own child. I find risk repugnant but our society appears not to. Risk to the lives of certain people has always been acceptable to our western civilization and culture. Until recently we drafted young men into a combat force against their will. We expect asbestos workers and coal miners to expose themselves to high risk. We tolerate cigarettes. So why proscribe the actions of an individual who voluntarily offers her uterus as a home to a cloned human? I suspect that labor unions will have more to say about who and who does not offer her womb for wages than do the commentators on the moral scene.

SOULS—FRAGMENTED OR INTACT?

A biologist treads on quicksand when he/she attempts to make pronouncements concerning the soul. Although it may seem difficult for the layperson to think of cloned humans as having a soul apart from the nuclear donor, I believe he/she would have as much soul as does each twin of an identical twin pair or each triplet of a triplet trio when descended from a common fertilized egg. For monozygotic twins or triplets are as much clones as the clones that would be produced by humans at the laboratory bench. I would never argue that an identical twin has less soul than its ordinary sibling—and, in precisely the same way, a cloned human would have no less soul than does a human who develops as a result of a sexual act.

I like to think of the biological significance of separated blastomeres and cloning. There is another procedure that is quite opposite. This procedure involves bringing together two early embryos to grow and develop as one. The fusion of two embryos to develop as one normal embryo is as interesting in a developmental sense as is cloning. It probably has happened spontaneously in humans—just as occasionally a cleaving human egg splits and forms twins. Only in this case, two fertilized eggs fuse to form one individual. Does that one individual have two souls? I doubt it. And, if a cloned individual were ever produced, I doubt if it would have less soul than anyone else.

HAZARDS

Today we know more about hazard than humans have ever known before. We know what kills. Lack of exercise and too much saturated fat in the diet probably contribute to cardiovascular disease. Smoking probably kills more individuals than any other environmental insult, taking its toll through cardiovascular disease and cancer. The United States and other nations have thermonuclear instruments of death ready for instant deployment, making thermonuclear conflict an ever present hazard.

I do not want to clone a human. I know of only one who has tried. I know of no one with the capability to clone a human. But what if a human were cloned? Would he or she be a hazard and would the act of cloning be a hazard? I doubt it. The cloned human would be a human just as the cloned frog is a frog. A human is not a hazard per se, although the acts of certain humans are hazardous. The cloned human might not be a hazard, but would the cloner be one? I doubt it. He or she would have an unusual skill—which would probably have little marketable value. If I had to limit myself to one skill, I would far rather be a machinist than a human cloner. There are many industries that make many useful products that will always have to employ machinists for the benefit of humans. I know of no industry now or in the future that will need the services of a human cloner.

Suggestions for Discussion and Writing

1. Is the title of McKinnell's essay well chosen?

2. How would you characterize the tone of the essay? How do the title and opening sentences help establish this tone?

3. What is the author's purpose (thesis) in this essay? How does the tone contribute to this purpose? Do you notice any pattern in the way McKinnell develops his case against human cloning?

4. Why, according to McKinnell, are "carbon copies" of human beings impossible?

5. Define the term "epigenesis."

6. What is McKinnell's case against the use of cloning to produce human offspring?

7. Compare McKinnell's essay with Weizenbaum's "Artificial Intelligence" (this chapter). In what ways are the concerns of the two authors similar or different?

8. In the final paragraph of his essay, McKinnell writes, "If I had to limit myself to one skill, I would far rather be a machinist than a human cloner." What is the force of this statement?

☐ ESCAPE FROM MODERNISM

Frederick Turner
(b. 1943)

Born in England and educated at Oxford University, Frederick Turner came to the United States in 1967. A poet, science-fiction writer, literary critic, and philosopher of science, he has taught at several institutions, including Kenyon College and the University of Texas at Dallas, where he was appointed Founders Professor of Art and Humanities in 1985. Among his many books are *Shakespeare and the Nature of Time* (1971), *Between Two Lives* (1972, poetry), *A Double Shadow* (1978, science fiction), and *Natural Classicism: Essays in Literature and Science* (1986). Turner has also published poems and essays in a variety of literary journals and national magazines and has twice appeared on "Smithsonian World" PBS documentaries.

Rejecting the notion that science and the humanities represent opposite ways of viewing, and understanding, the world, Turner in much of his work brings together an understanding of the sciences with the vision (and narrative skill) of the poet. The following essay, first published in *Harper's* (1984), illustrates this integrative thrust. Turner argues that modern science and technology are not the dehumanizing agents that "modernist" critics have made them out to be. Rather, he claims, they offer the promise of a more dynamic and integrated vision of nature and of man's role as "the supreme observer and shaper of the material world."

Consider the process by which a modern integrated circuit is made. A wafer of silicon is doped with impurities, exposed to light that is shone through a template to form a pattern of shadows, treated with new impurities that differentiate between the irradiated and unexposed areas, etched by a bath of corrosives, blanketed with a new surface of silicon, exposed to another pattern of light, and so on, until a marvelously complex three-dimensional system of switches, gates, resistors, and connections has been laid down. This system may be destined to become part of a computer that will in turn help design new integrated circuits. The technical term for this process is "photographic." An integrated circuit is essentially a very complex silicon photograph. Photographic techniques are now being used to make all kinds of tiny machines—solar energy collectors, pumps, and measuring devices.

We normally think of a photographic process as one that makes pictures of things rather than things themselves. A photograph is significant only as a record; as an object it's just a bit of sticky paper. But our silicon photograph doesn't merely *represent* something; it *does* what it is a photograph of. In a sense it is a miraculous picture, like that of Our Lady of Guadalupe: it not only depicts, but does; it is not just a representation, but reality; it is not just a piece of knowledge, but a piece of being; it is not just epistemology, but ontology.

Consider, moreover, the digital, or Soundstream, method of re-producing music. The music is scanned every forty-four thousandth of a second or so, and the sound wave activity in that forty-four thousandth of a second is given a numerical value. This value is recorded in terms of a binary sequence of laser-burned holes and unburned spaces on a record. To play the record you just scan the holes with another laser and synthesize a sound that corresponds to the number you get every forty-four thousandth of a second.

A digital recording is really just a sophisticated musical "score." It in no way reproduces the actual shape of the music, the way the grooves in the plastic of a normal record do, any more than the five parallel lines, the clef, and the little black ellipses with tails reproduce the sound of the music—or, indeed, than the letters on a page reproduce the sound of speech. In a sense, the digital recording harks back to an antiquated device for reproducing music: the player piano.

The interesting thing is that digital recordings are much more accurate than any analog recording could be. They are literally as accurate as you want: you could scan music every hundred thou-sandth of a second—though it would be useless, as the highest pitch we can hear is less than a twenty thousandth of a second in frequency. Moreover, a digital recording is theoretically almost in-vulnerable to wear, whereas an analog recording must suffer and shriek to give up its music.

Paradoxically, an analog recording, which is the actual reverber-ation of a performance of a piece of music—as if we were to put our ear against the wall of the Sistine Chapel choir—is less accurate than the entirely new performance generated by machinery from the meticulous numerical score of a digital recording. It is as if, knowing the right language, you could write the names of foods so that if you ate the paper on which they were written it would be more tasty and nourishing than the foods themselves.

So: photographs can now, magically, do what they are pictures of; and a score of a piece of music can give a more accurate recording than the sound of the music itself. We live once again in a world of runes and icons, efficacious and full of virtue; a world in which the distinction between how we know and what we know, statement and referent, meaning and object, has begun to break down. Indeed, quantum physics tells us that we are all made out of numerical likelihoods called electrons, photons, and so on; and the Big Bang theory says we are all made out of light.

*   *   *

Our children are growing up on computer programs and fantasy role-playing games—Voyager, Wizardry, Dungeons & Dragons. The space program was too slow to bring those other worlds to them, so they constructed them right here on earth. Play has become increasingly practical: it is almost as if an evolutionary necessity dictated that from our most infantile and unnecessary behaviors would come the solid future of the species. Just as it began to seem that political, economic, and technological forces were combining to organize the human race into a rational, centralized, and anonymous unity, and that the world was, as they say, becoming a small place, counterforces started taking us in completely new directions. The new electronic technology is by nature playful and individualizing. The strong hand of the corporation and the still stronger hand of the state, which were once able to coerce the population into service by cutting off the sources of energy and information, are losing their hold. Quite soon a family with its own solar power generator and its own computer will have the kind of practical sovereignty once possessed only by nations.

Remember the scene in *Close Encounters of the Third Kind* where the kids' mechanical toys all wake up and, in their dim electronic awareness, run about on the floor and clap their hands and flash their lights? And how the music of the aliens is actually a variation on the Disney tune "When You Wish Upon a Star"? We have met E.T., and he is our toys, our animated cartoons, our computer programs. We are re-entering at last the ancient animist universe, populated by genies and geniuses of place, in which every object possesses a demon that one might control and use. But the nymphs and dryads are now microprocessors inhabiting our cars, our stoves, our clocks, our chess sets, and our typewriters. Soon everything will have its own dedicated intelligence, its own nisus, or animating will.

We are at a curious juncture in the history of science and technology. The empiricism of the Renaissance gradually flattened out the ancient hierarchy of the universe and broke up the Great Chain of Being. But just when the world seemed to have been reduced to a collection of objective facts—the world view of modernism—a new order began to come into being.

The new Great Chain of Being, unlike the old one, is dynamic and fluid: it is the great branching tree of evolution. As long as evolution was confined to the realm of biology, it did not seriously threaten the modernist vision of the world as "value-flat"; it simply made of life a mystical anomaly, a "fever of matter" in the "frozen chastity" of the inorganic, as Thomas Mann put it. But now we can create viruses out of "dead" chemicals, proving they were not as dead as we thought. The link has been made. All of the world is alive.

The destruction of the old coherence is best illustrated by the collapse of the meaning of the word "art." In *The Tempest* it is Prospero's "art" that makes temporary sense of the airy nothing the world is made of, rendering it into cloud-capped towers, gorgeous palaces, solemn temples, even the Globe theater itself. For

Shakespeare "art" meant science, philosophy, technical power, craft, theatrical sleight of hand, liberal education, magic, and "art" in our modern meaning, all at once. The moment of *The Tempest* was the last moment of full cultural health and integrity. "Art," the word, was gradually torn to shreds, until in our century art and science, science and technology, philosophy and science, art and philosophy, magic and science, craft and art, education and art, have all been set against one another, like demons bred out of the corpse of the great mother.

But coherence is swiftly returning. The indeterminacy principle, which destroys the distinction between observation and action, makes all science into technology and all technology into science. Academic philosophy has died and passed its inheritance on to the theoreticians of science and the art critics. Anthropologists have revealed other cultures' magic as science and our own science as magic. In all the arts, the death of modernism has given birth to a rapprochement between craft and art, and art is, once more, properly required to be moral. All of these assertions are more prophetic than scholarly, but watch out.

Not that the empirical detour was necessary. Shakespeare's magic did not work outside the theater, and we needed three centuries of self-imposed alienation, of tearing things to pieces to see how they worked, to be able to come back to a coherent world, this time with the powers and knowledge we always felt were our birthright—powers and knowledge we had mimed with magic. But now that we have come back we must cast away the habits of exile—the self-contempt, the illusion of alienation, the hatred of the past, the sterile existentialism, the fear of the future, the willful imposition of meaninglessness on a universe bursting with meaning.

Another way of saying the same thing is that we are undergoing a religious revolution. In about 1600 a new religion, materialism, appeared on the scene. Its practice is what we usually call economic activity, and its higher emotions include a sense of the beauty of nature and awe at its workings, and a sense of triumph in technological achievement. Its theology is atomistic: like God, the atom of matter is indivisible, eternal, invulnerable, responsible for all events in the world. Unlike God, though, it is not conscious or personal. As with other great religions—and it is a great and in many ways noble religion, and much of our best and most significant behavior consists in its observance—it has given rise to magnificent heresies, moral systems, and even good science: dialectical materialism, existentialism, the theory of evolution.

If someone were to protest that materialism is not a religion, a cross-cultural view would rapidly convince him. Medieval people did not call their everyday rituals religious, or even rituals. They were just the way one lived one's life. Totemists, before contact with Europeans, would have said the same thing about their own practices, their own value systems. What enabled materialism to triumph was precisely the fact that it did not claim to be a religion at all, but labeled other systems as religious; and there are elements of materialism in all human value systems, just as there are elements of monotheism, polytheism, animism, totemism, and ancestor worship.

But materialism is now going through the same crisis Christianity went through 400 years ago. Christianity resolved its crisis by determining to coexist with the new religion, to the enrichment of both, while accepting certain limitations on its relevance, the chief of which was the recognition of itself as *a* religion, rather than "the way things are."

The main challenge to materialism was the discovery that the atom is not irreducible, and the consequent dissolution of matter into event, relation, and information. One of the advantages of materialism is that the further one goes in explaining the complex and ambiguous behavior of the apparent world in terms of simple atomic events, the more concrete and unambiguous it seems to be. Religion seeks certainty, and for a long time materialism delivered it. But one more reduction, one last simplification, spoiled everything. Suddenly the world, as it was revealed by quantum physics, became utterly ambiguous again.

Much that is good can be salvaged from the old religion. The world of matter, though it has been shown to be a provisional one, without the appealing absoluteness it once possessed, is still beautiful and exquisitely ordered; and surely we should give it a share of worship. But if we do so, we must give a greater share to ourselves, both as the supreme product of matter given the chance to do what comes naturally and as the supreme observer and shaper of the material world. That aspect of religion that appeals to the desire to worship something outside of, and superior to, ourselves will not be satisfied any longer with materialism.

And materialism has always carried a dangerous flaw: its fundamental parts, the atoms of matter, are impersonal, insentient, and unintelligent—that is precisely what makes them intelligible. But the elevation of matter implies the superiority of those characteristics—impersonality, insentience, unintelligence. The personal, the sensible, and the conscious came to be seen as a second-class reality that must face up to the impersonal "real world" and submit to the "reality principle": the blind forces of economic change, the dialectics of class struggle, the survival of the fittest. Perhaps our great political and technological monsters—communism, fascism, the hydrogen bomb—are the final expression of that suspicion of the personal: they promise to eradicate persons from the face of the earth.

The world is becoming a *bigger* place, more densely packed with information. A few years ago the amount of information stored in the world's libraries, computers, and so on doubled every ten years; now the doubling time is eight years, and it is continuing to shrink. This process has a cosmological significance, because the universe itself is made of information—matter and energy are only simple forms of it. And whereas matter and energy decay according to the laws of entropy, paying for their durability of form by their eventual death and transformation into more primitive states of organization, information is both immortal and self-propagating. On the level of matter and energy, the world is running down; on the level of information, the world is growing and becoming more elaborately organized. And *our* activities, tiny as they appear in space and time, are a significant part of that growth.

Pascal said that the silence of infinite spaces terrified him. But we now know that such spaces, large as they are, are not infinite; and that space itself is generated by an evolutionary process that preceded it. Once the universe was no bigger than a baseball, and before that it was smaller than an atom. What counted then was not how big it was but its capacity to generate information. Measured in terms of space and time, humankind is, indeed, a tiny speck in the vastness of the cosmos, as scientists have traditionally reminded us. Measured in a more fundamental way, in terms of density and complexity of information, we are already the largest things in the universe: we are its cortex, its skin, its bud, its growing surface. And our new laws—of morality, aesthetics, government, and games—have taken their appointed place next to their predecessors, the laws of biology, chemistry, physics, and mathematics. Our laws, though latecomers, are no less real for that. As Thoreau put it, punning on the leaves of trees, the leaves of books, and the "new leaf" we shall all turn over:

> No wonder that the earth expresses itself outwardly in leaves, it so labors with the idea inwardly. The atoms have already learned this law, and are pregnant by it. . . . The very globe continually transcends and translates itself, and becomes winged in its orbit. Even ice begins with delicate crystal leaves, as if it had flowed into moulds which the fronds of water plants had impressed on the watery mirror. The whole tree itself is but one leaf, and the rivers are still vaster leaves whose pulp is intervening earth, and towns and cities are the ova of insects in their axils.

The biologist A. G. Cairns-Smith recently suggested that there were, before the DNA-based life we know today, more primitive ways of self-replicating and metabolizing. In his book *Genetic Takeover and the Mineral Origins of Life* he postulates the existence of a silicon-based clay "organism," a halfway house between dead matter and life, which evolved until it was able to assemble and use complex carbon-based molecules—the forerunners of DNA—to perform necessary metabolic tasks. These molecules made up, as it were, a part of the "body" developed by the silicate "genes." In time they became independent of the clay organisms they had served and began to develop on their own. Thus the difficult question of the origins of DNA is answered.

Not least among the implications of this idea is the notion that what is now the genotype—the blueprint—of an organism was once only part of its phenotype—its blueprint expressed in physical terms. We do not need to go to Cairns-Smith's work for an illustration. There are many instances when the mechanism used by the genetic material of viruses or bacteria to promote its own survival has become incorporated into the material itself, as in the case of the plasmids; and the messengers of DNA often perform some of the functions of DNA itself, as when viral RNA takes on part of the responsibility for carrying the genetic inheritance.

A fascinating analogy suggests itself: perhaps our traditional ways of storing and passing on information, through speaking, writing, and data processing, are now taking over the genetic tasks of our species, just as, if Cairns-Smith's theory is correct, the organic molecules that were once its tools superseded the genetic functions of the clay.

To Descartes and Berkeley, the distinction between being and consciousness was so absolute as to require divine intervention to enable them to communicate. That distinction is now only a matter of degree. Being has dissolved before our eyes as we have examined it more closely, until, in quantum physics, matter proves less durable than the light in which we see it and evaporates into energy, pure event, if we try to take it apart any further.

That nature from which we are supposed to be alienated never existed. The great quantum experiments—the parallel-slits light experiment, the polarizing-filter light experiment—show that nature has not made up its mind about what it really is, and is quite happy to have us help it do so. The tradition of philosophy that saw us as cut off from our "true" way of being has collapsed, although it hasn't realized it yet. *We* are nature, and we are as at home here in the world as anything has ever been. For the whole world is made up of such as we; its physical components are, just as we are, tourists, outsiders, amateurs, getting by on a smile and a shoeshine, and deriving what being they have from the recognition of their fellows. All nature is second nature.

The new quantum theories of cosmology suggest that the chance-governed behavior of elementary particles is a sort of "living fossil" of the state of the entire universe in its first moments of existence. In other words, the order of the physical world as we know it through conventional physics and chemistry did not at first exist, but evolved out of chaos.

At the very beginning there existed an infinite number of possible states, each with a probability of one in infinity. Nothingness was one possibility, sharing with the others the same infinitesimal likelihood of being true. The fact that one cannot pin down an electron simultaneously in any one time and place is a remnant of that indeterminacy. The sharpness of reality is a result of the harmonious synchronization of many fuzzy events.

Technology is the continuation of the process of evolution by which the indefiniteness of the world gave rise to greater and greater certainty. It is the realizing of the possible, and our machines are only the end of a line that goes back through our own bodies, the persisting organization of crystals and stable molecules, and the durable coherence of elementary particles to that first moment when possibility resolved itself into a burst of identical photons.

In the heyday of high modernism the world of the future seemed impersonal, cool, centralized, inorganic, tidy, sharp-edged: a world-state with equal prosperity for all, tall rectilinear buildings, cool atonal music, abstract art, imagist free verse, novels purified of the fetishism and hierarchy of plot and character; a world-state without repression, alienation, and ego, free from the shibboleths of honor, beauty, sexual morality, patriotism, idealism, religion, and duty.

This future now appears dated, even dreary. It has been shown that yes, indeed, humankind *does* have a nature; there are cultural universals. There are rules to be followed if freedom—limitless-ness—is to come about. And those rules include not only the grammar of language, but also the classical laws of harmony, melody, color, proportion, rhythm, and balance. The modernists believed those classical qualities to be arbitrary and tried to sweep them away, thereby damaging the art forms they were trying to liberate and depriving them of their audience. But we are beginning to discover the nature of our humanity as well as the humanity of nature. To put it aphoristically: We have a nature; that nature is cultural; that culture is classical.

Of course we must redefine "classical" to include the tonality of Chinese and Indonesian and African music, the artistic conventions of the Tlingit and the Maori and the Navaho, the verse forms of the Eipo and the Inuit and the Yanomami. But there *are* rules to be culled from this panhuman study, and to break them is not a daring innovation but a pointless exercise—akin to shining a light in our eyes at a wavelength invisible to the retina, or to speaking a sentence whose grammar works on no comprehensible principle. We must change our romantic attitude toward the rules, too, and recognize them not as an imposition but as a biologically and culturally agreed-upon code of communication, our constitution, the foundation of our freedom. The great mistake of the modernists was to identify randomness with freedom. Freedom lies on the far side of order; it is an order that has got so complex that it has become self-referential, and thus autonomous. The random is the most complete of tyrannies.

The future now looks quite different from the way it once did. Not only is a world state, thank heavens, out of the question; we may even be in the last days of the nation-state. A much more decentralized world seems likely: personal, warm, custom-made, organic, untidy, decorated. Our music will be full of melody again, though it will be more incantatory, more rhythmic, with an Oriental quaver. Our visual arts will be mainly representational, with abstraction reserved for decoration. Our architecture will recapitulate the pan-human village clutter, and all functions—domestic, religious, commercial, industrial, educational, political—will be jumbled together. Our poetry will be, as all poetry was until seventy years ago, richly metrical and rhetorical, full of stories, ideas, moral energy, scientific speculation, theology, drama, history. Many of these changes have already begun, though a rear guard of modernist reactionaries still holds much political and economic power, and it will take decades to deprogram middlebrow taste from its masochistic preferences.

There will also be a refeminization of the arts. The modernists tended to write off sexual differences as trivial and imposed, and thus, paradoxically, re-formed their norms upon a masculine model. What followed was an attempt—pathetic as it now seems—to provide equality for women by demanding that they imitate the achievements of men. But the study of sexuality and gender, and of social and biological evolution, has shown distinct differences between men and women. A full, rich, and human culture built upon an exclusively masculine model is impossible, even if women could be trained to fit that model.

I suspect that some readers winced when I gave a list of values: honor, beauty, sexual morality, patriotism, idealism, religion, and duty. That reflex indicates a reaction to values and reward systems that has very rarely been examined.

In the nineteenth century, materialist ethics came together with materialist biology and agreed that there were only two types of rewards: those obviously associated with survival and those obviously associated with reproduction. Two brilliant value systems—Marx's, which reduced all value to the economics of survival, and Freud's, which reduced all value to libido—were the result. Existentialism struggles between accepting these rewards as preferable to the more complex value systems of a society and rejecting them, and all rewards, as bribes to make us give up our freedom.

Under the pressure of these theories, which postulated very coarse rewards even for very refined behavior, our value systems changed and coarsened. When people wince at the words "duty," "honor," and "beauty," they are doing exactly what Victorians would have done upon hearing the words "passion," "desire," and "sexuality," or even "money," "fees," and "honoraria." The Victorians, in a last-ditch defense of the older, more complex value system, would naturally have been pained by references to the enemy's rewards. We, the inheritors of D. H. Lawrence and Jean-Paul Sartre, feel the same old blush come to our faces when we are reminded of all the rewards—the joy of duty, the satisfaction of honorable conduct— that we have given up. Not that we are not, often, honorable and dutiful. But we are so in a spirit of taking nasty medicine with good grace, and we are deeply suspicious of those who enjoy doing their duty.

But new discoveries are forcing on us a new value system. The pleasures of eating and sex are not the only rewards. Scientists studying the chemistry of the brain have begun to uncover a remarkable variety of rewards, suppressors of rewards, suppressors of the suppressors, and so on. The pleasures of achievement, of insight into the truth, of heroic exertion or sacrifice, of good conscience, of beauty, are *real* pleasures in themselves, not repressed or sublimated derivatives of libido. Certainly the higher pleasures *enlist* the coarser and more obvious ones as reinforcement; and indeed society uses the coarser and more obvious ones—for example food, for children—to train the higher reward systems, to "prime the pump," so to speak. But the "endorphin high" is as real a reward as orgasm, or as food to a starving man.

Nor are hunger and sex the simple survival drives they seemed to the materialists. The study of evolution shows that the division of food played a central role in the religious rituals that defined the human community. What food *represents* has long been more important than the 2,000 calories a day required for survival. And the comparative study of sexual behavior shows that, far from possessing a feeble and watered-down version of brute sexuality, we are the most sexual of all animals—we are in heat all the time, we copulate face to face, our females have as powerful a libido as our males. Our sexuality is much more powerful than that of our closest relatives, the chimpanzees and gorillas; it is far more powerful than is needed for reproduction. Many anthropologists suspect that our sexuality evolved in tandem with our brains, and that it took on the important function of encouraging the creation of family and social groupings that could nurture the young and promote cooperation through affection. Nevertheless, without the discovery of the higher reward systems, the theories of sublimation and repression would still wash. It was the brain chemicals that broke the old ideology.

But there is a terrible tragedy here. Endorphins were discovered because certain scientists studying drug addiction asked the obvious, and brilliant question: Why does the brain have receptors designed precisely to respond with extreme sensitivity to the sap of an Oriental poppy? What was the evolutionary necessity? The answer, of course, is that those receptors were designed to respond to something else entirely. The poppy resins simply happened to possess a molecular resemblance to that something else—an opiate produced by the brain to reward itself for doing very hard work. The tragedy is this: the materialist theory of value has resulted in the cutting off of many of the pleasures produced by the brain chemicals. We are starved for the pleasures of the mind and spirit and soul. The twentieth century is full of *angst,* which has its source in a thirst for things like glory, sanctity, conscience, and heroism, things which have been forbidden to us. Worse: we have replaced those pleasures with counterfeits: and as the doctrines of materialism triumphed, first among intellectuals, then among the population at large, so did the use of opium, cocaine, mescaline, cannabis. (Of course those individuals at the bottom of society, who have always felt cast out, have always used such drugs when they could get them.)

We are only beginning to realize the horrible effects of tampering with the brain's own reward system by means of drugs. That realization touches us, with the hard thrill of permanent damage, in the very center of our will, our freedom, our selfhood. Who can forget those rats that would ignore females in heat and food, pressing the pedal that would deliver their shot of happiness? Or the teenage mugger, sniffing and shaking with his addiction, interested in nothing but the high?

But—turning again to the future—as the theory of reward expands to include endorphins, we will once again educate the young to create their own high, and the demand for the substitute will decline. After all, the real thing is, chemists say, fifty times more powerful than the false, though harder to obtain.

Any good teacher will recognize a gifted student whose capacity for self-reward has been stunted from birth by parents and teachers who would not challenge him and who feared to nurture in him an undemocratic pride and pleasure in achievement. As you force the unaccustomed juices of pleasure—in learning, in truth, in beauty, in work—to flow, the student is almost incredulous. Surely you can't mean him to *enjoy* it? It's obscene. You're teaching him vile and monstrous joys. In fact you're letting him into his inheritance, an inheritance paid for by millions of our ancestors, who humanized themselves by ritual, by claiming kin, by the agonizing and delicious effort to articulate the wordless.

Paradoxically, then, materialism as the supreme religion began to sicken when we began to make thinking machines, and died when we began to see ourselves as machines for the production of spirit, soul, value. Materialist politics is dying too, and we have come to see our traditional cultures as machines that support the process of soul-making. All over the world, revolutionary forces are championing complex and traditional value systems—ethnic, religious, and political—against materialism, whether it be liberal, fascist, capitalist, socialist, or communist. What makes the Vietnamese, the Poles, the Afghans, the Palestinians, and the Irish such dangerous adversaries is not a materialist ideology but religion, traditional education, blood ties, patriotism, a sense of beauty, honor, heroism, duty, and all the rest: the endorphins blazing in the head like a lantern, more fiercely than any sexual passion, or thirst, or hunger for bread.

To a materialist all those beliefs are only distracting games by which we hide the knowledge of death and the reality of our worldly condition from ourselves. But the human race is more deeply motivated by a game than by a reality, and fears losing more than it fears death. From the point of view with which I began—the collapse of the distinction between knowledge and being, information and reality, representing and doing—the paradox is no paradox. Reality has always been a game, and our games continue the evolution of reality. We evolved as idealists, teleologists, essentialists, because, by golly, we survive better that way. Teleology is the best policy. Less idealistic animals have less control over the future.

*   *   *

We have always been nature's insiders, and our solidarity with nature is based on the fact that nature, like us, is fallen and is still falling, outward from the chaos of the Big Bang into order and beauty and freedom.

Before the materialist revolution we robustly persisted in the belief that objects possessed the powers that the poetic imagination conferred on them: we believed in magic and magical properties. The rose was sick with love, the sword hated its enemies, jewels could enchant or heal, the moon was intelligent and a little mad. The world made more sense to us, even though it was inhabited by uncontrollable powers, than it does to the materialists.

For them, metaphor and symbol are terribly sad reminders of that world view that was lost, of our alienation from nature. The rose does not really love, nor the sword hate, nor the jewel heal, nor the moon enchant; they only arbitrarily symbolize those things. Metaphor is a technical failure. All significance is a pathetic fallacy, canals on Mars that we put there by the weakness and hopefulness of our eyes. There is no magic anymore.

We had to choose, as Freud saw but denied, between the power to do and psychic health.

That time is over. The nature of metaphor and symbol will change. We shall be making intelligent and crazy moons, and passionate roses, and fierce swords with microprocessors in their hilts, and jewels with the power to heal. No doubt we will build canals on Mars, if we want, and make it into exactly the place of Edgar Rice Burroughs's poetic visions. Metaphor and symbol will become programs for transformation, and technological inventions will become the new metaphors and symbols. Our poetry will become less obviously symbolic, for symbols will not be plastered onto the outside of reality but will be a concrete and accepted part of its plot, as the technical hardware is in a science-fiction novel. Facts will be significant, and symbols will be facts. It is not that we shall rise above nature—one of the goals of modernism. Rather, we shall *be* nature. We will once more see life, as Edgar says in *King Lear,* as a miracle, as magic; but we will see it too as an "art lawful as eating," like the enchantment that, in *The Winter's Tale,* brings the statue of the dead queen to life.

Suggestions for Discussion and Writing

1. What point is Turner making in his opening discussion of integrated circuits and the means by which they are produced? How does this point relate to his overall thesis?

2. What does Turner mean when he says that the new electronic technology is "playful and individualizing"? Do you agree with him?

3. Turner says that around the year 1600 "a new religion, materialism, appeared on the scene." What were some expressions of that "religion"? What were its values, contributions, ideals? What, according to Turner, was its "dangerous flaw"?

4. What does Turner mean when he says that "Technology is the continuation of the process of evolution by which the indefiniteness of the world gave rise to greater and greater certainty"?

5. How does Turner characterize the modernist's vision of the world? Can you think of a painter, a composer, or an architect whose work appears to conform to this vision? Write an essay defending your choice.

6. How does Turner characterize the "future," its arts, values, attitudes? Do you see any signs that he is right? Pick one aspect of his characterization and write an essay in which you agree or disagree with him.

7. In speaking of the "pathetic" attempt of modernists to provide equality for women, Turner asserts that "a full, rich, and human culture built upon an exclusively masculine model is impossible, even if women could be trained to fit that model." For Turner, a "refeminization of the arts" will be an essential ingredient of postmodernist culture. What does he mean by "refeminization"? Do you see any evidence that this change is already underway?

8. Turner states that "the study of sexuality and gender, and of social and biological evolution, has shown distinct differences between men and women." Would Fox Keller, Bleier, and Levin (Chapter 12) support or contradict this view? Write a brief essay in which you compare Turner's views with those of one or more of these authors.

9. Toward the end of his essay, Turner speaks of "an inheritance paid for by millions of our ancestors, who humanized themselves by ritual, by claiming kin, by the agonizing and delicious effort to articulate the wordless." What is the "inheritance"? In what sense do "ritual" and "claiming kin" humanize? Why is the "effort to articulate the worldless" both "agonizing and delicious"?

10. Do you agree with Turner that the new technology is liberating—that it can release our imagination and our spirit into a new (or regained) sense of our best selves and of our oneness with nature? Write an essay in which you develop your views.

☐ THE TWENTY-FIRST CENTURY

Freeman Dyson
(b. 1923)

Born in England and educated at Cambridge University, the physicist Freeman Dyson came to the United States in 1947 and became a citizen ten years later. Since 1953 he has conducted research at the Institute for Advanced Study at Princeton.

Although trained as a theoretical physicist, Dyson has been involved in a wide variety of practical concerns, including nuclear engineering, astronomy, and space technology among others. He strongly supports the idea of colonizing space and has proposed a number of schemes that might make this possible. Because space colonization would require a safe and economical means of transportation, he has long promoted the development of new propulsion systems.

In addition to his work as a practicing scientist, Dyson is keenly interested in the relationship between science and society and in the moral and social implications of today's technological advances. He has been a consultant to the Defense Department and the Arms Control and Disarmament Agency and an outspoken critic of nuclear arms proliferation, a subject he discussed in *Disturbing the Universe* (1979) and, at greater length, in *Weapons and Hope* (1984). Dyson has been widely praised for his ability to write about technical issues in a language that the general reader can understand. In 1984 he received the National Book Critics Circle Award for general nonfiction (for *Weapons and Hope*). In the following selection, taken from his most recent book, *Infinite in All Directions* (1988), he argues that technology is a liberating force that will dramatically alter our way of life in the twenty-first century.

T echnology is a gift of God. After the gift of life it is perhaps the greatest of God's gifts. It is the mother of civilizations, of arts and sciences. Nuclear weapons are a part of technology, but technology has outgrown nuclear weapons just as it has outgrown other less crude instruments of power. Technology continues to grow and to liberate mankind from the constraints of the past. Compared with the revolutions which technology is bringing to people and institutions all over the world, our quarrels with the Russians are small motes in the eye of history.

The most revolutionary aspect of technology is its mobility. Anybody can learn it. It jumps easily over barriers of race and language.

And its mobility is still increasing. The new technology of microchips and computer software is learned much faster than the old technology of coal and iron. It took three generations of misery for the older industrial countries to master the technology of coal and iron. The new industrial countries of East Asia, South Korea and Singapore and Taiwan, mastered the new technology and made the jump from poverty to wealth in a single generation. That is the reason why I call the new technology a technology of hope. It offers to the poor of the Earth a short-cut to wealth, a way of getting rich by cleverness rather than by back-breaking labor. The essential component of the new technology is information. Information travels light. Unlike coal and iron, it is available wherever there are people with brains to make use of it. Not only in East Asia but all over the planet, technology and the information on which it depends can be effective instruments for achieving a more just distribution of wealth among the nations of mankind. Without the hope of economic justice, mankind cannot realistically hope for lasting peace. If we view the world with a certain largeness of view, we see technology as the gift of God which may make it possible for us to live at peace with our neighbors on this crowded planet.

Such a largeness of view is conspicuous by its absence in the thinking of the Reagan administration. I dislike many things which this administration has done and said, but I dislike most of all the mean-spirited attempts to stop the export of technology and hamper the spread of information. These attempts reveal a mentality which is incompatible with any decent respect for the opinions of mankind. The idea that the United States should try to keep the Soviet Union in a state of technological backwardness excludes the possibility of comprehensive arms-control agreements; the Soviet Union will not negotiate upon any terms other than equality. The idea that the United States can play Nanny to the rest of the world and constrain the flow of technological goodies to reward our friends and punish our enemies is a puerile delusion. Technology is God's gift to all nations alike. The rest of the world will quickly learn whatever we attempt to keep hidden. And we will quickly lose the international goodwill which a more generous attitude has earned us in the past. If we are to lead the world toward a hopeful future, we must understand that technology is a part of the planetary environment, to be shared like air and water with the rest of mankind. To try to monopolize technology is as stupid as trying to monopolize air.

Technology as a liberating force in human affairs is more important than weapons. And that is why scientists speak about international political problems with an authority which goes far beyond their competence as bomb-builders. Forty years ago, scientists became suddenly influential in political life because they were the only people who knew how to make bombs. Today we can claim political influence for a better reason. We claim influence because we have practical experience in operating a genuinely international enterprise. We have friends and colleagues, people we know how to deal with, in the Soviet Union and in the People's Republic of China. We know what it takes to collaborate on a practical level with Soviet scientists, the bureaucratic obstacles that have to be overcome, the possibilities and limitations of personal contact. We know what it takes to operate an astronomical observatory in Chile, to launch an X-ray satellite from Tanzania, and to organize the eradication of the smallpox virus from its last stronghold in Ethiopia. Unlike our political leaders, we have first-hand knowledge of a business which is not merely multi-national but in its nature international. We know how difficult it is to get a piece of apparatus to work in the Soviet Union or in China, but we also know how with patience it can be done. As scientists we work every day in an international community. That is why we are not afraid of the technical difficulties of arms control. That is why we are appalled by the narrow-mindedness and ignorance of our political leaders. And that is why we are not shy to raise our voices, to teach mankind the hopeful lessons that we have learned from the practice of our trade.

It usually takes fifty to a hundred years for fundamental scientific discoveries to become embodied in technological applications on a large enough scale to have a serious impact on human life. One often hears it said that technological revolutions today occur more rapidly than they did in the past. But the apparent acceleration of techno-logical change is probably an illusion caused by perspective. Recent events are seen in greater detail than historical events of a century ago, and the loss of detail makes the more remote technological changes appear to proceed more slowly. In reality, the time elapsed between Maxwell's equations and the large-scale electrification of cities was no longer than the time between Thompson's discovery of the electron and the worldwide spread of television, or between Pasteur's discovery of microbes and the general availability of anti-biotics. In spite of the hustle and bustle of modern life, it still takes two or three generations to convert a new scientific idea into a major social revolution.

If it is true that the interval between discovery and large-scale application is still of the order of seventy years, this means that we should be able to foresee with some reliability the main technological changes that are likely to occur up to the middle of the twenty-first century. Until about the year 2050, large-scale technologies will be growing out of discoveries which have already been made. Only after 2050 are we likely to encounter technologies based on principles unknown to our contemporary science.

Here are my guesses for the dominant new technologies of the next seventy years. I look at contemporary science and see three main areas of existing knowledge not yet fully exploited. The first is molecular biology, the science of genetics and cellular physiology at the molecular level. The second is neurophysiology, the science of complex information-processing networks and brains. The third is space physics, the exploration of the solar system and the physical environment of the Earth. Each of these areas of science is likely to give rise to a profound revolution in technology. The names of the new technologies are genetic engineering, artificial intelligence and space colonization. This short list is not complete. No doubt there will be other innovations of equal importance. Whatever else may happen, these three technological revolutions will be changing the conditions of human life during the coming century. I will say a few words about each of them in turn.

Genetic engineering is already established as a tool of manufacture in the pharmaceutical industry. Bacteria can be infected with alien genes and cloned to produce in quantity the proteins which the alien genes specify. But the quantities that can be produced in this way are at present small. Genetic engineering makes economic sense today only for producing drugs which can be sold at a high unit price. Genetic engineering does not yet begin to compete with conventional industrial processes for the mass production of common chemicals. The fundamental limitation of genetic engineering as it now exists is the limitation of through-put. A genetically engineered bacterium in a tank produces about as much material in a day as a conventional combustion reactor in the same tank would produce in a second. Biological reactions are slow and require large volumes to produce substantial through-put of products. For this reason, genetic engineering will not replace conventional chemistry so long as the genetically engineered creatures are confined in tanks and retorts.

But why should genetically engineered production processes be confined in tanks? One reason for confinement is concern for environmental safety. Regulations in most countries forbid us to let genetically engineered creatures loose in the open air. It is reasonable to be cautious in relaxing regulations. Fears of genetically engineered monsters overrunning the Earth are often exaggerated, but the dangers may not be altogether imaginary. Newly engineered creatures must be studied and understood before they are released into the great outdoors. Still it seems likely that we shall learn in time to transfer genetic-engineering technology from the enclosed tank to the open field without serious danger. After all, farmers have been growing wheat in open fields for thousands of years, and wheat is also a product of human manipulation, just as artificial as genetically engineered *Escherichia coli.* Farmers long ago discovered that it is more profitable to grow wheat in open fields than in greenhouses. Genetic engineering will likewise become profitable for large-scale chemical production when the growing and harvesting of genetically engineered species can be moved outdoors. Chemical industry will then no longer be clearly distinguishable from agriculture. Crop plants will be engineered to produce food or to produce industrial chemicals according to demand.

Every technological revolution causes unplanned and unwelcome side effects. Genetic engineering will be no exception. One of the harmful side effects of genetic engineering might be the displacement of traditional agriculture by industrial crops. This effect would be a further extension of the displacement of subsistence farming by cash crops which happens today in developing countries. The disappearance of subsistence farming is deplorable for many reasons. It causes depopulation of the countryside and overgrowth of cities, it reduces the genetic diversity of our crop species, and it destroys the beauty of traditional rural landscapes. Already in 1924, J. B. S. Haldane saw what was coming and described it in his book *Daedalus*. Here is a passage quoted by Haldane from a term paper written by a fictitious undergraduate in the twenty-first century, summarizing the effects of genetic engineering in the twentieth:

> As a matter of fact it was not until 1940 that Selkovski invented the purple alga *Porphyrococcus fixator* which was to have so great an effect on the world's history. . . . *Porphyrococcus* is an enormously efficient nitrogen-fixer and will grow in almost any climate where there are water and traces of potash and phosphates in the soil, obtaining its nitrogen from the air. It has about the effect in four days that a crop of vetches would have had in a year. . . . The enormous fall in food prices and the ruin of purely agricultural states was of course one of the chief causes of the disastrous events of 1943 and 1944. The food glut was also greatly accentuated when in 1942 the Q strain of *Porphyrococcus* escaped into the sea and multiplied with enormous rapidity. When certain of the plankton organisms developed ferments capable of digesting it, the increase of the fish population of the seas was so great as to make fish the universal food that it is now. . . . It was of course as the result of its invasion by *Porphyrococcus* that the sea assumed the intense purple colour which seems so natural to us, but which so distressed the more aesthetically minded of our great grand-parents who witnessed the change. . . . I need not detail the work of Ferguson and Rahmatullah who in 1957 produced the lichen which has bound the drifting sand of the world's deserts, for it was merely a continuation of that of Selkovski, nor yet the story of how the agricultural countries dealt with their unemployment by huge socialistic windpower schemes. . . .

Haldane had his dates wrong by fifty years. He expected the genetic engineering revolution to come in the 1940s. In fact it is coming in the 1990s or later. But there is no doubt that it will come. Haldane also understood that it will not be an unmixed blessing. As he says at the end of his book:

> The scientific worker is brought up with the moral values of his neighbours. He is perhaps fortunate if he does not realize that it is his destiny to turn good into evil. An alteration in the scale of human power will render actions bad which were formerly good. Our increased

knowledge of hygiene has transformed resignation and inaction in face of epidemic disease from a religious virtue to a justly punishable offence. We have improved our armaments, and patriotism, which was once a flame upon the altar, has become a world-devouring conflagration.

One of the benefits of the genetic engineering revolution will be to allow us to make great areas of the globe economically productive without destroying their natural ecology. Instead of destroying tropical forests to make room for agriculture, we could leave the forests in place while teaching the trees to synthesize a variety of useful chemicals. Huge areas of arid land could be made fruitful either for agriculture or for biochemical industry. There are no laws of physics and chemistry which say that potatoes cannot grow on trees or that diamonds cannot grow in a desert. Moreover, animals can be genetically engineered as well as plants. There are no laws of nature which say that only sheep can produce wool or that only bees can harvest honey. In the end, the genetic engineering revolution will act as a great equalizer, allowing rich and poor countries alike to make productive use of their land. A suitably engineered biological community will be able to produce almost any desired chemical from air, rock, water and sunshine. Ultimately even water may be unnecessary, since the driest desert air contains enough water vapor to sustain a biological community if the community is careful not to waste it. Fixing water from the air should be a simpler biochemical problem than fixing nitrogen, and many existing plants know how to fix nitrogen. . . .

The second technological revolution is artificial intelligence. This revolution has already begun with the rapid development and proliferation of computers. I see the effects of the revolution already in the sociology of the Institute in which I work at Princeton. Until recently, our visiting members were usually assigned to offices with two members to an office. The offices are rather small but there was room in each office for two desks and two chairs. The members were generally content to share offices. It gave them a chance to make friends and to be drawn into scientific collaborations. If the office-mate smoked too much or talked too much, rearrangements could be peacefully negotiated. But, alas, this happy sociological pattern is now no more. A few years ago the Institute decided that in order to remain competitive with other research institutions, we must provide our members with computer terminals. In each office now there is a computer terminal which has to sit on one of the two desks. There is no longer enough room for two humans to work comfortably side by side. Each office now houses one human and one terminal, and the surplus members are exiled to another building.

Computer terminals in offices and homes are only the beginning of artificial intelligence. Artificial intelligence is an enterprise with grander aims. In discussing the future of artificial intelligence, I shall be following the script written by my friend Sir James Lighthill fifteen years ago. In 1972 Lighthill surveyed the field of artificial intelligence in an official report commissioned by the British Science Research Council. He was asked to evaluate the work done in the United Kingdom up to 1972 and to estimate the prospects for further progress up to the year 2000. We are now halfway between 1972 and 2000. So far, the development of the field has conformed closely to Lighthill's predictions. I consider it likely that Lighthill's estimates will remain valid up to the year 2000. But since I am interested in a longer future, I shall depart from Lighthill's script when I offer my guesses concerning what may happen later.

Lighthill begins by dividing artificial intelligence into three areas which he calls A, B, and C. A stands for advanced automation, the objective being to replace human beings by machines for specific purposes, for example, industrial assembly, military reconnaissance or scientific analysis. A large body of work in category A is concerned with pattern recognition, with the programming of computers to read documents or to recognize spoken words. C stands for computer-based central-nervous-system research. The objective here is to understand the functioning of brains, either human or animal, using the computer as a tool to complement and interpret the facts of experimental neurophysiology. A more remote aim is to understand the architecture of the brain so completely that we can borrow the brain's architecture in building a new generation of computers. Finally, B stands for bridge, an area of work which aims to make contact between A and C, to make use of neurophysiological models in designing machines to perform practical tasks. The main activity in area B has been the building of robots. Lighthill's main conclusion is that while work in areas A and C is promising and worthy of support, area B is largely illusory. Both advanced automation and neurophysiology are real sciences with concrete achievements, but the bridge linking them together is nonexistent. Insofar as artificial intelligence claims to be the unifying bridge, artificial intelligence has no real existence.

In the United Kingdom, Lighthill's sweeping condemnation of area B had the effect of a self-fulfilling prophecy. Funding of efforts in area B was withdrawn, and areas A and C continued their independent development. But in other parts of the world, and in particular in the United States, the same decline of area B occurred without Lighthill's intervention. I conclude that Lighthill's diagnosis was accurate, that his harsh words about area B were well founded.

Here is Lighthill's famous caricature of area B:

> Most robots are designed to operate in a world as like as possible to the conventional child's world as seen by a man: they play games, they do puzzles, they build towers of bricks, they recognize pictures in drawing-books, "bear on rug with ball," although the rich emotional character of the child's world is totally absent. Builders

of Robots can justly reply that while robots are still in
their infancy they can mimic only pre-adult functions and
a limited range of those at most, and that these will lead
on to higher things. Nevertheless, the view to which this
author has tentatively but perhaps quite wrongly come is
that a relationship which may be called pseudomaternal
comes into play between a Robot and its Builder.

As Lighthill predicted, the fruitful development of artificial intelligence during the last ten years has occurred in area A and not in
area B. The successful programs are utilitarian tools designed to
perform specific tasks without any pretensions of intelligence. They
are not supposed to understand what they are doing, nor to mimic
the operations of a human intelligence. Their software incorporates
large quantities of human knowledge, but this knowledge is supplied
to them from the outside, not generated on the inside by any process
of internal ratiocination. Artificial intelligence has been practically
useful only when it abandoned the illusion of being intelligent.

What of the future beyond the year 2000? I agree with Lighthill in
expecting advanced automation and neurophysiology to continue to
develop as separate sciences. They still must grow within their
separate domains before bridge building will be possible. But sooner
or later the two areas are bound to come into contact. The time will
come when brain-architecture in area C begins to be understood in
detail and program-architecture in area A begins to acquire some of
the sophistication of natural human language. At that stage the time
will be ripe for building bridges, and the further progress of the two
areas will be merged rather than separate. Machine builders will be
able to incorporate the structures of neurophysiology into their designs, and neurophysiologists will be able to monitor neural processes with properly matched connections between brains and
computers. When progress has reached this point, the grand claims
of artificial intelligence, so prematurely made and so justly ridiculed,
will at last be close to fulfillment. The building of truly intelligent
machines will then be possible. The artificial intelligence revolution
will be upon us in full force.

How long will this take to happen? My guess is about fifty years
from now, some time between the years 2000 and 2050. I am old
enough so that I do not need to worry about seeing my guess proved
wrong. What will be the human consequences of artificial intelligence? To guess the consequences is even more hazardous than to
guess the date of the revolution. I will say only that my view of the
consequences is not apocalyptic. I do not see any real danger that
human intelligence will be supplanted by artificial intelligence. Artificial intelligence will remain a tool under human control. To conclude my assessment of the future of artificial intelligence, I quote
again from Lighthill:

The intelligent problem-solving and eye-hand coordination and scene analysis capabilities that are much

studied in category B represent only a small part of the features of the human central nervous system that give the human race its uniqueness. It is a truism that human beings who are very strong intellectually but weak in emotional drives and emotional relationships are singularly ineffective in the world at large. Valuable results flow from the integration of intellectual activity with the capacity to feel and to relate to other people. Until this integration happens, problem-solving is no good, because there is no way of seeing which are the right problems. The over-optimistic category-B-dominated view of artificial intelligence not only fails to take the first fence but ignores the rest of the steeplechase altogether.

My verdict agrees with Lighthill's. I believe that artificial intelligence will succeed in jumping the first fence before the year 2050, but that human intelligence is far ahead and will remain far ahead in the rest of the steeplechase, as far into the future as I can imagine. Man does not live by problem solving alone. Artificial intelligence will not only help us with solving problems, but will also give us freedom and leisure for exercising those human qualities which computers cannot touch.

The third technological revolution which I see coming is the expansion of life's habitat from Earth into the solar system and beyond. This revolution may take a little longer than the other two. Perhaps it may take as long as a hundred years from now. In charting a possible course for this revolution, I take as my guide Ben Finney, an anthropologist at the University of Hawaii who has made a detailed study of the Polynesian navigators and their voyages of colonization from island to island across the Pacific Ocean. The Polynesians did not travel alone but carried with them as many helpful plants and animals as possible. And we shall too. Only for us, bringing life for the first time into a lifeless wilderness, the bringing along of a sufficient variety of plants and animals will be even more essential.

Finney and his friend Eric Jones wrote an essay with the title *From Africa to the Stars*, surveying the course of human history in the past and the future. Jones is not an anthropologist. He is a space scientist at the Los Alamos National Laboratory in New Mexico. Finney is an expert on the past and Jones is an expert on the future. They condense the whole of human history into four big steps. Step 1 was taken about four million years ago in East Africa. It was the step from the trees to open grassland. The new skills required for the change were walking and carrying. Step 2 was the move out of the warm, sunny climate of Africa to the more varied and generally hostile habitats of the remaining continents, Asia and Europe and America and Australia. This step began about 1 million years ago. The new skills required for it were hunting, firemaking and probably speech. Step 3 was the move from land out onto the open sea. This step began three thousand years ago and was taken first by the Polynesians, with the Europeans following hard on their heels. The new skills required were shipbuilding, navigation and science.

Step 4 is the step from Earth to the stars. This step is beginning now and will occupy us for at least the next few hundred years. The new skills required are to some extent already in hand: rocketry, radio communication, observation and analysis of remote objects. But Step 4 is a bigger enterprise than our present-day space technology can handle. Step 4 is the permanent and irreversible expansion of life's habitat from Earth into the cosmos. It will require other new skills which are not yet in hand. It will require genetic engineering, and probably artificial intelligence too. Genetic engineering to allow colonies of plants and animals to put down roots, to grow and spread in alien environments. Artificial intelligence to allow machines to go out ahead of life and prepare the ground for life's settlement. This is not to say that Step 4 cannot begin until the genetic engineering and artificial intelligence revolutions are complete. Step 4 is already in progress in a preliminary and tentative fashion. We are already started on our way to the stars. But this step, like the first three steps from trees to grassland, from Africa to the world, from land to sea, will not be finished within a century. . . .

Some of the first questions which come up in any practical discussion of space colonization are questions of economics. Suppose we go out and settle on a convenient asteroid with our little spaceship, what do we do when we get there? How do we make a living? What can we expect to export in order to pay for necessary imports? If space colonization makes any sense at all, these questions must have sensible answers. Unfortunately, we cannot hope to answer questions of economics until the asteroids have been explored. At present we know almost nothing about the chemical resources of asteroids and the physical conditions we shall find there. The most important of all resources is water, and the abundance of water is still unknown. No human instrument has ever touched an asteroid, or come close enough to make detailed observations. In this connection, it is interesting to compare the economics of asteroid settlement with the economics of early colonies in North America. The early American colonists knew almost as little about America as we know about asteroids, and their economic expectations almost always proved to be wrong. The first settlers in Virginia intended to find gold and instead grew rich by exporting tobacco. The Pilgrims in Massachusetts intended to live mainly by fishing and instead became farmers and fur traders. The most important prerequisite for economic survival is flexibility. Colonists should never believe economic forecasts and should be ready to switch to other means of livelihood when the forecasts are wrong.

In the circle of my own friends I have seen an example of a venture of colonization which may throw some light on the economic problems of asteroid settlers. My friends, a young man and his wife, established themselves on an uninhabited island in the North Pacific.

They built themselves a comfortable house and had no difficulty in growing enough food for the table. The husband was a skilled blacksmith and built a sawmill and other useful pieces of machinery. In most respects the colony was economically self-sufficient. But there were a few essential items which they could not produce for themselves and needed to import. Diesel fuel was the most essential import. They needed to sail down to Vancouver once or twice a year with a large barrel and fill it up with diesel fuel for their engines. The question then arose, What was the most convenient cash crop which they could produce for export? They had to find a crop which could be easily grown on their island, easily transported in their boat, and easily sold for a high price in Vancouver. They were law-abiding citizens of Canada, and they had no wish to become involved with the smuggling of illegal drugs. What then is the most convenient, legal, high-value cash crop for a small island in the North Pacific to export? The answer to this question was not obvious. My friends only found the answer by accident after a number of false starts. The answer was, pedigree Rhodesian Ridgeback pups. The dogs were easy to breed on the island. They did not need to be fenced since there was no danger of miscegenation. They fed mostly on leftovers from the farm. And the pups could be sold to dog-fanciers in Vancouver for a couple of hundred dollars each.

The economic problems of asteroid colonists must be solved in a similar fashion, by finding cash crops which conveniently exploit local opportunities. Rhodesian Ridgeback pups will not always be the answer. But it seems likely that the appropriate cash crops for asteroid colonies will often be products of specialized plant and animal breeding. Every asteroid colony must begin with a plant and animal breeding program aimed at the establishment of an ecology adapted to the local conditions. As a result, most colonies will possess varieties of plant and animal which are rare or nonexistent elsewhere. Just as on the North Pacific island, the isolation of an asteroid provides an ideal environment for maintaining purebred pedigrees. And every colony is likely to include not only a competent blacksmith but also an expert in genetic engineering.

[Elsewhere,] I mentioned two new technologies of space propulsion which may flourish in the next century, laser propulsion and solar sails. A third new technology for propulsion is the mass-driver. My friend Gerard O'Neill invented the mass-driver and built a working model of it at his Space Studies Institute in Princeton. The mass-driver is a long magnetic accelerator which pushes little buckets down a straight track. You put into the buckets any material which happens to be cheap and available. The contents of the buckets are thrown out into space at high speed. Like the exhaust of a rocket, they exert a thrust on the vehicle to which the mass-driver is attached. Unlike a rocket, the mass-driver can keep on running forever provided it is supplied with electric power. The Sun will supply enough power to keep a mass-driver running anywhere within the inner solar system. Ships propelled by mass-drivers would be an efficient and economical means of transport for voyagers moving around in the asteroid archipelago.

Like the Polynesian canoe, the mass-driver ship will be slow but will cover long distances cheaply. After arriving at an asteroid, the voyagers can use the local soil to reload the ship with propellant mass for the next leg of their journey. The main disadvantage of using mass-drivers in this way is that the bucketloads of dirt will gradually fill the space around the asteroids with rings of asteroidal dust like an attenuated version of the rings of Saturn. But the problem of the pollution of the solar system with dust has a remedy if ever it becomes serious. Oxygen is a major component of all asteroidal soils, the other major components being metals and silicon. Every asteroid colony will set up a process, either chemical or biological, for separating oxygen from the soil for breathing. Every colony is likely to maintain a large reserve supply of oxygen for emergencies. And liquid oxygen would be an ideal nonpolluting propellant for use in mass-drivers. The liquid oxygen thrown out into space would quickly evaporate and be carried harmlessly outward away from the Sun by the natural solar wind.

We cannot tell today whether mass-drivers, laser propulsion, solar sails or other propulsion systems still to be invented will prevail in the economic competition of the future. Probably each of these modes of propulsion will find its appropriate ecological niche. Each of these systems has the potential of being enormously cheaper than present-day chemical rockets. The space technology of today is absurdly expensive, for a variety of reasons. With today's technology there is not much incentive to reduce the costs of propulsion, since the payloads of most missions cost more than the propulsion systems. So long as space missions cost thousands of dollars per pound of payload, space colonies will remain an idle dream. The expansion of life into space will begin in earnest only when we are in command of radically cheaper technologies. Fortunately, the mass-driver and the laser and the solar sail give us a promise of radically cheaper propulsion, and genetic engineering and artificial intelligence give us a promise of radically cheaper payloads.

The next hundred years will be a period of transition between the metal-and-silicon technology of today and the enzyme-and-nerve technology of tomorrow. The enzyme-and-nerve technology will be the result of combining the tools of genetic engineering and artificial intelligence. We cannot hope to predict the concrete forms in which a mature enzyme-and-nerve technology would express itself. When I think of the space technology of tomorrow, I think of three concrete images in particular. First, the Martian potato, a succulent plant that lives deep underground, its roots penetrating layers of subterranean ice while its shoots gather carbon dioxide and sunlight on the surface under the protection of a self-generated greenhouse. Second, the comet creeper, a warm-blooded vine which spreads like a weed over the surfaces of comets and keeps itself warm with super-insulating fur as soft as sable. Third, the space butterfly, a creature truly at home in space, acting as our agent in exploration and reconnaissance, carrying pollen and information from world to world just as terrestrial insects carry pollen from flower to flower. It is easy to dream of other inhabitants of the celestial zoo, other images of a universe coming to life. The Martian potato, the comet creeper and the space butterfly are merely symbols, intended, like the pictures in a medieval bestiary, to edify rather than to enlighten.

I will not try to describe in detail the ways which space technology might follow when we look more than a hundred years into the future. Beyond the space butterfly is a further evolution as complicated and as unpredictable as the evolution of life on Earth. Only one thing is certain. The evolution of life in the universe will be like the evolution of life on Earth, an unfolding of weird and improbable patterns, an unfolding of ever-increasing richness and diversity.

When life spreads out and diversifies in the universe, adapting itself to a spectrum of environments far wider than any one planet can encompass, the human species will one day find itself faced with the most momentous choice that we have had to make since the days when our ancestors came down from the trees in Africa and left their cousins the chimpanzees behind. We will have to choose, either to remain one species united by a common bodily shape as well as by a common history, or to let ourselves diversify as the other species of plants and animals will diversify. Shall we be forever one people, or shall we be a million intelligent species exploring diverse ways of living in a million different places across the galaxy? This is the great question which will soon be upon us. Fortunately, it is not the responsibility of this generation to answer it.

Suggestions for Discussion and Writing

1. Dyson begins his essay by stating that "technology is a gift of God." What does he mean by this? Does he support his statement?

2. What does Dyson mean when he says that technology "is a part of the planetary environment"? Does he develop this point? What are the implications of this view?

3. Do you agree with Dyson's view that "scientists speak about international political problems with an authority which goes far beyond their competence as bomb-builders"?

4. Dyson identifies three "dominant new technologies" that will change "the conditions of human life during the coming century." What are these technologies? Can you think of a "new technology" that Dyson might have named but didn't? Choose one such technology and write an essay in which you explain some of the changes it might bring about.

5. What changes must take place, according to Dyson, before genetic engineering technology can become broadly "profitable"? What important aspects or implications of this technology does Dyson choose to ignore?

6. What three areas of artificial intelligence does Dyson discuss? Write an essay in which you compare his views on the possibility of building truly intelligent machines with those of Weizenbaum in "Artificial Intelligence" (this chapter).

7. What point(s) about the colonization of space is Dyson's example of his friends' "venture of colonization" designed to make?

8. Both Dyson and Turner ("Escape from Modernism," this chapter) see technology as a liberating force. Write an essay in which you compare their notions of "liberation" and the ways in which technology promotes it.

PRISONERS OF TECHNOLOGY: THE CASE OF NANCY CRUZAN

Marcia Angell
(b. 1939)

Marcia Angell is a pathologist and the executive editor of the *New England Journal of Medicine.* She graduated from Boston University School of Medicine and did postgraduate work in internal medicine as well as in pathology. With Dr. Stanley Robbins and, later, Dr. Vinay Kumar, she co-authored the first three editions of the textbook *Basic Pathology.* She frequently writes on ethical issues in medicine and biomedical research and is a lecturer in the Department of Social Medicine at Harvard Medical School.

In the following editorial from the *New England Journal of Medicine* (April 26, 1990), Angell discusses the ethical and legal dilemmas facing physicians who must decide whether patients alive in only a vegetative sense should be maintained on life-support systems.

L ife can now be sustained by medical technology under circumstances that just 15 to 20 years ago would have signified imminent death. This new power permits dramatic recoveries from some previously hopeless calamities. But, as with power in general, there is a dark side to it. Increasingly we find that life is being sustained indefinitely when there is no hope of recovery, simply because no one knows what else to do. Such a life may be filled with suffering, but sometimes it is devoid of anything—of pleasure, sensation, or comprehension.

This is the state of Nancy Cruzan, a 32-year-old woman who has been in what most agree is a persistent vegetative state since a car accident seven years ago. Although the diagnosis is not unanimous, the prognosis is. Everyone agrees that she will not recover; CT scans show that her cerebral cortex has already atrophied. But she is not dead, and she will probably live in her senseless state for many more years, thanks to sophisticated medical care and tube feeding through a gastrostomy. The costs are immeasurable anguish to her family and $130,000 yearly to the state of Missouri.

Three years ago, when it became apparent to even the most hopeful that Nancy Cruzan would not recover, her parents (who had become her legal guardians) requested that the feeding tube be removed so that she could die. The hospital insisted on a court order, and a trial court granted the parents' request. This decision accorded with a growing body of ethical and legal opinion, beginning with the case of Karen Ann Quinlan, which holds that life-sustaining treatment may be withheld from patients in a persistent vegetative state. With some exceptions, there is also a consensus that families may make this decision without review by the courts unless there is disagreement, and that artificial feeding is to be regarded as no different from any other form of medical care, such as the use of a respirator. It is understood that these patients would not experience the discomfort of dehydration, just as they would not experience the discomfort of suffocation if a ventilator was removed. In answer to the argument that no one can be absolutely certain of this, Nancy Cruzan's father said, "If Nancy is cognitively aware of pain, then it must be *hell* all the time. . . . The removal of hydration and nutrition might not generate any more pain than she's in now."

The Missouri Supreme Court, on appeal, reversed the lower court by a four-to-three majority. Although it acknowledged that Nancy Cruzan was in a persistent vegetative state and sympathized with her family, it based its decision on an unqualified state interest in the preservation of life. Other concerns of the court, including whether Nancy would have wanted the feeding tube removed and whether artificial feeding is different from other medical care, were clearly secondary. According to the court, "The state's interest is not in quality of life. . . . Instead, the state's interest is in life; that interest is unqualified."

The U.S. Supreme Court agreed to hear an appeal of the Missouri Supreme Court's decision. The arguments were presented in December 1989, and the decision is expected soon. The importance of the coming decision on the Cruzan case—the only case of its kind that the Supreme Court has agreed to hear—cannot be overestimated. In one way or another, it will affect nearly all of us, because it will influence profoundly the extent to which life-sustaining treatment is seen as optional, not only for our patients but for our family members and ourselves.

The U.S. Supreme Court should reverse the decision of the Missouri Supreme Court. The new problems created by the two-edged sword of medical technology require more sensitive consideration than was provided by the Missouri court. Its decision was at best sterile, applying a formula without regard for circumstances and seemingly without cognizance of the complexities of life and death in a modern hospital. Furthermore, the assertion of an unqualified interest in preserving life—which would seem to preclude anyone's refusing life-sustaining treatment for any reason—was unpersuasive. Nancy Cruzan's mother is herself not convinced that the state has evidenced an unqualified interest in preserving life. She pointed out that children in Missouri have been unable to obtain possibly life-saving bone marrow transplants for want of the $130,000 that the state is spending on Nancy yearly. Missouri also has a death penalty—hardly consonant with an unqualified interest in preserving life.

Competent adults have a generally recognized right to accept or refuse any medical treatment, the principal argument of the Missouri Supreme Court notwithstanding. In caring for patients like Nancy Cruzan, who cannot exercise this right, one should, I believe, consider three important questions. First, should we presume that most such patients would choose to live? Such a presumption is inherent in the view of some courts that life-sustaining treatment may be withheld only if the patient left unequivocal instructions to that effect. Yet, I doubt whether many of us would choose the life of Nancy Cruzan over death. There needs to be room in these deliberations for common sense. Second, if we grant that under some circumstances life-sustaining treatment may be withheld from patients who did not leave instructions, who is to make that decision? In the case of Nancy Cruzan, no one has doubted the motives of her parents, nor their understanding of her. Her parents believe that she would not have wanted to live in a persistent vegetative state. They also believe that they are the logical ones to speak on her behalf, and it is difficult to argue with that position. And third, should the courts be routinely involved in this sort of decision? Their procedures make them ill-equipped for such a role, and judges can certainly make no claim to any special understanding of the patient. The role of the courts might better be limited to appointing guardians or settling disputes when necessary.

State legislatures might deal with some of these issues by statute. Missouri's attorney general, William Webster, endorses a bill that would permit families to authorize the withdrawal of life-sustaining treatment from patients who have been in a persistent vegetative state for two or three years. An exception would be made for patients who had expressed a wish to be kept alive under all conditions. This would shift the burden of providing advance directives from those not wanting treatment in this situation to those wanting it. It is a proposal worth considering.

Nancy Cruzan is just 1 of about 10,000 patients in the United States who are in a persistent vegetative state, and this number will probably increase as our technology improves. Many more patients are not permanently unconscious, but are suffering from irreversible diseases and do not want to have their lives prolonged. In many of these cases, physicians agree with patients or their families that life-sustaining treatment is inappropriate. Yet, they—and the administrators of their institutions—are uncertain whether they have the authority to withhold treatment at the request of patients or families and often persist in treatment for this reason. Even among the healthy, the fear of being treated against one's wishes is widespread. Most of us have heard (or used) the phrase, "I wouldn't want to live like Karen Ann Quinlan"—sometimes said casually, but often seriously. The very high suicide rate among older Americans is probably due partly to their concern that they may be unable to stop treatment if they are hospitalized.

Here, then, is the tragic irony of our technological successes: some people now fear living more than dying because they dread becoming prisoners of technology. The Supreme Court will either alleviate or exacerbate this situation by its decision in the Cruzan case.*

Suggestions for Discussion and Writing

1. How would you summarize the author's views on the Nancy Cruzan case? Where does she state her thesis? In what ways does her diction help establish her point of view?

2. The author quotes the Missouri Supreme Court's opinion that "the state's interest is in life," and that this interest is "unqualified." Does she challenge this opinion?

3. What three important questions, according to the author, should be considered in cases such as that of Nancy Cruzan?

4. The United States Supreme Court rendered its decision on the Cruzan case in June 1990. In a brief report, summarize the

---

* **Editors' Note:** In June 1990 the United States Supreme Court, in a five-to-four decision, ruled to uphold the decision of the Missouri Supreme Court. Shortly thereafter Nancy Cruzan's parents introduced new evidence to the Missouri lower court, which had heard their original request. This new evidence established that before the accident Nancy Cruzan had frequently told friends that she would never want to "live like a vegetable." The court granted the parents' request that the feeding tube be removed. Nancy Cruzan died in December 1990.

majority and minority opinions. (You might wish to consult coverage of the decision in one or two major newspapers.)

5. Do you agree with the author that medical technology is a "two-edged sword"? What other aspects of this technology could be cited to support this view?

PART II

THE ENTERPRISE OF SCIENCE

OVERVIEW

Whereas the essays in Part I place science in the context of the larger society, those in Part II direct our attention to the activity of science itself—what it is, what it does, and how it does it. The following chapters address such issues as the limits of science, its values, and its obligations.

Chapters 5 and 6 discuss the nature of science. What, for instance, is physics? chemistry? biology? Rather than attempting to give a complete picture of each of the diverse but connected branches of science (such as anthropology, geology, astronomy, and zoology), these chapters focus on several major movements that have shaped the physical and biological sciences as they have come into the modern age. How, for example, did Lavoisier arrive at his ideas regarding the periodic table, the arrangement of the chemical elements according to their atomic numbers? In what ways did Einstein's theories change the direction taken by twentieth-century physics? In what sense can one say that the ideas of Charles Darwin provide the foundation for today's biosciences? In these chapters the intention is to examine broad issues and then move to more specific ones, to illustrate larger ideas through particular cases. For example, Chapter 5 ends with an essay on quantum mechanics, a specific branch of contemporary physics, Chapter 6 with a discussion of the harbor seal as an example of Darwinian adaptation.

Just as we may ask what science is, so we may ask how it goes about its business. What is unique about science as a way of knowing? What is the "scientific method"? In Chapter 7 we see that science has its own rigorous ways of proceeding in its search for truth, but that these ways involve more than our purely rational faculties. Yet if science has its own method(s), this very particularity implies other ways of knowing, other paths to understanding, for many important truths are beyond the reach of science. The boundaries imposed upon scientific knowledge both by nature itself and by the limitations of the human mind are the subject of Chapter 8. Finally, Chapter 9, with its concern for the ethical and moral constraints felt by the scientist, brings us back to the notion of science as an activity carried out within a larger community.

CHAPTER-BY-CHAPTER SUMMARY

Chapter 5

Chapter 5 centers on the revolutionary ideas that laid the groundwork for contemporary physical science. In the first essay, James Jeans reflects on the startling advances made in physics during the first part of the twentieth century. He goes on to ask whether, even in light of these advances, we can ever expect to know the universe. In the next essay, Douglas McKie traces the beginnings of modern chemistry back to the work of Antoine Lavoisier in the latter half of the eighteenth century. Lavoisier's discoveries, McKie tells us, created as profound a revolution in chemistry as Newton's did in physics. Einstein explains his revolutionary theories in the third essay, laying out the ideas that form the basis of his Special and General Theories of Relativity in a way that is accessible to the general reader. Bertrand Russell then sheds more light on Einstein's theories by showing that space and time, previously seen as separate elements in determining the position of an object or event in space, must, after Einstein, be seen as inseparable—that is, as two parts of a single entity, "space-time." Finally, Robert M. Hazen and James Trefil take us still farther along the revolutionary path of modern physics with their explanation of quantum mechanics, a specific branch of contemporary physics.

Chapter 6

If the changes in the physical sciences have been profound, those in the biological sciences have, in the opinion of many, been even more revolutionary. In the first essay, Jacob Bronowski sets the stage for the chapter by discussing the major breakthroughs that occurred in the biosciences soon after World War II—breakthroughs based on our new knowledge of the cell. This knowledge, he claims, has given us a far better understanding of the mechanics of evolution. But these new ideas are built on those of the nineteenth-century naturalist, Charles Darwin, who provided the broad framework that gives modern biology its coherence. Darwin speaks for himself in the next selections, taken from *The Origin of Species* (1859). He tells of his motivation for pursuing his research and recounts the observations that eventually led him to develop his theory of evolution, a theory that has had an incalculable impact, not only on science but on a whole range of intellectual disciplines. Taking the fundamental truth of Darwin's ideas as a given, Paul Colinvaux then examines the complex relationship between the individual species and its particular niche, as well as the place of both in the broader scheme of things. Focusing more sharply, Stephen Jay Gould looks at evolution as it affects the behavior of one species of bird on the Galapagos Islands, the location of much of Darwin's early work. Gould reports on his observations of nesting boobies and sees in the peculiarities of their behavior the creation and maintenance of the conditions necessary for their survival. Finally, reporting from a location far from the Galapagos, Deane Renouf recounts her study of harbor seals in Newfoundland. In the complex sensory functions developed by these mammals she sees an extraordinary response to the need to survive in not one but two environments.

Chapter 7

Chapter 7 offers a range of views on the scientific method. Thomas Huxley's essay emphasizes reason and logic and claims that the scientific method is merely a more rigorous and systematized version of common sense. Robert Pirsig's piece develops this idea further, stressing the interweaving of the inductive and deductive methods. Karl Popper supplements the more traditional view(s) by emphasizing hypothesis as the initiating force in scientific enquiry and pointing to disconfirmation (rather than verification) as being at the heart of the enquiring process. Hans Christian von Baeyer talks about the value of ballpark estimates at early stages of the investigative process and thus illustrates that in the scientific method even the "rough and ready approach" has its place. Robert S. Root-Bernstein moves away from the traditional emphasis on logic and reason by showing that a broad range of attitudes and activities helps set the stage for scientific discovery. For Root-Bernstein, the traditional definition of "method" must be broadened to include intuition and even the scientist's deep personal and sympathetic feelings for the object under investigation.

For him, "scientific objectivity" is not always the path to truth. In the final essay, Loren Eiseley focuses on the sense of awe and reverence that are, he believes, prerequisite to the fullest and highest understanding of nature. The separation of logic and reason from the impulses of the human spirit, he believes, signals the beginning of a slide to reductionism and a destructive dehumanization.

Chapter 8

As Loren Eiseley reminds us, the ability of science to understand nature is limited by its being a human enterprise. The essays in Chapter 8 take up this notion of limitation, starting with Carl Sagan's questioning the extent to which we can know the cosmos. He suggests that nature itself may place limitations on our capacity to know the universe. But it is not only the cosmos that refuses to yield itself completely to the powers of human reason. In his account of a simple smile, Alan Lightman suggests that, however much we may celebrate our knowledge of physiological and neurological responses, science can tell us nothing about the impulse that gives rise to this most ordinary of human acts. The theme of limitation is taken up next in a more global way by Loren Eiseley. Asking what our attitude toward the physical world should be, he answers that, in addition to a sense of reverence, we must bring to nature the humility which acknowledges that the ultimate mystery of life will always elude us. Further evidence of the elusiveness of truth can be found in the selection by James Gleick on chaos theory. Over the past several years, this new theory has caused scientists to reevaluate certain fundamental beliefs of modern physics, a reevaluation that calls into question the possibility of our ever understanding the physical world. A similar doubt arises in regard to the incident recounted by Richard Bergland. Lacking full knowledge of the mechanisms of pain, he and his colleagues performed neurosurgery that not only failed to improve the patient's condition but worsened it dramatically.

Chapter 9

Whereas the essays in Chapter 8 point to the limitations imposed on scientific knowledge by nature itself, Chapter 9 turns to another kind of constraint, one that has its roots in the practitioners of science. Because scientists work as members of a community, they are subject to the same moral and ethical imperatives as other members of that community. Thus, contrary to common belief, as Jacob Bronowski tells us, science is not without moral values. Indeed, by its very nature, scientific activity generates an overriding imperative: "truth to fact." Nevertheless, as Robert S. Root-Bernstein points out, scientists are sometimes guilty of "breaking faith," both with themselves and with the larger community. He cites several cases of scientific fraud and notes that, like any other fraud, it is rooted in the quintessentially human tendency to "believe what we want to believe." J. Robert Oppenheimer is also concerned with morality in science, but from a different perspective. In his final address to the scientists who worked with him in developing the atomic bomb, Oppenheimer reflects on the motivation that led them to devote themselves to a task whose final product was a weapon of previously unthinkable destructive power. That motivation, he suggests, was the "organic necessity" of the scientists' need to know. But given this new knowledge, they must recognize the new responsibilities imposed on them by the arrival of the atomic age. Motivation is also the concern of Richard Selzer in his account of one surgeon's attempt to correct a young girl's physical deformity. Motivation, his essay seems to suggest, is sometimes mixed. In the final essay, Abigail Zuger and Stephen H. Miles survey the behavior of physicians during the great plagues of the past and ask to what extent the lessons learned from that behavior can act as a guide for contemporary physicians faced with the AIDS epidemic.

Chapter 9, with its emphasis on the conscience of the scientist, directs our attention to the human aspects of the scientific enterprise. In doing so, it brings us full circle to Part I, where science is placed in the broad context of human concerns. Scientists do not work in a social or ethical vacuum. Their activities form part of the larger human experience and are subject to the uncertainty and error found in all walks of life. Contemporary science finds itself more and more frequently faced with issues that have extremely complex social and ethical implications. Four of these issues are taken up in Part III.

CHAPTER 5

The Physical Sciences

WHAT IS PHYSICS?

James Jeans
(1877–1946)

James Jeans, English astronomer and mathematical physicist, was educated at Trinity College, Cambridge, and went on to teach mathematics at Cambridge and Princeton and astronomy at the Royal Institution, London. Jeans received many awards and honors during his distinguished career, including knighthood in 1928 and the Order of Merit in 1939.

Jeans's intellectual interests were many and varied. He developed important applications of mathematics to problems in physics and astronomy. In physics he developed the kinetic theory of gases, which helped lay the groundwork for Planck's quantum theory and worked on the interrelation of radiation and free electrons. In astronomy he developed theories of the effect of gravitational motion on the motion of the stars, and of the formation and nature of binary stars and spiral nebulae. In a 1904 paper on radioactivity, he anticipated Einstein's prediction that matter might be convertible into energy and that this change might be the source of all stellar energy. Jeans's most important contribution to science was probably *Problems of Cosmogony and Stellar Dynamics* (1919).

In the last twenty years of his life, Jeans wrote many popular expositions of astronomy and cosmogony. In these books, including *The Universe Around Us* (1929) and *The Stars in Their Courses* (1931), he used telling imagery and apt analogies to explain clearly and precisely some of the most complex problems of modern science. In later years, Jeans pursued an interest in the philosophical implications of twentieth-century physics, an interest first seen in *The Mysterious Universe* (1930). There he first proposed his renowned—and startling—philosophical conclusion that reality is mental, that the universe consists of the thoughts of a Pure Mathematician, God. "The Great Architect of the Universe," he wrote, "now begins to appear as a pure mathematician." In the following selection taken from *Physics and Philosophy* (1942), Jeans returns to the problem of what we can know about the universe, and to the role that mathematics plays in our knowing it. Here he discusses the relationship between the inner world of the mind and the outer physical world of nature. Physics, he argues, is the attempt to understand the outer world in terms of its "patterns" (scientific laws) as expressed in mathematical formulae. He further contends that, although our minds are generally more suited to deal with concrete facts than with abstract concepts, twentieth-century physics has discovered that nature does not function in a way that can be "modelled" or "pictured" (i.e., in a way that can be made concrete). We are thus forced to accept a purely mathematical explanation of reality—an explanation that is by definition abstract. In this sense, the "true nature of reality" is ultimately beyond human understanding.

Both physics and philosophy had their beginnings in those dim ages in which man was first differentiating himself from his brute ancestry, acquiring new emotional and mental characteristics which were henceforth to be his distinguishing marks. Foremost among these were an intellectual curiosity out of which philosophy has grown, and a practical curiosity which was ultimately to develop into science.

For primitive man, thrown into a world which he did not understand, soon found that his comfort, his well-being, and even his life were jeopardized by this want of understanding. Inanimate nature seemed helpful and friendly to him at times, but could become hostile when the life-giving sunshine and gentle rain gave place to the thunderbolt and whirlwind; these inspired in him the same feelings of awe and fear as the wild beasts and human foes which threatened his life. His first reaction was to project his own human motives and passions on to the inanimate objects around him; he peopled his world with spirits and demons, with gods and goddesses great and small until, as Andrew Lang has said, 'all nature was a congeries of animated personalities'. Such imaginings were not confined to cavemen and savages; even Thales of Miletus (640–546 B.C.), astronomer, geometer and philosopher, maintained that all things were 'full of gods'.

Primitive man endowed these personalities with characteristics and qualities almost as definite as those of his real friends and foes. In so doing he was not altogether wrong, for they seemed to be creatures of habit; what they had done once they were likely to do again. Even the animals understand this; they avoid a place where they have suffered pain in the past, suspecting that what hurt them once may hurt them again, and they return to a place where they have once found food, considering it a hopeful place in which to look for more. What were mere associations of ideas in the brains of animals readily became translated into natural laws in the minds of thinking men, and led to the discovery of the principle of the uniformity of nature—what has happened once will, in similar circumstances, happen again; the events of nature do not occur at random but after an unvarying pattern. Once this discovery had been made, physical science became possible. Its primary aim is to discover that pattern of events, in so far as it governs the happenings of the inanimate world.

PHYSICAL KNOWLEDGE

We each live our mental life in a prison-house from which there is no escape. It is our body; and its only communication with the outer world is through our sense-organs—eyes, ears, etc. These form windows through which we can look out on to the outer world and acquire knowledge of it. A man lacking all five senses could know nothing of this outer world, because he would have no means of contact with it; the whole content of his mind would be an expansion of what had been in it at birth.

The sense-organs of a normal man receive stimuli—rays of light, waves of sound, etc.—from the outer world, and these produce electric changes which are propagated over his nerves to his brain. Here they produce further changes, as the result of which—after a series of processes we do not in the least understand—his mind acquires *perceptions*—to use Hume's terminology—of the outer world. These give rise to *impressions* and *ideas* in turn, an impression denoting a sensation, emotion or feeling at the moment when a perception first makes its appearance in the mind, and an idea denoting what is left of an impression when its first vigour is spent, including for instance the memory of an impression or the repetition of it in a dream.

Thus the whole content of a man's mind can consist of three parts at most—a part that was in his mind at birth, a part that has entered through his sense-organs, and a part which has been developed out of these two parts by processes of reflection and ratiocination. Some have denied that the first part exists at all, holding with Hobbes

(1588–1679) that 'there is no conception in a man's mind which hath not at first been begotten upon the organs of sense'—*nihil est in intellectu quod non fuerit in sensu.* Others have thought with Leibniz (1646–1716) that this should be amended by the addition of the words *nisi intellectus ipse*—there is nothing in the understanding that has not come through the senses, except the understanding itself. We shall discuss these questions more fully as the need arises.

Whenever a man increases the content of his mind he gains new knowledge, and this occurs each time a new relation is established between the worlds on the two sides of the sense-organs—the world of ideas in an individual mind, and the world of objects existing outside individual minds which is common to us all.

The study of science provides us with such new knowledge. Physics gives us exact knowledge because it is based on exact measurements. A physicist may announce, for instance, that the density of gold is 19.32, by which he means that the ratio of the weight of any piece of gold to that of a volume of water of equal size is 19.32; or that the wave-length of the line Hα in the spectrum of atomic hydrogen is 0.000065628 centimetre, by which he means that the ratio of the length of a wave of Hα light to that of a centimetre is 0.000065628, a centimetre being defined as a certain fraction of the diameter of the earth, or of the length of a specified bar of platinum, or as a certain multiple of the wave-length of a line in the spectrum of cadmium.

These statements import real knowledge into our minds, since each identifies a specific number, the idea of which is already in our minds, with the value of a ratio which has an existence in the world outside; this idea of a ratio is again something with which our minds are familiar. Thus the statements tell us something new in a language we can understand.

Each ratio expresses a relation between two things neither of which we understand separately, such as gold and water. Our minds can never step out of their prison-houses to investigate the real nature of the things—gold, water, atomic hydrogen, centimetres or wave-lengths—which inhabit that mysterious world out beyond our sense-organs. We are acquainted with such things only through the messages we receive from them through the windows of our senses, and these tell us nothing as to the essential nature of their origins. But our minds can understand and know ratios—which are pure numbers—even of quantities which are themselves incomprehensible. We can, then, acquire real knowledge of the external world of physics, but this must always consist of ratios, or, in other words, of numbers.

The raw material of every science must always be an accumulation of facts; the values of ratios of which we have just been speaking constitute the raw material of physics. But, as Poincaré remarked, an accumulation of facts is no more a science than a heap of stones is a house. When we set to work to build our house—i.e. to create a science—we must first coordinate and synthesize the accumulated piles of facts. It is then usually found that a great number of separate facts can be summed up in a much smaller number of general laws. This indeed is the most fundamental and also the most general fact disclosed by the experimental study of science—the stones fit together and combine, out of their intrinsic nature, to make a house. In brief, nature is rational. The house, being a rational structure and not a shapeless pile of stones, will show certain marked features. These express the pattern of events for which we are searching.

In physics the separate stones are numbers—the ratios just described—and the features of the house are relations between large groups of numbers. Clearly these relations will be most easily recorded and explained by embodying them in mathematical formulae, so that our scientific house will consist of a collection of mathematical formulae; in this way, and this alone, can we express the pattern of events. To take a simple illustration, the physicist finds that the spectrum of atomic hydrogen contains the line $H\alpha$ which we have already mentioned, and also a very great number of other lines which are usually designated as $H\beta$, $H\gamma$, $H\delta$, etc. The wave-lengths of these lines can be measured, and are found to be related with one another in a very simple way which can be expressed by a quite simple mathematical formula. This is typical of the way in which the particular scientific house of physics is built up; a great number of separate facts of observation are all subsumed in a single mathematical formula, and our knowledge of the physical world is expressed by a number of such formulae.

PICTORIAL REPRESENTATIONS

But now the complication intervenes that our minds do not take kindly to knowledge expressed in abstract mathematical form. Our mental faculties have come to us, through a long line of ancestry, from fishes and apes. At each stage the primary concern of our ancestors was not to understand the ultimate processes of physics, but to survive in the struggle for existence, to kill other animals without themselves being killed. They did not do this by pondering over mathematical formulae, but by adapting themselves to the hard facts of nature and the concrete problems of everyday life. Those who could not do this disappeared, while those who could survived, and have transmitted to us minds which are more suited to deal with concrete facts than with abstract concepts, with particulars rather than with universals; minds which are more at home in thinking of material objects, rest and motion, pushes, pulls and impacts, than in trying to digest symbols and formulae. The child who is beginning to learn algebra never takes kindly to x, y and z; he is only satisfied when he is told that they are numbers of apples or pears or something such.

In the same way, the physicists of a generation ago could not rest content with the x, y and z which were used to describe the pattern of events, but were for ever trying to interpret them in terms of something concrete. If, they thought, there is a pattern, there must be a loom for ever weaving it. They wanted to know what this loom was, how it worked, and why it worked thus rather than otherwise. And they assumed, or at least hoped, that it would prove possible to liken its ultimate constituents to such familiar mechanical objects as occur in looms, or perhaps to billiard-balls, jellies and spinning-tops, the workings of which they thought they understood. In time they hoped to devise a model which would reproduce all the phenomena of physics, and so make it possible to predict them all.

Such a model would, they thought, in some way correspond to the reality underlying the phenomena. No one seems to have considered the situation which would arise if two different models were found, each being perfect in this respect.

Yet this situation is of some interest. If it arose, there would be no means of choosing between the two models, since each would be perfect in the only property by which it could be tested, namely the power of predicting phenomena. Neither model could, then, claim to represent reality, whence it follows that we must never associate any model with reality, since even if it accounted for all the phenomena, a second model might appear at any moment with exactly the same qualifications to represent reality.

To-day we not only have no perfect model, but we know that it is of no use to search for one—it could have no intelligible meaning for us. For we have found out that nature does not function in a way that can be made comprehensible to the human mind through models or pictures.

If we are to explain the workings of an organization or a machine in a comprehensible way, we must speak to our listeners in a language they understand, and in terms of ideas with which they are familiar—otherwise our explanation will mean nothing to them. It is no good telling a crowd of savages that the time-differential of the electric displacement is the rotation of the magnetic force multiplied by the velocity of light. In the same way, if an interpretation of the workings of nature is to mean anything to us, it must be in terms of ideas which are already in our minds—otherwise it will be incomprehensible to us, and cannot add to our knowledge. We have already seen what types of ideas can be in our minds—ideas which have been in our minds from birth, ideas which have entered our minds as perceptions, and ideas which have been developed out of these primitive ideas by processes of reflection and ratiocination.

Such ideas as originated in perceptions, and so entered our minds through one or more of the five senses, may be classified by the sense or senses through which they entered. Thus the content of a mind will consist of visual ideas, auditory ideas, tactile ideas, and so on, as well as more fundamental ideas—such as those of number and quantity—which may be inborn or may have entered through several senses, and more complex ideas resulting from combinations and aggregations of simpler ideas, such as ideas of aesthetic beauty, moral perfection, maximum happiness, checkmate or free trade. It is useless to try to understand the workings of nature except in terms of ideas belonging to one or other of these classes.

For instance, the pitch, intensity and timbre of a musical sound are auditory ideas; we can explain the functioning of an orchestra in terms of them, but only to a person who is himself possessed of auditory ideas, and not to one who has been deaf all his life. Colour and illumination are visual ideas, but we could not explain a landscape or a portrait in such terms to a blind man, because he would have no visual ideas.

Clearly complex ideas of the kind exemplified above can give no help towards an understanding of the functioning of inanimate nature. The same is true of ideas which have entered through the senses of hearing, taste and smell—as for instance the memories of a symphony or of a good dinner. If for no other reason, none of these enter into direct relation with our perceptions of extension in space, which is one of the most fundamental of the things to be explained. We are left only with fundamental ideas such as number and quantity, and ideas which have entered our minds through the two senses of sight and touch. Of these sight provides more vivid and also more important ideas than touch—we learn more about the world by looking at it than by touching it. Besides number and quantity, our visual ideas include size or extension in space, position in space, shape and movement. Tactile ideas comprise all of these, although in a less vivid form, as well as ideas which are wholly tactile, such as hardness, pressure, impact and force. For an explanation of nature to be intelligible it must depend only on such ideas as these.

GEOMETRICAL EXPLANATIONS OF NATURE

Various attempts have been made to explain the workings of nature in terms of visual ideas alone, these depending mainly on the ideas of shape (geometrical figures) and motion. Three examples drawn from ancient, mediaeval and modern times respectively are:

1. The Greek explanation that all motion tends to be circular because the circle is the perfect figure geometrically, an explanation which remained in vogue at least until the fifteenth century notwithstanding its being contrary to the facts.
2. The system of Descartes, which tried to explain nature in terms of motion, vortices, etc. This also was contrary to the facts.
3. Einstein's relativity theory of gravitation, which is purely geometrical in form. This, so far as is known, is in complete agreement with the facts.

We shall discuss this last theory in some detail. In brief, it tells us that a moving object or a ray of light moves along a geodesic, which means that it takes the shortest route from place to place, or again, roughly speaking, that it goes as nearly in a straight line as circumstances permit. This geodesic is not in ordinary space, but in an ideal composite space of four dimensions, which results from blending space and time. This space is not only four-dimensional but is also curved; it is this curvature that prevents a geodesic being an ordinary straight line. Efforts have been made to explain the whole of electric and magnetic phenomena in a similar way, but so far without success.

It is perhaps doubtful whether such a curved four-dimensional space ought to be described as a visual idea which is already in our minds. It may be only ordinary space generalized, but if so it is generalized out of all recognition. The highly trained mathematician can visualize it partially and vaguely, others not at all. Unless we are willing to concede that the plain man has the idea of such a space in his mind, we must say that no appreciable fraction of the world has been really 'explained' in terms of visual ideas.

Even if it had, such an explanation would hardly carry any conviction of finality or completeness to our modern minds. To the Greek mind the supposed fact that the stars or planets moved in perfect geometrical figures provided a completely satisfying explanation of their motion—the world was a perfection waiting only to be elucidated, and here was a bit of the elucidation. Our minds work differently. Optimism has given place to pessimism, at least to the extent that we no longer feel any confidence in an overruling tendency to perfection, and if we are told that a planet moves in a perfect circle, or in a still more perfect geodesic, we merely go on to inquire: Why? When Giotto drew his perfect circle, his pencil was not guided by any abstract compulsion to perfection—if it were, we should all be able to draw perfect circles—but by the skill of his muscles. We want to know what provides the corresponding guidance to the planets, and this requires that the purely visual ideas of geometrical form shall be supplemented by the addition of tactile ideas.

MECHANICAL EXPLANATIONS OF NATURE

Explanations which introduce tactile ideas—forces, pressures and tensions—are of course dynamical or mechanical in their nature. It is not surprising that such explanations also should have been attempted from Greek times on, for, after all, our hairy ancestors had to think more about muscular force than about perfect circles or geodesics. Plato tells us that Anaxagoras claimed to be able to explain the workings of nature as a machine. In more recent times Newton, Huyghens and others thought that the only possible explanations of nature were mechanical. Thus in 1690 Huyghens wrote: 'In true philosophy, the causes of all natural phenomena are conceived in mechanical terms. We must do this, in my opinion, or else give up all hope of ever understanding anything in physics.'

To-day the average man probably holds very similar opinions. An explanation in any other than mechanical terms would seem incomprehensible to him, as it did to Newton and Huyghens, through the necessary ideas—the language in which the explanation was conveyed—not being in his mind. When he wants to move an object, he pulls or pushes it through the activity of his muscles, and cannot imagine that Nature does not effect her movements in a similar way.

Among attempted explanations in mechanical terms, the Newtonian system of mechanics stands first. This was supplemented in due course by various mechanical representations of the electromagnetic theories of Maxwell and Faraday. All envisaged the world as a collection of particles moving under the pushes and pulls of other particles, these pushes and pulls being of the same general nature as those we exert with our muscles on the objects we touch.

These and other attempted mechanical explanations have all failed. Indeed the progress of science has disclosed in detail the reasons why all failed, and all must fail. Two of the simpler of these reasons may be mentioned here.

The first is provided by the theory of relativity. The essence of a mechanical explanation is that each particle of a mechanism experiences a real and definite push or pull. This must be objective as regards both quantity and quality, so that its measure will always be the same, whatever means of measurement are employed to measure it—just as a real object must always weigh the same whether it is weighed on a spring balance or on a weighing-beam. But the theory of relativity shows that if motions are attributed to forces, these forces will be differently estimated, as regards both quantity and quality, by observers who happen to be moving at different speeds, and furthermore that all their estimates have an equal claim to be considered right. Thus the supposed forces cannot have a real objective existence; they are seen to be mere mental constructs which we make for ourselves in our efforts to understand the workings of nature.

A second reason is provided by the theory of quanta. A mechanical explanation implies not only that the particles of the universe move in space and time, but also that their motion is governed by agencies which operate in space and time. But the quantum theory finds, that the fundamental activities of nature cannot be represented as occurring in space and time; they cannot, then, be mechanical in the ordinary sense of the word.

In any case, no mechanical explanation could ever be satisfying and final; it could at best only postpone the demand for an explanation. For suppose—to imagine a simple although not very likely possibility—that it had been found that the pattern of events could be fully explained by assuming that matter consisted of hard spherical atoms, and that each of these behaved like a minute billiard-ball. At first this may look like a perfect mechanical explanation, but we soon find that it has only introduced us to a vicious circle; it first explains billiard-balls in terms of atoms, and then proceeds to explain atoms in terms of billiard-balls, so that we have not advanced a step towards a true understanding of the ultimate nature of either billiard-balls or atoms. All mechanical explanations are open to a similar criticism, since all are of the form 'A is like B, and B is like A'. Nothing is gained by saying that the loom of nature works like our muscles if we cannot explain how our muscles work. We come, then, to the position that nothing but a mechanical explanation can be satisfying to our minds, and that such an explanation would be valueless if we attained it. We see that we can never understand the true nature of reality.

THE MATHEMATICAL DESCRIPTION OF NATURE

In these and similar ways, the progress of science has itself shown that there can be no pictorial representation of the workings of nature of a kind which would be intelligible to our limited minds. The study of physics has driven us to the positivist conception of physics. We can never understand what events are, but must limit ourselves to describing the pattern of events in mathematical terms; no other aim is possible—at least until man becomes endowed with more senses than he at present possesses. Physicists who are trying to understand nature may work in many different fields and by many different methods; one may dig, one may sow, one may reap. But the final harvest will always be a sheaf of mathematical formulae. These will never describe nature itself, but only our observations on nature. Our studies can never put us into contact with reality; we can never penetrate beyond the impressions that reality implants in our minds.

Although we can never devise a pictorial representation which shall be both true to nature and intelligible to our minds, we may still be able to make partial aspects of the truth comprehensible through pictorial representations or parables. As the whole truth does not admit of intelligible representation, every such pictorial represen-tation or parable must fail somewhere. The physicist of the last generation was continually making pictorial representations and par-ables, and also making the mistake of treating the half-truths of pictorial representations and parables as literal truths. He did not see that all the concrete details of his picture—his luminiferous ether, his electric and magnetic forces, and possibly his atoms and electrons as well—were mere articles of clothing that he had himself draped over the mathematical symbols; they did not belong to the world of reality, but to the parables by which he had tried to make reality compre-hensible. For instance, when observation was found to suggest that light was of the nature of waves, it became customary to describe it as undulations in a rigid homogeneous ether which filled the whole of space. The only ascertained fact in this description is contained in the one word 'undulations', and even this must be understood in the narrowest mathematical sense; all the rest is pictorial detail, introduced to help out the limitations of our minds. Kronecker is quoted as saying that in arithmetic God made the integers and man made the rest; in the same spirit we may perhaps say that in physics God made the mathematics and man made the rest.

To sum up, physics tries to discover the pattern of events which controls the phenomena we observe. But we can never know what this pattern means or how it originates; and even if some superior intelligence were to tell us, we should find the explanation unintelligible. Our studies can never put us into contact with reality, and its true meaning and nature must be for ever hidden from us.

Suggestions for Discussion and Writing

1. Explain the principle of the "uniformity of nature." How did the discovery of this principle make physical science possible?

2. In what sense, according to Jeans, do we "live our mental life in a prison-house from which there is no escape"?

3. In a few paragraphs, explain how, according to Jeans, we gain new knowledge. What three elements are involved? What is the nature of their relationship?

4. What is the function of mathematics (numbers, ratios) in building the "house of physics"?

5. Why, according to Jeans, do we prefer pictures to "abstract mathematical forms"?

6. What kinds of ideas, according to the author, "help towards an understanding of the functioning of inanimate nature"? What kinds of ideas does the author exclude? Why?

7. Write a brief essay in which you discuss what the author means by a "mechanical explanation" of nature.

8. Jeans concludes his discussion of mechanical explanations with a paradox: "We come, then, to the position that nothing but a mechanical explanation can be satisfying to our minds, and that such an explanation would be valueless if we attained it." Briefly summarize the arguments by which Jeans supports his claim that a mechanical explanation would be valueless.

9. In the final section of his essay, Jeans states that "our studies can never put us into contact with reality" and that the "mathematical formulae" to which we are forced "will never describe nature itself, but only our observations on nature." What does this imply about the enterprise of science? About any attempt to understand the "whole truth" of nature?

10. Write an essay in which you discuss the views of Einstein and Planck (see Chapter 3) in the context of Jeans's ideas as expressed in the final section of his essay.

THE BIRTH OF MODERN CHEMISTRY

Douglas McKie
(1896–1967)

After a brief military career in the British Army cut short by wounds received in action, Douglas McKie entered the University of London to study chemistry, receiving his Ph.D. in 1927.

McKie spent his entire teaching career at the University of London, where he was a professor of the history and philosophy of science. He received several important awards, including the Dexter Award from the American Chemical Society (1963). He was named Chevalier de la Légion d'Honneur by the French government in 1957.

McKie wrote numerous articles on the history of science and several books, among them *Antoine Lavoisier, Scientist, Economist, Social Reformer* (1952). In the following essay from *The History of Science: Origins and Results of the Scientific Revolution (A Symposium)* (1951), he describes the process by which the foundations of modern chemistry were laid—a process that began with the discovery of the gases in the second half of the eighteenth century and ended with the publication of Lavoisier's classic work on the *Elements of Chemistry* (1789).

Great advances in astronomy, mechanics and physics were among the first results of the seventeenth century revolution in scientific thought. The science of chemistry was, however, not set on its modern road until almost the end of the eighteenth century. The reasons for this delay were, first, the ancient and at that time still acceptable theory of the composition of matter, and, second, the more recent theory of combustion that arose in the seventeenth and eighteenth centuries.

The ancient theory of the composition of matter was formulated in Greece and specially developed by Aristotle in the fourth century B.C. It regarded the vast multitude of different substances that we see in the world around us as consisting of compounds in different proportions of only four elements, earth and water, air and fire. A substance, for example, that burned more vigorously than another was therefore supposed to contain a higher proportion of the element of fire; and one that was more fluid than another was similarly supposed to contain a higher proportion of the element of water. There was, of course, during this long period of over two thousand years no chemical proof that earth and water and air and fire were elements, or that Nature's enormous variety of materials was made up of only four primary substances, but the theory helped to explain many facts in ways that were easily understood.

The other cause of delay in the reform of chemistry was a theory of combustion formulated by two German chemists, Becher and Stahl, in the seventeenth and eighteenth centuries, according to which all combustible and inflammable substances were assumed to contain a common principle of inflammability, which Stahl named 'phlogiston', so that, when a combustible substance was burnt, 'phlogiston' was said to have escaped from it in the form of fire and flame. Combustion was therefore a decomposition. It was a reasonable sort of explanation. Most of us today, without our present knowledge built on past discoveries, would be quite ready to agree that, when a match is struck or a candle burns, some 'fire-stuff' is released from each of them—and so likewise for other kinds of burning.

One application of the 'phlogiston' theory was eventually to lead chemists into much confusion and to help to bring about its downfall. It arose in this way. When a metal, such as copper or lead, is heated, it turns into a powdery substance and its metallic properties are lost. (The same thing happens in the familiar rusting of iron, but there without the application of heat.) The chemists of that time explained this by saying that a metal was a kind of combustible and that, when heated, it lost its 'phlogiston', leaving the powdery residue, which they called a calx. They knew that if this calx was heated afresh with charcoal, it was converted back again into metal; and charcoal, since it would burn away almost entirely, was held to be very rich in 'phlogiston'. The heating of the calx with charcoal had therefore restored enough 'phlogiston' to the calx to reconstitute the original metal. Thus a metal was a compound of its calx and 'phlogiston'; and the process of heating a metal to give its calx, called calcination, was a decomposition, a kind of combustion in which 'phlogiston' escaped from the metal.

It was known, on the other hand, that, when a metal was calcined, the weight of the residual calx or powder was greater than the original weight of the metal taken. But how could the weight increase, since something material, namely 'phlogiston', had been lost from the substance of the metal? In answer to this, some of the chemists who accepted the 'phlogiston' theory were driven to suppose that 'phlogiston' did not gravitate as other matter, but levitated—that it naturally rose upwards to the heavens whereas other substances naturally tended to fall to the earth—that it had a negative weight, as we might say. This contradiction was presently to be resolved in a simpler way than by supposing the existence of a kind of matter outside all experience.

So, until the four-element theory and the 'phlogiston' theory were rejected, modern chemistry remained unborn; for earth and air and water and fire are not the elements of which our world is made, and substances do not burn because of the presence in them of a common principle of inflammability or 'fire-stuff'.

The history of the rejection of these theories begins with the discovery of the gases, particularly the discovery of oxygen, which forms one-fifth of the common air. At first it was supposed that gases were mere varieties of common air, changed slightly in properties but still essentially the same. In 1755, however, Joseph Black differentiated one kind of air chemically from common air and gave it the name of 'fixed air'. (It is now known as carbon dioxide). Black showed that it was produced in the combustion of charcoal, in respiration when air is exhaled from the lungs, and in fermentation. In 1766 Henry Cavendish discovered another air, 'inflammable air', which we now call hydrogen; and from 1772 onwards Joseph Priestley discovered seven other gases, but still described them as 'different kinds of air'.

Joseph Priestley, a Nonconformist minister, was one of the greatest of all chemical experimenters. In August 1774, in one of his most remarkable experiments, made at Bowood House, Calne, Wiltshire, he obtained a new 'air', in which the flame of a candle burned much more brilliantly than in common air; and in March 1775, in studying this new 'air' in further experiments at Lansdowne House, Mayfair, London, he found that it was purer and better than common air for respiration. It was the gas we now call oxygen. Priestley soon suggested that it might be used to increase 'the force of fire' and that 'it might be peculiarly salutary to the lungs in certain morbid cases', two applications that were made later on. He had first used mice to test the respirability of the new 'air' and then he had tried it himself. 'Hitherto', he wrote, 'only two mice and myself have had the privilege of breathing it.'

In the autumn of 1774 Priestley visited Paris. There he met Antoine Laurent Lavoisier, the founder, indeed the Newton, of modern chemistry. In conversation with Lavoisier, Priestley described his latest discovery—the new 'air' in which the flame of a candle burned much more brilliantly than in common air; and he told Lavoisier that he had obtained it by heating the calx of mercury or the calx of lead.

Lavoisier had long been considering the related problems of combustion and calcination and, as early as 1772, he had concluded that air played an important part in combustion and that the two inflammable substances, phosphorus and sulphur, combined with air when they were burnt and that their weight was increased by this combination with air. Through many months of 1773 he made further experiments; and in 1774–75, after his talk with Priestley, he concluded that the gain in weight of metals on calcination was likewise due to their combination with air; but he still got no further than supposing that it was combination with common air in a pure state, not suspecting at this time that only a part or constituent of the common air was involved.

In 1777, in further experiments, Lavoisier concluded that only a part of the air was involved in combustion, respiration and calcination—the heavier part of the air—and that air itself was not a simple substance but consisted of two 'airs'. One of these was respirable, supported combustion and combined with metals on calcination—it was, he said, the 'salubrious part' of the air; the other part was incapable of supporting combustion or respiration, it was inimical both to fire and life, and it played no part in calcination.

Then, on 3 May 1777, Lavoisier read to the Paris Academy of Sciences an account of one of the most significant of all experiments in the long history of science. It is illustrated on page 236. He heated four ounces of mercury in the vessel A for twelve days and observed that the level of the water rose in the vessel B, connected as shown with vessel A, and that the rise in level corresponded to a decrease of about one-fifth of the total air contained in the apparatus. The residual air extinguished lighted candles and asphyxiated animals. He then removed the particles of calx of mercury formed in the vessel A by heating and heated them separately in a similar apparatus, collecting the so-called 'air' that they gave off. He had thus obtained from the calx of mercury, which was now reconverted into metallic mercury, the 'air' with which the mercury had combined in the first part of the experiment. This air was respirable. On mixing it with the air from which it had been removed, he obtained common air once again. He presently gave to this respirable air the name it still bears, oxygen. In this classic experiment, Lavoisier had shown that common air consisted of two 'airs' with strikingly different, indeed opposite, properties; and he had separated them one from the other.

Lavoisier's theory was not at all well received by his contemporaries, who were too much used to the older way of thinking. Even when, in 1783, he began to criticise the 'phlogiston' theory in the light of his own discoveries, he failed to make any serious inroad on the older beliefs.

But in this same year of 1783, from experiments made by Henry Cavendish, Lavoisier was able to carry his new theory much further—to an explanation of the composition of water. 'Inflammable air', or hydrogen as we now call it, was a combustible and therefore on burning it should, according to Lavoisier's theory, combine, as other combustibles did, with oxygen. Yet all attempts to obtain a product from this combustion failed until Cavendish found that, when 'inflammable air' was burnt in common air or oxygen, water was produced. On hearing of this in 1783, Lavoisier made a rough verification of the fact and concluded that water was a compound of oxygen and 'inflammable air', which he later re-named hydrogen (i.e. 'water-former'); and presently he confirmed this by decomposing water into its two constituent gases.

Soon the new theory of combustion with its satisfactory explanations of the role of air or oxygen in respiration and in calcination began to win acceptance and gradually, but not without much argument and struggle, the older theory was abandoned. Combustion, once thought to be the decomposition of a combustible with the release of its 'phlogiston', was now seen to be a process of chemical combination with oxygen—the oxygen of the air combined with the burning substance. And in respiration it was now seen that the oxygen taken into the lungs was converted into carbon dioxide. In collaboration with the mathematician, Laplace, Lavoisier concluded that respiration was a kind of slow combustion; and that the constant temperature of the animal organism was maintained by the heat liberated in the process of respiration through the combination of oxygen with carbonaceous matter in the blood.

And air was a mixture of two gases, while water was a compound—neither being an element.

Lavoisier also showed that, in chemical changes, matter was neither created nor destroyed; the total weight of the products of a chemical change was equal to the total weight of the substances

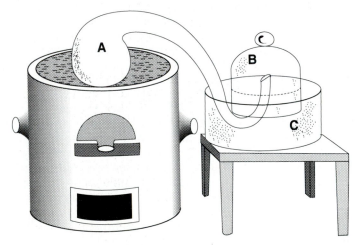

Apparatus Used by Lavoisier When He Isolated Oxygen
The neck of the glass vessel A (containing 4 oz. of mercury) was bent to connect with the air in the bell-jar B, inverted over mercury in trough C. After heating for twelve days on the charcoal furnace D, particles of the red calx or oxide of mercury formed in A and the volume of air in the apparatus decreased by about one-fifth. The residual air extinguished a flame and asphyxiated animals. It was nitrogen. Lavoisier then heated the red particles of mercuric oxide in a separate apparatus and collected the gas evolved from them. It amounted to about one-fifth of the original air and it supported combustion and respiration. It was oxygen.

originally taken. Chemistry was thus established on a quantitative basis and the first chemical balance sheet was now drawn up.

A most important immediate result of these great advances was the reform of the language of chemistry. The old names of substances had, of course, no relation to their chemical composition, since that was unknown; and their chemical composition could not be known until it had been discovered of what elements they were composed. Accordingly, Lavoisier applied a definition made by Robert Boyle in 1661 to the effect that an element was a substance that could not be decomposed into anything simpler; and he applied this idea in a very cautious way, not asserting that such substances as appeared to be incapable of further decomposition were, in fact, elements, but that they should be regarded as elements until evidence to the contrary was forthcoming. He therefore drew up our first table of chemical elements, which included oxygen, hydrogen and 'azote' (our modern 'nitrogen'), sulphur, phosphorus and carbon, and a large number of metals. Further discovery has, of course, since then greatly increased the number of elements known to us. Having thus determined what substances were to be regarded as elements, Lavoisier and some of the French chemists who had accepted his views set themselves the further task of devising a suitable system of chemical names by giving to every known substance a name that corresponded to its chemical composition. The old names had often been coined to indicate some physical property of a substance or its mode of preparation, or to perpetuate its discoverer's name or the place where it had been found as a mineral. They were often cumbersome. They were sometimes nonsensical; for instance, two very poisonous substances, compounds of arsenic and antimony, were known as 'butter of arsenic' and 'butter of antimony'!

The language of a science, Lavoisier insisted, was itself an analytical instrument; the new system of chemical names, which with slight modification is still in use today after more than a century and half of further discovery, gave us for every substance in a word or two a clear indication of its chemical nature and composition.

The revolution in chemistry was complete and modern chemistry dates from the publication of Lavoisier's great classic, the *Traité élémentaire de Chimie*, published in Paris in 1789, and translated into English and published in Edinburgh in 1790 under the title *Elements of Chemistry*, in which the new system was set out with all the penetrating lucidity characteristic of the French intellect. From this work, which ranks with Newton's *Principia* as one of the greatest of all scientific books, we may quote one sentence that particularly reveals the austere outlook of its author: 'I have imposed upon myself the law of never advancing but from the known to the unknown, of deducing no consequence that is not immediately derived from experiments and observations.'

The new chemistry soon began to yield results. In chemical industry, already beginning its modern development, processes were now better understood and improvements on the old ways followed.

Lavoisier himself applied his discoveries in the service of France, carrying out many investigations for the French Government and providing the first example of the scientist in the service of the nation. His earliest important national task was the reform of the manufacture of salt-petre and gun-powder, which he placed on a satisfactory scientific and economic basis; he investigated the principles of ballooning after the first balloon ascents by the Montgolfier brothers in 1783; he helped to draw up the first geological maps of France; he devised a system of lighting cities and large towns at night; and he studied a host of such problems, to all of which chemistry had something important to contribute, for chemistry is the one science that touches our lives at all points.

Science and the scientist are sometimes thought to be concerned only with scientific discovery and not greatly with its application, and still less with the more humane aspects of life. The founder of modern chemistry was one who proved that the finest practice is born of the finest theory; and he showed himself to be a great humanitarian. When the French Government called upon him as the most eminent chemist of his age to draw up reports on the hospitals and prisons, he went much further in his recommendations than dealing with ventilation and cleanliness in the light of the new chemistry; for the hospitals, he urged the classification of patients suffering from different diseases and the segregation of the feeble-minded from the sick; for prisons, he urged the separation of habitual criminals from first offenders and proclaimed his belief that the object of imprisonment was the reform of the prisoner and his return to daily life as a good citizen. His humanitarianism is very evident in his proposals for a state system of education, in which he called education 'a duty that society owes to the child', and for a system of voluntary contributory insurance against ill-health and old age. In the recollection of Lavoisier's reform of the science of chemistry, these other activities are worth recalling. So is his tragic end on the scaffold as a victim of the French Revolution through his former position as an official of the old régime.

Suggestions for Discussion and Writing

1. Why, according to McKie, was the birth of modern chemistry delayed?

2. Why were the theories of phlogiston and the four elements so attractive to seventeenth- and eighteenth-century chemists?

3. Name three scientists with whom Lavoisier worked closely. Describe the contribution of one of them.

4. Describe Lavoisier's classic experiment with mercury and air. What did he learn from it?

5. What do you understand the author to mean when he says that Lavoisier was "the Newton of modern chemistry"? What parallels do you see in their achievements?

6. What was the significance of Lavoisier's renaming "every known substance"?

7. Write an essay in which you illustrate the truth of McKie's assertion that chemistry "touches our lives at all points." You might wish to focus on some of the more surprising illustrations of this truth.

8. Briefly describe the ways in which Lavoisier's career confirmed the claim that "the finest practice is born of the finest theory."

9. In what ways is the final sentence of the essay ironic?

WHAT IS THE THEORY OF RELATIVITY?

Albert Einstein
(1879–1955)

For a biographical sketch of the author, see page 151.

In the following essay, written at the request of the editors of the *London Times* and subsequently reprinted in *Ideas and Opinions* (1954), Einstein attempts to provide the general reader with a better understanding of the theory of relativity. Without using mathematics, Einstein explains that relativity essentially involves the rejection of the traditional idea of a single, fixed coordinate system for measuring the position or motion of bodies in space.

I gladly accede to the request of your colleague to write something for *The Times* on relativity. After the lamentable breakdown of the old active intercourse between men of learning, I welcome this opportunity of expressing my feelings of joy and gratitude toward the astronomers and physicists of England. It is thoroughly in keeping with the great and proud traditions of scientific work in your country that eminent scientists should have spent much time and trouble, and your scientific institutions have spared no expense, to test the implications of a theory which was perfected and published during the war in the land of your enemies. Even though the investigation of the influence of the gravitational field of the sun on light rays is a purely objective matter, I cannot forbear to express my personal thanks to my English colleagues for their work; for without it I could hardly have lived to see the most important implication of my theory tested.

We can distinguish various kinds of theories in physics. Most of them are constructive. They attempt to build up a picture of the more complex phenomena out of the materials of a relatively simple formal scheme from which they start out. Thus the kinetic theory of gases seeks to reduce mechanical, thermal, and diffusional processes to movements of molecules—i.e., to build them up out of the hypothesis of molecular motion. When we say that we have succeeded in understanding a group of natural processes, we invariably mean that a constructive theory has been found which covers the processes in question.

Along with this most important class of theories there exists a second, which I will call "principle-theories." These employ the analytic, not the synthetic, method. The elements which form their basis and starting-point are not hypothetically constructed but empirically discovered ones, general characteristics of natural processes, principles that give rise to mathematically formulated criteria which the separate processes or the theoretical representations of them have to satisfy. Thus the science of thermodynamics seeks by analytical means to deduce necessary conditions, which separate events have to satisfy, from the universally experienced fact that perpetual motion is impossible.

The advantages of the constructive theory are completeness, adaptability, and clearness, those of the principle theory are logical perfection and security of the foundations.

The theory of relativity belongs to the latter class. In order to grasp its nature, one needs first of all to become acquainted with the principles on which it is based. Before I go into these, however, I must observe that the theory of relativity resembles a building consisting of two separate stories, the special theory and the general theory. The special theory, on which the general theory rests, applies to all physical phenomena with the exception of gravitation; the general theory provides the law of gravitation and its relations to the other forces of nature.

It has, of course, been known since the days of the ancient Greeks that in order to describe the movement of a body, a second body is needed to which the movement of the first is referred. The movement of a vehicle is considered in reference to the earth's surface, that of a planet to the totality of the visible fixed stars. In physics the body to which events are spatially referred is called the coordinate system. The laws of the mechanics of Galileo and Newton, for instance, can only be formulated with the aid of a coordinate system.

The state of motion of the coordinate system may not, however, be arbitrarily chosen, if the laws of mechanics are to be valid (it must be free from rotation and acceleration). A coordinate system which is admitted in mechanics is called an "inertial system." The state of motion of an inertial system is according to mechanics not one that is determined uniquely by nature. On the contrary, the following definition holds good: a coordinate system that is moved uniformly and in a straight line relative to an inertial system is likewise an inertial system. By the "special principle of relativity" is meant the generalization of this definition to include any natural event whatever: thus, every universal law of nature which is valid in relation to a coordinate system C, must also be valid, as it stands, in relation to a coordinate system C', which is in uniform translatory motion relatively to C.

The second principle, on which the special theory of relativity rests, is the "principle of the constant velocity of light in vacuo." This principle asserts that light in vacuo always has a definite velocity of propagation (independent of the state of motion of the observer or of the source of the light). The confidence which physicists place in this principle springs from the successes achieved by the electrodynamics of Maxwell and Lorentz.

Both the above-mentioned principles are powerfully supported by experience, but appear not to be logically reconcilable. The special theory of relativity finally succeeded in reconciling them logically by a modification of kinematics—i.e., of the doctrine of the laws relating to space and time (from the point of view of physics). It became clear that to speak of the simultaneity of two events had no meaning except in relation to a given coordinate system, and that the shape of measuring devices and the speed at which clocks move depend on their state of motion with respect to the coordinate system.

But the old physics, including the laws of motion of Galileo and Newton, did not fit in with the suggested relativist kinematics. From the latter, general mathematical conditions issued, to which natural laws had to conform, if the above-mentioned two principles were really to apply. To these, physics had to be adapted. In particular, scientists arrived at a new law of motion for (rapidly moving) mass points, which was admirably confirmed in the case of electrically charged particles. The most important upshot of the special theory of relativity concerned the inert masses of corporeal systems. It turned out that the inertia of a system necessarily depends on its energy-content, and this led straight to the notion that inert mass is simply latent energy. The principle of the conservation of mass lost its independence and became fused with that of the conservation of energy.

The special theory of relativity, which was simply a systematic development of the electrodynamics of Maxwell and Lorentz, pointed beyond itself, however. Should the independence of physical laws of the state of motion of the coordinate system be restricted to the uniform translatory motion of coordinate systems in respect to each other? What has nature to do with our coordinate systems and their state of motion? If it is necessary for the purpose of describing nature, to make use of a coordinate system arbitrarily introduced by us, then the choice of its state of motion ought to be subject to no restriction; the laws ought to be entirely independent of this choice (general principle of relativity).

The establishment of this general principle of relativity is made easier by a fact of experience that has long been known, namely, that the weight and inertia of a body are controlled by the same constant (equality of inertial and gravitational mass). Imagine a coordinate system which is rotating uniformly with respect to an inertial system in the Newtonian manner. The centrifugal forces which manifest themselves in relation to this system must, according to Newton's teaching, be regarded as effects of inertia. But these centrifugal forces are, exactly like the forces of gravity, proportional to the masses of the bodies. Ought it not to be possible in this case to regard the coordinate system as stationary and the centrifugal forces as gravitational forces? This seems the obvious view, but classical mechanics forbid it.

This hasty consideration suggests that a general theory of relativity must supply the laws of gravitation, and the consistent following up of the idea has justified our hopes.

But the path was thornier than one might suppose, because it demanded the abandonment of Euclidean geometry. This is to say, the laws according to which solid bodies may be arranged in space do not completely accord with the spatial laws attributed to bodies by Euclidian geometry. This is what we mean when we talk of the "curvature of space." The fundamental concepts of the "straight line," the "plane," etc., thereby lose their precise significance in physics.

In the general theory of relativity the doctrine of space and time, or kinematics, no longer figures as a fundamental independent of the rest of physics. The geometrical behavior of bodies and the motion of clocks rather depend on gravitational fields, which in their turn are produced by matter.

The new theory of gravitation diverges considerably, as regards principles, from Newton's theory. But its practical results agree so nearly with those of Newton's theory that it is difficult to find criteria for distinguishing them which are accessible to experience. Such have been discovered so far:

1. In the revolution of the ellipses of the planetary orbits round the sun (confirmed in the case of Mercury).
2. In the curving of light rays by the action of gravitational fields (confirmed by the English photographs of eclipses).
3. In a displacement of the spectral lines toward the red end of the spectrum in the case of light transmitted to us from stars of considerable magnitude (unconfirmed so far).[1]

[1]This criterion has since been confirmed.

The chief attraction of the theory lies in its logical completeness. If a single one of the conclusions drawn from it proves wrong, it must be given up; to modify it without destroying the whole structure seems to be impossible.

Let no one suppose, however, that the mighty work of Newton can really be superseded by this or any other theory. His great and lucid ideas will retain their unique significance for all time as the foundation of our whole modern conceptual structure in the sphere of natural philosophy.

Note: Some of the statements in your paper concerning my life and person owe their origin to the lively imagination of the writer. Here is yet another application of the principle of relativity for the delectation of the reader: today I am described in Germany as a "German savant," and in England as a "Swiss Jew." Should it ever be my fate to be represented as a *bête noire,* I should, on the contrary, become a "Swiss Jew" for the Germans and a "German savant" for the English.

Suggestions for Discussion and Writing

1. How would you characterize the tone of the opening paragraph? Is it consonant with Einstein's stature as a scientist? Does it contribute to his purpose?

2. Explain the distinction between "constructive theories" and "principle-theories." Why does Einstein identify these two kinds before turning to the theory of relativity?

3. In your own words, explain what is meant by a "coordinate system"; by an "inertial system."

4. Einstein asks the question, "What has nature to do with our coordinate systems and their state of motion?" Does he answer it?

5. Why does the rejection of a single, fixed coordinate system undermine the "precise significance" of the straight line and the plane?

6. Karl Popper says (see Chapter 7) that the best scientific theories make predictions and therefore risk "falsifiability." Does Einstein's theory of relativity meet this requirement?

7. In the final paragraph, Einstein refers to the "mighty work" of Newton. Is his view of Newton consistent with his attitude toward other scientists mentioned in the essay?

8. Look again at the final "Note." What do we learn here about Einstein the man?

☐ **SPACE–TIME**

Bertrand Russell
(1872–1970)

Born the son of Lord John Russell, Viscount Amberly, and succeeding his brother as third Earl of Russell, Bertrand Russell was anything but a conservative. A zealous reformer, his controversial social and political beliefs—from free love and open marriage to pacifism and unilateral disarmament—earned him a reputation as one of this century's most idiosyncratic thinkers.

Yet Russell's greatest contributions lie not in social or political thought but in mathematics and philosophy. His *Principles of Mathematics* (1903) and *Principia Mathematica* (1910–13), the latter written with Alfred North Whitehead, attempt to show how the laws of mathematics can be deduced from the basic axioms of logic. Russell's work has had enormous influence on the direction taken by twentieth-century mathematics, especially in the development of set theory. He has also profoundly influenced modern philosophy in the generation of logical positivism, particularly through the work of his student, Ludwig Wittgenstein. Russell was deeply committed to the scientific and philosophical postulates that individual facts are logically independent of one another and that knowledge is totally dependent on the data of original experience.

Though Russell's radicalism precluded a traditional academic career, he lectured frequently at universities from Los Angeles to Beijing and received numerous awards, including the Nobel Prize for Literature in 1950.

In the following essay, taken from *The ABC of Relativity* (1925, 1969), Russell attempts to resolve the apparent paradoxes posed by Einstein's special theory of relativity. Humankind has long held the notion that the position of an object or event in space can be defined by three measurements corresponding in some way to length, width, and height; a fourth and separate measurement gives the position in time. According to this view, space and time are independent of each other. If we understand, however, that the perceived position of an object or event is relative to the place of the observer in both space *and* time, we will recognize that space and time must be considered as interdependent, that is, as two parts of a whole, or space–time. As Russell assures us, to realize the implications of this newly perceived relationship is to understand the essential message of Einstein's theory.

Everybody who has ever heard of relativity knows the phrase "space–time," and knows that the correct thing is to use this phrase when formerly we should have said "space *and* time." But very few people who are not mathematicians have any clear idea of what is meant by this change of phraseology. Before dealing further with the special theory of relativity, I want to try to convey to the reader what is involved in the new phrase "space–time," because that is, from a philosophical and imaginative point of view, perhaps the most important of all the novelties that Einstein introduced.

Suppose you wish to say where and when some event has occurred—say an explosion on an airship—you will have to mention four quantities, say the latitude and longitude, the height above the ground, and the time. According to the traditional view, the first three of these give the position in space, while the fourth gives the position in time. The three quantities that give the position in space may be assigned in all sorts of ways. You might, for instance, take the plane of the equator, the plane of the meridian of Greenwich, and the plane of the 90th meridian, and say how far the airship was from each of these planes; these three distances would be what are called "Cartesian co-ordinates," after Descartes. You might take any other three planes all at right angles to each other, and you would still have Cartesian co-ordinates. Or you might take the distance from London to a point vertical below the airship, the direction of this distance (north-east, west-south-west, or whatever it might be), and the height of the airship above the ground. There are an infinite number of such ways of fixing the position in space, all equally legitimate; the choice between them is merely one of convenience.

When people said that space had three dimensions, they meant just this: that three quantities were necessary in order to specify the position of a point in space, but that the method of assigning these quantities was wholly arbitrary.

With regard to time, the matter was thought to be quite different. The only arbitrary elements in the reckoning of time were the unit, and the point of time from which the reckoning started. One could reckon in Greenwich time, or in Paris time, or in New York time; that made a difference as to the point of departure. One could reckon in seconds, minutes, hours, days, or years; that was a difference of unit. Both these were obvious and trivial matters. There was nothing corresponding to the liberty of choice as to the method of fixing position in space. And, in particular, it was thought that the method of fixing position in space and the method of fixing position in time could be made wholly independent of each other. For these reasons people regarded time and space as quite distinct.

The theory of relativity has changed this. There are now a number of different ways of fixing position in time, which do not differ merely as to the unit and the starting-point. Indeed, as we have seen, if one event is simultaneous with another in one reckoning, it will precede it in another and follow it in a third. Moreover, the space and time reckonings are no longer independent of each other. If you alter the way of reckoning position in space, you may also alter the time-interval between two events. If you alter the way of reckoning time, you may also alter the distance in space between two events. Thus space and time are no longer independent, any more than the three dimensions of space are. We still need four quantities to determine the position of an event, but we cannot, as before, divide off one of the four as quite independent of the other three.

It is not quite true to say that there is no longer any distinction between time and space. As we have seen, there are time-like intervals and space-like intervals. But the distinction is of a different sort from that which was formerly assumed. There is no longer a universal time which can be applied without ambiguity to any part of the universe; there are only the various "proper" times of the various bodies in the universe, which agree approximately for two bodies which are not in rapid motion, but never agree exactly except for two bodies which are at rest relatively to each other.

The picture of the world which is required for this new state of affairs is as follows: Suppose an event E occurs to me, and simultaneously a flash of light goes out from me in all directions. Anything that happens to any body after the light from the flash has reached it is definitely after the event E in any system of reckoning time. Any event anywhere which I could have seen before the event E occurred to me is definitely before the event E in any system of reckoning time. But any event which happened in the intervening time is not definitely either before or after the event E. To make the matter definite: suppose I could observe a person in Sirius, and he could observe me. Anything which he does, and which I see before the event E occurs to me, is definitely before E; anything he does after he has seen the event E is definitely after E. But anything that he does before he sees the event E, but so that I see it after the event E has happened, is not definitely before or after E. Since light takes many years to travel from Sirius to earth, this gives a period of twice as many years in Sirius which may be called "contemporary" with E, since these years are not definitely before or after E.

Dr. A. A. Robb, in his *Theory of Time and Space,* suggested a point of view which may or may not be philosophically fundamental, but is at any rate a help in understanding the state of affairs we have been describing. He maintained that one event can only be said to be definitely *before* another if it can influence that other in some way. Now influences spread from a centre at varying rates. Newspapers exercise an influence emanating from London at an average rate of about twenty miles an hour—rather more for long distances. Anything a man does because of what he reads in the newspaper is clearly subsequent to the printing of the newspaper. Sounds travel much faster: it would be possible to arrange a series of loud-speakers along the main roads, and have newspapers shouted from each to the next. But telegraphing is quicker, and wireless telegraphy travels with the velocity of light, so that nothing quicker can ever be hoped for. Now what a man does in consequence of receiving a wireless message he does *after* the message was sent; the meaning here is quite independent of conventions as to the measurement of time. But anything that he does while the message is on its way cannot be influenced by the sending of the message, and cannot influence the sender until some little time after he sent the message, that is to say, if two bodies are widely separated, neither can influence the other except after a certain lapse of time; what happens before that time has elapsed cannot affect the distant body. Suppose, for instance, that some notable event happens on the sun: there is a period of sixteen minutes on the earth during which no event on the earth can have influenced or been influenced by the said notable event on the sun. This gives a substantial ground for regarding that period of sixteen minutes on the earth as neither before nor after the event on the sun.

The paradoxes of the special theory of relativity are only paradoxes because we are unaccustomed to the point of view, and in the habit of taking things for granted when we have no right to do so. This is especially true as regards the measurement of lengths. In daily life, our way of measuring lengths is to apply a foot-rule or some other measure. At the moment when the foot-rule is applied, it is at rest relatively to the body which is being measured. Consequently the length that we arrive at by measurement is the "proper" length, that is to say, the length as estimated by an observer who shares the motion of the body. We never, in ordinary life, have to tackle the problem of measuring a body which is in continual motion. And even if we did, the velocities of visible bodies on the earth are so small relatively to the earth that the anomalies dealt with by the theory of relativity would not appear. But in astronomy, or in the investigation of atomic structure, we are faced with problems which cannot be tackled in this way. Not being Joshua, we cannot make the sun stand still while we measure it; if we are to estimate its size we must do so while it is in motion relatively to us. And similarly if you want to estimate the size of an electron, you have to do so while it is in rapid motion, because it never stands still for a moment. This is the sort of problem with which the theory of relativity is concerned. Measurement with a foot-rule, when it is possible, gives always the same result, because it gives the "proper" length of a body. But when this method is not possible, we find that curious things happen, particularly if the body to be measured is moving very fast relatively to the observer. The figure [on page 248] will help us to understand the state of affairs.

Let us suppose that the body on which we wish to measure lengths is moving relatively to ourselves, and that in one second it moves the distance OM. Let us draw a circle round O whose radius is the distance that light travels in a second. Through M draw MP perpendicular to OM, meeting the circle in P. Thus OP is the distance that light travels in a second. The ratio of OP to OM is the ratio of the velocity of light to the velocity of the body. The ratio of OP to MP is the ratio in which apparent lengths are altered by the motion. That

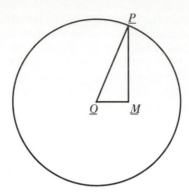

is to say, if the observer judges that two points in the line of motion on the moving body are at a distance from each other represented by MP, a person moving with the body would judge that they were at a distance represented (on the same scale) by OP. Distances on the moving body at right angles to the line of motion are not affected by the motion. The whole thing is reciprocal; that is to say, if an observer moving with the body were to measure lengths on the previous observer's body, they would be altered in just the same proportion. When two bodies are moving relatively to each other, lengths on either appear shorter to the other than to themselves. This is the Fitzgerald contraction, which was first invented to account for the result of the Michelson–Morley experiment. But it now emerges naturally from the fact that the two observers do not make the same judgment of simultaneity.

The way in which simultaneity comes in is this: We say that two points on a body are a foot apart when we can *simultaneously* apply one end of a foot-rule to the one and the other end to the other. If, now, two people disagree about simultaneity, and the body is in motion, they will obviously get different results from their measurements. Thus the trouble about time is at the bottom of the trouble about distance.

The ratio of OP to MP is the essential thing in all these matters. Times and lengths and masses are all altered in the proportion when the body concerned is in motion relatively to the observer. It will be seen that, if OM is very much smaller than OP, that is to say, if the body is moving very much more slowly than light, MP and OP are very nearly equal, so that the alterations produced by the motion are very small. But if OM is nearly as large as OP, that is to say, if the body is moving nearly as fast as light, MP becomes very small compared to OP, and the effects become very great. The apparent increase of mass in swiftly moving particles had been observed, and the right formula had been found, before Einstein invented his special theory of relativity. In fact, Lorentz had arrived at the formulae called the "Lorentz transformation," which embody the whole mathematical essence of the special theory of relativity. But it was Einstein who showed that the whole thing was what we ought to have expected, and not a set of makeshift devices to account for surprising experimental results. Nevertheless, it must not be forgotten that experimental results were the original motive of the whole theory, and have remained the ground for undertaking the tremendous logical reconstruction involved in Einstein's theories.

We may now recapitulate the reasons which have made it necessary to substitute "space–time" for space and time. The old separation of space and time rested upon the belief that there was no ambiguity in saying that two events in distant places happened at the same time; consequently it was thought that we could describe the topography of the universe at a given instant in purely spatial terms. But now that simultaneity has become relative to a particular observer, this is no longer possible. What is, for one observer, a description of the state of the world at a given instant, is, for another observer, a series of events at various different times, whose relations are not merely spatial but also temporal. For the same reason, we are concerned with *events,* rather than with *bodies.* In the old theory, it was possible to consider a number of bodies all at the same instant, and since the time was the same for all of them it could be ignored. But now we cannot do that if we are to obtain an objective account of physical occurrences. We must mention the date at which a body is to be considered, and thus we arrive at an "event," that is to say, something which happens at a given time. When we know the time and place of an event in one observer's system of reckoning, we can calculate its time and place according to another observer. But we must know the time as well as the place, because we can no longer ask what is its place for the new observer at the "same" time as for the old observer. There is no such thing as the "same" time for different observers, unless they are at rest relatively to each other. We need four measurements to fix a position, and four measurements fix the position of an event in space-time, not merely of a body in space. Three measurements are not enough to fix any position. That is the essence of what is meant by the substitution of space–time for space and time.

Suggestions for Discussion and Writing

1. What three traditional dimensions of space does Russell identify? Why are they "arbitrary"? Why are the traditional elements involved in the reckoning of time "trivial"?

2. In speaking of "the picture of the world which is required for this new state of affairs," Russell refers to the "intervening time" between an event and the perception of that event. What accounts for this intervening time?

3. In explaining ways of "reckoning time," Russell uses the example of an observer in Sirius. Summarize his explanation. Why does Russell frequently turn to examples to illustrate his points?

4. In explaining his diagram, Russell asserts that "the ratio of OP to MP is the essential thing in all these matters." How is this ratio determined? Why is it essential? (Sometimes the act of drawing can be helpful. You might wish to draw your own diagram following Russell's directions.)

5. What, according to Russell, was the relationship between the work of Lorentz and that of Einstein?

6. Explain in your own words why, after Einstein, space and time have become space–time.

7. In speaking of Einstein's work, Russell says that "the paradoxes of the special theory of relativity are only paradoxes because we are unaccustomed to the [relative] point of view, and in the habit of taking things for granted when we have no right to do so." Write an essay in which you explore the relevance of these ideas to a contemporary social or political issue.

☐ THE WORLD OF THE QUANTUM

Robert M. Hazen
(b. 1948)
James Trefil
(b. 1938)

A mineralogist and geologist, Robert Hazen was educated at the Massachusetts Institute of Technology and Harvard University. He has contributed more than one hundred articles and reviews to scientific journals and is the author or co-author of several books, including (with L. W. Finger) *Comparative Crystal Chemistry: Temperature, Pressure, Composition, and the Variation of Crystal Structure* (1982) and *The Poetry of Geology* (1982). Hazen is also a professional trumpet player and has performed with a number of well-known orchestras, including the Boston Symphony, the National Orchestra, and the Orchestre de Paris.

Educated at the University of Illinois, Oxford, and Stanford, James Trefil is the Clarence J. Robinson Professor of Physics at George Mason University. He has written a number of books on science for the general public, including *Physics as a Liberal Art*

(1978), *A Scientist at the Seashore* (1984), *Meditations at Ten Thousand Feet: A Scientist in the Mountains* (1986), and *Meditations at Sunset: A Scientist Looks at the Sky* (1987). These last three constitute a kind of trilogy in which Trefil explores common questions about our surroundings and applies physical laws to arrive at answers. Trefil has been widely praised for his ability to combine the knowledge of the expert with the enthusiasm of the beginner in his discussions of the physical world and the laws that govern it.

The following essay, taken from *Science Matters* (1990) and written with Robert Hazen, illustrates the authors' belief that a basic understanding of physical science, even of the complex world of the quantum, is within the grasp of the intelligent general reader willing to devote sufficient time and attention to it.

The word "quantum" is familiar to lay people—splashed on cars and bandied about by Madison Avenue. Pundits and newscasters talk about "quantum leaps," mostly in a context that has nothing to do with physics. But the ideas of quantum mechanics are neither familiar nor obvious, and the term can instill fear even in the hearts of otherwise knowledgeable scientists.

Most scientists understand quantum mechanics in a vague, non-mathematical sort of way, but very few can do anything practical with it. That's because quantum mechanics can be devilishly hard in all its quantitative rigor. Yet, in spite of this aura of complexity, the two basic ideas behind quantum mechanics—what you need to know to be scientifically literate—are quite simple: Everything—particles, energy, the rate of electron spin—comes in discrete units, and you can't measure anything without changing it. Together, these two basic facts explain the operation of atoms, things inside atoms, and things inside things inside atoms.

THE WORLD OF THE VERY SMALL

Quantum mechanics is the branch of science devoted to the study of the behavior of atoms and their constituents. *Quantum* is the Latin word for "so much" or "bundle," and "mechanics" is the old term for the study of motion. Thus, quantum mechanics is the study of the motion of things that come in little bundles.

A particle like the electron must come in a "quantized" form. You can have one electron, or two, or three, but never 1.5 or 2.7. It's not so obvious that something we usually think of as continuous, like light, comes in this form as well. In fact, the quantum or bundle of light is called the "photon" (you may find it useful to remember the "photon torpedoes" of *Star Trek* fame). It is even less obvious that quantities like energy and how fast electrons spin come only in discrete bundles as well, but they do. In the quantum world, *every-*

thing is quantized and can be increased or decreased only in discrete steps.

The behavior of quanta is puzzling at first. The obvious expectation is that when we look at things like electrons, we should find that they behave like microscopic billiard balls—that the world of the very small should behave in pretty much the same way as the ordinary world we experience every day. But an expectation is not the same as a commandment. We can *expect* the quantum world to be familiar to us, but if it turns out not to be, that doesn't mean nature is somehow weird or mystical. It just means that things are arranged in such a way that what is "normal" for us at the scale of billiard balls is not "normal" for the universe at the scale of the atom.

THE UNCERTAINTY PRINCIPLE

The strangeness of the quantum world is especially evident in the operation of the Uncertainty Principle, sometimes called the Heisenberg Uncertainty Principle after its discoverer, the German physicist Werner Heisenberg (1901–76). The easiest way to understand the Uncertainty Principle is to think about what it means to say that you "see" something. In order for you to see these words, for example, light from some source (the sun or a lamp) must strike the book and then travel to your eye. A complex chemical process in your retina converts the energy of the light into a signal that travels to your brain.

Think about the interaction of light with the book. When you look at the book you do not see it recoil when the light hits it, despite the fact that floods of protons must be bouncing off every second in order for you to see the page. This is the classic Newtonian way of thinking about measurement. It is assumed that the act of measurement (in this case, the act of bouncing light off the book) does not affect the object being measured in any way. Given the infinitesimal energy of the light compared to the energy required to move the book, this is certainly a reasonable way to look at things. After all, baseballs do not jitter around in the air because photographers are using flashbulbs, nor does the furniture in your living room jump every time you turn on the light.

But does this comfortable, reasonable, Newtonian viewpoint apply in the ultra-small world of the atom? Can you "see" an electron in the same way that you see this book?

If you think about this question for a moment, you will realize that there is a fundamental difference between "seeing" these two objects. You see a book by bouncing light off it, and the light has a negligible effect on the book. You "see" an electron, on the other hand, by bouncing another electron (or some other comparable bundle) off it. In this case, the thing being probed and the thing doing the probing are comparable in every way, and the interaction cannot leave the original electron unchanged. It's as if the only way you could see a billiard ball was to hit it with another billiard ball.

There is a useful analogy that will help you think about measurement in the quantum domain. Suppose there were a long, dark tunnel in a mountain and you wanted to know whether there was a car in the tunnel. Suppose further that you couldn't go into the tunnel yourself or shine a light down it—that the only way you could answer your question was to send another car down that tunnel and then listen for a crash. If you heard a crash, you could certainly say that there was another car in the tunnel. You couldn't say, however, that the car was the same after your "measurement" as it was before. The very act of measuring—in this case the collision of one car with the other—changes the original car. If you then sent another car down the tunnel to make a second measurement, you would no longer be measuring the original car, but the original car as it has been altered by the first measurement.

In the same way, the fact that to make a measurement on an electron requires the same sort of disruptive interaction means that the electron (or any other quantum particle) must be changed whenever it is measured. This simple fact is the basis for the uncertainty principle and, in the end, for many of the differences that exist between the familiar world and the world of the quantum.

The uncertainty principle is a statement that says, in effect, that the changes caused by the act of measurement make it impossible to know everything about a quantum particle with infinite precision. It says, for example, that you cannot know both the position (where something is) and velocity (how fast it's moving) exactly—the two pieces of data that are significant in describing any physical object.

The important thing about the uncertainty principle is that if you measure the position of a tiny particle with more and more precision, so that the error becomes smaller and smaller, the uncertainty in velocity must become greater to compensate. The more care you take to know one thing, the more poorly you know the other. The very act of measuring changes the thing you are measuring, so you must always be uncertain about something.

THE WAVE FUNCTION

The fact that one cannot measure a quantum system without changing it leads to an extremely important conclusion about the way that such systems must be described. Suppose that large objects, like airplanes, behaved the way electrons do. Suppose you knew that an airplane was flying somewhere in the Midwest and you wanted to predict where it would be a few hours later. Because of the uncertainty principle, you couldn't know both where the plane was and how fast it was going, and you'd have to make some compromise. You might, for example, locate the plane to within fifty miles and its velocity to within 100 miles per hour.

If you now ask where the plane will be in two hours, the only answer you can give is "It depends." If the plane is traveling 500 miles per hour, it will be a thousand miles away; if it's traveling 400 miles per hour, it will be only 800 miles away. And, since we don't know exactly where the plane started, there is an additional uncertainty about its final location.

One way to deal with this problem is to describe the final location of the plane in terms of probabilities: there's a 30 percent chance it will be in Pittsburgh, a 20 percent chance it will be in New York, and so on. You could, in fact, draw a graph that would show the probable location of the plane at any point east of the Mississippi. For historical reasons, a collection of probabilities like this is called the "wave function" of the plane.

We normally don't worry about wave function for airplanes, because in the everyday world the amount of change caused by a measurement is so small as to be negligible, so the uncertainties in the plane's position and speed are tiny. In the quantum world, however, *every* measurement causes appreciable change in the object being measured, and hence everything has to be described in terms of probabilities and wave functions. It was this unpredictable aspect of the quantum world that troubled Albert Einstein and caused him to remark that "God does not play dice with the universe." (His old friend Niels Bohr is supposed to have replied, "Albert, stop telling God what to do.")

WAVES OR PARTICLES?

We all run into trouble when we try to visualize a quantum object like an electron. Our inventory of mental images is limited to the sorts of things we can see in our familiar world, and, unfortunately, electrons just don't fit anywhere on our mental file cards. Nowhere is this problem of visualization more difficult than in discussion of particles and waves in the quantum world.

In our normal world, energy can be transferred by particle or by wave, as you can see by thinking about a bowling alley. Suppose there were one pin standing at the other end and you wanted to knock it down. You would have to apply energy to the pin to do this, of course, and might choose to expend some energy to get a bowling ball moving, and then let the ball roll down the alley and knock the pin over. This process involves a particle—the bowling ball—carrying energy from you to the pin. Alternatively, you could set up a line of pins and then knock the first one over. It would knock over the second, which would knock over the third, and so on like dominoes until the final pin fell. In this case, the energy would be transmitted by the wave of falling pins, and no single object travels from you to your target.

When scientists started to explore the subatomic world, they naturally asked "Are electrons particles or are they waves?" After all, an electron transfers energy, and if energy can be transferred only by particles and waves, then the electron must be one or the other.

Unfortunately, things aren't that simple. Experiments performed on electrons have found that in some situations they seem to act as particles, in other situations as waves. Similarly, something we normally consider to be a wave—light, for example—can appear to be a particle under certain circumstances. In the early years of this century, this seemingly inexplicable behavior was called "wave-particle duality" and was supposed to illustrate the strangeness of the quantum world.

There is, however, nothing particularly mysterious about "duality." The behavior of electrons and light simply tells us that in the quantum world, our familiar categories of "wave" and "particle" do not apply. The electron is not a wave, and it's not a particle—it's something else entirely. Depending on the experiment we do, we can see wave-like or particle-like behavior. The wave-particle problem lies not with nature, but with our own minds.

Suppose you were a Martian who, for some reason or other, had been able to pick up radio broadcasts from Earth only in the French and German languages. You might very well come up with a theory that every language on Earth was either French or German. Suppose then that you came to Earth and landed in the middle of an American city. You hear English for the first time, and you note that some of the words are like French and some are like German. You would have no problem if you realized that there was a third type of language of which you had been previously ignorant, but you could easily tie yourself in philosophical knots if you didn't. You might even develop a theory of "French-German duality" to explain the new phenomenon.

In the same way, as long as we are willing to accept that things at the atomic level are not like things in our everyday world, no problem arises with the question of whether things are waves or particles. The correct answer to the wave-particle question is simply "none of the above."

Of course, this means that we cannot visualize what an electron is like—we can't draw a picture of it. For creatures as wedded to visual imagery as we are, this is deeply troubling. Physicists and non-physicists alike rebel and try to make mental images, whether they are "real" or not. The authors are no different, and, for the record, we imagine the electron as something like a tidal wave, located in one general area, like a particle, but with crests and troughs, like a wave.

The length of the "tidal wave" associated with different kinds of particles varies tremendously. That of an electron, for example, is smaller than that of an atom, while a photon of ordinary visible light is about three feet long. Viewed this way, both "waves" like light and "particles" like electrons have the same basic structure. The distinction in classical physics between wave and particle turns out to be a meaningless distinction in the quantum world.

THE ATOM—QUANTUM MECHANICS IN ACTION

The most important role quantum mechanics plays in science is explaining how the atom is put together. [It is] the peculiar property of electrons in the Bohr atom to adopt fixed orbits. These fixed orbits are a consequence of quantized electron energies. Electrons can only have certain precise energies, and any quantum leap between orbits must correspond exactly to the difference in orbital energies. Each quantum leap by one electron leads to the absorption or the production of one photon.

Electrons moving up and down in their orbits are analogous to a person moving up and down a staircase: it requires energy to climb, and energy is released upon descent. And, like a person on a staircase, an electron cannot be found between "steps"—in other words, it can only be found in allowed orbits.

Although it is tempting to think of electrons in orbits as particles, like lumps of matter, scientists often picture them in terms of their wave functions. The peak in the electron "wave," corresponding to the highest probability of finding the electron, is at the place where the electron would be located if we pictured it as a particle.

Lasers

From grocery lines to rock concerts, compact discs to the most advanced weaponry, lasers are changing our world by changing the ways we use light.

"Laser" is an acronym for Light Amplification by Stimulated Emission of Radiation, an imposing name for a remarkable device. Lasers work like this: you start off with a collection of atoms, each with an electron in a high-energy orbit. The chromium atoms in crystals of ruby serve this function in many red lasers. Photons with exactly the same energy as the excited electrons are focused on those special atoms. When one of these photons comes near an atom it "stimulates" the electron in the atom to jump down, emitting another photon in the process—one that is not only of the same wavelength as the original, but is precisely aligned, crest-to-crest, trough-to-trough. The two photons now pass through the material, stimulating other atoms until a flood of precisely aligned photons results. In this way, one photon "amplifies" itself.

The energy needed to get the atoms into an excited state in the first place, and to get them to go back to it after they have emitted a photon, can be added to the system in many ways. Typically, scientists "pump" a laser by subjecting the material to heat, to a beam of energetic electrons, or to a bright light, from something like a flashbulb or even another laser.

Two precisely aligned mirrors at each end of the laser material causes the photons to move back and forth millions of times. Engineers design laser mirrors to allow a small fraction (maybe 5 percent) of the photons to escape on each bounce, and these leftover photons form the laser beam.

FRONTIERS
Visualizing the Quantum

There is a group of physicists who just can't seem to leave the quantum alone. Like a dog worrying a bone, they keep coming back to central issues like wave-particle duality, introducing new and highly innovative experiments to shed light on this (and other) issues of "quantum weirdness." The press often reports on these experiments because their results invariably present the kind of conflict between science and intuition we talked about earlier.

There are a large number of experiments being done in which the experimenters try to "trick" the quantum into revealing its true identity. For example, scientists have designed experiments that delay the decision of whether to test the wave- or particle-like aspects of a neutron until the neutron is actually in flight toward the apparatus. (For technical reasons, the electrically neutral neutron provides the best particles for these tests.) The results of such experiments are invariably in line with quantum mechanics—the "wave" experiment sees the neutron as a wave, while the "particle" experiment sees it as a particle. Nevertheless, the results run so counter to our intuition that they compel attention. It may be the only situation in science where we are more troubled when an experiment agrees with our theory than when it doesn't.

Quantum Detectors

Ronald Reagan often spiced his arms reduction rhetoric with the phrase "trust but verify." When pressed, Reagan revealed that verification would be accomplished, in part, by "technical means." Part of what he was really talking about were the most sensitive possible detectors, based on the principles of quantum mechanics.

The most sensitive detector responds to a single quantum—one photon, for instance. Among the most important of these tools is the SQUID, or Superconducting Quantum Interference Device. The SQUID stores a precise amount of electrical current in a tiny wire loop. Any slight change in magnetic field alters the current in the loop by one quantum unit, and that in turn triggers the detector. SQUIDs play a vital role in science, in medicine, and in detecting the small magnetic disturbances caused by a moving enemy submarine.

Suggestions for Discussion and Writing

1. At the beginning of their essay, the authors say that the term "quantum mechanics" can "instill fear even in the hearts of otherwise knowledgeable scientists." Point to some of the ways (diction, tone, etc.) by which the authors attempt to put their audience at ease.

2. How do the authors define quantum mechanics? In your own words, explain the two ideas that form the basis of this branch of physics.

3. Why must particles "come in a 'quantized' form"? What do the authors mean when they say that "in the quantum world, *everything* is quantized and can be increased or decreased only in discrete steps"?

4. In your own words, briefly explain the Uncertainty Principle.

5. Identify some of the more helpful analogies used by the authors to make their points. Choose one that is especially helpful and explain why it is successful.

6. Do the authors offer an explanation as to why analogies are especially useful in a discussion of quantum mechanics? Would Jeans agree that analogies are useful? (See "What Is Physics?" in this chapter.)

7. What did Einstein mean when he said that "God does not play dice with the universe"? In what sense was he "telling God what to do"?

8. Explain the distinction between waves and particles. How do the authors "resolve" the question of waves or particles?

9. Traditionally, "scientific objectivity" has implied a clear separation between the object (the thing being observed) and the subject (the observer). How does the world of the quantum imply a breakdown of this distinction?

CHAPTER 6

The Biosciences

TOWARD A PHILOSOPHY OF BIOLOGY

Jacob Bronowski
(1908–1974)

For a biographical sketch of the author, see page 30.

In the following selection, taken from *A Sense of the Future* (1977), Bronowski describes the revolution that has taken place in biology since World War II. He suggests that new knowledge about the nature of the cell has given us a far better understanding of the mechanisms of evolution.

The new biology has been built in the decades since World War II, in large part by young men whose careers the war had interrupted, and who had to make a fresh start at the end of it. Many of them had been employed on physical problems during the war, and physics had come to seem rather barren to them, surrounded with unpleasant hints of regimentation and secrecy. By comparison, biology looked invitingly like open country. Leo Szilard characterized his unspoken belief and theirs simply, as "What I brought into biology was an attitude: the conviction that mysteries can be solved. If secrets exist, they must be explainable." And the word was out that they were beginning to be explained: the chemists Linus Pauling and Desmond Bernal were already doing impressive work on the structure of proteins, and the physicist Max Delbrück led a program which might unravel the genetic tape or blueprint within the cell.

In moving to biology from physics, the newcomers naturally brought with them the habits of thought that had been successful in physics. For example, it had become commonplace in physics to think of any material body as an arrangement of large numbers of atoms, repeated in some regular way; and to explain the behavior of the body and derive its properties by going back to these basic units. Anyone now coming into biology was sure to look for a similar unit of structure there. Evidently, this unit of structure in living matter was the cell.

The most arresting discoveries that have been made in the biology of the cell concern the inborn instructions which regulate it—that is to say, the genetic material which goes from one generation to the next, and acts as a blueprint or program to direct the sequence of chemical processes that makes up the life cycle of each cell. The facts are now well known: the main activity of a cell is the manufacture of many specific proteins, and the instructions for the manufacturing process are carried in simpler material in the cell nucleus, the nucleic acids.

In 1950 bold men were asking themselves what could be the structure of the nucleic acids which would give them the power to copy themselves when the cell divides in two, and supply each daughter cell with an accurate copy. And in 1951 James Watson and Francis Crick revealed the starting simplicity of the double helix of the DNA molecule.

Since there are many varieties of living creatures, and many genes in each, there are many different forms of DNA, in each of which the sequence of bases is different and is characteristic for some chemical processes to make a protein in that creature. Crick and his colleagues have since shown that the sequence of bases in a molecule of DNA spells out the twenty amino acids, which in turn make the proteins. We have a simple hierarchy: the four bases are the four letters of the alphabet, each set of three letters makes up a word which is a fundamental amino acid, and the twenty words in their turn are assembled into different sentences which are the different proteins.

A cell is not at all a simple unit: and the very fact that there are creatures that consist of a single cell shows that it is effectively a microcosm of life. Since life is evidently not a thing but a process, it follows that we have to study the cell not merely as a structure, but as a changing structure. The cycle of events that follow one another within the cell is a life cycle, but more than that, it *is* life. But the basic structures and sequences of life follow from those of dead nature without the intervention of any special powers or acts. I want to make this point clearly and with force. There is no place for vitalism in the analysis of the cell. Certainly life, the perpetuation of form and process from generation to generation, is extraordinary: but whatever is extraordinary about it is not at the level of the atoms, or the molecules, or the genes and chromosomes and enzymes and electric discharges, the interlocking sequences of instructions and communications which actually make the body and the brain work. All that is understandable in physical terms, without the intervention of any mystic principles.

From the time of Henri Bergson and before, philosophers have been wrongheaded when they have tried to find a special sanction for the uniqueness of man in the mystery of life. What makes man unique is his command of cognitive knowledge, and that is not a property of life in the individual cell; on the contrary, it is precisely what man does not share with a cell—even with any other assembly of cells. The mystery is not in the cell: the mystery is that the cell is not a mystery to us—the mystery is that man can understand so much of nature.

None of this is to deny that life as a process has a different character from the other processes of the natural world. Life is a very specialized and accidental phenomenon: it derives its character (as well as its mystery) from the fact that it is improbable. I would put this forward as a philosophical principle, *that life is unique, and the forms of life are unique arrangements of matter, precisely because they are accidental.* I shall return to the statistical reasons and implications of that in good time.

If an arrangement of matter is unique, it must be accidental—that is, it must be singled out from all the other possible arrangements by an action which is arbitrary and highly improbable. Erwin Schrödinger took a similar idea from Max Delbrück, and Delbrück in his turn had been inspired to turn to biology by an essay on *Light and Life* by the greatest of all the quantum physicists, Niels Bohr.

Delbrück has recorded frankly what troubled him about physics in the 1930s and what he hoped to find in biology. Physics was exploring the behavior of matter on the minute scale of quantum changes. It seemed to Delbrück that there was something logically (and aesthetically) wrong in the disproportion between the tiny quantum effects and the vast apparatus which was required to demonstrate them. He hoped to find in living matter a kind of quantum resonator or multiplier, which would express new physical laws because it would display in visible form the impact of single quantum events.

In any simple sense, Delbrück turned out to be mistaken in his hope. Yet the crucial thought in Delbrück and Schrödinger is exactly right; as so often in science, the wrong guess is better and more creative than no guess at all. The cell is sensitive to single and unpredictable events which abruptly change its potential and that of the generations of cells that derive from it. The development of life from one form to another is unlike that of the rest of the physical world, because it is triggered by accidents, and they give each new form its unique character. Life is not an orderly continuum like the growing of a crystal. *The nature of life is only expressed in its perpetual evolution, which is another name for the succession (and the success) of its errors.*

*   *   *

Since I began this essay by analyzing the cell, I should now round it out by discussing the process of evolution. There are five distinct principles which make up the concept of evolution, as I interpret it. They are:

1. family descent
2. natural selection
3. Mendelian inheritance
4. fitness for change
5. stratified stability.

I shall present them in what is in effect their historical order. For evolution was not formed as an explanatory concept all in one leap; it grew by degrees from distinct strands, which came together one after another. The logic of evolution requires all five strands, in my view.

This first and central strand is simply the idea that the likenesses between different species of plants and animals are, literally, *family likenesses;* they derive from the fact that the species have a common family tree and ancestry. This idea is older than *The Origin of Species,* and goes back at least to Charles Darwin's grandfather Erasmus; yet (as a matter of history) this is what gave the book its shocking and decisive impact in 1859.

The principle of *natural selection* is the second strand in evolution; it is what gives the observations a structure and turns them into a theory. Selection is not strictly a causal mechanism, but a statistical one; and evolution is therefore the work of chance. Darwin was in no doubt about that—"Heaven forefend me from Lamarckian nonsense of a 'tendency to progression' "—and neither were his readers. We think of them now as outraged simply by the implication that man had not been specially created, as the Old Testament recorded, but was descended from the same stock as the apes and other mammals. But they were more deeply outraged, in their religious and their moral convictions, by the central place of chance in Darwin's theory of evolution.

Darwin had no theory of inheritance that could account for the persistence of a variant form from generation to generation. In this respect, his trust in natural selection as an agent that could form permanent species was an act of faith, backed only by the known experience of plant and animal breeders.

In essence, this difficulty was resolved by Gregor Mendel in the decade that followed the publication of *The Origin of Species,* and Darwin should have known that. Mendel guessed and then proved that every heritable trait is governed by a pair of discrete units, what we now call genes, one from each parent—of which one may mask or dominate the expression of the other, but both of which will be preserved and handed on to some of the offspring. This theory of *Mendelian inheritance* is a third and essential part of a soundly based theory of evolution.

In my view, it is necessary to add to a realistic account of evolution two further principles which govern its operation as we witness it. These two strands are *fitness for change* and *stratified stability.* That is to say, they are concerned, the one with the variability of living forms, and the other with their stability; and between them they explain how it comes about that biological evolution has a direction in time—and has a direction in the same sense that time has. The direction of evolution is an important and indeed crucial phenomenon, which singles it out among statistical processes. For in so far as statistical processes have a direction at all, it is usually a movement toward the average—and that is exactly what evolution is not. There is therefore something profound to be explained here, which goes to the heart of the mechanism of life; and it is natural that the disputes about the nature of life center on this. For the direction of evolution, which can be traced for about three thousand million years, gives it the appearance of a planned program: and the question is, How does this come about if there is no plan?

We need to be clear here what might be meant by a plan. For example, a vitalist who thinks it inconceivable that the orderly tree or pyramid of living forms could have evolved without a master plan might be content to say that the plan was conceived by a creator who simply understood the laws of chance better than we do. Indeed, he may claim (and no doubt he will, in time) that the two principles of variability and stability which I shall develop below demonstrate that the statistics of evolution have a scientific structure which an all-seeing creator understands at least as well as I do, and could employ to plan the future with perfect foresight.

Nevertheless, it is clear that such a statistical definition of a cosmic plan can satisfy no one, and is fundamentally pointless. For in the end it says no more than that the laws of nature take their course undisturbed, and move to their outcome with no other guidance than the edict which made them laws on the day of creation. Accordingly, we must suppose that those who believe that life follows some larger plan than the laws of physics constitute have in their minds a more literal picture of a plan.

For example, it is suggested that a living creature goes through a complex of cycles which are so matched to its environment that they have the manifest plan or purpose, they are patently *designed,* to preserve the life of the individual. But the fact that a living cell (for instance, a bacterium) is geared to go on living in the face of disturbance is no more supernatural than the fact that a falling stone is geared to go on falling, and a stone in free space is geared to go on moving in a straight line. This is its nature, and does not require explanation any more (or in any other sense) than does the behavior of a ray of light or the complex structure of an atom of uranium.

Therefore the vitalist must have some more sophisticated idea of a plan than the mere persistence of a cycle, or even of a linked sequence of cycles. Michael Polanyi, who claims that perpetuation of life cannot be understood except as an overall plan or purpose, uses a telling illustration. He says that to explain the machinery of a cell is like explaining the machinery of a watch; and that this misses the most important thing about a watch, which is that its machinery is planned for a purpose—to tell the time.

The design of a watch is the classical illustration for God's design in man that deists introduced in the eighteenth century. So what is telling is not that the illustration is fresh, but that it is oddly old-fashioned. Polanyi now gives the argument a new turn by saying that just as the design of the watch points to and is only understood in its purpose, so the design of the machinery of life points to and is only understood at a higher level of explanation by purpose.

However, the plan by which the watchmaker coordinates the totality of the machine from its subassemblies is not different in kind from the plan on which he forms a subassembly from its parts. They are all equally plans that are *closed,* in the sense that they describe the complete course or cycle which the operation runs. A closed plan is a rational sequence of instructions; the different levels of organization within it are merely levels of convenience; and there can be no level of design above the running of the machine, no overall purpose, unless there is an explicit designer outside the machine for whom it is a means to that purpose. We should have to believe in a creator with a conscious purpose, like a watchmaker who wants to tell the time.

Since I have stressed the character of what I call *closed* plans, it will be evident that I intend to contrast them with *open* plans. It is valid to regard an organism as a historical creation whose "plan" is explained by its evolution. But the plan of life in this sense is an open plan; only open plans can be creative; and evolution is the open plan which has created what is radically new in life, the dynamic of time.

So it is timely now to consider evolution as an open plan, and to ask what are the additional principles that are needed to make it capable of creating the new living forms that we know. For it is essential that we recognize these forms as new and as genuine creations. They arise naturally in and from the course of evolution, as a work of art or an ingenious move at chess arises naturally in and from the march or play of each successive step. Yet the work of art is not implied in its beginning, and the elegant mate at chess does not sleep like a seed in the first move of the game. They are open creations, and so is life; it is not a closed plan like that which runs its rigid course from the seed to the full-grown plant.

Put in this way, the issue is clear. There is a relation between the direction of evolution and the direction of time. In a history of three thousand million years, evolution has not run backward. Why is this? Why does evolution not run at random hither and thither in time? What is the screw that moves it forward—or at least, what is the ratchet that keeps it from slipping back? Is it possible to have such a mechanism which is not planned? What is the relation that ties evolution to the arrow of time, and makes it a barbed arrow?

The paradox to be resolved here is classical in science: How can disorder on the small scale be consonant with order on the large scale, in time or in space? Evolution must have a different statistical form in which there is an inherent potential for large-scale order to act as a sieve or selector on the individual chance events. The principle of a potential of order in the selection of chance events is clear, but what is never clear in advance is how it works. It is here that we need two additional mechanisms in evolution to turn the principle into natural selection as we know it, that is, with a natural order in time.

The first of the two additional mechanisms which we now see to underlie evolution is *fitness for change,* or (in more formal language) *selection for adaptability.* This important and unexpected process gives a special character to the variability which is inherent within any species. It is of course evident to our eyes that the members of a species are not identical; and in addition to this visible diversity, we know that there is an invisible diversity hidden in the mutant genes. This pool of hidden diversity supplies the variants which nature can select in order to modify the species. Thus we see that hidden diversity is an instrument for adaptation in the future.

But what is less easy to see, and is new and important, is that hidden diversity is the instrument for *adaptability* now, in the present. In order that a species shall be capable of changing to fit its environment tomorrow, it must maintain its fitness for change today. If this is to be done in the present, without some mysterious plan for the future, it must be by natural selection, not for this or that variant, but for variability itself.

And in fact it is evident that there is natural selection in favor of genetic variability. The selection is made by the small changes, up and down and up again and down again, by which the environment flutters about its mean. So the critical step in the conception of an open plan is certainly this: that "the survival of the fittest" must be understood as the *selection of those fitted for change* as part of the total concept of fitness to a changing environment.

Adaptation has to match the changes in the environment, but adaptability has to match the rates of change: it is (so to speak) the differential coefficient of adaptation, and expresses the second order of difference in the organism and its environment. It is of course characteristic of cooperative phenomena in nature that they involve higher orders of relation, and therefore the matching of higher orders of difference, than do isolated phenomena.

It is evident that we cannot discuss the variability of organisms and species without also examining their stability. We have therefore also to trace a mechanism for stability, as the second of the two balanced mechanisms that are needed to complete our understanding of evolution. I call this, the fifth and last strand in my analysis of evolution, the concept of *stratified stability.*

Evolution is commonly presented, even now, as if it required nothing but natural selection to explain its action, one minute step after another, as it were gene by gene. But an organism is an integrated system, and that implies that its coordination is easily disturbed. This is true of every gene: normal or mutant, it has to be incorporated into the ordered totality of the gene complex like a piece in a jigsaw puzzle.

Yet the analogy of the jigsaw is too rigid: we need a geometrical model of stability in living processes and the structures that carry them out which is not so landlocked against change. Moreover, the model must express the way in which the more complex forms of life arise from the simpler forms, and arise later in time. This is the model which I call *stratified* stability.

There are evolutionary processes in nature which do not demand the intervention of selective forces. Characteristic is the evolution of the chemical elements, which are built up in different stars step by step, first hydrogen to helium to carbon, and on to heavier elements. The most telling example is the creation of carbon from helium. Two helium nuclei which collide do not make a stable element, and fly apart again in less than a millionth of a millionth of a second. But if in that splinter of time a third helium nucleus runs into the pair, it binds them together and makes a stable triad which is a nucleus of carbon. And every carbon atom in every organic molecule in every cell in every living creature has been formed by such a wildly improbable triple collision in a star.

Here then is a physical model which shows how simple units come together to make more complex configurations. The stable higher forms cannot be reached in one leap: they have to be built up layer by layer, and each layer must be a stable form at which evolution can pause and accumulate enough raw material so that improbable encounters can happen to create still more complex stable forms.

The stratification of stability is fundamental in living systems, and it explains why evolution has a consistent direction in time. For the building up of stability in organization has a direction—the more complex stratum built on the next lower, and so on—which cannot be reversed.

There is therefore a peculiar irony in the vitalist claim that the progress of evolution from simple to complex cannot be the work of chance. On the contrary, as we see, exactly this is how chance works, and is constrained to work by its nature. The total potential of stability that is hidden in matter can only be evoked in steps, each higher layer resting on the layer below it. The stable units that compose one layer are the raw material for random encounters which will produce higher configurations, some of which chance to be stable. So long as there remains a potential of stability which has not become actual, there is no other way for chance to go.

It is often said that the progression from simple to complex runs counter to the normal statistics of chance which are formalized in the second law of thermodynamics. But this interpretation quite misunderstands the character of statistical laws in general. The second law of thermodynamics, for example (which is often quoted), describes the statistics of a system whose configurations are all equal, and it makes the obvious remark that chance can only make such a system fluctuate around its average. There are no stable states in such a system, and there is therefore no stratum that can establish itself; the system rests around its average only by a principle of indifference, because numerically the most configurations are bunched around the average.

Time in the large, open time, only has a direction when we mark and scale it by the evolutionary processes that climb from simple to more and more complex by steps. It is evolutionary processes that give time its direction; and no mystical explanation is required where there is nothing to explain. The progression from simple to complex, the building up of stratified stability, is the necessary character of evolution from which time takes its direction. And it is not a forward direction in the sense of a thrust toward the future, a headed arrow. What evolution does is to give the arrow of time a barb which stops it from running backwards; and once it has this barb, the chance play of errors will take it forward of itself.

Yet there is still a deeper question to be asked about time. It concerns our two experiences of time, one of which is the inner time of our body as an organism, and the other is the outer time of evolution. How does it come about that these two times, inner and outer, closed and open, have the same direction? Why does our sense of growing old and of going toward death point the same way as evolution, when we might well have expected the two to point in opposite directions?

The answer lies in the common mechanisms of life, which drive both the closed cycles of the organism and the open plan of evolution. In a living organism, growing old is not a thermal decay, and death is not a fall into the average such as the second law describes. As we understand old age, the cells in the organism age individually when they happen to make errors in their internal copying and when these errors are of a kind which repeat or perpetuate themselves. This is also and precisely the mechanism which underlies evolution. The cell cannot accommodate the errors because they do not fit into its organization, which is closed. But in the open field of evolution, the errors which are able to repeat or perpetuate themselves are the stuff of creation. The organism experiences the accumulation of errors in its cells as the direction of time toward its death. Evolution goes the same way because its mechanism is the same; and we perceive cosmic time as running the same way also because its direction is pointed by evolution.

Life as an evolutionary process is open, with no cycle in time; and it derives this openness from just such accidents or errors, at least in kind, as kill the individual. Here the mechanism is evolution, and evolution is that quantum resonator or multiplier, the exploitation of an accident to create a new and unique form, for which Delbrück was looking when he came into biology. *The closed cycle of an individual life and the open time of evolution are dual aspects of life, driven by the common mainspring of quantum accidents,* which are only properly understood when they are put side by side as complementary parts or processes of life.

The living creature and its evolution are the two matched faces of life. In this pairing, evolution is the creative partner: it does not solve a problem, as the cycles of the organism do, but makes a genuine creation—a creature. We can say of it what Piet Hein said of a work of art, in a penetrating phrase: that it solves a problem which we could not formulate until it was solved.

Suggestions for Discussion and Writing

1. In what way, according to Bronowski, did the focus of biology change after World War II?

2. In the fifth paragraph Bronowski appears to offer an analogy between amino acids and letters of the alphabet. Is this analogy successful? What other analogies does Bronowski use in his essay?

3. What does Bronowski mean when he says that "there is no place for vitalism in the analysis of the cell"? Does he explain what he means by "vitalism"?

4. Bronowski disputes philosophers who "have tried to find a special sanction for the uniqueness of man in the mystery of life." Where, for Bronowski, is the mystery? Could Bronowski be described as a religious man? Write an essay supporting your views. (You may, if you wish, use other essays by Bronowski in this volume to make your case.)

5. Explain the crucial difference between the development of life from one form to another and the development of other forms in the physical world, for example, the crystal.

6. Explain the difference between "closed" and "open" plans. Why can only "open" plans be "creative"? In what sense is evolution an "open plan"?

7. How does Bronowski resolve the paradox between the disorder of a process dependent upon chance and error and order "on the large scale"?

8. What "two experiences of time" does Bronowski identify? How are they similar? How are they different?

9. Bronowski divides his essay into four parts. What is the focus of each part? Does he offer an explicit thesis statement that holds these parts together?

10. Discuss Bronowski's use of the paragraph as an organized unit within the larger essay. Are his paragraphs typically governed by a topic sentence? Does he provide adequate support for his main ideas? Does he use transitions effectively?

FROM *THE ORIGIN OF SPECIES*: "INTRODUCTION" AND "STRUGGLE FOR EXISTENCE"

Charles Darwin
(1809–1882)

In his youth Charles Darwin showed no signs of the genius that would establish him as one of the giants of modern science and as the foundational figure in perhaps the most far-reaching intellectual revolution in the history of Western civilization.

After an undistinguished early schooling, Darwin went to Edinburgh University in 1825 to study medicine, but left in 1827 after discovering that he was not suited for a medical career. In that year, he entered Christ's College, Cambridge, with the intention of taking holy orders, but graduated without committing himself to the Church. At Cambridge, however, he had become interested in natural science and, through the help of his botany professor, took a post as a naturalist "without pay" aboard H.M.S. *Beagle,* which was about to leave on a five-year voyage of scientific exploration in the Southern Hemisphere. Darwin never received a systematic training in science, but this voyage (1831–1836) made a scientist of him, for it enabled him to make extensive observations of flora, fauna, and geological formations at widely separated points of the globe. These observations laid the foundation for many of his most important ideas and posed for him the momentous problem he would struggle with for the next twenty years: the problem of the origin of species.

When Darwin embarked on the *Beagle,* his opinions regarding the origin of species were entirely orthodox: he accepted without question the fixity of species and their special creation as described in Genesis. He began to doubt this version, however, as a result of his work in South America and the Galapagos Islands. Darwin was an exceptionally keen observer, and while in the Galapagos he noticed slight differences among the separated island populations of single species. This and other observations led him to the theory that species are not fixed but arise from previous species and are modified during descent—they evolve. In 1838, after reading Thomas Malthus's *Essay on Population,* he formulated the principle of "natural selection," which he identified as the primary mechanism by which evolution is effected.

During the next twenty years, Darwin carefully and painstakingly worked out his ideas, accumulating enormous masses of supporting detail to bolster his case. His friends, Sir Charles Lyell and Sir Joseph Hooker, saw short versions of his theory in the early 1840s, and in 1856 Lyell advised him to write a full-length account of his views. In 1858, however, with about half of his manuscript complete, Darwin was stunned when he received a paper from Alfred Russel Wallace (written in the Malay archipelago) setting out the very ideas that he himself had been working on for twenty-one years. The resulting crisis was resolved with the help of Lyell and Hooker, who arranged for a joint paper by the two men to be read before the Linnean Society on July 1, 1858. Faced with the possibility of being anticipated by Wallace's independent discoveries, Darwin quickly finished and published his classic work, *The Origin of Species,* in 1859. The entire edition of 1,250 copies was sold out on the day of issue.

Darwin's ideas aroused a storm of controversy. Popular reaction, led by the establishment, especially the Church, focused on the religious and ideological implications of his theory, and Darwin came to be seen as an enemy of the Bible, of the Church, of Christianity itself. Darwin shunned these controversies, however, and left the defense of "Darwinism" to his friends, especially Thomas Huxley ("Darwin's bulldog"), who willingly took on the antievolutionists. Huxley's debate with Bishop Wilberforce in 1860 was the most famous of the period. Within the scientific community, despite initial opposition, Darwin's ideas gained a fairly wide acceptance by about 1880.

Darwin wrote many important books in addition to his great classic, including *Fertilization in Orchids* (1862), *Variation in Animals and Plants under Domestication* (1868), and *The Expression of the Emotions in Man and Animals* (1872). The range of his interests and his work was enormous, and even if he had never written *The Origin* he would still be regarded as one of the great biologists of the nineteenth century.

But it was through the ideas laid out in *The Origin of Species* and augmented in *The Descent of Man* (1871) that Darwin established himself as one of the greatest scientists of all time. For with his theory of evolution he gave the biological sciences a set of unifying principles. In this sense we may say that he was to the biological sciences what Isaac Newton had been to the physical sciences.

Darwin's ideas, however, have reached far beyond science—to theology, philosophy, history, and sociology. Indeed, hardly a single field of human endeavor has *not* been influenced by his work. More than any thinker of the modern era, he changed man's thinking about himself and his place in nature.

Darwin himself was a humble and gentle man. "I have steadily endeavored," he wrote in his *Autobiography*, "to keep my mind free, so as to give up any hypothesis, however much beloved (and I cannot resist forming one on every subject), as soon as facts are shown to be opposed to it." Darwin died in 1882. He is buried in Westminster Abbey, a few feet from the grave of Sir Isaac Newton.

The following excerpts from *The Origin of Species* illustrate Darwin's direct and personal style. They illustrate, too, the careful and measured tone in which he lays out his revolutionary ideas.

INTRODUCTION

When on board H.M.S. 'Beagle,' as naturalist, I was much struck with certain facts in the distribution of the organic beings inhabiting South America, and in the geological relations of the present to the past inhabitants of that continent. These facts, as will be seen in the latter chapters of this volume, seemed to throw some light on the origin of species—that mystery of mysteries, as it has been called by one of our greatest philosophers. On my return home, it occurred to me, in 1837, that something might perhaps be made out on this question by patiently accumulating and reflecting on all sorts of facts which could possibly have any bearing on it. After five years' work I allowed myself to speculate on the subject, and drew up some short notes; these I enlarged in 1844 into a sketch of the conclusions, which then seemed to me probable: from that period to the present day I have steadily pursued the same object. I hope that I may be excused for entering on these personal details, as I give them to show that I have not been hasty in coming to a decision.

My work is now (1859) nearly finished; but as it will take me many more years to complete it, and as my health is far from strong, I have been urged to publish this Abstract. I have more especially been induced to do this, as Mr. Wallace, who is now studying the natural history of the Malay archipelago, has arrived at almost exactly the same general conclusions that I have on the origin of species. In 1858 he sent me a memoir on this subject, with a request that I would forward it to Sir Charles Lyell, who sent it to the Linnean Society, and it is published in the third volume of the Journal of that society. Sir C. Lyell and Dr. Hooker, who both knew of my work—the latter having read my sketch of 1844—honoured me by thinking it advisable to publish, with Mr. Wallace's excellent memoir, some brief extracts from my manuscripts.

This Abstract, which I now publish, must necessarily be imperfect. I cannot here give references and authorities for my several statements; and I must trust to the reader reposing some confidence in my accuracy. No doubt errors will have crept in, though I hope I have always been cautious in trusting to good authorities alone. I can here give only the general conclusions at which I have arrived, with a few facts in illustration, but which, I hope, in most cases will suffice. No one can feel more sensible than I do of the necessity of hereafter publishing in detail all the facts, with references, on which my conclusions have been grounded; and I hope in a future work to do this. For I am well aware that scarcely a single point is discussed in this volume on which facts cannot be adduced, often apparently leading to conclusions directly opposite to those at which I have arrived. A fair result can be obtained only by fully stating and balancing the facts and arguments on both sides of each question; and this is here impossible.

I much regret that want of space prevents my having the satisfaction of acknowledging the generous assistance which I have received from very many naturalists, some of them personally unknown to me. I cannot, however, let this opportunity pass without expressing my deep obligations to Dr. Hooker, who, for the last fifteen years, has aided me in every possible way by his large stores of knowledge and his excellent judgment.

In considering the Origin of Species, it is quite conceivable that a naturalist, reflecting on the mutual affinities of organic beings, on their embryological relations, their geographical distribution, geographical succession, and other such facts, might come to the conclusion that species had not been independently created, but had descended, like varieties, from other species. Nevertheless, such a conclusion, even if well founded, would be unsatisfactory, until it could be shown how the innumerable species inhabiting this world have been modified, so as to acquire that perfection of structure and coadaptation which justly excites our admiration. Naturalists continually refer to external conditions, such as climate, food, &c., as the only possible source of variation. In one limited sense, as we shall hereafter see, this may be true; but it is preposterous to attribute to mere external conditions, the structure, for instance, of the woodpecker, with its feet, tail, beak, and tongue, so admirably adapted to catch insects under the bark of trees. In the case of the mistletoe, which draws its nourishment from certain trees, which has seeds that must be transported by certain birds, and which has flowers with separate sexes absolutely requiring the agency of certain insects to bring pollen from one flower to the other, it is equally preposterous to account for the structure of this parasite, with its relations to several distinct organic beings, by the effects of external conditions, or of habit, or of the volition of the plant itself.

It is, therefore, of the highest importance to gain a clear insight into the means of modification and coadaptation. At the commencement of my observations it seemed to me probable that a careful study of domesticated animals and of cultivated plants would offer the best chance of making out this obscure problem. Nor have I been disappointed; in this and in all other perplexing cases I have invariably found that our knowledge, imperfect though it be, of variation under domestication, afforded the best and safest clue. I may venture to express my conviction of the high value of such studies, although they have been very commonly neglected by naturalists.

From these considerations, I shall devote the first chapter of this Abstract to Variation under Domestication. We shall thus see that a large amount of hereditary modification is at least possible; and, what is equally or more important, we shall see how great is the power of man in accumulating by his Selection successive slight variations. I will then pass on to the variability of species in a state of nature; but I shall, unfortunately, be compelled to treat this subject far too briefly, as it can be treated properly only by giving long catalogues of facts. We shall, however, be enabled to discuss what circumstances are most favourable to variation. In the next chapter the Struggle for Existence amongst all organic beings throughout the world, which inevitably follows from the high geometrical ratio of their increase, will be considered. This is the doctrine of Malthus, applied to the whole animal and vegetable kingdoms. As many more individuals of each species are born than can possibly survive; and as, consequently, there is a frequently recurring struggle for existence, it follows that any being, if it vary however slightly in any manner profitable to itself, under the complex and sometimes varying conditions of life, will have a better chance of surviving, and thus be *naturally selected.* From the strong principle of inheritance, any selected variety will tend to propagate its new and modified form.

This fundamental subject of Natural Selection will be treated at some length in the fourth chapter; and we shall then see how Natural Selection almost invariably causes much Extinction of the less improved forms of life, and leads to what I have called Divergence of Character. In the next chapter I shall discuss the complex and little known laws of variation. In the five succeeding chapters, the most apparent and gravest difficulties in accepting the theory will be given: namely, first, the difficulties of transitions, or how a simple being or a simple organ can be changed and perfected into a highly developed being or into an elaborately constructed organ; secondly; the subject of Instinct, or the mental powers of animals; thirdly, Hybridism, or the infertility of species and the fertility of varieties when intercrossed; and fourthly, the imperfection of the Geological Record. In the next chapter I shall consider the geological succession of organic beings throughout time; in the twelfth and thirteenth, their geographical distribution throughout space; in the fourteenth, their classification or mutual affinities, both when mature and in an embryonic condition. In the last chapter I shall give a brief recapitulation of the whole work, and a few concluding remarks.

No one ought to feel surprise at much remaining as yet unexplained in regard to the origin of species and varieties, if he make due allowance for our profound ignorance in regard to the mutual relations of the many beings which live around us. Who can explain why one species ranges widely and is very numerous, and why another allied species has a narrow range and is rare? Yet these relations are of the highest importance, for they determine the present welfare and, as I believe, the future success and modification of every inhabitant of this world. Still less do we know of the mutual relations of the innumerable inhabitants of the world during the many past geological epochs in its history. Although much remains obscure, and will long remain obscure, I can entertain no doubt, after the most deliberate study and dispassionate judgment of which I am capable, that the view which most naturalists until recently entertained, and which I formerly entertained—namely, that each species has been independently created—is erroneous. I am fully convinced that species are not immutable; but that those belonging to what are called the same genera are lineal descendants of some other and generally extinct species, in the same manner as the acknowledged varieties of any one species are the descendants of that species. Furthermore, I am convinced that Natural Selection has been the most important, but not the exclusive, means of modification. . . .

STRUGGLE FOR EXISTENCE

Before entering on the subject of this chapter, I must make a few preliminary remarks, to show how the struggle for existence bears on Natural Selection. It has been seen in the last chapter that amongst organic beings in a state of nature there is some individual variability: indeed I am not aware that this has ever been disputed. It is immaterial for us whether a multitude of doubtful forms be called species or sub-species or varieties; what rank, for instance, the two or three hundred doubtful forms of British plants are entitled to hold, if the existence of any well-marked varieties be admitted. But the mere existence of individual variability and of some few well-marked varieties, though necessary as the foundation for the work, helps us but little in understanding how species arise in nature. How have all those exquisite adaptations of one part of the organisation to another part, and to the conditions of life, and of one organic being to another being, been perfected? We see these beautiful co-adaptations most plainly in the woodpecker and the mistletoe; and only a little less plainly in the humblest parasite which clings to the hairs of a quadruped or feathers of a bird; in the structure of the beetle which dives through the water; in the plumed seed which is wafted by the gentlest breeze; in short, we see beautiful adaptations everywhere and in every part of the organic world.

Again, it may be asked, how is it that varieties, which I have called incipient species, become ultimately converted into good and distinct species which in most cases obviously differ from each other far more than do the varieties of the same species? How do those groups of species, which constitute what are called distinct genera, and which differ from each other more than do the species of the same genus, arise? All these results, as we shall more fully see in the next chapter, follow from the struggle for life. Owing to this struggle, variations, however slight and from whatever cause proceeding, if they be in any degree profitable to the individuals of a species, in their infinitely complex relations to other organic beings and to their physical conditions of life, will tend to the preservation of such individuals, and will generally be inherited by the offspring. The offspring, also, will thus have a better chance of surviving, for, of the many individuals of any species which are periodically born, but a small number can survive. I have called this principle, by which each slight variation, if useful, is preserved, by the term Natural Selection, in order to mark its relation to man's power of selection. But the expression often used by Mr. Herbert Spencer of the Survival of the Fittest is more accurate, and is sometimes equally convenient. We have seen that man by selection can certainly produce great results, and can adapt organic beings to his own uses, through the accumulation of slight but useful variations, given to him by the hand of Nature. But Natural Selection, as we shall hereafter see, is a power incessantly ready for action, and is as immeasurably superior to man's feeble efforts, as the works of Nature are to those of Art.

We will now discuss in a little more detail the struggle for existence. In my future work this subject will be treated, as it well deserves, at greater length. The elder De Candolle and Lyell have largely and philosophically shown that all organic beings are exposed to severe competition. In regard to plants, no one has treated this subject with more spirit and ability than W. Herbert, Dean of Manchester, evidently the result of his great horticultural knowledge. Nothing is easier than to admit in words the truth of the universal struggle for life, or more difficult—at least I have found it so—than constantly to bear this conclusion in mind. Yet unless it be thoroughly engrained in the mind, the whole economy of nature, with every fact on distribution, rarity, abundance, extinction, and variation, will be dimly seen or quite misunderstood. We behold the face of nature bright with gladness, we often see superabundance of food; we do not see or we forget, that the birds which are idly singing round us mostly live on insects or seeds, and are thus constantly destroying life; or we forget how largely these songsters, or their eggs, or their nestlings, are destroyed by birds and beasts of prey; we do not always bear in mind, that, though food may be now superabundant, it is not so at all seasons of each recurring year.

The Term, Struggle for Existence, Used in a Large Sense

I should premise that I use this term in a large and metaphorical sense including dependence of one being on another, and including (which is more important) not only the life of the individual, but success in leaving progeny. Two canine animals, in a time of dearth, may be truly said to struggle with each other which shall get food and live. But a plant on the edge of a desert is said to struggle for life against the drought, though more properly it should be said to be dependent on the moisture. A plant which annually produces a thousand seeds, of which only one of an average comes to maturity, may be more truly said to struggle with the plants of the same and other kinds which already clothe the ground. The mistletoe is dependent on the apple and a few other trees, but can only in a far-fetched sense be said to struggle with these trees, for, if too many of these parasites grow on the same tree, it languishes and dies. But several seedling mistletoes, growing close together on the same branch, may more truly be said to struggle with each other. As the mistletoe is disseminated by birds, its existence depends on them; and it may methodically be said to struggle with other fruit-bearing plants, in tempting the birds to devour and thus disseminate its seeds. In these several senses, which pass into each other, I use for convenience' sake the general term of Struggle for Existence.

Geometrical Ratio of Increase

A struggle for existence inevitably follows from the high rate at which all organic beings tend to increase. Every being, which during its natural lifetime produces several eggs or seeds, must suffer destruction during some period of its life, and during some season or occasional year, otherwise, on the principle of geometrical increase, its numbers would quickly become so inordinately great that no country could support the product. Hence, as more individuals are produced than can possibly survive, there must in every case be a struggle for existence, either one individual with another of the same species, or with the individuals of distinct species, or with the physical conditions of life. It is the doctrine of Malthus applied with manifold force to the whole animal and vegetable kingdoms; for in this case there can be no artificial increase of food, and no prudential restraint from marriage. Although some species may be now increasing, more or less rapidly, in numbers, all cannot do so, for the world would not hold them.

There is no exception to the rule that every organic being naturally increases at so high a rate, that, if not destroyed, the earth would soon be covered by the progeny of a single pair. Even slow-breeding man has doubled in twenty-five years, and at this rate, in less than a thousand years, there would literally not be standing-room for his progeny. Linnæus has calculated that if an annual plant produced only two seeds—and there is no plant so unproductive as this—and their seedlings next year produced two, and so on, then in twenty years there should be a million plants. The elephant is reckoned the slowest breeder of all known animals, and I have taken some pains to estimate its probable minimum rate of natural increase; it will be safest to assume that it begins breeding when thirty years old, and goes on breeding till ninety years old, bringing forth six young in the interval, and surviving till one hundred years old; if this be so, after a period of from 740 to 750 years there would be nearly nineteen million elephants alive, descended from the first pair.

But we have better evidence on this subject than mere theoretical calculations, namely, the numerous recorded cases of the astonishingly rapid increase of various animals in a state of nature, when circumstances have been favorable to them during two or three following seasons. Still more striking is the evidence from our domestic animals of many kinds which have run wild in several parts of the world; if the statements of the rate of increase of slow-breeding cattle and horses in South America, and latterly in Australia, had not been well authenticated, they would have been incredible. So it is with plants; cases could be given of introduced plants which have become common throughout whole islands in a period of less than ten years. Several of the plants, such as the cardoon and a tall thistle, which are now the commonest over the whole plains of La Plata, clothing square leagues of surface almost to the exclusion of every other plant, have been introduced from Europe; and there are plants which now range in India, as I hear from Dr. Falconer, from Cape Comorin to the Himalaya, which have been imported from America since its discovery. In such cases, and endless others could be given, no one supposes, that the fertility of the animals or plants has been suddenly and temporarily increased in any sensible degree. The obvious explanation is that the conditions of life have been highly favourable, and that there has consequently been less destruction of the old and young, and that nearly all the young have been enabled to breed. Their geometrical ratio of increase, the result of which never fails to be surprising, simply explains their extraordinarily rapid increase and wide diffusion in their new homes.

In a state of nature almost every full-grown plant annually produces seed, and amongst animals there are very few which do not annually pair. Hence we may confidently assert, that all plants and animals are tending to increase at a geometrical ratio,—that all would rapidly stock every station in which they could anyhow exist,—and that this geometrical tendency to increase must be checked by destruction at some period of life. Our familiarity with the larger domestic animals tends, I think, to mislead us: we see no great destruction falling on them, but we do not keep in mind that thousands are annually slaughtered for food, and that in a state of nature an equal number would have somehow to be disposed of.

The only difference between organisms which annually produce eggs or seeds by the thousand, and those which produce extremely few, is, that the slow-breeders would require a few more years to people, under favourable conditions, a whole district, let it be ever so large. The condor lays a couple of eggs and the ostrich a score, and yet in the same country the condor may be the more numerous of the two; the Fulmar petrel lays but one egg, yet it is believed to be the most numerous bird in the world. One fly deposits hundreds of eggs, and another, like the hippobosca, a single one; but this difference does not determine how many individuals of the two species can be supported in a district. A large number of eggs is of some importance to those species which depend on a fluctuating amount of food, for it allows them rapidly to increase in number. But the real importance of a large number of eggs or seeds is to make up for much destruction at some period of life; and this period in the great majority of cases is an early one. If an animal can in any way protect its own eggs or young, a small number may be produced, and yet the average stock be fully kept up; but if many eggs or young are destroyed, many must be produced, or the species will become extinct. It would suffice to keep up the full number of a tree, which lived on an average for a thousand years, if a single seed were produced once in a thousand years, supposing that this seed were never destroyed, and could be ensured to germinate in a fitting place. So that, in all cases, the average number of any animal or plant depends only indirectly on the number of its eggs or seeds.

In looking at Nature, it is most necessary to keep the foregoing considerations always in mind—never to forget that every single organic being may be said to be striving to the utmost to increase in numbers; that each lives by a struggle at some period of its life; that heavy destruction inevitably falls either on the young or old, during each generation or at recurrent intervals. Lighten any check, mitigate the destruction ever so little, and the number of the species will almost instantaneously increase to any amount. . . .

Suggestions for Discussion and Writing

1. In the opening paragraph of his Introduction, Darwin gives some "personal details" regarding his long-standing interest in the origin of species to show that he has "not been hasty" in arriving at his views. Can you think of at least two reasons why the issue of haste might have been important to him? Do you see evidence that Darwin published his work sooner than originally planned?

2. In the first sentence of his Introduction, Darwin speaks of the "geological relations of the present to past inhabitants" of South America. What does he mean by "geological relations"?

3. What explanations for "modification" and "coadaptation" did Darwin's study of domesticated animals and cultivated plants lead him to reject?

4. Why does Darwin prefer to use the term "natural selection" over Herbert Spencer's "survival of the fittest" which, he says, "is more accurate" and "sometimes equally convenient"?

5. Write an essay in which you explain what Darwin means by the term "struggle for existence." How is this notion related to natural selection? In what sense is Darwin's use of the word "struggle" metaphorical?

6. Why is extinction inevitably associated with natural selection?

7. Why does the "average number of any animal or plant" depend only indirectly on "the number of its eggs or seeds"? What other factors are involved?

8. What fundamental point about the origin of species is Darwin arguing? Does he clearly state the view he is rejecting?

9. Does Darwin use examples effectively? What should we infer from his selection of examples? Write an essay in which you discuss his particular selections to support your view.

10. *The Origin of Species* was a revolutionary work. (See Ernst Mayr's essay in Chapter 1.) Do you see evidence in either tone or content of his argument that Darwin expected strong opposition to his ideas?

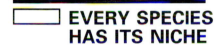 **EVERY SPECIES HAS ITS NICHE**

Paul Colinvaux
(b. 1930)

A celebrated teacher, British-born Paul Colinvaux has been a professor of zoology at Ohio State University since 1964. He earned degrees from Cambridge and Duke universities.

Colinvaux has done extensive field work at various locations throughout the world, including Alaska, the Galapagos, Peru, and Ecuador, and has served on the advisory subcommittee for ecological sciences of the National Science Foundation. In addition to his contributions to professional journals such as *Science*, *Nature*, and *Ecology*, Colinvaux has written several books, including *The Fates of Nations: A Biological Theory of History* (1980) and *Basic Ecology (1985)*. His book, *Why Big Fierce Animals Are Rare: An Ecologist's Perspective* (1978), has been described as "a model of scientific explanation." In the following excerpt from that book,

Colinvaux discusses the complex relationship between the individual species and its niche, and the place of both in "the grand scheme of things."

E very species has its niche, its place in the grand scheme of things.

Consider a wolf-spider as it hunts through the litter of leaves on the woodland floor. It must be a splendid hunter; that goes without saying for otherwise its line would long since have died out. But it must be proficient at other things too. Even as it hunts, it must keep some of its eight eyes on the look-out for the things that hunt it; and when it sees an enemy it must do the right thing to save itself. It must know what to do when it rains. It must have a life style that enables it to survive the winter. It must rest safely when the time is not apt for hunting. And there comes a season of the year when the spiders, as it were, feel the sap rising in their eight legs. The male must respond by going to look for a female spider, and when he finds her, he must convince her that he is not merely something to eat—yet. And she, in the fullness of time, must carry an egg-sack as she goes about her hunting, and later must let the babies ride on her back. They, in turn, must learn the various forms of fending for themselves as they go through the different moults of the spider's life until they, too, are swift-running, pouncing hunters of the woodland floor.

Wolf-spidering is a complex job, not something to be undertaken by an amateur. We might say that there is a profession of wolf-spidering. It is necessary to be good at all its manifold tasks to survive at it. What is more, the profession is possible only in very restricted circumstances. A woodland floor is necessary, for instance, and the right climate with a winter roughly like that your ancestors were used to; and enough of the right sorts of things to hunt, and the right shelter when you need it; and the numbers of natural enemies must be kept within reasonable bounds. For success, individual spiders must be superlatively good at their jobs and the right circumstances must prevail. Unless both the skills of spidering and the opportunity are present, there will not be any wolf-spiders. The "niche" of wolf-spidering will not be filled.

"Niche" is a word ecologists have borrowed from church architecture. In a church, of course, "niche" means a recess in the wall in which a figurine may be placed; it is an address, a location, a physical place. But the ecologist's "niche" is more than just a physical place: it is a place in the grand scheme of things. The niche is an animal's (or a plant's) profession. The niche of the wolf-spider is everything it does to get its food and raise its babies. To be able to do these things it must relate properly to the place where it lives and to the other inhabitants of that place. Everything the species does to survive and stay "fit" in the Darwinian sense is its niche.

The physical living place in an ecologist's jargon is called the *habitat*. The habitat is the "address" or "location" in which individuals of a species live: The woodland floor hunted by the wolf-spiders is the habitat, but wolf-spidering is their niche. It is the niche of wolf-spidering that has been fashioned by natural selection.

The idea of "niche" at once gives us a handle to one of those general questions that ecologists want to answer—the question of the constancy of numbers. The common stay common, and the rare stay rare, because the opportunities for each niche, or profession, are set by circumstance. Wolf-spidering needs the right sort of neighbors living in the right sort of wood, and the number of times that this combination comes up in any country is limited. So the number of wolf-spiders is limited also; the number was fixed when the niche was adopted. This number is likely to stay constant until something drastic happens to change the face of the country.

Likening an animal's niche to a human profession makes this idea of limits to number very clear. Let us take the profession of professing. There can only be as many professors in any city as there are teaching and scholarship jobs for professors to do. If the local university turns out more research scholars than there are professing jobs, then some of these hopeful young people will not be able to accept the scholar's tenure, however *cum laude* their degrees. They will have to emigrate, or take to honest work to make a living.

Likewise there cannot be more wolf-spiders than there are wolf-spider jobs, antelopes than there are antelope jobs, crab grass than there are crab grass jobs. Every species has its niche. And once its niche is fixed by natural selection, so also are its numbers fixed.

This idea of niche gets at the numbers problem without any discussion of breeding effort. Indeed, it shows that the way an animal breeds has very little to do with how many of it there are. This is a very strange idea to someone new to it, and it needs to be thought about carefully. *The reproductive effort makes no difference to the eventual size of the population.* Numerous eggs may increase numbers in the short term, following some disaster, but only for a while. The numbers that may live are set by the number of niche-spaces (jobs) in the environment, and these are quite independent of how fast a species makes babies.

But all the same each individual must try to breed as fast as it can. It is in a race with its neighbors of the same kind, a race that will decide whose babies will fill the niche-space jobs of the next generation. The actual number of those who will be able to live in that next generation has been fixed by the environment; we may say that the population will be a function of the *carrying capacity* of the land for animals of this kind in that time and place. But the issue of whose babies will take up those limited places is absolutely open. It is here that natural selection operates. A "fit" individual is, by definition, one that successfully takes up one of the niche-spaces from the limited pool, and the fitness of a parent is measured by how many future niche-spaces her or his offspring take up. "Survival of the fittest" means survival of those who leave the most living descendants. A massive breeding effort makes no difference to the future population, but it is vital for the hereditary future of one's own line. This is why everything that lives has the capacity for large families.

Yet there are degrees of largeness in wild families, and these degrees of largeness make sense when looked at with an ecologist's eye. The intuitively obvious consequence of a law that says "Have the largest possible family or face hereditary oblivion," is the family based on thousands of tiny eggs or seeds. This seems to be the commonest breeding strategy. Houseflies, mosquitoes, salmon, and dandelions all do it. I call it "the small-egg gambit." It has very obvious advantages, but there are also costs, which the clever ones with big babies avoid.

For users of the small-egg gambit, natural selection starts doing the obvious sums. If an egg is made just a little bit smaller, the parent might be able to make an extra egg for the same amount of food eaten, and this will give it a slight edge in the evolutionary race. It is enough. Natural selection will therefore choose families that make more and more of smaller and smaller eggs until a point of optimum smallness is reached. If the eggs are any smaller than this, the young may all die; if they are any larger, one's neighbor will swamp one's posterity with her mass-production. The largest number of the smallest possible eggs makes simple Darwinian sense.

But the costs of the small-egg gambit are grim. An inevitable consequence is that babies are thrown out into the world naked and tiny. Most of them as a result die, and early death is the common lot of baby salmon, dandelions, and the rest. In the days before Darwin, people used to say that the vast families of salmon, dandelions, and insects were compensations for the slaughter of the young. So terrible was the life of a baby fish that Providence provided a salmon with thousands of eggs to give it a chance that one or two might get through. It seems a natural assumption, and one that still confuses even some biologists. But the argument is the wrong way round. A high death rate for the tiny, helpless young is a consequence of the thousands of tiny eggs, not a cause. A selfish race of neighbor against neighbor leads to those thousands of tiny eggs, and the early deaths of the babies are the cost of this selfishness.

There is this to be said for the small-egg gambit, though; once you have been forced into it, there are the gambler's compensations. Many young scattered far and wide mean an intensive search for opportunity, and this may pay off when opportunity is thinly scattered in space. Weed and plague species win this advantage, as when the parachute seed of a dandelion is wafted between the trunks of the trees of a forest to alight on the fresh-turned earth of a rabbit burrow. The small-egg gambits of weeds may be likened to the tactics of a gambler at a casino who covers every number with a low-value chip. If he has enough chips, he is bound to win, particularly if big payoffs are possible. He does have to have very many chips to waste, though. This is why economists do not approve of gamblers.

To the person with an economic turn of mind, the small-egg gambit, for all its crazy logic, does not seem a proper way to manage affairs. The adherents of this gambit spend all their lives at their professions, winning as many resources as possible from their living places, and then they invest these resources in tiny babies, most of whom are going to die. What a ridiculously low return on capital. What economic folly. Any economist could tell these animals and plants that the real way to win in the hereditary stakes is to put all your capital into a lesser number of big strong babies, all of which are going to survive. A number of animals in fact do this. I call it "the large-young gambit."

In the large-young gambit one either makes a few huge eggs out of the food available, or the babies actually grow inside their mother, where they are safe. Either way, each baby has a very good chance of living to grow up. It is big to start with and it is fed or defended by parents until it can look after itself. Most of the food the parents collect goes into babies who live. There is little waste. Natural selection approves of this as much as do economists. Big babies who have a very good chance of long life mean more surviving offspring for the amount of food-investment in the end. This prudent outlay of resources is arranged by birds, viviparous snakes, great white sharks, goats, tigers, and people.

Having a few, large young, and then nursing them until they are big and strong, is the surest existing method of populating the future. Yet the success of this gambit assumes one essential condition. You must start with just the right number of young. If you lay too many monster hen's eggs or drop too many bawling brats, you may not be able to supply them with enough food, and some or all will die. You have then committed the economic wastefulness of those of the tiny eggs. So you must not be too ambitious in your breeding. But the abstemious will also lose out, because its neighbor may raise one more baby, may populate the future just that little bit better, and start your line on a one-way ride to hereditary oblivion. You must get it just right; not too many young, and not too few. Natural selection will preserve those family strains which are programmed to "choose" the best or optimum size of family.

Many ecologists have studied birds with these ideas in mind, and they have found that there is often a very good correlation between the number of eggs in a clutch and the food supply. In a year when food is plentiful a bird may lay, on the average, one or two eggs more than in a lean season. The trend may be slight but sometimes is quite obvious. Snowy owls, which are big white birds of the arctic tundra, build vast nests on the ground. They feed their chicks on lemmings, and the small brown arctic mice. When lemmings are scarce, there may be only one or two eggs in each owl's nest, but when the tundra is crawling with lemmings, the nests may well have ten eggs each. The owls are evidently clever at assessing how many chicks they can afford each year.

But people are cleverer than snowy owls and have brought the large-young gambit to its perfection. They can read the environment, guess the future, and plan their families according to what their intelligence tells them they can afford. Even the infanticide practiced by various peoples at various times serves the cause of Darwinian fitness, rather than acting as a curb on population. There is no point in keeping alive babies who could not be supported for long. Killing babies who could not be safely reared gives a better chance of survival to those who are left, and infanticide in hard times can mean that more children grow up in the end.

Thus, every species has its niche, its place in the grand scheme of things; and every species has a breeding strategy refined by natural selection to leave the largest possible number of surviving offspring. The requirement for a definite niche implies a limit to the size of the population because the numbers of the animal or plant are set by the opportunities for carrying on life in that niche. The kind of breeding strategy, on the other hand, has no effect on the size of the usual population, and the drive to breed is a struggle to decide which family strains have the privilege of taking up the limited numbers of opportunities for life. Every family tries to outbreed every other, though the total numbers of their kind remain the same. These are the principles on which an ecologist can base his effort to answer the major questions of his discipline.

Suggestions for Discussion and Writing

1. Good writing is usually concrete, particularized. At what point in his essay does Colinvaux first turn to a specific case? What does he achieve by his use of this particular example?

2. In the third paragraph the author says that "wolf-spidering is a complex job, not something to be undertaken by an amateur." Later, he likens an animal's "niche" to a human profession. Is this a helpful comparison? What other analogies does the author use?

3. Scientists must often define terms, especially when addressing the general reader. Does Colinvaux define his terms effectively?

4. Colinvaux says that "the way an animal breeds has very little to do with how many of it there are." Would Darwin agree? Why does the "reproductive effort" make "no difference to the eventual size of the population"?

5. Colinvaux uses the term "natural selection" several times. In what sense is selection "natural"?

6. Write an essay explaining what Colinvaux means by "Darwinian fitness."

7. Why, for a person "with an economic turn of mind," does the "small-egg gambit" not seem "a proper way to manage affairs"? Why, conversely, do both "natural selection" and "economists" approve of the "large-young gambit"?

8. The author says that "people are cleverer than snowy owls and have brought the large-young gambit to its perfection." Write an essay in which you explore the implications of this statement for human populations.

9. Compare the first and final paragraphs. What is the function of the final paragraph?

☐ THE GUANO RING

Stephen Jay Gould
(b. 1941)

Like many paleontologists, Stephen Jay Gould admits to having started his scientific life as a "dinosaur nut." Having received his doctorate from Columbia in 1967, Gould has since exercised his passion for dinosaurs as curator of paleontology and professor of zoology at Harvard University. He has become one of the most prominent advocates of the evolutionary theory known as "punctuated equilibrium," a modification of Darwinism that sees development and change in species not as the product of slowly accruing mutations (as the "gradualists" believe) but as the result of events that occur swiftly over a relatively short span of time. According to this theory, a species will return to equilibrium following these rapid changes, with natural selection acting to stabilize the species rather than alter it. One implication of this controversial hypothesis is that the "missing link" long sought by some traditional Darwinists does not exist.

The author of many scientific works, Gould has also written extensively for a wider audience. Books such as *The Panda's Thumb* (1980), *The Mismeasure of Man* (1981), and *Hen's Teeth and Horse's Toes* (1983) are much admired for their style and their accessibility to the general reader. For many years Gould has also written a monthly column, "This View of Life," for *Natural History* magazine.

In "The Guano Ring," from *Hen's Teeth and Horse's Toes*, Gould explores the complex social behavior of nesting boobies, birds found on the Galapagos Islands, and shows how this behavior creates an "evolutionary advantage" for the species.

When I first went to sea as a petrified urbanite who had never ridden anything larger than a rowboat, an old sailor (and Navy man) told me that I could chart my way through this *aqua incognita* if I remembered but one simple rule for life and work aboard a ship: if it moves, salute it; if it doesn't move, paint it.

If we analyze why such a statement counts as a joke (albeit a feeble one) in our culture, we must cite the incongruity of placing such a "mindless" model for making decisions inside a human skull. After all, the essence of human intelligence is creative flexibility, our skill in grasping new and complex contexts—in short, our ability to make (as we call them) judgments, rather than to act by the dictates of rigid, preset rules. We are, as Konrad Lorenz has stated, "specialists in nonspecialization." We do not behave as machines with simple yes-no switches, invariably triggered by definite bits of information present in our immediate environments. Our enlightened sailor, no matter how successful at combating rust or avoiding the brig, is not following a human style of intelligence.

Yet this inflexible model does represent the style of intelligence followed with great success by most other animals. The decisions of animals are usually unambiguous yeses or noes triggered by definite signals, not subtle choices based upon the assessment of a complex gestalt.

Many birds, for example, do not recognize their own young and act instead by the rule: care for what is inside the nest; ignore what is outside. British ethologist W. H. Thorpe writes: "Most birds, while they may be very attentive to their young in the nest, are completely callous and unresponsive to those same young when, as a result of some accident, they are outside the nest or the immediate nest territory."

This rule rarely poses evolutionary dilemmas for birds, since the objects in their nests are usually their own young (carrying their Darwinian heritage of shared genes). But this inflexible style of intelligence can be exploited and commandeered to a nefarious purpose by other species. Cuckoos, for example, lay their eggs in the nests of other birds. A cuckoo hatchling, usually larger and more vigorous than the rightful inhabitants, often expels its legitimate nest mates, which then die, frantically begging for food, while their parents follow the rule: ignore them for their inappropriate location, and feed the young cuckoo instead. We can intellectualize our anthropomorphism away, but we cannot expunge it from our aesthetic reactions. I must confess that no scene of organic activity makes me angrier about the world's injustice than the sight of a foster parent, its own young killed by a cuckoo, solicitously feeding a begging parasite that may be up to five times its own size (cuckoos often choose much smaller birds as their hosts, and the fledglings may be much larger than their foster parents).

During a recent trip to the Galápagos Islands, I encountered another, interestingly different, example of birds that twist this common rule to different uses. This time, both the victim and benefactor are true siblings and the end result, although condemning weaker siblings to death, is evolutionary advantage for family lines.

The boobies (along with their cousins, the gannets) form a small (nine species) but widespread family of seabirds, the Sulidae. (Everything, and more, that you will ever want to know about sulids you will find in J. Bryan Nelson's magnificent monograph: *The Sulidae: Gannets and Boobies,* 1978.) Earliest references in the Oxford English Dictionary indicate that boobies received their unflattering name, not for the distinctive waddling walk of one major display, big feet out and head held high in a behavior called "sky pointing," but for their remarkable tameness, which allowed sailors (bent only on destruction) to catch them so easily.

Three species of sulids inhabit the Galápagos Islands: the red-footed, the blue-footed, and the masked booby. The red-footed booby lays a single egg in a conventional nest built near the tops and edges of trees and bushes. By contrast, its cousin of markedly different natural pedicure, the blue-footed booby, lays its eggs on the ground and builds no true nest at all. Instead, it delimits the nesting area in a remarkable and efficient way: it squirts guano (birdshit to nonornithologists who have not read *Doctor No*) in all directions around itself, thus producing a symmetrical white ring as a symbolic marker of its nest.

Within this ring, the female blue-foot lays, not one (as in many boobies), but from one to three eggs. In his most impressive discovery, Nelson has explained much about the breeding behavior and general ecology of boobies by linking the production of eggs and young to the quality and style of feeding in parents. Boobies that travel long distances (up to 300 miles) to locate scarce sources of food, tend to lay but a single large egg, hatching into a resilient chick that can survive long intervals between parental feedings. On the other hand, when food sources are rich, dependable, and near, more eggs are laid and more young reared. At the extreme of this tendency lies the Peruvian booby, with its clutch of two to four eggs (averaging three) and its ability to raise all chicks to adulthood. Peruvian boobies feed on the teeming anchovies of their local waters, fish that may be almost as densely packed in the ocean as in the sardine cans that may become their posthumous home.

The blue-foot lies between these two tendencies. It is a nearshore feeder, but its sources have neither the richness nor the predictability of swarming anchovies. Consequently, conditions vary drastically from generation to generation. The blue-foot has therefore evolved a flexible strategy based on the exploitation by older siblings of their parents' intellectual style: yes-no decisions triggered by simple signals. In good times, parents may lay up to three eggs and successfully fledge all three chicks; in poor years, they may still lay two or three eggs and hatch all their chicks, but only one can survive. The death of nest (or, rather, ring) mates is not the haphazard result of a losing struggle to feed all chicks with insufficient food, but a highly systematic affair based on indirect murder by the oldest sibling.

I was reminded of the quip about painting and saluting while observing blue-footed boobies on Hood Island in the Galápagos. Their guano rings cover the volcanic surface in many places, often blocking the narrow paths that visitors must tread in these well protected islands. Parents sit on their eggs and young chicks, apparently oblivious to groups of visitors who gawk, gesticulate, and point cameras within inches of their territory. Yet I noticed, at first by accident, that any intrusion into a guano ring would alter the behavior of the adult birds from blissful ignorance to directed aggression. A single toe across the ring elicited an immediate barrage of squawking, posturing, and pecking. A few casual experiments led me to the tentative conclusion that the boundary is an invisible circle right in the middle of the ring. I could cautiously advance my toe across the outer part of the ring with no effect; but as I moved it forward, as slowly and as unobtrusively as possible, I invariably passed a central point that brought on the pronounced parental reaction all at once.

Three hours later, I learned from our excellent guides and from Bryan Nelson's popular book (*Galápagos: Islands of Birds*), how older siblings exploit this parental behavior. And, anthropomorphic as we all must be, it sent a shiver of wonder and disgust up my spine. (Science, to a large extent, consists of enhancing the first reaction and suppressing the second.) The female blue-foot lays her eggs several days apart, and they hatch in the same order. The firstborn sibling is thus larger and considerably stronger than its one or two ring mates. When food is abundant, parents feed all chicks adequately and the firstborn does not molest its younger siblings. But when food is scarce and only one chick can survive, the actions of younger sibs evoke (how, we do not know) a different behavior by big sister or brother. The oldest simply pushes its younger siblings outside the guano ring. As human mammals, our first reaction might be: so what? The younger sibs are not physically hurt and they end up but a few inches from the ring, where parents will surely notice their plaintive sounds and struggling motions and gather them quickly back.

But a parental booby does no such thing, for it operates like our proverbial sailor who made an either-or judgment by invoking the single criterion of movement. Parental boobies work by the rule: if a chick is inside the ring, care for it; if it is outside, ignore it. Even if the chick should flop, by happenstance, upon the ring, it will be rejected with all the vehemence applied to my transgressing toe.

We saw a chick on Hood Island struggling just a foot outside the ring in plain sight of the parent within, sitting (in an attitude that we tend to read as maternal affection) upon the triumphant older sibling (which did not, however, seem to be smirking). Every mother's son and daughter among us longed to replace the small chick, but a belief in noninterference must be respected even when it hurts. For if we understand this system aright, such a slaughter of the innocents is a hecatomb for success of the lineages practicing it. Older chicks only expel their siblings when food cannot be secured to raise them all. A parental struggle to raise three on food for one would probably lead to the death of all.

The rule of "nurture within, ignore or reject outside" cannot represent all the complexity of social behavior in nesting boobies. After all, most birds are noted "egalitarians" in their division of labor between sexes, and male boobies are almost as attentive as females in incubating eggs and chicks. Since each brooding stint lasts about a day, boobies must permit their mates to transgress the sanctity of the guano ring when exchanging roles of care and provision. Still, the basic rule remains in force; it is not flouted but rather overridden by specific and recognized signals that act as a ticket of admission. K. E. L. Simmons, working on Ascension Island with the related brown booby, described the extensive series of calls and landing rituals that returning mates use to gain admission to their territory. But when adults trespass upon the unattended territory of an unrelated bird (as they often do to scrounge nest material on the cheap), they enter as "silently and as inconspicuously as possible."

If chicks could perform the overriding behavior, they too could win readmission to the ring. Indeed, they learn these signals as they age, as well they must, for older chicks begin to wander from the ring as they gain sufficient mobility for such travels at about four to five weeks of age. (Nelson argues that they wander primarily to seek shade when both parents are foraging; overheating is a primary cause of death in booby chicks.) Yet hatchling boobies display only a few behaviors—little more than food begging and bill hiding (appeasement) gestures, as Nelson demonstrates—and the overriding signals for entrance into the ring are not among them.

The third species of the Galápagos, the white, or masked, booby, works on a more rigid system, but follows the same rules as its blue-footed cousin. Masked boobies are distant foragers, feeding primarily on flying fish. By Nelson's maxim, they should be able to raise but one chick. Sometimes, masked boobies lay only one egg, but usually they provision each nesting site with two. In this case, "brood reduction" (to use the somewhat euphemistic jargon) is obligatory. The older chick always pushes its younger sibling outside the nest (or occasionally stomps it to death within). This system seems, at first, to make no sense. The blue-foots, whatever our negative, if inappropriate, emotional reactions, at least use sibling murder as a device to match the number of chicks to the fluctuating supply of available food.

By what perverse logic should masked boobies produce two eggs, yet never rear more than one chick invariably branded with the mark of Cain? Nelson argues forcefully that clutches of two eggs represent an adaptation for generally increased success in raising *one* chick. The causes of death in eggs and young hatchlings are numerous— siblings intent upon murder being only one of many dangers to which booby flesh is heir. Eggs crack or roll from the nest; tiny hatchlings easily overheat. The second egg may represent insurance against death of the first chick. A healthy first chick cancels the policy directly, but the added investment may benefit parents as a hedge worth the expense of producing another egg (they will, after all, never need to expend much energy in feeding an unnecessary second chick). At Kure Atoll in the Hawaiian Archipelago, for example, clutches of two eggs successfully fledged one chick in 68 percent of nests examined during three years. But clutches of one egg fledged their single chick only 32 percent of the time.

Evolutionary biologists, by long training and ingrained habit, tend to discuss such phenomena as the siblicide of boobies in the language of adaptation; how does a behavior that seems, at first sight, harmful and irrational really represent an adaptation finely honed by natural selection for the benefit of struggling individuals? Indeed, I have (and somewhat uncharacteristically for me) used the conventional language in this essay, for Nelson's work persuades me that siblicide is a Darwinian adaptation for maximizing the success of parents in rearing the largest number of chicks permitted by prevailing abundances of food.

But I am most uncomfortable in attributing the basic behavior style, which permits siblicide as a specific manifestation, only to adaptation, although this too is usually done. I speak here of the basic mode of intelligence that permits siblicide to work: the sailor's system (of my opening paragraph) based on yes-no decisions triggered by definite signals. John Alcock, for example, in a leading contemporary text (*Animal Behavior: An Evolutionary Approach,* 1975) argues over and over again that this common intellectual style is, in itself and in general, an adaptation directly fashioned by natural selection for optimal responses in prevailing environments: "Programmed responses are widespread," he writes, "because animals that base their behavior on relatively simple signals provided by important objects in their environment are likely to do the biologically proper thing."

(On the overwhelming power of natural selection, no less a personage than H.R.H. Prince Philip, duke of Edinburgh, has written in the preface to Nelson's popular book on birds of the Galápagos: "The process of natural selection has controlled the very minutest detail of every feature of the whole individual and the group to which it belongs." I do not cite this passage facetiously to win an argument by saddling a position I do not accept with a mock seal of royal approval, but rather to indicate how widely the language of strict adaptation has moved beyond professional circles into the writing of well-informed amateurs.)

As I argued for siblicide and guano rings, I am prepared to view any specific manifestation of my sailor's intellectual style as an adaptation. But I cannot, as Alcock claims, view the style itself as no more than the optimized product of unconstrained natural selection. The smaller brain and more limited neural circuitry of nonhuman animals must impose, or at least encourage, intellectual modes different from our own. These smaller brains need not be viewed as direct adaptations to any prevailing condition. They represent, rather, inherited structural constraints that limit the range of specific adaptations fashioned within their orbit. The sailor's style is a constraint that permits boobies to reduce their broods by exploiting a behavioral repertoire based on inflexible rules and simple triggers. Such a system would not work in humans, for parents will not cease to recognize their babies after a small and simple change in location. In human societies that practice infanticide (for ecological reasons often quite similar to those inducing siblicide in boobies), explicit social rules or venerated religious traditions—rather than mere duplicity by removal—must force or persuade parental action.

Birds may have originally developed their brain, with its characteristic size, as an adaptation to life in an ancestral lineage more than 200 million years ago; the sailor's style of intelligence may be a nonadaptive consequence of this inherited design. Yet this style has set the boundaries of behavior ever since. Each individual behavior may be a lovely adaptation, but it must be fashioned within a prevailing constraint. Which is more important: the beauty of the adaptation or the constraint that limits it to a permissible path? We cannot and need not choose, for both factors define an essential tension that regulates all evolution.

The sources of organic form and behavior are manifold and include at least three primary categories. We have just discussed two: immediate adaptations fashioned by natural selection (exploitation by older booby siblings of their parents' intellectual style, leading to easy dispatch of nest mates); and potentially nonadaptive consequences of basic structural designs acting as constraints upon the pathways of adaptation (the intellectual style of yes-no decisions based on simple triggers).

In a third category, we find definite ancestral adaptations now used by descendants in different ways. Nelson has shown, for example, that boobies reinforce the pair-bond between male and female through a complex series of highly ritualized behaviors that include gathering objects and presenting them to mates. In boobies that lay their eggs upon the ground, these behaviors are clearly relics of actions that once served to gather material for ancestral nests—for some of the detailed motions that still build nests in related species are followed, while others have been lost. The egg-laying areas of masked boobies are strewn with appropriate bits of twigs and other nesting materials that adults gather for their mutual displays and then must sweep out of the guano ring to lie unused upon the ground. I have emphasized these curious changes in function in several other essays for they are the primary proof of evolution—forms and actions that only make sense in the light of a previous, inherited history.

When I wonder how three such disparate sources can lead to the harmonious structures that organisms embody, I temper my amazement by remembering the history of languages. Consider the amalgam that English represents—vestiges, borrowings, fusions. Yet poets continue to create things of beauty. Historical pathways and current uses are different aspects of a common subject. The pathways are intricate beyond all imagining, but only the hearty travelers remain with us.

Suggestions for Discussion and Writing

1. In the second paragraph Gould says that "the essence of human intelligence is creative flexibility" and that "we do not behave as machines with simple yes-no switches, invariably triggered by definite bits of information present in our immediate environments." What are the implications of this statement for the possibility of artificial intelligence? (You may wish to consult Joseph Weizenbaum's essay in Chapter 4.)

2. Gould says several times in his essay that scientists should not introduce anthropomorphic (for instance, moral and emotional) views into their judgments of events in the natural world. Is Gould himself entirely successful in this regard?

3. Gould refers to the killing of booby chicks as "a slaughter of the innocents." He later says that the surviving chicks are "invariably branded with the mark of Cain." What is the effect of such statements? (You might wish to look up the derivations of "slaughter of the innocents" and "mark of Cain.")

4. Why did Gould resist the temptation to place the struggling booby chick back inside the ring?

5. Why do masked boobies usually "produce two eggs, yet never rear more than one chick"?

6. Gould is persuaded that "siblicide is a Darwinian adaptation for maximizing the success of parents in rearing the largest number of chicks permitted by prevailing abundances of food." Why is he unwilling, though, to attribute "the basic mode of intelligence that permits siblicide to work" solely to adaptation fashioned by natural selection?

7. Do Gould and Colinvaux ("Every Species Has Its Niche," this chapter) agree on the function of infanticide in human societies? Why, according to Gould, is this practice associated with "explicit social rules or venerated religious traditions"?

8. Is Gould's analogy (in the final paragraph) between the evolutionary process and the English language a useful one? What points about evolution does it help Gould to make?

9. Write a brief essay in which you explore Gould's use of humor in "The Guano Ring." What purpose does this humor serve?

SENSORY FUNCTION IN THE HARBOR SEAL

Deane Renouf
(b. 1950)

Deane Renouf received her Ph.D. in 1975 from Dalhousie University in Nova Scotia and is currently a professor of biopsychology at Memorial University in Newfoundland. She has done extensive research into the behavior and physiology of seals and has published in numerous professional journals. Her first book, *The Behavior of the Pinnipeds,* appeared in 1991. In the following essay (from *Scientific American,* April 1989), Renouf describes the experiments she conducted to gain a better understanding of the extraordinary sensory adaptation of the harbor seal to its dark-water environment.

At night seals navigate through murky waters to find fish; during the day they often haul out on land, where they lie in the sun and, once a year, give birth to their young. Dividing time between land and water in such a fashion has its price: seals, like other members of the Pinnipedia (the order to which seals, sea lions, and walruses belong), have had to adapt to two separate sets of physical challenges. Sound and light behave differently in air and in water, and sensory organs that are adapted for one habitat tend to function differently in the other. Consider the seal's eye. How, if it is designed to function in water, does it also function on land? On what types of special sensory receptors does the seal rely on to find its way through turbid, choppy waters?

For the past 19 years I have been studying sensory function in the harbor seal, *Phoca vitulina.* The species is a good model for understanding how pinnipeds in general have adapted to an amphibious existence and is of special interest to me because it is found in coastal waters near my home in Newfoundland. Still, after many years of observing the animal—both in its natural habitat and in captivity—I continue to be puzzled by some of its sensory capabilities.

Although it is a common species along the northern coasts of the Atlantic and Pacific oceans, *P. vitulina* is notoriously difficult to study under natural field conditions. It is extremely skittish and flees into the ocean at the slightest provocation. Such behavior makes quantitative studies nearly impossible and has discouraged many investigators. I have been lucky, however, because I have found a site on Miquelon Island (some 18 kilometers off the southeast tip of Newfoundland) that is uniquely suited for observing seal colonies at close range.

During the reproductive season—in late spring and early summer—when the tide is low, about 800 seals (both male and female) cluster on exposed sand flats near the center of a large lagoon called the Grand Barachois. Females give birth at this time and remain with their pups until they are weaned at about four weeks of age. The seal's daily activities are synchronized with the tide: when the tide is high, the seals (including mothers and pups) are forced off the sand flats and into the water, where they stay until the tide recedes and the flats are again exposed. My colleagues and I have constructed elevated observation blinds adjacent to the sand flats, from which we can watch the seals at close range without disturbing them. We discovered that if we enter the blinds during high tide, the animals will pay us little or no attention when they return at low tide. From this vantage we have been able to observe how the seals have adapted to several crucial environmental challenges.

John W. Lawson, one of my graduate students, was the first to document controlled labor in the harbor seal, a physiological adaptation that allows females to accelerate or delay a pup's birth according to environmental conditions. On three occasions when a female in the final stages of labor was disturbed by the arrival of a group of tourists, Lawson saw the emerging head of the pup disappear back into the birth canal and labor come to a halt, resuming only after the disturbance had passed. We suspect that the ability of a seal to control the timing of her pup's birth is an adaptation that minimizes the risk of predation and enables seals to synchronize their labor with the onset of low tide.

While we were observing the breeding colony from our elevated blinds I became interested in the close relation that exists between females and their pups. The seal's amphibious habits and skittish behavior make bonding between mothers and their offspring somewhat problematic. I have seen a pup less than 15 minutes old follow its mother into the ocean, where visibility is often low, the current is strong and the level of ambient noise (caused by wind, choppy water and turbulence) is high. If a mother and her pup become separated, the likelihood of reunion is slim; this prediction is underscored by the fact that in some colonies as many as 10 percent of the unweaned pups starve to death every year when they are separated from their mothers.

How—if the seals rush into the ocean at the slightest disturbance—does a newborn pup manage to stay with its mother? It appears that a number of factors are responsible. The harbor seal pup demonstrates a following response (something like imprinting in birds) within the first few minutes of life and will follow its mother wherever she goes. The relationship is reciprocal: the mother in turn monitors the whereabouts of her pup. Females track their pups visually (in the water they can be seen stretching their heads backward to get an upside-down look at them) and also acoustically: a harbor seal pup vocalizes almost continuously when following its mother, emitting a call that is transmitted in air and underwater simultaneously; the call disappears from its repertoire soon after weaning.

To test whether a mother can recognize her pup by its call, Elizabeth Perry, one of my graduate students, and I recorded the calls of newborn pups and analyzed them sonographically. We found that each pup's call has a unique frequency pattern and wondered whether these differences could be discerned by a female seal.

To answer that question we devised an experiment to test a female's ability to distinguish among calls. At the Ocean Sciences Centre of Memorial University we trained a captive seal to open the door of a specific feeder when she heard one call and to open the door of another feeder when she heard a different call. Every time she made a correct association we rewarded her with herring. Six different calls were presented in various combinations; after a brief training period she was able to distinguish among the calls at least 80 percent of the time, a finding that leads us to believe females can recognize their pups in the ocean by their vocal emissions.

Vocalization is clearly an important means by which a mother and pup stay together, and yet the harbor seal lives in an environment dominated by high noise levels. How can a mother hear the call of her pup when the background noise (above water) may reach 80 decibels or more (a level comparable to that generated in an urban setting by heavy traffic)? When the ambient noise levels are high, can seals detect sounds that for human beings and other animals are masked by background noise?

I initiated a series of experiments to determine the extent to which noise affects the auditory threshold of the harbor seal. I trained two animals to swim to a paddle on one side of the tank when they heard a tone (a short burst of approximately 25 decibels, which was presented simultaneously with either 60-, 70-, or 80-decibel white noise) and to swim to a paddle on the other side if they did not hear a tone. I found that the auditory threshold of a harbor seal is raised when background noise levels are high and that the seal, like other mammals, has no special ability to compensate for noise. Extrapolating from these findings, I calculated that a pup can be heard only if it stays within about eight meters of its mother.

Within that radius of eight meters, however, females are adept at locating their young. I believe such an ability may be attributed to a unique quadraphonic hearing arrangement that enables them to determine from what direction a sound has come. On land sound reaches the seal's inner ear—as it does in most mammals—through the auditory meatus, or canal, and its direction is determined by the difference in arrival time at each ear. (In addition, certain sound characteristics such as volume and wave pattern are affected by arrival time.) In water, where sound travels about four times faster than it does in air, the difference in arrival time is much more difficult to detect.

Bertel Möhl of the Zoological Institute in Aarhus, Denmark, has shown, however, that in water sound is conducted to the seal's inner ear through a special vertical band of tissue that extends downward from the ear. When the mother's head is partially submerged, it is possible that sound passes through both the auditory meatus and the band of auditory tissue, enabling her to hear both the aerial and the underwater version of her pup's call. Because the call arrives at these receptors at slightly different times, she may be able to discern the direction from which it has come more precisely than if she relied only on the underwater or aerial versions of the call.

Harbor seals have interesting visual systems that reflect their amphibious habits. Behavioral studies by Ronald J. Schusterman and his colleagues at the University of California at Santa Cruz and anatomical studies by Glen Jamieson of the University of British Columbia and others show that the seal eye is remarkably well adapted for seeing both underwater and on land. The lens is large and spherical and its shape is suited for underwater acuity. The size and shape of the eye compensate for the fact that the refractive index of water is almost the same as that of the cornea. Consequently light waves entering a seal's eye in water do not refract, or bend, when they pass through the cornea as they do in air. Instead they are refracted only by the lens, which channels them to the retina, or focusing plane, at the back of the eye.

In contrast, human beings, whose eyes function best on land, where the cornea is refractive, see poorly underwater. Without the help of the cornea, light is refracted by the lens so that the visual image no longer forms on the retina and the image is therefore blurred. In seals the visual image forms on the retina and is in focus.

In air the seal's cornea is astigmatic: its curvature is distorted, particularly along the horizontal plane of the eye, and light waves are affected by the distortion as they pass through the eye. In water this astigmatism is of no importance because light there is not refracted as it passes through the cornea. On land the seal compensates by having a stenopaic (vertically contracting) pupil. Because the pupil closes down to a narrow vertical slit that is parallel to the axis of least astigmatism, the most astigmatic area of the cornea has little or no effect on the seal's vision. On foggy or dimly lit beaches the pupil does not contract and the seal has blurred vision. But when light levels are higher, as they usually are near the ocean or on ice, the pupil compensates for astigmatism and the seal's visual acuity in air should be comparable to that in water.

Underwater, harbor seals are extremely sensitive to low light levels; Douglas Wartzok of Purdue University has shown, for example, that on a moonlit night in clear water the seal can detect a moving object at depths as great as 466 meters.

How does the harbor seal, which spends much of its life in murky water where visibility is near zero and which feeds mostly at night, find the three kilograms or more of fish it must catch every day? In the 1960's Thomas C. Poulter of the Stanford Research Institute and others suggested that California sea lions (*Zalophus californianus*) can find and identify prey by echolocation. Echolocation, which was first discovered in bats and was later described in birds, porpoises and dolphins, is similar in principle to radar. Animals that echolocate emit a series of high-frequency sound pulses that reflect off anything they strike; the reflections in turn are processed by the animal's brain, where they form an image that effectively enables the animal to "see" in the dark.

Although no one has conclusively demonstrated that sea lions or other pinnipeds can echolocate, a growing amount of circumstantial evidence suggests that the harbor seal may indeed have the capability. Harbor seals emit click vocalizations: broad-frequency sounds that are produced in short, very fast bursts, most often at night. Recordings I have made of these vocalizations with special audio equipment reveal that many of the clicks are in the ultrasonic range (that is, above the upper limit of human hearing at 20 kilohertz). Working with captive seals, I have found that clicking increases when the seals are fed at night.

In 1968 Möhl was able to show that harbor seals can detect sound frequencies at least as high as 180 kHz and are most sensitive to frequencies of 32 kHz. (Human beings, in contrast, have a sensitivity range from .02 to 20 kHz.) Interestingly, some of the harbor seal clicks peaked in the range of 40 kHz, close to the seal's maximum sensitivity of 32 kHz. On land, where echolocation would be of little use to the seal (which feeds only in the water), the seal is unable to detect sound frequencies much greater than 16 kHz and emits no clicks, instead augmenting its vocabulary with low-frequency growls and snorts.

I devised an experiment with Benjamin Davis, one of my graduate students, to test echolocation in our captive seals. We wanted to see if they could distinguish between two doughnut-shaped rings that looked and weighed the same; one ring was filled with water and the other with air (and small weights), but they differed in their sound-reflecting characteristics. Because an object's density will affect the way sound waves reflect from it, we surmised that the only way the seals could differentiate between the rings was by echolocation.

We began the experiment by teaching a seal to retrieve just one of the rings at night: one of us would slip the ring into the water while the other distracted the seal at the opposite side of the training tank. The seal was then told to fetch; it quickly learned to do so, returning with the ring on its snout in an average of 34 seconds, whereupon we rewarded it with a piece of herring. Having determined that the seal could find a hidden ring and retrieve it without difficulty, we then tested the animal's ability to discriminate between the two rings. The same experimental procedure was followed except that when the seal returned with the air-filled ring, it was rewarded with a piece of herring; when it returned with the water-filled ring, a one-minute time-out (punishment for a hungry seal) was declared.

After 26 sessions the seal was able to correctly identify the air-filled ring from 75 to 80 percent of the time, a reasonable indication that it could distinguish between the two rings. We then removed the weights and added water to the air-filled ring, rendering it identical in every way with the other ring. When the experiment was repeated, the seal could no longer discriminate between them. Our results suggest that the seal can echolocate, but we are puzzled by one aspect of our study. Recordings showed that the seal vocalized very little during its search for the water-filled ring and that the clicks it emitted were intermittent and weak. Because of these findings, echolocation in the harbor seal remains unconfirmed.

Does something else explain the fact that harbor seals are extraordinarily adept at navigating and catching prey in their murky ocean habitat? For some years I have speculated that the seal's vibrissae, or whiskers, must be important sensory receptors. Vibrissae, which are present in almost all mammals (except human beings and a few other species), are unusually well developed in seals, sea lions and walruses. Research I have done with the help of my graduate student Fred Mills suggests that the vibrissae are highly sensitive to movement and thus might play a role in food capture.

We had four seals touch a small vibrating rod with their vibrissae while we varied both the frequency and the amplitude of the vibrations. By monitoring the animals' response (we gave them food when they responded to certain vibrations) we found they were most sensitive to higher frequencies (about 2.5 kHz). This finding was somewhat unexpected because it is the opposite of what occurs in other animals, whose tactile systems are most sensitive to lower frequencies. We calculated that at a distance of 43 centimeters the wave created by the tail beat of a herring-size fish would attenuate to the seal's lower threshold, theoretically enabling the seal to home in on the fish and capture it.

These predictions were given partial support when we clipped the seals' vibrissae (they grow back in a few weeks). In a set of before-and-after experiments we compared the speed at which seals could capture live fish when the vibrissae were intact with the speed at which they caught fish when the vibrissae were removed. The removal of the vibrissae had no significant effect on the length of time the seals needed to find and capture a fish in clear water. We repeated the experiment in murky water, and although they still showed no difference in prey-location time, with or without vibrissae, some dewhiskered seals took longer to actually capture fish in their mouth.

What other purpose might the vibrissae serve? In 1967 William Montagna of the Oregon Health Sciences University in Portland suggested they might function as a speedometer: their bending would correspond to the animal's swimming speed. My colleague Linda Gaborko and I set out to test this theory. We began by training a seal to swim at a speed of six kilometers per hour through hoops placed around a 17-meter course. The seal was rewarded with herring for each circuit in which it maintained a constant speed of six kilometers per hour. When it swam either too slowly or too fast, a buzzer sounded and no reward was given. Once we were convinced that the seal could maintain a steady speed (even after a 17-day break in the training), we clipped its vibrissae and repeated the trial. Its swimming speed was not affected; it thus appears that the vibrissae are important sensory receptors, but their precise function has yet to be determined.

Because the seals seem to function in many instances without conventional sensory channels, it occurred to me that they might be sensitive to magnetic fields. It is widely believed that birds can detect the earth's magnetic field and use it for compass orientation; why could the same not be true for seals? To test that hypothesis, we trained captive seals to swim through a hollow, double-walled fiberglass culvert in which we placed a Helmholtz coil: two hoops wrapped in copper wire through which a current is passed. By sending a current of 2.1 amperes at 70 volts through the coil, we were able to shift the earth's magnetic field within the culvert eastward by 60 degrees. Measurements with a magnetometer revealed that the field was uniformly shifted inside the coil and was not affected 30 centimeters outside it. Two buoys were anchored to a float three meters from the coil, one to the left of the coil, the other to the right. We hoped to train the seals to swim through the culvert on command and to touch the left buoy on emerging from the culvert when the magnetic field inside it was deflected eastward and to touch the right buoy when the coil was not powered.

The inside walls of the culvert were filled with fish oil (which prevented seawater from leaking in and also provided ballast). When the setup was complete, we conducted a number of sessions involving three seals. The first seal (a male) swam through the culvert 2,005 times in more than 30 separate sessions, the second seal (also a male) swam through it 927 times in 17 sessions and the third seal (a female) swam through it 1,227 times in 25 sessions. To our dismay the seals did not differentiate between the two electromagnetic fields.

We cannot conclude, however, that in their natural habitats seals are not sensitive to the earth's magnetic field. It must be emphasized that negative results are always difficult to interpret because they are often brought on by methodological omissions and errors. It could be that the seals failed to respond on the magnetic cues we provided because their environment (a small training tank) was artificial.

Although some aspects of seal biology are now known, many are still puzzling. It is clear that the animal, which traverses dark, murky waters in search of prey and spends considerable time on land, has either unusual sensory receptors or extraordinary cognitive abilities. Whether or not *Phoca vitulina* relies on echolocation in order to detect prey and other objects in the ocean and on the earth's magnetic field in order to navigate are questions awaiting resolution.

Suggestions for Discussion and Writing

1. In the first paragraph and throughout her essay, Renouf asks a number of questions. What rhetorical functions do these questions serve?

2. How does Renouf explain the female seal's ability to control the timing of her pup's birth? Does her explanation fit with the Darwinian notion of adaptation?

3. Briefly explain the extraordinary auditory and visual abilities of the harbor seal. In what way might these abilities be seen as mechanisms for survival?

4. What circumstantial evidence does the author cite to suggest that harbor seals can "echolocate"?

5. When describing a "genuinely empirical method," Karl Popper says in "Science: Conjectures and Refutations" (Chapter 7) that "confirming evidence should not count *except when it is the result of a genuine test of the theory;* and this means that it can be presented as a serious but unsuccessful attempt to falsify the theory." Describe Renouf's experiment to test echolocation in the harbor seal. What theory guided her experiment? Was the experiment a "serious" attempt "to falsify the theory"? Did she succeed? What does she conclude from her findings?

6. Why, according to Renouf, are negative results "always difficult to interpret"?

7. Renouf's tone throughout the essay is personal. Does this personal tone undermine the scientific objectivity of the essay?

8. Write an essay in which you discuss some of the interrelationships among the environment, behavior, and physiology of the harbor seal.

9. Jacob Bronowski, in "The Reach of Imagination" (Chapter 3), argues that creativity is essential to the practice of good science. Is Renouf a "creative" scientist? Write an essay defending your views.

CHAPTER 7

Science as a Way of Knowing

THE METHOD OF SCIENTIFIC INVESTIGATION

Thomas Henry Huxley
(1825–1895)

For Thomas Henry Huxley, the seventh child in an English family of modest means, formal education ended when he was 10 years old. During his adolescence, however, he acquired a broad background in both science and letters, largely through his own efforts. After medical studies at Charing Cross Hospital, he served in the Royal Navy as an assistant surgeon for several years, during which time he carried out extensive research on marine animals despite a lack of proper tools and books. By his late twenties he had established a reputation as a scientific investigator without rival. He was elected a Fellow of the Royal Society in 1851 at the age of 26.

In addition to his strictly scientific papers in the fields of biology and paleontology, Huxley wrote extensively on science, culture, and education. He was a tireless advocate of science in general and of Darwin's theory of evolution in particular. Indeed, he was often referred to as "Darwin's bulldog." He was also a formidable debater and an extremely popular public lecturer. His debate with Bishop Wilberforce on the subject of evolution (1860) was perhaps one of the most dramatic intellectual confrontations of the age.

Huxley's advocacy of science and his interest in education

came together in his famous "Lectures to Workingmen," delivered
in several series over a number of years. Excerpted from one of
these lectures, the following selection demonstrates Huxley's ability to demystify "scientific reasoning" by use of a plain, direct
style and by showing that it differs from ordinary common sense
not in kind, but simply in its rigor and its more systematized way
of proceeding. The scientist, he said elsewhere, "simply uses with
scrupulous exactness the methods which we all habitually use
carelessly."

T he method of scientific investigation is nothing but the expression
of the necessary mode of working of the human mind. It is
simply the mode at which all phenomena are reasoned about, rendered precise and exact. There is no more difference, but there is just
the same kind of difference, between the mental operations of a man
of science and those of an ordinary person, as there is between the
operations and methods of a baker or of a butcher weighing out his
goods in common scales, and the operations of a chemist in performing a difficult and complex analysis by means of his balance and
finely graduated weights. It is not that the action of the scales in the
one case, and the balance in the other, differ in the principles of their
construction or manner of working; but the beam of one is set on an
infinitely finer axis than the other, and of course turns by the addition
of a much smaller weight.

   You will understand this better, perhaps, if I give you some familiar
example. You have all heard it repeated, I dare say, that men of
science work by means of induction and deduction, and that by the
help of these operations, they, in a sort of sense, wring from Nature
certain other things, which are called natural laws, and causes, and
that out of these, by some cunning skill of their own, they build up
hypotheses and theories. And it is imagined by many, that the
operations of the common mind can be by no means compared with
these processes, and that they have to be acquired by a sort of
special apprenticeship to the craft. To hear all these large words, you
would think that the mind of a man of science must be constituted
differently from that of his fellow men; but if you will not be
frightened by terms, you will discover that you are quite wrong, and
that all these terrible apparatus are being used by yourselves every
day and every hour of your lives.

   There is a well-known incident in one of Molière's plays, where
the author makes the hero express unbounded delight on being told
that he had been talking prose during the whole of his life. In the
same way, I trust, that you will take comfort, and be delighted with
yourselves, on the discovery that you have been acting on the
principles of inductive and deductive philosophy during the same
period. Probably there is not one here who has not in the course of
the day had occasion to set in motion a complex train of reasoning,

of the very same kind, though differing of course in degree, as that which a scientific man goes through in tracing the causes of natural phenomena.

A very trivial circumstance will serve to exemplify this. Suppose you go into a fruiterer's shop, wanting an apple—you take up one, and, on biting it, you find it is sour; you look at it, and see that it is hard and green. You take up another one, and that too is hard, green, and sour. The shopman offers you a third; but, before biting it, you examine it, and find it is hard and green, and you immediately say that you will not have it, as it must be sour, like those that you have already tried.

Nothing can be more simple than that, you think; but if you will take the trouble to analyse and trace out into its logical elements what has been done by the mind, you will be greatly surprised. In the first place you have performed the operation of induction. You found that, in two experiences, hardness and greenness in apples went together with sourness. It was so in the first case, and it was confirmed by the second. True, it is a very small basis, but still it is enough to make an induction from; you generalise the facts, and you expect to find sourness in apples where you get hardness and greenness. You found upon that a general law that all hard and green apples are sour; and that, so far as it goes, is a perfect induction. Well, having got your natural law in this way, when you are offered another apple which you find is hard and green, you say, 'All hard and green apples are sour; this apple is hard and green, therefore this apple is sour.' That train of reasoning is what logicians call a syllogism, and has all its various parts and terms,—its major premiss, its minor premiss and its conclusion. And, by the help of further reasoning, which, if drawn out, would have to be exhibited in two or three other syllogisms, you arrive at your final determination, 'I will not have that apple.' So that, you see, you have, in the first place, established a law by induction, and upon that you have founded a deduction, and reasoned out the special particular case. Well now, suppose, having got your conclusion of the law, that at some time afterwards, you are discussing the qualities of apples with a friend: you will say to him, 'It is a very curious thing,—but I find that all hard and green apples are sour!' Your friend says to you, 'But how do you know that?' You at once reply, 'Oh, because I have tried them over and over again, and have always found them to be so.' Well, if we were talking science instead of common sense, we should call that an experimental verification. And, if still opposed, you go further, and say, 'I have heard from the people in Somersetshire and Devonshire, where a large number of apples are grown, that they have observed the same thing. It is also found to be the case in Normandy, and in North America. In short, I find it to be the universal experience of mankind wherever attention has been directed to the subject.' Whereupon, your friend, unless he is a very unreasonable man, agrees with you, and is convinced that you are quite right in the conclusion you have drawn. He believes, although perhaps he does not know he believes it, that the more extensive verifications are,—that the more frequently experiments have been made, and results of the same kind arrived at,—that the more varied the conditions under which the same results are attained, the more certain is the ultimate conclusion, and he disputes the question no further. He sees that the experiment has been tried under all sorts of conditions, as to time, place, and people, with the same result; and he says with you, therefore, that the law you have laid down must be a good one, and he must believe it.

In science we do the same thing;—the philosopher exercises precisely the same faculties, though in a much more delicate manner. In scientific inquiry it becomes a matter of duty to expose a supposed law to every possible kind of verification, and to take care, moreover, that this is done intentionally, and not left to a mere accident, as in the case of the apples. And in science, as in common life, our confidence in a law is in exact proportion to the absence of variation in the result of our experimental verifications. For instance, if you let go your grasp of an article you may have in your hand, it will immediately fall to the ground. That is a very common verification of one of the best established laws of nature—that of gravitation. The method by which men of science establish the existence of that law is exactly the same as that by which we have established the trivial proposition about the sourness of hard and green apples. But we believe it in such an extensive, thorough, and unhesitating manner because the universal experience of mankind verifies it, and we can verify it ourselves at any time; and that is the strongest possible foundation on which any natural law can rest.

So much, then, by way of proof that the method of establishing laws in science is exactly the same as that pursued in common life. Let us now turn to another matter (though really it is but another phase of the same question), and that is, the method by which, from the relations of certain phenomena, we prove that some stand in the position of causes towards the others.

I want to put the case clearly before you, and I will therefore show you what I mean by another familiar example. I will suppose that one of you, on coming down in the morning to the parlour of your house, finds that a tea-pot and some spoons which had been left in the room on the previous evening are gone,—the window is open, and you observe the mark of a dirty hand on the window-frame, and perhaps, in addition to that, you notice the impress of a hob-nailed shoe on the gravel outside. All these phenomena have struck your attention instantly, and before two seconds have passed you say, 'Oh, somebody has broken open the window, entered the room, and run off with the spoons and the tea-pot!' That speech is out of your mouth in a moment. And you will probably add, 'I know there has; I am quite sure of it!' You mean to say exactly what you know; but in reality you are giving expression to what is, in all essential particulars, an hypothesis. You do not *know* it at all; it is nothing but an hypothesis rapidly framed in your own mind. And it is an hypothesis founded on a long train of inductions and deductions.

What are those inductions and deductions, and how have you got at this hypothesis? You have observed in the first place, that the window is open; but by a train of reasoning involving many inductions and deductions, you have probably arrived long before at the general law—and a very good one it is—that windows do not open of themselves; and you therefore conclude that something has opened the window. A second general law that you have arrived at in the same way is, that tea-pots and spoons do not go out of a window spontaneously, and you are satisfied that, as they are not now where you left them, they have been removed. In the third place, you look at the marks on the window-sill, and the shoe-marks outside, and you say that in all previous experience the former kind of mark has never been produced by anything else but the hand of a human being; and the same experience shows that no other animal but man at present wears shoes with hob-nails in them such as would produce the marks in the gravel. I do not know, even if we could discover any of those 'missing links' that are talked about, that they would help us to any other conclusion! At any rate the law which states our present experience is strong enough for my present purpose. You next reach the conclusion that, as these kind of marks have not been left by any other animal than man, or are liable to be formed in any other way than a man's hand and shoe, the marks in question have been formed by a man in that way. You have, further, a general law, founded on observation and experience, and that, too, is, I am sorry to say, a very universal and unimpeachable one,—that some men are thieves; and you assume at once from all these premises—and that is what constitutes your hypothesis—that the man who made the marks outside and on the window-sill, opened the window, got into the room, and stole your tea-pot and spoons. You have now arrived at a *vera causa;*—you have assumed a cause which, it is plain, is competent to produce all the phenomena you have observed. You can explain all these phenomena only by the hypothesis of a thief. But that is a hypothetical conclusion, of the justice of which you have no absolute proof at all; it is only rendered highly probable by a series of inductive and deductive reasonings.

I suppose your first action, assuming that you are a man of ordinary common sense, and that you have established this hypothesis to your own satisfaction, will very likely be to go off for the police, and set them on the track of the burglar, with the view to the recovery of your property. But just as you are starting with this object, some person comes in, and on learning what you are about, says, 'My good friend, you are going on a great deal too fast. How do you know that the man who really made the marks took the spoons? It might have been a monkey that took them, and the man may have merely looked in afterwards.' You would probably reply, 'Well, that is all very well, but you see it is contrary to all experience of the way tea-pots and spoons are abstracted; so that, at any rate, your hypothesis is less probable than mine.' While you are talking the thing over in this way, another friend arrives, one of the good kind of people that I was talking of a little while ago. And he might say, 'Oh, my dear sir, you are certainly going on a great deal too fast. You are most presumptuous. You admit that all these occurrences took place when you were fast asleep, at a time when you could not possibly have known anything about what was taking place. How do you know that the laws of Nature are not suspended during the night? It may be that there has been some kind of supernatural interference in this case.' In point of fact, he declares that your hypothesis is one of which you cannot at all demonstrate the truth, and that you are by no means sure that the laws of Nature are the same when you are asleep as when you are awake.

Well, now, you cannot at the moment answer that kind of reasoning. You feel that your worthy friend has you somewhat at a disadvantage. You will feel perfectly convinced in your own mind, however, that you are quite right, and you say to him, 'My good friend, I can only be guided by the natural probabilities of the case, and if you will be kind enough to stand aside and permit me to pass, I will go and fetch the police.' Well, we will suppose that your journey is successful, and that by good luck you meet with a policeman; that eventually the burglar is found with your property on his person, and the marks correspond to his hand and to his boots. Probably any jury would consider those facts a very good experimental verification of your hypothesis, touching the cause of the abnormal phenomena observed in your parlour, and would act accordingly.

Now, in this supposititious case, I have taken phenomena of a very common kind, in order that you might see what are the different steps in an ordinary process of reasoning, if you will only take the trouble to analyse it carefully. All the operations I have described, you will see, are involved in the mind of any man of sense in leading him to a conclusion as to the course he should take in order to make good a robbery and punish the offender. I say that you are led, in that case, to your conclusion by exactly the same train of reasoning as that which a man of science pursues when he is endeavouring to discover the origin and laws of the most occult phenomena. The process is, and always must be, the same; and precisely the same mode of reasoning was employed by Newton and Laplace in their endeavours to discover and define the causes of the movements of the heavenly bodies, as you, with your own common sense, would employ to detect a burglar. The only difference is, that the nature of the inquiry being more abstruse, every step has to be most carefully watched, so that there may not be a single crack or flaw in your hypothesis. A flaw or crack in many of the hypotheses of daily life may be of little or no moment as affecting the general correctness of the conclusions at which we may arrive; but, in a scientific inquiry, a fallacy, great or small, is always of importance, and is sure to be in the long run constantly productive of mischievous if not fatal results.

Do not allow yourselves to be misled by the common notion that an hypothesis is untrustworthy simply because it is an hypothesis. It is often urged, in respect to some scientific conclusion, that, after all, it is only an hypothesis. But what more have we to guide us in nine-tenths of the most important affairs of daily life than hypotheses, and often very ill-based ones? So that in science, where the evidence of an hypothesis is subjected to the most rigid examination, we may rightly pursue the same course. You may have hypotheses, and hypotheses. A man may say, if he likes, that the moon is made of green cheese: that is an hypothesis. But another man, who has devoted a great deal of time and attention to the subject, and availed himself of the most powerful telescopes and the results of the observations of others, declares that in his opinion it is probably composed of materials very similar to those of which our own earth is made up: and that is also only an hypothesis. But I need not tell you that there is an enormous difference in the value of the two hypotheses. That one which is based on sound scientific knowledge is sure to have a corresponding value; and that which is a mere hasty random guess is likely to have but little value. Every great step in our progress in discovering causes has been made in exactly the same way as that which I have detailed to you. A person observing the occurrence of certain facts and phenomena asks, naturally enough, what process, what kind of operation known to occur in Nature applied to the particular case, will unravel and explain the mystery? Hence you have the scientific hypothesis; and its value will be proportionate to the care and completeness with which its basis had been tested and verified. It is in these matters as in the commonest affairs of practical life: the guess of the fool will be folly, while the guess of the wise man will contain wisdom. In all cases, you see that the value of the result depends on the patience and faithfulness with which the investigator applies to his hypothesis every possible kind of verification.

Suggestions for Discussion and Writing

1. This essay was originally delivered in the form of a lecture to an audience of workingmen. Can you identify any stylistic features suggestive of the essay's oral origins? In what ways did Huxley's audience influence his treatment of his subject?

2. Do you find it surprising that Huxley would address workingmen on the subject of the scientific method? What might we infer about his views on education? on workingmen? on science and its place in our daily lives?

3. Does Huxley introduce his subject effectively? Where does he state his thesis? How does he define the difference between the

"mental operations" of the scientist and those of the ordinary person?'

4. Discussing induction through the illustration of apple tasting in the fifth paragraph, Huxley says that "by the help of further reasoning, which, if drawn out, would have to be exhibited in two or three other syllogisms, you arrive at your final determination, 'I will not have that apple.' " What might one of these "other syllogisms" be?

5. Analyze and trace out into its logical elements a determination that you have made based upon common experience. State it in the form of a syllogism.

6. Huxley seems to be at pains to demystify scientific reasoning—to show that it differs only in degree, but not in kind, from common sense. How would you characterize his illustrations? Are they appropriate to his intention? Write an essay in which you develop your views with reference to three specific illustrations.

7. What is the function of the seventh paragraph?

8. Define the term "hypothesis." On what grounds does the scientist (or do we) choose one hypothesis over another in any given case? On what grounds does the nonscientist often choose a hypothesis? Write an essay developing your argument. Be sure to illustrate with examples.

9. Huxley was a friend of Darwin and a champion of Darwinism. Does this essay contribute to his defense of Darwin's theory of evolution? Should we attach any significance to his use of apple tasting to illustrate the scientific method?

☐ ON THE SCIENTIFIC METHOD

Robert M. Pirsig
(b. 1928)

Born in Minneapolis, Robert Pirsig has taught writing and has worked as a technical writer in industry. In his autobiographical *Zen and the Art of Motorcycle Maintenance: An Inquiry into Values* (1974), he uses a cross-country motorcycle trip as a framework within which to explore issues ranging from the proper way to care for tools to the quandaries facing high-energy physicists. Whatever the nature of his queries, Pirsig consistently stresses the wholeness of human experience, even amidst the vast complexity of our technological world. After a seventeen-year silence, Pirsig published *Lila* (1991), a novel that is as much concerned with metaphysics as it is with the fictional world of its characters.

In this selection from *Zen and the Art of Motorcycle Maintenance,* Pirsig extends Huxley's view of the scientific method by emphasizing the interweaving of induction and deduction and by placing his discussion in a broader philosophical context.

N ow we follow the Yellowstone Valley right across Montana. It changes from Western sagebrush to Midwestern cornfields and back again, depending on whether it's under irrigation from the river. Sometimes we cross over bluffs that take us out of the irrigated area, but usually we stay close to the river. We pass by a marker saying something about Lewis and Clark. One of them came up this way on a side excursion from the Northwest Passage.

Nice sound. Fits the Chautauqua. We're really on a kind of Northwest Passage too. We pass through more fields and desert and the day wears on.

I want to pursue further now that same ghost that Phaedrus pursued—rationality itself, that dull, complex, classical ghost of underlying form.

This morning I talked about hierarchies of thought—the system. Now I want to talk about methods of finding one's way through these hierarchies—logic.

Two kinds of logic are used, inductive and deductive. Inductive inferences start with observations of the machine and arrive at general conclusions. For example, if the cycle goes over a bump and the engine misfires, and then goes over another bump and the engine misfires, and then goes over another bump and the engine misfires, and then goes over a long smooth stretch of road and there is no misfiring, and then goes over a fourth bump and the engine misfires again, one can logically conclude that the misfiring is caused by the bumps. That is induction: reasoning from particular experiences to general truths.

Deductive inferences do the reverse. They start with general knowledge and predict a specific observation. For example, if, from reading the hierarchy of facts about the machine, the mechanic knows the horn of the cycle is powered exclusively by electricity from the battery, then he can logically infer that if the battery is dead the horn will not work. That is deduction.

Solution of problems too complicated for common sense to solve is achieved by long strings of mixed inductive and deductive inferences that weave back and forth between the observed machine and the mental hierarchy of the machine found in the manuals. The correct program for this interweaving is formalized as scientific method.

Actually I've never seen a cycle-maintenance problem complex enough really to require full-scale formal scientific method. Repair problems are not that hard. When I think of formal scientific method an image sometimes comes to mind of an enormous juggernaut, a huge bulldozer—slow, tedious, lumbering, laborious, but invincible. It takes twice as long, five times as long, maybe a dozen times as long as informal mechanic's techniques, but you know in the end you're going to *get* it. There's no fault isolation problem in motorcycle maintenance that can stand up to it. When you've hit a really tough one, tried everything, racked your brain and nothing works, and you know that this time Nature has really decided to be difficult, you say, "Okay, Nature, that's the end of the *nice* guy," and you crank up the formal scientific method.

For this you keep a lab notebook. Everything gets written down, formally, so that you know at all times where you are, where you've been, where you're going and where you want to get. In scientific work and electronics technology this is necessary because otherwise the problems get so complex you get lost in them and confused and forget what you know and what you don't know and have to give up. In cycle maintenance things are not that involved, but when confusion starts it's a good idea to hold it down by making everything formal and exact. Sometimes just the act of writing down the problems straightens out your head as to what they really are.

The logical statements entered into the notebook are broken down into six categories: (1) statement of the problem, (2) hypotheses as to the cause of the problem, (3) experiments designed to test each hypothesis, (4) predicted results of the experiments, (5) observed results of the experiments and (6) conclusions from the results of the experiments. This is not different from the formal arrangement of many college and high-school lab notebooks but the purpose here is no longer just busywork. The purpose now is precise guidance of thoughts that will fail if they are not accurate.

The real purpose of scientific method is to make sure Nature hasn't misled you into thinking you know something you don't actually know. There's not a mechanic or scientist or technician alive who hasn't suffered from that one so much that he's not instinctively on guard. That's the main reason why so much scientific and mechanical information sounds so dull and so cautious. If you get careless or go romanticizing scientific information, giving it a flourish here and there, Nature will soon make a complete fool out of you. It does it often enough anyway even when you don't give it opportunities. One must be extremely careful and rigidly logical when dealing with Nature: one logical slip and an entire scientific edifice comes tumbling down. One false deduction about the machine and you can get hung up indefinitely.

In Part One of formal scientific method, which is the statement of the problem, the main skill is in stating absolutely no more than you are positive you know. It is much better to enter a statement "Solve Problem: Why doesn't cycle work?" which sounds dumb but is correct, than it is to enter a statement "Solve Problem: What is wrong with the electrical system?'' when you don't absolutely *know* the trouble is *in* the electrical system. What you should state is ''Solve Problem: What is wrong with cycle?'' and *then* state as the first entry of Part Two: ''Hypothesis Number One: The trouble is in the electrical system.'' You think of as many hypotheses as you can, then you design experiments to test them to see which are true and which are false.

This careful approach to the beginning questions keeps you from taking a major wrong turn which might cause you weeks of extra work or can even hang you up completely. Scientific questions often have a surface appearance of dumbness for this reason. They are asked in order to prevent dumb mistakes later on.

Part Three, that part of formal scientific method called experimentation, is sometimes thought of by romantics as all of science itself because that's the only part with much visual surface. They see lots of test tubes and bizarre equipment and people running around making discoveries. They do not see the experiment as part of a larger intellectual process and so they often confuse experiments with demonstrations, which look the same. A man conducting a gee-whiz science show with fifty thousand dollars' worth of Frankenstein equipment is not doing anything scientific if he knows beforehand what the results of his efforts are going to be. A motorcycle mechanic, on the other hand, who honks the horn to see if the battery works is informally conducting a true scientific experiment. He is testing a hypothesis by putting the question to nature. The TV scientist who mutters sadly, ''The experiment is a failure; we have failed to achieve what we had hoped for,'' is suffering mainly from a bad scriptwriter. An experiment is never a failure solely because it fails to achieve predicted results. An experiment is a failure only when it also fails adequately to test the hypothesis in question, when the data it produces don't prove anything one way or another.

Skill at this point consists of using experiments that test only the hypothesis in question, nothing less, nothing more. If the horn honks, and the mechanic concludes that the whole electrical system is working, he is in deep trouble. He has reached an illogical conclusion. The honking horn only tells him that the battery and horn are working. To design an experiment properly he has to think very rigidly in terms of what directly causes what. This you know from the hierarchy. The horn doesn't make the cycle go. Neither does the battery, except in a very indirect way. The point at which the electrical system *directly* causes the engine to fire is at the spark plugs, and if you don't test here, at the output of the electrical system, you will never really know whether the failure is electrical or not.

To test properly the mechanic removes the plug and lays it against the engine so that the base around the plug is electrically grounded, kicks the starter lever and watches the spark-plug gap for a blue spark. If there isn't any he can conclude one of two things: (a) there is an electrical failure or (b) his experiment is sloppy. If he is experienced he will try it a few more times, checking connections, trying every way he can think of to get that plug to fire. Then, if he can't get it to fire, he finally concludes that *a* is correct, there's an electrical failure, and the experiment is over. He has proved that his hypothesis is correct.

In the final category, conclusions, skill comes in stating no more than the experiment has proved. It hasn't proved that when he fixes the electrical system the motorcycle will start. There may be other things wrong. But he does know that the motorcycle isn't going to run until the electrical system is working and he sets up the next formal question: "Solve problem: what is wrong with the electrical system?"

He then sets up hypotheses for these and tests them. By asking the right questions and choosing the right tests and drawing the right conclusions the mechanic works his way down the echelons of the motorcycle hierarchy until he has found the exact specific cause or causes of the engine failure, and then he changes them so that they no longer cause the failure.

An untrained observer will see only physical labor and often get the idea that physical labor is mainly what the mechanic does. Actually the physical labor is the smallest and easiest part of what the mechanic does. By far the greatest part of his work is careful observation and precise thinking. That is why mechanics sometimes seem so taciturn and withdrawn when performing tests. They don't like it when you talk to them because they are concentrating on mental images, hierarchies, and not really looking at you or the physical motorcycle at all. They are using the experiment as part of a program to expand their hierarchy of knowledge of the faulty motorcycle and compare it to the correct hierarchy in their mind. They are looking at underlying form.

Suggestions for Discussion and Writing

1. Is Pirsig's explanation of inductive and deductive reasoning effective? What technique(s) does he use to explain formal scientific method? Is his tone appropriate to his subject?

2. "Sometimes just the act of writing down the problems straightens out your head as to what they really are." Write an essay in which you describe how writing about a problem helped you to understand it.

3. Pirsig notes that statements entered into lab notebooks typically fall into six categories. Apply the six-step procedure suggested by these categories to an everyday problem that lends itself to simple experimentation. How well do your results match your hypotheses?

4. What, according to Pirsig, constitutes an experimental failure? Could an experiment that fails to achieve predicted results ever be considered a success?

5. In Pirsig's opinion what constitutes the "larger intellectual process" of which scientific experimentation is only a part?

6. "One must be extremely careful and rigidly logical when dealing with Nature: one logical slip and an entire scientific edifice comes tumbling down." Write an essay in which you compare Pirsig's view here with Eiseley's in "Science and the Sense of the Holy" (this chapter). Can the two views be reconciled?

7. Pirsig says, "When I think of formal scientific method an image sometimes comes to mind of an enormous juggernaut, a huge bulldozer—slow, tedious, lumbering, laborious, but invincible." Later in the same passage, he continues, "When you've hit a really tough one . . . and you know that this time Nature has really decided to be difficult, you say, 'Okay, Nature, that's the end of the *nice* guy,' and you crank up the formal scientific method." What view of nature—and the scientist's relationship to it—do these statements imply?

8. Early in the essay Pirsig speaks of rationality as "that dull, complex, classical ghost of underlying form." At the end of the essay he returns to this issue when he speaks of "underlying form" and the "correct hierarchy" of the mind. What does he mean by "underlying form"? In what sense is "ghost" an appropriate word here? What oppositions are implied in the statement?

SCIENCE: CONJECTURES AND REFUTATIONS*

Karl Popper
(b. 1902)

Karl Popper, Austrian philosopher of natural and social science, was born in Vienna and studied mathematics, physics, and philosophy at the University of Vienna. After teaching for several years at Canterbury University College in Christchurch, New Zealand, he was appointed Professor of Logic and Scientific

*A lecture given at Peterhouse, Cambridge, in Summer 1953, as part of a course on developments and trends in contemporary British philosophy, organized by the British Council; originally published under the title 'Philosophy of Science: a Personal Report' in *British Philosophy in Mid-Century*, ed. C. A. Mace, 1957.

Method in 1949 at the London School of Economics in the University of London. He was knighted in 1964. His books include *The Poverty of Historicism* (*1957*), *The Logic of Scientific Discovery* (*1959*), and *Conjectures and Refutations* (*1962*), from which the following essay is excerpted.

This selection illustrates two important aspects of Popper's contributions to modern theories of scientific method: 1) his views about "falsification" and the testing of scientific hypotheses, and 2) his use of the principle of falsification to distinguish science (and the scientific hypothesis) from nonscience (from, for example, Marxist economics and Freudian psychoanalytic theory).

I

When I received the list of participants in this course and realized that I had been asked to speak to philosophical colleagues I thought, after some hesitation and consultation, that you would probably prefer me to speak about those problems which interest me most, and about those developments with which I am most intimately acquainted. I therefore decided to do what I have never done before: to give you a report on my own work in the philosophy of science, since the autumn of 1919 when I first began to grapple with the problem, *'When should a theory be ranked as scientific?'* or *'Is there a criterion for the scientific character or status of a theory?'*

The problem which troubled me at the time was neither, 'When is a theory true?' nor, 'When is a theory acceptable?' My problem was different. I *wished to distinguish between science and pseudo-science;* knowing very well that science often errs, and that pseudo-science may happen to stumble on the truth.

I knew, of course, the most widely accepted answer to my problem: that science is distinguished from pseudo-science—or from 'metaphysics'—by its *empirical method,* which is essentially *inductive,* proceeding from observation or experiment. But this did not satisfy me. On the contrary, I often formulated my problem as one of distinguishing between a genuinely empirical method and a non-empirical or even a pseudo-empirical method—that is to say, a method which, although it appeals to observation and experiment, nevertheless does not come up to scientific standards. The latter method may be exemplified by astrology, with its stupendous mass of empirical evidence based on observation—on horoscopes and on biographies.

But as it was not the example of astrology which led me to my problem I should perhaps briefly describe the atmosphere in which my problem arose and the examples by which it was stimulated. After the collapse of the Austrian Empire there had been a revolution in Austria: the air was full of revolutionary slogans and ideas, and new and often wild theories. Among the theories which interested me

Einstein's theory of relativity was no doubt by far the most important. Three others were Marx's theory of history, Freud's psycho-analysis, and Alfred Adler's so-called 'individual psychology'.

There was a lot of popular nonsense talked about these theories, and especially about relativity (as still happens even today), but I was fortunate in those who introduced me to the study of this theory. We all—the small circle of students to which I belonged—were thrilled with the result of Eddington's eclipse observations which in 1919 brought the first important confirmation of Einstein's theory of gravitation. It was a great experience for us, and one which had a lasting influence on my intellectual development.

The three other theories I have mentioned were also widely discussed among students at that time. I myself happened to come into personal contact with Alfred Adler, and even to co-operate with him in his social work among the children and young people in the working-class districts of Vienna where he had established social guidance clinics.

It was during the summer of 1919 that I began to feel more and more dissatisfied with these three theories—the Marxist theory of history, psycho-analysis, and individual psychology; and I began to feel dubious about their claims to scientific status. My problem perhaps first took the simple form, 'What is wrong with Marxism, psycho-analysis, and individual psychology? Why are they so different from physical theories, from Newton's theory, and especially from the theory of relativity?'

To make this contrast clear I should explain that few of us at the time would have said that we believed in the *truth* of Einstein's theory of gravitation. This shows that it was not my doubting the *truth* of those other three theories which bothered me, but something else. Yet neither was it that I merely felt mathematical physics to be more *exact* than the sociological or psychological type of theory. Thus what worried me was neither the problem of truth, at that stage at least, nor the problem of exactness or measurability. It was rather that I felt that these other three theories, though posing as sciences, had in fact more in common with primitive myths than with science; that they resembled astrology rather than astronomy.

I found that those of my friends who were admirers of Marx, Freud, and Adler, were impressed by a number of points common to these theories, and especially by their apparent *explanatory power*. These theories appeared to be able to explain practically everything that happened within the fields to which they referred. The study of any of them seemed to have the effect of an intellectual conversion or revelation, opening your eyes to a new truth hidden from those not yet initiated. Once your eyes were thus opened you saw confirming instances everywhere: the world was full of *verifications* of the theory. Whatever happened always confirmed it. Thus its truth appeared manifest; and unbelievers were clearly people who did not want to see the manifest truth; who refused to see it, either because it was against their class interest, or because of their repressions which were still 'un-analysed' and crying aloud for treatment.

The most characteristic element in this situation seemed to me the incessant stream of confirmations, of observations which 'verified' the theories in question; and this point was constantly emphasized by their adherents. A Marxist could not open a newspaper without finding on every page confirming evidence for his interpretation of history; not only in the news, but also in its presentation—which revealed the class bias of the paper—and especially of course in what the paper did *not* say. The Freudian analysts emphasized that their theories were constantly verified by their 'clinical observations'. As for Adler, I was much impressed by a personal experience. Once, in 1919, I reported to him a case which to me did not seem particularly Adlerian, but which he found no difficulty in analysing in terms of his theory of inferiority feelings, although he had not even seen the child. Slightly shocked, I asked him how he could be so sure. 'Because of my thousandfold experience,' he replied; whereupon I could not help saying: 'And with this new case, I suppose, your experience has become thousand-and-one-fold.'

What I had in mind was that his previous observations may not have been much sounder than this new one; that each in its turn had been interpreted in the light of 'previous experience', and at the same time counted as additional confirmation. What, I asked myself, did it confirm? No more than that a case could be interpreted in the light of the theory. But this meant very little, I reflected, since every conceivable case could be interpreted in the light of Adler's theory, or equally of Freud's. I may illustrate this by two very different examples of human behaviour: that of a man who pushes a child into the water with the intention of drowning it; and that of a man who sacrifices his life in an attempt to save the child. Each of these two cases can be explained with equal ease in Freudian and in Adlerian terms. According to Freud the first man suffered from repression (say, of some component of his Oedipus complex), while the second man had achieved sublimation. According to Adler the first man suffered from feelings of inferiority (producing perhaps the need to prove to himself that he dared to commit some crime), and so did the second man (whose need was to prove to himself that he dared to rescue the child). I could not think of any human behaviour which could not be interpreted in terms of either theory. It was precisely this fact— that they always fitted, that they were always confirmed—which in the eyes of their admirers constituted the strongest argument in favour of these theories. It began to dawn on me that this apparent strength was in fact their weakness.

With Einstein's theory the situation was strikingly different. Take one typical instance—Einstein's prediction, just then confirmed by the findings of Eddington's expedition. Einstein's gravitational theory had led to the result that light must be attracted by heavy bodies (such as the sun), precisely as material bodies were attracted. As a consequence it could be calculated that light from a distant fixed star whose apparent position was close to the sun would reach the earth from such a direction that the star would seem to be slightly shifted away from the sun; or, in other words, that stars close to the sun would look as if they had moved a little away from the sun, and from one another. This is a thing which cannot normally be observed since such stars are rendered invisible in daytime by the sun's overwhelming brightness; but during an eclipse it is possible to take photographs of them. If the same constellation is photographed at night one can measure the distances on the two photographs, and check the predicted effect.

Now the impressive thing about this case is the *risk* involved in a prediction of this kind. If observation shows that the predicted effect is definitely absent, then the theory is simply refuted. The theory is *incompatible with certain possible results of observation*—in fact with results which everybody before Einstein would have expected. This is quite different from the situation I have previously described, when it turned out that the theories in question were compatible with the most divergent human behaviour, so that it was practically impossible to describe any human behaviour that might not be claimed to be a verification of these theories.

These considerations led me in the winter of 1919–20 to conclusions which I may now reformulate as follows:

1. It is easy to obtain confirmations, or verifications, for nearly every theory—if we look for confirmations.
2. Confirmations should count only if they are the result of *risky predictions;* that is to say, if, unenlightened by the theory in question, we should have expected an event which was incompatible with the theory—an event which would have refuted the theory.
3. Every 'good' scientific theory is a prohibition: it forbids certain things to happen. The more a theory forbids, the better it is.
4. A theory which is not refutable by any conceivable event is nonscientific. Irrefutability is not a virtue of a theory (as people often think) but a vice.
5. Every genuine *test* of a theory is an attempt to falsify it, or to refute it. Testability is falsifiability; but there are degrees of testability: some theories are more testable, more exposed to refutation, than others; they take, as it were, greater risks.
6. Confirming evidence should not count *except when it is the result of a genuine test of the theory;* and this means that it can be presented as a serious but unsuccessful attempt to falsify the theory. (I now speak in such cases of 'corroborating evidence'.)
7. Some genuinely testable theories, when found to be false, are still upheld by their admirers—for example by introducing *ad hoc* some auxiliary assumption, or

by re-interpreting the theory *ad hoc* in such a way that it escapes refutation. Such a procedure is always possible, but it rescues the theory from refutation only at the price of destroying, or at least lowering, its scientific status. (I later described such a rescuing operation as a *'conventionalist twist'* or a *'conventionalist stratagem'.*)

One can sum up all this by saying that *the criterion of the scientific status of a theory is its falsifiability, or refutability, or testability.*

II

I may perhaps exemplify this with the help of the various theories so far mentioned. Einstein's theory of gravitation clearly satisfied the criterion of falsifiability. Even if our measuring instruments at the time did not allow us to pronounce on the results of the tests with complete assurance, there was clearly a possibility of refuting the theory.

Astrology did not pass the test. Astrologers were greatly impressed, and misled, by what they believed to be confirming evidence—so much so that they were quite unimpressed by any unfavourable evidence. Moreover, by making their interpretations and prophecies sufficiently vague they were able to explain away anything that might have been a refutation of the theory had the theory and the prophecies been more precise. In order to escape falsification they destroyed the testability of their theory. It is a typical soothsayer's trick to predict things so vaguely that the predictions can hardly fail: that they become irrefutable.

The Marxist theory of history, in spite of the serious efforts of some of its founders and followers, ultimately adopted this soothsaying practice. In some of its earlier formulations (for example in Marx's analysis of the character of the 'coming social revolution') their predictions were testable, and in fact falsified. Yet instead of accepting the refutations the followers of Marx re-interpreted both the theory and the evidence in order to make them agree. In this way they rescued the theory from refutation; but they did so at the price of adopting a device which made it irrefutable. They thus gave a 'conventionalist twist' to the theory; and by this stratagem they destroyed its much advertised claim to scientific status.

The two psycho-analytic theories were in a different class. They were simply non-testable, irrefutable. There was no conceivable human behaviour which could contradict them. This does not mean that Freud and Adler were not seeing certain things correctly: I personally do not doubt that much of what they say is of considerable importance, and may well play its part one day in a psychological science which is testable. But it does mean that those 'clinical observations' which analysts naïvely believe confirm their theory cannot do this any more than the daily confirmations which astrologers find in their practice. And as for Freud's epic of the Ego, the Super-ego, and the Id, no substantially stronger claim to scientific status can be made for it than for Homer's collected stories from Olympus. These theories describe some facts, but in the manner of myths. They contain most interesting psychological suggestions, but not in a testable form.

At the same time I realized that such myths may be developed, and become testable; that historically speaking all—or very nearly all—scientific theories originate from myths, and that a myth may contain important anticipations of scientific theories. Examples are Empedocles' theory of evolution by trial and error, or Parmenides' myth of the unchanging block universe in which nothing ever happens and which, if we add another dimension, becomes Einstein's block universe (in which, too, nothing ever happens, since everything is, four-dimensionally speaking, determined and laid down from the beginning). I thus felt that if a theory is found to be non-scientific, or 'metaphysical' (as we might say), it is not thereby found to be unimportant, or insignificant, or 'meaningless', or 'nonsensical'. But it cannot claim to be backed by empirical evidence in the scientific sense—although it may easily be, in some genetic sense, the 'result of observation'.

(There were a great many other theories of this pre-scientific or pseudo-scientific character, some of them, unfortunately, as influential as the Marxist interpretation of history; for example, the racialist interpretation of history—another of those impressive and all-explanatory theories which act upon weak minds like revelations.)

Thus the problem which I tried to solve by proposing the criterion of falsifiability was neither a problem of meaningfulness or significance, nor a problem of truth or acceptability. It was the problem of drawing a line (as well as this can be done) between the statements, or systems of statements, of the empirical sciences, and all other statements—whether they are of a religious or of a metaphysical character, or simply pseudo-scientific. Years later—it must have been in 1928 or 1929—I called this first problem of mine the *problem of demarcation*. The criterion of falsifiability is a solution to this problem of demarcation, for it says that statements or systems of statements, in order to be ranked as scientific, must be capable of conflicting with possible, or conceivable, observations.

Suggestions for Discussion and Writing

1. In the second paragraph Popper says that "science is distinguished from pseudo-science—or from 'metaphysics'—by its empirical method, which is essentially inductive, proceeding from observation or experiment." Why was he not satisfied with this distinction?

2. Popper writes in terms of his struggle to distinguish "science" from "pseudo-science." What does he gain by focusing on the process by which he came to his views?

3. In 1919, Popper says, Arthur Eddington's findings dramatically confirmed Einstein's gravitational theory. What did that theory predict? How did Eddington confirm it? Why did this experience have "a lasting influence" on Popper's intellectual development?

4. What role does prediction play in scientific theories? What does Popper mean by a "risky prediction"?

5. In his list of conclusions, Popper says that "every 'good' scientific theory is a prohibition—it forbids certain things to happen." Why is this idea of prohibition essential to the "good" theory? Do you see a connection between "prohibition" and "prediction"?

6. One might sum up Popper's argument by saying that attempts to falsify a theory are more important than attempts to confirm it. Discuss.

7. Popper discusses several theories that do not meet the criterion of falsifiability. Write an essay in which you identify other such theories and explain how and why one of them fails to meet this criterion.

8. Consider the controversy of Evolution versus Creation in light of Popper's ideas. Does Popper help to clarify the nature of this debate?

9. Compare the first and last paragraphs. How are they similar? different? What role does summary play in the development of Popper's argument?

10. Write a brief essay in which you explain the notion of "pseudo-science."

☐ HOW FERMI WOULD HAVE FIXED IT

Hans Christian von Baeyer
(b. 1938)

Hans Christian von Baeyer was born in Berlin into a family of doctors and scientists. After schooling in Germany, Switzerland, Canada, and New York, he earned his Ph.D. at Vanderbilt University in Tennessee with a dissertation on theoretical particle physics. A professor of physics since 1968 at the College of

William and Mary in Virginia, von Baeyer has won the two high-est teaching awards of his university and in 1990 was selected as one of the outstanding faculty members of the Commonwealth of Virginia. In recognition of his contributions to mathematical phys-ics he was elected Fellow of the American Physical Society.

In recent years von Baeyer has increasingly turned his attention to science writing for the public. His essays in *The Sciences* (pub-lished by the New York Academy of Sciences), *Discover,* and other journals have won him the 1979 Science Writing Award of the American Institute of Physics, the 1990 Science Journalism Award of the American Association for the Advancement of Science, and a 1991 National Magazine Award in the category "Essays and Criticism." In 1991 von Baeyer wrote the script for a one-hour film entitled "The Quantum Universe," aired by the Public Broad-casting System as part of the series *Smithsonian World.* The film was nominated for an Emmy Award. His book *Taming the Atom: The Discovery of the Visible Microworld* was published by Random House in 1992.

In this essay from *The Sciences* (1988), von Baeyer offers the somewhat surprising view that even "rough-and-ready" calcula-tions have their place in scientific thinking.

A t twenty-nine minutes past five, on a Monday morning in July of 1945, the world's first atom bomb exploded in the desert sixty miles northwest of Alamogordo, New Mexico. Forty seconds later, the blast's shock wave reached the base camp, where scientists stood in stunned contemplation of the historic spectacle. The first person to stir was the Italian-American physicist Enrico Fermi, who was on hand to witness the culmination of a project he had helped begin.

Before the bomb detonated, Fermi had torn a sheet of notebook paper into small bits. Then, as he felt the first quiver of the shock wave spreading outward through the still air, he released the shreds above his head. They fluttered down and away from the mushroom cloud growing on the horizon, landing about two and a half yards behind him. After a brief mental calculation, Fermi announced that the bomb's energy had been equivalent to that produced by ten thousand tons of TNT. Sophisticated instruments also were at the site, and analyses of their readings of the shock wave's velocity and pressure, an exercise that took several weeks to complete, confirmed Fermi's instant estimate.

The bomb-test team was impressed, but not surprised, by this brilliant bit of scientific improvisation. Enrico Fermi's genius was known throughout the world of physics. In 1938, he had won a Nobel Prize for his work in elementary particle physics, and, four years later, in Chicago, had produced the first sustained nuclear chain reaction, thereby ushering in the age of atomic weapons and commercial nuclear power. No other physicist of his generation, and no one since, has been at once a masterful experimentalist and a leading theoretician. In miniature, the bits of paper and the analysis of their motion exemplified this unique combination of gifts.

Like all virtuosos, Fermi had a distinctive style. His approach to physics brooked no opposition; it simply never occurred to him that he might fail to find the solution to a problem. His scientific papers and books reveal a disdain for embellishment—a preference for the most direct, rather than the most intellectually elegant, route to an answer. When he reached the limits of his cleverness, Fermi completed a task by brute force.

To illustrate this approach, imagine that a physicist must determine the volume of an irregular object—say, Earth, which is slightly pear-shaped. He might feel stymied without some kind of formula, and there are several ways he could go about getting one. He could consult a mathematician, but finding one with enough knowledge and interest to be of help is usually difficult. He could search through the mathematical literature, a time-consuming and probably fruitless exercise, because the ideal shapes that interest mathematicians often do not match those of the irregular objects found in nature. Or he could set aside his own research in order to derive the formula from basic mathematical principles, but, of course, if he had wanted to devote his time to theoretical geometry, he wouldn't have become a physicist.

Alternatively, the physicist could do what Fermi would have done— compute the volume *numerically*. Instead of relying on a formula, he could mentally divide the planet into, perhaps, a large number of tiny cubes, each with a volume easily determined by multiplying the length times the width times the height, and then add together the answers to these more tractable problems. This method yields only an approximate solution, but it is sure to produce the desired result, which is what mattered to Fermi. With the introduction, after the Second World War, of computers and, later, of pocket calculators, numerical computation has become standard procedure in physics.

The technique of dividing difficult problems into small, manageable ones applies to many problems besides those amenable to numerical computation. Fermi excelled at this rough-and-ready modus operandi, and, to pass it on to his students, he developed a type of question that has become associated with his name. A Fermi problem has a characteristic profile: Upon first hearing it, one doesn't have even the remotest notion what the answer might be. And one feels certain that too little information exists to find a solution. Yet, when the problem is broken down into subproblems, each one answerable without the help of experts or reference books, an estimate can be made, either mentally or on the back of an envelope, that comes remarkably close to the exact solution.

Suppose, for example, that one wants to determine Earth's circumference without looking it up. Everyone knows that New York and Los Angeles are separated by about three thousand miles and that the time difference between the two coasts is three hours. Three hours corresponds to one-eighth of a day, and a day is the time it takes the planet to complete one revolution, so its circumference must be eight times three thousand, or twenty-four thousand miles—an answer that differs from the true value (at the equator, 24,902.45 miles) by less than four percent. In John Milton's words:

> so easy it seemed
> Once found, which yet unfound most would have thought
> Impossible.

Fermi problems might seem to resemble the brainteasers that appear among the back pages of airline magazines and other popular publications (Given three containers that hold eight, five, and three quarts, respectively, how do you measure out a single quart?), but the two genres differ significantly. The answer to a Fermi problem, in contrast to that of a brainteaser, cannot be verified by logical deduction alone and is always approximate. (To determine precisely Earth's circumference, it is necessary that the planet actually be measured.) Then, too, solving a Fermi problem requires a knowledge of facts not mentioned in the statement of the problem. (In contrast, the decanting puzzle contains all the information necessary for its solution.)

These differences mean that Fermi problems are more closely tied to the physical world than are mathematical puzzles, which rarely have anything practical to offer physicists. By the same token, Fermi problems are reminiscent of the ordinary dilemmas that nonphysicists encounter every day of their lives. Indeed, Fermi problems, and the way they are solved, not only are essential to the practice of physics; they teach a valuable lesson in the art of living.

How many piano tuners are there in Chicago? The whimsical nature of this question, the improbability that anyone knows the answer, and the fact that Fermi posed it to his classes at the University of Chicago have elevated it to the status of legend. There is no standard solution (that's exactly the point), but anyone can make assumptions that quickly lead to an approximate answer. Here is one way: If the population of metropolitan Chicago is three million, an average family consists of four people, and one-third of all families own pianos, there are two hundred and fifty thousand pianos in the city. If each piano is tuned every ten years, there are twenty-five thousand tunings a year. If each tuner can service four pianos a day, two hundred and fifty days a year, for a total of one thousand tunings a year, there must be about twenty-five piano tuners in the city. The answer is not exact; it could be as low as ten or as high as fifty. But, as the yellow pages of the telephone directory attest, it is definitely in the ball park.

Fermi's intent was to show that although, at the outset, even the answer's order of magnitude is unknown, one can proceed on the basis of different assumptions and still arrive at estimates that fall within range of the answer. The reason is that, in any string of calculations, errors tend to cancel out one another. If someone assumes, for instance, that every sixth, rather than third, family owns a piano, he is just as likely to assume that pianos are tuned every five, not ten, years. It is as improbable that all of one's errors will be underestimates (or overestimates) as it is that all the throws in a series of coin tosses will be heads (or tails). The law of probabilities dictates that deviations from the correct assumptions will tend to compensate for one another, so the final results will converge toward the right number.

Of course, the Fermi problems that physicists face deal more often with atoms and molecules than with pianos. To answer them, one needs to commit to memory a few basic magnitudes, such as the approximate radius of a typical atom or the number of molecules in a thimbleful of water. Equipped with such facts, one can estimate, for example, the distance a car must travel before a layer of rubber about the thickness of a molecule is worn off the tread of its tires. It turns out that that much is removed with each revolution of the wheels, a reminder of the immensity of the number of atoms in a tire. (Assume that the tread is about a quarter-inch thick and that it wears off in forty thousand miles of driving. If a quarter-inch is divided by the number of revolutions a typical wheel, with its typical circumference, makes in forty thousand miles, the answer is roughly one molecular diameter.)

More momentous Fermi problems might concern energy policy (the number of solar cells required to produce a certain amount of electricity), environmental quality (the amount of acid rain caused annually by coal consumption in the United States), or the arms race. A good example from the weapons field was proposed in 1981 by David Hafemeister, a physicist at the California Polytechnic State Universtity: For what length of time would the beam from the most powerful laser have to be focused on the skin of an incoming missile to ignite the chemical explosives in the missile's nuclear warhead? The key point is that a beam of light, no matter how well focused, spreads out like an ocean wave entering the narrow opening of a harbor, a phenomenon called diffraction broadening. The formula that describes such spreading applies to all forms of waves, including light waves, so, at a typical satellite-to-missile distance of, perhaps, seven hundred miles, a laser's energy will become considerably attenuated. With some reasonable assumptions about the temperature at which explosive materials ignite (say, a thousand degrees Fahrenheit), the diameter of the mirror that focuses the laser beam (ten feet is about right), and the maximum available power of chemical lasers (a level of a million watts has not yet been attained but is conceivable), the answer turns out to be around ten minutes.

Trying to keep a laser aimed at a speeding missile at a distance of seven hundred miles for that long is a task that greatly exceeds the capacity of existing technology. For one thing, the missile travels so rapidly that it would be impossible to keep it within range. For another, a laser beam must reflect back toward its source to verify that it is hitting its target (a process comparable to shining a flashlight at a small mirror carried by a running man at the opposite end of a football field so that the light reflected from the mirror stays in one's eyes).

The solution of this Fermi problem depends on more facts than average people, or even average physicists, have at their fingertips, but for those who do have them in mind, the calculation takes only a few minutes. And it is no less accurate for being easy to perform. So it is not surprising that Hafemeister's conclusion, which predated the President's 1983 Star Wars speech (research on laser weapons began two decades ago), agrees roughly with the findings of the American Physical Society's report entitled "Science and Technology of Directed Energy Weapons," which was the result of much more elaborate analysis. Prudent physicists—those who want to avoid false leads and dead ends—operate according to a long-standing principle: Never start a lengthy calculation until you know the range of values within which the answer is likely to fall (and, equally important, the range within which the answer is *un*likely to fall). They attack every problem as a Fermi problem, estimating the order of magnitude of the result before engaging in an investigation.

Physicists also use Fermi problems to communicate with one another. When they gather in university hallways, convention-center lobbies, or French restaurants to describe a new experiment or to discuss an unfamiliar subject, they often first survey the lay of the land, staking out, in a numerical way, the perimeter of the problem at hand. Only the timid hang back, deferring to the experts in their midst. Those accustomed to tackling Fermi problems approach the experiment or subject as if it were their own, demonstrating their understanding by performing rough calculations. If the conversation turns to a new particle accelerator, for example, they will estimate the strength of the magnets it requires; if the subject is the structure of a novel crystal, they will calculate the spacing between its atoms. Everyone tries to arrive at the correct answer with the least effort. It is this spirit of independence, which he himself possessed in ample measure, that Fermi sought to instill by posing his unconventional problems.

Questions about atom bombs, piano tuners, automobile tires, laser weapons, particle accelerators, and crystal structure have little in common. But the manner in which they are answered is the same in every case and can be applied to questions outside the realm of physics. Whether the problem concerns cooking, automobile repair, or personal relationships, there are two basic types of responses: the fainthearted turn to authority—to reference books, bosses, expert consultants, physicians, ministers—while the independent of mind delve into that private store of common sense and limited factual knowledge that everyone carries, make reasonable assumptions, and derive their own, admittedly approximate, solutions. To be sure, it would be foolish to practice neurosurgery at home, but mundane challenges—preparing chili from scratch, replacing a water pump, resolving a family quarrel—can often be sorted out with nothing more than logic, common sense, and patience.

The resemblance of technical problems to human ones was explored in Robert M. Pirsig's 1974 book, *Zen and the Art of Motorcycle Maintenance,* in which the repair and upkeep of a machine served as a metaphor for rationality itself. At one point, the protagonist proposed to fix the slipping handlebars of a friend's new BMW motorcycle, the pride of a half-century of German mechanical craftsmanship, with a piece of an old beer can. Although the proposal happened to be technically perfect (the aluminum was thin and flexible), the cycle's owner, a musician, could not break his reliance on authority; the idea had not originated with a factory-trained mechanic, so it did not deserve serious consideration. In the same way, certain observers would have been skeptical of Fermi's analysis, carried through with the aid of a handful of confetti, of a two-billion-dollar bomb test. Such an attitude demonstrates less, perhaps, about their knowledge of the problem than about their attitude toward life. As Pirsig put it, "The real cycle you're working on is a cycle called 'yourself.' "

Ultimately, the value of dealing with the problems of science, or those of everyday life, in the way Fermi did lies in the rewards one gains for making independent discoveries and inventions. It doesn't matter whether the discovery is as momentous as the determination of the yield of an atom bomb or as insignificant as an estimate of the number of piano tuners in a midwestern city. Looking up the answer, or letting someone else find it, actually impoverishes one; it robs one of the pleasure and pride that accompany creativity and deprives one of an experience that, more than anything else in life, bolsters self-confidence. Self-confidence, in turn, is the essential prerequisite for solving Fermi problems. Thus, approaching personal dilemmas as Fermi problems can become, by a kind of chain reaction, a habit that enriches life.

Suggestions for Discussion and Writing

1. Von Baeyer starts his essay with a brief narrative description. Is this an effective opening? Why?

2. In the third paragraph the author says that Fermi was at once "a masterful experimentalist and a leading theoretician." Explain the distinction. How does Fermi's measurement of the atom bomb's energy exemplify his "unique combination of gifts"?

3. What does the author mean when he says (in the fourth paragraph) that when Fermi reached the limits of his cleverness he "completed a task by brute force"?

4. What is implied (in the fifth paragraph) about mathematics (and mathematicians)?

5. What are the characteristics of a Fermi problem? What qualities and abilities was Fermi attempting to develop in his students by giving them Fermi problems? What, for instance, is the significance of the fact that "the answer to a Fermi problem . . . cannot be verified by logical deduction alone"?

6. Write a brief essay in which you discuss the usefulness in everyday life of the approach implicit in the "Fermi problem."

7. What is the practical value for a scientist of being able to attack every problem as a Fermi problem?

8. The essay is divided into three parts. Does this division seem appropriate to you? Why?

9. Fermi appears to have believed (and this author seems to agree) that the problems of science are in many ways akin to those of everyday life. Would Huxley (see "The Method of Scientific Investigation," this chapter) have agreed?

SETTING THE STAGE FOR DISCOVERY

Robert S. Root-Bernstein
(b. 1941)

A professor of natural science and physiology at Michigan State University, Robert Root-Bernstein studies the causes of autoimmune diseases and the interactions between drugs and neurotransmitters. In 1989 he published *Discovering,* a book on the strategies of scientific discovery. Root-Bernstein was one of the first MacArthur Prize Fellows and is a contributing editor of *The Sciences,* published by the New York Academy of Sciences.

In the following essay Root-Bernstein broadens the traditional definition of scientific method to include a range of attitudes and activities that can set the stage for discovery. In contrast to the traditional emphasis on logic and reason, he offers a view that stresses the importance of intuition and even of deep personal engagement as a means of achieving scientific insight.

Anyone familiar with the history or philosophy of science has heard some version of the story in which a researcher is going patiently about his daily grind—growing cell cultures or mixing chemicals or peering into a microscope—when, quite by accident, he makes some earthshaking discovery. Variations on the tale are myriad, but the moral is always the same: Great breakthroughs can be neither planned nor predicted; you just have to get lucky.

Consider, for example, the legend of how Louis Pasteur developed the cholera vaccine. According to the standard account, the French chemist might never have realized that weakened microorganisms can activate the immune system without causing serious illness had he not gone away on vacation during the summer of 1879. Pasteur had been experimenting with chicken cholera, the story goes, and happened to leave his germ cultures sitting out when he left Paris for more than two months. Upon his return, he found that the cultures, though still active, had become avirulent; they no longer could sicken a chicken. So he developed a new set of cultures from a natural outbreak of the disease and resumed his work. Yet he found, to his surprise, that the hens he had exposed to the weakened germ culture still failed to develop cholera. Only then did it dawn on Pasteur that he had inadvertently immunized them.

Equally fortuitous, according to conventional wisdom, was the German pathologist Oskar Minkowski's 1889 discovery that diabetes stems from a disorder of the pancreas. Minkowski had removed that organ from a dog to determine its role in the digestion of fat. After the operation, the dog happened to urinate on the laboratory floor. The urine drew flies, and the flies drew the attention of a sharp-eyed lab assistant. Puzzled, since flies are not normally attracted to urine, the assistant questioned Minkowski, who analyzed the urine and found it to be loaded with sugar. The obvious conclusion was that the pancreas was somehow involved in metabolizing that substance. (We now know that the pancreas contains islets of Langerhans, which secrete insulin, a hormone responsible for sugar metabolism.) The depancreatized dog turned out to be a perfect experimental model for diabetes. Yet, as legend has it, Minkowski would never have recognized this had the dog not relieved itself in the company of a swarm of flies and an alert lab assistant.

Still another breakthrough usually described as a fluke is the discovery of lysozyme—a bacteria-killing enzyme in tears, saliva, mucus, and other bodily fluids and tissues—by the British bacteriologist Alexander Fleming, in 1921. When Fleming began the work that led to this discovery, during the First World War, it was well known that the body had three lines of defense against infection—the skin (a physical barrier); macrophages (a type of white blood cell that ingests foreign material); and antibodies (proteins that neutralize toxins by adhering to them). But no one had even suggested there might be a fourth. Thus, we are told, Fleming was not looking for lysozyme; the discovery resulted from a series of chance occurrences. First, some contaminant from the air fell into a culture dish in

Fleming's laboratory, where it spawned a bacterial colony. Then, when Fleming leaned over his microscope to take a close look at this germ population, his nose dripped into it (he suffered from frequent winter colds). To his surprise, the drippings dissolved colonies of bacteria in the petri dish. He developed other cultures from the first one, subjected them to the same treatment, and obtained the same result. Further experiments confirmed that the mucus contained an antibacterial agent and showed that the agent was a proteinaceous substance that did not reproduce itself. He concluded it was an enzyme manufactured by the body.

Stories such as these (there are countless others, ranging from Wilhelm C. Röntgen's discovery of the X-ray to Jocelyn Bell Burnell's discovery of pulsars to Charles R. Richet's discovery of anaphylaxis—an extreme allergic reaction that can cause death) have led philosophers of science to draw a bold distinction between the process of *discovery* and that of *proof,* and to insist that logic and reason apply only to the latter. According to most standard texts— W. I. B. Beveridge's *Art of Scientific Investigation,* R. B. Braithwaite's *Scientific Explanation,* Carl Hempel's *Philosophy of Natural Science,* David Hull's *Philosophy of Biological Science,* Karl Popper's *Logic of Scientific Discovery*—discovery is a product not of particular methods of logical inquiry but of being in the right place at the right time. It could happen to anyone at any time. In contrast, the process of testing a hypothesis is said to be a more logical operation—one that only a rational inquirer, trained in the methods of science, can successfully perform. Unlike discovery, scientific validation is thought to consist of two distinct mental activities: induction (deriving general rules from particular instances) and deduction (making specific predictions based on general rules). The objective of science, according to this philosophy, is simply to validate or invalidate inexplicable insights.

By limiting themselves to explaining scientific validation, philosophers save themselves the trouble of trying to account for the rich, messy business of discovery. But this approach has drawbacks: It suggests, paradoxically, that illogical processes have led to the most logical constructs known to mankind—mathematics and science. And it fails to explain where problems come from, what scientists do from day to day, and how they actually think. Real scientists do not spend their lives cataloguing the facts that follow from established principles, or noting the principles that are implicit in particular facts. As the French mathematician Henry Poincaré argued in *Science and Method,* such exercises would be largely pointless and sterile and endlessly boring. The passion of any real scientist is to expand our knowledge of the world, not merely to confirm it. That means searching out instances in which the codified rules of science fail to account for our experience: looking for paradoxes, contradictions, anomalies—in short, for problems. It is only after a problem has been identified that induction or deduction can serve a purpose, and only in relation to such a problem that an observation becomes a discovery.

So something is clearly amiss. The notion of accidental discovery assumes that anyone else seeing what Pasteur, Minkowski, Fleming, Röntgen, Burnell, or Richet saw would have come to the same conclusions. Yet, in each case, someone else *was* there and did *not* make the discovery: Pasteur's collaborator Émile Roux, Minkowski's unidentified lab assistant, and Fleming's colleague V. D. Allison. Richet reports that the experiment that caused him to invent the concept of anaphylaxis was so bizarre, his collaborators refused even to countenance the results. And several people, including the English chemist William Crookes, observed the same phenomena that Röntgen did—fogged photographic plates and fluorescing barium plati-nocyanide screens—but did not appreciate the fact that these effects were created by previously unknown rays—X-rays—emitted by nearby cathode-ray tubes. Clearly, it is not sufficient simply to be in the right place at the right time. How a scientist interprets what he sees depends on what he expects. Discoveries do not just walk up and present themselves from time to time, disguised as chickens, dogs, or nasal drips.

Why not admit that discoveries derive from the ways in which particular scientists logically go about their work? Then, given that different scientists practice different styles of research, and that not all of them make discoveries, it should be possible to identify the styles that most often pay off. Surely, any mental activity that con-tributes directly to scientific discoveries should be recognized as scientific method. If such activities are not acknowledged by the prevailing view of how scientists use logic and reason, that does not mean the activities are illogical. It means that the prevailing view is too narrow to account for how scientists really think. The task, then, is to redefine the scientific method in a way that accounts for the process of discovery.

Were Pasteur's and Minkowski's and Fleming's breakthroughs really just accidents? A recent analysis of Pasteur's notebooks by the historian of science Antonio Cadeddu suggests that the discovery of the cholera vaccine was anything but. It was well known during the late nineteenth century that people who survive certain infectious diseases tend not to come down with them again. Pasteur had noted as much, and his experiments with chicken cholera were clearly designed to explore that phenomenon. He seems to have been consciously pursuing a problem: how to produce a microbe strong enough to cause some degree of illness (and thus to protect against future infection) yet not strong enough to kill. So he was not aimlessly inoculating chickens when he discovered the cholera vaccine; he was trying, to use his own term, to "enfeeble" the infectious agent.

Moreover, the breakthrough did not come about from his leaving flasks of germs unattended while he went on vacation. In fact, he left them in the care of Émile Roux. Pasteur did, upon his return, inoculate chickens with material from the flasks, and the birds did fail to become ill. But when the same chickens were later injected with a more virulent strain, they died. No discovery here. Indeed, the notebooks reveal that Pasteur did not even initiate his first successful enfeeblement experiment until a few months later, in October of 1879. He and Roux had tried to enfeeble the germs by passing them from one animal to another, by growing them in different media, by heating them, by exposing them to air—anything that conceivably might weaken them—and only after many such attempts did one of the experiments succeed.

That winter, Pasteur managed, by placing germ cultures in acidic mediums, to enfeeble them in varying degrees. For some time, the strains that failed to kill chickens were also too weak to immunize them. But by March of 1880, Pasteur had developed two cultures with the properties of vaccines. The trick, according to his notebooks, was to use a mildly acidic medium, not a strong one, and to leave the germ culture sitting in it for a long time. Thus, he produced an attenuated organism capable of inducing an immune response in chickens. The discovery, therefore, was not an accident at all; Pasteur had posed a question—Is it possible to immunize an animal with a weakened infectious agent?—and then systematically searched for the answer.

Minkowski, too, was less reliant on dumb luck than is widely presumed. He probably *was* surprised to find sugar in the urine of the depancreatized dog; he had, after all, set out to investigate the role of the pancreas in the metabolism of fat. But Minkowski's own account of the discovery, published long after the popular version took hold, suggests it was neither a swarm of flies nor an alert lab assistant that brought the undigested sugar to his attention. It was, rather, his own carefully honed skills of observation and diagnosis, which he applied to an unexpected change in the dog's behavior.

Minkowski recounts that the dog, though fully housebroken before the operation, became an inveterate floor wetter afterward. In medical terms, it developed polyuria—unusually frequent urination. Polyuria is a classic symptom of diabetes, and Minkowski had learned in medical school that if a patient developed that symptom, the way to find out whether he had diabetes rather than, say, a bladder infection was to test the urine for sugar. Once Minkowski had asked the right question—namely, Why does a depancreatized dog suddenly develop polyuria?—standard medical procedures provided a ready answer: the urine was found to contain sugar and, as expected, the dog eventually developed all the symptoms of diabetes. So it followed that diabetes stems from a pancreatic disorder.

Minkowski's discovery was clearly a surprise (he had not even set out to study diabetes), but that is not to say it was a random occurrence. The dog's indoor accidents did not just happen; they were an inevitable result of the pancreas experiment. Nor was it by fluke that Minkowski found the dog's problem significant. His response was a consequence of his expectations. Had he not known the dog, he might have assumed that it always urinated on the floor. And had he not been familiar with the symptoms of diabetes, he might never have suspected that he had induced it in the dog. In short, Minkowski's discovery consisted not of what he saw but of how he saw it.

What about Fleming's discovery of lysozyme? According to the accepted accounts, there was no logic whatever to this breakthrough; it grew out of at least three totally unpredictable occurrences: first, Fleming got a severe cold; second, at about the same time, his petri dish was mysteriously contaminated by one of the few bacteria sensitive to lysozyme; third, he happened to contaminate the same dish with a drip from his nose and still did not discard it. In fact, one need only consult Fleming's notebooks to see that he quite literally cultivated the circumstances surrounding his discovery. The initial contaminant turns out to have been a bacterium harvested from his own nose—and his fateful drip into this culture, part of a deliberate experiment.

The purpose of the experiment was to determine whether colds might be caused by bacteriophages—viruses that cause illness by destroying resident bacteria in a host's body. The bacteriologist Frederick W. Twort had discovered bacteriophages in 1915, and a few years later, another bacteriologist, Félix d'Hérelle, isolated them in locusts with diarrhea and in humans with dysentery. The cold-prone Fleming was personally interested in learning the cause of the common cold, and a simple, flippant play on words may have led him to suspect bacteriophages. Might not "runny noses" and "runny bottoms" be the work of related agents? The way to find out was to extract bacteria from normal nasal mucus and then determine whether a cold sufferer's mucus contains agents capable of destroying it.

Fleming reported that it took him four days to cultivate a suitable bacterial colony. (The chance-drip version of the story is further belied by his assistant W. Howard Hughes's recollection, in *Alexander Fleming and Penicillin,* that Fleming had attached a leather guard to his microscope to prevent such accidents from occurring.) A few drops of his cold-infected mucus ate holes into this lawn of bacteria— just as bacteriophages do. Fleming spent the next few weeks conducting additional tests to make sure. But things started going wrong.

The easiest way to find out whether a solution contains bacteriophages is to dilute it repeatedly. Because bacteriophages are self-replicating, a solution containing them will return to its original potency within a few hours. Thus, when Fleming's solutions did not regain their strength, he began to suspect that he was dealing with an enzyme. (Because enzymes are body products, not organisms, they are not self-replicating; the more an enzyme preparation is diluted, the less activity there is.) Furthermore, Fleming found that the agent he had isolated could be inactivated by heat, as other enzymes can, and chemical tests demonstrated that it had the proteinaceous composition of an enzyme. The original hypothesis was foiled: the antibacterial agent obviously was not an invading bacteriophage. Instead, Fleming had discovered a new enzyme. He soon published his discovery, adding lysozyme to the pantheon of recognized bodily defenses. But he never publicly explained how he had happened upon lysozyme, and, hence, the story of the contaminated cell culture and the accidental drip was invented to make up for historical ignorance.

As Minkowski and Pasteur did, Fleming succeeded only after failing, but he did not succeed by chance. Had he not conceived of a possible link between intestinal disease and the common cold, he would not have been looking for bacteriophages in his nasal mucus. And had he not expected his would-be bacteriophages to reproduce in solution, he would not have performed the tests that led to his recognition of a new enzyme.

Virtually every so-called chance discovery that has been reexamined in the light of additional historical evidence has had to be revised in the manner of the Pasteur, Minkowski, and Fleming stories. Again and again, the record reveals that the discovery is not a fluke but the inevitable, if unforeseen, consequence of a rational and carefully planned line of inquiry initiated by a scientist. It follows that, contrary to philosophical orthodoxy, the tests of an incorrect hypothesis often result in surprises that lead to discovery, and that discoverers are not just beneficiaries of fate. They seem to have ways of courting the unexpected, which improve their chances of making novel observations. So there must be a logic, or at least a set of strategies, in discovery. The question is, Why are discoveries made by certain scientists rather than others? Can their strategies be learned?

I think they can. But such strategies are not so easily codified as are the rules of scientific proof, for they pertain to everything from recognizing interesting problems to appreciating unexpected results. How a scientist handles these matters is a function of his entire personality—the sum of the interests, skills, experiences, and desires that define him as a human being. Still, it should be possible to identify some of the habits of thought that are particularly advantageous.

It is striking how many great scientists have incorporated play into their lives and work, how many have consciously avoided being overly cautious or orderly, or narrowly pragmatic. Fleming, for one, was famous for his love of games. He was raised in a family that played everything from poker and bridge to table tennis and quiz games. As an adult, he played croquet, bowls, and snooker at his club, and pitched pennies at his office whenever he lacked patients. He took up golf, too, but rarely played a straight game; he would putt holding the club as a snooker cue, or revise the rules to make the game more interesting. Life was essentially a game to him, and so was research. "I play with microbes," he once said, adding, "It is very plesant to break the rules."

In the laboratory, one of Fleming's favorite pastimes was to fashion art from germs. He would start with an assortment of microorganisms and, knowing which color each one would produce as it multiplied, paint them onto a petri dish. After incubating the dish for a day, he would unveil a picture of his house or a ballerina or a mother nursing a baby. Fleming was no great artist, but his hobby fostered a rare intimacy with the bacterial world. To paint his pictures, he had to know not only which germ would produce which color but also how rapidly each would proliferate at a given temperature. To maintain a diverse palette, he also had to be constantly on the lookout for bacteria that might suit his purposes. To this end, he made a point of creating environments in which unusual germs might crop up. V. D. Allison recalls in a lecture to the Ulster Medical Society, just how conscientiously Fleming practiced this method:

> At the end of each day's work I cleaned my bench, put it in order for the next day and discarded tubes and culture plates for which I had no further use. He, for his part, kept his cultures . . . for two or three weeks until his bench was overcrowded with forty or fifty cultures. He would then discard them, first of all looking at them individually to see whether anything interesting or unusual had developed.

Fleming was not alone in his tendency to mix things up a bit to see what would happen. Konrad Lorenz, the great animal behaviorist, was equally scrupulous about cultivating fruitful confusion. Lorenz lived among his research subjects: dozens of species of mammals, birds, reptiles, and fishes. He did not quantify, control, or consciously experiment. He got to know each creature individually, then threw them together, watching for the unexpected, the unusual, or the bizarre in the chaos that followed. For example, his interest in one of ethology's most important concepts, that of intention movements (motions with meaning, such as the head bobbing in birds that serves as an alarm signal before flight), derived from an inadvertent experiment. He had trained a free-flying raven to eat raw meat from his hand and had been feeding the bird on and off for several hours one day. He would reach into his pants pocket and take out a piece of meat, and the raven would swoop down to grab it in its bill. By and by, Lorenz went to relieve himself near a hedge. When the raven saw him put his hand into his pants and pull out another morsel of meat, it swooped down, hungrily grasping the new mouthful in its bill. Lorenz howled in pain. But the event left a deep impression on him—about how faithfully animals respond to intention movements, that is.

One mental quality that facilitates discovery, then, is a willingness to goof around, to play games, and to cultivate a degree of chaos aimed at revealing the unusual or the unexpected. Looking back on the scientists who missed discoveries—Allison in Fleming's lab; Richet's collaborators on the anaphylaxis experiments; Crookes, Röntgen's colleague—we see that, in each case, they refused to credit a phenomenon with significance because it was not what they were looking for. "It's just a contamination." "You must have injected the wrong solution." "Send the photographic plates back to the manufacturers and tell them they'd better deliver good ones tomorrow or we'll cancel our order."

A classic example of such a reaction was reported by Jocelyn Bell Burnell in an interview concerning her discovery of pulsars. She had been pointing her radio telescope toward a region of the heavens at a time when she expected to pick up only a weak signal, when the pen on the recording device started jiggling. Repeating the observation at weekly intervals yielded the same result, and test after test revealed nothing wrong with the equipment. Eventually, Burnell realized she had detected the presence of stellar sources of pulsating radio waves, or pulsars, which astronomers had hypothesized but never found. Sometime later, she heard that a colleague had observed the same phenomenon, given his equipment table a good kick, and written off the result as a mechanical aberration. We may presume he later kicked himself.

Not every anomaly or unexpected result leads to discovery, of course. As Sherlock Holmes once said, "It is of the highest importance in the art of detection to be able to recognize out of a number of facts which are incidental and which vital." However, Charles Richet, in *The Natural History of a Savant,* and the physicist George P. Thomson, in *The Strategy of Research,* both warn that there is no correlation between the difficulty of a problem and its importance. The most trivial observation can, in the mind of a scientist possessed of imagination, yield surprises of the greatest significance.

To elevate the trivial to the universal, the scientist must, first of all, be a global thinker; that is, he must be able to perceive how certain principles apply to diverse phenomena. The biochemist Albert Szent-Györgyi provides a good example. His discovery of the universal principles by which oxygen reacts with living tissue stemmed from his observation that bananas and lemons react differently with oxygen: bananas turn brown when they are bruised, but lemons do not. He concluded that lemons contain something that affects the way they react with oxygen and later found that something to be ascorbic acid—vitamin C. But Szent-Györgyi's insight did not end there. He realized that similar oxidative reactions must occur in all living organisms and went on to demonstrate how muscle tissue uses oxygen. "Looking back on this work today," he said years later, "I think that bananas, lemons, and men all have basically the same system of respiration, however different they may appear."

In the search for universal truths, a scientist is also wise to know intimately, even to identify with, the things or creatures he studies. Lorenz was fully aware of all his animals' normal behaviors—feeding, fighting, mating, nesting, impriting, rearing, and so on—so he could recognize when a behavior was exceptional. And Pasteur and Fleming had the same complete familiarity with microbes. But intimacy means more than mere knowledge. In an interview, the geneticist

Barbara McClintock, winner of the 1983 Nobel Prize in medicine, described her method of research as having "a feeling for the organism." Speaking of her work on the chromosomes of the *Neurospora* fungus, she said:

> I found that the more I worked with them, the bigger and bigger [they] got, and when I was really working with them I wasn't outside, I was down there. I was part of the system. . . . I even was able to see the internal parts of the chromosomes—actually everything was there. It surprised me because I actually felt as if . . . these were my friends. . . . As you look at these things, they become part of you. And you forget yourself. The main thing about it is you forget yourself.

The mathematician Jacob Bronowski, in an essay in *Scientific American,* wrote that it is this "personal engagement" of the scientist that differentiates him from a mere technician. The physicist-philosopher Michael Polanyi calls this "personal knowledge."

The reward for such internalization of subject matter is intuition. The scientist learns to sense what is expected, to *feel* how the world ought to work. Peter Debye, a Dutch-born American who won the 1936 Nobel Prize in chemistry for his work on molecular structure, said once that he would ask himself, "What did the carbon atom *want* to do?" The virologist Jonas Salk, discoverer of the polio vaccine, writes in *Anatomy of Reality,* "I would picture myself as a virus, or as a cancer cell, for example, and try to sense what it would be like to be either. I would also imagine myself as the immune system . . . engaged in combating a virus or cancer cell."

In essence, intuition is the ability to sense an underlying order in things, and thus is it related to still another mental tool that is indispensable to the working scientist: the perception of patterns, both visual and verbal. The Russian chemist Dmitri I. Mendeleyev's periodic table of elements is a classic example of how ordering facts yields new insights. Before he conceived it, in 1868, chemists had had great difficulty perceiving relationships between the elements. Mendeleyev noticed that when he arranged all the elements on a chart, according to their atomic weights, the chemically related elements appeared at regular, or periodic, intervals. (For example, magnesium, calcium, and strontium, all of which occur in the same column, have the same valence, or number of orbitals available for bonding.) His table had many gaps, but Mendeleyev correctly predicted the existence of missing elements, and scandium, gallium, and germanium, among others, were duly discovered during his lifetime.

All good theories contain, at heart, an ordering process that reveals hidden patterns. Consider how Pasteur discovered the phenomenon of molecular asymmetry—the way organic molecules exhibit what are called right-handed and left-handed forms. The discovery grew out of Pasteur's search for the molecular differences between racemic and tartaric acids, both of which are wine by-products that form crystals on the inner surfaces of casks during the fermentation process. The German chemist Eilhard Mitscherlich had concluded that the two acids not only had the same chemical composition and specific gravity but also seemed to form identical crystal structures. The only difference between them, he believed, was that a beam of polarized light would pass directly through a racemic acid crystal but would be bent, or deflected, as it passed through a crystal of tartaric acid.

Pasteur was puzzled by the notion that two crystals, identical in structure, would differ in this key respect, for studies of quartz crystals had suggested that differences in their ability to bend polarized light always corresponded to differences in crystal form. He hypothesized that Mitscherlich had been wrong and that the light-deflecting racemic molecules would turn out to be asymmetrical in structure and the tartaric ones, symmetrical. Pasteur placed samples of both acids under the microscope and noted that there were in fact slight irregularities in the racemic molecules. Yet he also discovered, to his surprise, that the tartaric molecules were slightly irregular. This finding shot down Pasteur's initial hypothesis—that a crystal's optical activity reveals whether its molecules are symmetrical or asymmetrical—but the paradox led him to a better theory. By designing further experiments, he figured out that tartaric acid had only one asymmetrical form, a right-handed form that caused it to bend polarized light, whereas racemic acid had two asymmetrical forms—right-handed and left-handed—which nullified each other's ability to deflect light.

Pasteur's advantage over the various crystallographers who had studied the same molecules and failed to detect their asymmetry was not that he had better eyesight (he was nearsighted) or that he was better at constructing hypotheses (indeed, his first one was wrong). It was that his logic and perceptual skills (as a teenager, he had been trained as an artist) gave him an edge. First, he insisted that the tartrates fit the pattern of previously studied compounds, and, second, he looked at molecules that other scientists regarded as identical, and he recognized differences in their structures.

Verbal patterns are sometimes just as suggestive as visual ones. Fleming, you will recall, had no reason beyond the verbal symmetry of runny bottoms and runny noses to seek a biological connection. And more than one valuable idea has begun as a pun. In 1943, when the biologist Ralph Lewis, of Michigan State University, started a study of how fungus is disseminated by insects, he could not get his flies to pick up the fungal spores he was placing in their midst, so his experiment came to a halt. The problem was that the spores were drying out in the laboratory. In nature, spores are released by the fungus in a sweet, moist substance called honeydew. Free-ranging insects are attracted to the fungus by the honeydew, and it sticks to their legs, carrying the embedded spores with it. The question that occurred to Lewis was, Would honey do? In fact, honey would do just fine, and the experiment could proceed. Lewis's idea was not a formal, logical inference, but it was a perfectly good one.

It should be clear by now that scientific discovery is never entirely accidental. It holds an element of surprise, to be sure, the effective surprise that changes a person's perception of nature. But the best scientists know how to surprise themselves purposely. They master the widest range of mental tools (including, but certainly not limited to, game playing, universal thinking, identification with subject matter, intuition, and pattern recognition) and identify deficiencies or inconsistencies in their understanding of the world. Finally, they are clever enough to interpret their observations in such a way as to change the perceptions of other scientists, as well. As Albert Szent-Györgyi put it, "Discovery consists of seeing what everybody has seen and thinking what nobody has thought."

We are forced to accept still another conclusion. The process of discovery is not distinguishable from that of logical testing. In each of the examples discussed above—Pasteur, Minkowski, Fleming, and all the rest—the tests neither validated nor invalidated the initial hypotheses but ended in surprise. What each of these scientists discovered was a new problem, an anomaly that led to the discovery of something else. Thus, it appears that the most important discoveries arise not from verification or disproof of preconceptions but from the unexpected results of testing them.

This has practical implications. At present, we fund experiments whose results are foreseeable rather than those that are most likely to surprise. Similarly, we train scientists almost solely in the methods of demonstration and proof. And students are evaluated on their ability to reach correct, accepted conclusions. This sort of education is necessary, but it is also insufficient, serving only to verify what we know, to build up the edifice of codified science without suggesting how to generate problems of the sort that lead to new discoveries.

A startling conclusion? Perhaps, but this is the message contained in the work of Pasteur, Minkowski, and Fleming, and dozens of other successful scientists. What is intriguing is how historians and philosophers persist in ignoring their testimony. Is it that we perceive only what we expect to see?

Suggestions for Discussion and Writing

1. The essay is divided into five parts; what is the specific function of the first part? What is the relationship of the second, third, and fourth paragraphs to the first paragraph? What is the author's purpose (and implied thesis)? Where does he state it?

2. Why, according to the author, have traditional discussions of scientific method been inadequate?

3. Why are the strategies of discovery less easily codified than the rules of scientific proof?

4. In the eighth paragraph the author writes: "Surely, any mental activity that contributes directly to scientific discoveries should be recognized as scientific method. If such activities are not acknowledged by the prevailing view of how scientists use logic and reason, that does not mean the activities are illogical. It means that the prevailing view is too narrow to account for how scientists really think." Later (at the start of the third part), in speaking of the strategies of discovery, he says, "how a scientist handles these matters is a function of his entire personality—the sum of the interests, skills, experiences, and desires that define him as a human being." Can these two statements be reconciled? Does the author establish a broader view of the way in which scientists use "logic and reason"?

5. What is the function of play? Why is it important? What mental processes or attitudes does it foster—or reflect? In what ways does play contribute to the scientist's ability to "court the unexpected"? Write an essay in which you develop your views.

6. Discuss the author's use of examples.

7. The author quotes several scientists, among them Barbara McClintock and Jonas Salk, to support his view that "a scientist is also wise to know intimately, even to identify with, the things or creatures he studies." How does the scientist achieve such intimacy? Does it involve a rejection of scientific objectivity?

8. Compare the author's statement, "All good theories contain, at heart, an ordering process that reveals hidden patterns," with Popper's (this chapter) that "every 'good' scientific theory is a prohibition—it forbids certain things to happen."

9. In the penultimate paragraph, the author suggests that the "training" and "education" of scientists is inadequate, given the way in which scientists actually work. What educational changes do you think he would recommend?

10. In a paragraph each, write an extended definition of "training" and "education."

☐ SCIENCE AND THE SENSE OF THE HOLY

Loren Eiseley *(1907–1977)*

Educated at the University of Nebraska, Loren Eiseley was for many years Benjamin Franklin Professor of Anthropology at the University of Pennsylvania and Curator of Early Man at the University Museum. During his distinguished career, he contributed to scientific journals such as *Science* and *American Anthropologist* as well as to magazines such as *Harper's* and *The Saturday Review of Literature.* Among his more well-known books are *The Immense Journey* (1957), *Notes of an Alchemist* (1972), and *The Star Thrower* (1978).

Frequently described as a scientist with the sensibilities of a poet, Eiseley's imagination and command of language are unquestionably extraordinary; his writings characteristically have a strong meditative quality. His literary gifts were recognized in 1971 with his election to the National Institute of Arts and Letters.

In the following selection from *The Star Thrower,* Eiseley speaks of the awe and reverence that the scientist must bring to the study of the physical world. The scientist who lacks a "sense of the holy" and relies exclusively on reasoning and logic, he believes, will never come to a full understanding of nature.

I

When I was a young man engaged in fossil hunting in the Nebraska badlands I was frequently reminded that the ravines, washes, and gullies over which we wandered resembled the fissures in a giant exposed brain. The human brain contains the fossil memories of its past—buried but not extinguished moments—just as this more formidable replica contained deep in its inner stratigraphic convolutions earth's past in the shape of horned titanotheres and stalking, dirk-toothed cats. Man's memory erodes away in the short space of a lifetime. Jutting from the coils of the earth brain over which I clambered were the buried remnants, the changing history, of the entire age of mammals—millions of years of vanished daylight with their accompanying traces of volcanic outbursts and upheavals. It may well be asked why this analogy of earth's memory should so preoccupy the mind of a scientist as to have affected his entire outlook upon nature and upon his kinship with—even his concern for—the plant and animal world about him.

Perhaps the problem can best be formulated by pointing out that there are two extreme approaches to the interpretation of the living world. One was expressed by Charles Darwin at the age of twenty-eight; one by Sigmund Freud in his mature years. Other men of science have been arrayed on opposite sides of the question, but the eminence of these two scholars will serve to point up a controversy that has been going on since science arose, sometimes quietly, sometimes marked by vitriolic behavior, as when a certain specialist wedded to his own view of the universe hurled his opponent's book into his wastebasket only to have it retrieved and cherished by a graduate student who became a lifelong advocate of the opinions reviled by his mentor. Thus it is evident that, in the supposed objective world of science, emotion and temperament may play a role in our selection of the mental tools with which we choose to investigate nature.

Charles Darwin, at a time when the majority of learned men looked upon animals as either automatons or creatures created merely for human exploitation, jotted thoughtfully into one of his early journals upon evolution the following observation:

"If we choose to let conjecture run wild, then animals, our fellow brethren in pain, disease, suffering and famine—our slaves in the most laborious works, our companions in our amusements—they may partake of our origin in one common ancestor—we may be all netted together."

What, we may now inquire, is the world view here implied, one way in which a great scientist looked upon the subject matter that was to preoccupy his entire working life? In spite of the fact that Darwin was, in his later years, an agnostic, in spite of confessing he was "in thick mud" so far as metaphysics was concerned, the remark I have quoted gives every sign of that feeling of awe, of dread of the holy playing upon nature, which characterizes the work of a number of naturalists and physicists down even to the present day. Darwin's remark reveals an intuitive sensitivity to the life of other creatures about him, an attitude quite distinct from that of the laboratory experimentalist who is hardened to the infliction of pain. In addition, Darwin's final comment that we may be all netted together in one gigantic mode of experience, that we are in a mystic sense one single diffuse animal, subject to joy and suffering beyond what we endure as individuals, reveals a youth drawn to the world of nature by far more than just the curiosity to be readily satisfied by the knife or the scalpel.

If we turn to Sigmund Freud by way of contrast we find an oddly inhibited reaction. Freud, though obviously influenced by the elegant medical experimenters of his college days, groped his way alone, and by methods not subject to quantification or absolute verification, into the dark realms of the subconscious. His reaction to the natural world, or at least his feelings and intuitions about it, are basically cold, clinical, and reserved. He of all men recognized what one poet has termed "the terrible archaeology of the brain." Freud states that "nothing once constructed has perished, and all the earlier stages of development have survived alongside the latest." But for Freud, convinced that childhood made the man, adult reactions were apt to fall under the suspicion of being childhood ghosts raised up in a disguised fashion. Thus, insightful though he could be, the very nature of his study of man tended to generate distrust of that outgoing empathy we observed in the young Darwin. "I find it very difficult to work with these intangible qualities," confessed Freud. He was suspicious of their representing some lingering monster of childhood, even if reduced in size. Since Freud regarded any type of religious feeling—even the illuminative quality of the universe—as an illusion, feelings of awe before natural phenomena such as that manfested by Darwin were to him basically remnants of childhood and to be dismissed accordingly.

In *Civilization and Its Discontents* Freud speaks with slight condescension of a friend who claimed a sensation of eternity, something limitless, unbounded—"oceanic," to use the friend's expression. The feeling had no sectarian origin, no assurance of immortality, but implied just such a sense of awe as might lie at the root of the religious impulse. "I cannot," maintained Freud, "discover this 'oceanic' impulse in myself." Instead he promptly psychoanalyzes the feeling of oneness with the universe into the child's pleasure ego which holds to itself all that is comforting; in short, the original ego, the infant's ego, included everything. Later, by experience, contended Freud, our adult ego becomes only a shrunken vestige of that far more extensive feeling which "expressed an inseparable connection . . . with the external world."

In essence, then, Freud is explaining away one of the great feelings characteristic of the best in man by relegating it to a childhood atavistic survival in adult life. The most highly developed animals, he observes, have arisen from the lowest. Although the great saurians are gone, the dwarfed crocodile remains. Presumably if Freud had completed the analogy he would have been forced to say that crocodilian adults without awe and with egos shrunken safely into their petty concerns represented a higher, more practical evolutionary level than the aberrant adult who persists in feelings of wonder before which Freud recoiled with a nineteenth-century mechanist's distaste, although not without acknowledging that this lurking childlike corruption might be widespread. He chose to regard it, however, as just another manifestation of the irrational aspect of man's divided psyche.

Over six decades before the present, a German theologian, Rudolf Otto, had chosen for his examination what he termed *The Idea of the Holy* (*Das Heilige*). Appearing in 1917 in a time of bitterness and disillusionment, his book was and is still widely read. It cut across denominational divisions and spoke to all those concerned with that *mysterium tremendum,* that very awe before the universe which Freud had sighed over and dismissed as irrational. I think it safe to affirm that Freud left adult man somewhat shrunken and misjudged—misjudged because some of the world's scientists and artists have been deeply affected by the great mystery, less so the child at one's knee who frequently has to be disciplined to what in India has been called the "opening of the heavenly eye."

Ever since man first painted animals in the dark of caves he has been responding to the holy, to the numinous, to the mystery of being and becoming, to what Goethe very aptly called "the weird portentous." Something inexpressible was felt to lie behind nature. The bear cult, circumpolar in distribution and known archaeologically to extend into Neanderthal times, is a further and most ancient example. The widespread beliefs in descent from a totemic animal, guardian helpers in the shapes of animals, the concept of the game lords who released or held back game to man are all part of a variety of a sanctified, reverent experience that extends from the beautiful rock paintings of South Africa to the men of the Labradorean forests or the Plains Indian seeking by starvation and isolation to bring the sacred spirits to his assistance. All this is part of the human inheritance, the wonder of the world, and nowhere does that wonder press closer to us than in the guise of animals which, whether supernaturally as in the caves of our origins or, as in Darwin's sudden illumination, perceived to be, at heart, one form, one awe-inspiring mystery, seemingly diverse and apart but derived from the same genetic source. Thus the *mysterium* arose not by primitive campfires alone. Skins may still prickle in a modern classroom.

In the end, science as we know it has two basic types of practitioners. One is the educated man who still has a controlled sense of wonder before the universal mystery, whether it hides in a snail's eye or within the light that impinges on that delicate organ. The second kind of observer is the extreme reductionist who is so busy stripping things apart that the tremendous mystery has been reduced to a trifle, to intangibles not worth troubling one's head about. The world of the secondary qualities—color, sound, thought—is reduced to illusion. The *only* true reality becomes the chill void of ever-streaming particles.

If one is a biologist this approach can result in behavior so remarkably cruel that it ceases to be objective but rather suggests a deep grain of sadism that is not science. To list but one example, a recent newspaper article reported that a great urban museum of national reputation had spent over a half-million dollars on mutilating experiments with cats. The experiments are too revolting to chronicle here and the museum has not seen fit to enlighten the public on the knowledge gained at so frightful a cost in pain. The cost, it would appear, lies not alone in animal suffering but in the dehumanization of those willing to engage in such blind, random cruelty. The practice was defended by museum officials, who in a muted show of scientific defense maintained the right to study what they chose "without regard to its demonstrable practical value."

This is a scientific precept hard to override since the days of Galileo, as the official well knew. Nevertheless, behind its seamless façade of probity many terrible things are and will be done. Blaise Pascal, as far back as the seventeenth century, foresaw our two opposed methods. Of them he said: "There are two equally dangerous extremes, to shut reason out, and to let nothing else in." It is the reductionist who, too frequently, would claim that the end justifies the means, who would assert reason as his defense and let that *mysterium* which guards man's moral nature fall away in indifference, a phantom without reality.

"The whole of existence frightens me," protested the philosopher Søren Kierkegaard; "from the smallest fly to the mystery of the Incarnation, everything is unintelligible to me, most of all myself." By contrast, the evolutionary reductionist Ernst Haeckel, writing in 1877, commented that "the cell consists of matter . . . composed chiefly of carbon with an admixture of hydrogen, nitrogen and sulphur. These component parts, properly united, produce the soul and body of the animated world, and suitably nourished become man. With this single argument the mystery of the universe is explained, the Deity annulled and a new era of infinite knowledge ushered in." Since these remarks of Haeckel's, uttered a hundred years ago, the genetic alphabet has scarcely substantiated in its essential intricacy Haeckel's carefree dismissal of the complexity of life. If anything, it has given weight to Kierkegaard's wary statement or at least heightened the compassionate wonder with which we are led to look upon our kind.

"A conviction akin to religious feeling of the rationality or intelligibility of the world lies behind all scientific work of a high order," says Albert Einstein. Here once more the eternal dichotomy manifests itself. Thoreau, the man of literature, writes compassionately, "Shall I not have intelligence with the earth? Am I not partly leaves and vegetable mould myself?" Or Walt Whitman, the poet, protests in his *Song of Myself:* "whoever walks a furlong without sympathy walks to his own funeral drest in a shroud."

> "Magnifying and applying come I"—he thunders—
> "Outbidding at the start the old cautious hucksters . . .
> Not objecting to special revelations, considering a curl of
>   smoke
>   or a hair
> on the back of my hand just as curious as any revelation."

Strange, is it not, that so many of these voices are not those of children, but those of great men—Newton playing on the vast shores of the universe, or Whitman touched with pity or Darwin infused with wonder over the clambering tree of life. Strange, that all these many voices should be dismissed as the atavistic yearnings of an unreduced childlike ego seeking in "oceanic" fashion to absorb its entire surroundings, as though in revolt against the counting house, the laboratory, and the computer.

II

Not long ago in a Manhattan art gallery there were exhibited paintings by Irwin Fleminger, a modernist whose vast lawless Martianlike landscapes contain cryptic human artifacts. One of these paintings attracted my eye by its title: "Laws of Nature." Here in a jumbled desert waste without visible life two thin laths had been erected a little distance apart. Strung across the top of the laths was an insubstantial string with even more insubstantial filaments depending from the connecting cord. The effect was terrifying. In the huge inhuman universe that constituted the background, man, who was even more diminished by his absence, had attempted to delineate and bring under natural law an area too big for his comprehension. His effort, his "law," whatever it was, denoted a tiny measure in the midst of an ominous landscape looming away to the horizon. The frail slats and dangling string would not have sufficed to fence a chicken run.

The message grew as one looked. With all the great powers of the human intellect we were safe, we understood, in degree, a space between some slats and string, a little gate into the world of infinitude. The effect was crushing and it brought before one that sense of the "other" of which Rudolf Otto spoke, the sense beyond our senses, unspoken awe, or, as the reductionist would have it, nothing but waste. There the slats stood and the string drooped hopelessly. It was the natural law imposed by man, but outside its compass, again to use the words of Thoreau, was something terrific, not bound to be kind to man. Not man's at all really—a star's substance totally indifferent to life or what laws life might concoct. No man would greatly extend that trifling toy. The line sagged hopelessly. Man's attempt had failed, leaving but an artifact in the wilderness. Perhaps, I thought, this is man's own measure. Perhaps he has already gone. The crepitation at my spine increased. I felt the mood of the paleolithic artists, lost in the mysteries of birth and coming, as they carved pregnant beasts in the dark of caves and tried by crayons to secure the food necessarily wrung from similar vast landscapes. Their art had the same holy quality that shows in the ivory figurines, the worship before the sacred mother who brought man mysteriously into the limited world of the cave mouth.

The numinous then is touched with superstition, the reductionist would say, but all the rituals suggest even toward hunted animals a respect and sympathy leading to ceremonial treatment of hunted souls; whereas by contrast in the modern world the degradation of animals in experiments of little, or vile, meaning, were easily turned to the experimental human torture practiced at Dachau and Buchenwald by men dignified with medical degrees. So the extremes of temperament stand today: the man with reverence and compassion in his heart whose eye ranges farther than the two slats in the wilderness, and the modern vandal totally lacking in empathy for life beyond his own, his sense of wonder reduced to a crushing series of gears and quantitative formula, the educated vandal without mercy or tolerance, the collecting man that I once tried to prevent from killing an endangered falcon, who raised his rifle, fired, and laughed as the bird tumbled at my feet. I suppose Freud might have argued that this was a man of normal ego, but I, extending my childlike mind into the composite life of the world, bled accordingly.

Perhaps Freud was right, but let us look once more at this brain that in many distinguished minds has agonized over life and the mysterious road by which it has come. Certainly, as Darwin recognized, it was not the tough-minded, logical inductionists of the early nineteenth century who in a deliberate distortion of Baconian philosophy solved the problem of evolution. Rather, it was what Darwin chose to call "speculative" men, men, in other words, with just a touch of the numinous in their eye, a sense of marvel, a glimpse of what was happening behind the visible, who saw the whole of the living world as though turning in a child's kaleidoscope.

Among the purely human marvels of the world is the way the human brain after birth, when its cranial capacity is scarcely larger than that of a gorilla or other big anthropoid, spurts onward to treble its size during the first year of life. The human infant's skull will soar to a cranial capacity of 950 cubic centimeters while the gorilla has reached only 380 cubic centimeters. In other words, the human brain grows at an exponential rate, a spurt which carries it almost to adult capacity at the age of fourteen.

This clever and specifically human adaptation enables the human offspring successfully to pass the birth canal like a reasonably small-headed animal, but in a more larval and helpless condition than its giant relatives. The brain burgeons after birth, not before, and it is this fact which enables the child, with proper care, to assimilate all that larger world which will be forever denied to its relative the gorilla. The big anthropoids enjoy no such expansion. Their brains grow without exponential quickening into maturity. Somewhere in the far past of man something strange happened in his evolutionary development. His skull has enhanced its youthful globularity; he has lost most of his body hair and what remains grows strangely. He demands, because of his immature emergence into the world, a lengthened and protected childhood. Without prolonged familial attendance he would not survive, yet in him reposes the capacity for great art, inventiveness, and his first mental tool, speech, which creates his humanity. He is without doubt the oddest and most unusual evolutionary product that this planet has yet seen.

The term applied to this condition is neoteny, or pedomorphism. Basically the evolutionary forces, and here "forces" stands for complete ignorance, seem to have taken a roughhewn ordinary primate and softened and eliminated the adult state in order to allow for a fantastic leap in brain growth. In fact, there is a growing suspicion that some, at least, of the African fossils found and ascribed to the direct line of human ascent in eastern Africa may never, except for bipedalism and some incipient tool-using capacities, have taken the human road at all.

Some with brains that seem to have remained at the same level through long ages have what amounts quantitatively to no more than an anthropoid brain. Allowing for upright posture and free use of the hand, there is no assurance that they spoke or in any effective way were more than well-adapted bipedal apes. Collateral relatives, in short, but scarcely to be termed men. All this is the more remarkable because their history can now be traced over roughly five if not six million years—a singularly unprogressive period for a creature destined later to break upon the world with such remarkable results after so long a period of gestation.

Has something about our calculations gone wrong? Are we studying, however necessarily, some bipedal cousins but not ancestral men? The human phylogeny which we seemed well on the way to arranging satisfactorily is now confused by a multiplicity of material contended over by an almost equal number of scholars. Just as a superfluity of flying particles is embarrassing the physicist, so man's evolution, once thought to be so clearly delineated, is showing signs of similar strain. A skull from Lake Rudolf with an estimated capacity of 775 cubic centimeters or even 800 and an antiquity ranging into the three-million-year range is at the human Rubicon, yet much younger fossils are nowhere out of the anthropoid range.

Are these all parts of a single variable subhumanity from which we arose or are some parts of this assemblage neotenous of brain and others not? The scientific exchanges are as stiff with politeness as exchanges between enemies on the floor of the Senate. "Professor so-and-so forgets the difficult task of restoring to its proper position a frontal bone trampled by cattle." A million years may be covertly jumped because there is nothing to be found in it. We must never lose sight of one fact, however: it is by neotenous brain growth that we came to be men, and certain of the South African hominids to which we have given such careful attention seem to have been remarkably slow in revealing such development. Some of them, in fact, during more years than present mankind has been alive seem to have flourished quite well as simple grassland apes.

Why indeed should they all have become men? Because they occupied the same ecological niche, contend those who would lump this variable assemblage. But surely paleontology does not always so bind its deliberations. We are here dealing with a gleam, a whisper, a thing of awe in the mind itself, that oceanic feeling which even the hardheaded Freud did not deny existed though he tried to assign it to childhood.

With animals whose precise environment through time may overlap, extinction may result among contending forms; it can and did happen among men. But with the first stirrings of the neotenous brain and its superinduced transformation of the family system a new type of ecological niche had incipiently appeared—a speaking niche, a wondering niche which need not have been first manifested in tools but in family organization, in wonder over what lay over the next hill or what became of the dead. Whether man preferred seeds or flesh, how he regarded his silent collateral relatives, may not at first have induced great competition. Only those gifted with the pedomorphic brain would in some degree have fallen out of competition with the real. It would have been their danger and at the same time their beginning triumph. They were starting to occupy, not a niche in nature, but an invisible niche carved into thought which in time would bring them suffering, superstition, and great power.

It cannot, in the beginning, be recognized clearly because it is not a matter of molar teeth and seeds, or killer instincts and ill-interpreted pebbles. Rather it was something happening in the brain, some blinding, irradiating thing. Until the quantity of that gray matter reached the threshold of human proportions no one could be sure whether the creature saw with a human eye or looked upon life with even the faint stirrings of some kind of religious compassion.

The new niche in its beginnings is invisible; it has to be inferred. It does not lie waiting to be discovered in a pebble or a massive molar. These things are important in the human dawn but so is the mystery that ordained that mind should pass the channel of birth and then grow like a fungus in the night—grow and convolute and overlap its older buried strata, while a 600-pound gorilla retains by contrast the cranial content of a very small child. When man cast off his fur and placed his trust in that remarkable brain linked by neural pathways to his tongue he had potentially abandoned niches for dreams. Henceforth the world was man's niche. All else would live by his toleration—even the earth from which he sprang. Perhaps this is the hardest, most expensive lesson the layers of the fungus brain have yet to learn: that man is not as other creatures and that without the sense of the holy, without compassion, his brain can become a gray stalking horror—the deviser of Belsen.

Its beginning is not the only curious thing about that brain. There are some finds in South Africa dating into immediately post-glacial times that reveal a face and calvaria more "modern" in appearance, more pedomorphic, than that of the average European. The skull is marked by cranial capacities in excess of 1700 cubic centimeters—big brained by any standards. The mastoids are childlike, the teeth reduced, the cranial base foreshortened. These people, variously termed Boskopoid or Strandlooper, have, in the words of one anthropologist, "the amazing cranium to face ratio of almost five to one. In Europeans it is about three to one. Face size has been modernized and subordinated to brain growth." In a culture still relying on coarse fare and primitive implements, the face and brain had been subtly altered in the direction science fiction writers like to imagine as the direction in which mankind is progressing. Yet here the curious foetalization of the human body seems to have outrun man's cultural status, though in the process giving warning that man's brain could still pass the straitened threshold of its birth.

How did these people look upon the primitive world into which they found themselves precipitated? History gives back no answer save that here there flourished striking three-dimensional art—the art of the brother animal seen in beauty. Childlike, Freud might have muttered, with childlike dreams, rushed into conflict with the strong, the adult and shrunken ego, the ego that gets what it wants. Yet how strangely we linger over this lost episode of the human story, its pathos, its possible meaning. From whence did these people come? We are not sure. We are not even sure that they derive from one of the groups among the ruck of bipdeal wandering apes long ago in Kenya that reveal some relationship to ourselves. Their development was slow, if indeed some of them took that road, the strange road to the foetalized brain that was to carry man outside of the little niche that fed him his tuberous, sandy diet.

We thought we were on the verge of solving the human story, but now we hold in our hands gross jaws and delicate, and are unsure of our direction save that the trail is longer than we had imagined twenty years ago. Yet still the question haunts us, the numinous, the holy in man's mind. Early man laid gifts beside the dead, but then in the modern unbelieving world, Ernst Haeckel's world, a renowned philosopher says, "The whole of existence frightens me," or another humble thinker says, "In the world there is nothing to explain the world" but remembers the gold eyes of the falcon thrown brutally at his feet. He shivers while Freud says, "As for me I have never had such feelings." They are a part of childhood, Freud argues, though there are some who counter that in childhood—yes, even Freud might grant it—the man is made, the awe persists or is turned off by blows or the dullness of unthinking parents. One can only assert that in science, as in religion, when one has destroyed human wonder and compassion, one has killed man, even if the man in question continues to go about his laboratory tasks.

III

Perhaps there is one great book out of all American literature which best expresses the clash between the man who has genuine perception and the one who pursues nature as ruthlessly as a hunted animal. I refer to *Moby Dick,* whose narrator, Ishmael, is the namesake of a Biblical wanderer. Every literate person knows the story of Moby Dick and his pursuit by the crazed Captain Ahab who had yielded a leg to the great albino whale. It is the whale and Ahab who dominate the story. What does the whale represent? A symbol of evil, as some critics have contended? Fate, destiny, the universe personified, as other scholars have protested?

Moby Dick is "all a magnet," remarks Ahab cryptically at one moment. "And be he agent or be he principal I will wreak my hate upon him." Here, reduced to the deck of a whaler out of Nantucket, the old immortal questions resound, the questions labeled science in our era. Nothing is to go unchallenged. Thrice, by different vessels, Ahab is warned away from his contemplated conquest. The whale does not pursue Ahab, Ahab pursues the whale. If there is evil represented in the white whale it cannot be personalized. The evils of self-murder, of megalomania, are at work in a single soul calling up its foreordained destruction. Ahab heartlessly brushes aside the supplications of a brother captain to aid in the search for his son, lost somewhere in a boat in the trail of the white whale's passing. Such a search would only impede the headlong fury of the pursuit.

In Ahab's anxiety to "strike through the mask," to confront "the principal," whether god or destiny, he is denuding himself of all humanity. He has forgotten his owners, his responsibility to his crew. His single obsession, the hidden obsession that lies at the root of much Faustian overdrive in science, totally possesses him. Like Faust he must know, if the knowing kills him, if naught lies beyond. "All my means are sane," he writes, like Haeckel and many another since. "My motive and my object mad."

So it must have been in the laboratories of the atom breakers in their first heady days of success. Yet again on the third day Starbuck, the doomed mate, cries out to Ahab, "Desist. Moby Dick seeks thee not. It is thou, thou, that madly seekest him." This then is not the pursuit of evil. It is man in his pride that the almighty gods will challenge soon enough. Not for nothing is Moby Dick a white snow hill rushing through Pacific nights. He carries upon his brow the inscrutability of fate. Agent or principal, Moby Dick presents to Ahab the mystery he may confront but never conquer. There is no harpoon tempered that will strike successfully the heart of the great enigma.

So much for the seeking peg-legged man without heart. We know he launched his boats and struck his blows and in the fury of returning vengeance lost his ship, his comrades, and his own life. If, indeed, he pierced momentarily the mask of the "agent," it was not long enough to tell the tale. But what of the sometimes silent narrator, the man who begins the book with the nonchalant announcement, "Call me Ishmael," the man whose Biblical namesake had every man's hand lifted against him? What did he tell? After all, Moby Dick is his book.

Ishmael, in contrast to Ahab, is the wondering man, the acceptor of all races and their gods. In contrast to the obsessed Ahab he paints a magnificent picture of the peace that reigned in the giant whale schools of the 1840s, the snuffling and grunting about the boats like dogs, loving and being loved, huge mothers gazing in bliss upon their offspring. After hours of staring in those peaceful depths, "Deep down," says Ishmael, "there I still bathe in eternal mildness of joy." The weird, the holy, hangs undisturbed over the whales' huge cradle. Ishmael knows it, others do not.

At the end, when Ahab has done his worst and the *Pequod* with the wounded whale is dragged into the depths amidst shrieking seafowl, it is Ishmael, buoyed up on the calked coffin of his cannibal friend Queequeg, who survives to tell the tale. Like Whitman, like W. H. Hudson, like Thoreau, Ishmael, the wanderer, has noted more of nature and his fellow men than has the headstrong pursuer of the white whale, whether "agent" or "principal," within the universe. The tale is not of science, but it symbolizes on a gigantic canvas the struggle between two ways of looking at the universe: the magnification by the poet's mind attempting to see all, while disturbing as little as possible, as opposed to the plunging fury of Ahab with his cry, "Strike, strike through the mask, whatever it may cost in lives and suffering." Within our generation we have seen the one view plead for endangered species and reject the despoliation of the earth; the other has left us lingering in the shadow of atomic disaster. Actually, the division is not so abrupt as this would imply, but we are conscious as never before in history that there is an invisible line of demarcation, an ethic that science must sooner or later devise for itself if mankind is to survive. Herman Melville glimpsed in his huge mythology of the white beast that was nature's agent something that only the twentieth century can fully grasp.

It may be that those childlike big-brained skulls from Africa are not of the past but of the future, man, not, in Freud's words, retaining an atavistic child's ego, but pushing onward in an evolutionary attempt to become truly at peace with the universe, to know and enjoy the sperm-whale nursery as did Ishmael, to paint in three dimensions the beauty of the world while not to harm it.

Yesterday, wandering along a railroad spur line, I glimpsed a surprising sight. All summer long, nourished by a few clods of earth on a boxcar roof, a sunflower had been growing. At last, the car had been remembered. A train was being made up. The box car with its swaying rooftop inhabitant was coupled in. The engine tooted and slowly, with nodding dignity, my plant began to travel.

Throughout the summer I had watched it grow but never troubled it. Now it lingered and bowed a trifle toward me as the winds began to touch it. A light not quite the sunlight of this earth was touching the flower, or perhaps it was the watering of my aging eye—who knows? The plant would not long survive its journey but the flower seeds were autumn-brown. At every jolt for miles they would drop along the embankment. They were travelers—travelers like Ishmael and myself, outlasting all fierce pursuits and destined to re-emerge into future autumns. Like Ishmael, I thought, they will speak with the voice of the one true agent: "I only am escaped to tell thee."

Suggestions for Discussion and Writing

1. In the opening paragraph Eiseley draws an analogy between the earth and the human brain. "It may well be asked," he writes, "why this analogy of earth's memory should so preoccupy the mind of a scientist as to have affected his entire outlook upon nature and upon his kinship with—even his concern for—the plant and animal world about him." Does this analogy make for an effective opening? Does Eiseley answer his own question? In what way does the analogy shape Eiseley's argument?

2. What rhetorical advantage does Eiseley gain by formulating the "problem" in terms of "two extreme approaches to the interpretation of the living world"?

3. In the second paragraph Eiseley says that "in the supposed objective world of science, emotion and temperament may play a role in our selection of the mental tools with which we choose to investigate nature." Would Huxley and Pirsig (this chapter) agree with this statement? Would Keller and Bleier (Chapter 12)?

4. Eiseley notes that, at a time when animals were seen "as either automatons or creatures created merely for human exploitation," Darwin made the following observation: "animals, our fellow brethren in pain, disease, suffering and famine . . . may partake of our origin in one common ancestor—we may be all netted together." Does Darwin's suggestion that "we may be all netted together" speak to contemporary concerns? Write an essay in which you explore this issue.

5. As Eiseley sees it, "that feeling of awe, of dread of the holy playing upon nature . . . characterizes the work of a number of naturalists and physicists down even to the present day." To which other authors in this book (for example, in Chapter 3) does this observation particularly apply?

6. In the seventh paragraph Eiseley speaks of those "feelings of wonder before which Freud recoiled with a nineteenth-century mechanist's distaste." What does Eiseley mean by the term "nineteenth-century mechanist"? What oppositions are implied in Eiseley's statement? Do you see a connection between the term "mechanist" and the metaphor of the watch in Bronowski's "Isaac Newton's Model" (Chapter 1)?

7. In the eighth paragraph Eiseley refers to Rudolf Otto's *The Idea of the Holy*, a work that apparently influenced the title of Eiseley's own essay. What is the significance of Eiseley's substitution of the word "sense" for "idea"? What does Eiseley mean by the word "holy"?

8. What does Eiseley mean when he writes, at the end of the ninth paragraph, that "skins may still prickle in a modern classroom"? What features of the paragraph (stylistic, allusive, thematic) give this sentence its force?

9. Eiseley says "science as we know it has two basic types of practitioners." What are these two types? Does Eiseley overstate his case when he says later in the essay that "the degradation of animals in experiments of little, or vile, meaning, was easily turned to the experimental human torture practiced at Dachau and Buchenwald by men dignified with medical degrees"?

10. Speaking of earliest man, Eiseley says: "The new niche in its beginnings is invisible; it has to be inferred. It does not lie waiting to be discovered in a pebble or a massive molar." Write

an essay in which you relate these statements to Eiseley's larger concerns in the essay.

11. In the first part of his essay, Eiseley focuses on the "two extreme approaches to the living world" represented by Darwin and Freud. In the second, he deals with questions of cranial capacity and the development of the human brain. In the final section, he turns to Herman Melville's *Moby Dick* and Captain Ahab's pursuit of the great white whale. What thematic relationship is there among the three parts?

12. Eiseley ends his essay with a story about a sunflower. What is his attitude to the sunflower? What details or devices (e.g., personification) help establish this attitude? How do you interpret Eiseley's statement that "a light not quite the sunlight of this earth was touching the flower"? Do you see any significance in the fact that Eiseley says that the flower "would not long survive its journey" but that its seeds would outlast "all fierce pursuits"? Using these questions as a starting point, write an essay exploring the force of this ending.

CHAPTER 8

The Limits of Science

CAN WE KNOW THE UNIVERSE? REFLECTIONS ON A GRAIN OF SALT

Carl Sagan
(b. 1934)

Few scientists have appeared on *The Tonight Show* and even fewer have created and hosted their own television series. *Cosmos,* which first aired in 1980, was a multimillion-dollar PBS production that explored subjects ranging from immense black holes in space to the intricacies of the living cell. The series catapulted Carl Sagan to a fame that outdid even his earlier renown as the best-selling author of *The Dragons of Eden* (1977) and *Broca's Brain* (1979). His provocative views on everything from nuclear disarmament to the possibility of life on other planets have made him one of modern science's most popular spokesmen.

A native of Brooklyn, Sagan earned his B.A., B.S., M.S., and Ph.D. at the University of Chicago before he was 26. He has been a professor of astronomy and astrophysics at Cornell since 1968 and is the director of its Laboratory for Planetary Studies. Much of his research has been devoted to exobiology (the possibility of extraterrestrial life); with his associates he has succeeded in creating amino acids from basic chemicals through the use of radiation, thus lending support to the possibility that life may exist elsewhere in the cosmos. He has played major roles in many

NASA projects, including the Mariner, Viking, and Voyager missions. His numerous scientific honors include the Apollo Achievement Award, given by NASA for distinguished accomplishment; his literary awards include the 1978 Pulitzer Prize for Literature.

In the following essay, taken from *Broca's Brain,* Sagan asks to what extent we can know the universe we inhabit. Does the very nature of the universe place limitations on our knowledge? How far can common sense take us in our drive to understand? We live in a world that includes much that is knowable and much that is not. And this, he suggests, is the way it should be.

> Nothing is rich but the inexhaustible wealth of nature. She shows us only surfaces, but she is a million fathoms deep.
> —*Ralph Waldo Emerson*

S cience is a way of thinking much more than it is a body of knowledge. Its goal is to find out how the world works, to seek what regularities there may be, to penetrate to the connections of things—from subnuclear particles, which may be the constituents of all matter, to living organisms, the human social community, and thence to the cosmos as a whole. Our intuition is by no means an infallible guide. Our perceptions may be distorted by training and prejudice or merely because of the limitations of our sense organs, which, of course, perceive directly but a small fraction of the phenomena of the world. Even so straightforward a question as whether in the absence of friction a pound of lead falls faster than a gram of fluff was answered incorrectly by Aristotle and almost everyone else before the time of Galileo. Science is based on experiment, on a willingness to challenge old dogma, on an openness to see the universe as it really is. Accordingly, science sometimes requires courage—at the very least the courage to question the conventional wisdom.

Beyond this the main trick of science is to *really* think of something: the shape of clouds and their occasional sharp bottom edges at the same altitude everywhere in the sky; the formation of a dewdrop on a leaf; the origin of a name or a word—Shakespeare, say, or "philanthropic"; the reason for human social customs—the incest taboo, for example; how it is that a lens in sunlight can make paper burn; how a "walking stick" got to look so much like a twig; why the Moon seems to follow us as we walk; what prevents us from digging a hole down to the center of the Earth; what the definition is of "down" on a spherical Earth; how it is possible for the body to convert yesterday's lunch into today's muscle and sinew; or how far is up—does the universe go on forever, or if it does not, is there any meaning to the question of what lies on the other side? Some of these questions are pretty easy. Others, especially the last, are mysteries to which no one even today knows the answer. They are natural questions to ask. Every culture has posed such questions in one way or another. Almost always the proposed answers are in the nature of "Just So Stories," attempted explanations divorced from experiment, or even from careful comparative observations.

But the scientific cast of mind examines the world critically as if many alternative worlds might exist, as if other things might be here which are not. Then we are forced to ask why what we see is present and not something else. Why are the Sun and the Moon and the planets spheres? Why not pyramids, or cubes, or dodecahedra? Why not irregular, jumbly shapes? Why so symmetrical, worlds? If you spend any time spinning hypotheses, checking to see whether they make sense, whether they conform to what else we know, thinking of tests you can pose to substantiate or deflate your hypotheses, you will find yourself doing science. And as you come to practice this habit of thought more and more you will get better and better at it. To penetrate into the heart of the thing—even a little thing, a blade of grass, as Walt Whitman said—is to experience a kind of exhilaration that, it may be, only human beings of all the beings on this planet can feel. We are an intelligent species and the use of our intelligence quite properly gives us pleasure. In this respect the brain is like a muscle. When we think well, we feel good. Understanding is a kind of ecstasy.

But to what extent can we *really* know the universe around us? Sometimes this question is posed by people who hope the answer will be in the negative, who are fearful of a universe in which everything might one day be known. And sometimes we hear pronouncements from scientists who confidently state that everything worth knowing will soon be known—or even is already known—and who paint pictures of a Dionysian or Polynesian age in which the zest for intellectual discovery has withered, to be replaced by a kind of subdued languor, the lotus eaters drinking fermented coconut milk or some other mild hallucinogen. In addition to maligning both the Polynesians, who were intrepid explorers (and whose brief respite in paradise is now sadly ending), as well as the inducements to intellectual discovery provided by some hallucinogens, this contention turns out to be trivially mistaken.

Let us approach a much more modest question: not whether we can know the universe or the Milky Way Galaxy or a star or a world. Can we know, ultimately and in detail, a grain of salt? Consider one microgram of table salt, a speck just barely large enough for someone with keen eyesight to make out without a microscope. In that grain of salt there are about 10^{16} sodium and chlorine atoms. This is a 1 followed by 16 zeros, 10 million billion atoms. If we wish to know a grain of salt, we must know at least the three-dimensional positions of each of these atoms. (In fact, there is much more to be known—for example, the nature of the forces between the atoms—

but we are making only a modest calculation.) Now, is this number more or less than the number of things which the brain can know?

How much *can* the brain know? There are perhaps 10^{11} neurons in the brain, the circuit elements and switches that are responsible in their electrical and chemical activity for the functioning of our minds. A typical brain neuron has perhaps a thousand little wires, called dendrites, which connect it with its fellows. If, as seems likely, every bit of information in the brain corresponds to one of these connections, the total number of things knowable by the brain is no more than 10^{14}, one hundred trillion. But this number is only one percent of the number of atoms in our speck of salt.

So in this sense the universe is intractable, astonishingly immune to any human attempt at full knowledge. We cannot on this level understand a grain of salt, much less the universe.

But let us look a little more deeply at our microgram of salt. Salt happens to be a crystal in which, except for defects in the structure of the crystal lattice, the position of every sodium and chlorine atom is predetermined. If we could shrink ourselves into this crystalline world, we would see rank upon rank of atoms in an ordered array, a regularly alternating structure—sodium, chlorine, sodium, chlorine, specifying the sheet of atoms we are standing on and all the sheets above us and below us. An absolutely pure crystal of salt could have the position of every atom specified by something like 10 bits of information.* This would not strain the information-carrying capacity of the brain.

If the universe had natural laws that governed its behavior to the same degree of regularity that determines a crystal of salt, then, of course, the universe would be knowable. Even if there were many such laws, each of considerable complexity, human beings might have the capability to understand them all. Even if such knowledge exceeded the information-carrying capacity of the brain, we might store the additional information outside our bodies—in books, for example, or in computer memories—and still, in some sense, know the universe.

Human beings are, understandably, highly motivated to find regularities, natural laws. The search for rules, the only possible way to understand such a vast and complex universe, is called science. The universe forces those who live in it to understand it. Those creatures who find everyday experience a muddled jumble of events with no predictability, no regularity, are in grave peril. The universe belongs to those who, at least to some degree, have figured it out.

It is an astonishing fact that there *are* laws of nature, rules that

---

*Chlorine is a deadly poison gas employed on European battlefields in World War I. Sodium is a corrosive metal which burns upon contact with water. Together they make a placid and unpoisonous material, table salt. Why each of these substances has the properties it does is a subject called chemistry, which requires more than 10 bits of information to understand.

summarize conveniently—not just qualitatively but quantitatively—how the world works. We might imagine a universe in which there are no such laws, in which the 10^{80} elementary particles that make up a universe like our own behave with utter and uncompromising abandon. To understand such a universe we would need a brain at least as massive as the universe. It seems unlikely that such a universe could have life and intelligence, because beings and brains require some degree of internal stability and order. But even if in a much more random universe there were such beings with an intelligence much greater than our own, there could not be much knowledge, passion or joy.

Fortunately for us, we live in a universe that has at least important parts that are knowable. Our commonsense experience and our evolutionary history have prepared us to understand something of the workaday world. When we go into other realms, however, common sense and ordinary intuition turn out to be highly unreliable guides. It is stunning that as we go close to the speed of light our mass increases indefinitely, we shrink toward zero thickness in the direction of motion, and time for us comes as near to stopping as we would like. Many people think that this is silly, and every week or two I get a letter from someone who complains to me about it. But it is a virtually certain consequence not just of experiment but also of Albert Einstein's brilliant analysis of space and time called the Special Theory of Relativity. It does not matter that these effects seem unreasonable to us. We are not in the habit of traveling close to the speed of light. The testimony of our common sense is suspect at high velocities.

Or consider an isolated molecule composed of two atoms shaped something like a dumbbell—a molecule of salt, it might be. Such a molecule rotates about an axis through the line connecting the two atoms. But in the world of quantum mechanics, the realm of the very small, not all orientations of our dumbbell molecule are possible. It might be that the molecule should be oriented in a horizontal position, say, or in a vertical position, but not at many angles in between. Some rotational positions are forbidden. Forbidden by what? By the laws of nature. The universe is built in such a way as to limit, or quantize, rotation. We do not experience this directly in everyday life; we would find it startling as well as awkward in sitting-up exercises, to find arms outstretched from the sides or pointed up to the skies permitted but many intermediate positions forbidden. We do not live in the world of the small, on the scale of 10^{-13} centimeters, in the realm where there are twelve zeros between the decimal place and the one. Our commonsense intuitions do not count. What does count is experiment—in this case observations from the far infrared spectra of molecules. They show molecular rotation to be quantized.

The idea that the world places restrictions on what humans might do is frustrating. Why *shouldn't* we be able to have intermediate rotational positions? Why *can't* we travel faster than the speed of light? But so far as we can tell, this is the way the universe is constructed. Such prohibitions not only press us toward a little humility; they also make the world more knowable. Every restriction corresponds to a law of nature, a regularization of the universe. The more restrictions there are on what matter and energy can do, the more knowledge human beings can attain. Whether in some sense the universe is ultimately knowable depends not only on how many natural laws there are that encompass widely divergent phenomena, but also on whether we have the openness and the intellectual capacity to understand such laws. Our formulations of the regularities of nature are surely dependent on how the brain is built, but also, and to a significant degree, on how the universe is built.

For myself, I like a universe that includes much that is unknown and, at the same time, much that is knowable. A universe in which everything is known would be static and dull, as boring as the heaven of some weak-minded theologians. A universe that is unknowable is no fit place for a thinking being. The ideal universe for us is one very much like the universe we inhabit. And I would guess that this is not really much of a coincidence.

Suggestions for Discussion and Writing

1. What does the author mean when he says that "science sometimes requires courage"? Can you think of a scientist who showed exceptional courage?

2. In what sense are the questions posed by Sagan in the second paragraph "natural"?

3. What does Sagan mean by "Just So Stories"? Write an essay in which you explain a currently accepted "story" in terms of this notion.

4. Briefly describe "the scientific cast of mind."

5. Is Sagan exaggerating when he says that "understanding is a kind of ecstasy"?

6. The poet William Blake wrote: "To see a World in a Grain of Sand/And a Heaven in a Wild Flower,/Hold Infinity in the palm of your hand/And Eternity in an hour." Would you say these lines are in accord with Sagan's views?

7. Why do the "prohibitions" of nature "make the world more knowable"?

8. Sagan says that "the testimony of our common sense is suspect at high velocities." What are some implications of this?

9. Sagan begins by asserting that "science is a way of thinking much more than it is a body of knowledge." Does the essay support this view?

☐ SMILE

Alan Lightman
(b. 1948)

Alan Lightman, whose scientific work has been largely in astrophysics, was born in Tennessee and received his Ph.D. in physics from the California Institute of Technology. A frequent contributor to scientific journals, Lightman has taught astronomy and physics at Harvard University and has worked as a physicist at the Smithsonian Astrophysical Observatory. He is currently a professor of science and writing at the Massachusetts Institute of Technology.

Lightman's essays have appeared in *Harper's, The New Yorker, Science 86,* and *Smithsonian,* among other publications. He has published two books of essays on science, *Time Travel and Papa Joe's Pipe* (1984) and *A Modern Day Yankee in a Connecticut Court* (1986), from which "Smile" is taken. In this brief essay, Lightman anatomizes in scientific terms a chance meeting between a man and a woman. In doing so, he celebrates the explanatory power of scientific knowledge at the very moment that he defines its limits. There are many important areas of our lives, he seems to be reminding us, about which science has nothing to say.

I t is a Saturday in March. The man wakes up slowly, reaches over and feels the windowpane, and decides it is warm enough to skip his thermal underwear. He yawns and dresses and goes out for his morning jog. When he comes back, he showers, cooks himself a scrambled egg, and settles down on the sofa with *The Essays of E. B. White.* Around noon, he rides his bike to the bookstore. He spends a couple of hours there, just poking around the books. Then he pedals back through the little town, past his house, and to the lake.

When the woman woke up this morning, she got out of bed and went immediately to her easel, where she picked up her pastels and set to work on her painting. After an hour, she is satisfied with the light effect and quits to have breakfast. She dresses quickly and walks to a nearby store to buy shutters for her bathroom. At the store, she meets friends and has lunch with them. Afterward, she wants to be alone and drives to the lake.

Now, the man and the woman stand on the wooden dock, gazing at the lake and the waves on the water. They haven't noticed each other.

The man turns. And so begins the sequence of events informing him of her. Light reflected from her body instantly enters the pupils of his eyes, at the rate of 10 trillion particles of light per second. Once through the pupil of each eye, the light travels through an oval-shaped lens, then through a transparent, jellylike substance filling up the eyeball, and lands on the retina. Here it is gathered by 100 million rod and cone cells.

Cells in the path of reflected highlights receive a great deal of light; cells falling in the shadows of the reflected scene receive very little. The woman's lips, for example, are just now glistening in the sunlight, reflecting light of high intensity onto a tiny patch of cells slightly northeast of back center of the man's retina. The edges around her mouth, on the other hand, are rather dark, so that cells neighboring the northeast patch receive much less light.

Each particle of light ends its journey in the eye upon meeting a retinene molecule, consisting of 20 carbon atoms, 28 hydrogen atoms, and 1 oxygen atom. In its dormant condition, each retinene molecule is attached to a protein molecule and has a twist between the eleventh and fifteenth carbon atoms. But when light strikes it, as is now happening in about 30,000 trillion retinene molecules every second, the molecule straightens out and separates from its protein. After several intermediate steps, it wraps into a twist again, awaiting arrival of a new particle of light. Far less than a thousandth of a second has elapsed since the man saw the woman.

Triggered by the dance of the retinene molecules, the nerve cells, or neurons, respond. First in the eye and then in the brain. One neuron, for instance, has just gone into action. Protein molecules on its surface suddenly change their shape, blocking the flow of positively charged sodium atoms from the surrounding body fluid. This change in flow of electrically charged atoms produces a change in voltage that shudders through the cell. After a distance of a fraction of an inch, the electrical signal reaches the end of the neuron, altering the release of specific molecules, which migrate a distance of a hundred-thousandth of an inch until they reach the next neuron, passing along the news.

The woman, in fact, holds her hands by her sides and tilts her head at an angle of five and a half degrees. Her hair falls just to her shoulders. This information and much much more is exactingly encoded by the electrical pulses in the various neurons of the man's eyes.

In another few thousandths of a second, the electrical signals reach the ganglion neurons, which bunch together in the optic nerve at the back of the eye and carry their data to the brain. Here the impulses race to the primary visual cortex, a highly folded layer of tissue about a tenth of an inch thick and two square inches in area, containing 100 million neurons in half a dozen layers. The fourth layer receives the input first, does a preliminary analysis, and transfers the information to neurons in other layers. At every stage, each neuron may receive signals from a thousand other neurons, combine the signals—some of which cancel each other out—and dispatch the computed result to a thousand-odd other neurons.

After about thirty seconds—after several hundred trillion particles of reflected light have entered the man's eyes and been processed—the woman says hello. Immediately, molecules of air are pushed together, then apart, then together, beginning in her vocal cords and traveling in a springlike motion to the man's ears. The sound makes the trip from her to him (twenty feet) in a fiftieth of a second.

Within each of his ears, the vibrating air quickly covers the distance to the eardrum. The eardrum, an oval membrane about .3 inch in diameter and tilted fifty-five degrees from the floor of the auditory canal, itself begins trembling and transmits its motion to three tiny bones. From there, the vibrations shake the fluid in the cochlea, which spirals snail-like two and a half turns around.

Inside the cochlea the tones are deciphered. Here, a very thin membrane undulates in step with the sloshing fluid, and through this basilar membrane run tiny filaments of varying thicknesses, like strings on a harp. The woman's voice, from afar, is playing this harp. Her hello begins in the low registers and rises in pitch toward the end. In precise response, the thick filaments in the basilar membrane vibrate first, followed by the thinner ones. Finally, tens of thousands of rod-shaped bodies perched on the basilar membrane convey their particular quiverings to the auditory nerve.

News of the woman's hello, in electrical form, races along the neurons of the auditory nerve and enters the man's brain, through the thalamus, to a specialized region of the cerebral cortex for further processing.

Eventually, a large fraction of the trillion neurons in the man's brain become involved with computing the visual and auditory data just acquired. Sodium and potassium gates open and close. Electrical currents speed along neuron fibers. Molecules flow from one nerve ending to the next.

All of this is known. What is not known is why, after about a minute, the man walks over to the woman and smiles.

Suggestions for Discussion and Writing

1. Through what senses does the man acquire his information about the woman?

2. How does the author prepare us for the man's walking over to the woman and smiling?

3. How would you characterize what is "known" and what is "not known" in this essay? Which is more important?

4. Do you see any similarities in tone and mood between the final paragraph and the opening three paragraphs?

5. In what sense does this brief essay define the limits of scientific knowledge?

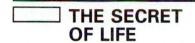

THE SECRET OF LIFE

Loren Eiseley
(1907–1977)

For a biographical sketch of the author, see page 340.
In the following selection from *The Immense Journey* (1957),
Loren Eiseley observes that, despite great advances in modern
chemistry and biology, the ultimate mystery of life still eludes us.

The notion that mice can be generated spontaneously from bundles of old clothes is so delightfully whimsical that it is easy to see why men were loath to abandon it. One could accept such accidents in a topsy-turvy universe without trying to decide what transformation of buckles into bones and shoe buttons into eyes had taken place. One could take life as a kind of fantastic magic and not blink too obviously when it appeared, beady-eyed and bustling, under the laundry in the back room.

It was only with the rise of modern biology and the discovery that the trail of life led backward toward infinitestimal beginnings in primordial sloughs, that men began the serious dissection and analysis of the cell. Darwin, in one of his less guarded moments, had spoken hopefully of the possibility that life had emerged from inorganic matter in some "warm little pond." From that day to this biologists have poured, analyzed, minced, and shredded recalcitrant protoplasm in a fruitless attempt to create life from nonliving matter. It seemed inevitable, if we could trace life down through simpler stages, that we must finally arrive at the point where, under the proper chemical conditions, the mysterious borderline that bounds the inanimate must be crossed. It seemed clear that life was a material manifestation. Somewhere, somehow, sometime, in the mysterious chemistry of carbon, the long march toward the talking animal had begun.

A hundred years ago men spoke optimistically about solving the secret, or at the very least they thought the next generation would be in a position to do so. Periodically there were claims that the emergence of life from matter had been observed, but in every case the observer proved to be self-deluded. It became obvious that the secret of life was not to be had by a little casual experimentation, and that life in today's terms appeared to arise only through the medium of preëxisting life. Yet, if science was not to be embarrassed by some kind of mind-matter dualism and a complete and irrational break between life and the world of inorganic matter, the emergence of life had, in some way, to be accounted for. Nevertheless, as the years passed, the secret remained locked in its living jelly, in spite of larger microscopes and more formidable means of dissection. As a matter of fact the mystery was heightened because all this intensified effort revealed that even the supposedly simple amoeba was a complex, self-operating chemical factory. The notion that he was a simple blob, the discovery of whose chemical composition would enable us instantly to set the life process in operation, turned out to be, at best, a monstrous caricature of the truth.

With the failure of these many efforts science was left in the somewhat embarrassing position of having to postulate theories of living origins which it could not demonstrate. After having chided the theologian for his reliance on myth and miracle, science found itself in the unenviable position of having to create a mythology of its own: namely, the assumption that what, after long effort, could not be proved to take place today had, in truth, taken place in the primeval past.

My use of the term *mythology* is perhaps a little harsh. One does occasionally observe, however, a tendency for the beginning zoological textbook to take the unwary reader by a hop, skip, and jump from the little steaming pond or the beneficient chemical crucible of the sea, into the lower world of life with such sureness and rapidity that it is easy to assume that there is no mystery about this matter at all, or, if there is, that it is a very little one.

This attitude has indeed been sharply criticized by the distinguished British biologist Woodger, who remarked some years ago: "Unstable organic compounds and chlorophyll corpuscles do not persist or come into existence in nature on their own account at the present day, and consequently it is necessary to postulate that conditions were once such that this did happen although and in spite of the fact that our knowledge of nature does not give us any warrant for making such a supposition . . . It is simple dogmatism—asserting that what you want to believe did in fact happen."

Yet, unless we are to turn to supernatural explanations or reinvoke a dualism which is scientifically dubious, we are forced inevitably toward only two possible explanations of life upon earth. One of these, although not entirely disproved, is most certainly out of fashion and surrounded with greater obstacles to its acceptance than at the time it was formulated. I refer, of course, to the suggestion of Lord Kelvin and Svante Arrhenius that life did not arise on this planet, but was wafted here through the depths of space. . . .

This theory had a certain attraction as a way out of an embarrassing dilemma, but it suffers from the defect of explaining nothing, even if it should prove true. It does not elucidate the nature of life. It simply removes the inconvenient problem of origins to far-off spaces or worlds into which we will never penetrate. Since life makes use of the chemical compounds of this earth, it would seem better to proceed, until incontrovertible evidence to the contrary is obtained, on the assumption that life has actually arisen upon this planet. The now widely accepted view that the entire universe in its present state is limited in time, and the apparently lethal nature of unscreened solar radiation are both obstacles which greatly lessen the likelihood that life has come to us across the infinite wastes of space. Once more, therefore, we are forced to examine our remaining notion that life is not coterminous with matter, but has arisen from it.

If the single-celled protozoans that riot in roadside pools are not the simplest forms of life, if, as we know today, these creatures are already highly adapted and really complex, though minute beings, then where are we to turn in the search for something simple enough to suggest the greatest missing link of all—the link between living and dead matter? It is this problem that keeps me wandering fruitlessly in pastures and weed thickets even though I know this is an old-fashioned naturalist's approach, and that busy men in laboratories have little patience with my scufflings of autumn leaves, or attempts to question beetles in decaying bark. Besides, many of these men are now fascinated by the crystalline viruses and have turned that remarkable instrument, the electron microscope, upon strange molecular "beings" never previously seen by man. Some are satisfied with this glimpse below the cell and find the virus a halfway station on the road to life. Perhaps it is, but as I wander about in the thin mist that is beginning to filter among these decaying stems and ruined spider webs, a kind of disconsolate uncertainty has taken hold of me.

I have come to suspect that this long descent down the ladder of life, beautiful and instructive though it may be, will not lead us to the final secret. In fact I have ceased to believe in the final brew or the ultimate chemical. There is, I know, a kind of heresy, a shocking negation of our confidence in blue-steel microtomes and men in white in making such a statement. I would not be understood to speak ill of scientific effort, for in simple truth I would not be alive today except for the microscopes and the blue steel. It is only that somewhere among these seeds and beetle shells and abandoned grasshopper legs I find something that is not accounted for very clearly in the dissections to the ultimate virus or crystal or protein particle. Even if the secret is contained in these things, in other words, I do not think it will yield to the kind of analysis our science is capable of making.

Imagine, for a moment, that you have drunk from a magician's goblet. Reverse the irreversible stream of time. Go down the dark stairwell out of which the race has ascended. Find yourself at last on the bottommost steps of time, slipping, sliding, and wallowing by scale and fin down into the muck and ooze out of which you arose. Pass by grunts and voiceless hissings below the last tree ferns. Eyeless and earless, float in the primal waters, sense sunlight you cannot see and stretch absorbing tentacles toward vague tastes that float in water. Still, in your formless shiftings, the *you* remains: the sliding particles, the juices, the transformations are working in an exquisitely patterned rhythm which has no other purpose than your preservation—you, the entity, the ameboid being whose substance contains the unfathomable future. Even so does every man come upward from the waters of his birth.

Yet if at any moment the magician bending over you should cry, "Speak! Tell us of that road!" you could not respond. The sensations are yours but not—and this is one of the great mysteries—the power over the body. You cannot describe how the body you inhabit functions, or picture or control the flights and spinnings, the dance of the molecules that compose it, or why they chose to dance into that particular pattern which is you, or, again, why up the long stairway of the eons they dance from one shape to another. It is for this reason that I am no longer interested in final particles. Follow them as you will, pursue them until they become nameless protein crystals replicating on the verge of life. Use all the great powers of the mind and pass backward until you hang with the dire faces of the conquerors in the hydrogen cloud from which the sun was born. You will then have performed the ultimate dissection that our analytic age demands, but the cloud will still veil the secret and, if not the cloud, then the nothingness into which, it now appears, the cloud, in its turn, may be dissolved. The secret, if one may paraphrase a savage vocabulary, lies in the egg of night. . . .

Every so often one encounters articles in leading magazines with titles such as "The Spark of Life," "The Secret of Life," "New Hormone Key to Life," or other similar optimistic proclamations. Only yesterday, for example, I discovered in the *New York Times* a headline announcing: "Scientist Predicts Creation of Life in Laboratory." The Moscow-datelined dispatch announced that Academician Olga Lepeshinskaya had predicted that "in the not too distant future, Soviet scientists would create life." "The time is not far off," warns the formidable Madame Olga, "when we shall be able to obtain the vital substance artificially." She said it with such vigor that I had about the same reaction as I do to announcements about atomic bombs. In fact I half started up to latch the door before an invading tide of Russian protoplasm flowed in upon me.

What finally enabled me to regain my shaken confidence was the recollection that these pronouncements have been going on for well over a century. Just now the Russian scientists show a particular tendency to issue such blasts—committed politically, as they are, to an uncompromising materialism and the boastfulness of very young science. Furthermore, Madame Lepeshinskaya's remarks as reported in the press had a curiously old-fashioned flavor about them. The protoplasm she referred to sounded amazingly like the outmoded *Urschleim* or *Autoplasson* of Haeckel—simplified mucoid slimes no longer taken very seriously. American versions—and one must remember they are often journalistic interpretations of scientists' studies rather than direct quotations from the scientists themselves—are more apt to fall into another pattern. Someone has found a new chemical, vitamin, or similar necessary ingredient without which life will not flourish. By the time this reaches the more sensational press, it may have become the "secret of life." The only thing the inexperienced reader may not comprehend is the fact that no one of these items, even the most recently discovered, is *the* secret. Instead, the substance is probably a part, a very small part, of a larger enigma which is well-nigh as inscrutable as it ever was. If anything, the growing list of catalysts, hormones, plasma genes, and other hobgoblins involved in the work of life only serves to underline the enormous complexity of the secret. "To grasp in detail," says the German biologist Von Bertalanffy, "the physico-chemical organization of the simplest cell is far beyond our capacity."

It is not, you understand, disrespect for the laudable and persistent patience of these dedicated scientists happily lost in their maze of pipettes, smells, and gas flames, that has led me into this runaway excursion to the wood. It is rather the loneliness of a man who knows he will not live to see the mystery solved, and who, furthermore, has come to believe that it will not be solved when the first humanly synthesized particle begins—if it ever does—to multiply itself in some unknown solution.

It is really a matter, I suppose, of the kind of questions one asks oneself. Some day we may be able to say with assurance, "We came from such and such a protein particle, possessing the powers of organizing in a manner leading under certain circumstances to that complex entity known as the cell, and from the cell by various steps onward, to mutliple cell formation." I mean we may be able to say all this with great surety and elaboration of detail, but it is not the answer to the grasshopper's leg, brown and black and saw-toothed here in my hand, nor the answer to the seeds still clinging tenaciously to my coat, nor to this field, nor to the subtle essences of memory, delight, and wistfulness moving among the thin wires of my brain.

I suppose that in the forty-five years of my existence every atom, every molecule that composes me has changed its position or danced away and beyond to become part of other things. New molecules have come from the grass and the bodies of animals to be part of me a little while, yet in this spinning, light and airy as a midge swarm in a shaft of sunlight, my memories hold, and a loved face of twenty years ago is before me still. Nor is that face, nor all my years, caught cellularly as in some cold precise photographic pattern, some gross, mechanical reproduction of the past. My memory holds the past and yet paradoxically knows, at the same time, that the past is gone and will never come again. It cherishes dead faces and silenced voices, yes, and lost evenings of childhood. In some odd nonspatial way it contains houses and rooms that have been torn timber from timber and brick from brick. These have a greater permanence in that midge dance which contains them than ever they had in the world of reality. It is for this reason that Academician Olga Lepeshinskaya has not answered the kind of questions one may ask in an open field.

If the day comes when the slime of the laboratory for the first time crawls under man's direction, we shall have great need of humbleness. It will be difficult for us to believe, in our pride of achievement, that the secret of life has slipped through our fingers and eludes us still. We will list all the chemicals and the reactions. The men who have become gods will pose austerely before the popping flashbulbs of news photographers, and there will be few to consider—so deep is the mind-set of an age—whether the desire to link life to matter may not have blinded us to the more remarkable characteristics of both.

As for me, if I am still around on that day, I intend to put on my old hat and climb over the wall as usual. I shall see strange mechanisms lying as they lie here now, in the autumn rain, strange pipes that transported the substance of life, the intricate seedcase out of which the life has flown. I shall observe no thing green, no delicate transpirations of leaves, nor subtle comings and goings of vapor. The little sunlit factories of the chloroplasts will have dissolved away into common earth.

Beautiful, angular, and bare the machinery of life will lie exposed, as it now is, to my view. There will be the thin, blue skeleton of a hare tumbled in a little heap, and crouching over it I will marvel, as I marvel now, at the wonderful correlation of parts, the perfect adaptation to purpose, the individually vanished and yet persisting pattern which is now hopping on some other hill. I will wonder, as always, in what manner "particles" pursue such devious plans and symmetries. I will ask once more in what way it is managed, that the simple dust takes on a history and begins to weave these unique and never recurring apparitions in the stream of time. I shall wonder what strange forces at the heart of matter regulate the tiny beating of a rabbit's heart or the dim dream that builds a milkweed pod.

It is said by men who know about these things that the smallest living cell probably contains over a quarter of a million protein molecules engaged in the multitudinous coördinated activities which make up the phenomenon of life. At the instant of death, whether of man or microbe, that ordered, incredible spinning passes away in an almost furious haste of those same particles to get themselves back into the chaotic, unplanned earth.

I do not think, if someone finally twists the key successfully in the tiniest and most humble house of life, that many of these questions will be answered, or that the dark forces which create lights in the deep sea and living batteries in the waters of tropical swamps, or the dread cycles of parasites, or the most noble workings of the human brain, will be much if at all revealed. Rather, I would say that if "dead" matter has reared up this curious landscape of fiddling crickets, song sparrows, and wondering men, it must be plain even to the most devoted materialist that the matter of which he speaks contains amazing, if not dreadful powers, and may not impossibly be, as Hardy has suggested, "but one mask of many worn by the Great Face behind."

Suggestions for Discussion and Writing

1. Why, according to Eiseley, was the "notion that mice can be generated spontaneously from bundles of old clothes" difficult to abandon? What traditional view regarding the origin of life is he dismissing here?

2. In your own words, explain the dilemma regarding "the secret of life" that science has been confronted with since the rise of modern biology.

3. What "mythology," according to Eiseley, was science obliged to create? Do you agree with him that the "term mythology is perhaps a little harsh"?

4. Having put aside supernatural possibilities, Eiseley asserts that "we are forced inevitably toward only two possible explanations of life upon earth." Summarize his reasons for dismissing the possibility that life "was wafted here through the depths of space."

5. Study the eleventh paragraph, in which Eiseley invites us to imagine that we "have drunk from a magician's goblet." What organizing principle governs the development of the paragraph? Identify specific words and phrases to support your view. What is the force of the final sentence?

6. What was Eiseley's reaction to the pronouncement that "Soviet scientists would create life"? What is his tone here? Why is "materialism" relevant to his point?

7. Why, in the author's view, is the search for the secret of life in the "ultimate virus or crystal or protein particle" misguided? Write an essay in which you explore Eiseley's definition of life.

8. At one point Eiseley admits that his refusal to believe "in the final brew or the ultimate chemical" is "a kind of heresy." Can his essay as a whole be seen as a critique of the aims and values of science as commonly understood and practiced? Write an essay developing your views.

9. Does Eiseley's apparent willingness to accept the mystery of life make him less of a scientist? Write an essay defending your views. You might wish to consult one or more of the essays in Chapter 3 or James Jeans's essay in Chapter 5 to develop your argument.

□ **CHAOS AND BEYOND**

James Gleick
(b. 1954)

Born in New York, James Gleick is a former science
writer for the *New York Times* and is currently its metropolitan editor. Nominated for a National Book Award, his *Chaos: Making a
New Science* (1987) has been widely praised for introducing non-
specialists to a fascinating new field of physics. The following selection from *Chaos* shows how traditional beliefs about the
physical world have undergone a dramatic reversal over the last
few years.

> "The classification of the constituents of a chaos,
> nothing less here is essayed."
> —Herman Melville, *Moby-Dick*

Two decades ago Edward Lorenz was thinking about the atmosphere, Michel Hénon the stars, Robert May the balance of
nature. Benoit Mandelbrot was an unknown IBM mathematician,
Mitchell Feigenbaum an undergraduate at the City College of New
York, Doyne Farmer a boy growing up in New Mexico. Most practicing scientists shared a set of beliefs about complexity. They held
these beliefs so closely that they did not need to put them into words.
Only later did it become possible to say what these beliefs were and
to bring them out for examination.

Simple systems behave in simple ways. A mechanical contraption
like a pendulum, a small electrical circuit, an idealized population of
fish in a pond—as long as these systems could be reduced to a few
perfectly understood, perfectly deterministic laws, their long-term
behavior would be stable and predictable.

Complex behavior implies complex causes. A mechanical device, an
electrical circuit, a wildlife population, a fluid flow, a biological organ,
a particle beam, an atmospheric storm, a national economy—a system that was visibly unstable, unpredictable, or out of control must
either be governed by a multitude of independent components or
subject to random external influences.

Different systems behave differently. A neurobiologist who spent a
career studying the chemistry of the human neuron without learning
anything about memory or perception, an aircraft designer who used
wind tunnels to solve aerodynamic problems without understanding
the mathematics of turbulence, an economist who analyzed the
psychology of purchasing decisions without gaining an ability to
forecast large-scale trends—scientists like these, knowing that the

components of their disciplines were different, took it for granted that the complex systems made up of billions of these components must also be different.

Now all that has changed. In the intervening twenty years, physicists, mathematicians, biologists, and astronomers have created an alternative set of ideas. Simple systems give rise to complex behavior. Complex systems give rise to simple behavior. And most important, the laws of complexity hold universally, caring not at all for the details of a system's constituent atoms.

For the mass of practicing scientists—particle physicists or neurologists or even mathematicians—the change did not matter immediately. They continued to work on research problems within their disciplines. But they were aware of something called chaos. They knew that some complex phenomena had been explained, and they knew that other phenomena suddenly seemed to need new explanations. A scientist studying chemical reactions in a laboratory or tracking insect populations in a three-year field experiment or modeling ocean temperature variations could not respond in the traditional way to the presence of unexpected fluctuations or oscillations— that is, by ignoring them. For some, that meant trouble. On the other hand, pragmatically, they knew that money was available from the federal government and from corporate research facilities for this faintly mathematical kind of science. More and more of them realized that chaos offered a fresh way to proceed with old data, forgotten in desk drawers because they had proved too erratic. More and more felt the compartmentalization of science as an impediment to their work. More and more felt the futility of studying parts in isolation from the whole. For them, chaos was the end of the reductionist program in science.

Uncomprehension; resistance; anger; acceptance. Those who had promoted chaos longest saw all of these. Joseph Ford of the Georgia Institute of Technology remembered lecturing to a thermodynamics group in the 1970s and mentioning that there was a chaotic behavior in the Duffing equation, a well-known textbook model for a simple oscillator subject to friction. To Ford, the presence of chaos in the Duffing equation was a curious fact—just one of those things he knew to be true, although several years passed before it was published in *Physical Review Letters*. But he might as well have told a gathering of paleontologists that dinosaurs had feathers. They knew better.

"When I said that? Jee-sus Christ, the audience began to bounce up and down. It was, 'My daddy played with the Duffing equation, and my granddaddy played with the Duffing equation, and nobody seen anything like what you're talking about.' You would really run across resistance to the notion that nature is complicated. What I didn't understand was the hostility."

Comfortable in his Atlanta office, the winter sun setting outside, Ford sipped soda from an oversized mug with the word CHAOS painted in bright colors. His younger colleague Ronald Fox talked about his own conversion, soon after buying an Apple II computer for his son, at a time when no self-respecting physicist would buy such a thing for his work. Fox heard that Mitchell Feigenbaum had discovered universal laws guiding the behavior of feedback functions, and he decided to write a short program that would let him see the behavior on the Apple display. He saw it all painted across the screen—pitchfork bifurcations, stable lines breaking in two, then four, then eight; the appearance of chaos itself; and within the chaos, the astonishing geometric regularity. "In a couple of days you could redo all of Feigenbaum," Fox said. Self-teaching by computing persuaded him and others who might have doubted a written argument.

Some scientists played with such programs for a while and then stopped. Others could not help but be changed. Fox was one of those who had remained conscious of the limits of standard linear science. He knew he had habitually set the hard nonlinear problems aside. In practice a physicist would always end up saying, *This is a problem that's going to take me to the handbook of special functions, which is the last place I want to go, and I'm sure as hell not going to get on a machine and do it, I'm too sophisticated for that.*

"The general picture of nonlinearity got a lot of people's attention—slowly at first, but increasingly," Fox said. "Everybody that looked at it, it bore fruit for. You now look at any problem you looked at before, no matter what science you're in. There was a place where you quit looking at it because it became nonlinear. Now you know how to look at it and you go back."

Ford said, "If an area begins to grow, it has to be because some clump of people feel that there's something it offers *them*—that if they modify their research, the rewards could be very big. To me chaos is like a dream. It offers the possibility that, if you come over and play this game, you can strike the mother lode."

Still, no one could quite agree on the word itself.

Philip Holmes, a white-bearded mathematician and poet from Cornell by way of Oxford: *The complicated, aperiodic, attracting orbits of certain (usually low-dimensional) dynamical systems.*

Hao Bai-Lin, a physicist in China who assembled many of the historical papers of chaos into a single reference volume: *A kind of order without periodicity.* And: *A rapidly expanding field of research to which mathematicians, physicists, hydrodynamicists, ecologists and many others have all made important contributions.* And: *A newly recognized and ubiquitous class of natural phenomena.*

H. Bruce Stewart, an applied mathematician at Brookhaven National Laboratory on Long Island: *Apparently random recurrent behavior in a simple deterministic (clockwork-like) system.*

Roderick V. Jensen of Yale University, a theoretical physicist exploring the possibility of quantum chaos: *The irregular, unpredictable behavior of deterministic, nonlinear dynamical systems.*

James Crutchfield of the Santa Cruz collective: *Dynamics with positive, but finite, metric entropy. The translation from mathese is:*

behavior that produces information (amplifies small uncertainties), but is not utterly unpredictable.

And Ford, self-proclaimed evangelist of chaos: *Dynamics freed at last from the shackles of order and predictability. . . . Systems liberated to randomly explore their every dynamical possibility. . . . Exciting variety, richness of choice, a cornucopia of opportunity.*

John Hubbard, exploring iterated functions and the infinite fractal wildness of the Mandelbrot set, considered chaos a poor name for his work, because it implied randomness. To him, the overriding message was that simple processes in nature could produce magnificent edifices of complexity *without* randomness. In nonlinearity and feedback lay all the necessary tools for encoding and then unfolding structures as rich as the human brain.

To other scientists, like Arthur Winfree, exploring the global topology of biological systems, chaos was too narrow a name. It implied simple systems, the one-dimensional maps of Feigenbaum and the two- or three- (and a fraction) dimensional strange attractors of Ruelle. Low-dimensional chaos was a special case, Winfree felt. He was interested in the laws of many-dimensional complexity—and he was convinced that such laws existed. Too much of the universe seemed beyond the reach of low-dimensional chaos.

The journal *Nature* carried a running debate about whether the earth's climate followed a strange attractor. Economists looked for recognizable strange attractors in stock market trends but so far had not found them. Dynamicists hoped to use the tools of chaos to explain fully developed turbulence. Albert Libchaber, now at the University of Chicago, was turning his elegant experimental style to the service of turbulence, creating a liquid-helium box thousands of times larger than his tiny cell of 1977. Whether such experiments, liberating fluid disorder in both space and time, would find simple attractors, no one knew. As the physicist Bernardo Huberman said, "If you had a turbulent river and put a probe in it and said, 'Look, here's a low-dimensional strange attractor,' we would all take off our hats and look."

Chaos was the set of ideas persuading all these scientists that they were members of a shared enterprise. Physicist or biologist or mathematician, they believed that simple, deterministic systems could breed complexity; that systems too complex for traditional mathematics could yet obey simple laws; and that, whatever their particular field, their task was to understand complexity itself.

"Let us again look at the laws of thermodynamics," wrote James E. Lovelock, author of the Gaia hypothesis. "It is true that at first sight they read like the notice at the gate of Dante's Hell . . ." But.

The Second Law is one piece of technical bad news from science that has established itself firmly in the nonscientific culture. Everything tends toward disorder. Any process that converts energy from one form to another must lose some as heat. Perfect efficiency is impossible. The universe is a one-way street. *Entropy must always increase in the universe and in any hypothetical isolated system within it.* However expressed, the Second Law is a rule from which there seems no appeal. In thermodynamics that is true. But the Second Law has had a life of its own in intellectual realms far removed from science, taking the blame for disintegration of societies, economic decay, the breakdown of manners, and many other variations on the decadent theme. These secondary, metaphorical incarnations of the Second Law now seem especially misguided. In our world, complexity flourishes, and those looking to science for a general understanding of nature's habits will be better served by the laws of chaos.

Somehow, after all, as the universe ebbs toward its final equilibrium in the featureless heat bath of maximum entropy, it manages to create interesting structures. Thoughtful physicists concerned with the workings of thermodynamics realize how disturbing is the question of, as one put it, "how a purposeless flow of energy can wash life and consciousness into the world." Compounding the trouble is the slippery notion of entropy, reasonably well-defined for thermodynamic purposes in terms of heat and temperature, but devilishly hard to pin down as a measure of *disorder*. Physicists have trouble enough measuring the degree of order in water, forming crystalline structures in the transition to ice, energy bleeding away all the while. But thermodynamic entropy fails miserably as a measure of the changing degree of form and formlessness in the creation of amino acids, of microorganisms, of self-reproducing plants and animals, of complex information systems like the brain. Certainly these evolving islands of order must obey the Second Law. The important laws, the creative laws, lie elsewhere.

Nature forms patterns. Some are orderly in space but disorderly in time, others orderly in time but disorderly in space. Some patterns are fractal, exhibiting structures self-similar in scale. Others give rise to steady states or oscillating ones. Pattern formation has become a branch of physics and of materials science, allowing scientists to model the aggregation of particles into clusters, the fractured spread of electrical discharges, and the growth of crystals in ice and metal alloys. The dynamics seem so basic—shapes changing in space and time—yet only now are the tools available to understand them. It is a fair question now to ask a physicist, "Why are all snowflakes different?"

Ice crystals form in the turbulent air with a famous blending of symmetry and chance, the special beauty of six-fold indeterminacy. As water freezes, crystals send out tips; the tips grow, their boundaries becoming unstable, and new tips shoot out from the sides. Snowflakes obey mathematical laws of surprising subtlety, and it was impossible to predict precisely how fast a tip would grow, how narrow it would be, or how often it would branch. Generations of scientists sketched and cataloged the variegated patterns: plates and columns, crystals and polycrystals, needles and dendrites. The treatises treated crystal formation as a classification matter, for lack of a better approach.

Growth of such tips, dendrites, is now known as a highly nonlinear unstable free boundary problem, meaning that models need to track a complex, wiggly boundary as it changes dynamically. When solidification proceeds from outside to inside, as in an ice tray, the boundary generally remains stable and smooth, its speed controlled by the ability of the walls to draw away the heat. But when a crystal solidifies outward from an initial seed—as a snowflake does, grabbing water molecules while it falls through the moisture-laden air—the process becomes unstable. Any bit of boundary that gets out ahead of its neighbors gains an advantage in picking up new water molecules and therefore grows that much faster—the "lightning-rod effect." New branches form, and then subbranches.

One difficulty was in deciding which of the many physical forces involved are important and which can safely be ignored. Most important, as scientists have long known, is the diffusion of the heat released when water freezes. But the physics of heat diffusion cannot completely explain the patterns researchers observe when they look at snowflakes under microscopes or grow them in the laboratory. Recently scientists worked out a way to incorporate another process: surface tension. The heart of the new snowflake model is the essence of chaos: a delicate balance between forces of stability and forces of instability; a powerful interplay of forces on atomic scales and forces on everyday scales.

Where heat diffusion tends to create instability, surface tension creates stability. The pull of surface tension makes a substance prefer smooth boundaries like the wall of a soap bubble. It costs energy to make surfaces that are rough. The balancing of these tendencies depends on the size of the crystal. While diffusion is mainly a large-scale, macroscopic process, surface tension is strongest at the microscopic scales.

Traditionally, because the surface tension effects are so small, researchers assumed that for practical purposes they could disregard them. Not so. The tiniest scales proved crucial; there the surface effects proved infinitely sensitive to the molecular structure of a solidifying substance. In the case of ice, a natural molecular symmetry gives a built-in preference for six directions of growth. To their surprise, scientists found that the mixture of stability and instability manges to amplify this microscopic preference, creating the near-fractal lacework that makes snowflakes. The mathematics came not from atmospheric scientists but from theoretical physicists, along with metallurgists, who had their own interest. In metals the molecular symmetry is different, and so are the characteristic crystals, which help determine an alloy's strength. But the mathematics are the same: the laws of pattern formation are universal.

Sensitive dependence on initial conditions serves not to destroy but to create. As a growing snowflake falls to earth, typically floating in the wind for an hour or more, the choices made by the branching tips at any instant depend sensitively on such things as the temperature, the humidity, and the presence of impurities in the atmosphere. The six tips of a single snowflake, spreading within a millimeter space, feel the same temperatures, and because the laws of growth are purely deterministic, they maintain a near-perfect symmetry. But the nature of turbulent air is such that any pair of snowflakes will experience very different paths. The final flake records the history of all the changing weather conditions it has experienced, and the combinations may as well be infinite.

Snowflakes are nonequilibrium phenomena, physicists like to say. They are products of imbalance in the flow of energy from one piece of nature to another. The flow turns a boundary into a tip, the tip into an array of branches, the array into a complex structure never before seen. As scientists have discovered such instability obeying the universal laws of chaos, they have succeeded in applying the same methods to a host of physical and chemical problems, and, inevitably, they suspect that biology is next. In the back of their minds, as they look at computer simulations of dendrite growth, they see algae, cell walls, organisms, budding and dividing.

From microscopic particles to everyday complexity, many paths now seem open. In mathematical physics the bifurcation theory of Feigenbaum and his colleagues advances in the United States and Europe. In the abstract reaches of theoretical physics scientists probe other new issues, such as the unsettled question of quantum chaos: Does quantum mechanics admit the chaotic phenomena of classical mechanics? In the study of moving fluids Libchaber builds his giant liquid-helium box, while Pierre Hohenberg and Günter Ahlers study the odd-shaped traveling waves of convection. In astronomy chaos experts use unexpected gravitational instabilities to explain the origin of meteorites—the seemingly inexplicable catapulting of asteroids from far beyond Mars. Scientists use the physics of dynamical systems to study the human immune system, with its billions of components and its capacity for learning, memory, and pattern recognition, and they simultaneously study evolution, hoping to find universal mechanisms of adaptation. Those who make such models quickly see structures that replicate themselves, compete, and evolve by natural selection.

"Evolution is chaos with feedback," Joseph Ford said. The universe is randomness and dissipation, yes. But randomness with direction can produce surprising complexity. And as Lorenz discovered so long ago, dissipation is an agent of order.

"God plays dice with the universe," is Ford's answer to Einstein's famous question. "But they're loaded dice. And the main objective of physics now is to find out by what rules were they loaded and how can we use them for our own ends."

Such ideas help drive the collective enterprise of science forward. Still, no philosophy, no proof, no experiment ever seems quite enough to sway the individual researchers for whom science must first and always provide a way of working. In some laboratories, the traditional ways falter. Normal science goes astray, as Kuhn put it; a piece of equipment fails to meet expectations; "the profession can no longer evade anomalies." For any one scientist the ideas of chaos could not prevail until the method of chaos became a necessity.

Every field had its own examples. In ecology, there was William M. Schaffer, who trained as the last student of Robert MacArthur, the dean of the field in the fifties and sixties. MacArthur built a conception of nature that gave a firm footing to the idea of *natural balance.* His models supposed that equilibriums would exist and that populations of plants and animals would remain close to them. To MacArthur, balance in nature had what could almost be called a moral quality—states of equilibrium in his models entailed the most efficient use of food resources, the least waste. Nature, if left alone, would be good.

Two decades later MacArthur's last student found himself realizing that ecology based on a sense of equilibrium seems doomed to fail. The traditional models are betrayed by their linear bias. Nature is more complicated. Instead he sees chaos, "both exhilarating and a bit threatening." Chaos may undermine ecology's most enduring assumptions, he tells his colleagues. "What passes for fundamental concepts in ecology is as mist before the fury of the storm—in this case, a full, nonlinear storm."

Schaffer is using strange attractors to explore the epidemiology of childhood diseases such as measles and chicken pox. He has collected data, first from New York City and Baltimore, then from Aberdeen, Scotland, and all England and Wales. He has made a dynamical model, resembling a damped, driven pendulum. The diseases are driven each year by the infectious spread among children returning to school, and damped by natural resistance. Schaffer's model predicts strikingly different behavior for these diseases. Chicken pox should vary periodically. Measles should vary chaotically. As it happens, the data show exactly what Schaffer predicts. To a traditional epidemiologist the yearly variations in measles seemed inexplicable—random and noisy. Schaffer, using the techniques of phase-space reconstruction, shows that measles follow a strange attractor, with a fractal dimension of about 2.5.

Schaffer computed Lyapunov exponents and made Poincaré maps. "More to the point," Schaffer said, "if you look at the pictures it jumps out at you, and you say, 'My God, this is the same thing.' " Although the attractor is chaotic, some predictability becomes possible in light of the deterministic nature of the model. A year of high measles infection will be followed by a crash. After a year of medium infection, the level will change only slightly. A year of low infection produces the greatest unpredictability. Schaffer's model also predicted the consequences of damping the dynamics by mass inoculation programs—consequences that could not be predicted by standard epidemiology.

On the collective scale and on the personal scale, the ideas of chaos advance in different ways and for different reasons. For Schaffer, as for many others, the transition from traditional science to chaos came unexpectedly. He was a perfect target for Robert May's evangelical plea in 1975; yet he read May's paper and discarded it. He thought the mathematical ideas were unrealistic for the kinds of systems a practicing ecologist would study. Oddly, he knew too much about ecology to appreciate May's point. These were one-dimensional maps, he thought—what bearing could they have on continuously changing systems? So a colleague said, "Read Lorenz." He wrote the reference on a slip of paper and never bothered to pursue it.

Years later Schaffer lived in the desert outside of Tucson, Arizona, and summers found him in the Santa Catalina mountains just to the north, islands of chaparral, merely hot when the desert floor is roasting. Amid the thickets in June and July, after the spring blooming season and before the summer rain, Schaffer and his graduate students tracked bees and flowers of different species. This ecological system was easy to measure despite all its year-to-year variation. Schaffer counted the bees on every stalk, measured the pollen by draining flowers with pipettes, and analyzed the data mathematically. Bumblebees competed with honeybees, and honeybees competed with carpenter bees, and Schaffer made a convincing model to explain the fluctuations in population.

By 1980 he knew that something was wrong. His model broke down. As it happened, the key player was a species he had overlooked: ants. Some colleagues suspected unusual winter weather; others unusual summer weather. Schaffer considered complicating his model by adding more variables. But he was deeply frustrated. Word was out among the graduate students that summer at 5,000 feet with Schaffer was hard work. And then everything changed.

He happened upon a preprint about chemical chaos in a complicated laboratory experiment, and he felt that the authors had experienced exactly his problem: the impossibility of monitoring dozens of fluctuating reaction products in a vessel matched the impossibility of monitoring dozens of species in the Arizona mountains. Yet they had succeeded where he had failed. He read about reconstructing phase space. He finally read Lorenz, and Yorke, and others. The University of Arizona sponsored a lecture series on "Order in Chaos." Harry Swinney came, and Swinney knew how to talk about experiments. When he explained chemical chaos, displaying a transparency of a strange attractor, and said, "That's real data," a chill ran up Schaffer's spine.

"All of a sudden I knew that that was my destiny," Schaffer said. He had a sabbatical year coming. He withdrew his application for National Science Foundation money and applied for a Guggenheim Fellowship. Up in the mountains, he knew, the ants changed with the season. Bees hovered and darted in a dynamical buzz. Clouds skidded across the sky. He could not work the old way any more.

Suggestions for Discussion and Writing

1. Summarize the traditional "beliefs about complexity" that, according to the author, have been overturned by the new concept of "chaos."

2. Briefly explain how the new ideas regarding complexity differ from the old.

3. What has been the reaction to the new ideas? Does the essay offer an explanation of that reaction?

4. At various points in the essay, the author's style could be characterized as colloquial, anecdotal, journalistic. Identify examples of this style. In what ways does it contribute to the author's purpose?

5. What does the author gain by quoting several different definitions of "chaos"? Does he offer his own definition?

6. Look up the meaning of "entropy" and of the First and Second Laws of Thermodynamics. How does entropy relate to the notion of chaos?

7. Why is the snowflake of special interest to Gleick? Write a brief explanation of why all snowflakes are different.

8. Toward the end of his essay, Gleick claims that the idea of chaos is now being recognized in the biological sciences. How does the work of William Schaffer support this claim?

9. Is there any connection between the ideas expressed in this essay and those expressed by Heisenberg or Bronowski in Chapter 1?

10. Gleick quotes Joseph Ford as saying, "Evolution is chaos with feedback." Do you see a connection between the notion of chaos and Bronowski's ideas in "Toward a Philosophy of Biology" (Chapter 6)?

☐ **CONFITEOR: NEUROSURGICAL MALFEASANCES**

Richard Bergland
(b. 1932)

Richard Bergland was formerly professor and head of neurosurgery at Harvard University Medical School. Born in Montana, he received his M.D. from Cornell in 1958, interned at New York's Bellevue Hospital, and did his residency at Columbia-Presbyterian Medical Center. Through his research and extensive publications, he has played a key role in convincing the scientific world that, because the brain is a gland, hormones and not electrical impulses determine the relationship between brain and body.

The following selection, taken from his book *The Fabric of Mind* (1985), offers a highly personal account of a professional failure, one which provided evidence that the paradigm of the brain-as-computer is tragically wrong.

L et me tell you about my involvement in a tragedy. Elise had been the leading dancer in one of the world's best ballet companies. She had given the best hours of every day since childhood to the dance and had come to love her lithe, strong legs. Born slightly bow-legged, she had recognized early on in her career that this gave her tremendous leaping ability.

At the age of thirty, at the pinnacle of her success, disaster struck. Over a two-day period she developed total paralysis of both legs. Her doctors, the best in the world, diagnosed her condition as 'transverse myelitis' and listed the possible causes. Some had been optimistic at the beginning, but as the weeks wore on and there was no sign of recovery the truth was clear; she would never move her legs again.

In the years that followed, the numb sensation in her paralysed legs was replaced by a sensation of pain. Woefully, any stimulation of her legs, the lightest touch, the weight of the bedclothes, a breeze, would cause a crescendo of pain so severe that she cried out in anguish.

The doctors, again the best in the world, called this 'anesthesia dolorosa', a condition in which the anesthetic parts of her body were painful.

Her pain separated her from her supportive friends and bound her more and more to her doctors. Soon an appetite for food was replaced by an appetite for narcotics. Then a love of narcotics became the driving force in her life but, even in doses strong enough to cause sleep, her pain never relented.

Fifteen years after the illness began I was asked to see her by a physician who was more conservative than most. He suggested that I surgically remove her spinal cord. He argued that it was no good to her, and that some kind of crooked regeneration had occurred within it that allowed touch sensation, or any sensation, to be interpreted by her brain as 'pain'. As I had done more than my share of spinal surgery, he selected me to perform this heroic, desperate procedure. The operation was intended to rid Elise of the unbearable, untreatable pain in her legs. She would trade her persistent pain for persistent numbness.

At operation, I made a lengthy midline incision in the upper back, removed the bones that formed the roof of the spinal canal and removed all the spinal cord below the level of the myelitis. The cord was abnormally small and abnormally coloured—certainly dead—and as I closed the wound I was confident that cord removal was the correct choice.

When Elise awoke from the operation her hopes, her husband's hopes, her personal physician's hopes, her nurse's hopes and my hopes were crushed. Her pain continued as before, not changed one bit by my heroic removal of her spinal cord.

The operation on Elise stemmed from the studies of anatomists who had located the 'pain pathway'. Knowing that many millions of nerves connected the body to the brain, they separated out the bundles that carried pain messages. They had reduced the problem of pain to a one-way signal, and my failed operation was based on that simplistic reduction of a very complex problem. It was my faith in that paradigm that led me to perform every kind of nerve-cutting operation for pain that has been devised.

Most of my operations for pain have failed in one way or another, and I have lost confidence in my ability to relieve pain by surgical procedures. Only in patients with facial pain—'trigeminal neuralgia'—can I confidently predict a successful outcome of a destructive operation.

Now, fifteen years after my operation on Elise, it is obvious to me and to most brain scientists that the brain is a gland. Pain is not something that can be effectively treated by dividing electrical circuits in the brain. Now we know that brain hormones modulate virtually every aspect of pain; the brain makes its own opiate-like hormones, enkephalin and endorphin, and has its own opiate receptors. It is the interaction of these hormones and receptors that underlies pain tolerance, pain intolerance and addiction to pain-relieving drugs. But many other brain hormones besides enkephalin and endorphin are involved in pain modulation; somatostatin, cholecystokinen, vasopressin, substance P, vasoactive intestinal peptide and neurotensin all may be involved. Each hormone appears to be effective by virtue of hormone and hormone receptor interaction in much the same way as the opiate and opiate receptor relationship. Each of the new brain peptides that are involved in pain modulation seems to interact with the others in patterns that are complex, but increasingly it is apparent that the electrical signals that are involved in pain are akin to the sparks that are produced by a fire. Hormones in the brain govern the fires that produce these sparks.

The reductionism of the paradigm that the brain is an electrically driven computer gave a narrowly focused, at best, half-true, starting premise to all brain doctors. Knowing now of the holistic relationships that are involved between brain and body hormones makes our electrically based reductionistic therapies appear not only wrong but also dumb.

My disastrous experience with Elise came shortly after the 'gate-control' theory of pain had been described in 1965. This revolutionary concept was advanced in that year by Patrick Wall and Ronald Melzack, and it provided a rational explanation for the failure of nerve-cutting operations to relieve pain.

The gate-control theory proposed that nature has set in place two very different systems that carry pain messages to the brain. Although they work together, nature has given us one system that protects us from outer injury during attack, and another that protects us from inner injury, from hurting ourselves.

This paradigm for pain modulation is named 'gate control' because one of these systems closes gates after the first news of pain reaches the brain. The other opens gates after the first pain message is sent to the brain.

Nature has given humans a wonderful mechanism that closes the gates through which pain signals must pass on their way to the brain. This mechanism is ordained to protect us from outside injury. If someone is attacked and physically wounded, for example, the initial pain serves as an alerting mechanism. But quickly the gates close, and the individual is able to carry on in defence without thinking of the painful wound. This mechanism is set in place for one purpose: to protect the body from external attack. The mechanism must be quick and is carried to the brain along the largest nerves, which carry the fastest signals. The mechanism must be sensitive and is carried by nerves that have the most sensitive hair triggers. But once the quick, sensitive mechanism is activated, it closes the gates through which it passed.

This gate-closing mechanism is seen commonly by those of us who man emergency rooms for accident victims or battalion hospitals for soldiers. There it is often observed that very severely injured people do not complain of pain. You have probably experienced the protection of the gate-closing mechanism: when the human thumb touches a hot stove or is slammed by a misdirected hammer, the initial pain pulls the hand back by reflex action. Then for a few minutes the gates are closed and the intensity of the pain is greatly diminished. It is later in the day, or in the night, when the gates are open again that the full intensity of the pain is appreciated by the brain. This is a common experience which did not rouse much scientific curiosity until 1965.

Nature carries pain originating inside the body by a different mechanism. This one is slow; there is no need for quick reflex movement, and it can be carried along thin, delicate nerve fibres at a slow rate. It is not very sensitive, and the stimuli that activate it must push against firm triggers, not hair triggers. But once these signals are carried by this mechanism to the brain, they open the gates through which they passed. Once open, these gates will allow even mild stimuli, those that ordinarily would not be at all bothersome, to reach the brain and to be interpreted as pain.

Together these two systems provide a beautifully balanced defence: the gate-closing mechanism protects against external injury, and the gate-opening mechanism protects against internal injury—against disease.

Most of the chronic pains that come to humans are carried by the slow-conducting mechanisms that open gates. Arthritis, disc disease, stomach cramps and angina are typical examples of internal causes of pain. Nature wants such patients to rest, not necessarily to take to their bed, but at least, to take it easy, confident that rest will cure the pain-causing problems. As patients with such pain know well, once the gate-opening mechanism is activated, all kinds of ordinary and non-noxious stimuli are perceived by the brain as painful.

The hinges of these gates can be controlled by the brain. Some signals flow out from the brain to set the tension of the gates. The gates can be adjusted by the brain to stay in the closed position. The Indian fakir lying on a bed of nails has developed such control over his pain-modulating gates that he can close them at will and limit the number of pain signals that reach his brain. The harried housewife who is insecure, lonely and depressed, on the other hand, cannot muster the brain energy to put any pressure on the brain side of the gates that control pain. Without that force coming from the brain, her gates stay open. Any sensation can pass through the gates and on to the brain. Backache, neckache and headache are the natural consequences of this situation. The pains are not imagined, they are real, but they result from a change in the threshold of gate opening and closing, not from any real disease in the back, the neck or the head.

The gate-control theory makes good sense, and for less than five years gate control appeared to be the best paradigm for understanding and treating pain. Like many others in my profession, I welcomed it, for it gave me a reason to slow down on nerve-cutting operations and a rational explanation for my failures.

During the time that the details of the gate-control paradigm were being worked out, America was racing to the moon. A crucial aspect of the moonshot programme was the ability of our scientists to broadcast radio signals to distant satellites.

The gate-control paradigm depended upon two kinds of nerves: one had a firm trigger and the other a hair trigger. The nerves that closed gates required only a one millivolt stimulus; the nerves that opened gates required a stimulus ten times as strong: ten millivolts.

This difference in threshold made electrical counterstimulation possible; brain scientists knew that a low-powered stimulus would close gates and not be interpreted as pain. To moonshot scientists, broadcasting radio signals into the brain or spinal cord was far less difficult than broadcasting to and from distant satellites. Knowing that there was a ten-fold difference between the gate-closing stimulus and the gate-opening stimulus made their task easier.

Two devices came off the NASA shelves and on to the shelves of neurosurgeons which allowed electrical counterstimulation to be used in patient care. Both depended upon the very sensitive nerves that closed gates; both were designed with the hope that a scarcely detectable 'buzz' could replace high-intensity pain.

The simplest of these is the 'transcutaneous electrical nerve stimulator', or TENS, a battery-operated device that delivers an electrical signal to a nerve located just below the skin. The TENS has the sophisticated space-age miniaturization that allows the patient to twist the dials of the device to a frequency and strength that closes gates and reduces the brain's perception of pain.

A more complicated device is the 'dorsal column stimulator', an ingenious radio receiver/transmitter that can be implanted permanently beneath the skin. The signal of this internal broadcasting station is carried along wires beneath the skin to platinum electrodes that are placed on the surface of the spinal cord. The radio does not have its own power supply; it is turned on by a battery-operated 'wand' or external coil that is held over the skin just above the receiver/transmitter. Activating the battery pack turns on the radio station, which sends its signal to the dorsal columns of the spinal cord.

It seemed then, in 1970, that the gate-control theory was a happy marriage of mankind's two greatest intellectual frontiers, the mind and space.

For the next few years, thousands of dorsal column stimulators were implanted with results that were far less impressive than the gate-control paradigm would have predicted. This electrically based paradigm for brain function looked wonderful in the laboratory but, at the bedside, didn't work well at all. The operation is seldom done today.

The TENS device, because it is innocuous, is still used widely, and many claim that it is the Western equivalent of acupuncture. In my experience it is helpful in about one third of patients, but placebo medications may match that level of effectiveness.

Dorsal column stimulation and percutaneous stimulation have been therapeutic failures, certainly not the panacea for pain. Despite those failures, the gate-control theory of pain modulation is valid. It is certainly the most useful paradigm that a patient in pain can know, for it encourages the use of the gate-closing ability that lies dormant in the brain.

My surgical failures—first in attempts to break the circuits of the brain and second in attempts to stimulate the circuits of the brain— are recounted to underscore the failure of the paradigm that the brain is an electrically driven computer. However easily electrical potentials can be measured on the surface of individual nerves or on the surface of the brain, when this paradigm is taken to the bedside it is not very helpful. Yet from the story of gate-control comes one of the best surprises in the history of the mind: as scientists sought an explanation for this phenomenon—for the pain tolerance of the Indian fakir and the pain-intolerance of the harried housewife—they came to realize that the brain is a gland. Hormones, not electricity, determine all brain/body and brain/behavioural relationships.

Suggestions for Discussion and Writing

1. In the title of his essay, Bergland uses the Latin word "confiteor" (I confess). To what is he confessing? In what sense is "malfeasance" an appropriate word?

2. What is the effect of the personal story with which the author begins his essay? In what sense was his operation on Elise "heroic"?

3. What paradigm led the author to perform the operation on Elise? How does he characterize this paradigm?

4. Write a brief explanation of the "gate-control theory" of pain?

5. What is the author's final assessment of the gate-control theory?

6. In what ways, according to Bergland, did the exploration of space influence medical efforts to control pain?

7. Could the author's surgical failures be said to have contributed to the advance of medical knowledge?

8. What implications follow from our understanding that the brain is a gland rather than an "electrically driven computer"?

9. What conclusions about the use of paradigms in science (and in medicine) might be drawn from Bergland's argument? Write a brief essay developing your views. You may wish to consult Jacob Bronowski's "Isaac Newton's Model" (Chapter 1) and James Jeans's "What Is Physics?" (Chapter 5).

 **THE VALUES
OF SCIENCE**

Jacob Bronowski
(1908–1974)

For a biographical sketch of the author, see page 30.

In the following selection, excerpted from *A Sense of the Future* (1977), Jacob Bronowski addresses the fear that science is without values. Examining first how values are evolved in any society, Bronowski goes on to show that a "scientific society," by the very nature of its activity, does indeed generate its own moral and ethical imperatives.

I t is standard good form nowadays in polite society to say that the civilized values are disappearing, and then to blame science for the change. People who say this are, of course, out of sympathy with modern life; but it would be foolish to ignore their sneer that science is destroying the values for which we all care, for some feeling of this kind haunts less prejudiced people too. There is a general sense that the traditional values form an a priori set of absolute judgments, which hang together in a permanent system. By contrast, it is felt, rightly, that there is nothing absolute about the concepts of natural science, which form a flexible framework that is always building and always being rebuilt; the only thing that the framework must fit, obstinately, is the facts. It is this tyranny of the facts, not as they ought to be but as they are, that distresses even intelligent people, who fear that the spread of science is robbing them of some freedom of judgment. They feel that scientists have no spiritual urges and no human scruples, because the only success that science acknowledges is success in conforming to the material facts of the world.

This latent opposition to science appears now whenever values are debated. It can be countered only by an unbiased study of values as they actually are displayed in the behavior of people. Nothing that we say in arguing about values is practical, nothing is even reasonable, if it neglects this empirical study; and I therefore propose to begin it here and now. This essay is a short but strictly empirical examination of the way in which some of the values in our society are evolved.

I shall confine myself to some human and, in a sense, social values such as inform and govern the relations between people. And I shall confine myself particularly to values that arise in the civilization in which we now live. The characteristic mark of this civilization, the special activity to which it is committed, is the practice of science. Science is the activity of finding facts and then arranging them in groups under general concepts, and these concepts are then judged and tested by the factual outcome of the further actions which we base on them. So, in all practical matters, ours is a society which judges belief by the outcome of the actions which it inspires. We believe in gravitation because we are thereby led to act in a way which works in our world. If we are to believe in values, they must lead us to act in a way that works in the society which hopes to live and to survive by them.

The concept of gravitation is, at bottom, a compact and orderly means to describe how things fall. In this sense, the concepts of science are all means to describe how things fall out. Therefore critics of science usually call it a neutral activity, because its concepts, however subtle we make them, still tell us only what happens and not what ought to happen.

This is a sad jumble of language, which confuses the activity of science with its findings. The findings of science are indeed neutral, if by this word is meant that they describe and do not exhort. It is difficult to see what else the findings could be, unless the critics still believe, as the alchemists did, that science ought to command and to overpower nature. If the criticism is that science discovers facts and not spells, then I gladly accept it.

But of course, the facts discovered must not be confused with the activity that discovers them. And the activity of science is not neutral: it is firmly directed and strictly judged. In practicing science, we accept from the outset an end which is laid down for us. The end of science is to discover what is true about the world. The activity of science is directed to seek the truth, and it is judged by the criterion of being true to the facts.

*   *   *

We can practice science only if we value the truth. This is the cardinal point that has never been seen clearly enough, either by critics or by scientists themselves. Because they have been preoccupied with the findings, they have overlooked that the activity of science is something different from its findings. When we practice science, we look for new facts, we find an order among the facts by grouping them under concepts, and we judge the concepts by testing whether their implications turn out to be true to other new facts. This procedure is meaningless, and indeed cannot be carried out, if we do not care what is true and what is fale.

When critics say that science is neutral, they mean that the findings are neither good nor bad in themselves; and they usually go on to say that therefore the use to which the findings are put must be determined by values which are not implied by the findings. So far, the argument is faultless; the use to which the facts are put must be determined by values which are brought in from outside the facts. But now the critics turn the argument into a verbal trick. To use the findings of science, we must have values from outside the findings; but the critics blandly read this to mean that we must have values from outside science. Even if this were true, it is certainly not implied by the argument.

What the critics are anxious to say, of course, is that the scientific civilization in which we live is not taught any values by the facts that science finds, by the machines that it builds, and even by the visions that it opens. The facts, the machines, the visions still require to be directed to an agreed end. But, of course, although the facts do not supply such an injunction or end, the activity of science does. The activity of science is committed to truth as an end in itself.

Here critics can argue, with justice, that men believed that truth is a value long before they heard of science. I could argue in turn that this belief had often defined truth very oddly; that truth as I define it, truth to fact, was not valued in dogmatic societies such as that which persecuted Galileo; and that the acceptance by any society of the material fact as an arbiter of truth really makes it a scientific society. But these are all debating points, and they are beside the point. It is beside the point to argue about the history of truth as a value: who discovered it, who brought it into our civilization. The point, the only point, is that truth is central to science. A scientific civilization like ours cannot exist unless it accepts truth to fact as its cardinal value. If our civilization did not have this value, then it would have to invent it, for it could not live without it.

I have established that the activity of science presupposes that truth is an end in itself. From this fundamental proposition, it is possible to go several ways. For example, it is possible to discuss what is implied by saying that a scientific description is true if it corresponds with the facts. For it is certain that such a correspondence cannot be perfect; in the nature of things, the description can match the facts only with a certain coarseness, with what engineers call some tolerance. A scientist therefore has to decide what coarseness he accepts, if he is ever to come to conclusions. This decision is itself an act of judgment, and I suspect that it has subtle things to teach us about how we judge and how we value. Certainly it should teach us what I miss most in the accusation that science is neutral— the sense that science involves the scientist as a person. A discovery has to be made by a man, not by a machine, because every discovery hinges on a critical judgment.

However, I want to go another way from my fundamental proposition that science must value truth. I want to take the proposition beyond the individual scientist, and ask what it implies in the society made up of men like him. This is a natural extension; we are all of us concerned not merely with our personal values but with the values of our whole society. But it is also an important extension for another reason. Many of the choices in which a man's values are expressed are precisely choices between what he would like to do as an individual and what he is asked to do as a member of a community. The social values are generated by this confrontation of individual wish and communal will. There are no conflicts of values until the man has to find a posture to his society, and the society has to find its attitude to him: until each has to adjust itself to the other.

Therefore we have only begun the elucidation of modern values when we have found that science must necessarily value truth. For truth is an individual value, which dictates the conduct of a scientist when he is alone with his work. It becomes a source of social values only when a whole society accepts the assumption that no belief will survive if it conflicts with factual truth. This is the unspoken assumption which our society makes. It is equivalent to setting up truth as the overriding value for our society, and to agreeing that the discovery of the truth is an end in itself, the supreme end, not only for individuals but for our society as a whole. It follows that a whole nexus of social values should be deducible, by logical steps, from the single injunction that society has a duty to seek the truth.

I have said that our scientific society takes it for granted that it should seek the truth: and this description is characteristic of it. For the description implies that the truth is still being sought, and will go on being sought always; the truth has not already been found. A society that believes that the truth has been finally found, for example in politics or in religion, simply imposes it; it is an authoritarian society. And what goes deeper, a society that believes that the truth has been found or revealed, that the truth is known, resists all change; for what is there to change for? When we say that our society seeks the truth, we imply that it acknowledges that it must itself change and evolve with the truth. The social values which I shall derive are, at bottom, a mechanism by which a society arranges that it shall evolve. They grow from the search for the truth in a scientific society, because the search demands that the society shall evolve.

*   *   *

A man who looks for the truth must be independent, and a society which values the truth must safeguard his independence. An age of reason may be anxious to persuade the unreasonable—and independent minds are always unreasonable—but it must be more anxious to ensure that they are not browbeaten. So Voltaire in his life was as belligerent for the independence of those who did not share his beliefs as for his own. A scientific society must set a high value on independence of mind, however angular and troublesome those who have it are to the rest of us.

We value independence of mind because it safeguards originality, and originality is the tool with which new discoveries are made. But although originality is only a tool, it has become a value in our society, because it is necessary to its evolution. So high is the value which a scientific society places on originality that it has ousted the value which the arts used to place on tradition. The strange and, to me, admirable result has been that the arts have become more and more imaginative, more eccentric and personal, in the last hundred years; and this has certainly been caused by the pressure for originality from what the critics still blindly call the impersonal field of science.

I do not claim that originality is always a virtue, any more than I claim that independence or even truth itself is always so. What I am showing is that originality has become a value in our society, as independence has, because both are means to foster its overriding value, the unending search for truth. There are occasions when originality, like the other values, becomes a bore. Whenever I go to an exhibition of children's paintings, I see several hundred examples of studied and uniform originality, and I sometimes suspect that originality is being taught as a classroom subject. I find this dull, but no more so than I should have found the studied and uniform conformity of children's paintings a hundred years ago, when tradition was taught as a classroom subject. The fact is that a child's painting is no more like art than a child's essay is like literature; what is dull in it today, what was dull a hundred years ago, is not the originality or the tradition, but the childishness. The child's painting has no more merit than an intelligence test; that is, it gives a hint of what the child's mind may do later; and as a scientist, I would rather be bored by the hint that it will dissent than by the conviction that it will conform.

Independence and originality are qualities of mind, and when a society elevates them to values, as ours has done, it must protect them by giving a special value to their expression. This is why we place a value on dissent. The high moments of dissent are monuments in our literature: the writings of Milton, the Declaration of Independence, the sermons of John Wesley, and the poetry of Shelley. True, we find it more comfortable if dissent takes place somewhere else: in the past or in another country. In the West, we like best to read about the dissent which Russian intellectuals have been expressing since the death of Stalin; and no doubt Russians prefer to praise the dissenting voices in the West. But when we have smiled at these human foibles, we recognize behind them that dissent is accepted as a value in the intellectual structure of our civilization. And it is a value which derives from the practice of science: from the experience that progress comes only when the accepted concepts are openly challenged, whether by Copernicus, by Charles Darwin, or by Albert Einstein, and when the challenger insists that the facts be looked at afresh because they have outgrown the old concepts. Dissent is an instrument of intellectual evolution.

A society which values dissent must provide safeguards for those who express it. These safeguards are the most familiar values in the repertory of the political orator: freedom of thought, freedom of speech and writing, and freedom of movement and assembly. But we must not take them for granted simply because lip service to them has become hackneyed, and we must not suppose that they are self-evident and natural values in any society. Plato did not offer freedom of speech and writing in his republic. Freedom is valued in a society only when the society wants to encourage dissent and to stimulate originality and independence. Freedom is therefore essential to a scientific society, a society in evolution. It is merely a nuisance, and is discouraged, in a static society. Yet freedom is the basic acknowledgment that the individual is more important than his society: and we see once again that science, in despite of its critics, prizes the individual as other systems do not.

So far, I have only deduced, from the conditions for the practice of science, those values which make for change. But a society must also have values which resist change; it must, in engineering terms, have a certain inertia, by which it resists the overthrow of what it holds to be true now, and makes the truth of tomorrow fight for life. These inertial values are, of course, more common in other, static societies; but they are also present and important in a scientific society. Respect, honor, and dignity are necessary to the stability of science as of any other social activity, and their value can therefore be demonstrated from the conditions for the practice of science, in the same way that I have demonstrated the evolutionary values. But because the inertial values hold in other societies, because they are necessary to the existence of any society at all, I shall not discuss them further here. Instead, I shall make only one point about them, which is this: in a scientific society, the inertial values are reached by a different path from that which leads to them in other societies.

In a scientific society such values as respect, honor, and dignity are approached across the value of tolerance, which forms as it were a bridge from the evolutionary values. Tolerance is a modern value, because it is a necessary condition for the coherence of a society in which different men have different opinions. Thus tolerance is essential to make a scientific society possible, and to link the work of the past with that of the future. Moreover, tolerance in this sense is not a negative value; it must grow out of an active respect for others. It is not enough in science to agree that other men are entitled to their opinions; we must believe that the opinions of others are interesting in themselves, and deserve our attention and respect even when we think them wrong. And in science, we often think that other men are wrong, but we never think that they are therefore wicked. By contrast, all absolute doctrines think (as the Inquisition did) that those who are wrong are deliberately and wickedly wrong, and may be subjected to any suffering to correct them. The tragedy of the political division of the world today is that it has this doctrinal intolerance: the statesmen of the West believe that those of the East are not merely wrong but wicked, and the statesmen of the East believe the same of us.

This is a good point at which to stop this exposition of some of the values of science. I have made no attempt to derive all the values which I believe a scientific society generates by the nature of its activity. And even if I had found logically all the values in science, I still would not claim that they exhaust all the human values, and that the practice of science gives man and society all the values that they need. This has not been my purpose.

My purpose has been to meet head-on the current mutiny against science that runs through so many discussions of values. This current always sets off with some harmless claim that science is neutral. But the harm is done by the confusion which is hidden in this innocent sentence. The findings of science are neutral, as every fact and every grouping of facts is neutral. But the activity of science which finds the facts and which orders them is not neutral. The activity of science is directed to one overriding end, which is to find the material truth. In our scientific society, this end is accepted as the supreme value.

From this cardinal value, some other values flow of necessity; and my purpose has been to show how this happens. It happens because a society which seeks the truth must provide means for its own evolution, and these means become values for it.

In deriving some of these values, by way of examples, I have shown that there is indeed an empirical procedure for studying the values of a society. What I have been doing is to make, in outline, a short empirical study of a few values. All values are subtle, and the values of science are as subtle as any others. A value is not a mechanical rule of conduct, nor is it a blueprint of virtue. A value is a concept which groups together some modes of behavior in our society. In this sense, when I say that originality is a value for our society, I am just as empirical and as descriptive as when I say that gravitation is a phenomenon of our planetary system. And when I seek the ground or reason for the value given to originality by tracing it back to the demand for truth, I am doing exactly what I should do if I were looking for the cause of gravitation in some more fundamental structure of matter.

This does not mean that values are mere descriptions of our

behavior: and that for two reasons. First, the interplay of values is more complex than any mechanical compounding of forces: it creates a tension which is the stuff of our lives. Second, and more simply, values are concepts which describe our behavior only when we understand what directs that behavior overall. Science is directed by the search for truth, and all societies are directed by the search for stability. The values of our scientific society describe our behavior as it is directed to make an evolving society which shall also be stable.

It is almost three hundred years since scientists first banded together in the Royal Society of England and the Academie Royale of France. What scientists thought to be true then seems very primitive to us now; Isaac Newton was still a youth then, and gravitation had barely been thought of. Every scientific theory has changed profoundly, and several times, in these three hundred years. Yet the society of scientists has remained stable, and binds together Englishmen and Frenchmen, and Americans and Chinese and Russians, in a unity of spirit, a community of principles, more profound than any other body of men. Does this impressive history really lend color to the myth that science is inhuman and impersonal? Does it really suggest that the activity of science generates no values to unite those who practice it?

The point of my analysis has not been to defend science from its critics. My point has been to attack what I believe to be a fundamental error of method in the critics: the error of looking for values outside our activity. If values are to be discussed in a useful way, then they must be discussed empirically, in the realistic setting of the world in which they operate. Values take their richness from the tension between each man and his society, and we should not be human if this tension disappeared: we should be a mechanical insect society. For this very reason, it is useless to accept or even to discuss values merely as absolute norms or as universal social injunctions; and equally it is useless to go to the opposite extreme and to discuss values as personal acts of faith while we disregard the society which must give them currency. If we take either of these one-sided courses, we shall always end by importing the values of some past tradition, and regretting that they do not fit us better. There are some traditional values alive in our scientific society today; but whether they are traditional or whether they are new, they are alive not by accident, but because they are appropriate: because they fit into, and grow from, the activity of science. It is time that those who discuss values learn the reach of that activity and the power of the values which spring from its modest search, personal and communal at the same time, for the factual truth.

Suggestions for Discussion and Writing

1. In the opening paragraph, Bronowski speaks of the "tyranny" of facts in the world of science. What does he mean by this? Can you think of some specific ways in which this tyranny shows itself?

2. What crucial distinction does Bronowski make in the first section of his essay?

3. At the end of the second paragraph, the author announces his intention: "This essay is a short but strictly empirical examination of the way in which some of the values in our society are evolved." In what ways do the tone and style of the essay reflect this announced intention? Point to specific examples.

4. By what logic does Bronowski shift from "truth" as a fundamental value of science to "truth as the overriding value for our society"?

5. Bronowski argues that discovering the material truth (i.e., to the facts) is "the supreme end . . . for our society as a whole." Is he open to the charge that this notion of truth is too limited to justify such a lofty claim? Is there, for instance, a place for "higher truths" in his system of values? Write an essay in which you explore these issues.

6. Bronowski claims that "the value which a scientific society places on originality" has led, over the last century or so, to art that is "more imaginative, more eccentric and personal." In what ways have the arts become more original and personal? What other factors might have contributed to this change?

7. The author says that "dissent is accepted as a value in the intellectual structure of our civilization." Do you agree? Write an essay in which you defend your views.

8. What does Bronowski mean by "inertial values"? Why are they important in a scientific society? Can you see a way in which this notion of inertia can be extended beyond personal qualities to the activity of science itself?

9. In the final section of his essay, Bronowski reasserts his claim that "there is indeed an empirical procedure for studying the values of a society." In what sense is Bronowski's method empirical? Do societal values lend themselves to empirical study? For instance, are his findings falsifiable? (You may wish to consult the essays in Chapter 7.)

10. Do you see a place for faith, for a sense of the holy, for religion in Bronowski's scientific society?

BREAKING FAITH

Robert S. Root-Bernstein
(b. 1941)

For a biographical sketch of the author, see page 327.

In the following essay from *The Sciences* (November/December 1989), Root-Bernstein discusses several cases of scientific fraud. He suggests that all fraud cases have certain things in common and indicates the path that science must follow to ensure its integrity.

N ational Institutes of Health researchers Walter Stewart and Ned Feder have reputations as fraud busters. In one of their most-publicized cases, they helped demonstrate that the Harvard University heart specialist John Darsee had fabricated data that provided the basis for more than a hundred articles and abstracts. So when postdoctoral fellow Margot O'Toole thought she had evidence that the Nobel laureate David Baltimore and his colleagues at the Massachusetts Institute of Technology and Tufts University had suppressed and misinterpreted data in a 1986 paper about their immunology research, a concerned co-worker turned to Stewart and Feder for help.

On the strength of seventeen pages of raw data supplied by O'Toole in April of 1987, Stewart and Feder circulated to a large number of scientists an article accusing Baltimore of making erroneous claims. When the two men attempted to publish the basis for their accusations in the journal *Cell,* in which Baltimore's results had appeared, their paper was rejected. Baltimore, meanwhile, denied any wrongdoing. MIT and Tufts officials had reviewed the allegations in 1986 and found them groundless. Dozens of scientists, including a who's who of biology, gave Baltimore moral support in the press and at subsequent NIH and congressional hearings. At the same time, a campaign was launched asserting that Stewart and Feder were muckraking only because they had become nonproductive in their own laboratories. Stories—apparently unfounded—circulated that the two were being pressured by NIH to resign.

Stewart and Feder would not back down. Baltimore suggested that the dispute be arbitrated by an independent panel of NIH scientists. Stewart and Feder refused, preferring to testify before House subcommittees of the Government Operations and the Energy and Commerce committees (to which Baltimore and his colleagues were not invited) during the following April. Congress had already requested a full-scale investigation and had taken the unprecedented step of assigning Secret Service personnel to examine the laboratory notebooks for signs of tampering.

Earlier this year, the Secret Service reported that a number of pages appeared to have been altered and that others had been inserted sometime after the original data had been recorded. The researcher who kept the notebooks, Thereza Imanishi-Kari, stated that she had done nothing wrong—that that was how she kept records. Various other apparently incriminating comments and letters were brushed aside as misunderstandings resulting from her poor command of English. Meanwhile, an NIH panel had confirmed that Baltimore and his co-workers had indeed misinterpreted and misrepresented some of their data, but the panel concluded that, while there was evidence of sloppy thinking, there was no evidence of intent to deceive and therefore no grounds for accusations of wrongdoing. Besides, according to Baltimore, the main points of the article had already been replicated by other researchers.

Congress, however, is not satisfied and is keeping the Baltimore case open as part of a massive investigation into the problem of scientific fraud in general. Recent studies, as well as such popularizations as William Broad and Nicholas Wade's book, *Betrayers of the Truth,* and a NOVA television program entitled "Do Scientists Cheat?" suggest that scientific fraud has increased dramatically in the past several decades—or at least has gained wider publicity. The government, as the most important patron of science, is justifiably concerned that it is being bilked of millions of dollars by con men in white coats.

Oddly, the only people who do not seem to be worried about scientific fraud are scientists themselves. "Fraud in science is so rare as to be negligible," is one standard line. "Besides, science is self-correcting," is another. "Absolutely," say those who would keep science independent of outside oversight. "If there is a problem, it is with peer review, and if we make peer review work more efficiently, then fraud will become impossible." A less polite but equally heartfelt belief is that "Congress has no business sticking its nose into things it doesn't understand. We'll handle it ourselves."

Such were the sentiments expressed by scientists to Congress when, two years ago, Harvard's dismissal of Darsee, along with a spate of other frauds, at Yale, Cornell, and several other institutions, drew national attention to the problem. With the emergence of the Baltimore case, such statements are again echoing in the chambers of Congress. Scientists, committed to the ethic of their profession, will protect their own. Indeed, if Stewart and Feder have transgressed, it is not in accusing Baltimore of misleading statements tantamount to fraud but in bringing their accusations into the public forum, where Baltimore, as well as all of science, may be embarrassed.

Yet scientists and Congress alike have missed the point. It probably *is* accurate to say that fraud cannot damage a healthy scientific system—though not necessarily for the reasons most scientists suppose. And it is also accurate to assert that, in such a system, no scientist in his right mind would attempt to deceive others; he would surely be caught. An increase in fraud, therefore, signals that some-thing is awry in the system itself. In a word, fraud is only a symptom; it derives its force and meaning from the conditions that make it possible.

All frauds, scientific or otherwise, have one thing in common: the perpetrators pander to the expectations of their audiences. Thus, while fraudulent science can misdirect small amounts of funding and take up a limited amount of journal space, it can have no long-term impact on the development of science, because it serves only to support ideas already accepted by the scientific community. The need to pander to expectation sets severe limitations on the kinds of fraud most likely to go unnoticed. Fraudulent individuals usually deceive only those whose expectations are known—those who have subor-dinated their skepticism to their desires. In any fraud, the gullibility of the audience is as much to blame as the dishonesty of the deceiver.

Among recent instances of scientific fraud, none demonstrates more clearly the tacit collaboration of deceiver and deceived than that of Cyril Burt, who died in 1971 at the age of eighty-eight. Regarded by many as Britain's most eminent psychologist, Burt had been a pro-fessor emeritus at the University of London, edited the *British Journal of Statistical Psychology* for many years, and been awarded the Thorndike Prize of the American Psychological Association for his contributions to the understanding of personality formation. He was also the first psychologist to be knighted.

Burt's studies of identical twins raised together and apart involved the largest test groups ever assembled and were considered definitive demonstrations that intelligence was mostly an inherited trait. Sim-ilarly, his research on the relationship between social class and mental ability became a bulwark for British upper-class prejudices and a mainstay for those in America, such as Arthur Jensen and Richard J. Herrnstein, who promote the idea that intelligence varies with race. Regrettably, Burt's most important contributions to psy-chology were fabricated.

No one doubted Burt's work while he was alive. But a year after his death, a student at Princeton University urged psychologist Leon Kamin to examine Burt's papers. "The immediate conclusion I came to after 10 minutes of reading," Kamin said, "was that Burt was a fraud." This was a strong statement, coming from a man with no background in the study of human intelligence, but Kamin's reasons for suspecting deceit also were strong. Burt had failed to provide details of how his studies were carried out, failed to document how the data were analyzed, and failed to discuss his conclusions in a scholarly fashion. But Kamin's clinching observation was that as Burt's group of twins increased from twenty-one pairs in 1955 to "over thirty" in 1958 to fifty-three in 1966, the correlation between the IQ scores of twins raised apart remained exactly 0.771, while the correlation between IQ scores of twins raised together remained exactly 0.994. Even if Burt had retested the same individuals at different ages, such consistency would be unlikely; that the scores would stay the same when the number and composition of the group changed was virtually impossible.

Kamin published his accusations in 1974. Once the gates of skepticism were opened, a flood of corroborating evidence poured in. Oliver Gillie, a medical correspondent for the London *Sunday Times,* reported in 1976 that he was unable to find any evidence of the existence of the two collaborators, Margaret Howard and Jane Conway, whom Burt claimed had aided him in his twins research. Further doubts emerged in 1979, when the historian Leslie S. Hearnshaw, of the University of Liverpool, published an official biography, in which he revealed that Burt's diaries and private papers demonstrated beyond a doubt that Howard and Conway, if they ever existed, did not help with Burt's research. He also verified that at least some of the data were fabricated and that many of Conway's letters and articles defending Burt's results in the *British Journal of Statistical Psychology* (as well as letters published under other names) were the work of Burt himself. Shortly thereafter, Stephen Jay Gould made a convincing case in his *Mismeasure of Man* that Burt's results were so statistically flawed as to have been useless anyway. Incredibly, none of these failings came to light during the five decades in which Burt was publishing—and others were poring over—his data.

The same pattern of uncritical acceptance of desirable results characterizes the 1979 case of Vijay R. Soman, a highly productive endocrinologist at the Yale University School of Medicine. The unraveling of his fraudulent activities began when his laboratory chief, Philip Felig, received a paper to review from *The New England Journal of Medicine.* The manuscript, by Helena Wachslicht-Rodbard, of the National Institutes of Health, was on the exact topic being studied in Felig's laboratory: insulin receptors in individuals with anorexia nervosa. After passing the manuscript to Soman, Felig recommended that it not be published.

A few months later, Wachslicht-Rodbard's laboratory chief, Jesse Roth, received a manuscript to review from *The American Journal of Medicine* written by Soman and Felig. He showed it to Wachslicht-Rodbard, who was shocked to find that several passages had been copied verbatim from her own, rejected manuscript. Further, analysis of the reported results suggested to her that they had been concocted from her own data, but in such a way as to make them appear too good to be true. She demanded an audit of Soman and Felig's research notebooks.

Unfortunately, Roth and Felig had worked in the same area of research for many years, and they were friends. Moreover, Felig held an endowed chair at Yale and was one of the most-published (with, at the age of forty-three, more than two hundred articles) and best-funded endocrinologists in the country. No one at NIH or Yale could seriously imagine that such a man would allow his collaborator to steal data, let alone do so himself. Roth asked Wachslicht-Rodbard to drop her complaint in return for concessions of priority. She refused. Her relationship with Roth deteriorated, and she resigned her increasingly uncomfortable job at NIH to take a position as a hospital physician.

For a while, it looked as if the fraud would succeed. Soman admitted to Felig that he had copied a few sentences from the Wachslicht-Rodbard paper and used an equation she had developed in it, but only, he insisted, because his knowledge of English was weak. He assured Felig that the studies had been conducted as reported, and Felig took him at his word. An audit by a Yale-approved scientist of the Soman–Felig notebooks, scheduled for 1979, never took place. Wachslicht-Rodbard persisted. Finally, in 1980, an independent investigator, the endocrinologist Jeffrey S. Flier, of Harvard Medical School, took the train from Boston to New Haven to look at Soman's notebooks.

Flier asked to see the original data. Soman provided a few pages of numbers that looked suspiciously incomplete. From these, Flier calculated the binding curves of the insulin. They did not match those published in the Soman–Felig paper. When pressed, Soman admitted having thrown out some "bad" data. When pressed further, he admitted "cooking" the remaining data to make them look more convincing, citing as his excuse the unbelievable pressures at Yale to publish fundable results.

When Flier reported his findings to the authorities at Yale, they asked Soman to leave the university. They also ordered fourteen of Soman's previous papers to be checked against his notebooks. Felig, who was coauthor of most of those publications, appeared shocked when the audit revealed that little of the original data existed. Meanwhile, he had secured a post at Columbia University's College of Physicians and Surgeons. But when letters went out to the journals retracting the previous Soman–Felig papers, news of the fraud finally reached Columbia, and Felig, too, was forced to resign.

The Burt and Soman cases illustrate at least two features of deceptive science. First, both frauds took place at esteemed institutions. Scientists so situated can rely on their positions, reputations, and authority to blind their colleagues to minor faults that probably would damn less eminent scientists. Second, each man reached his station by playing to the predispositions of his patrons. Burt told the aristocratic and academic elite what they wanted to hear about the heritability of intelligence and assured them that their sons and daughters would carry on the domination of society. They knighted him. Soman gave Felig the results Felig expected, so Felig never doubted the validity of the studies, and he then fed these results to his uncritical colleagues, who, expecting the same thing, rewarded him with publication, grants, and promotions. In each case, the resultant data were the envy of competitors. While other psychologists could hardly scrape together twenty pairs of identical twins for study, Burt was reporting on fifty. According to Morton Hunt, in an article on the Soman–Felig affair that appeared in the November 1,

1981, issue of *The New York Times Magazine,* Flier remembers thinking a year or two before being asked to audit the Soman–Felig papers that their results were almost too good to be true: "You'd shake your head and say, 'How did they ever get such beautiful data?' "

And that is precisely the point—the data had to be beautiful, because the perpetrator of a fraud cannot afford to be doubted. Thus, deceit in science is never groundbreaking, for the simple reason that anything truly original is usually met with a derisive laugh, followed by incredulity. Extraordinary ideas require extraordinary proofs. What Burt and Soman and Felig provided was not something new but the *best example* of results that had already met with scientific approval. Their publications simply consolidated existing dogma.

That frauds usually cater to expectation probably explains why specialists in the field overlook its signs. "Fraud," as Stewart has noted, "is almost never detected by peer review or by attempts at replication." Any psychologist from 1958 on could have spotted the statistical improbability in Burt's data. And any endocrinologist could have wondered why Soman and Felig always published better data than anyone else. But there was no reason to doubt. The data were exactly what one might hope to produce oneself, and they came from the best-funded and most-reputable laboratories in the world. How *could* one doubt?

That we, in fact, can, and should, but do not doubt is precisely what is wrong with the present system of science. Our methods of peer review, funding, and promotion reward to a much greater degree scientists who work on high-visibility problems using trendy techniques to produce predictable answers than they do controversy-prone mavericks who refuse to accept the current dogmas and who invent new and unforeseen fields of inquiry. To borrow from the historian Thomas Kuhn, the present system is devised to support *normal,* rather than *revolutionary,* science. In consequence, it also fosters fraudulent science. Every researcher working within a well-articulated paradigm knows what is expected and how to go about achieving it. Even those who would never consider perpetrating a fraud contribute to its possibility by encouraging such "safe" science; they, too, benefit from a reward structure that allows them to succeed without taking risks.

The failure to recognize the underlying causes of fraud is clear in the strategies offered to counteract it. Consider two of the preventive measures so far suggested: that all scientists be required to take seminars on scientific ethics, and that preemptive audits of original data be carried out by representatives of the scientific community, a proposal that is being reviewed by the U.S. Department of Health and Human Services. Both suggestions overlook basic aspects of fraud.

Dishonest individuals know they are being dishonest, and telling them not to be is likely to be as effective as telling a smoker his behavior is bad for his lungs. The effort wastes everyone's time. Audits also are unlikely to be effective. Soman showed Felig data sufficient to convince him the studies had been carried out, and initial investigations by Yale University officials corroborated Felig's opinion. The crucial data damning Burt came from personal material, such as letters and diaries, not laboratory notes. Indeed, initial reviews of most frauds have been unsuccessful, which is not surprising: One must believe that a fraud has occurred and know what to look for before spotting deceptive behavior.

A number of other ideas to control fraud have been recommended: that universities set policies for record keeping, including the archiving of results for several years after publication; that, in evaluating proposals, granting agencies emphasize quality rather than quantity of publications; that individuals alleging fraud on the part of other investigators be protected from retribution; that internal, non-adversarial means of dealing with such accusations be established; and that journals reach a consensus on how to deal with allegations of fraudulent publications as well as set guidelines to protect innocent coauthors by requiring signed statements outlining each individual's contributions to a paper. Clearly, these recommendations treat the symptoms of fraud rather than attack its root causes.

But that is not their only flaw. Because of the nature of fraud, the likely outcome of strengthening the peer-review and oversight functions of scientific institutions would be to define further, through homogenization, the expectations of the scientific community, which, in turn, would make deception even easier. Fraud thrives in an environment of rigorous control. Indeed, the less tolerant the system becomes of variety in the outlooks of scientists, the closer we edge toward the conditions that produced such grotesqueries as Nazi science. This may seem an extreme comparison, but it is a historical fact that fraud is least likely when scientists are stubbornly independent and the expectations of the community are heterogeneous.

Perhaps what each of us needs on our desks is a replica of the Piltdown skull that we can pick up and, like Hamlet, ruminate upon. It would remind us that even the experts are easy to fool when presented with the result they had hoped for. And it would remind us that in a system in which funding and promotion are determined by continual laboratory success and unusually large numbers of publications, it is inevitable that some scientists will take the easy path. The skull might also prompt us to conclude that every scientist who accepts counterfeit work at face value, along with every component of the system that gives such work its uncritical blessing, must accept a portion of the blame for creating an environment rife with the potential for fraud.

There is only one solution. We must reward scientists for their novelty, for creating problems that shake our faith in established patterns of thinking and research. Open controversy in the pages of journals must again be fostered, as it was in *Nature* and *Science* many decades ago, so that no result is taken for granted. And above all, we must learn to distrust most the results that best fit our expectations, since these are least valuable to the advancement of science and are easiest to forge. Part of the ethos that should be taught to all scientists is what the late philosopher Walter Kaufmann called the faith of the heretic: to doubt most that which one would most like to believe, and to believe only that which one has doubted. A system based on this approach has no need of policing, because the process itself is, by nature, self-regulating. Intelligent skeptics are difficult to fool.

The importance of these lessons is particularly clear in the Baltimore case. Baltimore and his colleagues have thus far been cleared of the charge of fraud, but some of their data have yet to be examined. That many of their results have been replicated does not, in itself, exonerate them, but neither does it implicate them. That they did modify and misreport some data to better fit the expected outcome is certainly telling. And regardless of whether there was any intent to mislead, it remains that had Margot O'Toole, an insider, not suggested improprieties, the results would never have been challenged. That a man of Baltimore's ability and reputation should even be called upon to explain such transgressions is a warning that much more is wrong with our system than meets the eye. Scientists should not need to obtain particular results to succeed as scientists.

Suggestions for Discussion and Writing

1. How did the scientific community initially react to the accusations of scientific fraud leveled against David Baltimore and his colleagues by Stewart and Feder?

2. Where does the author first state his thesis? What does he gain by starting his essay with a particular case?

3. Why, according to the author, can scientific fraud "have no long-term impact on the development of science"?

4. How does Root-Bernstein explain Cyril Burt's success in deceiving the scientific community for more than fifty years?

5. What features of "deceptive science" do the Burt and Soman cases illustrate?

6. What is "safe" science? What is its relation to "an environment of rigorous control"? How, according to the author, do such constraints contribute to scientific fraud? Write an essay developing your views.

7. Briefly describe the scientific environment that, according to the author, would eliminate (or at least dramatically reduce) scientific fraud.

8. What is "the faith of the heretic"?

9. Research the Piltdown controversy and write a brief essay summarizing it.

FAREWELL ADDRESS TO THE LOS ALAMOS SCIENTISTS

J. Robert Oppenheimer (1904–1967)

For a biographical sketch of the author, see page 70.

In this famous address, J. Robert Oppenheimer reflects on the motivations that led him and his fellow scientists to join the Manhattan Project and eventually develop the atomic bomb. He goes on to speak of the "grave crisis" created for humankind with the coming of the atomic age.

In considering what the situation of science is, it may be helpful to think a little of what people said and felt of their motives in coming into this job. One always has to worry that what people say of their motives is not adequate. Many people said different things, and most of them, I think, had some validity. There was in the first place the great concern that our enemy might develop these weapons before we did, and the feeling—at least, in the early days, the very strong feeling—that without atomic weapons it might be very difficult, it might be an impossible, it might be an incredibly long thing to win the war. These things wore off a little as it became clear that the war would be won in any case. Some people, I think, were motivated by curiosity, and rightly so; and some by a sense of adventure, and rightly so. Others had more political arguments and said, "Well, we know that atomic weapons are in principle possible, and it is not right that the threat of their unrealized possibility should hang over the world. It is right that the world should know what can be done in their field and deal with it." And the people added to that that it was a time when all over the world men would be particularly ripe and open for dealing with this problem because of the immediacy of the evils of war, because of the universal cry from everyone that one could not go through this thing again, even a war without atomic bombs. And there was finally, and I think rightly, the feeling that there was probably no place in the world where the development of atomic weapons would have a better chance of leading to a reasonable solution, and a smaller chance of leading to disaster, than within the United States. I believe all these things that people said are true, and I think I said them all myself at one time or another.

But when you come right down to it the reason that we did this job is because it was an organic necessity. If you are a scientist you cannot stop such a thing. If you are a scientist you believe that it is good to find out how the world works; that it is good to find out what the realities are; that it is good to turn over to mankind at large the greatest possible power to control the world and to deal with it according to its lights and its values.

There has been a lot of talk about the evil of secrecy, of concealment, of control, of security. Some of that talk has been on a rather low plane, limited really to saying that it is difficult or inconvenient to work in a world where you are not free to do what you want. I think that the talk has been justified, and that the almost unanimous resistance of scientists to the imposition of control and secrecy is a justified position, but I think that the reason for it may lie a little deeper. I think that it comes from the fact that secrecy strikes at the very root of what science is, and what it is for. It is not possible to be a scientist unless you believe that it is good to learn. It is not good to be a scientist, and it is not possible, unless you think that it is of the highest value to share your knowledge, to share it with anyone who is interested. It is not possible to be a scientist unless you believe that the knowledge of the world, and the power which this gives, is a thing which is of intrinsic value to humanity, and that you are using it to help in the spread of knowledge, and are willing to take the consequences. And, therefore, I think that this resistance which we feel and see all around us to anything which is an attempt to treat science of the future as though it were rather a dangerous thing, a thing that must be watched and managed, is resisted not because of its inconvenience—I think we are in a position where we must be willing to take any inconvenience—but resisted because it is based on a philosophy incompatible with that by which we live, and have learned to live in the past.

There are many people who try to wiggle out of this. They say the real importance of atomic energy does not lie in the weapons that have been made; the real importance lies in all the great benefits which atomic energy, which the various radiations, will bring to mankind. There may be some truth in this. I am sure that there is truth in it, because there has never in the past been a new field opened up where the real fruits of it have not been invisible at the beginning. I have a very high confidence that the fruits—the so-called peacetime applications—of atomic energy will have in them all that we think, and more. There are others who try to escape the immediacy of this situation by saying that, after all, war has always been very terrible; after all, weapons have always gotten worse and worse; that this is just another weapon and it doesn't create a great change; that they are not so bad; bombings have been bad in this war and this is not a change in that—it just adds a little to the effectiveness of bombing; that some sort of protection will be found. I think that these efforts to diffuse and weaken the nature of the crisis make it only more dangerous. I think it is for us to accept it as a very grave crisis, to realize that these atomic weapons which we have started to make are very terrible, that they involve a change, that they are not just a slight modification: to accept this, and to accept with it the necessity for those transformations in the world which will make it possible to integrate these developments into human life.

As scientists I think we have perhaps a little greater ability to accept change, and accept radical change, because of our experiences in the pursuit of science. And that may help us—that, and the fact that we have lived with it—to be of some use in understanding these problems. . . .

There are a few things which scientists perhaps should remember, that I don't think I need to remind us of; but I will, anyway. One is that they are very often called upon to give technical information in one way or another, and I think one cannot be too careful to be honest. And it is very difficult, not because one tells lies, but because so often questions are put in a form which makes it very hard to give an answer which is not misleading. I think we will be in a very weak position unless we maintain at its highest the scrupulousness which is traditional for us in sticking to the truth, and in distinguishing between what we know to be true from what we hope may be true.

The second thing I think it right to speak of is this: It is everywhere felt that the fraternity between us and scientists in other countries may be one of the most helpful things for the future; yet it is apparent that even in this country not all of us who are scientists are in agreement. There is no harm in that; such disagreement is healthy. But we must not lose the sense of fraternity because of it; we must not lose our fundamental confidence in our fellow scientists.

I think that we have no hope at all if we yield in our belief in the value of science, in the good that it can be to the world to know about reality, about nature, to attain a gradually greater and greater control of nature, to learn, to teach, to understand. I think that if we lose our faith in this we stop being scientists, we sell out our heritage, we lose what we have most of value for this time of crisis.

But there is another thing: we are not only scientists; we are men, too. We cannot forget our dependence on our fellow men. I mean not only our material dependence, without which no science would be possible, and without which we could not work; I mean also our deep moral dependence, in that the value of science must lie in the world of men, that all our roots lie there. These are the strongest bonds in the world, stronger than those even that bind us to one another, these are the deepest bonds—that bind us to our fellow men.

Suggestions for Discussion and Writing

1. How would you characterize the tone of Oppenheimer's address? Point to specific examples of diction, sentence structure, and other elements to support your view.

2. Why would Oppenheimer be concerned (as he clearly is in the first paragraph) about the motives of the scientists who joined the Manhattan Project?

3. Write an essay in which you explain how and why "secrecy strikes at the very root of what science is."

4. Do any of Oppenheimer's concerns here echo those of Bronowski in "The Values of Science" (this chapter) or of Oppenheimer himself in "The Sciences and Man's Community" (Chapter 2)?

5. Do you see any purpose in this address beyond the ostensible one of bidding farewell to colleagues?

6. At the start of his address, Oppenheimer speaks of "the situation of science." What is that situation? How has it been affected by the development of the atomic bomb? Are his reassurances at the end of the address adequate?

☐ IMELDA

Richard Selzer
(b. 1928)

Born in Troy, New York, Richard Selzer graduated from Union College, Albany Medical College, and the Surgical Training Program of Yale University. Since 1960 he has been in private practice as a surgeon. He is also on the faculty of the Yale School of Medicine.

Selzer has published essays and stories in a variety of popular magazines, including *Harper's, Esquire,* and *Redbook.* In 1975 he won the National Magazine Award from the Columbia University School of Journalism for essays published in *Esquire.* He has written several books, including *Rituals of Surgery* (short stories), 1974; *Mortal Lessons* (essays), 1977; and *Confessions of a Knife* (essays), 1979. In his stories and essays, Selzer takes us into hospital wards and operating rooms to give us an unadorned view of the world of medicine and surgery. For some readers, his realistic portrayal of the darker side of his profession—of disease and deformity, of patients' reactions to sickness and impending death—has at times seemed shocking, even grotesque. Others have seen his representations of suffering and death as an attempt to make his readers confront their own vulnerability and terror. "By dwelling on the mechanics of death," one critic has said, "Selzer celebrates life."

Selzer's prose style has been widely praised. "Imelda," taken from his fourth book, *Letters to a Young Doctor* (1982), illustrates his skillful use of detail and imagery. It shows, too, his interest in disease and deformity, and in the mind and motives of the surgeon who must encounter them.

I heard the other day that Hugh Franciscus had died. I knew him once. He was the Chief of Plastic Surgery when I was a medical student at Albany Medical College. Dr. Franciscus was the archetype of the professor of surgery—tall, vigorous, muscular, as precise in his technique as he was impeccable in his dress. Each day a clean lab coat monkishly starched, that sort of thing. I doubt that he ever read books. One book only, that of the human body, took the place of all others. He never raised his eyes from it. He read it like a printed page as though he knew that in the calligraphy there just beneath the skin were all the secrets of the world. Long before it became visible to anyone else, he could detect the first sign of granulation at the base of a wound, the first blue line of new epithelium at the periphery that would tell him that a wound would heal, or the barest hint of necrosis that presaged failure. This gave him the appearance of a prophet. "This skin graft will take," he would say, and you must believe beyond all cyanosis, exudation and inflammation that it would.

He had enemies, of course, who said he was arrogant, that he exalted activity for its own sake. Perhaps. But perhaps it was no more than the honesty of one who knows his own worth. Just look at a scalpel, after all. What a feeling of sovereignty, megalomania even, when you know that it is you and you alone who will make certain use of it. It was said, too, that he was a ladies' man. I don't know about that. It was all rumor. Besides, I think he had other things in mind than mere living. Hugh Franciscus was a zealous hunter. Every fall during the season he drove upstate to hunt deer. There was a glass-front case in his office where he showed his guns. How could he shoot a deer? we asked. But he knew better. To us medical students he was someone heroic, someone made up of several gods, beheld at a distance, and always from a lesser height. If he had grown accustomed to his miracles, we had not. He had no close friends on the staff. There was something a little sad in that. As though once long ago he had been flayed by friendship and now the slightest breeze would hurt. Confidences resulted in dishonor. Perhaps the person in whom one confided would scorn him, betray. Even though he spent his days among those less fortunate, weaker than he—the sick, after all—Franciscus seemed aware of an air of personal harshness in his environment to which he reacted by keeping his own counsel, by a certain remoteness. It was what gave him the appearance of being haughty. With the patients he was forthright. All the facts laid out, every question anticipated and answered with specific information. He delivered good news and bad with the same dispassion.

I was a third-year student, just turned onto the wards for the first time, and clerking on Surgery. Everything—the operating room, the morgue, the emergency room, the patients, professors, even the nurses—was terrifying. One picked one's way among the mines and booby traps of the hospital, hoping only to avoid the hemorrhage and perforation of disgrace. The opportunity for humiliation was everywhere.

It all began on Ward Rounds. Dr. Franciscus was demonstrating a cross-leg flap graft he had constructed to cover a large fleshy defect in the leg of a merchant seaman who had injured himself in a fall. The man was from Spain and spoke no English. There had been a comminuted fracture of the femur, much soft tissue damage, necrosis. After weeks of débridement and dressings, the wound had been made ready for grafting. Now the patient was in his fifth postoperative day. What we saw was a thick web of pale blue flesh arising from the man's left thigh, and which had been sutured to the open wound on the right thigh. When the surgeon pressed the pedicle with his finger, it blanched; when he let up, there was a slow return of the violaceous color.

"The circulation is good," Franciscus announced. "It will get better." In several weeks, we were told, he would divide the tube of flesh at its site of origin, and tailor it to fit the defect to which, by then, it would have grown more solidly. All at once, the webbed man in the bed reached out, and gripping Franciscus by the arm, began to speak rapidly, pointing to his groin and hip. Franciscus stepped back at once to disengage his arm from the patient's grasp.

"Anyone here know Spanish? I didn't get a word of that."

"The cast is digging into him up above," I said. "The edges of the plaster are rough. When he moves, they hurt."

Without acknowledging my assistance, Dr. Franciscus took a plaster shears from the dressing cart and with several large snips cut away the rough edges of the cast.

"*Gracias, gracias.*" The man in the bed smiled. But Franciscus had already moved on to the next bed. He seemed to me a man of immense strength and ability, yet without affection for the patients. He did not want to be touched by them. It was less kindness that he showed them than a reassurance that he would never give up, that he would bend every effort. If anyone could, he would solve the problems of their flesh.

Ward Rounds had disbanded and I was halfway down the corridor when I heard Dr. Franciscus' voice behind me.

"You speak Spanish." It seemed a command.

"I lived in Spain for two years," I told him.

"I'm taking a surgical team to Honduras next week to operate on the natives down there. I do it every year for three weeks, somewhere. This year, Honduras. I can arrange the time away from your duties here if you'd like to come along. You will act as interpreter. I'll show you how to use the clinical camera. What you'd see would make it worthwhile."

So it was that, a week later, the envy of my classmates, I joined the mobile surgical unit—surgeons, anesthetists, nurses and equipment—aboard a Military Air Transport plane to spend three weeks performing plastic surgery on people who had been previously selected by an advance team. Honduras. I don't suppose I shall ever see it again. Nor do I especially want to. From the plane it seemed a country made of clay—burnt umber, raw sienna, dry. It had a dead-weight quality, as though the ground had no buoyancy, no air sacs through which a breeze might wander. Our destination was Comayagua, a town in the Central Highlands. The town itself was situated on the edge of one of the flatlands that were linked in a network between the granite mountains. Above, all was brown, with only an occasional Spanish cedar tree; below, patches of luxuriant tropical growth. It was a day's bus ride from the airport. For hours, the town kept appearing and disappearing with the convolutions of the road. At last, there it lay before us, panting and exhausted at the bottom of the mountain.

That was all I was to see of the countryside. From then on, there was only the derelict hospital of Comayagua, with the smell of spoiling bananas and the accumulated odors of everyone who had been sick there for the last hundred years. Of the two, I much preferred the frank smell of the sick. The heat of the place was incendiary. So hot that, as we stepped from the bus, our own words did not carry through the air, but hung limply at our lips and chins. Just in front of the hospital was a thirsty courtyard where mobs of waiting people squatted or lay in the meager shade, and where, on dry days, a fine dust rose through which untethered goats shouldered. Against the walls of this courtyard, gaunt, dejected men stood, their faces, like their country, preternaturally solemn, leaden. Here no one looked up at the sky. Every head was bent beneath a wide-brimmed straw hat. In the days that followed, from the doorway of the dispensary, I would watch the brown mountains sliding about, drinking the hospital into their shadow as the afternoon grew later and later, flattening us by their very altitude.

The people were mestizos, of mixed Spanish and Indian blood. They had flat, broad, dumb museum feet. At first they seemed to me indistinguishable the one from the other, without animation. All the vitality, the hidden sexuality, was in their black hair. Soon I was to know them by the fissures with which each face was graven. But, even so, compared to us, they were masked, shut away. My job was to follow Dr. Franciscus around, photograph the patients before and after surgery, interpret and generally act as aide-de-camp. It was exhilarating. Within days I had decided that I was not just useful, but essential. Despite that we spent all day in each other's company, there were no overtures of friendship from Dr. Franciscus. He knew my place, and I knew it, too. In the afternoon he examined the patients scheduled for the next day's surgery. I would call out a name from the doorway to the examining room. In the courtyard someone would rise. I would usher the patient in, and nudge him to the examining table where Franciscus stood, always, I thought, on the verge of irritability. I would read aloud the case history, then wait while he carried out his examination. While I took the "before" photographs, Dr. Franciscus would dictate into a tape recorder:

"Ulcerating basal cell carcinoma of the right orbit—six by eight centimeters—involving the right eye and extending into the floor of the orbit. Operative plan: wide excision with enucleation of the eye. Later, bone and skin grafting." The next morning we would be in the operating room where the procedure would be carried out.

We were more than two weeks into our tour of duty—a few days to go—when it happened. Earlier in the day I had caught sight of her through the window of the dispensary. A thin, dark Indian girl about fourteen years old. A figurine, orange-brown, terra-cotta, and still attached to the unshaped clay from which she had been carved. An older, sun-weathered woman stood behind and somewhat to the left of the girl. The mother was short and dumpy. She wore a broad-brimmed hat with a high crown, and a shapeless dress like a cassock. The girl had long, loose black hair. There were tiny gold hoops in her ears. The dress she wore could have been her mother's. Far too big, it hung from her thin shoulders at some risk of slipping down her arms. Even with her in it, the dress was empty, something hanging on the back of a door. Her breasts made only the smallest imprint in the cloth, her hips none at all. All the while, she pressed to her mouth a filthy, pink, balled-up rag as though to stanch a flow or buttress against pain. I knew that what she had come to show us, what we were there to see, was hidden beneath that pink cloth. As I watched, the woman handed down to her a gourd from which the girl drank, lapping like a dog. She was the last patient of the day. They had been waiting in the courtyard for hours.

"Imelda Valdez," I called out. Slowly she rose to her feet, the cloth never leaving her mouth, and followed her mother to the examining-room door. I shooed them in.

"You sit up there on the table," I told her. "Mother, you stand over there, please." I read from the chart:

"This is a fourteen-year-old girl with a complete, unilateral, left-sided cleft lip and cleft palate. No other diseases or congenital defects. Laboratory tests, chest X ray—negative."

"Tell her to take the rag away," said Dr. Franciscus. I did, and the girl shrank back, pressing the cloth all the more firmly.

"Listen, this is silly," said Franciscus. "Tell her I've got to see it. Either she behaves, or send her away."

"Please give me the cloth," I said to the girl as gently as possible. She did not. She could not. Just then, Franciscus reached up and, taking the hand that held the rag, pulled it away with a hard jerk. For an instant the girl's head followed the cloth as it left her face, one arm still upflung against showing. Against all hope, she would hide herself. A moment later, she relaxed and sat still. She seemed to me then like an animal that looks outward at the infinite, at death, without fear, with recognition only.

Set as it was in the center of the girl's face, the defect was utterly hideous—a nude rubbery insect that had fastened there. The upper lip was widely split all the way to the nose. One white tooth perched upon the protruding upper jaw projected through the hole. Some of the bone seemed to have been gnawed away as well. Above the thing, clear almond eyes and long black hair reflected the light. Below, a slender neck where the pulse trilled visibly. Under our gaze the girl's eyes fell to her lap where her hands lay palms upward, half open. She was a beautiful bird with a crushed beak. And tense with the expectation of more shame.

"Open your mouth," said the surgeon. I translated. She did so, and the surgeon tipped back her head to see inside.

"The palate, too. Complete," he said. There was a long silence. At last he spoke.

"What is your name?" The margins of the wound melted until she herself was being sucked into it.

"Imelda." The syllables leaked through the hole with a slosh and a whistle.

"Tomorrow," said the surgeon, "I will fix your lip. *Mañana.*"

It seemed to me that Hugh Franciscus, in spite of his years of experience, in spite of all the dreadful things he had seen, must have been awed by the sight of this girl. I could see it flit across his face for an instant. Perhaps it was her small act of concealment, that he had had to demand that she show him the lip, that he had had to force her to show it to him. Perhaps it was her resistance that intensified the disfigurement. Had she brought her mouth to him willingly, without shame, she would have been for him neither more nor less than any other patient.

He measured the defect with calipers, studied it from different angles, turning her head with a finger at her chin.

"How can it ever be put back together?" I asked.

"Take her picture," he said. And to her, "Look straight ahead." Through the eye of the camera she seemed more pitiful than ever, her humiliation more complete.

"Wait!" The surgeon stopped me. I lowered the camera. A strand of her hair had fallen across her face and found its way to her mouth, becoming stuck there by saliva. He removed the hair and secured it behind her ear.

"Go ahead," he ordered. There was a click of the camera. The girl winced.

"Take three more, just in case."

When the girl and her mother had left, he took paper and pen and with a few lines drew a remarkable likeness of the girl's face.

"Look," he said. "If this dot is A, and this one B, this, C and this, D, the incisions are made A to B, then C to D. CD must equal AB. It is all equilateral triangles." All well and good, but then came X and Y and rotation flaps and the rest.

"Do you see?" he asked.

"It is confusing," I told him.

"It is simply a matter of dropping the upper lip into a normal position, then crossing the gap with two traingular flaps. It is geometry," he said.

"Yes," I said. "Geometry." And relinquished all hope of becoming a plastic surgeon.

In the operating room the next morning the anesthesia had already been administered when we arrived from Ward Rounds. The tube emerging from the girl's mouth was pressed against her lower lip to be kept out of the field of surgery. Already, a nurse was scrubbing the face which swam in a reddish-brown lather. The tiny gold earrings were included in the scrub. Now and then, one of them gave a brave flash. The face was washed for the last time, and dried. Green towels were placed over the face to hide everything but the mouth and nose. The drapes were applied.

"Calipers!" The surgeon measured, locating the peak of the distorted Cupid's bow.

"Marking pen!" He placed the first blue dot at the apex of the bow. The nasal sills were dotted; next, the inferior philtral dimple, the vermilion line. The *A* flap and the *B* flap were outlined. On he worked, peppering the lip and nose, making sense out of chaos, realizing the lip that lay waiting in that deep essential pink, that only he could see. The last dot and line were placed. He was ready.

"Scalpel!" He held the knife above the girl's mouth.

"O.K. to go ahead?" he asked the anesthetist.

"Yes."

He lowered the knife.

"No! Wait!" the anesthetist's voice was tense, staccato. "Hold it!"

The surgeon's hand was motionless.

"What's the matter?"

"Something's wrong. I'm not sure. God, she's hot as a pistol. Blood pressure is way up. Pulse one eighty. Get a rectal temperature." A nurse fumbled beneath the drapes. We waited. The nurse retrieved the thermometer.

"One hundred seven . . . no . . . eight." There was disbelief in her voice.

"Malignant hyperthermia," said the anesthetist. "Ice! Ice! Get lots of ice!" I raced out the door, accosted the first nurse I saw.

"Ice!" I shouted. "*Hielo!* Quickly! *Hielo!*" The woman's expression was blank. I ran to another. "*Hielo! Hielo!* For the love of God, ice."

"*Hielo?*" She shrugged. "*Nada.*" I ran back to the operating room.

"There isn't any ice," I reported. Dr. Franciscus had ripped off his rubber gloves and was feeling the skin of the girl's abdomen. Above the mask his eyes were the eyes of a horse in battle.

"The EKG is wild . . ."

"I can't get a pulse . . ."

"What the hell . . ."

The surgeon reached for the girl's groin. No femoral pulse.

"EKG flat. My God! She's dead!"

"She can't be."

"She is."

The surgeon's fingers pressed the groin where there was no pulse to be felt, only his own pulse hammering at the girl's flesh to be let in.

It was noon, four hours later, when we left the operating room. It was a day so hot and humid I felt steamed open like an envelope. The woman was sitting on a bench in the courtyard in her dress like a cassock. In one hand she held the piece of cloth the girl had used to conceal her mouth. As we watched, she folded it once neatly, and then again, smoothing it, cleaning the cloth which might have been the head of the girl in her lap that she stroked and consoled.

"I'll do the talking here," he said. He would tell her himself, in whatever Spanish he could find. Only if she did not understand was I to speak for him. I watched him brace himself, set his shoulders. How could he tell her? I wondered. What? But I knew he would tell her everything, exactly as it had happened. As much for himself as for her, he needed to explain. But suppose she screamed, fell to the ground, attacked him, even? All that hope of love . . . gone. Even in his discomfort I knew that he was teaching me. The way to do it was professionally. Now he was standing above her. When the woman saw that he did not speak, she lifted her eyes and saw what he held crammed in his mouth to tell her. She knew, and rose to her feet.

"Señora," he began, "I am sorry." All at once he seemed to me shorter than he was, scarcely taller than she. There was a place at the crown of his head where the hair had grown thin. His lips were stones. He could hardly move them. The voice dry, dusty.

"No one could have known. Some bad reaction to the medicine for sleeping. It poisoned her. High fever. She did not wake up." The last, a whisper. The woman studied his lips as though she were deaf. He tried, but could not control a twitching at the corner of his mouth. He raised a thumb and forefinger to press something back into his eyes.

"*Muerte,*" the woman announced to herself. Her eyes were human, deadly.

"*Sí, muerte.*" At that moment he was like someone cast, still alive, as an effigy for his own tomb. He closed his eyes. Nor did he open them until he felt the touch of the woman's hand on his arm, a touch from which he did not withdraw. Then he looked and saw the grief corroding her face, breaking it down, melting the features so that eyes, nose, mouth ran together in a distortion, like the girl's. For a long time they stood in silence. It seemed to me that minutes passed. At last her face cleared, the features rearranged themselves. She spoke, the words coming slowly to make certain that he understood her. She would go home now. The next day her sons would come for the girl, to take her home for burial. The doctor must not be sad. God has decided. And she was happy now that the harelip had been fixed so that her daughter might go to Heaven without it. Her bare feet retreating were the felted pads of a great bereft animal.

The next morning I did not go to the wards, but stood at the gate leading from the courtyard to the road outside. Two young men in striped ponchos lifted the girl's body wrapped in a straw mat onto the back of a wooden cart. A donkey waited. I had been drawn to this place as one is drawn, inexplicably, to certain scenes of desolation— executions, battlefields. All at once, the woman looked up and saw me. She had taken off her hat. The heavy-hanging coil of her hair made her head seem larger, darker, noble. I pressed some money into her hand.

"For flowers," I said. "A priest." Her cheeks shook as though minutes ago a stone had been dropped into her navel and the ripples were just now reaching her head. I regretted having come to that place.

"*Sí, sí,*" the woman said. Her own face was stitched with flies. "The doctor is one of the angels. He has finished the work of God. My daughter is beautiful."

What could she mean! The lip had not been fixed. The girl had died before he would have done it.

"Only a fine line that God will erase in time," she said.

I reached into the cart and lifted a corner of the mat in which the girl had been rolled. Where the cleft had been there was now a fresh line of tiny sutures. The Cupid's bow was delicately shaped, the vermilion border aligned. The flattened nostril had now the same rounded shape as the other one. I let the mat fall over the face of the dead girl, but not before I had seen the touching place where the finest black hairs sprang from the temple.

Adiós, adiós . . ." And the cart creaked away to the sound of hooves, a tinkling bell.

There are events in a doctor's life that seem to mark the boundary between youth and age, seeing and perceiving. Like certain dreams, they illuminate a whole lifetime of past behavior. After such an event, a doctor is not the same as he was before. It had seemed to me then to have been the act of someone demented, or at least insanely arrogant. An attempt to reorder events. Her death had come to him out of order. It should have come after the lip had been repaired, not before. He could have told the mother that, no, the lip had not been fixed. But he did not. He said nothing. It had been an act of omission, one of those strange lapses to which all of us are subject and which we live to regret. It must have been then, at that moment, that the knowledge of what he would do appeared to him. The words of the mother had not consoled him; they had hunted him down. He had not done it for her. The dire necessity was his. He would not accept that Imelda had died before he could repair her lip. People who do such things break free from society. They follow their own lonely path. They have a secret which they can never reveal. I must never let on that I knew.

How often I have imagined it. Ten o'clock at night. The hospital of Comayagua is all but dark. Here and there lanterns tilt and skitter up and down the corridors. One of these lamps breaks free from the others and descends the stone steps to the underground room that is the morgue of the hospital. This room wears the expression as if it had waited all night for someone to come. No silence so deep as this place with its cargo of newly dead. Only the slow drip of water over stone. The door closes gassily and clicks shut. The lock is turned. There are four tables, each with a body encased in a paper shroud. There is no mistaking her. She is the smallest. The surgeon takes a knife from his pocket and slits open the paper shroud, that part in which the girl's head is enclosed. The wound seems to be living on long after she has died. Waves of heat emanate from it, blurring his vision. All at once, he turns to peer over his shoulder. He sees nothing, only a wooden crucifix on the wall.

He removes a package of instruments from a satchel and arranges them on a tray. Scalpel, scissors, forceps, needle holder. Sutures and gauze sponges are produced. Stealthy, hunched, engaged, he begins. The dots of blue dye are still there upon her mouth. He raises the scalpel, pauses. A second glance into the darkness. From the wall a small lizard watches and accepts. The first cut is made. A sluggish flow of dark blood appears. He wipes it away with a sponge. No new blood comes to takes its place. Again and again he cuts, connecting each of the blue dots until the whole of the zigzag slice is made, first on one side of the cleft, then on the other. Now the edges of the cleft are lined with fresh tissue. He sets down the scalpel and takes up scissors and forceps, undermining the little flaps until each triangle is attached only at one side. He rotates each flap into its new position. He must be certain that they can be swung without tension. They can. He is ready to suture. He fits the tiny curved needle into the jaws of the needle holder. Each suture is placed precisely the same number of millimeters from the cut edge, and the same distance apart. He ties each knot down until the edges are apposed. Not too tightly. These are the most meticulous sutures of his life. He cuts each thread close to the knot. It goes well. The vermilion border with its white skin roll is exactly aligned. One more stitch and the Cupid's bow appears as if by magic. The man's face shines with moisture. Now the nostril is incised around the margin, released, and sutured into a round shape to match its mate. He wipes the blood from the face of the girl with gauze that he has dipped in water. Crumbs of light are scattered on the girl's face. The shroud is folded once more about her. The instruments are handed into the satchel. In a moment the morgue is dark and a lone lantern ascends the stairs and is extinguished.

*   *   *

Six weeks later I was in the darkened ampitheater of the Medical School. Tiers of seats rose in a semicircle above the small stage where Hugh Franciscus stood presenting the case material he had encountered in Honduras. It was the highlight of the year. The hall was filled. The night before he had arranged the slides in the order in which they were to be shown. I was at the controls of the slide projector.

"Next slide!" he would order from time to time in that military voice which had called forth blind obedience from generations of medical students, interns, residents and patients.

"This is a fifty-seven-year-old man with a severe burn contracture of the neck. You will notice the rigid webbing that has fused the chin to the presternal tissues. No motion of the head on the torso is possible. . . . Next slide!"

"Click," went the projector.

"Here he is after the excision of the scar tissue and with the head in full extension for the first time. The defect was then covered. . . . Next slide!"

"Click."

". . . with full-thickness drums of skin taken from the abdomen with the Padgett dermatone. Next slide!"

"Click."

And suddenly there she was, extracted from the shadows, suspended above and beyond all of us like a resurrection. There was the oval face, the long black hair unbraided, the tiny gold hoops in her ears. And that luminous gnawed mouth. The whole of her life seemed to have been summed up in this photograph. A long silence followed that was the surgeon's alone to break. Almost at once, like the anesthetist in the operating room in Comayagua, I knew that something was wrong. It was not that the man would not speak as that he could not. The audience of doctors, nurses and students seemed to have been infected by the black, limitless silence. My own pulse doubled. It was hard to breathe. Why did he not call out for the next slide? Why did he not save himself? Why had he not removed this slide from the ones to be shown? All at once I knew that he had used his camera on her again. I could see the long black shadows of her hair flowing into the darker shadows of the morgue. The sudden blinding flash . . . The next slide would be the one taken in the morgue. He would be exposed.

In the dim light reflected from the slide, I saw him gazing up at her, seeing not the colored photograph, I thought, but the negative of it where the ghost of the girl was. For me, the amphitheater had become Honduras. I saw again that courtyard littered with patients. I could see the dust in the beam of light from the projector. It was then that I knew that she was his measure of perfection and pain—the one lost, the other gained. He, too, had heard the click of the camera, had seen her wince and felt his mercy enlarge. At last he spoke.

"Imelda." It was the one word he had heard her say. At the sound of his voice I removed the next slide from the projector. "Click" . . . and she was gone. "Click" again, and in her place the man with the orbital cancer. For a long moment Franciscus looked up in my direction, on his face an expression that I have given up trying to interpret. Gratitude? Sorrow? It made me think of the gaze of the girl when at last she understood that she must hand over to him the evidence of her body.

"This is a sixty-two-year-old man with a basal cell carcinoma of the temple eroding into the bony orbit . . ." he began as though nothing had happened.

At the end of the hour, even before the lights went on, there was loud applause. I hurried to find him among the departing crowd. I could not. Some weeks went by before I caught sight of him. He seemed vaguely convalescent, as though a fever had taken its toll before burning out.

Hugh Franciscus continued to teach for fifteen years, although he operated a good deal less, then gave it up entirely. It was as though he had grown tired of blood, of always having to be involved with blood, of having to draw it, spill it, wipe it away, stanch it. He was a quieter, softer man, I heard, the ferocity diminished. There were no more expeditions to Honduras or anywhere else.

I, too, have not been entirely free of her. Now and then, in the years that have passed, I see that donkey-cart cortège, or his face bent over hers in the morgue. I would like to have told him what I now know, that his unrealistic act was one of goodness, one of those small, persevering acts done, perhaps, to ward off madness. Like lighting a lamp, boiling water for tea, washing a shirt. But, of course, it's too late now.

Suggestions for Discussion and Writing

1. Consider the title of Selzer's essay. Is it appropriate? What other title might the author have chosen?

2. What attitude toward Dr. Franciscus does the author establish in the first two paragraphs? Point to specific language to support your view.

3. Look closely at the passage in which Selzer describes his arrival in Comayagua. What impression predominates? How is it established? What is its significance?

4. In describing Franciscus's reaction to Imelda's "defect," Selzer writes that "in spite of all the dreadful things he had seen, [he] must have been awed by the sight of this girl." Why was Franciscus "awed" by the sight of Imelda? Write an essay in which you discuss the significance of her defect for him.

5. Selzer describes Dr. Franciscus at various times as being a "prophet," as someone both "heroic" and "arrogant," as a performer of "miracles." How do these perceptions of Franciscus help us to understand his response to Imelda and his decision to perform the surgery? What role does conscience play in his decision?

6. Write an essay on Dr. Franciscus as artist.

7. Describing Dr. Franciscus's conversation with Imelda's mother, Selzer writes, "Even in his discomfort I knew that he was teaching me." What did the author learn from Franciscus? How did the author change?

8. Look again at the section in which Selzer describes Dr. Franciscus's visit to the morgue. From whose point of view is this narrative told? What is achieved by adopting this point of view? What details of diction and syntax contribute to the force of this passage?

9. What do we learn about Franciscus at the slide show?

10. Do you agree with Selzer when he says, in the final paragraph, that even ordinary acts, like "lighting a lamp, boiling water for tea, washing a shirt," help "ward off madness"?

☐ PHYSICIANS, AIDS, AND OCCUPATIONAL RISK

Abigail Zuger
(b. 1955)

Stephen H. Miles
(b. 1950)

Born in New York City, Abigail Zuger received her M.D. from Case Western Reserve University in 1981. She did her internship and residency at Bellevue Hospital, where she currently specializes in internal medicine and infectious diseases. Zuger has written frequently on ethics in medicine.   .

Like Abigail Zuger, Stephen H. Miles specializes in internal medicine. He was born in Minneapolis, received his M.D. from the University of Minnesota in 1976, and currently practices in his native city. He has published extensively on questions of medical ethics.

The following article, originally published in the *Journal of the American Medical Association*, examines the history of physicians' behavior during the great plagues of the past and asks whether that behavior can provide a model for contemporary physicians facing the AIDS epidemic.

B eneath all its layered horrors, the acquired immunodeficiency syndrome (AIDS) epidemic—that Pandora's box of the 20th century—has left us with one small gift. It has forced our attention toward issues that, over the last century, we have grown unaccustomed to facing; it is making us relearn lessons we had almost forgotten.

Acquired immunodeficiency syndrome has provoked a set of particularly unfamiliar questions in the medical community. Physicians are analyzing their own obligations in this epidemic, weighing them against the personal risk that some fear the care of these patients necessarily entails. Of all the complex and contagious modern diseases we face, AIDS alone has prompted this kind of self-examination.

Repeatedly, in these discussions, analogies are drawn between AIDS and other great historic epidemics. In fact, AIDS has little in common with these, least of all in the personal risk it poses to physicians. The risks physicians took in caring for the victims of smallpox, yellow fever, or the bubonic plague were poorly understood and often quite large. The risks AIDS poses to most physicians have been, in comparison, exhaustively evaluated; infection control measures make these risks manageable, if not negligible. Nonetheless, inevitably, past epidemics are recalled and historic traditions stressed in most discussions of physicians' duties toward persons with AIDS.

The urgent need for a coherent professional ethic governing the care of human immunodeficiency virus (HIV)–infected persons prompted us to review medicine's tradition in times of pestilence more closely. We were forced to conclude that past epidemics, which posed far more significant personal risks to physicians, do not provide us with a tradition strong or consistent enough for our present needs. In this article, we review some examples of the profession's past confrontations with the medical and ethical realities of pestilential disease. We then examine several alternative structures for a professional ethic in the care of patients with AIDS.

THE BLACK DEATH

The Black Death, the second great pandemic of bubonic plague, arrived in Europe in the autumn of 1347. In the next four years, by most estimates, at least one fourth of the population of Europe died. The resulting social devastation was compounded by the general agreement among Europe's physicians that the disease was contagious. "The breath of the sick man alone," wrote one chronicler, "may corrupt the healthy, who will suffer from the same plague. . . . To hide is of no avail; flight only protects. . . ."

The great physicians of Greece and Rome had left medieval physicians no specific reflections about a professional duty to accept personal risk. Galen himself had admitted to fleeing from Rome when plague struck that city in 166 A.D. Most of the evidence argues that the Black Death did not instill the medical profession with a new tradition of self-sacrifice. Medieval physicians ranged enormously in education and social importance. For many of them, religious obligations to treat victims of the plague shaped their professional duties. Nonetheless, the dominant impression that this diverse group left among its contemporaries was not one of heroism.

Among the medieval chroniclers, "writer after writer lamented the avarice and cowardice of doctors in times of plague. . . ." Physicians all over Europe appear to have fled from incurable disease and incurable patients alike. When the plague first arrived in Venice, "nearly all physicians withdrew out of fear and terror." Some of the doctors who did not actually leave the city locked themselves in their houses and refused to come out. There is evidence that the prestige of the medical profession suffered considerably during the plague. Physicians' fears, the futility of their treatments, and the rather dispassionate scientific interest some of them took in the disease itself, all came to alarm and horrify the public.

Medieval physicians themselves left few records of how they understood their professional duties. Some of them did not flee the plague but actually sought it out for its extraordinary financial opportunities. Others remained in infected areas for patriotic rather than professional reasons. ("I would rather die here than live elsewhere," said a physician who remained in plague-ridden Venice.) In addition, many physicians at medical schools and royal courts across Europe appear to have stayed at their jobs, for they died of the plague themselves.

The *Plague Tractates,* documents written by medieval physicians concerning the plague, do not discuss ethical obligations. Nonetheless, their existence itself—nearly 300 of them still survive—has been taken as good evidence of the duty some physicians felt to cope with the disease. Several tractate authors repeatedly mentioned that physicians *"debent curare infirmos"*—must, ought to, care for the sick. This small phrase has been interpreted as a denial of a powerful tradition in ancient Roman and Greek medicine against accepting hopelessly sick cases. It fails to answer the question of whether the individual physician is obliged to accept a risky patient.

Guy de Chauliac, one of Pope Clement VII's surgeons, left an introspective and revealing paragraph for posterity. "The plague was useless and shameful for the doctors," he wrote.

> They dared not visit the sick, for fear of becoming infected. And when they did visit, they did nothing, and earned nothing, for all the sick died. . . . To survive there

was nothing better than to flee the region before becoming infected. . . . And I, to avoid infamy, did not dare remove myself, but with continuous fear preserved myself as best I could. . . .

The plague lingered in Europe for several centuries after its dramatic arrival. Signs of physicians' ambivalence regarding their duties to plague victims persist. In 1382, Venice passed a law forbidding physicians to flee the city during times of plague. Similar laws were enacted in the 1400s in Barcelona and Cologne. The figure of "the plague doctor" became a convenient institution in many cities. He was a municipal employee who was given a home, a salary, and citizenship; in return he agreed to "treat all patients and visit infected places as it shall be found to be necessary," thus relieving his colleagues of this obligation. Meanwhile, medical writings regarding the plague continued to be quite pragmatic. "If you are asked to treat a patient with no chance of recovery," wrote one surgeon in a late 14th-century book of advice for medical students, "say that you will be leaving town shortly and cannot take the case."

THE GREAT PLAGUE OF LONDON

From May to December 1665, at least 68,000—probably many more—of London's 400,000 citizens died in one of the last great epidemics of bubonic plague in Europe. The record of London's physicians during this epidemic is, again, a checkered one. Four "plague doctors" were appointed by the city council; as the summer progressed, nine other physicians volunteered for this duty. Most sources agree that most of the rest of London's physicians, apothecaries and surgeons—including Thomas Sydenham, who was just beginning his illustrious career as a student of contagious diseases—fled the city as quickly as they could, not to return until the danger was past.

Only a few popular reactions to this mass exodus survive. The printer who compiled the city Bills of Mortality at the end of the year voiced a hope that, should the plague ever return, "neither the physicians of our souls or bodies may hereafter in such great numbers forsake us." The foremost of the municipal plague doctors, Nathanael Hodges, mentioned his vanished colleagues in a plague memoir only to excuse them: ". . . in a Plague . . . many Physicians retire (not so much for their own Preservation, as the Service of those whom they attend). . . ." It was generally accepted that when wealthy families traveled, whatever the reason, their physicians would naturally accompany them.

Daniel Defoe describes the public's reaction to the departed doctors as follows: "Great was the reproach thrown on those physicians who left their patients during the sickness, and now they came to town again nobody cared to employ them. They were called deserters. . . ." Yet many medical men who stayed in town suffered a similar fate: they were called "quacks," castigated for the useless medicines and useless treatments they provided. And even more villified were the nurses who stayed in the city and hired themselves out to tend the dying. In one anonymous poem about the plague, an entire stanza is devoted to the nurses,

> . . . A cursed crew
> Which did more mischief than the plague could do
> Nurses! who slew so fast as if they meant
> To make the Pestilence innocent. . . .

As in the middle ages, those doctors who did not flee from the plague left no coherent philosophy behind them. Only one appears to have pondered his ethical obligations for posterity. He was William Boghurst, an apothecary who wrote a small plague memoir in 1666. For a page of his manuscript (unpublished until 1894), Boghurst considered who should be encouraged to flee from a plague. Children, he decided, should go, as well as all others that "are free and not obliged to stay either by their office, relations or necessity, such as Magistrates, Ministers, and Physitians, Apothecaries, Surgeons, Midwives." He elaborated:

> Every man that undertakes to bee of a profession or takes upon him any office must take all parts of it, the good and the evill, the pleasure and the pain, the profit and the inconvenience altogether, and not pick and chuse; for ministers must preach, Captains must fight, Physitians attend upon the Sick, etc.

Boghurst's paragraph is an eloquent recreation of that medieval statement that physicians "must" care for the sick. It is the only echo of this duty easily found in the literature of the London plague.

THE YELLOW FEVER IN PHILADELPHIA

When yellow fever broke out in Philadelphia in the summer of 1793, one observer wrote, "the consternation of the people was carried beyond all bounds. Most people who could, fled the city." Although Philadelphia's physicians debated the source of the epidemic, they nonetheless advised the citizenry to "avoid every infected person, as much as possible." Forced to decide whether to comply with their own recommendations, their response was variable. Three of the city's best-known physicians fled to the healthy countryside. Other physicians—probably most others—remained in town. Of those who stayed, many sickened and died of the fever.

During this epidemic, those doctors who fled the city were the subjects of bitter public mockery. This time, they were the ones to attract poetic notice:

On prancing steed, with spunge at nose
From town behold [the doctor] fly . . .
Safe in an atmosphere of scents,
He leaves us to our own defense.
. . . Some soldiers, thus, to honour lost
In day of battle quit their post.

Military metaphors abounded in the pages of the daily newspaper. "Physicians are justly considered as public property," wrote the editor, "and like military men, it pertains to their profession to be occasionally in the way of danger. . . ." (*Federal Gazette,* Philadelphia, Oct. 2, 1793, p. 3). The physicians of the time, however, do not speak of themselves as either soldiers or public servants. Rather, those who stayed spoke of a more private, usually religious obligation to the sick. The metaphor Benjamin Rush used to describe his obligations to the plague-stricken was a different one. If he should get sick, he wrote to his wife, "it would be as much your duty not to desert me in that situation, as it is mine not to desert my patients." His patients were his extended family; in that paternal role he treated the yellow fever victims tirelessly through the summer, although he became ill several times himself.

LATER PROFESSIONAL CODES AND CONDUCT

In 1847 the newly formed American Medical Association (AMA) drew up its first code of medical ethics. At the end, deep in the section entitled "The Duties of the Profession to the Public," came the following statement: ". . . and when pestilence prevails, it is their [physicians'] duty to face the danger, and to continue their labors for the alleviation of the suffering, even at the jeopardy of their own lives." (American Medical Association: *Code of Ethics Adopted May 1846.* Philadelphia, Turner Hamilton, 1871, p. 32).

In the history of ethical codes for the medical profession, this statement is unprecedented. None of the early codifiers of Anglo-American medical ethics, including Sir Thomas Percival, John Gregory, and Samuel Bard, mentioned this duty. Even the Royal College of Physicians, who issued an "ethical code" in 1543, in the midst of London's intermittent visitations of plague, had not attempted to regulate its members' duties in this way. The AMA's strong statement probably owes more to a determination to establish the honor and prestige of the profession than to physicians' actual abilities, at this time, either to understand or cure epidemic diseases.

Still, the sense of duty formalized by the AMA was sustained. From the second half of the 19th century through the present, despite the continuing visitation of epidemic diseases, it becomes far more difficult to find recorded instances of physicians' reluctance to accept the risks that epidemics entailed for them. The stories of the cholera pandemics of the 19th century, the plague in the Orient, the influenza pandemic of 1918, polio in the 1950s, are largely ones of medical heroism.

The short phrase formally reminding American physicians that their profession was a risky one remained in the AMA's Code of Ethics for over 100 years. When the Code was shortened in 1957, the section discussing physicians' duties during epidemics was deleted. The present Code emphasizes physicians' duties to society and calls on them to provide "competent medical service with compassion and respect for human dignity." Nonetheless, a phrase that first appeared in the Code in 1912, and remains in Section VI in its most recent revision, seems most pertinent to the issue: "A physician shall, in the provision of appropriate patient care, except in emergencies, be free to choose whom to serve. . . ." Similarly, none of the other modern ethical codes that now govern American physicians' behavior in multiple contexts mentions the physician's duty to accept personal risk in the care of patients.

AIDS AND A NEW PROFESSIONAL TRADITION

These examples illustrate the difficulties of grounding a professional ethic for the care of HIV-infected persons exclusively in historic precedent and existing ethical codes. First, the professional tradition has not been consistent: in all epidemics some physicians have fled and some have stayed, in most cases impelled by individual conscience rather than professional ethic. Second, past epidemics resemble AIDS very little, save only in the fear they have provoked among some physicians. Finally, our ethical language differs enormously from that of past centuries. Respect for individual civil rights and autonomy now protects the discretionary freedoms of physicians as well as their patients. Laws like those of Venice, revoking the citizenship of physicians who fled the plague, are no longer possible. Medical paternalism is unacceptable to most modern critics. A professional ethic can no longer be grounded on presumedly universal religious beliefs, nor do the soldierly metaphors of the past speak clearly to our time.

These historic models of professional duty have been replaced by many modern alternatives. Each of them has specific implications for the medical care of patients with contagious diseases. In the remainder of this essay we will examine three of these models and the conclusions each provides regarding physicians' obligations to HIV-infected persons.

THE RIGHT TO HEALTH CARE AND THE PATIENT–PHYSICIAN CONTRACT

Of all the modern ethical models of medical care, two are particularly familiar to modern clinicians. The first is the "rights model," [see table below] in which a patient's right to health care creates a correlative duty on the part of physicians, institutions, or society to provide health care. The second is the "contract model," in which patient and physician are implicitly bound by a voluntary contract governing the patient's care. Although each of these models makes provision for the medical care of the contagious patient, each also gives individual physicians considerable freedom to accept or refuse an individual patient who asks for treatment.

The principle of an individual's right to health care was inspired by John Locke's affirmations of man's natural rights in the 17th century. It has evolved enormously since then: its modern interpretation translates health care into a public good, which the state has a duty to allocate fairly. Inextricably bound to questions of health policy and resource allocation, the rights model of medical care has generated a good deal of controversy. Nonetheless, "a right of equitable access to health care for all" has been twice affirmed by the executive branch of the American government. Public assistance programs and public hospitals cite this model to provide basic health care to any ill person. Recent legislation has, in effect, confirmed the right of all Americans to emergency medical care from any hospital.

In its complete form, the rights model of medical care obliges the profession to care for ill patients, but imposes only indirect obligations on individual practitioners. Section VI of the AMA's Code of Ethics has been used to illustrate this distinction. Affirming that a physician is free, except in emergencies, "to choose whom to serve," Section VI emphasizes that an ill patient does not create an immediate duty on the part of an individual physician to care for that patient. Physicians' relationships with contagious patients are no exception to this principle. While society must make provision for the medical care of contagious patients, individual practitioners have no duty to do so. The quantity of risk patients pose to physicians enters into this calculation only minimally. Physicians who are unwilling to

PROFESSIONAL ETHICS FOR PROFESSIONAL RISK

Model	Addresses Profession?	Addresses Practitioners?	Condemns Refusal to Treat?	Addresses New Therapeutic Affiliation?
Rights	Yes	Mainly indirectly	Rarely	No
Contract	Yes	Directly	Existing relationships only	No
Virtue	Yes	Directly	Yes	Yes

assume even tiny risks of exposure to contagious patients, such as HIV-infected persons, are exercising a civil liberty, not violating a patient's right.

In the rights model, an HIV-infected person's right to health care creates a specific duty to provide this care on the part of only two classes of physicians. The first are physicians employed in emergency departments; the second are physicians employed in public hospitals. Both groups are immediate agents of society's duty to fulfill the right to medical care. Other physicians, free to choose their work settings and patients, are free to choose not to treat HIV-infected persons.

More widely accepted than the rights model, the contract model of medical care has come to dominate the social and legal understanding of the modern physician's obligation to patients. The contract, voluntarily created by patient and physician, imposes a fiduciary obligation on the physician to act in the patient's interest and to provide the patient with a standard of competent medical care. Voluntariness is preserved after the contract is formed: the patient can leave the physician at any time. The physician is similarly free to sever the relationship, provided the patient is given sufficient opportunity to find another physician. The legal standards of informed consent, negligence, and abandonment buttress this model of the patient–doctor relationship.

The contract model of medical care imposes certain constraints on the physician in dealing with contagious patients. Primarily, it prohibits physicians from engineering variations on standard medical care to minimize their own risks of infection. Since patients cannot contract for negligent care, contagious patients will receive from their physicians medical care indistinguishable from that received by other patients.

The contract model, however, allows physicians virtually complete freedom in choosing to enter into a treatment contract. Magnitude of risk again does not enter into the calculation. Risk-averse physicians need not expose themselves to even minimal risks. The recent statement on AIDS issued by the AMA clearly illustrates the obligations physicians incur to HIV-infected patients under the contract model of medical care. The formation of new treatment contracts with HIV-infected persons is not discussed, but is tacitly left up to the preferences of the individual physician. Termination of treatment contracts with HIV-infected patients is permitted, limited only by the customary protections against abandonment.

Both the contract and the rights model thus offer the individual physician considerable freedom to refuse to care for HIV-infected patients. Physicians who avail themselves of this freedom have, nonetheless, attracted a certain notoriety and concern (*The New York Times,* March 13, 1987, p. 11.). Widely accepted though they are, both models have been widely criticized as well. One critic of the contract model has eloquently condemned it for reducing patient care to a commodity, relieving the physician of responsibility to the moral art of medicine. The moral art of medicine is addressed by the next model of medical care.

THE VIRTUOUS PHYSICIAN

A virtue-based medical ethic is less familiar to modern clinicians than the contract or rights-based ethics. Though the concept of the virtuous physician has a long history, it has recently fallen from favor. In its simplest sense, an ethic of virtue requires a virtuous moral agent whose character can be nurtured and trained and who can be held morally accountable for his actions. Virtues necessary to the physician have included honesty, compassion, fidelity, courage: in general, moral attributes that sustain the moral purpose of medical care.

The moral implications of a professional commitment to medicine were examined in some detail in the first century A.D. by Scribonius Largus, a Roman physician. Scribonius concluded in *Professio Medici* that to be in a profession implied a commitment to a certain end (*professio*), and thus an obligation to perform certain functions or duties (*officia*) necessary to attain that end. In the case of medicine, the *professio* is healing, the *officia* is treatment of sick persons presenting for care. Professional virtues are the attributes of character needed to honor the commitment to healing.

A virtue-based medical ethic has powerful implications for the care of contagious patients in general, and HIV-infected patients in particular. It recognizes that all HIV-infected persons are in need of the healing art—for counseling and reassurance, if nothing else. It mandates, as well, that because of their prior voluntary commitment to the *professio* of healing, physicians are obliged to undertake the *officia* of caring for these patients. Individual physicians who decline to perform these *officia* are falling short of an excellence in practice implicit in their professional commitment.

In a virtue-based medical ethic, the magnitude of risk posed by a contagious patient is taken into consideration, for it determines the nature of the virtues required in the medical care of that patient. The risk posed to a physician by an HIV-infected person is not of the same order of magnitude as those posed during other epidemics. The latter would necessarily evoke virtues on the order of heroism, self-sacrifice, and daring. The risks posed by HIV are small, and the virtues demanded on a smaller scale: courage and intellectual integrity.

Commentators note that the virtues can coexist with other systems of medical ethics. In the case of contagious patients and the other more familiar medical-ethic models, this point is particularly valid. The Table summarizes the implications each of the models of medical care has for the medical care of contagious patients. Although a rights-based ethic commits the profession to the care of these patients, it leaves individual clinicians free to refuse to care for them.

Although a contract-based ethic sets quality standards for the care these patients receive, it also allows individual clinicians to refuse to establish relationships with them. A virtue-based ethic supplements both these models, addressing individual practitioners as well as the profession, honoring physicians who treat contagious patients for practicing excellent medicine, and condemning those who fail to do so for failure to live up to their professional commitments.

CONCLUSION

The issue of physicians' obligations to contagious patients has complex ethical and philosophic overtones. It encompasses questions of beneficence, philanthropy, and altruism, as well as the issues of rights, duties, and virtues outlined previously herein. Despite this complexity, however, our society no longer has the leisure to think the theory through at a scholarly pace. The medical needs of HIV-infected persons will soon seriously strain America's health care system; all physicians will encounter these patients in the course of a day's work. In the face of these realities, professional ethics that emphasize the rights of physicians to decline to treat these patients seem to us particularly inadequate and incomplete.

These ethics should be supplemented with a virtue-based component—one that derives its credibility not from physicians' historical aspirations. A virtue-based ethic would mandate that physicians commit themselves to obligations beyond those narrowly required by law or contract. It would remind us that medicine is an inherently moral enterprise, the success and future of which depend to a great extent on the integrity of individual professionals as they face the duties the calling of healer entails.

Suggestions for Discussion and Writing

1. What is the purpose of the authors' investigation? What do they gain by stating it where they do?

2. The authors delay the statement of their thesis until the final paragraphs of the essay. What argumentative advantage do they gain from this strategy?

3. What rhetorical purpose is served by the brief section at the center of the essay entitled "AIDS and a New Professional Tradition"?

4. What do the authors conclude about the value of historical precedent as a guide to ethical conduct within the medical profession?

5. Write an essay in which you discuss some of the ways in which history and tradition influence our moral values.

6. Do you believe that physicians should be bound by a professional code of ethics that requires them to take personal risks in the treatment of their patients? What are the arguments for and against such a code? Write an essay developing your views.

7. Compare the relative force of a "professional ethic" and the "individual conscience." Which of these two imperatives is more likely to lead a physician to accept personal risk in the care of patients? Why?

8. The AIDS epidemic "has forced our attention toward issues that, over the last century, we have grown unaccustomed to facing; it is making us relearn lessons we had almost forgotten." What, in your opinion, are some of those issues and lessons? Write an essay in which you argue your case.

PART III

SOME ISSUES FOR THE NINETIES

OVERVIEW

Part II asked what science is, how it "knows," what its limits are, and its values and obligations. Part III extends this discussion by focusing on these concerns in the context of four contemporary social issues—the role of science as it relates to the unborn, to the environment, to gender, and to education. These four issues are by no means the only ways in which science is involved in important national debates. But they are representative of the ways in which science influences and is influenced by the broader range of human concerns—social, political, and ethical. Part III, then, brings us back once again to the beginning of this anthology: In its continuing interchange with the broader community, science defines itself as an element of culture.

CHAPTER-BY-CHAPTER SUMMARY

Chapter 10

Chapter 10 pursues the question of limits and values by asking what role science should play in the treatment of the unborn. In the opening essay, Clifford Grobstein discusses the developmental stages through which a fetus passes and shows how they complicate the problem of establishing a fetus's "status." Establishing status is important, he argues, because status determines treatment. Leon R. Kass looks at this issue from a somewhat different

431

perspective, voicing his concern that technological advances will override moral considerations in our drive to produce perfect babies. Focusing on the pro-choice/pro-life debate, Mary B. Mahowald argues that the discussion has centered largely on legal questions since *Roe v. Wade*, thus polarizing the two sides and obscuring important moral issues. Because so much of the public debate regarding the unborn centers on abortion, and because for most of us abortion is a deeply emotional as well as political and philosophical issue, the chapter concludes with two essays (by Gerald Weissmann and by Richard Selzer, practicing physicians both) that combine personal as well as professional views.

Chapter 11

The relationship of living things to each other and to their environment is a central issue in evolutionary theory; Chapter 11—on the environment—thus builds on the earlier discussion of the biosciences (with its emphasis on Darwin's contribution) but adds a disturbing dimension. For man has had an enormous (and enormously destructive) impact on the environment in the last hundred years or so. And the assault continues. As Edward O. Wilson points out, man's impact has already led to a massive extinction of species, thus undermining the evolutionary process itself—the very process of which we ourselves are a product. For Wilson, "every species extinction diminishes humanity." Broadening the focus, Eric J. Barron discusses Earth's problematic future in light of the vastly increasing emission of destructive gases into the atmosphere. For him that future is shrouded in uncertainty. Clive Agnew and Andrew Warren look at environmental damage from yet another perspective, arguing that much of the world's marginally arable land is threatened more by advancing civilization and its technology than by the natural cycles of drought and shifting desert sands.

We usually look to science for help in understanding the nature and extent of environmental damage, and for ways to remedy it. Sometimes, however, science itself in its search for knowledge is part of the problem. Michael Tobias cites such a case in his account of the scientific exploration of Antarctica, perhaps the world's most fragile environment. According to Tobias, the human (largely scientific) presence on that continent is destroying not only a fragile ecosystem but also an "extraordinary global laboratory." The exploration of space offers a further example of such damage. In the final essay, Isaac Asimov and Frederick Pohl argue that even regions far above the earth are now littered with the debris of our modern space age.

Chapter 12

Chapter 12 turns to the issue of gender and thus examines science in the context of one of the most important social revolutions of the last twenty years. Does gender have a bearing on a student's aptitude for science? Does it influence the way science gets done, and the kind of science that gets done? These are three of the many questions engaged in this chapter. In the first essay, Vera Rubin describes the treatment of women in the field of astronomy over the last century and argues that though more women are entering this field of astronomy they still constitute only a tiny fraction of its tenured professors. The second and third essays offer a more radical feminist critique. After reviewing the range of feminist criticism, Evelyn Fox Keller argues that a masculine bias has dictated the prevailing attitudes and practices of science and thereby limited its findings. Ruth Bleier, arguing from a similar perspective, attacks the "patriarchal structure of science" and calls for a more "humane" approach. Responding to these and other radical views, Margarita Levin challenges the basic assumptions of the feminist position, claiming that they are fundamentally flawed. In the final essay, Sherry Turkle reports on her study of children working with computers. Though boys and girls tend to approach this technology differently, she argues, they are equally able to "master" it.

Chapter 13

A great deal of evidence accumulated over the last decade or so suggests that science education is in serious trouble. Chapter 13 explores this issue from a variety of perspectives. In the first essay, Alan Lightman, recalling his experience in a science lab, humorously describes his discovery that he was better suited for theoretical than for experimental physics. Turning to the science textbook, Stephen Jay Gould reviews the treatment of Darwin's theory of evolution in high school texts. For him, the history of this treatment illustrates the degree to which religious and social pressures can undermine the teaching of science. John S. Rigden and Sheila Tobias explore the problem of teaching from another perspective, this time at the college level. Noting that many students abandon science after their introductory courses, these authors argue that the subject must be placed in a broader context and that students must be helped to see science not simply as a rigorous exercise of the mind but as an exciting—if challenging—adventure. This notion of adventure is central to Lewis Thomas's view of science. Calling for a fundamental revision of introductory courses, he proposes that such courses focus on questions rather than on answers, on what is not known rather than on established facts. This broadened vision also informs the final essay, in which N. David Mermin addresses the graduating class of St. John's College. In an imaginative and humorous piece, he shows that the habits of mind encouraged by a liberal education are precisely those required of the practicing physicist. For Mermin, as for the other authors in this chapter, science education (like all education) must challenge not only the faculty of rational thought but the more open terrain of the creative imagination.

CHAPTER 10

Science and the Unborn

THE SIGNIFICANCE OF STATUS

Clifford Grobstein
(b. 1916)

Born in New York, Clifford Grobstein was educated at City College and the University of California, Los Angeles. He has taught since 1965 at the University of California, San Diego, where he is Professor Emeritus of Biological Science and Public Policy. A noted embryologist, Grobstein is a member of the National Academy of Sciences and has served as a consultant to the National Institutes of Health. He has written several books, including *A Double Image of the Double Helix* (1979) and *From Chance to Purpose: An Appraisal of External Human Fertilization* (1981). Much of Grobstein's recent work has focused on the impact of advancing biomedical science on questions of public policy, especially as that policy affects the regulation of genetic technology and of external human fertilization and embryo transfer.

In the following selection, excerpted from *Science and the Unborn* (1988), Grobstein discusses some of the scientific and ethical issues involved in establishing the status of the unborn, and explains why resolving the problem of status is important.

For most people, the unborn are an enigma. They both illustrate a general problem and have their own special difficulty. The general problem is: How does a new phenomenon arise when nothing resembling it seems to precede it, that is, when it seems to originate *de novo?*

An astrophysical example is the origin of a star out of interstellar dust. Astrophysicists have proposed on theoretical grounds that this happens, and astronomers are now observing what appear to be stages in the process. Dust falls together as the result of gravitational attraction, heating up as it condenses until the mass ignites to temperatures at which nuclear reactions begin. The result is a blazing star—for example, our sun. A star is not budded from an earlier star; it undergoes its own genesis from nonstar materials—some of which may be products of disintegration from earlier stars.

An anthroposocial instance is the initiation of a settled community at the intersection of two or more trade routes. When the numbers of travelers passing through the intersection reach some critical level, services provided to and paid for by the travelers can become the economic base for a population of nontravelers, the beginning of a community.

A developmental example is a seedling breaking out of its protective coats to become a tree. Without previous experience, who would guess that the tiny generative part of the seed is the progenitor of a massive sequoia?

In each case something entirely new seems to arise out of almost nothing—the source of the process does not even remotely resemble the end point. How do complex phenomena arise as if out of nothing? Is this evidence of divine guidance—a miracle without natural cause? Can it happen by chance? Or is the whole phenomenon already preformed at the beginning, in miniature, needing only to be scaled up in size to be visible?

Choice among these explanations has been debated for centuries. Today we are beginning to understand how the seeming miracle occurs. I shall say much more about that in later discussion. For the moment I note only that the transformations undergone by the human unborn provide this kind of enigma, and undoubtedly in the most complex and difficult form that we know.

In roughly nine calendar months a single human cell, the zygote produced at conception, or fertilization, multiplies in cell number, becomes cohesive, reorders, grows further, differentiates, and forms a multiplicity of functioning parts. Throughout this orderly and as-yet only incompletely comprehended process, the developing entity maintains its initial endowment of individuality and elaborates it into a human infant composed of billions of cells that are organized into one of the most intricate entities known to science. It is this emerging human entity, during its profound transformations, that must be given its due and appropriate place in the social fabric. An appropriate place means that it should have an accepted and commonly understood status, or site and role in its community. This is simple enough to declare; it proves to be no mean task to accomplish.

Status is the issue for the unborn because for them it is incompletely and poorly defined. Whether codified in law, usage, or tradition, status helps people to know how to treat and relate to each other. It may be as formal as military rank or as informal as the establishment of leadership by a strong personality on a playground. However established, there is no more fundamental status in moral, legal, and policy terms than membership in a human community. A formally defined status for the unborn is therefore essential to provide guidelines on how these nascent individuals should be treated throughout their developmental course from fertilized egg to birth.

The assignment of status to the unborn is especially difficult because not only are they an enigma, but they are, in effect, rapidly moving targets. They are undergoing fundamental transformations; they are continually changing and becoming something new. The pervasiveness, the magnitude, and yet the seamlessness of the changes during human development defy sharp and convenient classification. Moreover, this radical metamorphosis of properties and characteristics normally takes place while hidden in the seclusion of the womb. The process of creative becoming is interactive between the mother and the offspring-to-be; it is a powerful transaction that merits a private sanctum not to be rudely or casually invaded.

Is the single zygote cell that begins the profound transformation human? Scientifically there is no question; the zygote is certainly human to its core. But does the zygote display all of the characteristics of a human being? Can a single cell be a human being, a person, an entity endowed with unalienable right to life, liberty, and the pursuit of happiness? This question cannot be answered on scientific grounds alone. Human being, person, and human rights are not terms stemming from scientific definition. But one trained and accustomed to think as a scientist cannot fail to note significant disparity between the common meaning of these terms and a single cell.

When we view the public world of real people dealing with each other in the complex and subtle interactions of social life, it seems ludicrous to suggest that concepts appropriate to that realm should be extended to an individual cell at the bare limit of ordinary visibility. It makes as much sense as declaring acorns to be oak trees and selling them at oak tree prices. Less ludicrous, but much more difficult to answer, are questions about what should, in fact, be the status of the zygote and—most difficult of all to answer—exactly when in the course of development full human status should be assigned.

Controversy over these questions continues to agitate many minds—of presidents, justices, and legislators as well as physicians, scientists, lawyers, philosophers, and theologians. No answer has yet proven universally persuasive; the questions clearly pose a number of imponderables. Having been unresolvable to the full satisfaction of all so far, the questions toss in a sea of uncertainty and debate, leaving the unborn without clearly defined status. As one consequence, medical effort to improve treatment of the unborn is hampered and growth of scientific knowledge about them is constrained.

In democratic society, status confers rights protective of the interests of individual members. In the United States, equality before the law is constitutionally guaranteed and every adult citizen has the right to vote. Internationally, freedom from deliberately inflicted pain and suffering is the subject of solemn covenants not always observed. Such human rights are aspects of status, especially in countries that vest fundamental value in each individual human being. Status may change in the course of life, as in acquiring the right to drive at the age of assumed responsibility or losing the right to be free on conviction of a felony.

Therefore, if the status of the unborn is unclear in national jurisprudence, their rights are also ill defined. In the United States, the situation is part cause and part effect of dissension as to how to treat the unborn in the politically tense area of abortion. The tension has infected consideration of other reproductive issues, including such innovative technologies as external or *in vitro* fertilization (IVF) and fetal research in general. The tension and dissension also have widening effects in the whole area of public reproductive health policy.

While there is no simple answer as to why this tension has come to pass, in no small measure it is because the unborn have for so long been cloistered within the maternal womb where they are not accessible for direct interaction with others. Even when the mother becomes big with child, the fetus itself remains unperceived.

The normally covert existence of the unborn is, of course, derived from our origins as mammals. All mammals reproduce by internal fertilization and temporarily nurture their offspring within the uterus of the mother (gestation or pregnancy). This arrangement can be interpreted as an advantage in human evolution because it entails minimal conscious attention, proceeding largely through involuntary mechanisms. Except in very late stages or in abnormal cases, the pregnant woman can go about other duties with little or no handicap.

These mammalian facts of life have profoundly shaped values and customs in all human societies. They have particularly shaped the role and lives of women, all of whom carry the mark and the burden of this mammalian heritage. It therefore comes as no surprise that women's rights to reproductive choice, especially with respect to decisions about the maintenance of pregnancy versus abortion, mobilize the efforts and concerns of activist feminists.

Moreover, it follows that during the close mutual interaction of mother and developing offspring in pregnancy the status of the unborn is difficult to separate from that of the mother. For some time neither the status nor welfare of the one can be altered without affecting the other. This has tended even further to suppress attention to the status of the invisible "insider" who is at first little more than a part of the socially much more firmly established "outsider."

In recent years, however, the situation has been changing noticeably in several significant respects. One example is a fact that increasing knowledge and altered reproductive practices have taught us. The earliest phase of human development, while it normally occurs in the oviduct of the mother, is actually quite independent of her. In the IVF procedure these same stages proceed quite normally outside the mother and in an artificially prepared solution that is incubated in a suitable gaseous environment. Clearly, early dependence on the mother is actually relatively minimal in that it is readily satisfied in other ways.

This phase of relative independence begins at ovulation, when the egg is discharged from the nurturing ovarian follicle and starts its journey down the oviduct or fallopian tube into the uterus. If the egg meets sperm in the oviduct and is successfully fertilized, in a few days the developing entity—the preembryo—reaches the uterus and implants in its wall. Implantation may be thought of as the physiological beginning of actual maternal pregnancy as well as of the offspring's significant dependency on its mother. Until that time the developing entity is within the "mother" but not importantly interactive with her, as the following facts indicate.

First, the woman within whom the egg is fertilized is normally unaware of when fertilization occurs. The union of the male and female gametes is a complex and fascinating story in its own right, but there are no signals to either parent as it happens. Moreover, there is no discernible effect on maternal functions until about a week later when the first detectable hormonal changes occur, in association with implantation of the preembyro in the uterine wall. If implantation does not occur, which is perhaps half the time in human species, the woman never shows any signs of pregnancy, nor does she have any knowledge or recall of the temporary presence within her of a potential offspring. It follows that there is no easy way to assign status of any kind to so transient an entity when its very existence is unrecognized.

In terms of maternal effect, therefore, pregnancy begins not with conception but with implantation. Measures that inhibit implantation (the intrauterine device or the "morning after" pill) are more accurately called contragestive (antipregnancy) than contraceptive (anticonception). This does not change the fact that both block production of an offspring resulting from sexual intercourse, the objective of all methods of birth control.

Second, as noted, the conditions necessary for preembryo development external to the mother are readily supplied in the laboratory, as is done in the IVF procedure. They involve only incubation at controlled temperature in a relatively simply physiological solution. However, this creates an entirely new situation with respect to status. The preembryo is now fully revealed, there is no uncertainty about its existence. On the contrary, we shall see that very real questions and issues of status arise in connection with it—quite separately from those that arise in connection with abortion.

Third, also as already noted, in the normal process within the mother it is not until implantation that hormonal changes announce the beginning of the pregnant state. Roughly concurrently, complex interactions and exchanges between the developing entity and the maternal circulation are initiated. With these events independence of mother and offspring is terminated and a relationship between two living entities begins that is as complex, intimate, and complete as any known to biological science, or to ethics and philosophy.

Fourth, the independence of the preimplantation phase is dramatically demonstrated in the few IVF cases in which an externally developing offspring has been transferred to the uterus of a woman who is not its genetic mother. Development continues in such a substitute gestational mother. Thus *genetic* and *gestational* motherhood can be separated, and the potential developmental history of the early offspring can be realized totally independently of the genetic mother.

Fifth, preservation by freezing (cryopreservation) further extends the gestational independence of external preembryos. At least theoretically they might be maintained indefinitely in the frozen state, even well beyond the life of the genetic mother. Who, then, is responsible for their welfare and their fate?

The five circumstances outlined indicate that the earliest phase of human development can occur separately from and independently of the genetic mother. Under some circumstances, therefore, the status of this phase must be addressed as an entity physically separable from its mother. The point is dramatized and becomes pressing with the practice of frozen storage, through which the preembryo may survive even beyond the death of both parents.

In the early stages of development of human IVF (in the late 1970s), pregnancies and births were obtained but at unsatisfactorily low rates. However, when the earlier developed technique of superovulation was applied, success rates were significantly raised. Superovulation involves pharmacological stimulation of the woman's ovaries so that they produce more than one egg in a given month. Several eggs can then be recovered, fertilized, and transferred to the uterus, increasing the chances that at least one will implant.

But such stimulation of a woman's ovaries often produces an embarrassment of riches—four or even more eggs. Transfer of all of them not only increases the pregnancy rate but also the frequency of multiple pregnancy. In turn, multiple pregnancy, particularly more than two, elevates obstetrical risk to both mother and offspring and imposes rearing burdens that understandably daunt many couples.

The freezing of "surplus" preembryos, beyond the several that seem optimal for transfer, therefore offers possible advantages. For example, it allows storage of the surplus to await a possible second transfer attempt if the first fails. However, in the early trials it quickly became apparent that frozen storage also heightened and sharpened issues raised by the uncertain status of preimplantation stages. In one instance, at an Australian infertility center in Melbourne where frozen storage was first practiced successfully, two frozen preembryos were stored pending success or failure of a first attempt at transfer to a patient's uterus. Unfortunately, before a second attempt was made, the American donor couple was killed in an airplane accident, thus inadvertently abandoning and "orphaning" their two "offspring." How to dispose of these offspring became the subject of intense debate in Melbourne and in the international press. The incident significantly affected the course of IVF legislation then pending in the Australian state of Victoria where Melbourne is located, and the case remained unresolved some five years later.

The crux of the issue, of course, is that cryopreservation results in reversible suspension of life activities, essentially a pause in biological time. So far as is known, the state of suspended animation can be maintained indefinitely without significant change in the frozen material. Whatever the status, or its lack, prior to freezing, it too remains frozen. The result is a classic dilemma. The longer the passage of time, the more attenuated becomes the connection between the static offspring and the aging genetic parents.

Indeed, the same kind of disparity between siblings has been reported by the press from England. A first transfer was successful but frozen preembryos from the same "litter" were used in a later, also successful, transfer. Although the two offspring were of the same age in time elapsed from fertilization (in this sense fraternal twins), they were several years apart in developmental age (and thus like ordinary siblings).

Such situations offer a number of speculative issues that will be returned to later. In the Melbourne case, the status question became acute because the genetic connection with the parents as gamete donors was abruptly interrupted. The question then arose as to who has the right or responsibility of decision regarding what happens next.

The dilemma is not made easier by the opinion, strongly held by right-to-life community leaders in Melbourne, that to discard potential offspring, whether prior to freezing or after, would be a wrongful violation of their fundamental right to continued life. This view stems, of course, from the contention, forcefully advanced in the abortion debate, that an individual life begins at conception (fertilization). Almost as if it were contrived to do so, this contention underlines the ambiguous and unresolved status of the preimplantation stage of human development.

Thus the pro-life contention sidesteps the difficult and delicate questions of appropriate status at particular stages, as well as in particular circumstances, by declaring that a person exists fully and absolutely from the first initiation at conception. Such a definition precludes induced abortion at any time or under any circumstance, which is the objective of the right-to-life movement. However, it also places severe constraints on other reproductive options such as IVF, which seeks to generate life rather than to terminate it.

This inevitable policy linkage of a right to life that begins at conception with limitation of reproductive options was made crystal clear in the recent document issued by the Vatican's Congregation for the Doctrine of Faith. It is an instruction to members of the Catholic faith that reasserts a rigid doctrine in the face of advancing reproductive knowledge and its derivative technology, even though the technology is designed to yield a clear human benefit.

Moreover, the central issue, as the Vatican document perceives it, is not only the moral but the *public* status of the unborn at all stages, including the preembryo. The document requires brief quotation to convey both its substance and its flavor. It deals successively with "fundamental principles," "respect for the human being," "moral questions raised by technical interventions on human procreation," and "the relationship between moral law and civil law."

Under fundamental principles, the Vatican document notes that "thanks to the progress of the biological and medical sciences, man has at his disposal ever more effective therapeutic resources; but he can also acquire new powers, with unforeseeable consequences, over human life at its very beginning and in its first stages. Various procedures now make it possible to intervene not only in order to assist but also to dominate the processes of procreation. These techniques can enable man to 'take in hand his own destiny,' but they also expose him 'to the temptation to go beyond the limits of a reasonable dominion over nature.' They might constitute progress in the service of man, but they also involve serious risks."

To cope with the risks, "science and technology require, for their own intrinsic meaning, an unconditional respect for the fundamental criteria of the moral law; that is to say, they must be at the service of the human person, of his inalienable rights and his true and integral good according to the design and will of God. . . . science without conscience can only lead to man's ruin."

The caveat applies especially "in the field of sexuality and procreation, in which man and woman actualize the fundamental values of love and life. . . . Such values and meanings are of the personal order and determine from the moral point of view the meaning and limits of artificial interventions on procreation and on the origin of human life. These interventions are not to be rejected on the grounds that they are artificial. As such, they bear witness to the possibilities of the art of medicine. But they must be given a moral evaluation in reference to the dignity of the human person, who is called to realize his vocation from God to the gift of love and the gift of life."

Human procreation differs from all other. "The transmission of human life is entrusted by nature to a personal and conscious act and as such is subject to the all-holy laws of God; immutable and inviolable laws which must be recognized and observed. For this reason one cannot use means and follow methods which could be licit in the transmission of life of plants and animals."

With respect to "interventions upon embryos and human fetuses," the Vatican document draws a major conclusion: "The human being must be respected—as a person—from the very first instant of his existence. . . . Life once conceived, must be protected with the utmost care; abortion and infanticide are abominable crimes. . . . Human life must be absolutely respected and protected from the moment of conception. . . . This teaching remains valid and is further confirmed, if confirmation were needed, by recent findings of human biological science which recognize that in the zygote resulting from fertilization the biological identity of a new human individual is already constituted. . . . Thus the fruit of human generation, from the first moment of its existence . . . demands the unconditional respect that is morally due to the human being in his bodily and spiritual totality."

The position taken by the Vatican document, with passionate finality, sharply poses certain central questions in setting public status for the unborn, particularly in communities containing significant Catholic or other groups whose reproductive morality proceeds from religious doctrine or other fixed tradition. What are the purposes to be served in a pluralistic community by *public* policy as against group or personal morality? Should any *particular* morality be made the basis of public policy? What are the appropriate targets for public policy? Can the impacts of a formulated policy be confined to consensually selected targets or will policy have unintended consequences beyond its target area?

Given the complexity and profound importance of reproduction in human society, it seems clear that assignment of status to any particular stage of reproductive realization is likely to have multiple and complex consequences, some of which may be foreseeable and intentional; but others may not. To assign status rigidly on the basis of a morality subscribed to by only a fraction of the population will seem arbitrary to all others and will only invite continued dissension. The purpose of public policy should be acknowledged to be limited and limiting—that is, to set consensual limits within which particular moralities can be practiced with respect and tolerance.

In the matter of abortion, as a case in point, many people regard the procedure as regrettable at best but nonetheless justifiable under special circumstances—for example, pregnancy resulting from rape. Such persons, who might favor contraceptives and contragestives as a means of family planning, might strongly reject abortion for the same purposes, particularly if the intention were to select the sex of offspring by aborting the undesired sex. Rigid right-to-life definitions of unborn status, as exemplified by the Vatican document, exclude realization of all of these purposes—a result certainly not generally acceptable in the pluralistic ethos of the United States.

Thus a general issue is joined by the Vatican document: Can status of the unborn be effectively defined for contemporary purposes if the status is founded in absolute and rigid criteria that are largely derived from past tradition and incorporate assertions of faith that appear to take little account of the findings of contemporary developmental science?

For example, contemporary knowledge has revealed that there is no *instant* of conception; the *process* of fertilization (or syngamy) extends over many hours. This precise fact has become an issue in another continuing controversy in Melbourne with respect to the legitimacy of surgically introducing a sperm into a human egg as a possible alleviation of male infertility. The issue is whether the actual intervention occurs *prior* to conception and is, therefore, allowable. One cannot help recalling the medieval issue of the number of angels able to dance on the head of a pin.

. . . Scientifically, conception is only a partial boundary (albeit a significant one) when one views the entire continuous and complex process of genesis of a person. Beyond even that question, however, definitive founding of so central a matter as social status on a single biological aspect fails to take into account the varied and often subtly different social contexts within which the concept of person is applied. Rigid and overly simplistic criteria may seem gratifyingly final, but their simplicity often proves illusory when confronted by complex reality.

What we require are status criteria based in *contemporary* knowledge of the nature of developmental change combined with sensitive appraisal of specific social circumstances and contexts, such as are invariably associated with decisions as grave as abortion or assignment of rearing responsibility for a child. The general policy dichotomy thus presented is between *absolute* criteria based on traditional concepts and *relative* criteria appropriate to the current state of knowledge and *specific* currently formulated purposes.

Status based on relative criteria obviously offers greater flexibility and wider opportunity for accommodation of differing views—both of which are advantages for reaching consensus in a pluralistic society. To the degree that consensual dominant objectives can be articulated by such a society, assuming the society to be committed to mutual tolerance, status can then be crafted politically to meet even a diverse set of consensual objectives.

It is worth recalling in this connection that the current status of adults has had a long and continuing history of contention—social, political, and even military (consider slavery, doctrines of racial and ethnic superiority, the relative status of the sexes, and the violence of religious wars). Fortunately, processes of negotiation and accommodation have been able to resolve at least some of these status issues. The same processes need now to be applied assiduously to the status of the unborn.

What realistic opportunities are there to achieve some degree of accommodation with respect to the status of the unborn? How might an accommodative process be set in motion? What current consensus exists that might provide a launching platform for such an effort? Several objectives that have been articulated and have reechoed in the abortion debate and in discussion of new reproductive options deserve consideration as a possible accommodative base.

First, and probably foremost, is the widely expressed need to

preserve the special quality and dignity of human life. Shared in general by most persons, it is the most strongly pressed objective of the right-to-life position. As it is often formulated in religious terms, it cannot be incorporated directly into U.S. public policy without breaching the fundamental and strongly supported doctrine of separation of church and state. However, it is in fact also a primary secular value in the United States, an objective that permeates our national philosophy—as do individual rights and freedom. Suitably framed, a consensus position assuring respect and dignity to the human quality of the unborn might easily be included in their status assignment.

Second, many people are uneasy about the increasingly powerful and precise ability of science and medicine to intervene in and modify natural human reproduction. The uneasiness is over whether this capability may advance more rapidly than our wisdom in employing it—that it may be used either inadvertently or deliberately to diminish human beings. This concern could be made an accommodative objective in considering such questions as: How should the principle of informed consent, as developed by adults for adults, be translated to fit the unborn who are not yet capable of deliberation or decision about their own fate? (The question is not a new one, of course, but it is increasingly applicable not only to the now arising generation but to the subsequent generations that will be their offspring.) Given the possibility of even a limited impact on future generations, what interventive reproductive options are sanctionable and which ones should be constrained? How can the range of tolerable intervention be delimited without excessively confining advancing knowledge and practice?

In general, I believe that in assigning status to the unborn, consensus should be sought to recognize and protect their critical human potential, both immediately and for the longer-term future. The unborn should be valued not only as offspring but as ancestors of generations-to-be. Policy decisions about them must therefore enlist the highest standards of human concern and wisdom.

Third, there is general concern about whether and when the unborn may suffer pain and discomfort. It should be a shared objective among contending points of view to better understand the developmental maturation of pain mechanisms and to apply that understanding to definitions of status that leave margins of safety when there is uncertainty. . . .

Fourth, general support exists in the United States for the advancement of knowledge and the expansion of technology as means to further health and control disease, providing that the process does not threaten other major objectives. The motivation is perhaps strongest among health professionals. Some nonprofessionals are concerned that the strength of personal professional motivation may sometimes outweigh other important considerations, particularly in connection with research on human subjects. This is an important factor in the debate over status of the unborn. To deal with these matters, a national consensus statement might be developed to assure commitment to increase biomedical knowledge and its application, balanced against specified essential considerations such as informed consent and avoidance of imposed suffering on human and other sentient beings. Such a statement might reduce existing tension and distrust and facilitate accommodation and realistic consensus on status of the unborn.

Finally, the prospect of what has been called human engineering generates concern about scenarios similar to the Brave New World. With respect to the status of the unborn, the thrust of such scenarios is illustrated by the question of whether, given the current capability to produce human embryos externally, the technique might be used in future "people farms" to create human embryos solely for experimentation, as a source of cells and tissues for transplantation therapy, or to provide an underclass of slaves and servants for a dominant stratum of aristocrats. It would be a useful objective to develop consensual guidelines on such prospects before they become possible. The general presumption might be that interventions practiced on human beings at any stage are unwarranted unless *specifically sanctioned* for consensually derived purposes through a formal process of decision which is accessible to all interests.

This list of possible consensual objectives is substantial but is not intended to be exhaustive. Rather it is a sample, to be modified and expanded during a broad and continuing deliberation. One generalization from the sample is that specified concerns and objectives should be formulated first; then they can be the targets for specific proposals for status definition. The proposals should be evaluated in relation to their effects on their targets, not only in terms of the expected mitigating effects but for their possible unintended and unanticipated effects as well. Moreover, the political feasibility of the proposals must be examined along with their probable effects. Nothing will be gained by defining a status that cannot be implemented because of unexpressed but deeply entrenched moral objections.

Also, the defined status must be realistic and not overly ambitious in objective. In the abortion debate, right-to-life and right-to-choice groups have rallied to their opposing slogans because they believe that most people see both continued life and free choice as desirable objectives. But neither indefinitely continued life nor unlimited choice are assured even to adult persons. To try to assure both in the intimate conjunction of pregnancy necessarily sets the stage for conflict.

More modest and less confrontational concepts and language are needed for accommodative solutions, especially since the phenomenon of pregnancy involves what may be the ultimate in human mutuality—for both the mother and the unborn fetus. The concept of status for the unborn must not only placate the concerns of individuality but assure the benefits and value of the profound mutual experience of pregnancy—experience that locks into place one of the most powerful human bondings, that between mother and child.

Suggestions for Discussion and Writing

1. Does the author use paragraphs effectively? Point to two or three examples to make your case.

2. To help us understand why "the unborn are an enigma," Grobstein, at the start of his essay, gives three examples of new phenomena arising "as if out of nothing." Are his examples helpful? Are they equally appropriate to his discussion of the unborn?

3. Early in his essay Grobstein refers to "the developing entity" and "this emerging human entity" when discussing the process that begins with conception (fertilization). What is the significance of this language for his more general argument?

4. What does the author mean by "status"? Why is the issue of status important to a discussion of the unborn?

5. How, according to Grobstein, is the problem of status complicated by our mammalian heritage?

6. What are some of the implications (medical, ethical, moral) of the author's point that "the earliest phase of human development, while it normally occurs in the oviduct of the mother, is actually quite independent of her" and that "in terms of maternal effect . . . pregnancy begins not with conception but with implantation"?

7. Write an essay in which you discuss some of the ways in which science/technology has complicated the ethical/moral issues involved in the treatment of the unborn.

8. The author characterizes the position on the unborn taken by the Vatican's Congregation for the Doctrine of the Faith as rigid, simplistic, and absolutist. Does he make his case?

9. According to the author, among the questions posed by the position taken in the Vatican document regarding the setting of public status for the unborn is the following: "Should any *particular* morality be made the basis of public policy?" Write an essay in which you discuss this issue.

10. What role should science play in the formulation of a public policy regarding the status of the unborn?

11. Grobstein quotes the Vatican document: "Science without conscience can only lead to man's ruin." Could Grobstein here be said to represent "science without conscience"?

PERFECT BABIES

Leon R. Kass
(b. 1939)

After receiving his M.D. from the University of Chicago, Leon R. Kass interned at Beth Israel Hospital in Boston and then went on to earn his Ph.D. in biochemistry and molecular biology at Harvard University in 1967. He then did research at the National Institute for Arthritis and Metabolic Diseases at the National Institutes of Health. After serving on the Committee for Life Sciences and Social Policy at the National Academy of Sciences, Kass was appointed Research Professor in Bioethics at the Kennedy Institute of Georgetown University. He returned to the University of Chicago in 1976, where he is currently Professor of the College and Committee on Social Thought.

The recipient of numerous awards, Kass is considered a major figure in the field of bioethics. He was a founding fellow and is on the board of directors of the Hastings Center, which is dedicated to the study of social and ethical questions arising out of contemporary medicine.

In the following selection, taken from his *Toward a More Natural Science* (1985), Kass explores the ethical issues raised by prenatal diagnosis of and abortion for genetic defects.

The [essay] you are about to read might never have been written. The same, of course, could be said about *any* work of writing, for the usual and obvious reasons—not least, because the author might never have been born. But for the present author and the present readers of the present [essay], the accident of our births may now be seen to have been more than usually accidental. Reflect a moment, gentle reader, and take stock of yourself: I suppose that you, too, will discover how fortunate we are to be here. For we were conceived after the discovery of antibiotics yet before amniocentesis, late enough to have benefited from medicine's ability to prevent and control fatal infectious diseases, yet early enough to have escaped from medicine's ability to detect, and to prevent us from living to suffer, our genetic diseases. To be sure, my own genetic vices are, as far as I know them, rather modest, taken individually—myopia, asthma and other allergies, bilateral forefoot adduction, bowleggedness, loquacity, and pessimism, plus some four to eight as yet undiagnosed recessive lethal genes in the heterozygous condition—but, taken together, and if diagnosable prenatally, I might never have made it.

Over the past decade, thousands of our might-have-been friends and relations have, in fact, *not* made it. For but a single (albeit more serious) genetic fault, itself no fault of theirs, they were prematurely sentenced to death (or nonbirth, if you prefer), through amniocentesis and abortion. Their genetic offenses had become capital—somewhat arbitrarily, since others equally grave have not—only because scientists had developed tests that could detect them prenatally.

Genetic counseling had previously been limited to teaching couples at risk for having children with genetic abnormalities—usually, in families already known to have one or more such offspring—the probabilities of an afflicted child and helping them consider what to do with the knowledge. Only adoption or artificial insemination (with donor semen) stood as practical alternatives to taking the risk or abstaining from further procreation. Amniocentesis and the devising of sophisticated cytological and biochemical tests have changed the situation dramatically; today, though still selectively used, prenatal diagnosis is becoming an integral part of obstetrical care. Early in gestation, cells of the prospective child are obtained by withdrawing samples of the amniotic fluid in which it is suspended *in utero.* From studies on these fetal cells, a large and growing number of chromosomal and functional abnormalities (as well as biological gender) can be accurately diagnosed. Some day, probably in the distant future, genetic screening and prenatal diagnosis may be coupled to techniques of genetic engineering that would seek to correct these abnormalities, treating either the fetus *in utero* or, perhaps, the egg and sperm before fertilization. Eventually, efforts to make perfect babies may go beyond treating known diseases to include also engineering desired improvements in biological capacities. But, for the present, abortion of the defective child-to-be is the only remedy medicine has to offer once the defect is prenatally diagnosed.*

ABORTION AND GENETIC ABORTION

Any discussion of the ethical issues of prenatal diagnosis will be unavoidably haunted by a ghost called the morality of abortion. This ghost I shall not vex. Neither shall I vex the reader by telling ghost stories. However, I would be neither surprised nor disappointed if my

---

*Relief of anxiety, if tests are negative, is, of course, a remedy for the apprehensive parents-to-be—though it must be said that the availability of genetic testing is itself probably responsible for much of our increased anxiety about genetic disease, especially where there has been no previous family history.

discussion of an admittedly related matter, the ethics of aborting the genetically defective, summons that hovering spirit to the reader's mind. For the morality of abortion is a matter not easily laid to rest, recent efforts to do so notwithstanding. A decision of the Supreme Court of the United States can indeed legitimate the disposal of fetuses, but not of the moral questions. The questions remain, and there is likely to be little new that can be said about them, and certainly not by me.

Yet before leaving the general question of abortion, let me pause to drop some anchors for the discussion that follows. Despite great differences of opinion regarding what to think and how to reason about abortion, nearly everyone agrees that abortion *is* a moral issue.* What does this mean? Formally, it means that a woman choosing or refusing an abortion (or a physician performing or refusing to perform an abortion) can expect to be asked (at least by herself) to justify her action. A moral choice begs for justification, whereas a mere preference, say for strawberry over vanilla, neither needs nor can get one. In other words, we expect that the woman (or physician) choosing abortion should be able to give reasons for her choice, beyond "I want it" or "I don't want it." Substantively, to say abortion is a moral issue means that, absent good reasons for termination, there is some presumption in favor of allowing the pregnancy to continue once it has begun. A common way, but by no means the only way, of expressing this presumption is to say that "a fetus has a right to continued life."† In this context, disagreement concerning the moral permissibility of abortion concerns what rights

---

*This strikes me as by far the most important inference to be drawn from the fact that human beings in different times and cultures have answered the abortion question differently. Seen in this light, the differing and changing answers themselves suggest that it is a question not easily put under, at least not for very long.

†Other ways include: one should not do violence to living or growing things; life is sacred; life is good; respect nature; respect life; fetal life has value; refrain from taking innocent life; protect and preserve life. It is evident that the terms chosen are of different weight and would require reasons of different weight to tip the balance in favor of abortion. My choice of the "rights" terminology is not meant to beg the questions of whether such rights really exist, or of where they come from. The notion of a "fetal right to life" presents only a little more difficulty in this regard than does the notion of a "human right to life," since the former does not depend on a claim that the human fetus is already "human." In my sense of the terms "right" and "life," one might even say that a dog or a fetal dog has a "right to life," and that it would be cruel and immoral for a man to go around performing abortions even on dogs for no good reason.

While on the subject of terminology, I note that the choice of words to describe the intrauterine being may also be morally charged. Consider, for example, the differing pictures conjured by "embryo," "fetus," "potential child," "nascent life," "child-to-be," "unborn child," "child," or "baby," or by the pronoun "he" or "she" as opposed to "it." My usual choice will be "fetus"; my reason, a wish not to beg any questions nor to gain by naming what cannot be had by reasoned argument.

(or interests or needs), and whose, override (take precedence over, or outweigh) this fetal right. Even most of the opponents of abortion agree that the mother's right to live takes precedence, and that abortion to save her life is permissible, perhaps obligatory. Some believe that a woman's right to determine the number and spacing of her children takes precedence, while others argue that the need to curb population growth is, at least at this time, overriding.

This brief analysis of what it means to say that abortion is a moral issue should suffice to establish two points. First, the fetus is a living thing with some moral claim on us not to do it violence, and, therefore, second, justification must be given for destroying it.

Let us turn now from the ethical questions of abortion in general, to focus on the special ethical issues raised by the abortion of "defective" fetuses (so-called abortion for fetal indications or genetic abortion). I shall consider only the cleanest cases—those cases in which well-characterized genetic diseases are diagnosed with a high degree of certainty by means of amniocentesis—in order to sidestep the added moral dilemmas posed when the diagnosis is suspected or possible, but unconfirmed. However, much of the discussion will also apply to cases in which genetic analysis gives only a statistical prediction about the genotype of the fetus, and also to cases in which the defect has an infectious or chemical rather than a genetic cause (e.g., rubella, thalidomide).

My first and possibly most difficult task is to show that there is something left to discuss once we have agreed not to discuss the morality of abortion in general. There is a sense in which abortion for genetic defect is, after abortion to save the life of the mother, perhaps the most defensible kind of abortion. Certainly, it is a serious and not a frivolous reason for abortion, defended by its proponents in sober and rational speech—unlike justifications based upon the false notion that a fetus is a mere part of a woman's body, to be used and abused at her pleasure. Standing behind genetic abortion are serious and well-intentioned people, with reasonable ends in view: the prevention of genetic diseases; the elimination of suffering in families; the preservation of precious financial and medical resources; the protection of our genetic heritage. No profiteers, no profligates, no racists. No arguments about the connection of abortion with pro-miscuity and licentiousness, no perjured testimony about the mental health of the mother, no arguments about the seriousness of the population problem. In short, clear objective data, a worthy cause, decent men and women. If abortion, what better reason for it?

If we consider only the *fact* of abortion, that is, the emptying of the womb and the destruction of fetal life, genetic abortion would seem to raise no new questions. But if we attend to the *reason* for abortion, that is, the genetic defectiveness of the fetus, we confront an entirely new set of issues. Precisely because the quality of the fetus is central to the decision to abort, the practice of genetic abortion has implications beyond those raised by abortion in general. The new focus on quality challenges the old presumption of equality. At stake here is the belief in the radical moral equality of all human beings, the belief that all human beings possess equally and independent of merit certain fundamental rights, one among which is, of course, the right to life.

EQUALITY AND EQUAL RIGHTS

The fate of belief in the equality of fundamental rights must be regarded as a weighty matter, and especially by Americans—regardless of their race, religion, or genotype of origin. For although one may claim that the principle of the sanctity of life, arguably violated in abortion as such, finally requires specific religious justification, no one can deny that the principle of human equality and equal rights has a secular and political-philosophical ground. Moreover this ground is the foundation of the American Republic. The Declaration of Independence states that the American people hold as a self-evident truth "that all men are created equal." Not equal in *all* respects, not created the *same,* but nonetheless equal in certain politically crucial ways. The politically relevant meaning of equality comes out in the next two clauses: "that they are endowed by their Creator with certain unalienable rights, that among these are Life, Liberty and the pursuit of Happiness." Human beings are equal in the equal and equally unalienable possession of rights. These rights are said to belong to us by nature, by mere membership in the human species, without qualification according to differences in intelligence, virtue, wisdom, beauty, strength, health, or genetic endowment.

To be sure, the belief that fundamental human rights belong equally to all human beings has been but an ideal, never fully realized,* often ignored, sometimes shamelessly. Yet it has been perhaps the most powerful moral idea at work in the world for at least two centuries. It is this idea and ideal that animates most of the current political and social criticism around the globe, and that has inspired much progressive legislation and social change in our own country. It is ironic that we should acquire the power to detect and eliminate the genetically unequal at a time when we have finally succeeded in removing much of the stigma and disgrace previously attached to victims of congenital illness, in providing them with improved care and support, and in preventing, by means of education, feelings of guilt on the part of their parents. One might even wonder whether the development of amniocentesis and prenatal

*In the Gettysburg Address, Lincoln calls the principle of human equality a "proposition" to which our Fathers dedicated the nation, rather than, as the Declaration had it, a self-evident truth. Self-evident truths (axioms) neither require nor admit of proof; propositions require it. Lincoln appears to teach that the American Republic is founded to test or prove the truth of the proposition of equal rights, by realizing that ideal through practice dedicated to that end.

diagnosis may represent a backlash against these same humanitarian and egalitarian tendencies in the practice of medicine, which, by helping to sustain to the age of reproduction persons with genetic disease, has itself contributed to the increasing incidence of genetic disease, and with it, to increased pressures for genetic screening, genetic counseling, and genetic abortion.

No doubt our humanitarian and egalitarian principles and practices have caused us some new difficulties. I myself have argued that compassionate humanitarianism is an insufficient guide to wise practice, and that its logical conclusion would be the dehumanization of a Brave New World. Also, our current egalitarianism has wandered excessively far from that foundational equality of rights, and even foolishly threatens to sacrifice those rights (especially liberty) to achieve equality of condition. But these excesses ought not to lead us to reject the principles of human equality, equal rights, or generous humaneness. And, in any case, if we do mean to weaken or turn our backs on these beliefs and practices, we should do so consciously and thoughtfully. If, as I believe, the way in which genetic abortion is described, discussed, and justified is perhaps of even greater consequence than its practice for our notion of human rights and their equal possession by all human beings, we should pay special attention to questions of language and, in particular, to the question of justification. Before turning full attention to these matters, two points should be clarified.

First, moral questions surrounding genetic abortion, as well as the implications of this practice for the principle of human equality, are largely independent of the question, Who decides? The vast majority of genetic counselors endorse (and, for the most part, in practice adhere to) the principle that the decision to abort an abnormal fetus belongs solely to the woman (or couple).* When challenged about their practice, counselors and obstetricians have tended either to deny that they make any moral choices ("We just provide information; the decision is the woman's") or to assert that they serve the moral good of enhancing freedom ("We give the information *in order* to permit free choice"), thus transforming the substantive moral question ("*What* to do?") into a procedural one ("*Who* should *decide* what to do?"). Yet the substantive questions—What decision, and why—do not disappear simply because the decision is left in the hands of each pregnant woman (or couple); they remain *her* (their) moral questions. And because of the nature of the moral questions of genetic abortion, her decision has consequences that affect more than herself and her fetus. The moral and political health of the community, and, indirectly, of each of its members, is as likely to be affected by the aggregate of purely private and voluntary decisions on

*However, some physicians refuse to perform amniocentesis unless the woman first indicates that she will elect abortion if an abnormality is discovered.

genetic abortion as by a uniform policy dictated by physicians or imposed by statute. Further, it seems especially disingenuous and even irresponsible for physicians and scientists to finesse the moral questions of genetic abortion and its implications and to take refuge behind the issue of who decides or behind the not-yet-widened skirts of their pregnant patients. For it is we who are responsible for choosing to develop the technology of prenatal diagnosis, for informing and promoting this technology among the public, and for the actual counseling of individual patients to avail themselves of this procedure.

Second, I wish to distinguish my discussion of what ought to be done from a descriptive account of what in fact is being done, and also from a consideration of what I myself might do if faced with the difficult decision. I cannot know with certainty what I would think, feel, do, or want done faced with the knowledge that my wife was carrying a child branded with Down's syndrome or Tay–Sachs disease. But an understanding of the issues is not advanced by personal anecdote or confession. We all know that what we and others actually do is often done out of weakness, rather than conviction. It is all too human to make an exception in one's own case (consider, e.g., busing our own child, doing national service, taking income tax deductions, claiming or paying a just wage, drinking before driving).

For what it is worth, I confess to feeling more than a little sympathy with would-be parents who choose abortions for severe genetic defects. Nevertheless, as I shall indicate later, in seeking for reasons to justify this practice, I can find none that are in themselves fully satisfactory and none that do not simultaneously justify the killing of "defective" infants, children, and adults. I am mindful that my arguments will fall far from the middle of the stream, yet I hope that the oarsmen of the flagship will pause and row more slowly while we all consider whither we are going.

GENETIC ABORTION AND THE LIVING DEFECTIVE

The practice of abortion of the genetically defective will no doubt affect our view of and our behavior toward those abnormals who escape the net of detection and abortion. A child with Down's syndrome or hemophilia or muscular dystrophy born at a time when most of his (potential) fellow sufferers were destroyed prenatally is liable to be looked upon by the community as one unfit to be alive, as a second- (or even lower) class human type. He may be seen as a person who need not have been and who would not have been if only someone had gotten to him in time.

The parents of such children are also likely to treat them differently, especially if the mother would have wished but failed to get an amniocentesis because of ignorance, poverty, or distance from the testing station, or if the prenatal diagnosis was in error. In such cases, parents are especially likely to resent the child. They may be disinclined to give it the kind of care they might have before the advent of amniocentesis and genetic abortion, rationalizing that a second-class specimen is not entitled to first-class treatment. If pressed to do so, say by physicians, the parents might refuse, and the courts may become involved. This has already begun to happen, and with increasing frequency.

In one of the earliest cases, in the early 1960s in Maryland, parents of a child with Down's syndrome refused permission to have the child operated on for an intestinal obstruction present at birth. The physicians and the hospital sought an injunction to require the parents to allow surgery. The judge ruled in favor of the parents, despite what was then the weight of precedent to the contrary, on the grounds that the child was "Mongoloid"—i.e., had the child been "normal," the decision would have gone the other way. Although the decision was not appealed and hence not affirmed by a higher court, one could already see through the prism of this case the possibility that the new powers of human genetics would strip the blindfold from the lady of justice and would make official the dangerous doctrine that some men are more equal than others. A steady parade of such "Baby Jane Doe" cases and similar court decisions during the past decade seem to be establishing precisely this doctrine.

The abnormal child may also feel resentful. A child with Down's syndrome or Tay–Sachs disease will probably never know or care, but what about a child with hemophilia or with Turner's syndrome?* In the past two decades, with medical knowledge and power over the prenatal child increasing and with parental authority over the postnatal child decreasing, we have seen the appearance of a new type of legal action, suits for wrongful life. Children have brought suit against their parents (and others) seeking to recover damages for physical and social handicaps inextricably tied to their birth (e.g., congenital deformities, congenital syphilis, illegitimacy). Recently, genetic counselors and laboratories have been sued for not correctly diagnosing prenatally the disease now suffered by the child plaintiff, who, in the absence of such negligence, would have been prevented by abortion from being born to suffer. Most American courts, though recognizing justice in the child's claim (that he suffers now through someone's negligence), have refused to award damages, due to policy considerations. But even this precedent has been overturned. In the *Curlender* case in California, damages were awarded to a child with Tay–Sachs disease whose birth would have been prevented had accurate genetic information been provided her parents. With the

---

*Turner's syndrome, caused by a defect or absence of a second sex (X) chromosome (genotype XO, phenotype female), comprises short stature, undifferentiated gonads (and hence sterility), and other variably associated abnormalities.

spread of amniocentesis and genetic abortion, we can only expect such cases to increase. And here it will be the soft-hearted rather than the hard-hearted judges who will establish the doctrine of second-class human beings because of their compassion for the mutants who escaped the traps set out for them.

It may be argued that I am dealing with a problem that, even if it is real, will affect very few people. It may be suggested that very few will escape the traps once we have set them properly and widely, once people are informed about amniocentesis, once the power to detect prenatally grows to its full capacity, and once our allegedly "superstitious" opposition to abortion dies out or is extirpated. But in order even to come close to this vision of success, amniocentesis or some other technique for prenatal diagnosis* will have to become part of every pregnancy—either by making it mandatory, like the test for syphilis, or by making it routine medical practice, like the Pap smear. Leaving aside the other problems with universal amniocentesis, we must expect that the problem for the few who escape is likely to be even worse precisely because they will be few.

The point, however, should be generalized. How will we come to view and act toward the many abnormals that will remain among us—the retarded, the crippled, the senile, the deformed, and the true mutants—once we embark on a program to root out genetic abnormality? For it must be remembered that we shall always have abnormals—some who escape detection or whose disease is undetectable *in utero,* others whose defects are a result of new mutations, birth injuries, accidents, maltreatment, or disease—who will require our care and protection. The existence of "defectives" cannot be fully prevented, not even by totalitarian breeding and weeding programs. Is it not likely that our principle with respect to these people will change from "we try harder" to "why accept second best?" The idea of "the unwanted because abnormal child" may become a self-fulfilling prophecy whose consequences may be worse than those of the abnormality itself.

GENETIC AND OTHER DEFECTIVES

The mention of other abnormals points to a second danger of the practice of genetic abortion. Genetic abortion may come to be seen

---

*Amniocentesis is not the only means of gathering information about the genetic state of the fetus. New techniques that biopsy the chorionic villi (the fetal portion of the placenta) are already in clinical use, and others that depend on finding fetal cells in the maternal bloodstream are under investigation. Also, direct inspection of the fetus (fetoscopy) provides other information about the normality of development. The issues discussed in this chapter are, however, independent of the technique used for prenatal evaluation: they concern only the implications of and justifications for the practice of aborting those deemed abnormal (by whatever means).

not so much as the prevention of genetic diseases, but as the prevention of defective or abnormal children—and, in a way, understandably so. *For in the case of what other diseases does preventive medicine consist in the elimination of the patient at-risk?* Moreover, the very language used to discuss genetic disease leads us to the easy but wrong conclusion that the afflicted fetus or person *is* rather than *has* a disease. True, one is partly defined by his genotype, but only partly. A person is more than his disease. And yet we slide easily from the language of possession to the language of identity, from "he has hemophilia" to "he is a hemophiliac," from "she has diabetes" through "she is diabetic" to "she is a diabetic," from "the fetus has Down's syndrome" to "the fetus is a Down's." This way of speaking encourages the belief that it is defective persons (or potential persons) that are being eliminated, rather than the diseases.

If this is so, then it becomes simply accidental that the defect has a genetic cause. Surely, it is only because of the high regard for medicine and science, and for the accuracy of genetic diagnosis, that genotypic defectives are likely to be the first to go. But once the principle, "defectives should not be born," is established, grounds other than cytological and biochemical may very well be sought. Even ignoring racialists and others equally misguided—of course, they cannot be ignored—we should know that there are social scientists, for example, who believe that one can predict with a high degree of accuracy how a child will turn out from a careful, systematic study of the socioeconomic and psychodynamic environment into which he is born and in which he grows up. They might press for the prevention of sociopsychological "disease," even of criminality, by means of prenatal *environmental* diagnosis and abortion. A crude unscientific form of eliminating potential, "phenotypic defectives" may already be operative in some cities in the sense that submission to abortion is allegedly being made a condition for the receipt of welfare payments. " 'Defectives' should not be born" is a principle without limits. We can ill-afford to have it established.

Up to this point, I have been discussing the possible implications of the practice of genetic abortion for our belief in and adherence to the idea that, at least in fundamental human matters such as life and liberty, all men are to be considered as equals, and that, for these matters, we should ignore as irrelevant the real qualitative differences among men, however important these differences may be for other purposes. Those who are concerned about abortion in general fear that the permissible time of eliminating the unwanted will be moved forward along the time continuum, against newborns, infants, and children. Analogously, I suggest that we should be concerned lest the attack on gross genetic inequality in fetuses be advanced both along the continuum of quality and into the later stages of life.

I am not engaged in predicting the future; the point is not that amniocentesis and genetic abortion *will* lead down the road to Nazi Germany. Rather, by examining the logic of justification, we discover that the principles underlying genetic abortion simultaneously justify many further steps down that road. The point was very well made by Abraham Lincoln:

> If A. can prove, however conclusively, that he may, of right, enslave B.—why may not B. snatch the same argument, and prove equally, that he may enslave A?—
>
> You say A. is white, and B. is black. It is *color,* then; the lighter, having the right to enslave the darker? Take care. By this rule, you are to be slave to the first man you meet, with a fairer skin than your own.
>
> You do not mean *color* exactly?—You mean the whites are *intellectually* the superiors of the blacks, and, therefore have the right to enslave them? Take care again. By this rule, you are to be slave to the first man you meet, with an intellect superior to your own.
>
> But, say you, it is a question of *interest;* and, if you can make it your *interest,* you have the right to enslave another. Very well. And if he can make it his interest, he has the right to enslave you.

Perhaps I have exaggerated the dangers; perhaps we will not abandon our inexplicable preference for generous humanitarianism and equal treatment over consistency. But we should indeed be cautious and move slowly as we give serious consideration to the question: What price the perfect baby? In particular, we should attend carefully to the principles and standards that might guide and justify our practice.

STANDARDS FOR JUSTIFYING GENETIC ABORTION

What would constitute an adequate justification of the decision to abort a genetically defective fetus? Let me suggest the following formal characteristics, each of which still leaves open many questions.

1. The reasons given should be logically consistent and should lead to relatively unambiguous guidelines—note that I do not say rules—for action in most cases.
2. The justification should be made evident to a reasonable person that the interest or need or right being served by abortion is sufficient to override the otherwise presumptive claim on us to protect and preserve the life of the fetus.
3. The justification ought to be such as to help provide intellectual support for drawing distinctions between acceptable and unacceptable kinds of genetic abortion, and between genetic abortion itself and the further practices we would all find abhorrent.

4. The justification ought to be generalizable to cover all persons in identical circumstances.
5. The justifications should not lead to different actions from month to month or from year to year.
6. The justification should be grounded on standards that can, both in principle and in fact, sustain and support our actions in the case of genetic abortion without contradicting or subverting our notions of fundamental and equal human rights.

The reader would do well to consider all these criteria, but I shall focus here primarily on the last. According to what standards can and should we judge a fetus with genetic abnormalities unfit to live (i.e., abortable)? It seems to me that there are at least three dominant standards to which we are likely to repair.

The Social Standard

The first is social or public good. The needs and interests of society are often invoked to justify the practices of prenatal diagnosis and abortion of the genetically abnormal. The argument, full blown, runs something like this. Society has an interest in the genetic fitness of its members. It is foolish for society to squander its precious resources ministering to and caring for the unfit, especially for those who will never become "productive," or who will never in any way benefit society. Therefore, the interests of society are best served by the elimination of the genetically defective prior to their births.

The social standard is all too often reduced to its lowest common denominator: money. Thus, one physician, claiming that he has "made a cost-benefit analysis of Tay–Sachs disease," notes that "the total cost of carrier detection, prenatal diagnosis, and termination of at-risk pregnancies for all Jewish individuals in the United States under thirty who will marry is $5,730,281. If the program is set up to screen only one married partner, the cost is $3,122,695. The hospital costs for the 990 cases of Tay–Sachs disease these individuals would produce over a thirty-year period in the United States is $34,650,000." Another physician, apparently less interested or able to make such a precise audit, has written: "Cost benefit analyses have been made for the total prospective detection and monitoring of Tay–Sachs disease, cystic fibrosis (when prenatal detection becomes available for cystic fibrosis), and other disorders, and in most cases, the expenditures for hospitalization and medical care far exceed the cost of prenatal detection in properly selected risk populations, followed by selective abortion." Yet a third physician has calculated that the costs to the state of caring for children with Down's syndrome is more than three times that of detecting and aborting them. (These authors all acknowledge the additional nonsocial [i.e., private] costs of personal suffering, but insofar as they consider *society,* the costs are purely economic.)

Many questions can be raised about this approach. First, how accurate are the calculations? Not all the costs have been reckoned. The aborted "defective" child will in most cases be "replaced" by a "normal" child. In keeping the ledger, the costs to society of his care and maintenance cannot be ignored—costs of educating him, or removing his wastes and pollutions, not to mention the costs in nonreplaceable natural resources that he consumes. Who is a greater drain on society's precious resources, the average inmate of a home for the retarded or the average graduate of Berkeley? I doubt that we know or can even find out. Then there are the costs of training the physicians and genetic counselors, equipping their laboratories, supporting their research, and sending them and us to conferences to worry about what they are doing. An accurate economic analysis seems to me to be impossible, even in principle. (And even were it possible, the economic argument must still face or silence the challenge posed by the ordinary language philosopher. Andy Capp, who, when his wife said that she was getting really worried about the cost of living, replied: "Sweet'eart, name me one person who wants t'stop livin' on account of the cost.")

A second, more serious, defect of the economic analysis: There are matters of social importance that are not reducible to financial costs, and others that may not be quantifiable at all. How does one quantify the costs of real and potential social conflict, either between children and parents, or between the community and the "deviants" who refuse amniocentesis and continue to bear abnormal children? Can one measure the effect on racial tensions of government-supported programs to screen for and prevent the birth of children homozygous (or heterozygous) for sickle cell anemia? What numbers does one attach to any decreased willingness or ability to take care of the less fortunate, or to cope with difficult problems? And what about the costs of rising expectations? Will we become increasingly dissatisfied with anything short of the "optimum baby"? How does one quantify anxiety? Humiliation? Guilt? Might not the medical profession pay an unmeasurable price if genetic abortion and other revolutionary activities bring about changes in medical ethics and medical practice that lead to the further erosion of trust in the physician? Finally, who is able accurately to compute the costs of weakening our dedication to the proposition of equal rights?

An appeal to social worthiness or usefulness is a less vulgar form of the standard of social good. It is true that great social contributions are unlikely to be forthcoming from persons who suffer from most serious genetic diseases, especially since many of them die in childhood. Yet consider the following remarks by Pearl Buck on the subject of being a mother of a child retarded from phenylketonuria (PKU):*

*PKU is a genetic disorder (autosomal recessive in inheritance) due to an inborn absence of an enzyme that catalyzes the conversion of the amino acid

My child's life has not been meaningless. She has indeed brought comfort and practical help to many people who are parents of retarded children or are themselves handicapped. True, she has done it through me, yet without her I would not have had the means of learning how to accept the inevitable sorrow, and how to make that acceptance useful to others. Would I be so heartless to say that it has been worthwhile for my child to be born retarded? Certainly not, but I am saying that even though gravely retarded it has been worthwhile for her to have lived.

It can be summed up, perhaps, by saying that in this world, where cruelty prevails in so many aspects of our life, I would not add the weight of choice to kill rather than to let live. A retarded child, a handicapped person, brings its own gift to life, even to the life of normal human beings. That gift is comprehended in the lessons of patience, understanding, and mercy, lessons which we all need to receive and to practice with one another, whatever we are.

The standard of potential social worthiness is little better in deciding about abortion in particular cases than is the standard of economic cost. To drive home the point, each one of us might consider retrospectively whether he would have been willing, when he was a fetus, to stand trial for his life, pleading only his worth to society as he now can evaluate it. How many of us are not socially "defective" and with none of the excuses possible for a child with PKU? If there is to be human life at all, potential social worthiness cannot be its entitlement.

Finally, we should take note of the ambiguities in the very notion of social good. Some use the term "society" to mean their own particular political community, others to mean the whole human race, and still others speak as if they mean both simultaneously, following that all-too-human belief that what is good for me and mine is good for mankind. Who knows what is genetically best for mankind, even with respect to Down's syndrome? And even if we knew, we are unlikely to secure it through prenatal diagnosis and abortion. For the genetic heritage of the human species is largely in the care of persons who do not live, and may never live, along the amniocentesis frontier. Moreover, for those who live in the industrialized West, it is certainly a mistake to regard genetic abortion as our first duty to the human gene pool. If we are truly serious about the genetic future of the entire species, we should concentrate our attack

phenylalanine to tyrosine. The children are fair-skinned and suffer from mental retardation, other neurological symptoms (e.g., epilepsy), and eczema, unless they are treated by a diet low in phenylalanine.

on mutagenesis, and especially on *our* large contribution to the pool of environmental mutagens.

But even the more narrow definition of society is ambiguous. Do we mean our society as it is today? Or do we mean our society as it ought to be? If the former, our standards will be ephemeral, for ours is a faddish society. (By far the most worrisome feature of the changing attitudes on abortion is the suddenness with which they changed.) Any such socially determined standards are likely to provide too precarious a foundation for decisions about genetic abortion, let alone for our notions of human rights. If we mean the latter, then we have transcended the social standard, since the good society is not to be found in society itself, nor is it likely to be discovered by taking a vote. In sum, social or public good as a standard for justifying genetic abortion seems to be unsatisfactory. It is hard to define in general, difficult to apply clearly to particular cases, susceptible to overreaching and abuse (hence, very dangerous), and not sufficient unto itself if considerations of the *good* community are held to be automatically implied.

The Familial Standard

A second major alternative is the standard of parental or familial good. Here the argument of justification might run as follows: Parents have a right to determine, according to their own wishes, and based upon their own notions of what is good for them, the qualitative as well as the quantitative character of their families. If they believe that the birth of a seriously deformed child will be the cause of great sorrow and suffering to themselves and to their other children and a drain on their time and resources, then they may ethically decide to prevent the birth of such a child, even by abortion.

This argument, I expect, is more attractive to most people than the argument appealing to the good of society. For one thing, we are more likely to trust a person's conception of what is good for him than his notion of what is good for society. Also, for each decision, the number of persons involved is small, making it seem less impossible to weigh all the relevant factors in determining the good of the family. Most powerfully, one can see and appreciate the possible harm done to healthy children if the parents are obliged to devote most of their energies to caring for the afflicted child.

Yet there are ambiguities and difficulties perhaps as great as with the standard of social good. In the first place, it is not entirely clear what *would* be good for the other children. In a strong family, the experience with a suffering and dying child might help the healthy siblings learn to face and cope with adversity. Some have even speculated that the lack of experience with death and serious illness in our affluent young people is responsible for their immaturity and lack of gravity and their inability to respond patiently and steadily to the serious problems they encounter, in private or community life.

Doubtless many American parents have unwittingly fostered child-ishness by their well-meaning efforts to spare their children any confrontation with harsh reality. Still, I suspect that one can not generalize. In some children, and in some families, experience with suffering may be strengthening, and in others, disabling. My point here is that the matter is uncertain, and that parents deciding *on this basis* are as likely as not to be mistaken.

The familial or parental standard, like the social standard, is unavoidably elastic because suffering does not come in discontinuous units, and because parental wishes and desires know no limits. Both are utterly subjective, relative, and notoriously subject to change. Some parents claim that they could not tolerate raising a child of the undesired sex: I know of one case where, in the delivery room, the mother, on being informed that her child was a son, told the phy-sician that she did not even wish to see it and that he should get rid of it. We may judge her attitude to be pathological, but even patho-logical suffering is suffering. Would such suffering justify aborting her normal male fetus?

Or take the converse case of two parents, who for their own very peculiar reasons, wish to have an abnormal child, say a child who will suffer from the same disease as grandpa or a child whose arrested development would preclude the threat of adolescent rebel-lion and separation, or a dwarf who could work with them in the circus. Are these acceptable grounds for the abortion of "normals"?

Granted, such cases will be rare. But they serve to show the dangers inherent in talking about a parental right to determine, according to their wishes, the quality of their children. Indeed, the whole idea of parental rights with respect to children strikes me as problematic. It suggests that children are like property, that they exist *for* the parents. One need only look around to see some of the results of this notion of parenthood. The language of duties to children—including, at minimum, the duty not to violate their unalienable rights as human beings—would be more in keeping with the heavy re-sponsibility we bear in affirming the continuity of life with life, and in trying to transmit what wisdom we have acquired to the next generation. Our children are not *our* children. Reflection on these matters could lead to a greater appreciation of why it is people do and should have children. No better consequence can be hoped for from the advent of amniocentesis and other technologies for con-trolling human reproduction.

If one speaks of familial good in terms of parental duty, one could still argue that parents have an obligation to do what they can to insure that all their children are born healthy and sound. But this formulation transcends the limitation of parental wishes and desires. As in the case of the good society, the idea of healthy and sound requires a nonarbitrary or so-called objective standard, a standard in the nature of things. Hard as it may be to uncover it, this is what we are seeking.

The Natural Standard

Nature as a standard is thus the third alternative. The justification according to the natural standard might run like this: As a result of our knowledge of genetic diseases, we know that persons afflicted with certain diseases will never be capable of living the full life of a human being. Just as a no-necked giraffe could never live a giraffe's life, or a needleless porcupine would not attain true "procupine-hood," so a child or fetus with Tay-Sachs disease or Down's syndrome, for example, will never be truly human. He will never be able to care for himself, nor have even the potential for developing, to any significant extent, the distinctively human capacities for thought or self-consciousness. Nature herself has aborted many similar cases and has provided for the early death of many who happen to get born. There is no reason to keep them alive; instead, we should prevent their birth by contraception or sterilization if possible, and abortion if necessary.

The advantages of this approach are clear. The standards are "objective" and in the fetus itself, thus avoiding the relativity and ambiguity we observed in the notions of social and parental good. The standard can be easily generalized to cover all such cases and will be resistant to the shifting sands of public opinion.

This standard, I would suggest, is the one that most physicians and genetic counselors appeal to in their heart of hearts, no matter what they say or do about letting the parents choose. Why else have they developed genetic counseling and amniocentesis? Indeed, the notions of disease, of abnormal, of defective, make no sense at all in the absence of a natural norm of health. This norm is the foundation of the art of the physician and of the inquiry of the health scientist. Yet the standard is elusive. Ironically, we are gaining increasing power to manipulate and control our own nature at a time in which we are increasingly confused about what is normal, healthy, and fit.

Although possibly acceptable in principle, the natural standard runs into problems in application, when attempts are made to fix the boundary between potentially human and potentially not human. Professor Jerome Lejeune has demonstrated the difficulty, if not the impossibility, of setting clear molecular, cytological, or developmental signposts for this boundary. Attempts to obtain such signposts by induction, say by considering the phenotypes of the worst cases, are equally difficult. Which features would we take to be the most relevant in, say, Tay-Sachs disease, Lesch–Nyhan syndrome, Cri du chat,* Down's syndrome? Certainly severe mental retardation. But

---

*Lesch–Nyhan syndrome is an inherited (sex-linked) severe neurological disease (of males), characterized by mental retardation, involuntary writhing motions, and compulsive self-mutilation through biting of lips and fingertips; it is due to an absence of an enzyme in purine metabolism. Cri du chat is a hereditary condition characterized by severe mental deficiency, skull abnormalities, and a plaintive cat-like cry; it is due to a deletion of a specific chromosome.

how severe is severe? As Abraham Lincoln and I argued earlier, mental retardation admits of degree. It, too, is highly variable and relative. Moreover, it is not clear that certain other defects and deformities might not equally foreclose the possibility of a truly or fully human life. What about blindness or deafness? Quadriplegia? Aphasia? Several of these in combination? Not only does each kind of defect admit a continuous scale of severity, but it also merges with other defects on a continuous scale of defectiveness. Where on this scale is the line to be drawn: after mental retardation? Blindness? Muscular dystrophy? Cystic fibrosis? Hemophilia? Diabetes? Galactosemia? Turner's syndrome? XYY? Clubfoot? Asthma? Moreover, the identical two continuous scales—of kind and severity—are found also among the living. In fact, it is this natural standard that most threatens the notion of human equality. For it leads most directly to the idea that there are second-class human beings and subhuman human beings, not equally entitled to the rights of life or the pursuit of their own happiness.

But the story is not complete. The very idea of "nature" is ambiguous. According to one view, the one I have been using, nature points to or implies a peak, a fullness, a perfection. According to this view, human rights depend upon attaining the status of full humanness. The fetus is only potential; it has no rights, according to this view. But all kinds of people also fall short of the norm: children, idiots, "defective" adults. It is this understanding of nature that has been used to justify not only abortion and infanticide, but also slavery.

There is another notion of nature, less splendid, more humane, and, though less able to sustain a notion of health, more acceptable to the findings of modern science: nature not as the norm or perfection, but nature as the innate, the given, the inborn. Our animal nature is characterized by impulses toward self-preservation and by the capacity to feel pleasure and to suffer pain. On this understanding of nature, man is fundamentally like the other animals, differing only in his conscious awareness of these inborn impulses, capacities, and concerns. The right to life rests on the fact that we are self-preserving and suffering creatures.* Yet on this understanding of nature, the fetus—even a "defective" fetus, not to speak of a child, "defective" or no—is not potential, but actual. The right to life belongs to him.

---

*The whole tradition of natural rights, in which the American Founders firmly stand, goes back to Thomas Hobbes, the first to speak of natural right in this now commonplace sense. "The right of nature, which writers commonly call *jus naturale*, is the liberty each man hath, to use his own power, as he will himself, for the preservation of his own nature; that is to say, of his own life; and consequently, of doing any thing, which in his own judgment, and reason, he shall conceive to be the aptest means thereunto" (*Leviathan*, Chapter XIV). As the example of Hobbes plainly shows, the doctrine of natural and equal rights is connected with a nonteleological view of nature, that is, with a view of nature that knows not natural perfection or fullness.

For this reason, this understanding of nature does not provide and seems even to deny us what we are seeking, namely, a justification for genetic abortion, adequate unto itself, which does not simultaneously justify infanticide, homicide, and enslavement of the genetically abnormal.

There is a third understanding of nature, nature as sacrosanct, nature as created by a Creator. Indeed, to speak about this reminds us that there is a fourth possible standard for judgments about genetic abortion: the religious standard. I shall leave the discussion of this standard to those who are able to speak of it in better faith. I suspect, however, that it, too, will not answer our justificatory needs.

Now that I am at the end, the reader can better share my sense of frustration. I have failed to provide myself with a satisfactory intellectual and moral justification for the practice of genetic abortion. Perhaps the pragmatists can persuade me that we should abandon the search for principled justification, that if we just trust people's situational decisions or their gut reactions, everything will turn out fine. Maybe they are right. but we should not forget the sage observation of Bertrand Russell: "Pragmatism is like a warm bath that heats up so imperceptibly that you don't know when to scream." Before we submerge ourselves irrevocably in amniotic fluid, we should note its connection to our own baths, into which we have started the hot water running.

Suggestions for Discussion and Writing

1. What is the tone of the first three paragraphs? What specific language helps establish this tone? What, for instance, is the effect of the author's reference to his own "genetic vices"? Do you find the tone of these paragraphs appropriate to his subject?

2. The author says that "any discussion of the ethical issues of prenatal diagnosis will be unavoidably haunted by a ghost called the morality of abortion" but that this is a ghost he will not "vex." What is meant by "ethics"? by "morality"? by "vex"? Does the author keep his promise?

3. In the eighth paragraph Kass says that "there is a sense in which abortion for genetic defect is . . . perhaps the most defensible kind of abortion" and that "standing behind genetic abortion are serious and well-intentioned people, with reasonable ends in view." What does he gain rhetorically by engaging perhaps the most "defensible" case? What is the effect of the sentence beginning "No profiteers . . ."?

4. In discussing the "moral questions surrounding genetic abortions," Kass takes up the issue of "who decides?" Who, ac-

cording to Kass, *should* decide? Who, in fact, does? Do you agree with the author's suggestion that by supplying genetic counseling and prenatal diagnosis physicians and scientists are inevitably morally involved? Write an essay defending your views.

5. In making his case against genetic abortion, the author raises the issue of how "abnormals who escape the net of detection and abortion" are likely to be treated. Do you find his argument here persuasive? Write an essay developing your views.

6. Early in his essay Kass discusses the importance of terminology and the degree to which it can be "morally charged." He himself, however, could be said to use such language (e.g., "might-have-been friends . . . were prematurely sentenced to death"). Cite other examples and show how they contribute to his rhetorical purpose.

7. Kass says that "an understanding of the issues is not advanced by personal anecdote or confession." What does he mean? Do you agree? Would Selzer and Weissmann (this chapter)?

8. The author quotes Pearl Buck's remarks regarding her retarded daughter. Write an essay in which you engage some of the issues she raises.

9. In discussing "the natural standard" as a possible justification for genetic abortion, the author distinguishes among three notions of nature. Explain these distinctions. Which idea of nature does he prefer? Why is one "more acceptable to the findings of modern science"?

10. Look at the final two sentences. In what sense, according to Kass, are we in danger of submerging "ourselves irrevocably in amniotic fluid"? What is the connection between that statement and the quotation by Russell? Explain the force of this ending.

☐ IS THERE LIFE AFTER *ROE v. WADE?*

Mary B. Mahowald (b. 1935)

A professor of biomedical ethics and a member of the Department of Pediatrics at Case Western Reserve School of Medicine, Mary B. Mahowald has written extensively on the ethical issues associated with the transplantation of fetal tissue. She is also the editor of *Philosophy of Woman: An Anthology of Classic and Current Concepts* (1983).

In the following essay, she examines the debate between "pro-choice" and "pro-life" activists and suggests that the preoccupation of both groups with the legal status of abortion has led to their ignoring other, more fundamental issues.

I t has been sixteen years since the landmark case *Roe v. Wade* was decided by a majority vote of the United States Supreme Court. Sixteen years is enough time for humans and their laws to be conceived, embodied, and grow to maturity, but *Roe* still threatens to abort. In fact, by the time this article appears, it may have been overturned by a new decision that vitiates its main provisions. Is there any way of saving its life? Is its life worth saving?

"Pro-life" activists would probably answer both questions negatively, and "pro-choice" activists would probably answer them affirmatively. For each side the answer to the second question is likely to be more definitive. Those whose views on the legality or morality of abortion are somewhere between absolute permissiveness and absolute condemnation, a position held by the majority of the American people, may look for ways of saving what seems worth saving of *Roe.*

Why has the debate raged on without abatement for so long? Is it possible to find some areas of agreement that dissidents on the issue might acknowledge? While addressing these questions, I will also briefly sketch my own views on possible changes in *Roe* and the morality of abortion.

THE LONG DEBATE

Laws often have a settling as well as regulative influence on individuals. For example, legal enactments such as the Emancipation Proclamation and the Nineteenth Amendment granting women the vote eventually became settled opinion in American consciousness despite initial controversies. One might have thought, therefore, that by now the cool rationale of the *Roe* decision in 1973 would have quelled the heat of public debate about abortion. Instead, the heat has escalated from fiery words to clinic bombings.

Intransigence on opposite sides of the issue, coupled with misleading and emotionally charged rhetoric, are partly to blame for prolongation of the controversy. For the most part, the rhetoric of abortion aims at different targets: "pro-lifers" focus on abortions for trivial reasons, performed even when the fetus is well-developed; "pro-choice" proponents tend to discuss abortions undertaken early for compelling reasons such as rape, or threat to a woman's health or life. One side refers to embryos as babies, and abortions as (therefore?) murder; the other describes a second trimester fetus as a blob of cells, and compares abortion to removal of a wart or tumor.

The phrase "abortion on demand" is used prevalently to describe the current legal status of abortion; yet the text of the *Roe* ruling fails to support that interpretation.

Beyond simplistic rhetoric and intransigence, thoughtful, well-developed arguments and openness to further consideration have helped to keep the debate constructively alive. Increased knowledge of fetal development and advances in neonatology, along with the incidence of infertility and shortage of adoptable babies, have caused some to wane in their initial enthusiasm for *Roe*. Those whose main concern in legalizing safe abortions was to promote the health of poor women may be comforted by the reduction of morbidity and mortality related to abortions, but disturbed by the overall increase in the number of abortions performed.

COMPLEXITIES OF THE ISSUE

Fortunately or unfortunately, I cannot honestly align myself with either "pro-choice" or "pro-life" activists. Either side betrays, to me, the enormous complexity of the issue. This complexity is in part a function of the following features associated with abortion decisions: duration of gestation, circumstances of conception, age and competence of the pregnant woman, health status of the fetus, and health status of the pregnant woman. Regardless of the outcome of *Webster*, recognition of this complexity could be a beginning point for discussion between dissidents.

Duration of gestation. For most people, abortion decisions become more difficult to justify as gestation progresses. For example, an intrauterine device, usually viewed as a contraceptive despite its abortifacient effect, is hardly controversial. RU 486, a drug that induces abortion very early in pregnancy, has evoked controversy because it allows a woman to abort herself; if the drug could be used effectively late in pregnancy its availability would surely be more disturbing to some individuals. Physicians who have no moral qualms about early abortions tend to avoid performing them during the second trimester. Legal and emotional factors may trigger such avoidance more than moral concerns. In general, however, the more advanced the gestation, the more likely it is that significant moral factors are introduced, such as the onset of fetal brain activity (at about 8 weeks), and of fetal sentiency (probably during the second trimester).

Roe maintains that fetal viability, "the ability (of the fetus) to survive ex utero, albeit with artificial aid," occurs during the third trimester, at which point the states may thereafter promote their interest in the "potentiality of human life" by proscribing abortion unless it is necessary for maternal health. Because of advances in perinatal and neonatal medicine, and greater availability of technology, the duration of gestation required for viability has been reduced since 1973. Accordingly, the trimester breakdown by which abortion is permissible until the third trimester no longer provides an adequate guide to decisions based on fetal viability. Moreover, in a forty-week (full-term) gestation, just when second trimester ends and third trimester begins is unclear even to practicing physicians.

Technically, abortion is no longer possible after viability, because termination of pregnancy, whether spontaneous or induced, is then clinically defined as premature birth. However, *Roe* uses the term abortion to refer to termination of pregnancy both before and after viability, and many people, including practitioners, construe abortion as the termination of the fetus prior to birth, whether the fetus is viable or not. On that interpretation, if the fetus is considered viable or possibly viable, a method may be chosen to insure fetal demise in utero. If abortion is defined as termination of pregnancy rather than termination of the fetus, the method selected may be one that maximizes the chance of fetal survival.

From a medical standpoint, the choice of method is partly determined by the duration of gestation: vacuum aspiration or suction curettage are appropriate during the first trimester, while induction methods (using saline, urea, or prostaglandin) or dilatation and evacuation (D&E) are appropriate during the second trimester. *Roe* says nothing about methods of abortion and their different effects on the fetus as well as the pregnant woman. Yet surely the possibility of fetal survival, of pain, and of risk to the pregnant woman's health are morally relevant factors influenced by the method selected.

Circumstances of conception. Many opposed to legal abortion generally make exceptions for cases of rape or incest. Requiring a woman to maintain a pregnancy caused by rape imposes on her a constant reminder of the violence committed against her. Pregnancy due to incest may also have its origins in violence, and ordinarily entails social stigma and risk of birth defect. Abortion in such circumstances is more likely to be morally justified than when intercourse occurs voluntarily in a nonincestuous relationship.

Voluntariness, as a crucial component of moral behavior, applies not only to intercourse but also to conception. Accordingly, we may wonder about responsibility for pregnancies that occur in spite of careful contraceptive practice, when intercourse is clearly voluntary but conception is not. The voluntariness of intercourse may imply responsibility for conception, at least on the part of those aware that contraception sometimes fails. If contraception were faithfully practiced and fully reliable, neither pregnancy nor abortion could occur. When appropriate contraception fails, however, those who practice it are less responsible for the resultant pregnancy than those who don't.

Additional circumstances associated with abortion decisions include the marital and economic status of the pregnant woman, and responsibilities to others, such as a spouse, parents, or children already born. In most cases, however, the moral relevance of these circumstances rests on an assumption that commitment to parenthood is essentially linked with carrying a pregnancy to term. (I will return to this point later.) Moreover, different circumstances may influence the morality of the agent without altering the morality of the act. Abortion construed as the killing of an innocent person would thus be a morally wrong act, but mitigating circumstances would reduce the culpability of the agent committing the act.

Age and competence of the pregnant woman. The age at which pregnancy occurs is relevant for medical as well as psychological reasons. Pregnancy and childbirth are not only particularly hazardous as discrete events for those who are not yet fully mature, but they also tend to impede such persons from reaching their full measure of development. Moreover, the younger the individual, the less likely it is that she has fully and freely consented to the pregnancy or to abortion.

Maternal age is also a risk factor for the fetus. The incidence of prematurity is greatest for the oldest and youngest age groups. Women over thirty-five are often aware of their increased risk of conceiving a child with Down syndrome, and the incidence of medical complications for pregnant women as well as fetuses escalates as the age of the pregnant woman advances beyond the mid-thirties. A forty-five-year-old woman whose children are already raised, may become pregnant when she fails to practice birth control because she mistakenly believes herself menopausal. Because of the risk factor, this suggests a morally different picture than the unplanned pregnancy of a twenty-five-year-old.

Competence, often related to age, is another morally relevant factor in abortion decisions. Partly because of laws against involuntary sterilization, incompetent and questionably competent adults become pregnant. Here a pro-choice argument for abortion is hardly adequate. Here too, the possibility that the pregnant woman can or will be permitted to raise her offspring is remote. Competence thus applies not only to the capability for moral decision making, but also to capability for parenthood. So long as a child can be raised by others who are competent, the absence of competence for parenthood is not an adequate reason for abortion.

Health status of the fetus. In normal pregnancy, the health of the pregnant woman and of the fetus are interdependent. Nonetheless, early spontaneous abortions occur, sometimes before women realize they are pregnant, often because embryos or fetuses are abnormal. Spontaneous abortions are thus a kind of natural eugenic event. Because of improvements in high-risk obstetrics, infertility treatment, and perinatology, some fetuses that previously would have succumbed in utero now survive. By means of prenatal diagnostic techniques we can detect fetal anomalies, some of which are treatable in utero and some ex utero. Through legal access to safe abortions, an elective eugenic procedure is thus available.

Although clinicians may refer to elective abortion for fetal anomaly as "therapeutic," the procedure is not usually medically therapeutic for the pregnant woman. A rationale of fetal euthanasia may be applied to cases where the abnormality is so severe that survival seems worse than death (for example, Tay–Sachs disease or Lesch–Nyhan syndrome). In most cases of abnormality, however, survival presents a greater burden to the family than to the child. It also entails a burden to society, which ordinarily subsidizes the treatment, education, and social supports necessary for disabled persons throughout their lifetimes. Down syndrome, a condition that is mentally debilitating but not generally emotionally or physically debilitating, is a clear example of a prenatally detectable anomaly that usually prompts abortion. The procedure may be defended as a means by which to avoid the psychosocial burdens that care for a person with Down syndrome entails; it can hardly be justified on the basis of the interests of the fetus.

Health status of the pregnant woman. Some pregnancies are life-threatening to some women. Since self-defense seems so basic a human right, few would argue that a woman is morally obliged to sacrifice her life for the sake of a fetus. However, some women in fact choose to risk their health for the sake of their fetuses, while others may decline to do so for unselfish reasons. Consider, for example, the following cases:

> CASE A:
> A twenty-six-year-old married woman had Eisenmenger's syndrome, a condition that is life-threatening in association with late pregnancy and childbirth. The cardiologist who had warned her against childbearing advised her to have an abortion when she became pregnant. The woman was aware that her chance of survival was about 50 percent, but insisted that she wanted to have the baby. Although her husband and parents preferred that she abort the fetus in order to maximize her own prospect of survival, she chose to continue the pregnancy. In conformity with the woman's wishes the infant was delivered by cesarean section. Despite aggressive efforts to support her throughout the medical crisis, she died four days later.

> CASE B:
> A thirty-two-year-old woman with multiple sclerosis became pregnant despite use of a diaphragm. She and her husband had two children, four and six years old, for whom she was the principal caregiver. Although the couple were generally opposed to abortion, both were extremely concerned that continuation of the pregnancy would further compromise the woman's health. Previous pregnancies had resulted in permanent aggravation of her condition, to a point where she required a wheelchair. One week after learning she was pregnant the woman requested an abortion. She hoped, she said, to

preserve her ability to care for the children she already had.

The woman described in Case A showed a heroic degree of self-sacrifice in behalf of the fetus. Poignant and appealing as it is, however, such self-sacrifice or virtue lies beyond the moral requirements of the law. Until and unless our society is willing to coerce some persons to risk their health for the sake of others—to donate bone marrow, blood, or a kidney, for example—we surely should not force pregnant women to do this for their fetuses. Even then, the argument in behalf of those who are uncontroversially persons is more compelling than the argument made for fetuses. Accordingly, the woman who chose abortion in Case B may also be acting virtuously, pursuing an alternative that may in fact be the most loving and responsible course to follow.

Generally, the lesser the threat, the less convincing the self-defense rationale. At a certain point in the development process, the medical risk of elective abortion is equal to the risk of continuing the pregnancy to term and birth. Psychological, social, and economic risks are also prevalently associated with pregnancy. Although these may influence the condition of the fetus, they directly affect the life of the pregnant woman. Unlike the fetus, however, she is able to communicate her priorities regarding her own interests or those of the fetus. In situations of conflict, whether or not her autonomy is socially supported depends on whether pro-choice or pro-life values prevail.

POSSIBLE AREAS OF AGREEMENT

Should the values of one perspective prevail, or are there points of convergence that both sides might acknowledge? In addition to recognizing that abortion is a complex issue, I believe dissidents might agree on the following points.

Abortion is a bad thing. Ordinarily, pregnancy represents a natural, healthy process that abortion interrupts. Elective abortion entails an actively invasive procedure for the woman undergoing the termination of her pregnancy. But whether the abortion is spontaneous or deliberate, the interruption signifies termination of a physiological relationship that has supported a developing human life, which is a positive human value. Unfortunately, Roe fails to acknowledge this "fact of life," confusing the philosophically controversial concept of person with the relatively simple biological concept of human life.

Often the circumstances that trigger abortion are themselves tragic, and the decision is an effort to minimize the harm done to those affected, including others besides the pregnant woman. It may of course be argued that the harm done to a fetus through abortion is always greater than that done to others by continuing an unwanted but healthy pregnancy. Nonetheless, one can acknowledge the harm of abortion while holding that in some circumstances it entails less harm than alternatives.

The term "pro-abortion" is a misleading label for those who argue for its permissibility only in certain circumstances. To limit those circumstances by providing alternatives to women is an appropriate objective of "pro-choice" as well as "pro-life" supporters. The Bush administration's proposal that adoption be more widely encouraged is an obvious possibility in this regard. Some argue, however, that adoption is more psychologically costly for pregnant women than abortion. More social supports for childrearing, especially when children are disabled, is another practical means of expanding the alternatives of pregnant women. Probably the most effective way to avoid abortions, however, is to improve the practice of contraception. If pregnancy were prevalently voluntary, the incidence of abortion would surely be reduced.

There are differences between the right to terminate a pregnancy, the right to terminate a fetus, and parental responsibility. Neither morally nor practically is termination of pregnancy equivalent to termination of a fetus. This is obviously true when the termination of pregnancy occurs through the birth of a live infant. It may also be true of procedures in which a nonviable fetus is removed for treatment of a condition that gravely threatens the life or health of a pregnant woman, such as ectopic pregnancy or cancer of the uterus. It is clearly not true when termination occurs because of fetal anomaly. In normal pregnancies, abortions may be elected with the intention of ending the pregnancy, terminating the fetus, and/or avoiding the responsibilities of motherhood. The last intention is also achievable by continuing the pregnancy, giving birth, and then surrendering the newborn into the care of others. *Roe* seems to ignore the latter possibility in arguing that "the problem of bringing a child into a family already unable, psychologically and otherwise, to care for it" provides grounds for abortion.

Several supporters of a woman's right to abortion explicitly limit their support to an understanding of abortion as termination of pregnancy rather than termination of a fetus. In interpreting *Roe* with regard to survivors of legal "abortions," the states have assumed the same distinction. If termination of pregnancy occurs either spontaneously or electively after viability, a living survivor must be provided with the same medical care as is appropriate for any premature newborn. Even if the infant is nonviable, such terminations of pregnancy are technically considered live births rather than abortions. As already mentioned, if the fetus in utero is considered viable or possibly viable, the practitioner may choose a procedure that will insure fetal or newborn demise, or a procedure that is most conducive to survival. At that point, the moral and practical difference between termination of pregnancy and termination of a fetus is inescapable.

Disclosure of accurate information is as morally requisite here as in other treatment situations. Ordinarily, few people question the moral significance of full and accurate disclosure by caregivers presenting treatment options to competent, conscious patients. Free and informed consent is not possible without such disclosure. Nonetheless, communication is often influenced by the subjective biases of the communicator, and this is especially so in discussions of abortion. An important and obvious way of reducing bias is to use technically correct language rather than controversial terminology. For example, to refer to a pregnant woman as a mother is not technically correct unless she has already given birth; nor is the male whose sperm has fertilized a woman's ovum a father until the fertilized ovum produces a neonate. Neither embryos nor fetuses are yet babies, and should not therefore be characterized as such. Nor should fetuses be referred to as embryos, as in Luker's account, because the term "embryo" understates the reality of fetal development, providing valid grounds for criticism by "pro-life" advocates.

But disclosure is not simply a matter of using correct terminology; it also involves selection of the content to be disclosed. Efforts to require disclosure of the developmental status of the fetus and alternatives to abortion (adoption, for example) have been rebuffed by Supreme Court decisions following *Roe*. In June 1986, the majority opinion in *Thornburgh* upheld a ruling of the Pennsylvania Court of Appeals on the unconstitutionality of requiring that certain information be provided to women seeking abortion. The information included the name of the physician who would perform the abortion, the probable gestational age of the fetus, a description of the medical risks associated with the procedure and with carrying the fetus to term, and an offer of materials to review regarding "the probable anatomical and physiological characteristics of the unborn child at two-week gestational increments from fertilization to full term, including any relevant information on the possibility of the unborn child's survival."

In writing for the majority, Justice Blackmun argued that the above description of fetal characteristics was "overinclusive," that it is "not medical information that is always relevant to the woman's decision, and it may serve only to confuse and punish her anxiety, contrary to accepted medical practice." It is also possible that such information could lead to some women's changing their mind about abortion. Selig Neubardt and Harold Schulman observed that when second trimester abortion patients were informed that the procedure (saline or prostaglandin infusion) would induce labor and delivery of a formed fetus, one fourth declined the procedure.

In a dissenting opinion, Chief Justice Burger, who voted with the majority in *Roe*, expressed concerns about "abortion on demand" as a practice he believes the Court never supported. *Roe*, he claimed, was based on the State's interest in preserving and protecting the health of the pregnant woman. Burger found it astonishing that the Court would deny that the state could "require that a woman contemplating an abortion be provided with accurate medical information concerning the risks inherent in the medical procedure which she is about to undergo and the availability of alternatives if she elects not to run those risks." Ironically, his critique of the majority opinion is based on its failure to be sufficiently "pro-choice": denial of information pertinent to abortion decisions reduces the autonomy of pregnant women.

Pregnant women have rights at least equivalent to those of non-pregnant people. Presumably, this claim is uncontroversial because the personhood of pregnant women is generally accepted. The fact of their pregnancy, whether deliberately undertaken or not, does not diminish their personhood. Accordingly, pregnant women ought not to be subjected to coercive treatment that others might effectively refuse, such as blood transfusion, surgery, or even hospitalization. Even if treatment were imposed on an adult for the sake of minor children, further argument is needed to justify its imposition for the sake of fetuses. Minor children are uncontroversially persons, and fetuses are not.

With regard to induced abortion, a request for the procedure is not equivalent to refusal of treatment. Hence the request, while legally or morally legitimate, does not morally oblige a practitioner to perform the abortion. The pregnant woman's right to treatment, like the comparable right of nonpregnant persons, is contingent on the right of others to refuse to provide the treatment. To the extent that the pregnant woman's health or welfare is threatened by continuation of the pregnancy, her right to (the treatment of) abortion becomes stronger, and the right of others to refuse assistance becomes weaker.

Viability and sentience of fetuses are morally relevant to abortion decisions. Viability allows others to care for the fetus after an abortion has been performed. The situation seems comparable to the obligation of someone who finds an abandoned newborn. When others can and are willing to care for the fetus-that-may-be-aborted the distinction between the right to terminate a pregnancy and the right to terminate a fetus is reintroduced. Even in cases of serious genetic defect, viable fetuses may be adopted after abortion. This provides *prima facie* grounds for requiring a method of terminating pregnancy that maximizes the chance of fetal survival.

Regarding sentience, the obligation to avoid inflicting pain on others, even animals or criminals who may legally be killed, is surely applicable to fetuses also. While little data are available concerning the capacity of the fetus to experience pain, it seems clear that the sentient capacity of a late gestation fetus resembles that of a neonate, and that the earlier the point of development, the more diminished that capacity. Even the possibility of sentient capacity is morally relevant, and thus clearly has implications for decisions about techniques of abortion.

Legality and morality are related but not equivalent. This may be the most telling point of all regarding the continuation of the abortion controversy. Although many of those who oppose abortion recognize that *Roe* takes no stand on the morality of abortion, their efforts have apparently concentrated on overturning the law rather than emphasizing their moral position. Yet their advocacy of moral decision making about abortion entails the possibility that their position can and should be implemented regardless of whether the law is changed. A golden opportunity wrought by *Roe* has thus been missed, that of educating people more broadly about the fact that legality is not equivalent to morality, and about the morality of affirming life in all its forms and states. Clearly, the moral force of a "pro-life" movement is weakened by failure to support other life-affirming efforts, such as opposition to a nuclear arms race or capital punishment.

The moral force of either "pro-life" or "pro-choice" arguments is weakened by failure on either side to expand the moral options of women who are or may be pregnant. Preoccupation with the legal status of abortion seems to have compromised efforts in this regard, strengthening the erroneous tendency to define morality in terms of legality. Admittedly, if women are legally coerced to continue pregnancies, the autonomy necessary for moral decision making is thus reduced. But if *Roe* is substantially reaffirmed in *Webster*, the challenge to pro-choice advocates will remain what it has been all along: to insure that women's choices are not simply legal but morally informed and socially supported.

POSSIBLE CHANGES IN *ROE v. WADE*

As the preceding account suggests, I don't consider *Roe* a model ruling. I believe the Court should retain certain features, such as its emphasis on viability of the fetus, implying certain obligations on the part of others, as well as its affirmation that women's health or life provides adequate reason for terminating pregnancy even in its later stages. But specification of trimesters, and of twenty-four weeks' gestation, as points for determining whether to honor women's requests for abortion, should be abandoned because of their ambiguity and inadequacy in establishing viability.

Although the majority opinion in *Roe* was based primarily on the pregnant woman's right to privacy, Justice Stewart argued in his concurring opinion that liberty rather than privacy should be emphasized. I agree with Stewart that personal liberty provides a clearer and more convincing rationale for women's right to choose abortion. In keeping with that rationale, instead of stating that "the abortion decision and its effectuation must be left to the medical judgment of the pregnant woman's attending physician," the Court should affirm the pregnant woman as primary decision maker, limiting the physician's role to medical aspects of the decision. If and when RU 486 is available, physicians will not be necessary for performance of safe early abortion. Support for state proscription of "any abortion by a person who is not a physician" therefore needs to be deleted from *Roe*.

Clarifications should be introduced regarding the distinction between controversial meanings of personhood and a living (human) embryo or fetus, as well as the difference (and relation) between a decision about pregnancy and a decision to raise a child. In addition, a number of points not addressed in *Roe* need to be articulated. These include acknowledgment that the right to terminate pregnancy is not necessarily equivalent to the right to terminate a fetus, and that a right to abortion applies to the former but not to the latter if the two are separable (as in cases of possible viability); recognition of obligations to a sentient fetus to reduce or eliminate pain unless the woman's health is thereby compromised; and affirmation that informed consent requirements should be satisfied, including full and accurate disclosure of pertinent information concerning the procedure.

These recommendations reflect in part my own moral point of view, but they do not represent it in its entirety. Consideration of the complexity of abortion decisions, and possible areas of agreement between dissidents leads me to articulate the following as a summary of that position:

1. Abortion is rarely if ever virtuous, sometimes morally justified, and sometimes immoral.
2. Such claims are neither negated nor affirmed by *Roe v. Wade,* that is, by the legality of abortion.
3. Our society is one in which the circumstances that occasion abortion are often immoral, sometimes more immoral than abortion, and one in which people do not now agree about the morality of abortion, nor do they appear likely to agree in the future.
4. The immoral conditions that sometimes occasion abortion include poverty, lack of social and medical supports for pregnancy and parenthood, stereotypic views of sex roles and biological parenthood, and a eugenic mentality that welcomes only "premium babies." Clearly, greater societal effort is needed to rectify these conditions. In addition, the following practices would facilitate moral decisions about pregnancy:
   - broader education regarding the distinction between legality and morality, using pregnancy decisions as an example of but one area where the distinction is important;
   - broader education concerning responsibility for contraception, encouragement of positive social attitudes toward and expansion of practical possibilities for adoption, information regarding the developmental status of the human embryo/fetus, and the various methods of abortion and their effects on pregnant women and fetuses;
   - insistence that a pregnant woman's autonomy in decisions that affect her is as binding on others as is

the autonomy of nonpregnant persons in decisions affecting them;

■ broader regard for human life throughout the spectrum of development.

So long as social disagreement about the morality of abortion remains, the law should not preempt the right and responsibility of individuals to make their own moral decisions. However, if the law were to become more restrictive (for example, by excluding late or second trimester abortions for nonmedical reasons), it might still reflect the moral sentiment of most people. If overturning *Roe* led to illegalization of abortions in extreme circumstances such as pregnancy due to rape and incest, or pregnancies that are life-threatening for women or fetuses, it would clearly betray the moral sentiment of most people.

I don't pretend to have developed all of the above points adequately, but most if not all have been well-developed elsewhere. This account might serve as a springboard for further discussion among those who recognize not only that contradictory positions cannot both be true, but also that truth doesn't necessarily lie in the middle.

Suggestions for Discussion and Writing

1. What is the purpose of the author's questions in the first three paragraphs? How would you respond to the question: "Why has the debate [regarding abortion] raged on without abatement for so long?" Write an essay developing your response.

2. Mahowald says that "the rhetoric of abortion aims at different targets" and that both sides tend to choose simplified cases for rhetorical purposes. Could Selzer and Weissmann (this chapter) be accused of rhetorical shenanigans in this regard?

3. Early in her essay the author says that she cannot align herself with either "pro-choice" or "pro-life" activists because both groups betray "the enormous complexity of the issue." In your view, does her subsequent discussion justify her position? Is there a sense in which political struggles inevitably involve a simplification of the issues?

4. Explain Mahowald's statement that "different circumstances may influence the morality of the agent without altering the morality of the act." Does this principle apply to matters other than abortion?

5. In her discussion of abortion as a "bad thing," the author says that "it may of course be argued that the harm done to a fetus through abortion is always greater than that done to others by continuing an unwanted but healthy pregnancy." On the other

hand, she observes that "in some circumstances [abortion] entails less harm than alternatives." How might Kass (this chapter) respond to these statements?

6. Do you agree with the majority opinion written by Justice Blackmun (in the Thornburgh case) that a description of fetal characteristics is "overinclusive," that it is not relevant "medical information," and that it "may serve only to confuse and punish" pregnant women? Why might such information be confusing? Do you agree that "denial of information pertinent to abortion decisions reduces the autonomy of pregnant women"?

7. How might Selzer (this chapter) respond to the issues raised in Question 6 above?

8. Explain the author's distinction between legality and morality. Do you agree that the moral force of the arguments on both sides of the abortion debate "is weakened by failure . . . to expand the moral options of women who are or may be pregnant"? Write an essay in which you defend your views.

9. In arguing that liberty rather than privacy offers "a clearer and more convincing rationale for women's right to choose abortion," the author says that "the [Supreme] Court should affirm the pregnant woman as primary decision maker, limiting the physician's role to medical aspects of the decision." Do you agree? Would Kass agree that the physician's role can be thus limited?

☐ TO THE NOBSKA LIGHTHOUSE

Gerald Weissmann
(b. 1930)

For a biographical sketch of the author, see page 108.
In "To the Nobska Lighthouse," taken from *The Doctor with Two Heads* (1990), Weissmann remembers his attempts to save Kate, a young woman dying of toxic shock after an illegal abortion. Placing the issue of abortion in the context of America's Puritan legacy, he argues that, though this legacy has had much to do with the tradition of learning and the advancement of medical science, it has also fostered an attitude toward women and a moralism reflected in current attempts to make abortion illegal.

The Nobska lighthouse stands guard over shoals at Woods Hole where the Atlantic runs between Vineyard Sound and Buzzards Bay. The bluff on which the lighthouse sits is the highest of that stretch of the coast and on fair days yields splendid views of upper

Cape Cod and its islands. The prospect is never fairer from Nobska point than on early mornings in October, when—in the words of Justice Oliver Wendell Holmes—"the wind blows from the west and the air is clear." Recently, such a morning found me running uphill to the Nobska lighthouse. A plangent sea was on my left, thickets of wild grape and bittersweet were on my right. In the distance across the sound, the highlands of Martha's Vineyard flashed pink in the dawn. Nearer by, the hillocks of Naushon Island flickered mauve and green. A few cirrus clouds were backlit on the eastern horizon, the sky above was clear. On the crest of the hill the westerly breeze rustled low conifers and floated a strike force of gulls. Breathless, I stopped at the top of the bluff, convinced that the shores of Arcadia could offer nothing so bracing as this New England sunrise.

The Nobska light station is placed on a tidy promontory seventy-six feet above sea level. Its lawns are closely mowed and its hedges tightly clipped, its buildings display the prudent ordinates of Yankee architecture. The horizontal axis is defined by the keeper's house: twin, gabled saltboxes joined into a single cottage. Modest vertical accents are provided by three chimneys, a steel radio antenna, and a signal tower from which small-craft warnings flutter on stormy days. The chief vertical axis is announced by the monumental shaft of the lighthouse, a tapered tower some forty feet high made of whitewashed steel-encased brick. The tower is topped by a black lacework cupola in which the light source is housed behind a ten-sided cage of window panes. A single 150-watt bulb refracted by a cunning Fresnel lens generates 7,000 candlepower and can be seen for more than ten miles.

With stars and stripes fluttering from a freestanding flagpole, with deep shadows cast by morning light under the cottage eaves, the scene was an Edward Hopper canvas brought to life. Other themes sprang to mind. I had read that the lens of the lighthouse had been ground in 1828 by New England craftsmen from designs by Augustin-Jean Fresnel (1788–1827). Fresnel was a Jansenist from the Vendée who in the post-Napoleonic restoration pursued his optical theories while on tours of duty with the civil service. He was convinced that light was a wave rather than a particle, as Newton had taught. The young Frenchman arrived at his equations in settings fit for making waves of light: the Lighthouse Commission and the *Corps des Ponts et Chausées* (Bridge and Road Corps). His more practical work resulted in the replacement of mirrors by lenses in lighthouses the world over. Fresnel's early death from tuberculosis ended a blossoming reputation not only in physics but also in moral philosophy; he had become a keen apologist for the puritanical doctrines of his sect. He might have been pleased to know, were he among the elect, that for more than a century and a half his lens had cast light over waters that the stern Pilgrims had mastered. He might also have subscribed to the closing sentiments of "Fair Harvard":

> Let not moss-covered error moor thee by its side,
> While the world on truth's current glides by;
> Be the herald of light and the bearer of love,
> 'Til the stock of the Puritans die.

Reasoning that I had been diverted from matters Arcadian to refrains academic by the anoxia of uphill running, I started downhill with relief. Arcadia had waited. Nobska beach, in the cove below the lighthouse, was at low tide. Its sands reflected the morning sun and the breeze played with tendrils of seaweed at the tidemark. By the roadway, bracken on the low dunes glowed in autumn paisley. The beach was empty, the only artifact visible an old Corvair parked some thirty yards away. The single object in motion was on the water: the first ferry to Vineyard Haven had rounded the point of Woods Hole harbor. It made a dashing sight, with its white hull, black smoke, and frothy wake against a turquoise sea. Exhilarated, I kept running along the short length of the beach back to the center of town.

I had almost left the Corvair behind me when I noticed a striking bumper sticker placed prominently on the flivver's rear. It showed the abortion rights symbol, a black coathanger on which the red international logo for "prohibited" had been superimposed. NEVER AGAIN was the legend, and NARAL (the National Abortion Rights Action League) was noted as the sponsor. The car was empty and bore no other identification except its Massachusetts plate. At that moment, I spied what must have been the owner of the car emerging from behind a bend of the cove. At that distance I could see she was a fit, middle-aged woman with short gray hair, dressed in khaki shorts and a blue denim work shirt. She was busy gathering seashells: stopping, stooping, starting, she looked like a busy shore bird. Suddenly she halted and, shielding her eyes, looked straight out at the sea and the passing ferry. Her trim form echoed the vertical of the lighthouse above; the sun caught her face and was reflected by the galvanized tin bucket she had put down beside her. Solitary against the beach, her Keds in the sand, she could have served, I thought, as a model for a low-keyed statue of Reason.

The woman in her Keds, the NARAL logo, the lighthouse—the Enlightenment?—spurred associations that turned the rest of my outing into a rumination on the days of the rusty coathanger. My mind was, literally, jogged back to Bellevue Hospital in 1959 and the era when abortion was illegal. Coathangers, rusty or not, were not the chief instruments of botched home abortions. The victims treated by my generation of house officers had been invaded by knitting needles, rat-tailed combs, and—sad to say—the metal probes used by plumbers. It is not true that only poor women bore the brunt of injury; fear of parents, fear of their partners, and fear of professional abortionists often brought daughters of the middle class to the emergency room. Rich and poor alike were at risk for the major complications of all that clumsy instrumentation: bleeding and sepsis, frequently both. For reasons not hard to imagine, the patients arrived most often at midnight and too often in shock.

Sometime after midnight on a warm Labor Day weekend thirty years ago, the Keds that I remember to this day were neatly stowed side by side under the bed of a young woman who lay febrile, breathless, and barely conscious in the emergency ward of Bellevue. One white sneaker was immaculate, the other was stained by two splotches of blood that had soaked into the canvas uppers and dried on the rubber of the instep. Most of what I recall of the larger scene was also in primary colors. The three doctors and two nurses at the bedside were in white, as were the curtains around the bed, the sheets, and the patient's gown. The blankets alone were gray, city issue, but the young woman had flushed, freckled cheeks and flame-red hair. Her lips were blue and her temperature was 104. Trying to rouse her, the nurse called her Kate; I have forgotten her last name. She was a nineteen-year-old nursing student from the school across the street and had been brought in after a fumbled attempt at self-abortion. I was the chief medical resident of Bellevue Hospital and all of ten years older than the patient. I ordered some epinephrine, diluted it, and injected a tenth of a cc in her skin.

"We're going to look for the Thomas lesion," I said, as I pointed to the pale forearm taped to a plank with white gauze. "If there is endotoxin on board, that little spot should be necrotic in a few hours." First white, then red, then black; color and then the absence of color.

The human details of the case are less clear in memory than the stark tableau of the emergency room. I seem to recall that Kate was a farm kid from Duchess County. She had missed a period, turned positive in a furtive rabbit test of the day, and tried to instrument herself with the help of a friend late on Saturday night. The procedure would have involved a hand mirror, some stolen local anesthetic, and a steel knitting needle sterilized over a candle. But it hadn't worked, all that happened was a cervical tear and diffuse bleeding, which the kids tried to stop with gauze. Shaken and afraid, Kate had gone to ground in the student nurse's dorm all day Sunday. By Sunday night she was again oozing large amounts of blood and had developed shaking chills. She was brought to the receiving area of Bellevue by her friend, who also provided all the details of Kate's history. By the time I saw her early on Labor Day morning, she should have been better. The gynecologists had typed, cross-matched, and transfused three pints of blood, performed a dilation-and-curettage, and sutured her cervical wounds to stop the bleeding. But complications arose. Her temperature climbed, her white cell and platelet counts dropped, bleeding started again from every needle and suture site. Suspecting that their patient was bleeding from disseminated intravascular coagulation due to gram-negative sepsis—a disorder of blood clotting caused by bacterial endotoxin—the surgeons paged the medical resident on call. He in turn knew that I was in the house, that I was working with bacterial endotoxin, and that I was up to date on gram-negative shock. I had been briefed by an expert, Lewis Thomas, our chief of service.

So there we were, like doctors before us and after, up to date but quite at sea, at the bedside of a young woman, searching in the only way known at the time for endotoxin in blood. We gave her more blood transfusions, intravenous broad-spectrum antibiotics (Aureomycin? Chloromycetin?), and prayed that her kidneys wouldn't shut down. I forget now what bug it was that grew out of her blood cultures the next afternoon, *Aerobacter* or *Pseudomonas*. I do remember that by then things could not have gotten worse. Her kidneys had failed, she never brought her oxygen up, she kept bleeding. We could not pull her out of shock and she died before we found out whether the Thomas lesion had turned positive.

I also remember meeting her parents the next day in the squalid waiting room of the old hospital. A postmortem examination by the Office of the Chief Medical Examiner, which was mandatory in such cases, had shown that she had died of septic shock with bilateral renal cortical necrosis and pulmonary edema with blood in the lungs. The parents appeared grief-stricken but not entirely surprised by the news that their daughter had died from a fumbled abortion. They were stern fundamentalists, American Gothics, and deep in their rustic hearts they seemed to have expected that sin would catch up with Kate, who was the "fastest" of their three daughters. She had broken their hearts when she had run away to the big city to become a nurse; the profession in those days was tainted by a touch of the profane in the minds of small-town folk. As we spoke of their daughter's death, they looked at me as coldly as if I myself had raped and killed her. In cool fury, directed at cities, hospitals, doctors, nurses, women—who knows what—the father permitted himself to say, "God punished her. She must have deserved it. She's better off this way." He took his wife's hand, asked the way to the mortuary, and left the building. Through the glass-paneled door I saw him stop, carefully fit a black felt hat to his pate, and proceed up East Twenty-sixth Street with his wife in tow.

Absorbed in those ancient recollections on my morning ramble I almost failed to notice that I had come abreast of another Woods Hole landmark, the seaside Church of the Messiah. Its new copper gutters shone in the glory of fall. Morning light also caught the salmon and gray of its cemetery stones; the green lawns had not yet been cleared of overnight leaves. I reckoned that poor Kate had been born a generation too soon on two counts: these days abortion is legal, and we know much more about the cause and treatment of endotoxin shock. Young women like Kate need not die. She would have been forty-nine by now; I imagined her standing under the Nobska light, her Keds in the sand, her Corvair parked down the road. More power to NARAL. But as I looked up at the New England steeple, it struck me that the Puritan fathers would have been as stern on abortion as Kate's father. I'm not sure how they would feel about endotoxin.

The meliorist path of our secular republic is not the road mapped out by the elders of Plymouth. The Yankee patriarchs found it easy in the name of their God to blame His victims and easier still if their names be women. Dr. Cotton Mather would have been pleased by President Bush's veto of a bill permitting the use of federal funds to pay for abortions of indigent women who have been the victims of rape or incest. Governor Bradford of Plymouth Colony might have gone a touch further. On September 8, 1642, some thirty miles north of the Church of the Messiah, a sixteen-year-old youth named Thomas Granger was convicted of unnatural sexual acts and executed by order of the magistrates of Plymouth. According to Governor Bradford's journal of the event, *Of Plymouth Plantation 1620–1647,* the lad had been

> detected of buggery, and indicted for the same, with a mare, a cow, two goats, five sheep, two calves and a turkey. . . . A very sad spectacle it was. For first the mare and then the cow and the rest of the lesser cattle were killed before his face, according to the law, Leviticus xx.15; and then he himself was executed. The cattle were all cast into a great and large pit that was digged for the purpose of them, and no use made of any part of them.

No mention is specifically made of the turkey, but Bradford tells us that the elders were worried that innocent sheep might be slaughtered. They forced young Granger not only to confess, but to identify his former playmates: "And whereas some of the sheep could not so well be known by his description of them, others with them were brought before him and he declared which they were and which were not."

The Pilgrims' attention to details of sexual conduct was coupled to a strict regard for biblical authority. Shortly before Granger's execution, Bradford asked three local divines to find legal and scriptural precedents for the death penalty in cases of sexual deviance. He asked several specific questions related to offenses of sex and received appropriate answers in which no graphic detail of plumbing was omitted. As one might expect from a future president of Harvard, Charles Chauncy's reply had more citations in Latin and English than the other two responses, and the most from the Old Testament. His answer was also the strongest in rhetoric, the freest of sentiment, and the sternest in tone.

The Answer of Mr. Charles Chauncy
An contactus et fricatio usque ad seminis effusionem
sine penetratione corporis sit sodimia morte plectenda?
Question: The question is, What sodomitical acts are to
be punished with death, and what very fact committed
(ipso facto) is worthy of death, or if the fact itself be not

capital, what circumstances concurring may make it capital? The same question may be asked of rape, incest, bestiality, unnatural sins, presumptuous sins. These be the words of the first question. The answer unto this I will Lay down (as God shall direct by His Word and Spirit) in these following conclusions.

Chauncy answered that the Mosaic laws are "immutable and perpetual" and grounded on the law of nature, indeed, that all the sins enumerated are punishable by death. Quoting extensively from Luther, Melanchthon, Calvin, and other fathers of the Reformation, he reassured the governor that

> Then we may reason . . . what grievous sin in the sight of God it is, by the instigation of burning lusts, set on fire of hell, to proceed to *contactum et fricationem ad emissionem seminis,* etc. and that *contra naturam,* or to attempt the gross acts of unnatural filthiness. Again, if that unnatural lusts of men with men, or woman with woman, or either with beasts be to be punished with death, then *a pari* natural lusts of men toward children under age are so to be punished.

These themes, and their canonic variation, were also sounded by the two other elders of the Church, Mr. Raynor and Mr. Partridge. The Old Testament called for the death penalty for "unnatural vices" or offenses to God, and the Puritan preachers found ample precedent in Mosaic law for divine retribution. But a closer reading of Charles Chauncy's reply to Governor Bradford yields a remarkable passage, which must contain the first—and most severe—American argument for the prohibition of abortion. The "pro-life" movement may be said to have begun in 1642; it was announced in concert with a call for death:

> In concluding punishments from the judicial law of Moses that is perpetual, we must often proceed by analogical proportion and interpretation, as *a paribus similibus, minore ad majus,* etc.; for there will still fall out some cases, in every commonwealth, which are not in so many words extant in Holy Writ, yet the substance of the matter in every kin (I conceive under correction) may be drawn and concluded out of the Scripture by good consequence of an equivalent nature. *As, for example, there is no express law against destroying conception in the womb by potions, yet by analogy with Exodus xxi.22, 23, we may reason that life is to be given for life* [italics mine].

Perhaps Chauncy's doctrine that life is to be given for life found its highest expression in the era of the rusty coathanger. Social historians have traced some of the prohibitions against abortion in the days before *Roe v. Wade* to the severe Mosaic laws of Plymouth Plantation. Puritan values and Catholic teaching made Massachusetts the last state in the union to permit doctors to prescribe birth control for married women (1966). The prohibition of unpopular private behavior has a long history in New England; not only sodomized cattle have been sacrificed in Massachusetts. The Puritans' preoccupation with sexual offenses, their obsession with anal coitus and seminal emissions, their fear of filthiness and the unnatural have set the darker themes of political and religious discourse in America for more than three centuries. H. L. Mencken defined Puritanism as "the haunting fear that someone, somewhere might be happy." A more dynamic interpretation of the excess attention paid to pudenda by the Pilgrims might explain why the life that was to be given for a life was invariably a woman's.

More agreeable aspects of the Puritan legacy came to mind as I loped the last mile home. My path took me to the back of Eel Pond, a natural marina around which the village is disposed. The last yachts of the season and assorted skiffs were berthed in the small harbor; its periphery was ablaze with autumn elm and maple. Cormorants ruffled the pond. Across the water, the sun shone on the colonial cupola of the Woods Hole Ocenographic Institute (WHOI). A flag snapped in the breeze above the pediments of the Marine Biological Laboratory; the early sun was reflected from windows of its library. The hum of machinery which carried softly from the labs reminded me that both of those scientific institutions are in their halcyon days. That summer, deep-water submersibles from WHOI had found the battleship *Bismarck* at the bottom of the Atlantic, while with the spiffiest of new microscopes scientists of the MBL had discovered the molecular motors of mitosis. The morning panorama of a maritime campus, neat and shipshape, already busy at work, was a hardedged illustration of Puritan values. Bradford and Winthrop would have approved: their land still housed heralds of light and bearers of love; truth's current had not passed Woods Hole by.

Governor Winthrop expressed a millenarian vision of the New Jerusalem when he spoke of the colony "as a City upon a Hill, the eyes of all people are upon us." The eyes of all people were no less important to the elders than the ears, for the Puritan leaders were preachers of the Word. But above all, they were men who worshipped ideas. "Every man makes his God," wrote Dr. Oliver Wendell Holmes to Harriet Beecher Stowe; "the South Sea Islander makes him out of wood, the Christian New Englander out of ideas." Holmes—son of a Cambridge minister, professor of anatomy at Harvard, and father of the Supreme Court justice—knew that he and his kind, the sons of the Puritans, could never "get the iron of Calvin out of our souls." The other sentiment he could not erase was a Calvinist sense of the elect, of belonging to an elite whose sainthood was made visible by the products of mind.

Historians of the Puritan revolution teach us that a ministry of educated men was required in order to replace the sacramental priesthood of the Roman Church. Education based on the Word of the Bible, and not the authority of a church, was expected to assure the victory of Puritan mind over papal matter. What was less expected was that biblical education, especially in the New World, would also lead to a democratic, individual response to society: all this and the rise of the middle class. Friedrich Engels, writing in 1892, pointed out that Calvin's creed was one fit for the most advanced bourgeoisie of the Puritans' time and that Calvin's constitution was "thoroughly democratic and republican." Almost a century later, the historian Michael Walzer has described the Puritan clergy in England and America as "educated (or self-educated) and aggressive men who wanted a voice in church government, who wanted a church, in effect open to talent. . . . Decisions would be made by prolonged discussion and natural criticism, and finally by a show of hands. Somber, undecorated clothing would suggest the supremacy of the mind. . . . The Puritan ministers provide perhaps the first example of 'advanced' intellectuals in a traditional society. . . . Its first manifestation was the evasion of traditional authority and routine."

A disproportionate number of these advanced intellectuals came to New England; between 1629 and 1640 some one hundred Cambridge men arrived in America. Charles Chauncy would have returned to a chair by the Cam, in England, had not the new Cambridge made him its master. One suspects that Chauncy, like other intellectuals since, may have evaded traditional authority and routine in order to impose an authority and routine of his own.

Traditional authority and routine do not rule Woods Hole today. From the Nobska lighthouse to Eel Pond, moss-covered error keeps no one at its side; the Yankee landscape and the learned institutions throbbing by its sea bear witness to the nobler side of the Puritan effort. From the Charles to the Housatonic, New England considers itself, perhaps rightly, as the intellectual arsenal of our democracy. The darker side of the Puritan endeavor—patriarchal, bigoted, severe—seems for the moment to be under wraps. Indeed, even the history of Puritan terror, the tradition of Chauncy, Cotton Mather, et al., are in good hands these days. Historian Gordon Wood, writing in *The New York Review of Books,* contends that the two leading scholars of Puritan life and letters, successors to such Puritan stock as Perry Miller and Samuel Eliot Morison, are Sacvan Bercovitch (Harvard) and Andrew Delbanco (Columbia). From Bercovitch and Delbanco one gathers that the Puritan terror was at least in part a response to the alienating experience of absolute power in the face of absolute wilderness. Those scholars remind us that the men who hanged witches in Salem also founded Harvard. Nowadays that university is neither bigoted nor severe. It remains a place for the worship of ideas, and in that sense its scholars are all sons of the Puritans.

A future historian may judge that our era, with its free-and-easy social arrangements, our uncommitted youth, casual sex, foul manners, terrifying streets, our infatuation with the gaudy, the rich, the drugged, the besotted, the violent—our culture of Lawrence Taylor, Mick Jagger, and Donald Trump—is not a happier place than the strict New England of 1642. Young men have died for sodomy in both societies, young women have been murdered then and now. If the traditions of Chauncy and company were distantly responsible for the death of Kate in the Bellevue of 1959, one might ask what religious or secular orthodoxy is responsible for deaths at Bellevue in 1990, for the victims of rape, murder, addiction, and AIDS?

Looking at the peaceful scenes of New England, I thought of the new Bellevue, where I work most of the year. An unshaven derelict named Steven Smith, discharged after "treatment" for violent behavior, "dressed like a doctor" in a scruffy scrub suit, put a stethoscope around his neck and roamed around the hospital at will. On Saturday night, January 7, 1989, he raped and murdered a young pathologist who was working late in her office. I was reminded at the time of the death of young Kate thirty years earlier: a life for a life. Kathryn Hinnant was also pregnant. For whose life did she pay? Steven Smith's? That same future historian might find that we are unknowing accomplices in Kathryn Hinnant's death as Charles Chauncy was in the execution of Thomas Granger. He might, if conservative, argue that Dr. Hinnant died for our liberal creed. He might be able to find evidence that our closed asylums, our practice of permitting the mad and violent to prowl the streets, had results more lethal than the Puritan terror.

Saturday nights in Bellevue Hospital were less hazardous for young doctors in my day. The chief resident, like all house officers, lived in the house staff dormitory; if lucky, one saw one's family on alternate evenings. This arrangement gave one a goodly amount of time in the hospital and made it possible not only to follow patients but also to do simple research. In the summer and fall of 1959 one of my projects was to study how epinephrine caused necrosis of skin in rabbits treated with endotoxin. Lewis Thomas had established a small animal room on the sixth floor of the old Bellevue, and there he put me to work measuring fever in rabbits—another bioassay for endotoxin. The procedure involved the frequent insertion of small thermosensitive probes into the rectums of bunnies; I am persuaded that my postdocs who do density gradient experiments with clean gloves have a better deal these days.

In the event, the epinephrine project was part of an effort to find out the mechanism of the Schwartzman phenomenon, the thorough exploration of which had made my mentor's scientific reputation. Here is his account of the *local* phenomenon in *The Youngest Science:*

> A small quantity of endotoxin is injected into the abdominal skin of a rabbit, not enough to make the animal sick, but just enough to cause mild, localized inflammation at the infected site, a pink area the size of a quarter. If nothing else is done the inflammation subsides and

vanishes after a day. But if you wait about eighteen
hours after the skin injection, and then inject a small
non-toxic dose of endotoxin into one of the rabbit's ear
veins, something fantastic happens: within the next two
hours, small, pinpoint areas of bleeding appear in the
prepared skin, and these enlarge and coalesce until the
whole area, the size of a silver dollar, is converted into
a solid mass of deep-blue hemorrhage and necrosis.

Kate, the nursing student, had died of the *generalized* Schwartzman
phenomenon, in which two appropriately timed injections of bacterial
endotoxin produce bilateral renal cortical necrosis, pulmonary edema,
and—too frequently—death. Whether local or generalized, the
Schwartzman phenomenon leads to the clumping of platelets and
especially neutrophils within the circulation. These tend to become
sequestered in the small capillaries of kidney and lung or to attach
to the sticky walls of blood vessels of the prepared skin site. By 1959
Thomas and coworkers knew that if white cells were removed from
the equation, the lesions did not develop. A few years before, he had
discovered that small amounts of adrenalin—epinephrine—which
alone had little effect, would cause hemorrhagic necrosis in the skin
of rabbits prepared with a previous injection of endotoxin. His
younger disciples, and soon the whole house staff of Bellevue, came
to call this lesion "the Thomas test" since we applied it to humans
to judge whether they had endotoxin in the circulation. Ironically, on
the night Kate was admitted I had returned to Bellevue to check on
the skin of some rabbits whose "Thomas lesion" had been abrogated
by endotoxin tolerance.

Nowadays, thanks to a generation of investigators, but especially
to Drs. Timothy Springer, Ramzi Cotran, Michael Gimbrone, and
Micahel Bevilacqua of the Harvard Medical School, we have a pretty
good notion of why exactly the Schwartzman phenomenon comes
about. Indeed, we know so many of the proteins and genes involved
that we are at the point of dotting the *i*s in ic3b and crossing the *t*s
of its TATA box (these are abbreviations for the relevant molecules).
When endotoxin is injected, the walls of blood vessels (endothelial
cells) are made receptive and sticky, because the endothelial cells
display specific adhesive molecules for white cells. In turn, white cells
display specific adhesive molecules which permit them to stick to
each other and to blood vessel walls (iC3b). In the process, molecules
such as interleukin 1, tumor necrosis factor, and complement split
products are let loose in the circulation. Those gymnastics of cell
regulation produce the effects that Lewis Thomas knew by 1959:

In the Schwartzman phenomenon, cell death is caused
by a shutting off of the blood supply to the target tissue.
After the second injection, the small veins and capillaries
in the prepared skin area become plugged by dense

masses of blood platelets and white cells, all stuck to each other and to the lining of the vessels; behind these clumped cells the blood clots, and the tissue dies of a sort of strangulation. Then the blood vessels suddenly dilate, the plugs move away into the larger veins just ahead, the walls of the necrotic capillaries burst, and the tissue is filled up, engorged by the hemorrhage.

We never did figure out how epinephrine worked. But when, at the end of my Woods Hole run, I thought about poor young Kate and her botched abortion that Labor Day weekend in 1959, I had an idea for an experiment. What if endotoxin were to increase the number of epinephrine receptors on the surface of endothelial cells, as it increases the number of adhesive molecules? What if that poor young woman died because the blood vessels of her kidneys closed in an overeager response to epinephrine? What if . . . ?

Looking at the gracious landscape of the Puritans, I realized that the pursuit of ideas in that university seventy miles to the north—by Bevilacqua, by Holmes, and yes, by Chauncy—had provided the facts I needed to ask those questions. Not only Fresnel lenses project light. I also realized, of course, that I was looking for a scientific solution to a social problem. The Kates of today need not die, because abortion is still legal, and as a doctor I strongly resent those movements that would permit return of the rusty coathanger. I have no idea when life begins, but I am sure when it ends. Absent a new Puritan terror, young women—children, indeed—will become pregnant. Absent recourse to safe abortion, some of those, and mainly the poor, will die in blood and pain. Liberal programs, when they go wrong, may disrupt social *order*. But the error that fundamentalists make is to value creed over social *justice*. Mosaic laws are laws for old men. In the slogans of the campaign against legal abortion, I hear echoes from the Plymouth of 1642: A life for a life is a call for revenge by elders on the bodies of young women.

In advocating the cause of keeping abortion legal and safe, I am drawn to the finer side of the Puritan temper. Dr. Oliver Wendell Holmes, after an apprenticeship in Paris, brought home not only a French microscope but also the enlightened Gallic habit of clinical investigation in urban hospitals. Discovering that young Boston mothers died of puerperal fever because doctors carried the infection from bed to bed, he defined the problem, described the obvious solution, and was roundly renounced by the traditionalists. In 1855 Holmes replied to his elders on behalf of the young women of Massachusetts much as I would speak on behalf of those who will surely die if *Roe v. Wade* is further diluted: "I am too much in earnest for either humility or vanity, but I do entreat those who hold the keys of life and death to listen to me also for this once. I ask no personal favor; but I beg to be heard in behalf of women whose lives are at stake, until some stronger voice shall plead for them."

Suggestions for Discussion and Writing

1. Is the essay appropriately titled? Analyze Weissmann's description of the light station. How does it contribute to his larger concerns in the essay?

2. The essay is a distillation of thoughts and memories associated with sights and places the author comes across during his morning run. What are the consequences of this narrative device for the development of his argument?

3. Like Selzer (this chapter), Weissmann is a physician writing about abortion. Compare their essays in terms of focus, style, tone, and so forth. Which is more personal? Which more "scientific"?

4. How does the author portray Kate? What specific language establishes this portrayal?

5. Write an essay in which you analyze Weissmann's attitude toward Puritanism and the Puritan legacy. How does that legacy play itself out in terms of Kate's story and its aftermath?

6. After considering an idea for an experiment to find out how epinephrine works, Weissmann realized that he "was looking for a scientific solution to a social problem." In what sense(s) can science provide solutions to social problems?

7. Do you agree with the author's statement that "the error that fundamentalists make [in their attitude toward abortion] is to value creed over social *justice*"? Write an essay developing your views.

8. In the final paragraph, Weissmann tells the story of Dr. Oliver Wendell Holmes's discovery of the transmission and prevention of puerperal fever, for which he was "roundly denounced by the traditionalists." Are science and tradition inevitably at odds? Write an essay developing your views.

 **ABORTION**

Richard Selzer
(b. 1928)

For a   biographical sketch of the author, see page 406.
In the following essay, taken from *Mortal Lessons* (1974), Selzer dramatizes his feelings about abortion in an emotionally charged essay that focuses on two specific events.

Horror, like bacteria, is everywhere. It blankets the earth, endlessly lapping to find that one unguarded entryway. As though
narcotized, we walk beneath, upon, through it. Carelessly we touch
the familiar infected linen, eat from the universal dish; we disdain
isolation. We are like the newborn that carry immunity from their
mother's wombs. Exteriorized, we are wrapped in impermeable membranes that cannot be seen. Then one day, the defense is gone. And
we awaken to horror.

In our city, garbage is collected early in the morning. Sometimes
the bang of the cans and the grind of the truck awaken us before our
time. We are resentful, mutter into our pillows, then go back to sleep.
On the morning of August 6, 1975, the people of 73rd Street near
Woodside Avenue do just that. When at last they rise from their beds,
dress, eat breakfast and leave their houses for work, they have
forgotten, if they had ever known, that the garbage truck had passed
earlier that morning. The event has slipped into unmemory, like a
dream.

They close their doors and descend to the pavement. It is mid-
summer. You measure the climate, decide how you feel in relation to
the heat and the humidity. You walk toward the bus stop. Others,
your neighbors, are waiting there. It is all so familiar. All at once you
step on something soft. You feel it with your foot. Even through your
shoe you have the sense of something unusual, something marked by
a special "give." It is a foreignness upon the pavement. Instinct pulls
your foot away in an awkward little movement. You look down, and
you see . . . a tiny naked body, its arms and legs flung apart, its head
thrown back, its mouth agape, its face serious. A bird, you think,
fallen from its nest. But there is no nest here on 73rd Street, no bird
so big. It is rubber, then. A model, a . . . joke. Yes, that's it, a joke.
And you bend to see. Because you must. And it is no joke. Such a
gray softness can be but one thing. It is a baby, and dead. You cover
your mouth, your eyes. You are fixed. Horror has found its chink and
crawled in, and you will never be the same as you were. Years later
you will step from a sidewalk to a lawn, and you will start at its
softness, and think of that upon which you have just trod.

Now you look about; another man has seen it too. "My God," he
whispers. Others come, people you have seen every day for years,
and you hear them speak with strangely altered voices. "Look," they
say, "it's a baby." There is a cry. "Here's another!" and "Another!"
and "Another!" And you follow with your gaze the index fingers of
your friends pointing from the huddle where you cluster. Yes, it is
true! There *are* more of these . . . little carcasses upon the street. And
for a moment you look up to see if all the unbaptized sinless are
falling from Limbo.

Now the street is filling with people. There are police. They know
what to do. They rope off the area, then stand guard over the
enclosed space. They are controlled, methodical, these young po-
licemen. Servants, they do not reveal themselves to their public
master; it would not be seemly. Yet I do see their pallor and the

sweat that breaks upon the face of one, the way another bites the lining of his cheek and holds it thus. Ambulance attendants scoop up the bodies. They scan the street; none must be overlooked. What they place upon the litter amounts to little more than a dozen pounds of human flesh. They raise the litter, and slide it home inside the ambulance, and they drive away. You and your neighbors stand about in the street which is become for you a battlefield from which the newly slain have at last been bagged and tagged and dragged away. *But what shrapnel is this? By what explosion flung, these fragments that sink into the brain and fester there?* Whatever smell there is in this place becomes for you the stench of death. The people of 73rd Street do not then speak to each other. It is too soon for outrage, too late for blindness. It is the time of unresisted horror.

Later, at the police station, the investigation is brisk, conclusive. It is the hospital director speaking: "... fetuses accidentally got mixed up with the hospital rubbish ... were picked up at approximately eight fifteen A.M. by a sanitation truck. Somehow, the plastic lab bag, labeled HAZARDOUS MATERIAL, fell off the back of the truck and broke open. No, it is not known how the fetuses got in the orange plastic bag labeled HAZARDOUS MATERIAL. It is a freak accident." The hospital director wants you to know that it is not an everyday occurrence. Once in a lifetime, he says. But you have seen it, and what are his words to you now?

He grows affable, familiar, tells you that, by mistake, the fetuses got mixed up with the other debris. (Yes, he says *other*; he says *debris*.) He has spent the entire day, he says, trying to figure out how it happened. He wants you to know that. Somehow it matters to him. He goes on:

Aborted fetuses that weigh one pound or less are incinerated. Those weighing over one pound are buried at a city cemetery. He says this. Now you see. It *is* orderly. It *is* sensible. The world is *not* mad. This is still a civilized society.

There is no more. You turn to leave. Outside on the street, men are talking things over, reassuring each other that the right thing is being done. But just this once, you know it isn't. You saw, and you know.

And you know, too, that the Street of the Dead Fetuses will be wherever you go. You are part of its history now, its legend. It has laid claim upon you so that you cannot entirely leave it—not ever.

I am a surgeon. I do not shrink from the particularities of sick flesh. Escaping blood, all the outpourings of disease—phlegm, pus, vomitus, even those occult meaty tumors that terrify—I see as blood, disease, phlegm, and so on. I touch them to destroy them. But I do not make symbols of them. I have seen, and I am used to seeing. Yet there are paths within the body that I have not taken, penetralia where I do not go. Nor is it lack of technique, limitation of knowledge that forbids me these ways.

*   *   *

It is the western wing of the fourth floor of a great university hospital. An abortion is about to take place. I am present because I asked to be present. I wanted to see what I had never seen.

The patient is Jamaican. She lies on the table submissively, and now and then she smiles at one of the nurses as though acknowledging a secret.

A nurse draws down the sheet, lays bare the abdomen. The belly mounds gently in the twenty-fourth week of pregnancy. The chief surgeon paints it with a sponge soaked in red antiseptic. He does this three times, each time a fresh sponge. He covers the area with a sterile sheet, an aperture in its center. He is a kindly man who teaches as he works, who pauses to reassure the woman.

He begins.

A little pinprick, he says to the woman.

He inserts the point of a tiny needle at the midline of the lower portion of her abdomen, on the downslope. He infiltrates local anesthetic into the skin, where it forms a small white bubble.

The woman grimaces.

That is all you will feel, the doctor says. Except for a little pressure. But no more pain.

She smiles again. She seems to relax. She settles comfortably on the table. The worst is over.

The doctor selects a three-and-one-half-inch needle bearing a central stylet. He places the point at the site of the previous injection. He aims it straight up and down, perpendicular. Next he takes hold of her abdomen with his left hand, palming the womb, steadying it. He thrusts with his right hand. The needle sinks into the abdominal wall.

Oh, says the woman quietly.

But I guess it is not pain that she feels. It is more a recognition that the deed is being done.

Another thrust and he has speared the uterus.

We are in, he says.

He has felt the muscular wall of the organ gripping the shaft of his needle. A further slight pressure on the needle advances it a bit more. He takes his left hand from the woman's abdomen. He retracts the filament of the stylet from the barrel of the needle. A small geyser of pale yellow fluid erupts.

We are in the right place, says the doctor. Are you feeling any pain? he asks.

She smiles, shakes her head. She gazes at the ceiling.

In the room we are six: two physicians, two nurses, the patient, and me. The participants are busy, very attentive. I am not at all busy—but I am no less attentive. I want to see.

I see something! It is unexpected, utterly unexpected, like a disturbance in the earth, a tumultuous jarring. I see a movement—a small one. But I have seen it.

And then I see it again. And now I see that it is the hub of the needle in the woman's belly that has jerked. First to one side. Then to the other side. Once more it wobbles, is *tugged,* like a fishing line nibbled by a sunfish.

Again! And I *know!*

It is the *fetus* that worries thus. It is the fetus struggling against the needle. Struggling? How can that be? I think: *that cannot be.* I think: the fetus feels no pain, cannot feel fear, has no *motivation.* It is merely reflex.

I point to the needle.

It is a reflex, says the doctor.

By the end of the fifth month, the fetus weighs about one pound, is about twelve inches long. Hair is on the head. There are eyebrows, eyelashes. Pale pink nipples show on the chest. Nails are present, at the fingertips, at the toes.

At the beginning of the sixth month, the fetus can cry, can suck, can make a fist. He kicks, he punches. The mother can feel this, can *see* this. His eyelids, until now closed, can open. He may look up, down, sideways. His grip is very strong. He could support his weight by holding with one hand.

A reflex, the doctor says.

I hear him. But I saw something in that mass of cells *understand* that it must bob and butt. And I see it again! I have an impulse to shove to the table—it is just a step—seize that needle, pull it out.

We are not six, I think. We are *seven.*

Something strangles *there.* An effort, its effort, binds me to it.

I do not shove to the table. I take no little step. It would be . . . well, madness. Everyone here wants the needle where it is. Six do. No, *five* do.

I close my eyes. I see the inside of the uterus. It is bathed in ruby gloom. I see the creature curled upon itself. Its knees are flexed. Its head is bent upon its chest. It is in fluid and gently rocks to the rhythm of the distant heartbeat.

It resembles . . . a sleeping infant.

Its place is entered by something. It is sudden. A point coming. A needle!

A spike of *daylight* pierces the chamber. Now the light is extinguished. The needle comes closer in the pool. The point grazes the thigh, and I stir. Perhaps I wake from dozing. The light is there again. I twist and straighten. My arms and legs *push.* My hand finds the shaft—grabs! I *grab.* I bend the needle this way and that. The point probes, touches on my belly. My mouth opens. Could I cry out? All is a commotion and a churning. There is a presence in the pool. An activity! The pool colors, reddens, darkens.

I open my eyes to see the doctor feeding a small plastic tube through the barrel of the needle into the uterus. Drops of pink fluid overrun the rim and spill onto the sheet. He withdraws the needle from around the plastic tubing. Now only the little tube protrudes from the woman's body. A nurse hands the physician a syringe loaded with a colorless liquid. He attaches it to the end of the tubing and injects it.

Prostaglandin, he says.

Ah well, prostaglandin—a substance found normally in the body. When given in concentrated dosage, it throws the uterus into vigorous contraction. In eight to twelve hours, the woman will expel the fetus.

The doctor detaches the syringe but does not remove the tubing.

In case we must do it over, he says.

He takes away the sheet. He places gauze pads over the tubing. Over all this he applies adhesive tape.

I know. We cannot feed the great numbers. There is no more room. I know, I know. It is a woman's right to refuse the risk, to decline the pain of childbirth. And an unwanted child is a very great burden. An unwanted child is a burden to himself. I know.

And yet . . . there is the flick of that needle. I *saw* it. I saw . . . I *felt*—in that room, a pace away, life prodded, life fending off. I saw life avulsed—swept by flood, blackening—then *out.*

There, says the doctor. It's all over. It wasn't too bad, was it? he says to the woman.

She smiles. It is all over. Oh, yes.

And who would care to imagine that from a moist and dark commencement six months before there would ripen the cluster and globule, the sprout and pouch of man?

And who would care to imagine that trapped within the laked pearl and a dowry of yoke would lie the earliest stuff of dream and memory?

It is a persona carried here as well as a person, I think. I think it is a signed piece, engraved with a hieroglyph of human genes.

I did not think this until I saw. The flick. The fending off.

Later, in the corridor, the doctor explains that the law does not permit abortion beyond the twenty-fourth week. That is when the fetus may be viable, he says. We stand together for a moment, and he tells of an abortion in which the fetus *cried* after it was passed.

What did you do? I ask him.

There was nothing *to* do but let it live, he says. It did very well, he says. A case of mistaken dates.

Suggestions for Discussion and Writing

1. Describe as precisely as you can the purpose of the opening paragraph. What details are significant? What is the effect, for example, of saying that "we are like the newborn . . ."?

2. Selzer speaks of the morning of August 6, 1975, as a "time of unresisted horror." By what means does he intensify the horror? What part does his choice of tense play in the description?

3. What does the author mean when, speaking as a surgeon, he says that "there are paths within the body that I have not taken, penetralia where I do not go"? What "forbids [him] these ways"?

4. What explanations are given to account for the wobbling of the needle during the abortion? Who gives them? How do they add to the dramatic tension?

5. Selzer describes the appearance and abilities of a fetus at the end of the fifth and the beginning of the sixth months. What is the effect of that description? of its placement? Is his use of the personal pronoun significant?

6. How does Selzer use point of view to influence our response to the abortion?

7. Consider the last two sections of the essay (starting with "There, says the doctor. It's all over"). What attitudes toward abortion are posed in these sections? What is the effect of the author's question, "And who would care to imagine that trapped within the laked pearl and a dowry of yoke would lie the earliest stuff of dream and memory"? What is the force of the final exchange about the fetus that cried after it was passed?

8. Is Selzer fair in his treatment of abortion? Should he be? In what sense can this be considered a personal essay?

9. One critic has said of *Mortal Lessons* (the book from which "Abortion" is taken), "Dr. Selzer's vision and words are poetic." Could this be said specifically of "Abortion"? Write an essay developing your views.

10. Abortion has been the subject of a national debate as a social, political, and moral issue for some years now. Is Selzer's essay a helpful contribution to that debate? Write an essay developing your views.

CHAPTER 11
Science and the Environment

THREATS TO BIODIVERSITY

Edward O. Wilson
(b. 1929)

Educated at the University of Alabama and Harvard University, Edward Wilson teaches biology and zoology at Harvard and is Curator of Entomology at the Museum of Comparative Zoology. Wilson has received many awards during his career, including the Distinguished Service award from the American Institute of Biological Sciences and the National Medal of Science. In 1979 he was awarded the Pulitzer Prize in general nonfiction for his book *On Human Nature* (1978). His other books include *Sociobiology: The New Synthesis* (1975) and *Biophilia: The Human Bond to Other Species* (1984).

One of America's leading experts on the insect world, Wilson is most widely known as a spokesman for sociobiology, a controversial scientific discipline whose central concept is that all behavior, including human behavior, is genetically based. According to this theory, even our most apparently altruistic actions (such as helping the poor) are essentially selfish because they are ultimately dictated by our need to survive. In his more recent work he has emphasized man's natural attraction to other living things and has used this idea to promote conservation.

In the following essay, published in 1989, he argues that the destruction of habitats is driving thousands of species to extinction each year, a process that can threaten a country's potential material wealth as well as its evolutionary heritage.

T he human species came into being at the time of greatest biological diversity in the history of the earth. Today as human populations expand and alter the natural environment, they are reducing biological diversity to its lowest level since the end of the Mesozoic era, 65 million years ago. The ultimate consequences of this biological collision are beyond calculation and certain to be harmful. That, in essence, is the biodiversity crisis.

In one sense the loss of diversity is the most important process of environmental change. I say this because it is the only process that is wholly irreversible. Its consequences are also the least predictable, because the value of the earth's biota (the fauna and flora collectively) remains largely unstudied and unappreciated. Every country can be said to have three forms of wealth: material, cultural and biological. The first two we understand very well, because they are the substance of our everyday lives. Biological wealth is taken much less seriously. This is a serious strategic error, one that will be increasingly regretted as time passes. The biota is on the one hand part of a country's heritage, the product of millions of years of evolution centered on that place and hence as much a reason for national concern as the particularities of language and culture. On the other hand, it is a potential source for immense untapped material wealth in the form of food, medicine and other commercially important substances.

It is a remarkable fact, given the interdependence of human beings and the other species that inhabit the planet, that the task of studying biodiversity is still in an early stage. Although systematics is one of the two oldest formal disciplines of biology (the other is anatomy), we do not even know to the nearest order of magnitude the number of species of organisms on the earth. With the help of other specialists, I have estimated the number of species that have been formally described (given a Latinized scientific name) to be about 1.4 million. Even conservative guesses place the actual number of species at four million or greater, more than twice the number described to date.

Terry L. Erwin of the Smithsonian's National Museum of Natural History believes the number of species to be even greater. With the help of co-workers, he applied an insecticidal fog to the forest canopy localities in Brazil and Peru in order to obtain an estimate of the total number of insect and other arthropod species in this rich but still relatively unexplored habitat. By extrapolating his findings to moist tropical forests around the world and by including a rough estimate of the number of ground-dwelling species in his calculations, Erwin arrived at a global total of 30 million species. Even if this number proves to be a considerable overestimate, the amount of biodiversity in the world is certain to be projected sharply upward in other, compensatory ways.

Groups such as the mites and fungi, for example, are extremely rich and also very underexplored, and habitats such as the floors of the deep sea are thought to harbor hundreds of thousands of species, most of which remain undescribed. Even the number of bacterial species on the earth is expected to be many times greater than the 3,000 that have been characterized to date. To take one example, an entirely new flora of bacteria has recently been discovered living at depths of 350 meters or more beneath the ground near Hilton Head, South Carolina. Even new species of birds continue to turn up at an average rate of two per year.

Systematists are in wide agreement that whatever the absolute numbers, more than half of the species on the earth live in moist tropical forests, popularly referred to as rain forests. Occupying only 6 percent of the land surface, these ecosystems are found in warm areas where the rainfall is 200 centimeters or more per year, which allows broad-leaved evergreen trees to flourish. The trees typically sort into three or more horizontal layers, the canopy of the tallest being 30 meters (about 100 feet) or more from the ground. Together the tree crowns of the several layers admit little sunlight to the forest floor, inhibiting the development of undergrowth and leaving large spaces through which it is relatively easy to walk.

The belief that a majority of the planet's species live in tropical rain-forest habitats is not based on an exact and comprehensive census but on the fact that the two overwhelmingly species-rich groups, the arthropods (especially insects) and the flowering plants, are concentrated there. Other extremely species-rich environments exist, including the coral reefs and abyssal plains of the oceans and the heathlands of South Africa and southwestern Australia, but these appear to be outranked substantially by the rain forests.

Every tropical biologist has stories of the prodigious variety in this one habitat type. From a single leguminous tree in Peru, I once retrieved 43 ant species belonging to 26 genera, approximately equal to the ant diversity of all of the British Isles. In 10 selected one-hectare plots in Kalimantan in Indonesia, Peter S. Ashton of Harvard University found more than 700 tree species native to all North America. The current world record at this writing (certain to be broken) was established in 1988 by Alwyn H. Gentry of the Missouri Botanical Garden, who identified approximately 300 tree species in each of two one-hectare plots near Iquitos, Peru.

Why has life multiplied so prodigiously in a few limited places such as tropical forests and coral reefs? It was once widely believed that when large numbers of species coexist, their life cycles and food webs lock together in a way that makes the ecosystem more robust. This diversity–stability hypothesis has given way during the past 20 years to a reverse cause-and-effect scenario that might be called the stability–diversity hypothesis: fragile superstructures of species build up when the environment remains stable enough to support their evolution during long periods of time. Biologists now know that biotas, like houses of cards, can be brought tumbling down by relatively small perturbations in the physical environment. They are not robust at all.

The history of global diversity is reflected in the standing diversity of marine animals, the group best represented in the fossil record. The trajectory can be summarized as follows: after the initial "experimental" flowering of multicellular animals there was a swift rise in species number in early Paleozoic times (some 600 million years ago), then plateaulike stagnation for the remaining 200 million years of the Paleozoic era and finally a slow but steady climb through the Mesozoic and Cenozoic eras to diversity's present all-time high.

The overall impression from examining these and comparable sets of data for other groups of organisms is that biological diversity was hard won and a long time in coming. Furthermore, the procession of life was set back by five massive extinction episodes during the Ordovician, Devonian, Permian, Triassic and Cretaceous periods. The last of these is by far the most famous, because it ended the age of dinosaurs, conferred hegemony on the mammals and ultimately, for better or worse, made possible the origin of our own species. But the Cretaceous crisis was minor compared with the great Permian crash some 240 million years ago, which extinguished between 77 and 96 percent of all marine animal species. As David M. Raup of the University of Chicago has observed, "If these estimates are even reasonably accurate, global biology (for higher organisms, at least) had an extremely close call." It took five million years, well into Mesozoic times, for species diversity to begin a significant recovery.

What lessons can be drawn from these extinction episodes of the past? It is clear that recovery, given sufficient time, is sometimes possible. It is also true that in some cases new species can be created rapidly. A large minority of flowering-plant species have originated in a single generation by polyploidy—a multiplication of chromosome sets, either within a single individual or following the hybridization of two previously distinct species. Even geographic speciation, in which populations diverge genetically after being separated by a barrier such as a strait or desert, can in extreme cases lead to the evolution of new species in as few as from 10 to 100 generations. Hence, it might be argued that when a mass extinction occurs the deficit can be made up in a relatively short time. But under such circumstances pure *numbers* of species mean little. What matters more, in terms of the spread of genetic codes and the multiple ways of life they prescribe, is diversity at the higher taxonomic levels: the number of genera, families and so on.

A species is most interesting when its traits are sufficiently unique to warrant its placement in a distinct genus or even a higher-level taxon, such as a family. A concrete example helps to illustrate my point. In western China a new species of muntjac deer was recently discovered, which appears to differ from the typical muntjac of Asia only in chromosome number and in a few relatively minor anatomical traits. Human beings intuitively value this slightly differentiated species, of course, but not nearly so much as they value the giant panda, which is so distinctive as to be placed in its own genus (*Ailuropoda*) and family (Ailuropodidae).

Within the past 10,000 years biological diversity has entered a wholly new era in the turbulent history of life on the earth. Human activity has had a devastating effect on species diversity, and the rate of human-induced extinctions is accelerating. The heaviest pressure has hitherto been exerted on islands, lakes and other isolated and strongly circumscribed environments. Fully one half of the bird species of Polynesia have been eliminated through hunting and the destruction of native forests. In the 1800's most of the unique flora of trees and shrubs on St. Helena, a tiny island in the South Atlantic, was lost forever when the island was completely deforested. Hundreds of fish species that are endemic to Lake Victoria, formerly of great commercial value as food and aquarium fish, are now threatened with extinction as the result of the careless introduction of one species of fish, the Nile perch. The list of such biogeographic disasters is extensive.

Serious as the episodes of pinpoint destruction are, they are minor compared with the species hecatomb caused by the clearing and burning of tropical rain forests. Already the forest has been reduced to approximately 55 percent of its original cover (as inferred from soil and climate profiles of the land surface), and it is being further reduced at a rate in excess of 100,000 square kilometers a year. This amount is 1 percent of the total cover, or more than the area of Switzerland and the Netherlands combined.

What is the effect of such habitat reduction on species diversity? In archipelago systems such as the West Indies and Polynesia, the number of species found on an individual island corresponds roughly to the island's area: the number of species usually increases with the size of the island, by somewhere between the fifth and the third root of the area. Many fall close to the central value of the fourth root. The same relation holds for "habitat islands," such as patches of forest surrounded by a sea of grassland. As a rough rule of thumb, a tenfold increase in area results in a doubling of the number of species. Put the other way, if the island area is diminished tenfold, the number of species will be cut in half.

The theory of island biogeography, which has been substantiated at least in broad outline by experimental alterations of island biotas and other field studies, holds that species number usually fluctuates around an equilibrium. The number remains more or less constant over time because the rate of immigration of new species to the island balances the extinction rate of species already there, and so diversity remains fairly constant. The relation between the theory of island biogeography and global diversity is an important one: if the area of a particular habitat, such as a patch of rain forest, is reduced by a given amount, the number of species living in it will subside to a new, lower equilibrium. The rich forest along the Atlantic coast of Brazil, for example, has been cleared to less than 1 percent of its original cover; even in the unlikely event that no more trees are cut, the forest biota can be expected to decline by perhaps 75 percent, or to one quarter of its original number of species.

I have conservatively estimated that on a worldwide basis the ultimate loss attributable to rain-forest clearing alone (at the present 1 percent rate) is from .2 to .3 percent of all species in the forests per year. Taking a very conservative figure of two million species confined to the forests, the global loss that results from deforestation could be as much as from 4,000 to 6,000 species a year. That in turn is on the order of 10,000 times greater than the naturally occurring background extinction rate that existed prior to the appearance of human beings.

Although the impact of habitat destruction is most severely felt in tropical rain forests, where species diversity is so high, it is also felt in other regions of the planet, particularly where extensive forest clearing is taking place. In the U.S. alone, some 60,000 acres of ancient forests are being cut per year, mostly for lumber that is then exported to Japan and other countries in the Pacific rim. Most severely affected are the national forests of the Pacific Northwest, from which some 5.5 billion board-feet of timber were harvested in 1987, and Alaska's Tongass National Forest, where as much as 50 percent of the most productive forestland has been logged since 1950. Although reforestation in these areas is possible, the process of regrowth may last 100 years or more.

How long does it take, once a habitat is reduced or destroyed, for the species that live in it to actually become extinct? The rate of extinction depends on the size of the habitat patch left undisturbed and the group of organisms concerned. In one ingenious study, Jared M. Diamond of the University of California at Los Angeles and John W. Terborgh of Duke University counted the number of bird species on several continental-shelf islands, which until about 10,000 years ago had been part of the mainland but then became isolated when the sea level rose. By comparing the number of species per island with the number of species on the adjacent mainland, Diamond and Terborgh were able to estimate the number of species each island had lost and to correlate the rate of species loss with island size.

Their model has been reasonably well confirmed by empirical studies of local bird faunas, and the results are sobering: in patches of between one and 20 square kilometers, a common size for reserves and parks in the tropics and elsewhere, 20 percent or more of the species disappear within 50 years. Some of the birds vanish quickly. Others linger for a while as the "living dead." In regions where the natural habitat is highly fragmented, the rate of species loss is even greater.

These extinction rates are probably underestimates, because they are based on the assumption that the species are distributed more or less evenly throughout the forests being cut. But biological surveys indicate that large numbers of species are confined to very limited ranges; if the small fraction of the forest habitat occupied by a species is destroyed, the species is eliminated immediately. When a single ridge top in Peru was cleared recently, more than 90 plant species known only from that locality were lost forever.

Ecologists have begun to identify "hot spots" around the world— habitats that are rich in species and also in imminent danger of destruction. Norman Myers, an environmental consultant with wide experience in the tropics, has compiled a list of threatened rain-forest habitats from 10 places: the Chocó of western Colombia, the uplands of western Amazonia, the Atlantic coast of Brazil, Madagascar, the eastern Himalayas, the Philippines, Malaysia, northwestern Borneo, Queensland and New Caledonia. Other biologists have similarly classified certain temperate forest patches, heathlands, coral reefs, drainage systems and ancient lakes. One of the more surprising examples is Lake Baikal in Siberia, where large numbers of endemic crustaceans and other invertebrates are endangered by rising levels of pollution.

The world biota is trapped as though in a vise. On one side it is being swiftly reduced by deforestation. On the other it is threatened by climatic warming brought on by the greenhouse effect. Whereas habitat loss is most destructive to tropical biotas, climatic warming is expected to have a greater impact on the biotas of the cold temperate regions and polar regions. A poleward shift of climate at the rate of 100 kilometers or more per century, which is considered at least a possibility, would leave wildlife preserves and entire species ranges behind, and many kinds of plants and animals could not migrate fast enough to keep up.

The problem would be particularly acute for plants, which are relatively immobile and do not disperse as readily as animals. The Engelmann spruce, for example, has an estimated natural dispersal capacity of from one to 20 kilometers per century, so that massive new plantings would be required to sustain the size of the range it currently occupies. Margaret Davis and Catherine Zabinski of the University of Minnesota predict that in response to global warming four North American trees—yellow birch, sugar maple, beech and hemlock—will be displaced northward by from 500 to 1,000 kilometers. Hundreds of thousands of species are likely to be similarly displaced; how many will adapt to the changing climate, not having migrated, and how many will become extinct is, of course, unknown.

Virtually all ecologists, and I include myself among them, would argue that every species extinction diminishes humanity. Every microorganism, animal and plant contains on the order of from one million to 10 billion bits of information in its genetic code, hammered into existence by an astronomical number of mutations and episodes of natural selection over the course of thousands or millions of years of evolution. Biologists may eventually come to read the entire genetic codes of some individual strains of a few of the vanishing species, but I doubt that they can hope to measure, let alone replace, the natural species and the great array of genetic strains composing them. The power of evolution by natural selection may be too great even to conceive, let alone duplicate. Without diversity there can be no selection (either natural or artificial) for organisms adapted to a particular habitat that then undergoes change. Species diversity—the world's available gene pool—is one of our planet's most important and irreplaceable resources. No artificially selected genetic strain has, to my knowledge, ever outcompeted wild variants of the same species in the natural environment.

It would be naive to think that humanity need only wait while natural speciation refills the diversity void created by mass extinctions. Following the great Cretaceous extinction (the latest such episode), from five to 10 million years passed before diversity was restored to its original levels. As species are exterminated, largely as a result of habitat destruction, the capacity for natural genetic regeneration is greatly reduced. In Norman Myers's phrase, we are causing the death of birth.

Wild species in tropical forests and other natural habitats are among the most important resources available to humankind, and so far they are the least utilized. At present, less than one tenth of 1 percent of naturally occurring species are exploited by human beings, while the rest remain untested and fallow. In the course of history people have utilized about 7,000 plant species for food, but today they rely heavily on about 20 species, such as wheat, rye, millet and rice—plants for the most part that Neolithic man encountered haphazardly at the dawn of agriculture. Yet at least 75,000 plant species have edible parts, and at least some of them are demonstrably superior to crop species in prevalent use. For example, the winged bean, *Psophocarpus tetragonolobus*, which grows in New Guinea, has been called a one-species supermarket: the entire plant—roots, seeds, leaves, stems and flowers—is edible, and a coffeelike beverage can be made from its juice. It grows rapidly, reaching a height of 15 feet in a few weeks, and has a nutritional value equal to that of soybeans.

Wild plant and animal species also represent vast reservoirs of such potentially valuable products as fibers and petroleum substitutes. One example is the babassú palm, *Orbignya phalerata*, from the Amazon basin; a stand of 500 trees produces about 125 barrels of oil a year. Another striking example is the rosy periwinkle, *Catharanthus roseus*, an inconspicuous little plant that originated in Madagascar. It yields two alkaloids, vinblastine and vincristine, that are extremely effective against Hodgkin's disease and acute lymphocytic leukemia. The income from these two substances alone exceeds $100 million a year. Five other species of *Catharanthus* occur on Madagascar, none of which have been carefully studied. At this moment one of the five is close to extinction due to habitat destruction.

*   *   *

Biological diversity is eroding at a swift pace, and massive losses can be expected if present rates continue. Can steps be taken to slow the extinction process and eventually bring it to a halt? The answer is a guarded "yes." Both developed and developing (mostly tropical) countries need to expand their taxonomic inventories and reference libraries in order to map the world's species and identify hot spots for priority in conservation. At the same time, conservation must be closely coupled with economic development, especially in countries where poverty and high population densities threaten the last of the retreating wildlands. Biologists and economic planners now understand that merely setting aside reserves, without regard for the needs of the local population, is but a short-term solution to the biodiversity crisis.

Recent studies indicate that even with a limited knowledge of wild species and only a modest effort, more income can often be extracted from sustained harvesting of natural forest products than from clear-cutting for timber and agriculture. The irony of cutting down tropical forests in order to grow crops or graze cattle is that after two or three years the nutrient-poor topsoil can no longer support the agricultural activity for which it was cleared in the first place.

Thomas Eisner of Cornell University has suggested that in addition to the compilation of biological inventories, programs should be established to promote chemical prospecting around the world as part of the search for new products. The U.S. National Cancer Institute has begun to do just that: their natural products branch is currently screening some 10,000 substances a year for activity against cancer cells and the AIDS virus.

It has become equally clear that biological research must be tied to zoning and regional land-use planning designed not only to conserve and promote the use of wild species but also to make more efficient use of land previously converted to agriculture and mono-culture timber. More efficient land use includes choosing commercial species well suited to local climatic and soil conditions, planting mixtures of species with yields higher than those of monocultures and rotating crops on a regular basis. These methods relieve pressure on natural lands without reducing their overall productivity. No less important are social studies and educational programs that focus directly on the needs of people who live on the land.

I have enough faith in human nature to believe that when people are economically secure and aware of the value of biological wealth they will take the necessary measures to protect their environment. Out of that commitment will grow new knowledge and an enrichment of the human spirit beyond our present imagination.

Suggestions for Discussion and Writing

1. What is the function of the first two paragraphs? Point to specific passages to support your view.

2. What does the author mean when he says that the loss of biological diversity "is the only [environmental] process that is wholly irreversible"?

3. Explain the difference between the "diversity–stability" hypothesis and the "stability–diversity" hypothesis. What condition do they attempt to explain? Why do scientists now prefer the latter hypothesis?

4. Does the author use definitions effectively?

5. Good writing involves striking an appropriate balance between general statements and particular cases. Does Wilson strike the right balance?

6. The author names several "hot spots" around the world—"habitats that are rich in species and also in imminent danger of destruction." Investigate one of the "spots" and write a paper in which you discuss its contribution to the "biodiversity crisis."

7. Write an essay explaining the "vise" in which the world biota is trapped.

8. "Every species extinction diminishes humanity." What do you understand the author to mean here? Write an essay in which you support or challenge the statement.

9. What is the function of the final section of the essay?

☐ EARTH'S SHROUDED FUTURE

Eric J. Barron
(b. 1951)

A climatologist, Eric Barron received his Ph.D. in geophysics from the University of Miami in 1980. He has worked as a scientist at the National Center for Atmospheric Research and currently teaches at Pennsylvania State University, where he is also the director of the Earth System Science Center. Barron's research has focused on global change, specifically the development of numerical models of the climate system, and on climate change throughout the Earth's history.

In the following essay, published in 1989, Barron discusses the scientific debate over global warming, and some of the difficulties involved in the development of models than can predict global climatic change.

T he prophecy of global warming—a scorched planet—has the ring of apocalypse. By the middle of the next century, according to meteorologists around the world, a thick blanket of air pollution will have unfurled across the sky, further insulating the atmosphere and compounding its natural tendency to act as a greenhouse. Scientists suspect that man-made gases will raise the planet's temperature by a few degrees, triggering climatic change as severe as that which occurred during the last ice age, only this time the earth will resemble not a freezer but a furnace.

In forecasting what the future holds, many scientists point no further than the summer of 1988 in North America—three months of blistering drought and record heat. Throughout the Great Plains, crops withered and lakes evaporated, while, in urban areas, reservoirs dropped to precariously low levels. In the midst of the searing temperatures, a few climatologists—notably James Hansen, of NASA, who testified before Congress—flatly asserted that the weather was a signal that global warming is under way. Hansen had been convinced by the uncanny correspondence between the overall global patterns and what computer models had predicted: areas closer to the poles underwent greater increases in temperature than the tropics, whereas the hearts of continents became parched. This year, bolstering Hansen's case, scientists at the Climatic Research Unit, in Norwich, England, reported that 1988 was not the first year of the decade in which record warm temperatures occurred; in fact, 1980, 1981, 1983, 1986, and 1987 also ranked among the hottest of the century.

As often happens when scientific debate enters the public arena, the eye-catching headlines that Hansen's assertion generated were followed by more skeptical comments. An article in the August 18, 1988, issue of *The Wall Street Journal* quoted meteorologist Peter Leavitt, of the Weather Services Corporation, in Bedford, Massachusetts, who suggested that the prophets of climatic doom were motivated by the need for financial support. "Tying . . . theories to disasters is a matter of survival for these theorists," Leavitt said. Others dissented on purely scientific grounds, contending that, although the eighties saw unusually warm years, the meteorological past and present do not provide incontrovertible evidence that the elevated temperatures were due to a man-made amplification of the greenhouse effect. In this view, the decade's seemingly anomalous weather was not qualitatively different from previous climatic fluctuations—the heat wave of the thirties, for example, or the cooling trend of the forties. After studying the air and water dynamics of the tropical Pacific, Kevin E. Trenberth and Grant W. Branstator, of the National Center for Atmospheric Research, in Boulder, Colorado, and

Philip A. Arkin, of the National Oceanic and Atmospheric Administration, blamed the weather of 1988 on "natural variations" in circular patterns. Despite the criticism, Hansen stood by his original assertion: global warming had started.

The longer the debate wore on, the more it seemed to warrant Mark Twain's droll remark, "The researches of many commentators have already thrown much darkness on this subject, and it is probable that, if they continue, we shall soon know nothing at all about it." Without question, the disagreement inside the scientific community confused those outside it—government officials and policy makers, in particular. But the most regrettable outcome of the debate over the summer of 1988 was how it obscured the issue about which most climatologists agree: that, given man's growing impact on the atmosphere, global warming is a virtual certainty. Opinions vary only regarding when the climate will change, how much, and where, and how life on Earth will be affected.

The single greatest obstacle to predicting, in detail, the weather of the future is the complexity of the climate. Even the most sophisticated computer models fall far short of fully representing the elements—oceans, landmasses, vegetation, pollutants—that determine weather patterns at a particular time and place. What's more, it is difficult to distinguish, on the basis of the models alone, between man-made trends in global climate and manifestations of large-scale natural cycles, about which little is known. And neither the mathematical equations that underlie the models nor the available meteorological data can be used to project with certainty how global warming itself, once it sets in, will alter other aspects of the climate. Might some of the additional warmth be absorbed by the oceans? Might higher temperatures lead to greater cloud cover, which could act to cool the planet? Until such questions can be answered, we must accept a measure of uncertainty about the climate's future. It would be a mistake, however, to use this uncertainty as an excuse to avoid taking measures that would limit man's modification of the atmosphere.

The machine that drives Earth's weather is the sun. Depending upon changes in the tilt of the planet's axis and position during any one season, the sun's rays strike different parts of the globe at various angles; tropical regions tend to receive more direct light than the poles, which are hit so obliquely that massive glaciers have formed on the continents. Every day, as the planet spins, the sun's heat warms the air and water, generating wind and ocean currents. By constantly helping water evaporate, the sun also creates clouds, which shield the land from solar radiation.

Because of the sun's particular surface temperature (ten thousand eight hundred degrees Fahrenheit), it generates energy of relatively short wavelengths, mostly in the visible and ultraviolet segments of the electromagnetic spectrum, which easily pierce the layer of gases that constitutes Earth's atmosphere. On reaching the planet's surface, the energy is absorbed by rocks, soil, and water, which, as they cool, release it in the form of infrared radiation, or heat. But because this energy has a much longer wavelength than that of visible light, it is then absorbed by gases in the atmosphere, which re-emit the energy in all directions—much of it back toward the planet's surface. Thus, in the manner of a greenhouse, the atmosphere, by preventing heat from escaping into space, maintains Earth's thermal environment.

In the nineteenth century, scientists came to believe that Earth's distinctive heat-trapping ability depends on the composition of its atmosphere. Yet the atmosphere is three-quarters nitrogen and one-fifth oxygen, and neither gas absorbs much heat. Later, at the turn of the twentieth century, the Swedish chemist and Nobel laureate Svante Arrhenius investigated both the dynamics of heat absorption on Earth and the outpouring of energy from the sun and discovered that traces of two other gases, carbon dioxide and water vapor, could trap enough heat to maintain the planet's thermal environment. He understood that the secret of this atmospheric blanket lay in the nature of its molecular fabric, for atoms of different airborne compounds vibrate at different energy levels as they are bombarded by heat from the planet's surface. (The quantity of carbon dioxide accounts for the difference between the blazing temperature of Venus, which has a thick layer of the gas, and the frozen surface of Mars, which has almost none.) A handful of other gases—methane, chlorofluorocarbons, and nitrous oxide—also trap warmth efficiently and, thus, contribute to the greenhouse effect, even though they, like carbon dioxide, are present in the atmosphere in minuscule amounts.

Arrhenius was also among the first to recognize that human activities had begun to generate greenhouse gases in considerable quantities. The first major source of carbon dioxide was the coal furnace, the centerpiece of the Industrial Revolution. Today, factories, locomotives, trucks, automobiles, and electric generators—burning oil and gasoline—disgorge carbon dioxide at the rate of more than five billion tons a year. The citizens of the United States, the Soviet Union, and the rest of the industrialized world account for more than half the human output of carbon dioxide; less developed countries, such as China, also have begun to produce the compound in earnest. And in addition to the fumes emanating from cities, approximately a billion tons of carbon dioxide wafts into the atmosphere from the burning of tropical rain forests (wood, like coal and gas, is a rich source of carbon), which are being cleared at the rate of forty thousand square miles annually.

The scientific community did not become concerned about carbon dioxide pollution until it was confronted with real measurements of atmospheric levels of the gas. In 1958, Charles D. Keeling, a chemist at the Scripps Institution of Oceanography, in La Jolla, California, established a sampling station on the slope of a volcano on the pristine island of Hawaii, where data were unaffected by local sources of pollution. During the thirty years that he took readings, the concentration of carbon dioxide in the atmosphere climbed from three hundred and fifteen parts per million to three hundred and forty-eight.

Climatologists have used Keeling's data to extrapolate backward in time, estimating that the preindustrial level of the gas was only two hundred and eighty parts per million. That figure has been corroborated by studies of ice samples extracted from glaciers in Greenland and Antarctica, where ancient air bubbles, frozen under layers of snow for thousands of years, show exactly the same concentration. The numbers indicate that the level of carbon dioxide in the atmosphere has risen twenty-five percent during the past hundred years alone. Taking the entire progression of measurements into account, and assuming a conservative rate of industrial growth throughout the world, most atmospheric chemists predict that the quantity of carbon dioxide in the atmosphere will almost double by the middle of next century, reaching six hundred parts per million.

Carbon dioxide is not the only form of pollution that threatens to alter the planet's temperature budget. Just as ominous is the more recently documented buildup of methane, a gas that absorbs twenty times as much heat, per molecule, as carbon dioxide. Methane is produced naturally, as an effluvium of swamps and marshes, in which strains of aquatic bacteria generate the gas as they digest organic material. Bacteria in the stomachs of ruminants, such as cattle and sheep, also liberate methane—up to half a pound a day for each animal—during the metabolism of cellulose.

Lately, however, mankind has begun to rival nature's production, as Reinhold Rasmussen and M. A. K. Khalil, of the Institute of Atmospheric Sciences, in Beaverton, Oregon, discovered when they began to monitor methane a decade ago. Their studies suggest that the atmospheric level of the gas is rising at the rate of one percent a year. Evidence from ice samples suggests further that the level is three hundred percent higher than it was two centuries ago. Part of this accumulation may be traced to the cultivation, chiefly in eastern Asia and in India, of more than six hundred thousand square miles of rice paddies, where two crops a year often are grown in areas that previously supported one; besides pouring from the marshy land itself, methane is vented to the surface by the rice plants as part of the growing process. Raising and maintaining vast herds of cattle (farmers around the world now manage one and a half billion head) also have contributed to methane pollution. According to estimates by Ralph Cicerone, a chemist at the National Center for Atmospheric Research, the global production of methane may be as high as six hundred million tons a year, enough to double the atmospheric concentration of the gas during the next hundred years. And scientists have only begun to quantify how much methane might be released as the organic matter in arctic tundra thaws and decays after being exposed to the first wave of global warming.

As if carbon dioxide and methane were not enough to disturb Earth's thermal balance, man has also produced chlorofluorocarbons, a class of compounds widely used in plastics, industrial processes, and refrigerators and air conditioners. Each molecule of a CFC can absorb ten to twenty thousand times as much heat as a molecule of carbon dioxide, and the concentration of CFCs in the atmosphere is growing by as much as eleven percent a year. This surge, like the rising concentrations of carbon dioxide and methane, is not disputed by the scientists studying global warming. The question is, Exactly what effects will the greenhouse gases have?

Recent historical data on climatic change are not particularly helpful in this regard. Earth's climate system experiences a considerable amount of natural variability, which can easily be confused with change caused by man. Temperature, humidity, and every other facet of weather continually fluctuate as a consequence of seemingly negligible shifts in the orbit and tilt of the planet. Other fluctuations arise from geological changes: the accumulation of vast clouds of volcanic ash may obscure the sun; rising mountain ranges can interrupt prevailing winds; glaciers reflect a sunlight, cooling the planet. As the fossil record of microorganisms sensitive to temperature makes clear, such cycles can range in duration from thousands to millions of years. It has proved exceedingly tricky to distinguish the natural swings from those induced by man.

Even when it comes to assessing the extent of climatic fluctuation during the past hundred years, for which a wealth of weather data is available, scientists must accept a considerable amount of ambiguity, because these data are, for the most part, not precise enough to sense long-term climatic change. For the purposes of greenhouse research, in which a change of a few degrees over a century is regarded as evidence of a global trend, the accuracy of measurements is of utmost importance, but not all readings have been taken with scientific precision. Many of the daily weather measurements from around the globe have been collected by sailors on ships, with a view toward describing what caused today's cold snap or toward forecasting tomorrow's thunderstorm. Thus, it was not considered a problem if they failed to record temperatures exactly at noon or if old thermometers were replaced with new models that were not calibrated to preserve the continuity of measurements. And it took a long time to appreciate that, as cities grew more dense, and such heat-absorbing materials as concrete and steel proliferated, thermometer readings from urban locations were being artificially elevated.

As a consequence of the shortcomings of the historical data, which effectively prevent one from ascribing a specific degree of warming to the elevated levels of carbon dioxide in the atmosphere, scientists have tried instead to forecast the climate on the basis of first principles—on computer models, whose equations are derived from physical laws that govern the circulation of the ocean and the atmosphere. Unlike weather models, which rely on thousands of facts but are limited to anticipating conditions in a particular area for only a few days, climate models use a few facts about the conditions that control climate (the carbon dioxide level, say, or the solar angle) to make predictions regarding large regions for long periods. Driven by supercomputers, which perform hundreds of millions of computations every second, they can forecast global patterns for the next several decades.

Five climate models, including the one at the National Center for Atmospheric Research, have been used to project what will occur if, as expected, the carbon dioxide level in Earth's atmosphere doubles by the year 2050. According to all five, global temperatures will rise between four and ten degrees Fahrenheit. The warming trend probably will not visit all parts of the world with equal intensity; rather, the greatest change is expected to occur at high latitudes, where the increased heat will melt the upper layers of glaciers. Once these begin to thaw, ocean levels could rise slightly; which might be enough to dislodge the West Antarctic ice sheet. As that massive glacier thaws further, and ocean water expands (it becomes less dense at higher temperatures), sea levels might, in a matter of decades, surge by five yards or more. Major coastal cities—New York, Los Angeles, London, Venice, Shanghai—could eventually be flooded.

According to what the models tell us, the hydrologic cycle—the ceaseless evaporation and precipitation of water—may be especially sensitive to global warming. Rainfall and snowfall are expected to increase by seven to fifteen percent, and as the magnitude of precipitation shifts, so will the distribution. The greatest increases are likely to occur in the tropics—especially over the equatorial oceans—and to the poleward sides of present-day midlatitude rain belts. Canada and Siberia might experience unusually high levels of heat and moisture, while the American Midwest probably will become more arid. (Even climatologists who disagree with Hansen's views on the advent of global warming concede that the summer of 1988 was at least a dress rehearsal.)

Yet, in considering these harrowing scenarios, there is good reason for caution: the models themselves are imperfect. One problem is that the earth system is, on the whole, too complicated to be reduced to a group of equations, no matter how well conceived. Although every cloud, mountain range, factory, and passing gust of wind can affect the weather, most cannot be included in a single model, much less digested by a computer whose capabilities are already strained. Each of the two thousand or so sectors into which climatologists have partitioned the globe is about the size of Minnesota yet is represented by a small set of variables—temperature, humidity, atmospheric pressure, and the like. Thus, the models do not reflect real, local weather patterns.

Even if it were possible to incorporate the many aspects of today's climate that might affect weather in the years ahead, there still would be the difficulty of accounting for the little-understood feedback effects of climatic change itself—the ways in which individual facets of global warming are likely to modify the broader trend. Some feedback effects will accelerate the heating: if greenhouse gases play a greater role in the melting of the ice caps, for instance, and oceans rise, the amount of ice and snow, which are highly reflective, will decrease, resulting in the entire planet's becoming hotter than is forecast on the basis of accumulating greenhouse gases alone. On the other hand, because the seas absorb carbon dioxide (the gas is soluble in salt water, and algae, plankton, and other microorganisms use it during photosynthesis), they might dampen the rate of accumulation of the gas in the atmosphere. Deep ocean currents, which carry large amounts of heat (from sunlight), might be another factor in the forecast; by circulating throughout the globe, they could drastically influence climatic change from one region to the next.

An elevation in global temperature might also increase cloud cover—which already blankets sixty percent of the planet's surface— because more water evaporates in hot weather. But in the absence of detailed information about the type and extent of clouds, determining their role in the larger, mathematical framework of global warming has been controversial. Moreover, it has so far proved impossible to process simultaneously, in computer models, our understanding of the feedback effects associated with cloud cover (which forms and dissipates by the hour), global vegetation (whose nature and extent change over seasons and decades), and the oceans (in which transformations can take thousands of years).

Given the great tangle of data now available on Earth's weather, and the many unknowns about how global warming will proceed, climatologists can only do their best to simplify the climate system in such a way as to mimic, with some accuracy, real change. Naturally, they would like to be able to check how well their simulations work, but the only periods that offer a comparable shift in climate are ancient epochs, for which no complete records exist. One can incorporate into a model the conditions that presumably existed then and see whether the model simulates a realistic change in global temperatures. But reliable meteorological information from the past is limited, and only a few predictions can be verified.

Accompanying the uncertainty about global warming in scientific circles is a good measure of indecision in the world of politics— indecision fueled partly by concerns about the costs of controlling the production of greenhouse gases and partly by the scientific debate itself.

Any of the proposals to be presented at an international conference on global warming in Washington, D.C., this October—installing catalytic converters in automobiles, stopping the destruction of rain forests, curbing the release of CFCs, developing energy sources based on elements other than carbon—would certainly reduce the emission of greenhouse gases, but they would be expensive to implement and would require dramatic changes in the ways billions of people live and work. So it will be difficult, to say the least, to convince all countries of the wisdom of making such changes.

It is naïve to suppose that Third World countries, with their rapidly growing populations, would agree to reductions in carbon-based energy sources and methane-related food sources without receiving assurances that alternative sources will be made available. And developing countries feel that they risk political chaos if they retard expansion; debt-ridden Brazil has already bridled at suggestions that it cease clearing its forests, pointing out that England and all other industrial countries did the same thing during the early stages of their development. China, along with other countries that possess ample reserves of fossil fuels, is understandably reluctant to foreclose the possibility of ever tapping inexpensive sources of energy. Despite their comparative material advantages, the three largest producers of greenhouse gases—the United States, the Soviet Union, and western Europe—are hardly eager to stall their own economies. And some northern countries, such as Canada and the Soviet Union, may welcome a climatic change that could result, for them, in milder temperatures and greater rainfall.

Politicians in the United States and elsewhere have also justified their hesitation on the ground that scientists themselves seem divided about the advent of global warming. But, in doing so, they have missed the point. Few climatologists dispute that the billions of tons of carbon dioxide, methane, and CFCs pouring into the atmosphere every year will eventually warm the climate. By the time researchers can fill in the picture—when models and data are refined to the point at which we know exactly where and to what degree climate patterns will change—it may be too late to avoid global trauma, particularly with regard to water. Postponing any action could be the costliest decision of all. Just repairing the erosion of U.S. coastlines, in the aftermath of rising seas, has been estimated to cost tens of billions of dollars. Protecting or moving cities would be unimaginably expensive.

In delaying attempts to combat the intensification of the greenhouse effect, or to moderate its impact on human life, the government is taking a greater risk than is tolerated in other areas of public policy. We maintain fire stations not because we are certain that fires will occur but because there is a reasonable probability they will. Despite our inability to specify the extent to which a virus will spread if left unchecked, we vaccinate large segments of the population. And though we cannot predict when, or even if, the Soviet navy will attack the United States, we prepare for such a grim possibility by building and maintaining our own battleships. Why adopt a different approach to the greenhouse effect, which imperils not just buildings, people, and nations, but the entire planet?

Suggestions for Discussion and Writing

1. Is this essay well titled? In what sense(s) is "shrouded" an appropriate word?

2. In the opening paragraphs Barron discusses the scientific debate surrounding global warming. What are the elements of this

debate? What does the author gain rhetorically by presenting both sides of the debate at the outset? In what way has the outcome of the debate been regrettable?

3. In your own words, summarize the author's explanation of the process by which the atmosphere maintains Earth's thermal environment.

4. In a brief essay, define and explain the process of global warming.

5. How have scientists estimated the pre-industrial level of carbon dioxide in the atmosphere?

6. Does the author use paragraphs effectively? Point to several paragraphs (identifying their topic sentences) to support your view.

7. The essay is divided into four parts. Identify the thematic concern of each part and state it in a single sentence. Can the four sentences be easily linked to form a unified statement?

8. In noting the inadequacy of scientific models to help predict global warming trends, Barron says "the earth system is, on the whole, too complicated to be reduced to a group of equations, no matter how well conceived." Write an essay in which you explore this statement in light of one or more of the essays in Chapter 8.

9. Write an essay in which you discuss some of the factors—economic, political, social—that complicate the solution to the problem of global warming. You might want to consult outside sources.

SAND TRAP

Clive Agnew
(b. 1960)
Andrew Warren
(b. 1942)

A lecturer in geography at University College, London, Clive Agnew is an applied climatologist who has worked extensively in the drylands of sub-Saharan Africa, North Africa, and the Middle East. His primary interest is in environmental change, particularly drought and desertification. He is the author (with E. Anderson) of *Water Resources in the Arid Realm* (1992).

Andrew Warren is a geomorphologist with three decades of experience in the arid realm, working from Pakistan to sub-Saharan Africa. He is currently a senior lecturer in geography at University College, London, where he is head of the Arid Lands Research Group. Originally trained as a soil scientist, Warren has conducted research in both environmental conservation and aeolian processes. He has published a number of books on ecology and conservation, including *Conservation in Practice* (1974) and *Conservation in Perspective* (1983), both edited with F. B. Goldsmith. His most recent publication (with M. Khogali) is *Desertification and Drought in the Sudano-Sahelian Region, 1985–1992* (1992).

In the following essay, Agnew and Warren argue that the greatest threat to arid land is not encroaching desert but agriculture.

T he arable land of our planet, by some reputable accounts, will soon be buried under sand. Vast deserts are said to be advancing across millions of acres in Africa, Asia and Australia, despoiling farms and villages and leaving starvation and desolation in their wake. By some reckonings the desert edge will move into certain forests and fields as fast as six miles a year; the obliterated territory will be immense. According to one oft-cited report prepared by the United Nations 80,000 square miles of productive land—an area the size of Nebraska—is being reduced to wasteland every year. Another third of the earth's land surface, or more than seventeen million square miles, is now officially deemed at risk from the approaching deserts.

Typical of the dire predictions that herald the desertification of the world are two bulletins collected for the 1989 edition of the *State of the World Report*, an annual compendium of ecological catastrophes. Patricia A. Jacobberger, a geologist from the Smithsonian Institution in Washington, D.C., who has studied arid lands in Mali, notes that "on the Landsat maps, there is now—and there wasn't in 1976—a bright ring of soil around villages. Those areas are now 90 percent devoid of vegetation, the topsoil is gone, and the surface is disrupted and cracked." Sidy Gaye, a journalist familiar with Mauritania, has observed, "There were only 43 sandstorms in the whole country between 1960 and 1970. The number increased tenfold in the following decade, and in . . . 1983 alone a record 240 sandstorms darkened the nation's skies."

Most of the evidence cited for the growth of the deserts seems irrefutable. Local accounts, scientific monographs, aerial photographs and voluminous questionnaires all appear to suggest that deserts are on the march. To cite just one example, Harold E. Dregne, a soil scientist at Texas Tech University in Lubbock, working from a survey of deserts throughout the world, estimated that four-fifths of the world's rangeland and three-quarters of its cropland have been transformed into desert since agriculture began. Critics of such assessments are referred to maps summarizing data from satellites, which portray the devastation in stark lines that creep outward around the Sahara and other major deserts. The starvation of thousands of people, according to conventional wisdom, grimly corroborates this view: forced to flee the sands, millions migrate to barely inhabitable refugee camps that soon become as barren as the desert itself.

The early signs of invading dunes have not escaped the notice of politicians, who have tended to respond with proposals for heroic measures. Taking the personal approach, Senyi Kountche, late president of Niger, asked his countrymen to "join the fight against the advancing Sahara" and exploited the specter of encroaching deserts as a pretext for cracking down on merchants and civil servants. The governments of Algeria, Sudan and Somalia have planted grass seed and saplings on sand dunes in an effort to contain the onward-creeping Sahara. One plan under consideration calls for planting a green belt, or thin strip of trees, across the Sahel, a broad band of arid but vegetated terrain spanning more than 2,000 miles. The United Nations and other international organizations meanwhile have annually allocated at least $400 million to antidesertification efforts in Africa alone and have devised dozens of programs to study and combat the shifting sands. Like the greenhouse effect and the burning of tropical forests, the fight against desertification seems a matter that deserves the immediate attention and financial support of every nation in the world.

But the world's arid lands, while troubled, are not doomed. The facts needed to buttress the case for a desertified earth are few and dubious, and reliable geographic indications of a long-term trend toward drier conditions and an expansion of arid lands do not exist. In sober scientific circles the reports of marching deserts now seem exaggerated, and the expensive remedies needed to address such a problem appear inappropriate and even destructive. Although substantial difficulties are still posed by arid lands, few of them are related to the lack of rainfall or the advance of sand. Indeed, prodigious irrigation in many places is actually hastening the deterioration of the land. Fretting about deserts on the march will only distract scientists and citizens from far more immediate threats to the land that have nothing to do with shifting dunes. And governments ought to abandon the convenient mythology that nature's deserts are moving inexorably toward man and begin to consider the possibility that civilization is responsible for a more ominous kind of terrestrial desolation.

Because geographers agree that arid lands cover a third of the earth's land, it is amusing to learn that official predictions expect deserts to invade an area of the same size. Such regions are already dry, and they are likely to remain so. But defining what portion of the arid terrain is "desert" and what is not has vexed every geographer and climatologist who has studied arid terrain. The lack of a definition is much more than an academic concern: it has bollixed all efforts to gauge the extent of deserts worldwide.

In seeking some consensus about what makes a desert, geographers and climatologists have considered and rejected several obvious generalizations. One common standard is that a desert gets no more than four inches of rain annually. But any such index is arbitrary and tells little about the utility of the land: some areas receiving four inches of rainfall annually can be relatively lush, whereas others are wasted, depending on latitude, altitude, prevailing winds and human pressures on the land. Nor are deserts necessarily vast regions of undulating dunes: only 20 percent of all deserts, properly speaking, fit that description, and just 25 percent of the Sahara is covered with sand. More common are wide, barren expanses of flat rock, gravel, clay or some mixture of all three. And deserts may or may not be hot: the Arctic and the Antarctic, for example, get very low levels of precipitation each year, and the South Pole may be the driest spot on earth. Finally, deserts are generally not devoid of plants: most geographers would consider a region to be a desert even if vegetation covers as much as 35 percent of the land. When the coverage is less than that, the topsoil itself begins to get swept away by wind and even by the infrequent rain. Without topsoil all land becomes barren and incapable of supporting plant life. In contrast, many arid or semiarid regions are covered with sparse but hardy vegetation that renders them reasonably stable.

In the absence of a clear, scientific consensus about what constitutes a desert, the popular understanding has focused instead on drought. As it happens, droughts and deserts have been associated with each other so routinely that many people assume that droughts propel the march of deserts. Actually there is no clear relation between the two. Given the scant and variable precipitation of the arid lands, droughts are inevitable from time to time and must be expected. Slight advances of a desert brought on by drought are invariably pushed back by later periods of rain, when grasslands regain whatever territory was lost. Although long-term climatic patterns are clear from the geological record, the short-term climatic cycles of more interest to farmers have proved difficult to identify. Since the climatological data are poor, and since there is no clear evidence from computer models that drought causes desertification, drought ought to be treated as conceptually independent of longer-term land degradation.

Charged with describing a process that specialists cannot define unequivocally and that the public does not fully understand, U.N. officials have chosen to adopt their own definition of desertification. To the layman the term may suggest the sequence of changes whereby arid land becomes barren. But the official definition is a model of ambiguity: ''the diminution or destruction of the biological potential of the land [that] can lead ultimately to desert-like conditions." It turns out that this definition is the shifting foundation on which the international response of the past ten years has been built. The lack of any common definition of desert terrain has enabled experts to evade the simple fact that, by any definition, the so-called desert lands are not advancing.

Judging from all the evidence, the U.N. definition of desertification is so broad that virtually any change in the climate or vegetation of arid lands can be considered a calamity in the making. This problem was clear as long ago as 1975, when the ecologist Hugh Lamprey, now of the World Wildlife Fund and one of the first scientists to entangle himself in the vagaries of defining the process, reported his findings on a survey done in Africa. Lamprey compared data on a seventeen-year-old map of western Sudan with the results of his own reconnaissance of the same area from a small plane. His discovery was dramatic and alarming: the edge of the desert had moved more than fifty-five miles since the map was drawn.

Subsequent surveillance from the air has shown no such advance. Lamprey apparently failed to distinguish between temporary damage from an ongoing drought in 1975 and the longer-term devastation that could be expected from "advancing" sand. Moreover, as other geographers have noted, his work was based on climatic data, from which the vegetation had been inferred. The map itself was an extrapolation from readings made at a few weather stations and therefore could only approximate where the desert began. Yet according to the U.N. definition, what Lamprey reported was, strictly speaking, a form of desertification, even though it turned out to be irrelevant to any process of lasting and severe land degradation. Other geographers have since found fleeting damage from droughts in western Sudan, although they report that the boundary between the vegetated arid land and the desert is in flux. But there is no indication that barren wasteland as a whole is spreading.

Other reports of desertification have been based on written surveys, and they have had equally frustrating problems with terminology. In 1977 and 1982, for example, the United Nations distributed a questionnaire to determine whether deserts were spreading; most governments reported they were. But those years were dry, and the survey lacked a precise standard for estimating the extent of desert growth beyond what would be expected under normal drought conditions. Six years ago the agronomist Lance E. Woods of the Department of Primary Industries and Energy in Canberra encountered similar problems of shifting definitions in Australia. There, as in the U.N. surveys of Africa, estimates of damage were based on surveys of local experts considered familiar with the landscape. Theoretically such observations should provide an accurate portrait of an area at any given time. But Woods discovered that the respondents to the survey, mostly local agricultural officials, had varying ideas about what constituted degraded lands. Without a consensus among the people completing the survey, its findings seem only marginally useful at best.

Even evidence that once seemed incontrovertible, which might have been expected to establish desertification once and for all, has turned out to be ambiguous. Electronic sensors aboard surveillance satellites can measure the light reflected from thousands of patches of desert, rain forest, permafrost and other kinds of terrain. Since every habitat reflects its own characteristic amount of light, called its reflectance, the readings should in principle be able to be compiled into reliable maps of the underlying terrain.

Under scrutiny, alas, the satellite images seem to measure nothing more than the effects of rainfall on a patch of land, not the extent to which that land resembles desert or prairie. In Mali, for example, geographers relying on satellite information might quickly notice a sharp boundary between the Sahel, which has a relatively high reflectance, and the darker savanna, which is a lush green expanse to the south and has a lower reflectance. One might assume that the savanna, since it is greener, would support more livestock. Yet the drier Sahelian pastures nurture grasses that are far more nutritious than the abundant vegetation just to the south. In short, the usually accepted correlations between satellite pictures and ground-based reality are often reversed.

As the experience in Mali suggests, attempts to map and analyze the deserts of the world according to the kinds of flora they support have proved problematic. Two years ago in central Sudan Eva Ahlcrona of the University of Lund in Sweden discovered that pastures were being invaded by weeds that cattle avoid. *Calatropis procera*, for instance, contains a white rubbery liquid that even parched and starving cows disdain. But the weeds caused no change in the reflectance, as recorded in satellite imagery, because the plants are large and leafy and reflect light comparable to that from more nutritious plants. Thus the estimate of total vegetation remained the same even as the habitat deteriorated. Similarly, the comparatively lush Negev desert region of Israel would at first seem more productive than the relatively desolate reaches of the Sinai just across the border in Egypt. (Bedouin herdsmen have been ousted from what is now Israeli territory, but nomads remain on the Egyptian lands.) Botanists now suspect, however, that sparse desert pastures such as the ones in the Sinai yield *more* grazing material when lightly grazed and infrequently watered. A small amount of grazing stimulates growth, partly because smaller and tougher plants are more likely to survive in arid conditions.

Geographers have found it equally troublesome to make long-range forecasts of the extent and duration of various kinds of terrestrial change. The effects of some climatic events, such as a drought or deluge, may last a season; but long-term shifts, such as the destruction of a layer of topsoil, may persist for thousands of years. Perhaps the most notorious miscalculation was made during the Dust Bowl. The U.S. Soil Conservation Service tried to estimate the extent of the erosion in various parts of the American West. Its predictions were generally accurate on a broad scale, but they were far off target at local and regional levels. Making such forecasts in Africa today is hard enough without the confusion added by the hopelessly vague definition of what constitutes a desert. Such confusion has contributed substantially to misconceptions about exactly what is happening to the planet's driest lands.

Although the arid lands of the world are not being overrun with deserts, they face an assault from man, who is severely taxing the capacity of the terrain. The dangers of agriculture cannot be easily reduced to a single term such as *desertification*, but collectively they threaten the lives of millions of people in Africa and elsewhere. The most appropriate term for describing the threat is *degradation*, or the steady deterioration of the land until it becomes useless. The crux of the distinction between desertification and degradation is that the former, more popular term applies to the undocumented advance of sand dunes. Our concern—the proper concern for the long-term benefit of humanity—is the deterioration of arid soils.

Perhaps the most publicized threat to the soil is the nomads who graze herds far larger than the land previously supported. According to reports by countless observers, these shepherds supervise herds that consume large portions of the thin vegetative cover on arid lands, while trampling what they do not eat. Eventually, of course, the nomads must move their animals to new sites, where the process begins anew. Given an opportunity to expand their herds—when the government drills for water or when a well-meaning charitable organization trains a veterinarian—the herdsmen invariably make a choice that adds to the burden on the land. One result is that the herds often trample the soil around watering holes, further accelerating erosion. In fact, though such problems are serious, they tend to be confined to small areas. Moreover, they are generally an outcome of national or regional land-use policies that allocate large portions of land to farmers; the nomads are not as culpable as those who are taking their place.

A far more harmful influence on the land is overcultivation: the relentless use of land despite numerous signs that it needs a rest. In Iran and eastern Sudan, for example, the thin layer of soil that lies just above the sand, clay or rock in arid lands has been torn up with heavy plows, tractors, harrows, rollers and other mechanized equipment, which accelerates the process of erosion. In this regard, the Dust Bowl in the United States is instructive: that disaster was accelerated, it is now believed, by the imprudent use of large farm machinery. Nigel Twose, director of the Panos Institute, an English relief organization, has pointed out that in West Africa the fervor to earn foreign currencies has inspired the cultivation of cash crops, such as peanuts, cotton and sugarcane, all of which further deplete the soil of its vital nutrients.

Strangely enough, when cultivation involves irrigation, the practice often leaves the soil saturated. Improper watering has become a severe problem where vast agricultural projects have been hastily planned and built. In many parts of Africa and Asia the canals that bring water to the fields are rarely lined with concrete, and so they leak huge quantities of precious water. The water collects below the surface, usually above a largely impermeable layer of clay or rock. Other fields are poorly drained, partly because proper drainage is extremely expensive to install, with the cumulative effect that the water table begins to rise. When the level of the water rises too high the roots of plants rot, and when the plants die the soil tends to blow away. The agronomist Alastair R. Grieve of the Department of Agriculture in New South Wales has studied this sequence of events in Australia, and he has estimated that nearly a third of the 1987 harvest was lost because of waterlogged fields and leaky irrigation channels.

Rising water levels also start another form of irreversible damage to arid soils. A small amount of salt accumulates naturally after a rain, when dirt and water mix, and during the weathering of rock, which produces salt as a byproduct. But modern agriculture and irrigation can exacerbate the process when millions of gallons of water are pumped through a field. When the water evaporates, small amounts of salt begin to accumulate on the surface of the soil. In countries such as India, Pakistan and Israel governments are considering the construction of elaborate pumping systems that funnel some of the salt out to sea. But the flat wastes of southeastern Iraq—barren since biblical times but believed to have been fertile a thousand years earlier—offer silent testimony to the permanent sterility that is the final stage of salinization.

Ultimately most of the practices that lead to the degradation of arid lands can be traced not to specific farmers but to poorly conceived politics. Many African nations, in an effort to develop their economies, have encouraged practices the land cannot support: In Senegal farmers who fail to cultivate pieces of land for three years lose their rights to farm them; yet some lands can be planted prudently only with less frequency. Politicians and farmers in Australia are beginning to appreciate the folly of their massive irrigation projects, which threaten not only to waterlog the soil but also—through salinization—to kill it. In fairness, it must also be noted that a few Third World countries have undertaken some of the most effective measures for restoring their land: the Kenyan green belt movement, which aims at planting hardy native trees in small woodlots, has excellent prospects for guarding the soil.

Many Third World nations have also recognized that some of their problems were foisted on them by advisers from the West—well-intentioned experts who assumed that techniques from more temperate climates could be extended to arid regions. When the techniques were introduced, hazards such as erosion and salinization were not pressing concerns: the goal was to quickly transplant the techniques that had worked well in wetter, cooler climates. Traditional methods of roaming and foraging were abandoned and virtually lost long before scientists began to realize how little they understood about dry lands—less, in fact, than they do about any other habitat on earth. This rather paternalistic attitude endures: the Club of Rome, a major international aid agency, has proposed sending U.N. military personnel to build roads and wells and providing other logistical support in the Sahel, a measure that will only further degrade the region.

In the broadest sense, both local and multinational policies have failed to address the cultural roots of land degradation. To westerners the grazing habits of Bedouin shepherds may seem almost mad; to the shepherds themselves the practices are part of a tradition far more likely to provide sustenance than the latest Western agricultural fashion. Unfortunately, few people are willing to acknowledge the inconvenient fact that many cultures, seeking to maximize the likelihood of survival, have been forced to deplete communal resources. Individuals gain in the short run by exploiting every nearby asset. But if millions of people act in a similar fashion over the long run society at large will lose. The most hopeful scenario—provided societies and individuals agree to preserve what remains—is that both might begin to appreciate the limits and possibilities of arid lands.

Suggestions for Discussion and Writing

1. What is the dominant tone of the opening paragraph? How does this tone serve the authors' purpose? Do you see any ways in which the tone is qualified?

2. Do you agree with the authors that the United Nations' definition of "desertification" is a "model of ambiguity"? In what sense is this definition a "shifting foundation"? Is the phrase "shifting foundation" well chosen?

3. Can technology be said to have contributed to the confusion regarding desertification?

4. The authors appear to give up on the term "desertification." What term do they prefer? Why?

5. To advance understanding, scientists must often clear away misconceptions. What misconceptions about arid land—its condition, treatment, uses—do the authors debunk? Write an essay developing your views.

6. In the final two paragraphs, the authors discuss conflicts between Third World nations and "well-intentioned experts" who show a "paternalistic attitude" toward countries coping with arid land. In an essay, discuss some of the reasons for these conflicts. What role should "westerners" play in the solution of arid-land problems?

☐ THE NEXT WASTELAND

Michael Tobias
(b. 1951)

Michael Tobias, a former professor of environmental studies at Dartmouth College and author of *Deep Ecology* (1985) and *Mountain People* (1986), has produced and directed numerous documentary films, including *Antarctica: The Last Continent*. In the following essay, Tobias tells of the biological and geological richness of Antarctica, while warning of the dangers posed to its fragile ecosystem by pollution, most of which is produced by the scientists working there.

A ntarctica has always been a place of the mind, a land more often frozen into the imagination than visited in the flesh. Long before explorers ventured there, the ancient Greeks suspected that a lush southern *terra australis incognita* might balance the weight of continents to the north. Later, Polynesian sailors, hazarding across the Pacific toward the pole, incorporated sightings of mist-shrouded icebergs into their folk songs. Even the man credited with discovering Antarctica, the English seaman James Cook, circumnavigated the continent but never saw a speck of land on his famous voyage of 1772. Another fifty years would pass before navigators broke through miles of ice and gazed upon Antarctica itself.

Cook could only guess that the seals he saw drifting on ice floes in the open sea had originated on some undiscovered terrain. But his journals, widely circulated in England, inspired the poet Samuel Taylor Coleridge, who never traveled farther south than the Mediterranean, to write his epic *Rime of the Ancient Mariner*. Published in 1798, the poem tells of a ship blown to the South Pole and haunted by an albatross:

> And now there came both mist and snow,
> And it grew wondrous cold:
> And ice, mast-high, came floating by,
> As green as emerald.

As an idea, Antarctica still exists mostly as Coleridge evoked it: serene, primeval, unreachable. But the real Antarctica is no longer so pristine. Though isolated by hundreds of miles of ocean, the seventh continent has been irreversibly marked by man. Antarctica has never been burdened by more than four thousand human inhabitants at once but it supports fifty-seven permanent encampments for research, each with teams of scientists and contingents of support personnel. Nearly every base has its own harbor, helipad, and landfill;

the Antarctic shoreline is littered with abandoned vehicles and deserted buildings, rusting fuel tanks and fifty-five-gallon drums. Since almost nothing rots in the cold, dry air, piles of garbage simply grow higher and higher. (At the Argentine station known as Primavera, the trash on the shore is so deep that snow petrels hatch amid beer cans, plastic, and steel scrap.) Supply ships pump oily bilge and sewage into coastal inlets, where raging winds disperse the pollutants; polychlorinated biphenyls, the toxic chemicals known as PCBs, are embedded in the tissues of the continent's penguins and seals. Only Poland thoroughly filters human waste from its base. Other nations are not so conscientious; Chile, for example, has been discovered using a rare Antarctic lake as a dump.

Civilization has also come to Antarctica by way of the United States. At McMurdo Station, the largest of three permanent American bases, trash is burned in open pits that stretch for acres, and the levels of particulate matter in the atmosphere have been rising as a result. Unburned garbage winds up in a landfill, which is prohibited by international agreement, but even that could not hold the twelve truckloads of scrap metal that base commanders recently deposited in nearby McMurdo Sound. (When the metal would not fall through the ice on its own, dynamite was used to send it to an underwater grave.) According to a study released last year by the Environmental Defense Fund, the waters near the U.S. station are so contaminated with PCBs that levels of the pollutant exceed those found in several major U.S. harbors. And as long as fifteen years ago, Paul K. Dayton, a biologist now at the Scripps Institution of Oceanography, in La Jolla, California, pronounced the bay so fouled with diesel fuel as to be "essentially dead." The National Science Foundation, which administers the American presence in Antarctica, estimated last year that a cleanup of U.S. areas alone would cost thirty million dollars, or approximately one-quarter of the budget for all the nation's programs on the continent. Unlikely as it may seem, coastal Antarctica may someday resemble the fouled beaches of New Jersey.

The continent was not supposed to become an icy eyesore: in 1961, twelve nations ratified the Antarctic Treaty, which established Antarctica as a preserve for science and outlawed military maneuvers and the storage of nuclear weapons or waste. Another two dozen countries have since signed the pact, and later treaties, also adopted by dozens of nations, have attempted to protect much of the marine life in the surrounding seas. Even though enormous reserves of petroleum, coal, uranium, and precious metals are thought to lie beneath Antarctica's ice cap and oceans, their exploitation was likewise delayed, in an effort to protect the only place on Earth that had never been transformed by man. Indeed, the continent's pristine condition was part of what appealed most to biologists, meteorologists, and geologists, who frequently sought to study some unspoiled facet of the natural world—a shoal of shrimplike krill, a flask of unadulterated air, a block of immaculate ice.

Yet as the research stations at McMurdo and Primavera demonstrate, the treaties have not protected the continent at all. The coldest place on Earth, in fact, seems likely to become more developed in the years ahead: there are indications of expanding tourism, such as the construction of small Argentine and Chilean hotels, and a treaty proposed last summer would allow exploratory drilling for precious metals, natural gas, and oil. Scientists, too, are finding more reasons to work on the continent, and all the visitors will ensure that less and less of it remains unaffected by man.

Because the Antarctic Treaty may be renegotiated on its thirtieth anniversary, in 1991, and because the original twelve parties to the pact are expected to allow more extensive fishing and mining than in the past, Antarctica's future—as a natural sanctuary and a unique global laboratory—is soon to be determined. The outlook is so bleak that the only way to preserve the continent, in the end, may be to create a world park, a wilderness where research, but not commerce, could proceed undisturbed.

Antarctica was not always isolated at the end of the earth. Two hundred million years ago, geologists believe, it was the keystone of a vast supercontinent that spanned much of the Southern Hemisphere. The contours of the landmass were first deduced by scientists who noticed that the coasts of eastern South America and western Africa fit snugly together, like pieces of a puzzle, a suspicion later confirmed by the discovery of the fossil seed fern *Glossopteris* in Antarctica and, indeed, throughout the rest of the Southern Hemisphere. Then scientists found closely matching layers of rock, containing identical sediments and fossils, that stretched through South America, Africa, India, Australia, and Antarctica. This single great expanse came to be called Gondwanaland, after the Indian region in which the rock layers were first identified.

The supercontinent split apart as the crustal plates beneath it began to shift, about one hundred and seventy million years ago. Some of the world's richest mineral deposits lie in the more northern sections of Gondwanaland, and most geologists believe that such reserves may extend to the South Pole. The gold and platinum that South Africans discovered in Witwatersrand, for example, may be present in analogous rock formations in eastern Antarctica's Queen Maude Land; extensive deposits of iron and zinc in southern Australia, as well as copper in Chile, may correspond to similar geological strata in the Transantarctic Mountains and the Antarctic Peninsula.

For millions of years, even after Gondwanaland had begun to fracture, Antarctica lay to the north of its present position and was blessed with warm weather: large amphibians and reptiles thrived, and massive coal deposits, formed over aeons from decayed plants, attest to once extensive vegetation. But since Antarctica holds no fossils of mammals, it must have pulled away from Africa and South America by fifty million years ago (when mammals began to evolve), eventually drifting over the South Pole, where it received the sun's rays only obliquely, if at all.

Antarctica grew still chillier when the strait now known as the Drake Passage formed between it and South America. Meteorologists studying satellite photographs have concluded that the breach between the two continents allowed violent circumpolar winds and ocean currents to swirl unimpeded around the globe for the first time. These eddies skirt the bottom of the planet in a twenty-four-thousand-mile circuit—the longest uninterrupted current in the world—and routinely generate thirty-foot waves and forty-mile-an-hour winds. The effects of polar weather extend throughout Antarctica, where temperatures on inland glaciers often reach ninety degrees Fahrenheit below zero during the coldest parts of the year. Ice sheets more than a mile and a half thick, on average, now cover all but two percent of Antarctica, or more than five million square miles (an area ten times as large as Alaska), and contain at least two-thirds of all the freshwater on the planet. As radar soundings have revealed, the ice is so heavy that it has pressed large portions of the continent's landmass *below* sea level.

Paradoxically, the glaciers account for both the desolation of the interior and the profusion of marine life in the surrounding seas. The continent's frozen inland reaches are arid, sterile plains, receiving just two inches of precipitation a year. Only lichens, mosses, and a few insects survive there. But the coasts are another matter: By cooling the waters of the southern Pacific, Atlantic, and Indian oceans, which meet in a ring called the Antarctic Convergence, the ice fosters unusually fertile seas. The incessant, turbulent mixing of warm waters from more northerly latitudes and icy currents from the pole thrust plankton, algae, and microorganisms up toward the surface. And pack ice extending hundreds of miles beyond the shore suspends algae through the winter, then releases them, in astonishing numbers, upon melting. Together, these rich sources of nutrients feed billions of Antarctic krill, which, in turn, nourish perhaps sixty-five million penguins and thirty-five million seals, as well as three hundred species of sponges, one hundred and twenty-six kinds of fishes, and whales of every description. Antarctic seas may be nearly frozen, but they teem with life.

It was inevitable that this biological and geological abundance would lure mankind and thereby usher in a period of exploration and exploitation. Soon after Captain Cook's account of vast herds of seals was published, in the late 1770s, American and British hunters arrived to harvest the resource. The Antarctic fur seal, treasured for its soft, luxuriant pelt, was driven to near-extinction by the early nineteenth century and has begun to recover only in the past several decades. As the stocks of seals dwindled, hunters forged farther south in search of prey, though their wooden boats often were crushed by the thick ice pack encircling the continent. By 1820, three men had finally ventured beyond the ice to sight the continent itself. Nathaniel Palmer was an American sealing captain; Edward Bransfield, a British sailor; and Fabian von Bellingshausen, a Russian admiral and explorer.

For the remainder of the nineteenth century, the continent was visited mainly by whalers, who systematically harvested most of the cetaceans, and by a few explorers, who mapped the perimeter. Journeys to the interior were rare, and it was not until 1911 that the Norwegian explorer Roald Amundsen beat the English adventurer Robert F. Scott in their celebrated—and, for Scott, fatal—race to the pole. A few explorers, from Great Britain, Norway, and Argentina, attempted to claim territories in Antarctica, stumbling ashore briefly and planting flags before beating hasty retreats to the warmth and comfort of their ships. Nazi aviators had a less exhausting idea; they dropped thousands of stakes emblazoned with swastikas. And the Argentines have gone so far as to shift their nation's capital temporarily to a base at Marambio, on the Antarctic Peninsula, and to import a pregnant woman to the continent, where she gave birth to the first Antarctic "native." But, until recently, the continent remained essentially unsettled.

The latest chapter in Antarctica's story has been written not by sailors or sealers but by diplomats. Despite conflicting claims to various wedge-shaped sections of the continent, a few countries—the United States and the Soviet Union among them—have maintained that it belongs to no government. After the Second World War, various international groups began to advocate a treaty to settle questions of sovereignty, and in 1952, the International Council of Scientific Unions, a body of scientists from around the world, proposed that a multidisciplinary investigation of the Antarctic (part of the International Geophysical Year) be conducted. Employing thousands of scientists from sixty-six countries, the research spawned a measure of global goodwill that resulted, in 1961, in ratification of the Antarctic Treaty.

The agreement neither grants nor disputes any nation's claims to territory on the continent and, in the spirit of international cooperation, declares that the pursuit of science shall be the principal endeavor there. To ensure that no facilities are used for military purposes, the treaty allows any individual to conduct surprise inspections of any buildings. Even today, the parties to the pact cooperate in Antarctica to a degree seldom found anywhere else. Soviet and American negotiators have met to discuss the continent even when international discord, such as the Russian invasion of Afghanistan, could have been expected to derail their talks.

The international harmony surrounding the continent has not, regrettably, inspired measures to protect it. Scientists are flocking to the Antarctic to pursue opportunities that exist nowhere else. High-altitude weather balloons and satellites have provided meteorologists with their only glimpse of a "hole," or deficiency, in the blanket of ozone that protects the planet from damaging ultraviolet radiation. And air samples are being used to determine levels of carbon dioxide and other gases, which trap heat and create the so-called greenhouse effect, the global warming that could someday melt the Antarctic ice pack and raise the world's sea level by two hundred feet or more—enough to swamp all but the highest coastlines. Geologists, meanwhile, are prospecting to gauge exactly how much oil, natural gas, and minerals lie under the continent and its oceans. Psychologists are investigating the effects of isolation and sensory deprivation upon scientists during the long Antarctic winter. And marine biologists, attracted by a profusion of aquatic life uniquely adapted to cold, hope to understand the protective metabolic mechanisms in creatures such as Weddell seals and Antarctic cod. Most of these researchers do not deliberately harm the Antarctic environment; they are simply too consumed with their own projects to take steps to protect it.

The scientists are just part of the growing human presence in Antarctica. The logistics of feeding, housing, and transporting researchers in the bitter polar climate require support staffs two to three times as large as the research contingents at a typical base. (In 1986, nine percent of the U.S. budget for Antarctica was devoted to research; the remainder was earmarked for the maintenance of bases.) If they were spread evenly across the continent, none of these individuals would leave a notable imprint. But because ninety-eight percent of the continent is buried in ice, nature and man must battle for control of a few rocky outcrops. Throughout Antarctica, there are only three hundred miles of ice-free shore, where fragile wildlife—birds, seals, grasses, lichens—frequently must compete with human beings for living space. Chilean and Argentine research stations have been constructed smack in the middle of dense bird breeding colonies, and the French Dumont d'Urville station was built three hundred yards from the rookeries of eight species. The constant plane and helicopter traffic, shuttling scientists and their gear around the continent, further disrupts the birds, which abandon their young as aircraft approach. At Argentina's Esperanza base, packs of huskies once were allowed to run wild, even though the dogs had destroyed one hundred thousand penguins over a four-year period. Impossible as it may seem to deplete a stock of tens of millions of birds, the record in Antarctica and the rest of the world shows that even species that seem infinite in number can be eradicated. Whales still have not made complete recoveries a century after their decimation in Antarctic seas

The same settled two percent of the continent must now bear a new burden, for researchers and their assistants are for the first time outnumbered by tourists. Some seven thousand tourists arrived in Antarctica during the most recent austral summer. And over the past three decades, more than seventy thousand people have visited the Antarctic Peninsula alone. Even one of the most remote points on the planet, the South Pole, is now within reach: last year a dozen North Americans spent thirty-five thousand dollars apiece to walk the ice and visit the U.S. station there. Some needed bottled oxygen, and those unable to walk the several hundred feet from the airstrip to the pole were *driven* in a military vehicle.

Tourists, in fact, are now present in such numbers that many scientists view them as an unwelcome distraction during the four brief months in which their research projects must be finished. Besides taking scientists from their work, the camera-toting travelers are so persistent in their search for seals and penguins and other birds that in many locations, they disrupt mating and nesting by scattering the animals as they approach. And they trample delicate lichens and mosses, the so-called redwoods of Antarctica, which are hundreds of years old.

Garbage and debris from tour ships add to the mess in coastal waters. Crews throw just about everything—fluorescent bulbs, plastic water jugs, scrap metal—overboard. Tourists themselves leave cigarette butts, wine bottles, and empty film canisters. And the situation hardly will improve when the Chilean and Argentine hotels, on the mainland and an offshore island, become popular.

There is also pressure from businessmen. The annual harvest of krill has grown more than twentyfold since 1973. The Soviet Union, Japan, Poland, Norway, and West Germany all harvest the species; the 1986 catch totaled nearly five hundred thousand tons. While present in prodigious quantities, krill is such an excellent source of protein that its depletion can never be ruled out; biologists estimate the crustacean could supply twice the protein found in the present catch of fish throughout the rest of the world. Corporate geologists and petroleum engineers have also started to arrive in Antarctica. Troves of cobalt, chromium, manganese, uranium, platinum, coal, iron, molybdenum, gold, and nickel are thought to exist. With present techniques, mining in the interior seems unlikely because of the glaciers' extraordinary depth and constant shifting. But developers are actively prospecting for petroleum in coastal waters: the U.S. Geological Survey estimated, in 1974, that the continent and adjacent seas might hold as much as forty-five billion barrels of oil and one hundred and fifty trillion cubic feet of natural gas—quantities roughly comparable to the existing reserves in the United States. (The extraction of these reserves is not thought profitable, given the low price of oil prevailing today, but the situation will change if the market for petroleum rebounds.) Last summer, in an attempt to identify such reserves, treaty members decided to allow more extensive exploration and established procedures for drilling and extracting rock from the continent and its seabed, where the Japanese are already searching.

Much of the human activity that exploits the continent is either expressly prohibited by, or, at the least, contrary to the spirit of, the Antarctic Treaty. The problem is that the treaty nations have never found a way of enforcing the prohibitions against killing Antarctic wildlife or, for that matter, any provision of any accord; no penalties have ever been imposed. Even flagrant violations go unpunished. The United States, to take one example, built and briefly operated a nuclear-powered electrical plant in Antarctica, importing nuclear fuel, generating atomic waste, and contaminating soil and McMurdo Station, activities never sanctioned by international agreement. The Soviet Union, to take another example, has harvested four thousand seals (whose pelts are not left behind) for allegedly scientific purposes, and Japan runs an "experimental" whaling operation that annually manages to take three hundred minke whales—the only cetacean present in numbers sufficient for a profitable harvest. In these and other instances, treaty nations have been so concerned with bonhomie in Antarctica, they have failed to notice that the health of the continent is at stake. The result is that, as the treaty's thirtieth anniversary approaches, its members are expected to allow larger catches and more extensive mineral exploration.

There is, however, an alternative to the gradual degradation of the continent. For fifteen years, various environmental organizations have led a popular movement to declare Antarctica a world park—an enclave in which only science would proceed unhindered—and citizens of sixty-five countries have signed a petition supporting the idea. As currently envisioned, the park would be closed to efforts to extract oil, natural gas, and minerals, but tourism, tightly controlled, might continue. Most members of the Antarctic Treaty oppose a world park, even though, as a few diplomats have conceded, it embodies the original spirit of the treaty, which sought to protect and preserve the continent for science and all mankind.

The day-to-day administration of an Antarctic world park has not yet been planned, even by its most ardent supporters. But unlike the present arrangement, a world park might allow treaty nations to set limits on the extent to which any activity—tourism, mining, research—would be allowed to affect the continent's environment. Wardens or rangers, presumably, might be authorized to monitor what is hunted, dumped, or burned in Antarctica and its oceans; penalties might be levied against scientists, corporations, or entire nations. Indeed, compared with the private Antarctic Treaty tribunal, which meets only biannually, any bureaucratic presence might better ensure that the continent is not defiled.

If, on the other hand, no conservation measures are taken, the consequences of an expanded human presence in Antarctica are not pleasant to imagine. Considering the ineffective treaties that now govern the continent, and the reductions in stocks of marine life elsewhere in the world, the fishing industry could eventually decimate the krill, which would have dire consequences for every aquatic species around Antarctica. An oil spill in Antarctic seas could have a similarly devastating effect: massive icebergs, traveling as fast as forty miles a day in the swift currents, could topple platforms or rupture tankers, fouling the waters with slicks that ice- and fog-bound cleanup crews could never contain.

Beyond damaging the continent's ecosystems, continued human

migration to Antarctica could ultimately destroy the extraordinary global laboratory the continent has become. A good measure of the pole's appeal lies in its being a place that has not yet been spoiled by man. It is a sort of "clean room" for a range of experiments impossible to conduct in parts of the world affected by large populations and pollution. Already, however, some biologists must venture farther and farther from their base camps in order to find unspoiled terrain. In the end, by ruining Antarctica for no evident reason, scientists and others may relive the fate of the anguished sailor in Coleridge's poem, whose sin was shooting a solitary albatross—a seemingly minor offense, but one that would haunt him forever.

Suggestions for Discussion and Writing

1. What does Tobias mean when he says that "Antarctica has always been a place of the mind"? How does this idea serve his rhetorical purpose? Why does he return to this notion at the very end of his essay?

2. The author says that "the Antarctic Treaty may be renegotiated on its thirtieth anniversary" (1991). Using outside sources, report on the status of these negotiations.

3. What evidence suggests that Antarctica was once part of a vast continent spanning much of the Southern hemisphere? How are scientists able to date the breaking away of Antarctica from that continent?

4. What, according to the author, fosters the fertility of the Antarctic seas?

5. Do you find it surprising that scientists are contributing so massively to the polluting of Antarctica?

6. In speaking of the richness of Antarctica, Tobias says that "it was inevitable that this biological and geological abundance would lure mankind and thereby usher in a period of exploration and exploitation." Why is "exploration and exploitation" inevitable? Does the author himself suggest an answer? Write an essay exploring this issue.

7. Should Antarctica be "preserved"—declared a "world park"? Write an essay developing your views.

☐ THE POLLUTION OF SPACE

Isaac Asimov
(1920–1992)
Frederik Pohl
(b. 1919)

The *New York Times Book Review* once labeled Isaac Asimov a "writing machine." With more than 450 books to his name, the label seems appropriate—if not altogether descriptive of the quality of his writing. Even more astonishing than the bulk of his writing is its incredible range—from science fiction, mystery, and humor to philosophy, history, and science—writing for both adults and children. Among his most famous science fiction works are the Foundation trilogy, the Robot series, and the Empire stories. His "Nightfall" is judged by many to be the best science fiction short story of all time. Asimov's science writing for juveniles has enjoyed immense popularity, with his "How Did We Find Out" series being perhaps the best known.

Born in Russia, Asimov was brought to the United States at the age of 3 and was raised in Brooklyn, New York. He received his B.S. and M.A. in chemistry from Columbia University. He then worked as a civilian chemist at the U.S. Navy Air Experimental Station in Philadelphia and served in the U.S. Army. He returned to Columbia to earn his Ph.D. in chemistry in 1948 and then joined the faculty of the Boston University School of Medicine, where he taught until the early 1980s.

Asimov received many awards, fourteen honorary degrees among them. His science fiction writing was awarded virtually every prize possible, including the Hugo Award in 1973 for *The Gods Themselves* and again in 1983 for *Foundation's Edge*. His science writing received the James T. Grady Award of the American Chemical Society in 1965 and the American Association for the Advancement of Science–Westinghouse Award in 1967.

Like Isaac Asimov, Frederik Pohl grew up in Brooklyn and is a renowned science fiction writer. But unlike Asimov he was a high school dropout who never pursued higher education. His work as an editor and writer has earned him major honors such as the Hugo Award in 1966, 1967, and 1968, the H.G. Wells Award in 1975, and the John W. Campbell Award in 1978. His best-known novel, *Gateway*, received the Nebula Award of the Science Fiction Writers of America in 1978.

The following selection, taken from Asimov and Pohl's *Our Angry Earth* (1991), addresses the danger posed to future space travellers by the littering of space.

I t's hard to believe that empty space itself can be polluted by human efforts. It's true, though. We have trashed the orbits our spacecraft travel through. So much so that, before every launch of a space shuttle, NASA's high-speed computers run for a full twenty-four hours on just one element of the flight: to choose a safe orbit, so that the shuttle won't destroy itself by colliding with some other man-made orbiting body.

Space is in fact fairly empty. But it is no longer empty *enough*. As of the last announced count (in early 1989) there were 7,119 man-made objects in Low Earth Orbit big enough to be tracked by surface radar. A handful of them are working satellites—communications, intelligence, weather. Some are satellites which have run out of energy or lost communication and are now "dead"—but remain in orbit because the laws of orbiting ballistics don't give them any other place to go. Some are pieces of scrap metal from broken-up satellites, launch vehicles or fuel tanks. A few are simply objects that the astronauts or cosmonauts have dropped—a wrench, a screwdriver, a Hasselblad camera. They range from the size of a baseball to the size of a school bus, and they are moving at high speeds—around four miles a second, fast enough so that even the smallest of them could seriously damage any object they happened to hit, even the shuttle.

Taken all together, what these abandoned spaceborne objects amount to is a sort of orbital minefield, left there by the spacefaring nations of the Earth. They are space junk, and their number is still increasing. Two German scientists—Peter Eichler and Dietrich Rex of the Technical University of Braunschweig—have estimated that the chance of a "catastrophic" collision in space is now about 3.7% per year, and predict that if the present rate of increase of space debris continues, by the middle of the next century any such collision could set off a chain reaction.

Is there any way of cleaning up this garbage belt? There have been plenty of proposals for doing so, ranging from passive "vacuum cleaners" (a windmill-like satellite with huge plastic vanes, or a huge, miles-across ball of sponge plastic, either of which would simply soak up all the smaller objects in their path) to active robot spacecraft, remote-controlled, that would be flown ahead of the Shuttle through its orbit, as tanks shelter advancing infantry. None of these is likely to be put into practice for three reasons. First, they are all terribly expensive. Second, none of them would work as well as simply keeping the trash out of orbit in the first place. And third, most of them might actually produce *more* small particles after a collision.

For those large objects are only the beginning. In addition to the big ones, there is an uncounted multitude of tinier objects in those same orbits, too small for the radar search at Goddard Flight Center to detect. There are somewhere around forty or fifty thousand of these smaller things from the size of a marble up—as well as a much larger number of tinier objects still. Perhaps there are a million of the least bits of trash: flecks of paint from old fuel tanks, fragments of metal tinier than a fingernail, odds and ends of litter of all kinds.

Even the tiniest of these bits of cosmic shrapnel are dangerous to anything they collide with. Small as they are, they are *fast*. Because of their velocities the kinetic energy—which is to say, the destructive power—of even the least of them in a head-on collision can do as much damage as a cannonball at sixty miles an hour. It is certainly enough, for instance, to kill an astronaut if he were unlucky enough to have his suit punctured by one.

Here, too, there is no end to the technological fixes that have been proposed. If the space station is ever built, for example, NASA has already made plans to surround it with a double wall of thin sheet aluminum—hopefully to absorb the kinetic energy before it hits anything important. Two engineers, Cyrus Butner and Charles Garrell, have patented a "Method and Apparatus for Orbit Debris Mitigation" which consists of a honeycomb of cone-shaped buffers lined with some energy-absorbing substance, and there are dozens of other ideas which have been put forth more tentatively.

Whether any of them would work is unclear. That they would add mass to every launch, and thus reduce the amount of payload that could be carried, is unquestionable. In any case, even if they worked there are many cases where they couldn't be used. The mirror of a space telescope or the receptors of many kinds of instruments simply could not function with any sort of shield between them and the things they are launched to observe.

The danger from these tiniest bits is no longer theoretical, either. It has already been proven to be enough to destroy a working satellite.

Consider the case of the Solar Maximum satellite.

Solar Max was launched in 1980 as a scientific instrument, charged with measuring the radiation from the sun. That is important research, because its purpose was to study the indispensable ultimate source of energy possessed by the human race.

Solar Max did its job very well for a while, but the good time lasted only for a few months. On September 23, 1980, the data from Solar Max stopped coming, and its ground controllers could not tell why.

For three and a half years after that date, Solar Max circled the Earth in silence.

Then, in April, 1984, the shuttle astronauts repaired it. They did it while both they and it were in orbit, and that was a truly remarkable feat. First they had to find the dead satellite and maneuver the shuttle to approach it as closely as possible. Then one of them had to put on a spacesuit, launch himself out into space to Solar Max, open the satellite up, remove the damaged parts and replace them with new ones. All of this had to be done while floating in empty space, more than a hundred miles above the Earth. It was a complex and exhausting job, and the astronauts did it beautifully.

They were successful. At once Solar Max came alive again. It took up its interrupted task; its reports began to come back down to the ground stations, and they kept on doing so until at last, five years later, Solar Max came to the end of its working life. It wasn't any kind of instrument failure that finally did it in. It was atmospheric friction. In the normal course of the solar cycle the Sun's heat had warmed the Earth's atmosphere to the point where thermal expansion brought air molecules up to Solar Max's level. The drag of the atmosphere slowed Solar Max down until it fell out of orbit. It finally crashed into the Indian Ocean, near Sri Lanka, on December 3, 1989.

What was it that had knocked Solar Max out of service for three and a half years of its working life?

The answer to that came when NASA's scientists studied the broken parts. The delicate instrument panels had been riddled with tiny holes, 150 of them in a surface area about the size of a card table. Solar Max had been struck with a blast of cosmic buckshot. Some of those tiniest bits of orbiting junk, impossible either to see or to avoid, had collided with it and killed its instrumentation.

So the risk of collision with orbiting trash is real. It has not happened to just that one satellite, either. At least three others are known to have been, or are suspected of having been, damaged the same way; and, on at least one flight, so was the space shuttle itself.

On the third day of its July, 1983, flight, the shuttle *Challenger*—yes, the same one that was destroyed a few years later when it exploded after launch—was hit with an object too small to be seen, but big enough to pit the glass in the pilot's windscreen with a crater the size of a pea. Again, NASA's analysis showed the culprit: *Challenger* had been struck by a tiny flake of white paint, no doubt chipped off some old booster. Fortunately it had been only a glancing blow, but even so the screen had to be replaced (at a cost of $50,000) before *Challenger* could fly again.

So the number of objects in the trash belt in space continues to grow, and most of them will remain in orbit for decades or even centuries, and there isn't any technological fix in prospect.

Worse still, if we should be unfortunate enough to see some current military projects grow to fruition—Star Wars, for instance—that orbiting minefield may fence us in so thoroughly as to prohibit future space projects from being accomplished at all.

Star Wars—officially termed the Strategic Defense Initiative, or SDI— was the bill of goods Edward Teller sold Ronald Reagan in 1983. It was supposed to put a "nuclear umbrella" over America; its backers invested a fortune in TV commercials, showing a sweet little girl sleeping in perfect security, with the Russians presumably gnashing their teeth in thwarted rage.

The opinion of most qualified scientists—at least, of those not employed by the project itself—is that there's no hope in the world that Star Wars can ever fulfill that promise. Even the project's own authorities have now cut their claims back, saying only that it can probably be used to protect some of our own missile launch pads against many of the ICBMs that would be launched against them. (The cities where sweet little girls sleep will have to take their chances.)

Whether even that claim is true, and whether that sort of limited defense is worth its staggering cost, is questionable. Some experts suggest that, in fact, Star Wars is more likely to provoke a nuclear attack than to prevent it . . . yet the project won't die. In spite of everything, in spite of the changed relationships between the USSR and the USA, in spite of all the evidence that Star Wars is a bad idea, it still continues to be funded with billions of dollars every year. Twenty-two percent of the increase in federally funded research and development from 1983 to 1989 went to Star Wars-related projects, as did eleven percent of *all* American R&D, public and private. Although, before the war in the Persian Gulf, the future of many new high-tech weapons systems was in some doubt, with much talk of cancelling them for a "peace dividend," Star Wars had a charmed life. Then, of course, the swift and total American military victory in the Gulf revived all the high-tech warriors' hopes. The Patriot missile, the use of laser-guided "smart" bombs and many another new wonder weapon was hailed as a direct result of Star Wars research, and a justification for all its efforts.

None of those claims, of course, was true. Just how successful the new super-weapons were is hard to assess; all reports were censored by the military, and often colored for their own purposes. (For instance, although the bulk of naval missiles were launched from cruisers and destroyers, almost the only ones allowed to be reported were those launched from submarines and battleships—because the Navy wants them funded.) But to use laser to guide a bomb is nothing like using a laser to blow up an enemy missile; and the Patriot (which was originally designed to attack enemy aircraft, not missiles, because it is totally useless against anything more sophisticated than the slow, clumsy Scud) was actually commissioned long before Star Wars was even a gleam in Ronald Reagan's eye.

All the same, the high-pressure public-relations of the military and the defense contractors has certainly obscured the issue. It now seems highly likely that at least some elements of Star Wars will be built and put into orbit within the next five years.

What will the effects of that bad idea be on the ecology of Low Earth Orbit?

We can get some idea by looking at past history—for instance, at the sorrowful story of the satellite called Solwind.

The astronomical research satellite designated P78-1—called "Solwind" for short—was launched from Vandenberg in February, 1979. The principal instrument Solwind carried was a coronagraph—which is to say, a telescope equipped with an "occulter" to block out the direct light of the Sun, so that the solar corona can be observed.

For six and a half years Solwind did the job it was designed for, churning out its pictures of the Sun's corona; it even did more than had been hoped, in fact, for example discovering a whole new class of sun-grazing comets. At times there were other science satellites observing the Sun. Some of them—the aforementioned Solar Max for one—were larger, newer and more sophisticated. But for the three and a half years while Solar Max was out of commission, Solwind was the only dedicated source of coronal data scientists had.

It was Star Wars that finally killed Solwind.

The Star Wars people have a history of conducting meaningful public-relations "tests" to make the taxpayer feel they're getting somewhere. Some of the tests are silly, if not even fraudulent ("destroying" a target with a laser, without mentioning that the target was surrounded with mirrors to concentrate the radiation; "targeting" one of the shuttle flights with a radar impulse—as though an enemy missile would be as obliging as the shuttle in announcing its orbital plans). However meaningless, all of them are hyped as major breakthroughs. When, in 1985, they needed another "breakthrough" to keep the appropriations flowing, they decided to destroy a satellite in orbit.

They picked old Solwind as the victim.

They made it a point, of course, to tell the world that the satellite they had chosen to zap was not only obsolete but no longer working. Of course, neither statement was true. Nevertheless they went ahead, pulverizing the Solwind satellite on September 13, 1985. The scientists who had depended on it for data protested vigorously, but of course the Star Wars people simply ignored them.

Solwind doesn't deliver any data any more. Still, it isn't entirely gone. Of those 7,119 trackable trash fragments in orbit, about a hundred are the remaining blown-up pieces of Solwind.

If, against all common sense, Star Wars is sooner or later even partially deployed, the trash belt in Low Earth Orbit will be multiplied many times over—even if no orbital war is ever actually fought. For instance, if the Star Wars X-ray laser (which requires nuclear blasts for power) were ever deployed, it would necessitate a hundred or more nuclear reactors in orbit.

That isn't likely to happen; even the Star Warriors seem to have given up on the X-ray laser. Currently their best bet for *some* kind of orbital defense is the "brilliant pebbles" scheme proposed by the Lawrence Livermore scientist Lowell Wood. Each pebble would be a complicated and expensive satellite about ten feet long, weighing 350 pounds, guided to attack the first enemy missile it sees by its own on-board computer—a very *good* computer, comparable to Cray-1, but less than a thousandth its size, filled with (as Wood says) "so much prior knowledge and detailed battle strategy and battle tactics" that "it can perform its purely defensive mission with no external supervision or coaching."

That is to say, the computer will decide for itself what to attack, and when. No human being will control it. (No such wonderful computer exists at present, either, but the Star Warriors are always hopeful.) And there will be thousands of these smart pebbles in orbit.

As we have seen from the studies of the two German scientists above (which were presented at the 1989 International Astronautical Federation meeting in Torremolinos) just adding all those additional bodies in orbit may make collisions almost inevitable, after which one big smashup could produce so much space junk that it could set off a chain reaction. It is not clear how many brilliant pebbles and associated hardware, even if never fired at an enemy in combat, could bring the number up to that point.

But some things are clear, and one of them is what happens if Star Wars actually is deployed, is committed to combat and actually works.

What happens then? How many tens or hundreds of thousands of trackably-large hunks of junk (never mind the millions of tiny ones) would be left in orbit from the use or destruction of all those communications and control satellites, missile casings, even nuclear charges; of popup lasers, smart rocks or brilliant pebbles and all the rest of the wonderland of high-tech, high-mass gadgets the Star Warriors wish to set spinning around the Earth over our heads?

How many centuries would it then be before a space program is possible again, without unacceptable risks of collision with some of those hurtling hunks of scrap?

Our space exploration has not merely trashed the Low Earth Orbits, it has done a job on the surface and the atmosphere of the planet as well. The two solid rockets for each Shuttle launch burn seven hundred tons of ammonium perchlorate. The chlorine this contains makes acid rain, for which reason the Shuttle is only permitted to launch when the winds are blowing offshore, to keep the stuff from falling on Florida's cities and farmlands.

The chlorine in it may also contribute to ozone-layer destruction, and the fuel, which is a hundred and sixty tons of aluminum, definitely does. It produces aluminum oxide. That chemical isn't naturally found in the upper air, but when we put it there it produces particles which are just the right size to form "seeds" on which the ice crystals that facilitate ozone destruction can form.

Elsewhere in the world, the Soviets are right now trying to clean up several million acres of land in the district called Dzhezkazgan, just east of their rocket launch pads at the space base of Tyuratam.

Rockets have to be launched toward the east, to take advantage of the boost they get from the rotation of the Earth. The Soviets didn't happen to own a usable eastward-facing coast like Cape Canaveral, so they launched from the middle of the continent. That meant that the 890 launch-stage boosters launched from Tyuratam fell to the ground in the Dzhezkazgan region, where they still remain. They contain pumps and other parts which hold toxic fluids, so much of them that the soil there is now too contaminated to allow cattle to graze on it.

Of course, our American space program didn't have quite the same problem. Our own boosters and toxic chemicals all fell into the Atlantic Ocean. The difference, of course, is that ours are not visible, and so can't be cleaned up.

The space program is, by and large, one of the most wonderful and promising endeavors ever undertaken by the human race. It would be folly to abandon it. But it is even greater folly to fail to exercise caution in how we carry it out . . . if only because if we don't, we may reach a point when we can't have a space program at all.

Suggestions for Discussion and Writing

1. How would you characterize the authors' style—as formal, informal? Do they, for example, use overstatement or subtlety to make their case? Point to specific aspects of the essay (diction, sentence structure, tone, etc.) to support your view.

2. Compare this essay to "The Next Wasteland" by Michael Tobias (this chapter). Do the two essays contain similar attitudes toward our physical world? What are those attitudes? Write a brief essay developing your views.

3. "If the present rate of increase of space debris continues," the authors say, "by the middle of the next century [a catastrophic] collision could set off a chain reaction." What is this "chain reaction"? Do the authors offer evidence to help us understand how it could occur?

4. Does the discussion of Stars Wars divert the reader from (or support) the main topic?

5. What is the authors' attitude toward Star Wars and its proponents? What specific language helps establish this attitude?

6. Several essays in this chapter seem to suggest that the scientific enterprise itself is placing an enormous—and perhaps unsustainable—burden on the natural world. Is the nature of modern science such that it can be practiced only at some cost to the world it studies? Develop your views in an essay, focusing on a few specific cases.

CHAPTER 12

Science and Gender

☐ WOMEN'S WORK

Vera Rubin
(b. 1928)

That "dark matter" has become a major focus of contemporary astronomy is due in no small measure to Vera Rubin's
studies of galactic motion. She is a staff member of the Department of Terrestrial Magnetism at the Carnegie Institution in Washington, D.C., and is one of three female astronomers in the
National Academy of Sciences (to which seventy-five women have
been elected since its founding in 1863).

Rubin's success in a field dominated by men has not come easily. When she was considering applying to Swarthmore College as
an astronomy major, she was told by an admissions officer that
she would be better off painting pictures of stars than studying
them. Rubin enrolled instead at Vassar College and graduated as
an astronomy major within three years. After obtaining a master's
degree at Cornell University, she hoped to pursue a Ph.D. at
Princeton University but learned that women were not allowed
into the graduate physics or astronomy programs (a policy that
was changed in the 1970s). She entered Georgetown University
and there earned a Ph.D. in astronomy in 1954.

Published widely in her field, Rubin has received numerous honors, including appointments as Distinguished Visiting Astronomer at
Chile's Cerro Tololo Observatory in 1978 and as Chancellor's

Distinguished Professor of Astronomy at the University of California, Berkeley, in 1981.

In the following essay from *Science* (1986) she places the obstacles she faced in pursuing her own career in the context of the difficulties encountered by women scientists of the past.

I was an astronomy student at Vassar College on October 1, 1947, 100 years after the night that Maria Mitchell discovered a comet. Only recently have I realized that no note whatsoever was taken of the centennial of this discovery by the first prominent female astronomer in the United States. Perhaps on that day one of my friends or I irreverently tied a bright scarf around the stern-looking bust of Mitchell in a niche of the observatory building, where she taught for many years. But she deserved more.

What I do remember of 1947 is that I wrote a postcard to Princeton University asking for a catalog of the graduate school. Sir Hugh Taylor, the eminent chemist and dean of the graduate school, took the effort to answer by writing back that as Princeton did not accept women in the graduate physics and astronomy program, he would not send a catalog. Princeton did not accept women in graduate physics until 1971, in graduate astronomy until 1975, and in graduate math programs until 1976.

For me as a youngster, the account of Mitchell's comet discovery that I found in library books was an exciting part of the lore from the scientific past, along with Benjamin Franklin's kite. Like the kite, it should be a part of every American child's heritage. Yet in 1976, when the Smithsonian Air and Space Museum presented as its first planetarium show a history of 200 years of American astronomy, only male astronomers—all but one of them white—were included. Little boys learned that they could become astronomers. But little girls, who also streamed into the show in enormous numbers, saw that only men were astronomers. After months of effort to have the planetarium show corrected, I received a statement that the talk was recorded and could not be altered.

All of us, men and women alike, need permission to enter and continue in the world of science. In high school and college, students need the permission of parents and teachers. During graduate and postgraduate years, young scientists need the permission of college officials, funding officers, mentors, and colleagues. While such permission has generally been granted to bright men, it has always been less readily granted to young women and continues to be denied to many women even today. In many fields of science, women constitute such a distinct minority—less than five percent of all physicists and seven percent of all astronomers—that they suffer many of the social ills common to minorities.

*   *   *

In colonial America, public education for women was practically nonexistent. But starting about 1820, women's academies came into vogue, and science was a part of the curriculum. By 1871, 18 of these schools had observatories and offered a course in astronomy. Nevertheless, throughout most of the 19th century, women in the United States were usually dependent upon a supportive male relative to introduce them to the world of science. For Maria Mitchell it was no different.

The daughter of an intellectual Nantucket family, Maria Mitchell learned from her father how to search the sky with a telescope and how to calculate orbits. Employed during the 1840s and 1850s as the librarian of the Nantucket Athenaeum—the intellectual center of Nantucket and home of literary and philosophical societies, where giants like Thoreau, Agassiz, and Audubon lectured—she studied the advanced astronomical and mathematical texts available to her. Evenings she spent with her father on the roof of their home studying the sky with a telescope. On October 1, 1847, while her parents were downstairs entertaining guests at dinner, the 29-year-old librarian discovered a comet. She promptly announced her discovery to her parents, and Mr. Mitchell immediately posted a note to William Bond, director of the Harvard College Observatory. In 1831, the king of Denmark had offered a gold medal to the next person who discovered a comet with a telescope. (Comets were then generally discovered by eye.) Though the comet was also spotted in Europe, Mitchell's discovery was adjudged to be the first, and the medal was hers.

For the United States, Maria Mitchell became the symbol of women's emergence into the public world of science. In 1848 she became the first woman elected into the American Academy of Arts and Sciences—95 years were to go by until the next woman was admitted. And she was an active member of the American Association for the Advancement of Science. Nevertheless, when Joseph Henry, the first secretary of the Smithsonian Institution, announced in 1848 an "account of a new comet, the discovery of which is one of the finest additions to science ever made in this country," he never identified the "American lady" who made the discovery.

When Vassar Female College opened in 1865, Maria Mitchell was invited to become director of the college observatory and professor of astronomy. She accepted the positions and remained at Vassar until her retirement in 1888. Like many other women professors then teaching in women's colleges, she had no college education, but she had developed her skills working at the Athenaeum and as a "computer" for the United States Coast Survey, making calculations of planet and star positions from her home.

By the 1880s, more women were being hired as computers to do calculations and make measurements of photographic plates in observatories. A male graduate student of mine once quipped that American astronomy became preeminent over European astronomy because of two discoveries: Hale discovered money and Pickering discovered women.

George Ellery Hale, an eminent astronomer and organizational genius, learned how to raise money for building large, powerful telescopes by going to wealthy friends and others interested in revolutionizing American astronomy. Hale built the 40-inch refractor at Yerkes Observatory in Wisconsin, the 60- and 100-inch telescopes at Mt. Wilson in California, and the 200-inch telescope on Palomar Mountain in California. Though Hale's efforts helped put Americans at the forefront of astronomy, Hale harked back to the 19th century in his attitudes toward women. He and other astronomers dubbed the living quarters on Mt. Wilson (and later Palomar) The Monastery and banned women from using the telescopes—a restriction not lifted until the mid-1960s.

Edward C. Pickering, as director of the Harvard College Observatory from 1877 to 1919, responded to the competitive forces in astronomy by combining observational astronomy and physics into a new technology—the field of astrophysics. Photographing the heavens each clear evening, astronomers used spectroscopy—examining the constituent wavelengths of a star's light through a prism attached to a telescope—to distinguish between different types of stars. Pickering needed helpers to search the thousands of photographic plates his equipment was generating and to carry out long, detailed calculations to determine the positions and other information about those heavenly bodies recorded on the plates. Planning and directing the science was a man's job; tedious detail work was considered suitable work for women amateurs. While his style of doing astronomy opened the door for employing women, Pickering's attitudes were nonetheless financially motivated. He learned that the women he hired were "capable of doing as much good routine work as astronomers who would receive much larger salaries. Three or four times as many assistants can thus be employed," he reported in Harvard College Observatory's annual report of 1898, "and the work done correspondingly increased for a given expenditure."

Eminent women too shared the view that women were less suited for scientific tasks involving creative thinking. In 1893 physician Mary Putnam Jacobi sent a paper to the World's Congress of Representative Women held in Bogota, Colombia: "Modern science," she said, requires "a great number of assistants to perform manipulations involving much labor and time, requiring intelligence and great accuracy, but not necessitating original mental power. . . . This is a most useful and important field of work for women."

Of all the observatories hiring women, Harvard College Observatory hired the greatest number—a total of 45 during Pickering's years as director. Along with Pickering's new approach to astonomy, the establishment of the Henry Draper Memorial also contributed directly to this surge in jobs for women.

Henry Draper, a wealthy New York doctor and amateur astronomer, took the first photograph of the spectrum of a star in 1872.

Spectral lines in stars—a series of dark lines appearing across a continuous band of color that corresponds to the radiation emitted by a star—had been observed through spectroscopes attached to telescopes since the early 1800s. Later, stars were classified into several types according to these spectral lines, which indicate the star's various chemical elements. When Draper started photographing stellar spectra using a spectrograph attached to the telescope, he could make a detailed photograph of the spectrum of a single star. With that innovation, the possibilities for studying the stars took a giant leap.

Historians have dubbed the women Pickering hired to perform such meticulous study "Pickering's harem." Modifying Draper's technique, they produced telescopic images of many stars, each spread out to form a spectrum, on a single photographic plate. Using a magnifying glass, they studied the spectrum of each star in order to classify it. They recorded their observations, identified other heavenly bodies photographed with the stars, and checked the results with charts. Working with incredible patience and unflagging industry, they were observers, computers, and discoverers. Some became full-fledged mathematical astronomers, computing orbits of planets and asteroids. Some compiled star catalogs, devising systems to estimate stellar brightnesses. Some, like Williamina Fleming, were put in charge of managing the staff and hiring other women assistants.

An entry from Williamina Fleming's diary, dated March 12, 1900, tells something of her attitudes toward Pickering's policies on promotions and raises:

> During the morning's work on correspondence etc. I had some conversation with the Director regarding women's salaries. He seems to think that no work is too much or too hard for me, no matter what the responsibility or how long the hours. But let me raise the question of salary and I am immediately told that I receive an excellent salary as women's salaries stand. . . . Sometimes I feel tempted to give up and let him try some one else, or some of the men to do my work, in order to have him find out what he is getting for $1,500 a year from me, compared with $2,500 from some of the other assistants. Does he ever think that I have a . . . family to take care of as well as the men? But I suppose a woman has no claim to such comforts. And this is considered an enlightened age!

Many of the women working at the Harvard observatory were outstanding. Annie Jump Cannon established the system with which she classified the spectra of more than 350,000 stars. Cannon would examine the plate with a magnifying lens, mentally classify the star into a number of alphabetical categories depending on the pattern of lines she saw, and call out her identifications to an assistant, who would write them down. She learned to identify the line patterns almost instantaneously, at a rate of more than three stars a minute. Arranging the spectral types of stars in order of decreasing temperature, she originated an alphabetical sequence that was ultimately rearranged into the hottest to coolest sequence O, B, A, F, G, K, M—the Oh Be A Fine Girl Kiss Me sequence that every beginning astronomy student today must learn. The result of her classifications are published in a work named, ironically, *The Henry Draper Catalogue*. This compilation laid the groundwork for modern stellar spectroscopy.

In 1925, Cannon received, among other honors, the first honorary degree Oxford University ever bestowed on a woman. But through four decades of work at the observatory, she received no academic recognition from Harvard. Not until 1938, shortly before her death, was she made a professor of astronomy. As early as 1911, a visiting committee of the observatory reported: "It is an anomaly that, though she is recognized the world over as the greatest living expert in this line of work . . . she holds no official position in the university."

Henrietta Swan Leavitt joined the observatory staff permanently in 1902. In 1910 she made perhaps the greatest discovery of the Harvard women of this era. She identified the Cepheids—stars in the Magellanic Clouds whose brightnesses vary. In so doing, she discovered that the period of a star's variability was related to the star's intrinsic brightness. The longer the cycle from faint to bright to faint, the truly brighter the star. This discovery evolved into the most fundamental method of calculating distances in the universe: by observing the period of variability of stars in other galaxies and thus obtaining their true brightness to compare with their apparent brightness. This made it possible for Edwin Hubble to later demonstrate that our galaxy is only one of billions in the universe. Obtaining distances to other galaxies by this method will be one of the prime tasks for the Hubble Space Telescope.

However, Leavitt was not permitted to pursue her discovery; her job was to identify and catalog the variables. Pickering also assigned her the difficult job of comparing color indices and magnitudes on plates from different telescopes. According to Cecelia Payne-Gaposchkin, another of the eminent women astronomers who came later to the observatory, this was a "harsh decision, which probably set back the study of variable stars for several decades, and condemned a brilliant woman to uncongenial work." She died at a young age, before Professor Mittag-Leffler of the Swedish Academy of Sciences would be able to nominate her for the Nobel Prize he thought she deserved.

By 1920, American women could study science, though generally only in women's colleges; a few could get graduate degrees; and a dozen or so women had earned Ph.D.'s in astronomy. But the belief persisted that the role of women in doing science was different from the role of men. In a graduation address delivered to the 1921 class of Bryn Mawr College, Simon Flexner, Director of Laboratories at the Rockefeller Institute, discussed "The Scientific Career for Women." He distinguished discoveries based on "genius" or "imaginative insight"—and here the scientists he mentioned were men—from the predictable discovery demanding "knowledge, often deep and precise, and method, but not the highest talent." Here his example was Madame Curie.

Cecilia Payne-Gaposchkin received in 1925 the first Ph.D. in astronomy Harvard granted. Her thesis on stellar atmospheres was described by Otto Struve, an eminent astronomer at Yerkes Observatory at the time, as "undoubtedly the most brilliant Ph.D. thesis ever written in astronomy." She chose to remain at Harvard, since few other positions were available to her. But her career there was orchestrated by the observatory directors. She virtually never obtained the freedom to choose her own research directions, and her achievements were less remarkable than they might have been. For most of her professional career she remained untenured. Like Cannon, she was made a professor of astronomy and granted tenure at the end of her career.

Late in her life and early in my career, I attended an international astronomy meeting at the National Academy of Sciences at which she was present, and one evening found myself helping her fix her zipper in the ladies' room. Impulsively I took the opportunity to ask her many questions concerning her experience as a woman in a scientific field dominated by men. Oh, no, she replied to each of my questions, being a woman had made no difference.

But the next evening she sought me out as we were socializing in the Great Hall before the banquet. "You know those questions you asked me last night?" she asked. "Well, I decided that I gave you all the wrong answers." Then she proceeded to describe many of the difficulties that had plagued her throughout her career at Harvard. Her autobiography, *The Dyer's Hand,* published after her death, tells a tale of disappointment after disappointment, of opportunities denied. One of the most brilliant astronomers of her time, Payne-Gaposchkin was never permitted to work on astronomy's significant problems and never elected to the National Academy of Sciences.

By 1950, women astronomers with Ph.D.'s from American universities numbered about 50 in a total community of about 300. Almost all of them were employed by women's colleges; a few had access to other opportunities through a father, uncle, or brother who could sponsor them in the world of science. Almost all were single. They could look back on 100 years of American women doing astronomy and note that limited opportunities had generally restricted the contributions women had made. They could not know that as a total percentage of the astronomy community their numbers would soon begin to shrink. At the founding of the American Astronomical Society in the 1890s, the 11 female charter members constituted about 10 percent of the society. By 1985 women members numbered about 300 out of 4,000—about seven percent.

SInce the 1950s, opportunities for women in astronomy have increased, but serious problems have not disappeared. Women whose brilliance is apparent at an early age can study at prestigious undergraduate universities, be accepted to graduate schools, accomplish important research, and obtain university or observatory positions. But, as with their male counterparts, such brilliance is rare. The remainder suffer because of their small numbers.

A student who thinks she might like to be an astronomer will often enter a department where she will be the only woman student; there will be no women on the faculty. If fortunate, she will find a sympathetic adviser and congenial colleagues with whom to study. Even so, she will be treated differently from male students. One faculty member may proclaim openly that he doesn't want a woman to work with him. Her work will be scrutinized with a care that most of her male counterparts will be lucky enough to escape. She will stand out in everything that she does. And if she persists and obtains a degree, her adviser may well sit her down and suggest that she not set her sights too high in seeking a postdoctoral position.

This kind of gatekeeping also serves to limit opportunities. The letters of recommendation that her adviser writes will not be discriminatory but may be subtly different and tentative. If she is married, she may not receive job offers: "We thought her husband would not want to move" is the usual excuse. And when she goes to a meeting, she is likely to be the only woman attending.

Permanent jobs in astronomy are scarce and hard to get for young men and women alike. Affirmative action seems to have made few inroads in the filling of academic positions. It is common for an astronomy department to receive 100 or more applications for a job; usually no more than one or two of the candidates are women.

Women constitute only a tiny fraction of tenured professors of astronomy. Many important astronomy departments, such as Harvard's, and the Mt. Wilson and Las Campanas Observatories of my own Carnegie Institution of Washington, have no women on their permanent staffs. I think this is in part because the field of astronomy is still so dominated by a male establishment. A single member of a department search committee who is reluctant to add a woman to his staff can have an enormous influence for many years. Cases have occurred in which an application list of many has been carefully narrowed down to three: two men and one woman, in that order. Following job offers to the top two, who decline the offer, the decision is then made to reopen the competition rather than offer the job to the third. Rarely does this happen when the top three candidates are male. Unfortunately, as the job market becomes even tighter, it is unlikely that the number of women in tenured academic positions will increase.

The saddest part, of course, is that only about one-fifth of the women who enter college intend to study science. Lack of support and encouragement at an early age has by then taken its toll. A young woman who enters graduate school to study science is a rare creature indeed, to be encouraged and supported. But instead, the colleges are often a part of the problem rather than part of the solution.

In spite of these difficulties, women are becoming astronomers—and successful ones. They are asking important, imaginative questions about the universe and getting answers no less often than their male colleagues. Only for the past 20 years or so have they been permitted to apply for telescope time on all telescopes—time being allotted on the basis of the excellence of the proposal. Now about one-third of the telescope time of the national facilities, which include Kitt Peak Observatory outside of Tucson, Arizona, and Cerro Tololo Observatory in Chile, is assigned to women.

A cable that was sent to me in 1978 is a testament to that. "Dear Madame," it reads, "You might appreciate hearing that four women astronomers are observing on Cerro Tololo tonight, on the four largest telescopes! We are M. H. Ulrich, M. T. Ruiz, P. Lugger, and L. Schweizer." I hope the sky was very clear that night.

Suggestions for Discussion and Writing

1. What is Rubin's purpose in this essay? Does she achieve it?

2. Do you see any irony in the title of this essay? in the mnemonic device (Oh Be A Fine Girl Kiss Me) astronomy students use to remember the spectral sequence of stars?

3. The author says, "All of us, men and women alike, need permission to enter and continue in the world of science." What are some of the forms that this "permission" takes? How does the permission needed by men differ from that needed by women?

4. Write an essay in which you explore some of the reasons why Cecilia Payne-Gaposchkin might have denied that being a woman in a scientific field dominated by men had affected her career. Do you see a connection between this denial and the author's belated realization that "no note whatsoever" was taken of the centennial of Maria Mitchell's discovery of a comet?

5. Rubin's essay is narrative in form and strongly autobiographical. What does she gain by this approach? Would an explicitly argumentative essay have enabled her to make her case more forcefully?

FEMINISM AND SCIENCE

Evelyn Fox Keller
(b. 1936)

Educated at Brandeis, Radcliffe, and Harvard, Evelyn Fox Keller has worked in mathematical biology, and, more recently, in the history, philosophy, and psychology of science. She has taught at a number of institutions, including New York University and Northeastern University, and is currently a professor of rhetoric, women's studies, and history of science at the University of California, Berkeley. Best known for her work on women and science, Keller has contributed numerous articles to professional journals and is the author of two books, *A Feeling for the Organism: The Life and Work of Barbara McClintock* (1983) and *Reflections on Gender and Science* (1985).

In the following essay, published in 1982, Keller reviews the range of criticisms brought by feminists against science and discusses the nature and origins of what she takes to be its masculine bias.

In recent years, a new critique of science has begun to emerge from a number of feminist writings. The lens of feminist politics brings into focus certain masculinist distortions of the scientific enterprise, creating, for those of us who are scientists, a potential dilemma. Is there a conflict between our commitment to feminism and our commitment to science? As both a feminist and a scientist, I am more familiar than I might wish with the nervousness and defensiveness that such a potential conflict evokes. As scientists, we have very real difficulties in thinking about the kinds of issues that, as feminists, we have been raising. These difficulties may, however, ultimately be productive. My purpose in the present essay is to explore the implications of recent feminist criticism of science for the relationship between science and feminism. Do these criticisms imply conflict? If they do, how necessary is that conflict? I will argue that those elements of feminist criticism that seem to conflict most with at least conventional conceptions of science may, in fact, carry a liberating potential for science. It could therefore benefit scientists to attend closely to feminist criticism. I will suggest that we might even use feminist thought to illuminate and clarify part of the substructure of science (which may have been historically conditioned into distortion) in order to preserve the things that science has taught us, in order to be more objective. But first it is necessary to review the various criticisms that feminists have articulated.

The range of their critique is broad. Though they all claim that science embodies a strong androcentric bias, the meanings attached to this charge vary widely. It is convenient to represent the differences in meaning by a spectrum that parallels the political range characteristic of feminism as a whole. I label this spectrum from right to left, beginning somewhere left of center with what might be called the liberal position. From the liberal critique, charges of androcentricity emerge that are relatively easy to correct. The more radical critique calls for correspondingly more radical changes; it requires a reexamination of the underlying assumptions of scientific theory and method for the presence of male bias. The difference between these positions is, however, often obscured by a knee-jerk reaction that leads many scientists to regard all such criticism as a unit—as a challenge to the neutrality of science. One of the points I wish to emphasize here is that the range of meanings attributed to the claim of androcentric bias reflects very different levels of challenge, some of which even the most conservative scientists ought to be able to accept.

First, in what I have called the liberal critique, is the charge that is essentially one of unfair employment practices. It proceeds from the observation that almost all scientists are men. This criticism is liberal in the sense that it in no way conflicts either with traditional conceptions of science or with current liberal, egalitarian politics. It is, in fact, a purely political criticism, and one which can be supported by all of us who are in favor of equal opportunity. According to this point of view, science itself would in no way be affected by the presence or absence of women.

A slightly more radical criticism continues from this and argues that the predominance of men in the sciences has led to a bias in the choice and definition of problems with which scientists have concerned themselves. This argument is most frequently and most easily made in regard to the health sciences. It is claimed, for example, that contraception has not been given the scientific attention its human importance warrants and that, furthermore, the attention it has been given has been focused primarily on contraceptive techniques to be used by women. In a related complaint, feminists argue that menstrual cramps, a serious problem for many women, have never been taken seriously by the medical profession. Presumably, had the concerns of medical research been articulated by women, these particular imbalances would not have arisen. Similar biases in sciences remote from the subject of women's bodies are more difficult to locate—they may, however, exist. Even so, this kind of criticism does not touch our conception of what science is, nor our confidence in the neutrality of science. It may be true that in some areas we have ignored certain problems, but our definition of science does not include the choice of problem—that, we can readily agree, has always been influenced by social forces. We remain, therefore, in the liberal domain.

Continuing to the left, we next find claims of bias in the actual design and interpretation of experiments. For example, it is pointed out that virtually all of the animal-learning research on rats has been performed with male rats. Though a simple explanation is offered—namely, that female rats have a four-day cycle that complicates experiments—the criticism is hardly vitiated by the explanation. The implicit assumption is, of course, that the male rat represents the species. There exist many other, often similar, examples in psychology. Examples from the biological sciences are somewhat more difficult to find, though one suspects that they exist. An area in which this suspicion is particularly strong is that of sex research. Here the influence of heavily invested preconceptions seems all but inevitable. In fact, although the existence of such preconceptions has been well documented historically, a convincing case for the existence of a corresponding bias in either the design or interpretation of experiments has yet to be made. That this is so can, I think, be taken as testimony to the effectiveness of the standards of objectivity operating.

But evidence for bias in the interpretation of observations and experiments is very easy to find in the more socially oriented sciences. The area of primatology is a familiar target. Over the past fifteen years women working in the field have undertaken an extensive reexamination of theoretical concepts, often using essentially the same methodological tools. These efforts have resulted in some radically different formulations. The range of difference frequently reflects the powerful influence of ordinary language in biasing our theoretical formulations. A great deal of very interesting work analyzing such distortions has been done. Though I cannot begin to do justice to that work here, let me offer, as a single example, the following description of a single-male troop of animals that Jane Lancaster provides as a substitute for the familiar concept of "harem": "For a female, males are a resource in her environment which she may use to further the survival of herself and her offspring. If environmental conditions are such that the male role can be minimal, a one-male group is likely. Only one male is necessary for a group of females if his only role is to impregnate them."

These critiques, which maintain that a substantive effect on scientific theory results from the predominance of men in the field, are almost exclusively aimed at the "softer," even the "softest," sciences. Thus they can still be accommodated within the traditional framework by the simple argument that the critiques, if justified, merely reflect the fact that these subjects are not sufficiently scientific. Presumably, fair-minded (or scientifically minded) scientists can and should join forces with the feminists in attempting to identify the presence of bias—equally offensive, if for different reasons, to both scientists and feminists—in order to make these "soft" sciences more rigorous.

It is much more difficult to deal with the truly radical critique that attempts to locate androcentric bias even in the "hard" sciences, indeed in scientific ideology itself. This range of criticism takes us out of the liberal domain and requires us to question the very assumptions of objectivity and rationality that underlie the scientific enterprise. To challenge the truth and necessity of the conclusions of natural science on the grounds that they too reflect the judgment of men is to take the Galilean credo and turn it on its head. It is not true that "the conclusions of natural science are true and necessary, and the judgment of man has nothing to do with them"; it is the judgment of woman that they have nothing to do with.

The impetus behind this radical move is twofold. First, it is supported by the experience of feminist scholars in other fields of inquiry. Over and over, feminists have found it necessary, in seeking to reinstate women as agents and as subjects, to question the very canons of their fields. They have turned their attention, accordingly, to the operation of patriarchal bias on ever deeper levels of social structure, even of language and thought.

But the possibility of extending the feminist critique into the foundations of scientific thought is created by recent developments in the history and philosophy of science itself. As long as the course of scientific thought was judged to be exclusively determined by its own logical and empirical necessities, there could be no place for any signature, male or otherwise, in that system of knowledge. Furthermore, any suggestion of gender differences in our thinking about the world could argue only too readily for the further exclusion of women from science. But as the philosophical and historical inadequacies of the classical conception of science have become more evident, and as historians and sociologists have begun to identify the ways in which the development of scientific knowledge has been shaped by its particular social and political context, our understanding of science as a social process has grown. This understanding is a necessary prerequisite, both politically and intellectually, for a feminist theoretic in science.

Joining feminist thought to other social studies of science brings the promise of radically new insights, but it also adds to the existing intellectual danger a political threat. The intellectual danger resides in viewing science as pure social product; science then dissolves into ideology and objectivity loses all intrinsic meaning. In the resulting cultural relativism, any emancipatory function of modern science is negated, and the arbitration of truth recedes into the political domain. Against this background, the temptation arises for feminists to abandon their claim for representation in sceintific culture and, in its place, to invite a return to a purely "female" subjectivity, leaving rationality and objectivity in the male domain, dismissed as products of a purely male consciousness.

Many authors have addressed the problems raised by total relativism; here I wish merely to mention some of the special problems added by its feminist variant. They are several. In important respects, feminist relativism is just the kind of radical move that transforms the political spectrum into a circle. By rejecting objectivity as a masculine ideal, it simultaneously lends its voice to an enemy chorus and dooms women to residing outside of the realpolitik modern culture;

it exacerbates the very problem it wishes to solve. It also nullifies the radical potential of feminist criticism for our understanding of science. As I see it, the task of a feminist theoretic in science is twofold: to distinguish that which is parochial from that which is universal in the scientific impulse, reclaiming for women what has historically been denied to them; and to legitimate those elements of scientific culture that have been denied precisely because they are defined as female.

It is important to recognize that the framework inviting what might be called the nihilist retreat is in fact provided by the very ideology of objectivity we wish to escape. This is the ideology that asserts an opposition between (male) objectivity and (female) subjectivity and denies the possibility of mediation between the two. A first step, therefore, in extending the feminist critique to the foundations of scientific thought is to reconceptualize objectivity as a dialectical process so as to allow for the possibility of distinguishing the objective effort from the objectivist illusion. As Piaget reminds us:

> Objectivity consists in so fully realizing the countless intrusions of the self in everyday thought and the countless illusions which result—illusions of sense, language, point of view, value, etc.—that the preliminary step to every judgment is the effort to exclude the intrusive self. Realism, on the contrary, consists in ignoring the existence of self and thence regarding one's own perspective as immediately objective and absolute. Realism is thus anthropocentric illusion, finality—in short, all those illusions which teem in the history of science. So long as thought has not become conscious of self, it is a prey to perpetual confusions between objective and subjective, between the real and the ostensible.

In short, rather than abandon the quintessentially human effort to understand the world in rational terms, we need to refine that effort. To do this, we need to add to the familiar methods of rational and empirical inquiry the additional process of critical self-reflection. Following Piaget's injunction, we need to "become conscious of self." In this way, we can become conscious of the features of the scientific project that belie its claim to universality.

The ideological ingredients of particular concern to feminists are found where objectivity is linked with autonomy and masculinity, and in turn, the goals of science with power and domination. The linking of objectivity with social and political autonomy has been examined by many authors and shown to serve a variety of important political functions. The implications of joining objectivity with masculinity are less well understood. This conjunction also serves critical political functions. But an understanding of the sociopolitical meaning of the entire constellation requires an examination of the psychological processes through which these connections become internalized and perpetuated. Here psychoanalysis offers us an invaluable perspective, and it is to the exploitation of that perspective that much of my own work has been directed. In an earlier paper, I tried to show how psychoanalytic theories of development illuminate the structure and meaning of an interacting system of associations linking objectivity (a cognitive trait) with autonomy (an affective trait) and masculinity (a gender trait). Here, after a brief summary of my earlier argument, I want to explore the relation of this system to power and domination.

Along with Nancy Chodorow and Dorothy Dinnerstein, I have found that branch of psychoanalytic theory known as object relations theory to be especially useful. In seeking to account for personality development in terms of both innate drives and actual relations with other objects (i.e., subjects), it permits us to understand the ways in which our earliest experiences—experiences in large part determined by the socially structured relationships that form the context of our developmental processes—help to shape our conception of the world and our characteristic orientations to it. In particular, our first steps in the world are guided primarily by the parents of one sex—our mothers; this determines a maturational framework for our emotional, cognitive, and gender development, a framework later filled in by cultural expectations.

In brief, I argued the following: Our early maternal environment, coupled with the cultural definition of masculine (that which can never appear feminine) and of autonomy (that which can never be compromised by dependency) leads to the association of female with the pleasures and dangers of merging, and of male with the comfort and loneliness of separateness. The boy's internal anxiety about both self and gender is echoed by the more widespread cultural anxiety, thereby encouraging postures of autonomy and masculinity, which can, indeed may, be designed to defend against that anxiety and the longing that generates it. Finally, for all of us, our sense of reality is carved out of the same developmental matrix. As Piaget and others have emphasized, the capacity for cognitive distinctions between self and other (objectivity) evolves concurrently and interdependently with the development of psychic autonomy; our cognitive ideals thereby become subject to the same psychological influences as our emotional and gender ideals. Along with autonomy the very act of separating subject from object—objectivity itself—comes to be associated with masculinity. The combined psychological and cultural pressures lead all three ideals—affective, gender, and cognitive—to a mutually reinforcing process of exaggeration and rigidification. The net result is the entrenchment of an objectivist ideology and a correlative devaluation of (female) subjectivity.

This analysis leaves out many things. Above all it omits discussion of the psychological meanings of power and domination, and it is to those meanings I now wish to turn. Central to object relations theory is the recognition that the condition of psychic autonomy is double edged: it offers a profound source of pleasure, and simultaneously of potential dread. The values of autonomy are consonant with the values of competence, of mastery. Indeed competence is itself a prior condition for autonomy and serves immeasurably to confirm one's sense of self. But need the development of competence and the sense of mastery lead to a state of alienated selfhood, of denied connectedness, of defensive separatness? To forms of autonomy that can be understood as protections against dread? Object relations theory makes us sensitive to autonomy's range of meanings; it simultaneously suggests the need to consider the corresponding meanings of competence. Under what circumstances does competence imply mastery of one's own fate and under what circumstances does it imply mastery over another's? In short, are control and domination essential ingredients of competence, and intrinsic to selfhood, or are they correlates of an alienated selfhood?

One way to answer these questions is to use the logic of the analysis summarized above to examine the shift from competence to power and control in the psychic economy of the young child. From that analysis, the impulse toward domination can be understood as a natural concomitant of defensive separateness—as Jessica Benjamin has written, "A way of repudiating sameness, dependency and closeness with another person, while attempting to avoid the consequent feelings of aloneness." Perhaps no one has written more sensitively than psychoanalyst D. W. Winnicott of the rough waters the child must travel in negotiating the transition from symbiotic union to the recognition of self and other as autonomous entities. He alerts us to a danger that others have missed—a danger arising from the unconscious fantasy that the subject has actually destroyed the object in the process of becoming separate.

Indeed, he writes, "It is the destruction of the object that places the object outside the area of control. . . . After 'subject relates to object' comes 'subject destroys object' (as it becomes external); then may come '*object survives* destruction by the subject.' But there may or may not be survival." When there is, "because of the survival of the object, the subject may now have started to live a life in the world of objects, and so the subject stands to gain immeasurably; but the price has to be paid in acceptance of the ongoing destruction in unconscious fantasy relative to object-relating." Winnicott, of course, is not speaking of actual survival but of subjective confidence in the survival of the other. Survival in that sense requires that the child maintain relatedness; failure induces inevitable guilt and dread. The child is poised on a terrifying precipice. On one side lies the fear of having destroyed the object, on the other side, loss of self. The child may make an attempt to secure this precarious position by seeking to master the other. The cycles of destruction and survival are reenacted while the other is kept safely at bay, and as Benjamin writes, "the original self assertion is . . . converted from innocent mastery to mastery over and against the other." In psychodynamic terms, this particular resolution of preoedipal conflicts is a product of oedipal consolidation. The (male) child achieves his final security by identification with the father—an identification involving simultaneously a denial of the mother and a transformation of guilt and fear into aggression.

Aggression, of course, has many meanings, many sources, and many forms of expression. Here I mean to refer only to the form underlying the impulse toward domination. I invoke psychoanalytic theory to help illuminate the forms of expression that impulse finds in science as a whole, and its relation to objectification in particular. The same questions I asked about the child I can also ask about science. Under what circumstances is scientific knowledge sought for the pleasures of knowing, for the increased competence it grants us, for the increased mastery (real or imagined) over our own fate, and under what circumstances is it fair to say that science seeks actually to dominate nature? Is there a meaningful distinction to be made here?

In his work *The Domination of Nature* William Leiss observes, "The necessary correlate of domination is the consciousness of subordination in those who must obey the will of another; thus properly speaking only other men can be the objects of domination." (Or women, we might add.) Leiss infers from this observation that it is not the domination of physical nature we should worry about but the use of our knowledge of physical nature as an instrument for the domination of human nature. He therefore sees the need for correctives, not in science but in its uses. This is his point of departure from other authors of the Frankfurt school, who assume the very logic of science to be the logic of domination. I agree with Leiss's basic observation but draw a somewhat different inference. I suggest that the impulse toward domination does find expression in the goals (and even in the theories and practice) of modern science, and argue that where it finds such expression the impulse needs to be acknowledged as projection. In short, I argue that not only in the denial of interaction between subject and other but also in the access of domination to the goals of scientific knowledge, one finds the intrusion of a self we begin to recognize as partaking in the cultural construct of masculinity.

The value of consciousness is that it enables us to make choices—both as individuals and as scientists. Control and domination are in fact intrinsic neither to selfhood (i.e., autonomy) nor to scientific knowledge. I want to suggest, rather, that the particular emphasis Western science has placed on these functions of knowledge is twin to the objectivist ideal. Knowledge in general, and scientific knowledge in particular, serves two gods: power and transcendence. It aspires alternately to mastery over and union with nature. Sexuality serves the same two gods, aspiring to domination and ecstatic communion—in short, aggression and eros. And it is hardly a new insight to say that power, control, and domination are fueled largely by aggression, while union satisfies a more purely erotic impulse.

To see the emphasis on power and control so prevalent in the

rhetoric of Western science as projection of a specifically male consciousness requires no great leap of the imagination. Indeed, that
perception has become a commonplace. Above all, it is invited by the
rhetoric that conjoins the domination of nature with the insistent
image of nature as female, nowhere more familiar than in the
writings of Francis Bacon. For Bacon, knowledge and power are one,
and the promise of science is expressed as "leading to you Nature
with all her children to bind her to your service and make her your
slave," by means that do not "merely exert a gentle guidance over
nature's course; they have the power to conquer and subdue her, to
shake her to her foundations." In the context of the Baconian vision,
Bruno Bettelheim's conclusion appears inescapable: "Only with phal-
lic psychology did aggressive manipulation of nature become possible."

The view of science as an oedipal project is also familiar from the
writings of Herbert Marcuse and Norman O. Brown. But Brown's
preoccupation, as well as Marcuse's, is with what Brown calls a
"morbid" science. Accordingly, for both authors the quest for a
nonmorbid science, an "erotic" science, remains a romantic one.
This is so because their picture of science is incomplete: it omits from
consideration the crucial, albeit less visible, erotic components already present in the scientific tradition. Our own quest, if it is to be
realistic rather than romantic, must be based on a richer understanding of the scientific tradition, in all its dimensions, and on an understanding of the ways in which this complex, dialectical tradition
becomes transformed into a monolithic rhetoric. Neither the oedipal
child nor modern science has in fact managed to rid itself of its
preoedipal and fundamentally bisexual yearnings. It is with this
recognition that the quest for a different science, a science undis-
torted by masculinist bias, must begin.

The presence of contrasting themes, of a dialectic between aggressive and erotic impulses, can be seen both within the work of
individual scientists and, even more dramatically, in the juxtaposed
writings of different scientists. Francis Bacon provides us with one
model; there are many others. For an especially striking contrast,
consider a contemporary scientist [Barbara McClintock] who insists
on the importance of "letting the material speak to you," of allowing
it to "tell you what to do next"—one who chastises other scientists
for attempting to "impose an answer" on what they see. For this
scientist, discovery is facilitated by becoming "part of the system,"
rather than remaining outside; one must have a "feeling for the
organism." It is true that the author of these remarks is not only from
a different epoch and a different field (Bacon himself was not actually
a scientist by most standards), she is also a woman. It is also true
that there are many reasons, some of which I have already suggested, for thinking that gender (itself constructed in an ideological
context) actually does make a difference in scientific inquiry. Nevertheless, my point here is that neither science nor individuals are
totally bound by ideology. In fact, it is not difficult to find similar

sentiments expressed by male scientists. Consider, for example, the following remarks: "I have often had cause to feel that my hands are cleverer than my head. That is a crude way of characterizing the dialectics of experimentation. When it is going well, it is like a quiet conversation with Nature." The difference between conceptions of science as "dominating" and as "conversing with" nature may not be a difference primarily between epochs, nor between the sexes. Rather, it can be seen as representing a dual theme played out in the work of all scientists, in all ages. But the two poles of this dialectic do not appear with equal weight in the history of science. What we therefore need to attend to is the evolutionary process that selects one theme as dominant.

Elsewhere I have argued for the importance of a different selection process. In part, scientists are themselves selected by the emotional appeal of particular (stereotypic) images of science. Here I am arguing for the importance of selection within scientific thought—first of preferred methodologies and aims, and finally of preferred theories. The two processes are not unrelated. While stereotypes are not binding (i.e., they do not describe all or perhaps any individuals), and this fact creates the possibility for an ongoing contest within science, the first selection process undoubtedly influences the outcome of the second. That is, individuals drawn by a particular ideology will tend to select themes consistent with that ideology.

One example in which this process is played out on a theoretical level is in the fate of interactionist theories in the history of biology. Consider the contest that has raged throughout this century between organismic and particulate views of cellular organization—between what might be described as hierarchical and nonhierarchical theories. Whether the debate is over the primacy of the nucleus or the cell as a whole, the genome or the cytoplasm, the proponents of hierarchy have won out. One geneticist has described the conflict in explicitly political terms:

> Two concepts of genetic mechanisms have persisted side by side throughout the growth of modern genetics, but the emphasis has been very strongly in favor of one of these. . . . The first of these we will designate as the "Master Molecule" concept. . . . This is in essence the Theory of the Gene, interpreted to suggest a totalitarian government. . . . The second concept we will designate as the "Steady State" concept. By this term . . . we envision a dynamic self-perpetuating organization of a variety of molecular species which owes its specific properties not to the characteristic of any one kind of molecule, but to the functional interrelationships of these molecular species.

Soon after these remarks, the debate between "master molecules" and dynamic interactionism was foreclosed by the synthesis provided by DNA and the "central dogma." With the success of the new molecular biology such "steady state" (or egalitarian) theories lost interest for almost all geneticists. But today, the same conflict shows signs of reemerging—in genetics, in theories of the immune system, and in theories of development.

I suggest that method and theory may constitute a natural continuum, despite Popperian claims to the contrary, and that the same processes of selection may bear equally and simultaneously on both the means and aims of science and the actual theoretical descriptions that emerge. I suggest this in part because of the recurrent and striking consonance that can be seen in the way scientists work, the relation they take to their object of study, and the theoretical orientation they favor. To pursue the example cited earlier, the same scientist who allowed herself to become "part of the system," whose investigations were guided by a "feeling for the organism," developed a paradigm that diverged as radically from the dominant paradigm of her field as did her methodological style.

In lieu of the linear hierarchy described by the central dogma of molecular biology, in which the DNA encodes and transmits all instructions for the unfolding of a living cell, her research yielded a view of the DNA in delicate interaction with the cellular environment—an organismic view. For more important than the genome as such (i.e., the DNA) is the "overall organism." As she sees it, the genome functions "only in respect to the environment in which it is found." In this work the program encoded by the DNA is itself subject to change. No longer is a master control to be found in a single component of the cell; rather, control resides in the complex interactions of the entire system. When first presented, the work underlying this vision was not understood, and it was poorly received. Today much of that work is undergoing a renaissance, although it is important to say that her full vision remains too radical for most biologists to accept.

This example suggests that we need not rely on our imagination for a vision of what a different science—a science less restrained by the impulse to dominate—might be like. Rather, we need only look to the thematic pluralism in the history of our own science as it has evolved. Many other examples can be found, but we lack an adequate understanding of the full range of influences that lead to the acceptance or rejection not only of particular theories but of different theoretical orientations. What I am suggesting is that if certain theoretical interpretations have been selected against, it is precisely in this process of selection that ideology in general, and a masculinist ideology in particular, can be found to effect its influence. The task this implies for a radical feminist critique of science is, then, first a historical one, but finally a transformative one. In the historical effort, feminists can bring a whole new range of sensitivities, leading to an equally new consciousness of the potentialities lying latent in the scientific project.

Suggestions for Discussion and Writing

1. Keller ranges feminist critiques of science along a spectrum "from right to left, beginning somewhere left of center with what might be called the liberal position." In your own words, summarize the critique of each identified group. Where does the author herself belong on this spectrum? Where does Vera Rubin (this chapter) belong? Is it appropriate to give feminist views on science a political cast?

2. What evidence does the author offer to support the view that the health and biological sciences have been negatively affected by male bias? Is this evidence convincing? Can you think of other evidence? Why might evidence from psychology and the "soft" sciences be easier to find?

3. In what ways does Jane Lancaster's description of a "single-male troop of animals" differ from the "familiar concept of 'harem' "? Is it significant that the author contrasts Lancaster's description simply with a "familiar concept"?

4. Keller recognizes the difficulty of dealing with "the truly radical critique that attempts to locate androcentric bias even in the 'hard' sciences, indeed in scientific ideology itself." What is this difficulty? Does it influence the direction of her subsequent argument?

5. What does the author mean when she says that an "understanding of science as a social process . . . is a necessary prerequisite . . . for a feminist theoretic in science"? What "intellectual danger" is inherent in viewing science as a social process?

6. In a brief essay, explain how, according to Keller and psychoanalytic "object relations" theory, "objectivity" comes to be associated with "masculinity."

7. Keller relies on psychoanalytic theory to establish "objectification," "domination," "power," and so on as essentially "masculine" preoccupations that have shaped "the very logic of science." Does the fact that she relies on what Popper would call "pseudoscience" (see Chapter 7) to support her argument undermine her position? Write an essay defending your views.

8. What does the author mean when she says that the "quest for a different science" must begin with the recognition that "neither the oedipal child nor modern science has in fact managed to rid itself of its preoedipal and fundamentally bisexual yearnings"?

9. At the end of her essay, Keller says that the task for a radical feminist critique is "finally a transformative one." Has she established that science as currently practiced needs to be

transformed? What evidence does she offer? Do you find it convincing? Pointing to specific examples, write an essay defending your views.

☐ **FEMINIST SCIENCE: CHANGE, COMPLEXITY, CONTEXTUALITY, INTERACTION**

Ruth Bleier
(1923–1988)

Ruth Bleier was among the first to call for a critical reexamination of the biological sciences from a feminist perspective. Her *Science and Gender: A Critique of Biology and Its Theories on Women* (1984) and her anthology *Feminist Approaches to Science* (1986) are regarded as major contributions to feminist scholarship.

Politically committed throughout her life, Bleier began her career in the early 1950s as a physician working in Baltimore's inner city. Her activity in the peace movement attracted the unfavorable attention of the House Un-American Activities Committee, and she was called to testify. She refused to cooperate with the Committee and was subsequently denied hospital privileges, an action designed to curtail her medical practice. During this period, however, Bleier was studying neurophysiology at Johns Hopkins School of Medicine and, in 1961, gave up her medical practice to become an instructor of neuroanatomy there. Her reputation as a scientist was established by her studies of the hypothalamus in animals, a subject on which she published three widely respected books.

Joining the Department of Neurophysiology at the University of Wisconsin at Madison in 1967, Bleier helped create the Association of Faculty Women, a group committed to ensuring equal pay for women faculty members as well as full compliance with affirmative action requirements. She also played a key role in establishing the Women's Studies Program at Wisconsin in the mid-1970s. She was stricken with cancer in the summer of 1987 and died six months later.

In the following selection, taken from *Science and Gender*, Bleier discusses the "dualistic" modes of thought that, in her view, have damaged not just science but "our social world and women's place in it." She calls for breaking down the "patriarchal structure of science" and "the changing of boundaries and definitions" within it.

A first task in science is to examine the modes of thought that structure science's methodologies and its views of the world. As both Fee and O'Brien have also suggested, the historical separation of human experience into mutually contradictory realms, female and male, engendered our culturally inherited dualistic modes of thought, and that male–female dichotomy was built into our ways of perceiving truth. An important task for feminist scientists and, I believe, all feminist scholars is to question and examine *all* dualisms, all dichotomous ways in which nature, human "nature," and human activities are described, analyzed, and categorized. The dualistic mode defines science itself, describes and prescribes participants as well as objects of study and orders and explains the world that science purports to analyze and explain. Not only is the dualistic mode of organizing thought a cultural construction, but the oppositions and universals it poses are themselves culture-bound concepts. Hierarchies, relations of domination, subordination, power, and control are not necessarily inherent in nature but are an integral part of the conceptual framework of persons bred in a civilization constructed on principles of stratification, domination, subordination, power, and control, all made to appear natural. The relationship of culture to nature is not necessarily oppositional; the relationship of the knowing subject to the studied object is not necessarily the dualistic one of activity and passivity or domination and subordinance. These dualisms resonate interchangeably and metaphorically with the female–male dichotomy throughout our literary, artistic, scientific, and other cultural expressions.

Science need not be permitted to specify who does science by defining itself as the expression and epitomy of the male mind, which *it* defines as self-evidently objective, impersonal, and creative. Science need not be permitted to define objectivity and creativity as that which the male mind does and subjectivity and emotionality as that which the female mind is. It need not be permitted to claim that science is or even can be objective, transcendent, neutral, and value-free.

Such dualistic and universalistic concepts and modes of thinking have not only damaged science as well as scholarship in other areas such as anthropology, psychology, and sociology, but they have also structured our social world and women's place in it. They provided the intellectual structure to accommodate the subordinate status of women required by patriarchal ideologies and institutions. Thus, feminist critiques and transformations of science, like feminist scholarship in other fields, will not simply restore missing subjects and points of view, will not simply make science better and capable of a more complete appreciation of the world; they will also transform ideological bases for our Western civilization and for women's place in it.

The problems with a dualistic mode of thought are several. It structures our approach to knowledge of the world, it structures the world itself in an *a priori* fashion and imposes, as premises, dualisms and dichotomies, onto the organization of the natural world that do not exist. Most basically, it obscures a fundamental characteristic of life and matter, perhaps first enunciated by Heraclitus over 2000 years ago: everything is in a constant state of flux, change, interaction. With such a view of reality, we cannot separate genes from environment, culture from nature, subject from object. We cannot view science as an act of domination and objectivity, but rather as one of mutuality and interaction with nature.

Some may view this as an easy mode of thought for women, whose lives are nearly always contextual and interrelational rather than transcendent. As Hein points out, the requirement to be self-effacing, egoless, objective, and transcendent in order to be a good scientist or scholar is an inappropriate exhortation for women. Since woman's ego or "self has not been abstractly affirmed to begin with, it does not stand in transcendent opposition to its object." So are women's relationships to knowledge, to objects of study and knowing, more usually ones of mutuality rather than invasion or dominance. While women certainly are, as Hein says, educable to male-defined rules, they are more attuned to the fluidity of life, an acceptance of change, fusion, and interaction. Such experiencing of life more easily generates a sense of inclusiveness and contextuality as cognitive frameworks and modes of perceiving and understanding the world, as contrasted with aloofness, exclusiveness, separateness, impersonality. Women's experience, Hein suggests, places them in a perspectival framework different from but no less legitimate than that of men:

> That male categories and rules of understanding should appear to have greater legitimacy than those of women can be due only to the political dominance which men have enjoyed. There can be no absolute basis for comparing distinct modes of experiencing, let alone for evaluating them.

This is not the same as claiming for women a particular "inherent" or "innate" way of thinking. We cannot make the important claims, basic feminist insights, that little girls in our Western cultures are socialized from birth to be nurturant, loving, responsive and dependent; that they become, consequently, exquisitely sensitive to the social cues from those on whom they are taught to depend for love and approval; that they learn to define themselves only or primarily in relation to a multitude of others; and, at the same time, believe that such learning has no effect on our modes and frameworks of thinking, and the values and judgments that are an integral part of the process of science and scholarship. If there is a general difference between women and men in their approach to science, it may lie in their different relationships to the concept and practice of control. To

be in control of things, people, phenomena, information, and institutions, is an essence of our Western industrial class culture. Since
men are the designated actors in patriarchal cultures, they are the
ones who must be and are taught to be in control. To know, to be
certain, is part of being in control. It is important to know *causes* for
events and phenomena, for without that "knowledge" one cannot
know how to intervene effectively in order to remain or be in control.
To be concerned with understanding process, change, and interaction, rather than causes and effects, is to relinquish the need for
control or to acknowledge the implicit irrelevance of the issue of
control. For women in general, control has been a non-issue. Just as
men were not taught or expected to think about parenting as a
relevant issue for their lives or their self-definition before the contemporary women's movement, the question of being in control (of
anything or anyone, including their own selves) was never part of
women's frame of reference for conceptualizing or realizing their
own relationships to others or to nature. Since interaction and
concern with process characterize the generally accepted (if not
required) mode of women's social responses and interchanges, they
are seemingly our natural modes of thought and conceptualizations.

Other philosophies and methods—Hegelian dialectics, Marxist dialectical materialism, phenomenology, hermeneutics—also appreciate
the realities of change, interconnectedness, and contextuality, but
they are not modes of thought that are part of mainstream biological
and social science. Hein believes both that women's experiences of
life generally engender such modes of thought and that their experiencing of life, of nature, of the world is yet to find expression, since

> female frameworks have been so profoundly devalued
> that neither women nor men have found it worthwhile to
> try to transmit them, and so there is not even a lan-
> guage in which they might be expressed. Since women
> have been dispersed throughout the dominant culture,
> they have not formulated a distinctive and common tool
> of communication.

If nondualistic, contextual, interrelational cognitive modes were to
prevail, if women were to find expression for *their* experiencing of
life, a process that has begun, sciences could become whole.

Whether one is attempting to explain the development of tuberculosis in humans (the majority of whom in the United States are
exposed during their lifetime to the tubercle bacillus but do not
acquire active tuberculosis), the gradual development of sedentarism
and villages, or the development of patriarchal ideologies and cultures, it is important to recognize that there can be no single
"correct" explanation, no simple, dramatic "cause." Rather, there
will be an array of factors, some more important than others, each
factor having its own historical course of development and its own
situational specificities, interacting with other such factors over time

and eventually leading to the phenomenon under scrutiny. We can use the example of lung cancer. There are people who get lung cancer who have never smoked and others who smoke two packs a day and don't get lung cancer. In the smoker who gets lung cancer, smoking has interacted with a particular combination of biological and environmental factors that may very well be a unique combination for each person. Biological factors would include immunological, anatomical, hormonal, and genetic characteristics; environmental factors could include air and occupational toxins and pollutants, viral and bacterial infections of the lungs and bronchial tree, nutrition, drugs, and stress. Environmental factors all have an effect on one or another of the biological characteristics. Some particular coincidence of several such factors constitutes the complex "causation" of cancer in any particular person.

It follows from this that no single individual scientist, scholar, or theorizer can produce the "whole truth" about a given phenomenon. Each of us brings to the inquiry, to the investigation of a particular phenomenon, our own life history of experiences, knowledge, and attitudes as well as our particular skills and training, and, consequently, each illuminates one or another facet of the complex phenomenon we are trying to explain. Together we illuminate many different facets, all varied aspects of the "truth." It is through this plurality of shared views and voices that we come to some understanding of nature, society, and ourselves.

After this critical examination of the dualistic/universalistic mode of thought and the limitations on its usefulness, as compared with concepts of change and interaction, it is important to examine particular dualisms that mold our approaches to science and knowledge and our perceptions of natural phenomena. Two that leap to mind in association with doing science are the dualisms of objectivity–subjectivity and dominance–subordinance. As one approach to knowledge of nature and society, science relies on methods of rationality, logic, empirical testing, and objectivity. Like others elsewhere, I have criticized particular scientists and sciences for their false claims to objectivity and neutrality and for their role in providing unwarranted "scientific" authority as legitimization for social and political beliefs. However, both Fee and Keller warn against a nihilistic retreat into cultural relativism and a wholesale rejection of science and the possibility of comprehending the world in rational terms; and Fee outlines the characteristics of an ideal and useful scientific approach:

> The concept of creating knowledge through a constant process of practical interactions with nature, the willingness to consider all assumptions and methods as open to question, the expectation that ideas will be tested and refined in practice, and that results and conclusions of research will be subjected to the most unfettered critical evaluation—all these are aspects of scientific objectivity which should be preserved and defended. The hope of

learning more about the world and ourselves by such collective process is not one to be abandoned.

While in most scientific efforts we cannot exclude the self (i.e., subjectivity), we can at least insist that our thoughts become "conscious of self," that "critical self-reflection" be part of our scholarly inquiry. A part of this process is recognizing the degree to which investment of ego and pride in one's previously stated beliefs and theories may corrupt the scientific approach outlined above by Fee. Objectivity and subjectivity are inseparable parts of the thought processes and inquiries of women and men, scientists and nonscientists alike. To believe otherwise is to believe in myths. Individuals differ primarily in the levels of their consciousness and acknowledgment of self (with its history, experiences, values, beliefs, hopes, and desires) in their private and public judgments and acts and their scholarly productions. The experiences, values, and ideas embodied in the self can, as an integral part of any scholarly inquiry, help to illuminate some facet of truth or reality or, on the other hand, act to distort and torture reality in the service of personal, social, or political needs. In the former case, the "critical self-reflection" can be and usually is a freely acknowledged (and clearly unavoidable) part of scholarly inquiry and has been an important feature of feminist scholarship. In the latter case, the experiences, values, and beliefs of the self are not acknowledged as such but rather are universalized as objective truths about society, nature, and human nature and have been an important feature of Sociobiological and other biological determinist theorizing.

The other important dualism that has molded scientific thought and methodology is that of dominance and subordinance. I have provided examples of the extent to which dominance and dominance hierarchies have served as organizing principles and causal explanations in the fields of anthropology, primatology, and Sociobiology. Evelyn Fox Keller also discusses the importance of the ideas of power, control, and domination, both over nature and other humans, in the goals, theory, and practice of modern Western science. She documents the early expression in our modern scientific tradition of the combined patriarchal view of gender relations and science with a quotation from the philosopher of science, Francis Bacon (1561–1626), who spoke of science as "leading to you Nature with all her children to bind her to your service and make her your slave." The themes of domination permeate the sciences both as explicit principles of social organization assumed to exist among primates and other species of animals, as though inherent in nature, and also as metaphoric assumption, such as in the "Master Molecule" concept of the action of genes. Through this concept, Keller nicely illustrates two different ways of conceptualizing and approaching the investigation of natural phenomena. In the face of a dominant paradigm in the field of molecular biology that posits a linear hierarchy in which genetic DNA encodes and transmits all instructions for cellular development, the research of biologist Barbara McClintock, who spoke to Keller of her scientific approach of "letting the material speak to you" and having "a feeling for the organism," led her to a different view. In this view, DNA is "in delicate interaction with the cellular environment"; master control is not found in a single component of the cell; rather, "control resides in the complex interactions of the entire system." The focus of importance is on the organism and its environment, not on a Master Molecule.

Over the past several years, the fields of biological development and ecology have undergone dramatic change in their concepts and approach from mechanistic and deterministic explanations to a fuller understanding of the importance of change, context, and interaction. It is recognized that genes do not *determine* events, but that genetic mechanisms are "turned on" by environmental events and constantly influenced by them. Historians or scientists in these disciplines may be interested in discovering the degree to which these trends have been influenced by the work of scientists like McClintock and Rachel Carson and other women active in these scientific fields, which may have a larger than ordinary proportion of women.

Both Fee and Haraway suggest that it may not be possible for us, immersed and marginalized in a patriarchal capitalist system and ideology of dominance, to conceptualize a feminist science. It would be, Fee says, "like asking a medieval peasant to imagine the theory of genetics or the production of a space capsule." On the other hand, certain themes emerge from the work of Fee and Haraway and other feminist philosophers and historians I have discussed, which reflects my own perspective as a feminist scientist. These are themes that point toward a better science, one that includes and encompasses women, but these themes do not by themselves constitute a feminist science with a uniquely, radically feminist philosophy and approach. It does not seem unreasonable to expect that the development of feminist scientific theory and philosophy will proceed hand-in-hand with the feminist struggle to change the conditions of our lives and work and with the development of feminist theory in general: a theory that articulates the new self-conscious destiny of women, points to the abolition of barriers "between public and private, between production and reproduction, between women and men," and makes impossible both the appropriation of women and children and all systems of dominance by any group over others.

Doing science well requires what women, in general, have: the ability to listen and hear, to be aware and perceptive, to understand and appreciate process and interaction. It is "letting the material speak to you" and having "a feeling for the organism," whether that material or organism is another human being, a chimpanzee, genes, or the unexpected signals from a radiotelescope. It has to do with not imposing the ego in the form of preconceived, unalterable, unacknowledged, and constraining belief systems on the subject matter, but rather creating the circumstances that permit the matter to reveal some of its characteristics to you. This means the courageous and difficult task of examining and questioning all of our assumptions and the very structure of our thought processes, all clearly born and bred within a profoundly stratified, hierarchical, patriarchal culture. These include assumptions about dominance and subordinance, women and men, objectivity and subjectivity; about causation, truth and reality; about what is "normal" and "natural"; about control and power; about reproduction and motherhood. Doing good science involves an appreciation of the complexity of all phenomena and the constancy of only the process of change.

While similar critiques of science have been made by scientists of the political left who would not necessarily call themselves feminists, what is potentially and ultimately revolutionary in the feminist critique is that the patriarchal structure of science, its theory and practice, will not be left intact. What is developing as a unique emphasis in feminist scholarship is the value of and the necessity for the plurality of our views. If indeed the phenomena we examine are multifaceted in their complex reality and their causal forces, if indeed we are validly different from one other, each bringing our unique coincidence of history, experience, belief, and skills to our joint efforts, then we know we must turn our enormous learned capacities to listen and nurture to an attentive appreciation of each other and our different views and approaches, which, together, will illuminate important realities. The answer to Haraway's question, "How can feminism, a political position about love and power, have anything to do with science as I have described it?" involves the idea of our collective approach to knowledge of nature and ourselves and the survival of both. It involves the breaking down of hierarchies, the changing of boundaries and definitions, since, as Fausto-Sterling suggests, women entering a non-hierarchical science in large numbers will have their own ideas about the subject matter of science and the language it will use. "The ideal of individual creativity subjected to the constraints of community validation through a set of recognized procedures" can guide us toward a better and more humane science; and the contours of a feminist science will emerge as more feminist scientists, scholars, and practitioners turn their attention to the problem.

Suggestions for Discussion and Writing

1. Which adjective(s) best describes Bleier's style: "discussive," "argumentative," "declarative"? (If you wish, choose another adjective.) Support your choice by pointing to stylistic and tonal features of the essay.

2. How, according to the author, have women's lives affected their "relationships to knowledge" and their "modes of thought"?

3. What does Bleier mean by "dualistic modes of thought"?

4. Bleier uses lung cancer to illustrate her point that a variety of interacting factors are often (or usually) involved in the development of a particular situation or condition. What is the connection between this point and her broader argument that, by bringing "nondualistic, contextual, and interrelational cognitive modes" to science, women could help make it "whole"?

5. One of the best ways to support an argument is through the use of examples. Does the author use examples effectively?

6. Bleier says that "over the past several years, the fields of biological development and ecology have undergone dramatic change in their concepts and approach from mechanistic and deterministic explanations to a fuller understanding of the importance of change, context, and interaction." To what does she attribute this change? In what ways has twentieth-century physics undergone a similar change? You may wish to consult (in Chapter 1) Heisenberg, and/or (in Chapter 5) Einstein, Russell, Hazen/ Trefil.

7. At the end of her essay, the author suggests the need for a "more humane science." In what ways can science be made more humane? Write an essay developing your views.

CARING NEW WORLD: FEMINISM AND SCIENCE

Margarita Levin
(b. 1945)

Margarita Levin, a native New Yorker of Cuban descent, teaches philosophy at Yeshiva College and Stern College for Women, both part of Yeshiva University in New York City. Her bachelor's degree is in mathematics, her Ph.D. in the philosophy of mathematics. Among her published articles are "Tymoczko's Argument for Mathematical Empiricism" and "In Defense of Objectivity." In the following essay, first published in *The American Scholar* (1988), Levin examines the feminist critique of science, arguing that it is flawed in three fundamental ways.

The past decade has seen one academic discipline after another re-interpreted by feminist scholars. The process began with the rediscovery and re-evaluation of female authors, and the championing of art unique to women, such as quilts and embroidery. It moved on to attacks on psychology, sociology, history, political science, anthropology, and of course biology as it concerns sex differences. Common to all such feminist revisionism has been an insistence on examining every discipline through the lens of a belief in the past and present unfair treatment of women.

By this point probably every academic in the humanities or social sciences has some acquaintance with the feminist version of his field of inquiry. It would, however, be natural to assume that feminists could not seriously undertake to accuse the physical sciences of "sexism" since those disciplines do not study human beings at all. But, it seems, a number of recent books and articles have launched just such an attack. Among the more important are Sandra Harding's book-length study *The Science Question in Feminism* and Evelyn Fox Keller's collection of essays *Reflections on Gender and Science,* as well as her earlier essay "Feminism and Science."

Sandra Harding explains why feminists have now begun to analyze science:

> Once we begin to theorize gender—to define gender as an analytic category within which humans think about and organize their social activity rather than as a natural consequence of sex difference . . . we can begin to appreciate the extent to which gender meanings have suffused our belief systems [and] institutions. . . . When feminist thinking about science is adequately theorized, we will have a clearer grasp of how scientific activity is and is not gendered in this sense.

The impetus for such an analysis arises from the need for completeness—"gender" must be shown to be a social artifact suffusing *all* "belief systems"—and, of course, from the need to explain away particular scientific studies that confirm innate sex differences that feminists deny are "natural." But the real threat to feminist ideology, it turns out, is the scientific method itself, with its promise of objectivity no matter who the scientist is.

At first feminists did not find it necessary to "reconceptualize" science so thoroughly. They were interested in restoring the reputations of (it was assumed) unjustly neglected "women worthies," in determining the distribution and status of contemporary female scientists, and in discovering what types of "social conditioning" prevented girls from pursuing or even wanting to pursue careers in science. At this preliminary stage—what Sandra Harding calls "the 'Woman Question' in science"—it was assumed that science was sex-neutral and that women could be just as proficient at it as men when allowed their rightful place.

It soon became clear, however, that—unlike art and literature—science has very few female worthies, neglected or otherwise. All that this was taken to prove, when viewed through the feminist lens, was that, in Harding's words, "women have been more systematically excluded from doing serious science than from performing any other social activity except, perhaps, frontline warfare." The idea that women have been completely excluded from science led naturally to the question of, in Evelyn Fox Keller's words, whether "the predominance of men in the sciences has led to a bias in the choice and definition of problems." (An example of such bias is scientists' ignoring such uniquely female problems as menstrual cramps.) But how a question is posed can determine the range of possible answers. If bias entered in the *definition* of problems, there might, as Keller notes, be "bias in the actual design and interpretation of experiments" as well.

This ever-widening hunt for bias was sustained by an unwillingness to admit that, as a natural consequence of innate sex differences, men might have a greater aptitude for the abstract, analytic thinking required for scientific discovery. That such a sex difference does exist in mathematics, which is at the core of modern science, appears to have been definitively verified by the Benbow–Stanley study at Johns Hopkins of tens of thousands of mathematically precocious junior-high-school-age boys and girls. Girls in the very top of their age group in mathematical ability, as determined by age-appropriate tests, are vastly outperformed by precocious boys of the same age on tests of mathematical ability meant for high school seniors. This study, and others like it, is unanimously disputed by feminists. In other words, the idea that science is a valuable activity that reveals the truth about the world, and is one in which many more men than women naturally excel, was unavailable to feminists. If men are better at science, science itself must be a distortion or an outright evil; something, in any case, must be wrong. Thus feminists reached the " 'Science Question' in feminism"—whether science as practiced is so set in a masculine framework that women have been correct not to participate in it. "That the scientific worldview had its dangers was not a new idea," Hester Eisenstein writes. "But what a feminist perspective contributed was the realization that this stance was linked to male psychology and male dominance."

Feminist ideology has been seesawing between the claim that women's unique viewpoint will bring a *different* conceptual framework to bear on the world, and the claim that women will bring a *better, truer* set of concepts. The weight now seems to be shifting toward the latter, more radical end. Or, as Harding puts it, "The feminist standpoint . . . argues that man's dominating position in social life results in partial and perverse understandings, whereas women's subjugated position provides the possibility of more complete and less perverse understandings." Feminists have not yet explained how subjugation produces wider and clearer vision, a problem they share with Marxists. But, then, many feminists embrace the Marxist view of science as one more "social product" determined by economic factors, although they add a few slogans of their own. A good example is to be found in Lynda Birke's *Women, Feminism and Biology:*

> [Can] we achieve a more socialist science? This would, it
> is generally agreed, be a science geared more to human
> need than to corporate greed; it would be a science that
> is accountable to society, rather than elitist and mystify-
> ing. It would certainly not be a science that serves a gi-
> ant military-industrial complex in the exploitation of
> nature, but would attempt to cooperate with nature. . . .
> [Feminists] would add that a more progressive science
> should be one that did not perpetuate in any way the
> subordination and oppression of women.

Many feminists who write about science from a Marxist perspective seem wholly uninformed about science, and identify "male"
science with weapons and strip-mining, all intended for use, as
Harding writes, "in the service of sexist, racist, homophobic and
classist projects." No claim is judged too bizarrely reductive for them
to defend. The feminist theoretician Alison Jaggar approvingly cites
Alfred Sohn-Rethel's claim that "the emergence of capitalism, which
necessitates the unending movement of money . . . generat[ed] the
Galilean concept of inertial motion which is the fundamental category
of Newtonian physics."

Some feminist writers possess quite respectable credentials. Evelyn Fox Keller received her B.S. in physics and is professor of
mathematics and humanities at Northeastern. She has written a
competent biography of Barbara McClintock, the 1983 Nobel Prize
winner in medicine. Sandra Harding teaches philosophy at the University of Delaware. Their technical backgrounds, however, have not
prevented either from reaching the most radical conclusions:

> Male scientific investigations were meant to pacify, con-
> trol, exploit and manipulate women or to glorify males
> and their domination (Harding, unpublished paper).

> If the conception of objectivity is a parochial one, influ-
> enced by a particular ideology about gender, it is one
> which has served our particular economic and political
> history well. . . . It is therefore not likely to be radically
> transformed without, simultaneously, a thoroughgoing po-
> litical and economic re-organization (Keller, essay in *In-
> ternational Journal of Women's Studies*).

> The Science Question critiques appear skeptical that we
> can locate anything morally and politically worth redeem-
> ing or reforming in the scientific worldview, its underly-
> ing epistemology, or the practices these legitimate
> (Harding).

These feminist epistemologists see male dominance at work in, for
instance, the "master molecule" theory of DNA functioning; in the
notion of forces "acting on" objects; in the description of evolution

as the result of a "struggle" to survive; in the view that scarcity of resources results in "competition" between animals—in short, in any theory positing what they deem destructive, violent, uni-directional or hierarchical relations. The idea of dominance is directly linked to the notion of scientific objectivity, which, in current feminist thinking, is understood as synonymous with "distancing oneself" from nature. Harding writes:

> [Science] is inextricably connected with specifically mas-
> culine—and perhaps uniquely Western and bourgeois—
> needs and desires. Objectivity vs. subjectivity, the
> scientist as knowing subject vs. the objects of his inquiry,
> reason vs. the emotions, mind vs. body—in each case the
> former has been associated with masculinity and the lat-
> ter with femininity. In each case it has been claimed that
> human progress requires the former to dominate the
> latter.

Despite the enormous scope of these claims, the actual evidence offered for the androcentric distortion of science is extremely thin. The centerpiece of historical support is, in Harding's book, the "rape and torture metaphors in the writings of Sir Francis Bacon and others (e.g., Machiavelli) enthusiastic about the scientific method." Referring to the new post-alchemy science, for instance, Bacon wrote, "I am come in very truth leading you to Nature with all her children to bind her to your service and make her your slave." Notwithstanding Bacon's quite marginal status in the actual development of modern science, to say nothing of Machiavelli's, Harding seizes on these turns of phrase:

> Traditional historians have said that these metaphors are
> irrelevant to the *real* meanings and referents of scientific
> concepts. . . . But when it comes to regarding nature as a
> machine, they have quite a different analysis . . . the
> mataphor provides the interpretations . . . it directs in-
> quiries to fruitful ways to apply [Newton's] theories. . . .
> [If] we are to believe that mechanistic metaphors were a
> fundamental component of the explanations the new sci-
> ence provided, why should we believe that the gender
> metaphors were not? . . . [Why] is it not as illuminating
> and honest to refer to Newton's laws as "Newton's rape
> manual" as it is to call them "Newton's mechanics"?

Harding is unaware that she has already answered her own rhetorical questions. The machine metaphor is fruitful; the rape metaphor is not. Consider the lesson that machines teach: what at first glance seems a complex jumble of parts can be analyzed into repetitions and rearrangements of simpler machines, such as levers, pulleys, and gears. In the same way, the seemingly irregular shape of a mollusk's shell turns out to result from the repetition of a simpler shape. Harding would not want to maintain, presumably, that rape metaphors have led to any comparable increase in knowledge. That is why rape metaphors are irrelevant to any analysis of extant scientific concepts, and why no one today speaks of Newton's rape manual.

The feminist case against traditional science also relies heavily on the observation that scientists are influenced by extra-logical considerations. And it is true—as no honest scientist will deny—that personal beliefs and desires can influence the research topics and even the methods chosen by scientists. (Lysenko's foray into genetics is a notorious instance.) Such deviations from the ideal of objectivity occur because science is done by human beings, not robots. But the self-correcting character of the scientific method, with its emphasis on observation, the replication of experiments, and open discussion, insures that such deviation will eventually be seen as such. Furthermore, as one moves away from such touchy topics as heritable traits and sex differences, the closer to the ideal scientific practice tends to come. For this reason, the physical sciences, traditionally seen as approaching this ideal most closely, pose the greatest difficulty for feminist theory. Harding, at least, acknowledges that critics will say that feminism "will not succeed in 'proving' that science is as gendered as any other human activity unless it can show that the specific problematics, concepts, theories, language and methods of modern physics are gender-laden—especially . . . that the mathematical expressions of Newton's laws of mechanics and Einstein's relativity theory are gender-laden."

Her reply to this challenge is, in effect, to refuse to consider it. Instead of actually attempting to show in detail that physics is "gender-laden," she asks, "Why should we continue to regard physics as the paradigm of scientific knowledge?" There is, in fact, a perfectly good reason why physics is so regarded: other sciences—like astronomy and geology and, increasingly, chemistry—are usually thought to concern special cases of the basic and universal processes that physics has discovered. Harding does not consider this crucial point. Instead she simply asserts that "we should understand physics not as the model for all scientific inquiry, but as atypical of inquiry just insofar as its ontological and methodological assumptions can in fact secure value-free research." In other words, physics is not science because it does not fit what feminists say must be true of science. At best, then, the feminist analysis is circular. But Harding goes further, and adds, "Perhaps in the science of the future, physics will be relegated to the backwaters of knowledge-seeking and thought to be concerned only with esoteric problems that have little impact on how we live."

This suggestion may appear plausible, because physics, like scientific theories generally, is not uppermost in the minds of nonscientists. That any two bodies attract each other with a force inversely proportional to the square of the distance between them makes no difference to people solving everyday problems. But imagine the law of gravity suddenly suspended, and you realize that all those practical decisions do indeed depend on physical laws being what they are. Ironically, Harding, the radical feminist, appears to agree with the traditional "sexist" who thinks that women's thinking is best confined to the practical while men should be off exploring the abstract and fundamental.

If physics seems devoid of "social fingerprints," mathematics seems even more so—more indeed than any other discipline. The absoluteness of mathematical truth also contrasts sharply with the vulnerability of conjectures in other sciences to revision in the light of experience. As one trained in mathematics, this writer was curious to see how feminist epistemologists would analyze mathematical reasoning, and indeed, the feminist treatment of mathematics is particularly uninformed and unconvincing. Feminists have not so far claimed that there is anything androcentric about arithmetic or militaristic about geometry: Harding draws back from arguing that mathematics is "*male*-biased." However, "it [is] plausible to regard as mythical the possibility of *pure* mathematics." She then goes on to give some examples that supposedly show mathematics to be subject to the social assumptions and conceptual frameworks of a particular culture:

> The ancient Greeks . . . did not regard one, the first in a series of integers, as a number, nor did they consider it odd or even. We, of course, think of it as a number, and as an odd number, because unlike the ancient Greeks, we are not mathematically interested in the distinction between the first . . . of a lineage . . . and the lineage itself.

This first example is unsuccessful because it involves a purely terminological point. Whether they considered 1 a number or not, the Greeks agreed with us that $3 + 1 = 4$. There are no arithmetical calculations in which the Greeks got one answer and we get another. Whether "1" is honored with the name "number" makes no difference. Let us, then, look at a second example.

> Common sense tells us that a part cannot be equal to the whole. Thus it is only relatively recently that mathematicians have been able to countenance the idea that the numbers could be infinite in number. Earlier mathematicians' problem was as follows: one can match each sequential integer with an even integer (1–2, 2–4, 3–6, 4–8, . . .) resulting in an infinite series in which there are as many even integers as there are integers—at first glance an absurdity. How was this paradox resolved? Mathematicians were willing to let go of the common sense truth that a part cannot be equal to the whole. They did so by replacing the social image of numbers as counting units with the social image of numbers as divi-

sions on a line. . . . A whole field of mathematical inquiry
was made possible by the substitution of a different kind
of social image for thinking about what numbers are. . . .
Such a process of socially negotiating cultural images in
mathematics is similar to what we do when we exclude
patriotic killing in wartime from the moral and legal category of murder.

That last line is characteristically tendentious, but let it go. This
passage is full of errors. To begin with, it was old news to Euclid that
there were infinitely many *prime* numbers, let alone numbers (see
Book IX, proposition 20 of his *Elements*). Second, modern mathematicians do not claim, as Harding implies they do, that a part is equal
to the whole in the sense of being identical to the whole. Rather, they
claim that a part and the whole can be the *same size*. What Harding
may be trying to describe with her two "social images" is the entirely
irrelevant distinction between ordinality and cardinality, between
objects arranged in a particular order and the size of the set these
objects form independent of the order. (Two infinite sets may differ
in their ordinality but agree in cardinality.) The fairly recent discovery
Harding has muddled is that there are different sizes of infinity, but
she has certainly not shown that this discovery was influenced by any
social consideration, and in fact there is no reason to think it was.

Most revealing of all Harding's confusions is her use of the word
social. She has evidently run together the true and not very controversial statement that mathematical concepts began in attempts by
"social" beings to solve practical problems, with the more dramatic
but utterly unsubstantiated claim that mathematical truth somehow
depends upon or is relative to social concepts. It is as if one
concluded that, since art may have begun as a way of ensuring that
what was depicted would in fact happen, therefore Dalí intended to
have his surreal images come alive.

This claim about mathematics' alleged social heritage is, in turn,
an instance of the first of three fundamental errors that form the basis
of the feminist account of science. It is what logicians call the genetic
fallacy: to confuse something with its origin and reject it on that
basis. Even if, for the sake of argument, Bacon's rape and torture
metaphors actually had been crucial for the beginning of modern
science, that would have been completely irrelevant to the verifiabil-
ity and accuracy of scientific theories inspired by those metaphors.
Early astronomers hoped to predict men's future by recording the
positions of heavenly bodies, but that does not invalidate the successful prediction of eclipses or the discovery of Pluto. Medicine
began with attempts to cast out the demons causing illness. That
viruses and bacteria have turned out to harbor no evil intentions does
not invalidate the efficacy of vaccines and antibiotics. It is the same
fallacy to infer from any male bias in the selection of scientific
problems that the solutions to these problems offered by men are
also necessarily "biased." Even if masculine interests may have led

to investigation of falling bodies before the study of personal relations, it hardly follows that "masculine" dynamics itself is in any way distorted.

Feminists' reliance on the genetic fallacy is related to their second basic error, which is their failure to take seriously the fact that so-called masculine science *works*. Science makes predictions that can be and are verified every day. Whenever we throw a light switch, photocopy an article, or drive a car, we not only see technology in action, but also witness additional confirmation of the theories behind the technology. Feminists deal with this stumbling block by refusing, in one way or another, to admit that they have tripped and fallen headlong. As noted earlier, many feminists seem unaware that science is anything more than MX missiles conceived as embodiments of male aggression. What they overlook is that those missiles would not present a danger to humanity if scientific theories about atomic fission and ballistics were not literally and absolutely true.

Of a piece with feminist unwillingness to confront the success of science is a glaring failure to give any concrete account of what a feminist science would be like. Attempts to address this question have so far been evasive, to put it charitably. We find Elizabeth Fee writing in the *International Journal of Women's Studies* that "[We] can say that a feminist science should not create artificial distinctions between the production and uses of knowledge, between thought and feeling, between subject and object, or between expert and non-expert." And Virginia Held, in a review for *Philosophy and Public Affairs,* writes:

> Many feminists reject the goal of conquering or dominating an alien nature. A concern for living at peace with nature often characterizes feminism as well as ecologically sensitive thought. . . . [That] special closeness to nature that women are said to have . . . may provide possibilities for special conceptualizing and knowing, through the more relational approaches of women.

These promissory notes address only the more morally elevated attitudes that feminist scientists would, presumably, have and the applications of scientific results they would make (or refrain from making). One still wants to know whether feminists' airplanes would stay airborne for feminist engineers.

The only specific revisions in any currently accepted scientific theories that feminists have offered are no more than changes in *vocabulary*. This is the third and most serious error in feminist writing on science. They think that a change in words amounts to a change in thought. Consider the following passage, in which Michael Gross and Mary Beth Averill propose a replacement for the "patriarchal" images of scarcity and competition in evolutionary theory.

> Why not see nature as bounteous, rather than parsimonious, and admit that opportunity and cooperation are

more likely to abet novelty, innovation and creation than are struggle and competition? Evolution in this perspective can be seen not as a constant struggle for occupation and control of territory but as a successive opening of new opportunities, each new mode of biological organization providing a new opportunity for still more diverse forms of life.

This reads almost like a parody of what female science might be expected to be like—all that has happened is that "caring" words have been substituted for "dominating" words. No new facts about evolution are being presented to challenge standard theories, nor can new words change the old facts (although they will certainly obscure them). Are the life-forms that become extinct as nature "provides new opportunities" to be thought of as happily yielding their places so that others may have a chance? Is the predator-prey relation one of cooperation? Did the apparently successful attempt on the part of "masculine" science to eradicate smallpox threaten the diversity and bounty of nature?

In fact, the whole idea of a "masculine" theory or problem is extremely dubious. If masculine scientific vocabulary and masculine modes of thought can only admit hierarchical and uni-directional relationships, how did male scientists discover mutualism and symbiosis in nature? Or consider another male discovery, the concept of feedback, in which a system constantly changes in response to signals it both receives from and sends to the environment—a very complex interaction. Or, again, consider the male discovery of catalysis, in which one substance triggers a chemical reaction between other substances without being affected itself. Could this not be said to resemble the behavior of a good hostess who introduces two guests to each other at her party and then moves on while they engage in conversation?

The point is that one can play "the gendered metaphor" with any scientific discovery. While it may well be true (although not for reasons feminists would admit) that on average men are more suited than women for constructing abstract theories about the extra-social world, the labels "masculine" and "feminine" as applied to those theories are themselves purely arbitrary. You could argue that Einstein's theory of relativity is more masculine than Newton's classical mechanics because relativity uses non-Euclidean geometry, a more abstract mathematical construction. Or you could argue that Einstein's theory is more feminine than Newton's because it offers no *absolute* reference frame for calculating time or mass, and it offers each moving object its own personal reference frame. One can play this game forever. Newton's conception of gravity as involving a *mutual* attraction between every two objects is much less hierarchical than Aristotle's, which placed the Earth at the center of everything. The Copernican revolution has generally been seen as replacing a human-centered universe with a more impersonal one, but Alison

Jaggar claims that "Copernican theory replaced the female (earth)-centered universe with a male (sun)-centered universe." The big question is: does Jaggar think we have a *choice* about which theory is correct? Masculine or feminine, the solar system is the way it is.

One suspects that feminists themselves sense the emptiness of their enterprise. Those confident of their product do not strain to oversell it, yet much of feminist scholarly writing consists of wildly extravagant praise of other feminists. A's "brilliant analysis" supplements B's "revolutionary breakthrough" and C's "courageous undertaking." More disconcerting is the penchant of many feminists to praise themselves most fulsomely. Harding ends her book on the following self-congratulatory note:

> When we began theorizing our experience . . . we knew our task would be a difficult though exciting one. But I doubt that in our wildest dreams we ever imagined we would have to reinvent both science and theorizing itself to make sense of women's social experience.

This megalomania would be disturbing in a Newton or Darwin; in the present context it is merely embarrassing.

If feminist writing on science is so insubstantial, why pay it any attention? What harm can feminists do preaching to one another? If feminist theory had as little influence on the real world as the real world has on it, it could be ignored with impunity. Unfortunately, feminist theory has so far had all too great an influence in academia. Many colleges have yielded to feminist demands for special departments, courses, and requirements, none with greater legitimacy than "feminist science." If science goes the way of other disciplines, there will presently be demands for "subjective" science courses, for the adoption by scientific journals of guidelines for non-masculinist writing, for grading of female students that would be sensitive to their presumed non-dominant attitudes, and for denial of funding for "masculinist" research. Lest this be considered alarmist, consider the threat implicit here in Sandra Harding's book:

> If we regarded science as a totally social activity we could begin to understand the myriad ways in which it too is structured by expressions of gender. All that stands between us and that project are inadequate theories of gender, the dogmas of empiricism, and a good deal of political struggle.

Unfortunately, feminist theorizing is never far removed from "political struggle."

Suggestions for Discussion and Writing

1. In light of your readings of Keller and Bleier (this chapter), does Levin summarize the feminist view of traditional science fairly?

2. How does Levin establish a tone early in her essay? How would you characterize this tone? Point to particular examples of diction to support your view.

3. Levin acknowledges that "extra-logical considerations" sometimes influence the methods and direction of science. She goes on to argue, however, that the "self-correcting character of the scientific method . . . insures that such deviation will eventually be seen as such." How might Keller respond? In a brief essay, support or challenge Levin's argument.

4. Summarize the reasoning process by which Levin comes to the conclusion that the feminist analysis regarding the status of physics as "the paradigm of scientific knowledge" is "circular."

5. Why does mathematics (the fundamental language of physics) present the most difficult case for feminists? In what sense does it seem devoid of "social fingerprints"? Why is the presence or absence of "social fingerprints" significant?

6. Summarize the three "fundamental errors" that, according to Levin, form the basis of the feminist account of science. Do you agree that they are "fundamental" errors, and, if so, that the third is the most serious?

7. Does Levin use evidence and examples to support her argument effectively? Focusing on a particular instance, show how it does or does not support her case.

8. Levin ends her essay with the observation that "feminist theorizing is never far removed from 'political struggle.' " What do you understand her to mean by this? Do you agree with her? In what sense is the feminist critique of traditional science political? Write an essay in which you explore these issues.

CHILD PROGRAMMERS: THE FIRST GENERATION

Sherry Turkle
(b. 1948)

Sherry Turkle is a professor in the Department of Technology and Human Affairs at the Massachusetts Institute of Technology. Born in New York City, she earned a Ph.D. in clinical psychology from Harvard. Her awards include a Rockefeller Foundation Fellowship in 1980 and a Guggenheim Fellowship in 1981. She is widely known for her research into the effects of computer use on our ways of thinking.

In the following selection, taken from her book *The Second Self: Computers and the Human Spirit* (1984), Turkle reports on her study of the way children of both sexes learn to deal with the complexities of the computer.

C onsider Robin, a four-year-old with blond hair and a pinafore, standing in front of a computer console, typing at its keyboard. She is a student at a nursery school that is introducing computers to very young children. She is playing a game that allows her to build stick figures by commanding the computer to make components appear and move into a desired position. The machine responds to Robin's commands and tells her when it does not understand an instruction. Many people find this scene disturbing. First, Robin is "plugged into" a machine. We speak of television as a "plug-in drug," but perhaps the very passivity of what we do with television reassures us. We are concerned about children glued to screens, but, despite what we have heard of Marshall McLuhan and the idea that "the medium is the message," the passivity of television encourages many of us to situate our sense of its impact at the level of the content of television programming. Is it violent or sexually suggestive? Is it educational? But Robin is not "watching" anything on the computer. She is manipulating—perhaps more problematic, *interacting with*—a complex technological medium. And the degree and intensity of her involvement suggests that (like the children at the video games) it is the medium itself and not the content of a particular program that produces the more powerful effect. But beyond any specific fear, so young a child at a computer conflicts with our ideal image of childhood. The "natural" child is out of doors; machines are indoors. The natural child runs free; machines control and constrain. Machines and children don't go together.

Something else feels discordant, and that is the nature of Robin's interaction with the computer. She is not manipulating the machine by turning knobs or pressing buttons. She is writing messages to it by spelling out instructions letter by letter. Her painfully slow typing seems laborious to adults, but she carries on with an absorption that makes it clear that time has lost its meaning for her. Computers bring writing within the scope of what very young children can do. It is far easier to press keys on a keyboard than to control a pencil. Electronic keyboards can be made sensitive to the lightest touch; more important, they permit instant erasure. The computer is a forgiving writing instrument, much easier to use than even an electric typewriter.

That a four-year-old or a three-year-old might learn to make a fire poses a real physical danger, but it does not call anything about childhood into question. We find it easy to accept, indeed we are proud, when children develop physical skills or the ability to manipulate concrete materials earlier than we expect. But a basic change in the child's manipulation of symbolic materials threatens something deep. Central to our notion of childhood is the idea that children of Robin's age and younger speak but do not write.

Many people are excited by the possibility that writing may be brought within the range of capabilities of very young children. But others seem to feel that setting a four-year-old to writing does violence to a natural process of unfolding. For them, what is most disturbing about Robin is not her relationship to the machine, but her relationship to writing, to the abstract, to the symbolic. Opening the question of children and writing provokes a reaction whose force recalls that evoked by Freud's challenge to the sexual innocence of the child.

In the eighteenth century, Jean-Jacques Rousseau associated writing with moral danger in the most direct way. He saw the passage from nature to culture as the end of a community of free, spontaneous communication. Writing marked the point of rupture. In Rousseau's mind, this story of loss of community and communication projects itself onto the life of each individual. Each growing up is a loss of innocence and immediacy, and the act of writing symbolizes that the loss has taken place. To a certain extent, each of us reenacts the fall. Our first marks of pen on paper retrace the introduction of a barrier between ourselves and other people. Childhood, innocence, is the state of not writing.

The computer has become the new cultural symbol of the things that Rousseau feared from the pen: loss of direct contact with other people, the construction of a private world, a flight from real things to their representations. With programming, as for so many other things, the computer presence takes what was already a concern and gives it new form and new degree. If our ideas about childhood are called into question by child writers, what of child programmers? If childhood innocence is eroded by writing, how much more so by programming?

What happens when young children, grade-school children, become programmers? Faced with the reality of child experts who have appropriated the computers that dot grade schools and junior highs across the country, there is talk of a "computer generation" and of a new generation gap.

Sarah, a thirty-five-year-old lawyer and mother of three, feels an unbridgeable gap between herself and her son, and she alternates between agitation and resignation:

> I could have learned that "new math." I could under-
> stand, respect my son if his values turn out to be differ-
> ent than mine. I mean, I think I could handle the kinds
> of things that came up between parents and kids in the
> sixties. I would have talked to my son; I would have
> tried to understand. But my ten-year-old is into program-
> ming, into computers, and I feel that this makes his
> mind work in a whole different way.

Do computers change the way children think? Do they open children's minds or do they dangerously narrow their experience, making their thinking more linear and less intuitive? There is a temptation to look for a universal, isolable effect, the sort that still eludes experts on the effect of television.

The problem here is the search for a universal effect. I have found that different children are touched in remarkably different ways by their experience with the computer. However, by looking closely at how individual children appropriate the computer we can build ways to think about how the computer enters into development, and we begin to get some answers to our questions. In a sense, I turn the usual question around: instead of asking what the computer does to children I ask what children, and more important, what different kinds of children make of the computer. . . .

JEFF AND KEVIN

Jeff, a fourth grader, has a reputation as one of the school's computer experts. He is meticulous in his study habits, does super-lative work in all subjects. His teachers were not surprised to see him excelling in programming. Jeff approaches the machine with deter-mination and the need to be in control, the way he approaches both his schoolwork and his extracurricular activities. He likes to be, and often is, chairman of student committees. At the moment, his pre-occupation with computers is intense: "They're the biggest thing in my life right now." He speaks very fast, and when he talks about his programs he speaks even faster, tending to monologue. He answers a question about what his program does by tossing off lines of computer code that for him seem to come as naturally as English. His typing is expert—he does not look at the code as it appears on the screen. He conveys the feeling that he is speaking directly to an entity inside. "When I program I put myself in the place of the sprite. And I make it do things."

Jeff is the author of one of the first space-shuttle programs. He does it, as he does most other things, by making a plan. There will be a rocket, boosters, a trip through the stars, a landing. He conceives the program globally; then he breaks it up into manageable pieces. "I wrote out the parts on a big piece of cardboard. I saw the whole thing in my mind just in one night, and I couldn't wait to come to school to make it work." Computer scientists will recognize this global "top-down," "divide-and-conquer" strategy as "good programming style." And we all recognize in Jeff someone who conforms to our stereotype of a "computer person" or an engineer—someone who would be good with machines, good at science, someone organized, who approaches the world of things with confidence and sure intent, with the determination to make it work.

Kevin is a very different sort of child. Where Jeff is precise in all of his actions, Kevin is dreamy and impressionistic. Where Jeff tends to try to impose his ideas on other children, Kevin's warmth, easy-going nature, and interest in others make him popular. Meetings with Kevin were often interrupted by his being called out to rehearse for a school play. The play was *Cinderella,* and he had been given the role of Prince Charming. Kevin comes from a military family; his father and grandfather were both in the Air Force. But Kevin has no intention of following in their footsteps. "I don't want to be an army man. I don't want to be a fighting man. You can get killed." Kevin doesn't like fighting or competition in general. "You can avoid fights. I never get anybody mad—I mean, I try not to."

Jeff has been playing with machines all his life—Tinkertoys, motors, bikes—but Kevin has never played with machines. He likes stories, he likes to read, he is proud of knowing the names of "a lot of different trees." He is artistic and introspective. When Jeff is asked questions about his activities, about what he thinks is fun, he answers in terms of how to do them right and how well he does them. He talks about video games by describing his strategy breakthroughs on the new version of Space Invaders: "Much harder, much trickier than the first one." By contrast, Kevin talks about experiences in terms of how they make him feel. Video games make him feel nervous, he says. "The computer is better," he adds. "It's easier. You get more relaxed. You're not being bombarded with stuff all the time."

Kevin too is making a space scene. But the way he goes about it is not at all like Jeff's approach. Jeff doesn't care too much about the detail of the form of his rocket ship; what is important is getting a complex system to work together as a whole. But Kevin cares more about the aesthetics of the graphics. He spends a lot of time on the shape of his rocket. He abandons his original idea ("It didn't look right against the stars") but continues to "doodle" with the scratch-pad shape-maker. He works without plan, experimenting, throwing different shapes onto the screen. He frequently stands back to inspect his work, looking at it from different angles, finally settling on a red shape against a black night—a streamlined, futuristic design. He is excited and calls over two friends. One admires the red on the black. The other says that the red shape "looks like fire." Jeff happens to pass Kevin's machine on the way to lunch and automatically checks out its screen, since he is always looking for new tricks to add to his toolkit for building programs. He shrugs. "That's been done." Nothing new there, nothing technically different, just a red blob.

Everyone goes away and Kevin continues, now completely taken up by the idea that the red looks like fire. He decides to make the ship white so that a red shape can be red fire "at the bottom." A long time is spent making the new red fireball, finding ways to give it spikes. And a long time is spent adding detail to the now white ship. With the change of color, new possibilities emerge: "More things will show up on it." Insignias, stripes, windows, and the project about which Kevin is most enthusiastic: "It can have a little seat for the astronaut." When Jeff programs he puts himself in the place of the sprite; he thinks of himself as an abstract computational object. Kevin says that, as he works, "I think of myself as the man inside the rocket ship. I daydream about it. I'd like to go to the moon."

By the next day Kevin has a rocket with red fire at the bottom. "Now I guess I should make it move . . . moving and wings . . . it should have moving and wings." The wings turn out to be easy, just some more experimenting with the scratchpad. But he is less certain about how to get the moving right.

Kevin knows how to write programs, but his programs emerge—he is not concerned with imposing his will on the machine. He is concerned primarily with creating exciting visual effects and allows himself to be led by the effects he produces. Since he lets his plans change as new ideas turn up, his work has not been systematic. And he often loses track of things. Kevin has lovingly worked on creating the rocket, the flare, and a background of twinkling stars. Now he wants the stars to stay in place and the rocket and the flare to move through them together.

It is easy to set sprites in motion: just command them to an initial position and give them a speed and a direction. But Kevin's rocket and red flare are two separate objects (each shape is carried by a different sprite) and they have to be commanded to move together at the same speed, even though they will be starting from different places. To do this successfully, you have to think about coordinates and you have to make sure that the objects are identified differently so that code for commanding their movement can be addressed to each of them independently. Without a master plan Kevin gets confused about the code numbers he has assigned to the different parts of his program, and the flare doesn't stay with the rocket but flies off with the stars. It takes a lot of time to get the flare and the ship back together. When Jeff makes a mistake, he is annoyed, calls himself "stupid," and rushes to correct his technical error. But when Kevin makes an error, although it frustrates him he doesn't seem to resent it. He sometimes throws his arms up in exasperation: "Oh no, oh no. What did I do?" His fascination with his effect keeps him at it.

In correcting his error, Kevin explores the system, discovering new special effects as he goes along. In fact, the "mistake" leads him to a new idea: the flare shouldn't go off with the stars but should drop off the rocket, "and then the rocket could float in the stars." More experimenting, trying out of different colors, with different placements of the ship and the flare. He adds a moon, some planets. He tries out different trajectories for the rocket ship, different headings, and different speeds; more mistakes, more standing back and admiring his evolving canvas. By the end of the week Kevin too has programmed a space scene.

STYLES OF MASTERY

Jeff and Kevin represent cultural extremes. Some children are at home with the manipulation of formal objects, while others develop their ideas more impressionistically, with language or visual images, with attention to such hard-to-formalize aspects of the world as feeling, color, sound, and personal rapport. Scientific and technical fields are usually seen as the natural home for people like Jeff; the arts and humanities seem to belong to the Kevins.

Watching Kevin and Jeff programming the same computer shows us two very different children succeeding at the same thing—and here it must be said that Kevin not only succeeded in creating a space scene, but, like Jeff, he learned a great deal about computer programming and mathematics, about manipulating angles, shapes, rates, and coordinates. But although succeeding at the same thing, they are not doing it the same way. Each child developed a distinctive style of mastery—styles that can be called hard and soft mastery.

Hard mastery is the imposition of will over the machine through the implementation of a plan. A program is the instrument of premeditated control. Getting the program to work is more like getting "to say one's piece" than allowing ideas to emerge in the give-and-take of conversation. The details of the specific program obviously need to be "debugged"—there has to be room for change, for some degree of flexibility in order to get it right—but the goal is always getting the program to realize the plan.

Soft mastery is more interactive. Kevin is like a painter who stands back between brushstrokes, looks at the canvas, and only from this contemplation decides what to do next. Hard mastery is the mastery of the planner, the engineer, soft mastery is the mastery of the artist: try this, wait for a response, try something else, let the overall shape emerge from an interaction with the medium. It is more like a conversation than a monologue.

Hard and soft mastery recalls anthropologist Claude Lévi-Strauss' discussion of the scientist and the *bricoleur*. Lévi-Strauss used the term *bricolage*, tinkering, to make a distinction between Western science and the science of preliterate societies. The former is a science of the abstract, the latter is a science of the concrete. Like the *bricoleur,* the soft master works with a set of concrete elements. While the hard master thinks in terms of global abstractions, the soft master works on a problem by arranging and rearranging these elements, working through new combinations. Although the *bricoleur* works with a closed set of materials, the results of combining elements can lead to new and surprising results.

MASTERY AND PERSONALITY

Computer programming is usually thought of as an activity that imposes its style on the programmer. And that style is usually presumed to be closer to Jeff and his structured, "planner's" approach than to Kevin and his open, interactive one. In practice, computer programming allows for radical differences in style. And looking more closely at Jeff and Kevin makes it apparent that a style of dealing with the computer is of a piece with other things about the person—his or her way of facing the world, of coping with problems, of defending against what is felt as dangerous. Programming style is an expression of personality style.

For example, the hard masters tend to see the world as something to be brought under control. They place little stock in fate. In child's terms, they don't believe much in a rabbit's foot or a lucky day. Jeff is popular and sociable, but he likes to be committee chairman, the one who controls the meeting. From the earliest ages most of these children have preferred to operate on the manipulable—on blocks, on Tinkertoys, on mechanisms. It is not surprising that the "hards" sometimes have more difficulty with the give-and-take of the playground. When your needs for control are too great, relationships with people become tense and strained. The computer offers a "next-best" gratification. The Tinkertoy is inert. The computer is responsive. Some children even feel that when they master it they are dominating something that "fights back." It is not surprising that hard masters take avidly to the computer. It is also not surprising that their style of working with the computer emphasizes the imposition of will.

The soft masters are more likely to see the world as something they need to accommodate to, something beyond their direct control. In general, these children have played not with model trains and Erector sets but with toy soldiers or with dolls. They have taken the props (cowboy hats, guns, and grownup clothes for dress-up) from the adult world and used them in fantasy play with other children. In doing so, they have learned how to negotiate, compromise, empathize. They tend to feel more impinged upon, more reactive. As we have seen, this accommodating style is expressed in their relational attitude toward programming as well as in their relationships with people. . . .

MASTERY AND GENDER

I have used boys as examples in order to describe hard and soft mastery without reference to gender. But now it is time to state what might be anticipated by many readers: girls tend to be soft masters, while the hard masters are overwhelmingly male. At [the Austen school] girls are trying to forge relationships with the computer that bypass objectivity altogether. They tend to see computational objects as sensuous and tactile and relate to the computer's formal system not as a set of unforgiving "rules," but as a language for communicating with, negotiating with, a behaving, psychological entity.

There are many reasons why we are not surprised that girls tend to be soft masters. In our culture girls are taught the characteristics of soft mastery—negotiation, compromise, give-and-take—as psychological virtues, while models of male behavior stress decisiveness and the imposition of will. Boys and girls are encouraged to adopt these stances in the world of people. It is not surprising that they show up when children deal with the world of things. The girl child plays with dolls, imagined not as objects to command but as children to nurture. When the boy unwraps his birthday presents they are most likely to be Tinkertoys, blocks, Erector sets—all of which put him in the role of builder.

Thinking in terms of dolls and Erector sets, like talking about teaching negotiation and control, suggests that gender differentiation is a product of the social construction that determines what toys and what models of correct behavior are given to children of each sex. Psychoanalytic thought suggests many ways in which far earlier processes could have their role to play; styles of mastery may also be rooted in the child's earliest experiences. One school of thought, usually referred to as "object relations theory," is particularly rich in images that suggest a relation between styles of mastery and gender differences.

It portrays the infant beginning life in a closely bonded relationship with the mother, one in which boundaries between self and other are not clear. Nor does the child experience a separation between the self and the outer world. The gradual development of a consciousness of separate existence begins with a separation from the mother. It is fraught with conflict. On the one hand, there is a desire to return to the comfort of the lost state of oneness. On the other hand, there is the pleasure of autonomy, of acting on independent desire. Slowly the infant develops the sense of an "objective" reality "out there" and separate from the self. Recently, there has been serious consideration of the ways in which this process may take on a sense of gender. Since our earliest and most compelling experiences of merging are with the mother, experiences where boundaries are not clear become something "female." Differentiation and delineation, first worked through in a separation from the mother, are marked as "not-mother," not-female.

Up to this point the experiences are common to girls and boys. But at the Oedipal stage, there is a fork in the road. The boy is involved in a fantasized romance with the mother. The father steps in to break it up and, in doing so, strikes another blow against fusional relationships. It is also another chance to see the pressure for separation as male. This is reinforced by the fact that this time the boy gives up the idea of a romance with the mother through identifying himself with his father. Thus, for the boy, separation from the mother is more brutal, because in a certain sense it happens twice: first in the loss of the original bonded relationship, then again at the point of the Oedipal struggle.

Since separation from the mother made possible the first experiences of the world as "out there," we might call it the discovery of the "objective." Because the boy goes through this separation twice, for him objectivity becomes more highly charged. Boys feel a greater desire for it: the objective, distanced relationship feels like safe, approved ground. There is more of a taboo on the fusional, along with a correspondingly greater fear of giving in to its forbidden pleasures. According to this theory the girl is less driven to objectivity because she is allowed to maintain more elements of the old fusional relationship with the mother, and, correspondingly, it is easier for her to play with the pleasure of closeness with other objects as well.

ANNE AND MARY

In the eyes of a true hard programmer like Jeff, his classmate Anne, also nine, is an enigma. On the one hand, she hardly seems serious about the computer. She is willing to spend days creating shimmering patterns on the screen in a kind of "moiré effect" and she doesn't seem to care whether she gets her visual effects with what Jeff would classify as technically uninteresting "tricks" or with what he would see as "really interesting" methods. Jeff knows that all the children anthropomorphize the computer to a certain extent; everyone says things like "My program knows how to do this" or "You have to tell the computer what speed you want the sprites to go," but Anne carries anthropomorphizing to what, to Jeff, seems like extreme lengths. For example, she insists on calling the computer "he," with the explanation "It doesn't seem right to call it an it." All the same, this doesn't keep her from getting down to serious programming. She has made some technical inventions, and Jeff and the other male hard masters recognize that if they want to keep abreast of the state of the art at Austen they must pay attention to what Anne is doing. And Anne knows how to take advantage of her achievements. She analogizes the spread of programming ideas to the game of telephone and enjoys seeing versions of her ideas on half a dozen screens. "They didn't copy me exactly, but I can recognize my idea." Jeff's grudging acknowledgment of Anne's "not quite serious" accomplishments seems almost a microcosm of reactions to competent women in society as a whole. There, as at Austen, there is appreciation, incomprehension, and ambivalence.

When Jeff talks with the other male experts about the computer, they usually talk "shop" about technical details. Anne, on the other hand, likes to discuss her strong views about the machine's psychology. She has no doubt that computers have psychologies: they "think," as people do, although they "can't really have emotions." Nevertheless, the computer might have preferences. "He would like it if you did a pretty program." When it comes to technical things, she assumes the computer has an aesthetic: "I don't know if he would rather have the program be very complicated or very simple."

Anne thinks about whether the computer is alive. She says that the computer is "certainly not alive like a cat," but it is "sort of alive," it has "alive things." Her evidence comes from the machine's responsive behavior. As she types her instructions into the machine, she comments, "You see, this computer is close to being alive because he does what you are saying."

This remark is reminiscent of the talk among the somewhat younger children who were preoccupied with sorting out the computer's status as a living or a not living thing. There is, however, a difference. For the younger children, these questions have a certain theoretical urgency. For Anne, they are both less urgent and part of a practical philosophy: she has woven this way of seeing the computer into her style of technical mastery.

Anne wants to know how her programs work and to understand her failures when they don't. But she draws the line between understanding and not understanding in a way that is different from most of the hard-master boys at a similar degree of competence. For them, a program (like anything else built out of the elements of a formal system) is either right or wrong. Programs that are correct in their general structure are not "really correct" until the small errors, the bugs, are removed. For a hard programmer like Jeff, the bugs are there to ferret out. Anne, on the other hand, makes no demand that her programs be perfect. To a certain degree, although to put it too flatly would be an exaggeration, when she programs the computer she treats it as a person. People can be understood only incompletely: because of their complexity, you can expect to understand them only enough to get along, as well as possible for maintaining the kind of relationship you want. And when you want people to do something, you don't insist that it be done exactly as you want it, but only "near enough." Anne allows a certain amount of negotiation with the computer about just what should be an acceptable program. For her, the machine is enough alive to deserve a compromise.

This "negotiating" and "relational" style is pervasive in Anne's work but is more easily described by an example from her classmate Mary, another soft-mastery programmer and an even stauncher lobbyist for the use of personal pronouns to refer to computers. Mary differs strikingly from Anne in having a soft style that is verbal where Anne's is consistently visual.

Mary wanted to add a few lines of dialogue to the end of a game program. Her original idea was that the computer would ask the player, "Do you want to play another game?" If the player typed "Yes," a new game would start. If the player typed "No," the machine would print out the final score and "exit" the program—that is, put the machine back into a state where it is ready for anything, back to "top level." She writes a program that has two steps, captured in the following English-language rendition of the relevant Logo instructions:

> If what-the-user-types is "Yes," start a new game.
> If what-the-user-types is "No," print score and stop.

As instructions to an intelligent person, these two statements are unambiguous. Not so as instructions to a computer. The program "runs," but not quite as Mary originally planned. The answer "Yes" produces the "right" behavior, a new game. But in order to get the final score and exit, it is necessary to type "No" twice. Mary knew this meant there was an "error," but she liked this bug. She saw the behavior as a humanlike quirk.

What was behind the quirk? The computer is a serial machine; it executes each instruction independently. It gets up to the first instruction that tells it to wait until the user types something. If this something is "Yes," a new game is started up. If the user doesn't type "Yes," if, for example, he or she types "No," the computer does nothing except pass on to the next instruction without "remembering" what has come before. The second instruction, like the first, tells the computer to wait until the user has typed something. And if this something is "No," to print the score and stop.

Now the role of the two "Nos" is clear. A single "No" will leave the computer trying to obey the second instruction—that is, waiting for the user to type something. There are ways of fixing this bug, but what is important here is the difference in attitude between a programmer like Jeff, who would not rest until he fixed it, and a programmer like Mary, who could figure out how to fix it but decides not to. Mary *likes* this bug because it makes the machine appear to have more of a personality. It lets you feel closer to it. As Mary puts it, "He will not take no for an answer" unless you really insist. She allows the computer its idiosyncrasies and happily goes on to another program.

Mary's work is marked by her interest in language. Anne's is equally marked by her hobby, painting. She uses visual materials to create strategies for feeling "close to the machine."

Anne had become an expert at writing programs to produce visual effects of appearance and disappearance. In one, a flock of birds flies through the sky, disappears at the horizon and reappears some other place and time. If all the birds are the same color, such as red, then disappearance and appearance could be produced by the commands "SETCOLOR :INVISIBLE" to get rid of them and "SETCOLOR :RED" to make them appear. But since Anne wants the birds to have different colors, the problem of the birds' reappearing with their original color is more complicated.

There is a classical method for getting this done: get the program to "store away" each bird's original color before changing that color to "invisible," and then to recall the color when the birds are to reappear. This method calls for an algebraic style of thinking. You have to think about variables and use a variable for each bird—for example, letting A equal the color of the first bird, B the color of the second bird, and so on. Anne will use this kind of method when she has to, but she prefers another kind, a method of her own invention that has a different feel.

She likes to feel that she is there among her birds, manipulating them much in the way she can manipulate physical materials. When you want to hide something on a canvas, you paint it out, you cover it with something that looks like the background. This is Anne's solution. She lets each bird keep its color, but she makes her program "hide it" by placing a screen over it. She designs a sprite that will screen the bird when she doesn't want it seen, a sky-colored screen that makes it disappear. Just as the computer can be programmed to make a bird-shaped object on the screen, it can be programmed to make an opaque sky-colored square act as a screen.

Anne is programming a computer, but she is thinking like a painter. She is not thinking about sprites and variables. She is thinking about birds and screens. Anne's way of making birds appear and disappear doesn't make things technically easy. On the contrary, to maintain her programming aesthetic requires technical sophistication and ingenuity.

For example, how does the program "know" where the bird is so as to place the screen on it? Anne attaches the screen to the bird when the bird is created, instead of putting it on later. The screen is on top of the bird at all times and moves with the bird wherever it goes. Thus she has invented a new kind of object, a "screened bird." When Anne wants the bird to be seen, the screen is given the "invisible" color, so the bird, whatever its color, shows right through it. When she wants the bird to disappear, the screen is given the color of the sky. The problem of the multiplicity of bird colors is solved. A bird can have any color. But the screens need only two colors, invisible or sky blue. A bird gets to keep its color at all times. It is only the color of its screen that changes. The problem of remembering the color of a particular bird and reassigning it at a particular time has been bypassed.

Anne's bird program is particularly ingenious, but its programming style is characteristic of many of the girls in her class. Most of the boys seem driven by the pleasures of mastering and manipulating a formal system: for them, the operations, the programming instructions, are what it is all about. For Anne, pleasure comes from being able to put herself into the space of the birds. Her method of manipulating screens and birds allows her to feel that these objects are close, not distant and untouchable things that need designation by variables. The ambivalence of the computational sprite—an object at once physical and abstract—allows it to be picked up differently by hards and softs. Anne responds to the sprites as physical objects. Her work with them is intimate and direct. The formal operations need to be mastered, but they are not what drive her.

No one would find Anne's relation to the birds and the screens surprising if it were in the context of painting or making collages with scraps of this and that. There we expect to find "closeness to the object." But finding a sensual aesthetic in the development of a computer program surprises us. We tend to think of programming as the manipulation of a formal system which, like the objects for scientific inquiry, is "out there" to be operated on as something radically split from the self.

GENDER AND SCIENCE

Evelyn Keller has coined the phrase "the genderization of science." She argues that what our culture defines as the scientific stance toward the world corresponds to the kind of relationships with the object world that most men (if we follow psychoanalytic theories of development) would be expected to find most comfortable. It is a relationship that cuts off subject from object.

Scientific objects are placed in a "space" psychologically far away from the world of everyday life, from the world of emotion and relationships. Men seem able, willing, and invested in constructing these separate "objective" worlds, which they can visit as neutral observers. In this way the scientific tradition that takes objectivity as its hallmark is also defined as a male preserve. Taking it from the other side, we can see why men would be drawn to this construction of science. Men are highly invested in objective relationships with the world. Their earliest experiences have left them with a sense of the fusional as taboo, as something to be defended against. Science, which represents itself as revealing a reality in which subject and object are radically separated, is reassuring. We can also see why women might experience a conflict between this construction of science and what feels like "their way" of dealing with the world, a way that leaves more room for continuous relationships between self and other. Keller adds that the presentation of science as an extreme form of objective thinking has been reinforced by the way in which male scientists traditionally write and speak about their work. A characterization of science that appears to "gratify particular emotional needs" may "give rise to a self-selection of scientists—a self-selection which would in turn lead to a perpetuation of that characterization."

In Anne's classroom, nine- and ten-year-old girls are just beginning to program. The fact that they relate to computational objects differently from boys raises the question of whether with growing expertise they will maintain their style or whether we are simply seeing them at an early stage before they become "recuperated" into a more objective computational culture. In my observation, with greater experience soft masters, male and female, reap the benefits of their long explorations, so that they appear more decisive and more like "planners" when they program on familiar terrains. But the "negotiating" and "relational" style remains behind the appearance and resurfaces when they tackle something new.

Lorraine is the only woman on a large team working on the design of a new programming language. She expresses her sense of difference with some embarrassment.

> I know that the guys I work with think I am crazy. But we will be working on a big program and I'll have a dream about what the program feels like inside and somehow the dream will help me through.
>
> When I work on the system I know that to everybody else it looks like I'm doing what everyone else is doing, but I'm doing that part with only a small part of my mind. The rest of me is imagining what the components feel like. It's like doing my pottery. . . . Keep this anonymous. I know this sounds stupid.

Shelley is a graduate student in computer science who corrects me sharply when I ask her when she got interested in electronics and machines. "Machines," she responds, "I am definitely not into machines." And she is even less involved with electronics:

> My father was an electrician and he had all of these machines around. All of these wires, all of this stuff. And he taught my brothers all about it. But all I remember him telling me was, "Don't touch it, you'll get a shock." I hate machines. But I don't think of computers as machines. I think of moving pieces of language around. Not like making a poem, the way you would usually think of moving language around, more like making a piece of language sculpture.

These words are reminiscent of women in other scientific disciplines. Barbara McClintock, an eminent biologist, describes her work as an ongoing "conversation" with her materials, and she speaks of frustration with the way science is usually done: "If you'd only just let the materials speak to you . . ." In an interview with her biographer, Evelyn Keller, McClintock described her studies of neurospora chromosomes (so small that others had been unable to identify them) in terms that recall Anne's relationship with the birds and the screens. "The more she worked with the chromosomes, the bigger they got; until finally, 'I wasn't outside, I was down there—I was part of the system.' . . . As 'part of the system' even the internal parts of the chromosomes become visible. 'I actually felt as if were down there and these were my friends.' "

Keller comments that McClintock's "fusion" with her objects of study is something experienced by male scientists. But perhaps Mc-Clintock was able to exploit this less distanced model of scientific thought, far from the way science was discussed in the 1950s, more fully, visibly, and less self-consciously, because she is a woman. This is surely the case for the girls in the Austen classrooms. Their artistic, interactive style is culturally sanctioned. Of course, with children, as in the larger world, the lines of division are not rigid. Some girls are hard masters and I purposely took a boy as the first case of a soft master—Kevin, who did not see the sprites as "outside" but who is right there with them, who imagines himself a traveler in the rocket ship, taking himself and his daydreams with him.

Children working with computers are a microcosm for the larger world of relations between gender and science. Jeff took the sprite as an object apart and in a world of its own. When he entered the sprite world, it was to command it better. Kevin used the sprite world to fantasize in. Anne does something more. She moves further in the direction I am calling "feminine," further in the direction of seeing herself as in the world of the sprite, further in the direction of seeing the sprite as sensuous rather than abstract. When Anne puts herself into the sprite world, she imagines herself to be a part of the system, playing with the birds and the screens as though they were tactile materials.

Science is usually defined in the terms of the hard masters: it is the place for the abstract, the domain for a clear and distinct separation between subject and object. If we accept this definition, the Austen classroom, with its male hard masters, is a microcosm of the male genderization of science. But what about Anne and Mary? What about the other girls like them who are exploring and mastering the computer? Should we not say that they too are "little scientists"? If we do, then we see at Austen not only a model of the male model that characterizes "official science," but a model of how women, when given a chance, can find another way to think and talk about the mastery not simply of machines but of formal systems. And here the computer may have a special role. It provides an entry to formal systems that is more accessible to women. It can be negotiated with, it can be responded to, it can be psychologized.

Suggestions for Discussion and Writing

1. What is Turkle's true subject in this essay? Where does it first become clear? What argumentative advantage does she gain by revealing it when she does?

2. The author identifies two styles of "mastery." Does she define these terms effectively? In a paragraph each, define these terms in your own words.

3. Turkle develops her argument through narrative. Is narrative an appropriate way to substantiate scientific findings? Is it an appropriate way for the author to substantiate her views on the relationship between science and gender? Is Turkle's work here that of a "hard" or "soft" master?

4. Is the distinction between "hard" and "soft" mastery a useful one? What kind of "masters" are Renouf (Chapter 6), Darwin (Chapter 6), Galileo (as presented by Bronowski, Chapter 1), and Fleming (as presented by Root-Bernstein, Chapter 7)?

5. Does Turkle's essay foster sexual stereotyping?

6. Write an essay about your own experience with computers. Would you describe yourself as a "hard" or "soft" master?

CHAPTER 13

Science and Education

☐ A FLASH OF LIGHT

Alan Lightman
(b. 1948)

For a biographical sketch of the author, see page 360.

In the following essay, taken from *A Modern Day Yankee in a Connecticut Court* (1984), Lightman humorously recalls a project he worked on in a college physics course, a project that led to his discovery that he would be a theoretical rather than an experimental physicist.

M y serious interest in physics began in my freshman year of college. In the dining hall that year, one of the upperclassmen smugly announced that, on the strength of mechanics alone, he could predict where to strike a billiard ball so that it would roll with no sliding. I was mightily impressed and decided this was a subject worth looking into.

Although I didn't realize it at the time, scientists generally divide into two camps, theorists and experimentalists. The abstractionists and the tinkerers. Especially in the physical sciences, the distinction can be spotted straight off. It has since been my observation that, in addition to their skills in the lab, the experimentalists (particularly the males) can fix things around the house, know what's happening under the hood of a car, and have a special appeal to the opposite sex. Theorists stick to their own gifts, like engaging themselves for hours with a mostly blank sheet of paper and discussing chess problems at lunch. Sometime in college, either by genes or by accident, a budding scientist starts drifting one way or the other. From then on, things are pretty much settled.

My path was decided in junior year. For some reason, the physics department had gotten into its head that we students should have a practical knowledge of our subject. To this end, an ungraded electronics workshop, to be tackled in the fall of that year, was strongly encouraged. Most of my colleagues leaped at the opportunity. This was particularly true of those scholars shaky in course work, who could be heard muttering such quips as, "This will separate the men from the boys." (My college was all male in those days.) I had an inkling of trouble, but was not one to tuck in my tail. I signed up.

This electronics workshop was considerably different from the routine laboratory exercises attached to most courses. In the latter, you were always measuring something where you knew damn well what the right answer was. One experiment I remember involved determining the speed of light. The equipment consisted of two mirrors, one of them stationary and the other rotating rapidly. Light making a round trip between the two mirrors would be slightly deflected on its return path by the rotation of the moving mirror, and from the amount of deflection you could deduce the speed of light. Of course, you could also look up the speed of light in any number of books. If your own measured value came out shy of the mark, you could nudge the mirrors and try again. With enough stamina, you eventually got the result you were looking for, at which point everything was carefully recorded, the experiment was declared a success, and you strode out of the laboratory in search of other mountains to climb.

But this electronics project was different. Each of us was provided with a large stock of transistors, capacitors, and so forth, a description of what the final thing had to *do,* and let loose. The stated aim of my gadget, as I recall, was to light up for several seconds when pure tones above middle C were offered to it but to maintain a state of torpor otherwise. (The state of torpor I had no problem with.) To help us get started with the fundamentals, we were given a textbook titled *Basic Electronics for Scientists,* which I immediately recognized as a friendly ally, took with me everywhere for months, and pored over deep into the night, at the expense of my own and my roommate's sleep.

The next couple of months were miserable. I discovered that what worked in the book didn't necessarily work on the lab table, at least under my supervision. In this regard, I lagged far behind most of my classmates. When they looked at the wavy line of an oscilloscope, it spoke to them, and they knew just how to fix up their circuits to get the desired results. I badly wanted my project to succeed. But I did not possess that peculiar knack for making things work. I could write poetry, I could play "Clair de Lune" on the piano, and I loved talking about ideas. But I could not make things work.

One day that term, through some odd misdirection of the postal service, I received in my mail slot a catalog for a home electronics course. Normally, I throw such things out. But to me, at that time, this catalog seemed like a greeting from providence. I took the thing back to my dormitory room, discreetly, and began reading. The front page said something to the effect that, with no prior training or aptitude, you would in six weeks be designing working circuits, mending broken televisions, and presenting yourself to the electronics industry as a force to be reckoned with. There were a few sample diagrams, some pictures of robust-looking devices, and glowing statements of successful graduates. What caught my eye was the provision that, during the course, you could mail in detailed sketches for an electrical project of your own design and be promptly and accurately informed whether the thing would, in fact, work. This last feature was absolutely guaranteed. Mending televisions didn't much interest me, but the chance of securing a foolproof verdict on my floundering electrical enterprise was nothing to be sneered at.

I enrolled without delay in this mail-order electronics course. The cost was $200, and you had to furnish your own parts, of which I had ample supply. My plan was to send in furtively a series of intermediate designs for my college project until one of them received the seal of approval. I could then prance into the physics lab and assemble the contraption in short order. My colleagues, meanwhile, were reporting to the lab daily, laboriously testing out each little step of their assigned projects. I had tried this method and failed. It was a great relief to me that I could now suffer through all the preliminary defeats in private, without humiliating myself in front of the others.

Eventually one of my designs was certified. I spent the last few days before the project deadline calmly at work in the lab, soldering each part into its approved position. My fellow students watched my miraculous progress with the kind of respect that is never verbalized. We were all equals, and I basked in my satisfaction. However, I never had the courage to put the device through a dry run.

The final judgments of the projects were pronounced on a day in December by a highly competent member of the faculty named Professor Pollock. Pollock was a man of few words, but a fair man. He was partially bald, as I remember, wore thick glasses, and usually held his head lowered below eye level. When something you said or did amused him, he would look up briefly and grin, without making the slightest sound or the tiniest movement of his head. Pollock was someone who could make things work. He had large hands. He had built cyclotrons.

On that day in the lab, the various projects and students stood at attention, like dogs and their masters in a dog show. When it came time to put my pet through its paces, I played a note to it—I forget now whether above or below middle C—and it answered with a single, blinding flash of light followed by the unmistakable odor of an electrical fire. The flash going off seemed like a shotgun blast, and I instinctively ducked for cover. It was amazing that no one was hurt. Pollock stood grinning longer than usual.

The following summer Armstrong and Aldrin walked on the moon. As I sat watching them on television in my family house, I had enormous respect for the parts that had worked to get them there: the rocket propellant, the computers, the space suits. And I was filled with admiration for the people behind all that, people good with their hands. Pollock may have been one of them and, undoubtedly, the handy students in my physics class would work on similar things in the future. But it also occurred to me that we theorists were needed to make sure the moon would be there at the same time the astronauts were. There are abstractionists and there are tinkerers, and I was not unhappy to have discovered my lot.

Suggestions for Discussion and Writing

1. How does Lightman present himself in this essay? In what ways does this presentation contribute to the overall tone?

2. In a paragraph, explain the difference between the "abstractionists" and the "tinkerers." What kind of scientist is Lightman? Where would you place yourself?

3. Do you see any connection between the two categories of scientist (abstractionist/theorist and tinkerer/experimentalist) described by Lightman and the gender approaches to science discussed by Keller (Chapter 12) and Turkle (Chapter 12)?

4. What is the author's view of Professor Pollock? What is your view? Is he the kind of science teacher you would want for your college science course(s)? In a brief essay describe the ideal science teacher.

5. At the end of his essay, Lightman recognizes that both theorists and experimentalists are necessary to the practice of science. He clearly places himself in one camp. Where would you place Charles Darwin (see Mayr, Chapter 1, and the essays in Chapter 6)? Where would you place Lavoisier (see McKie, Chapter 5)?

MOON, MANN, AND OTTO

Stephen Jay Gould
(b. 1941)

For a biographical sketch of the author, see page 285.

In the following essay, taken from *Hen's Teeth and Horses Toes* (1983), Gould discusses the effects of religious belief on the teaching of Darwin's theory of evolution as reflected in high school textbooks, and he praises those teachers who, over the years, have stood firm for the principles of science and of their profession.

Little Rock, Arkansas
December 10, 1981

This morning's *Arkansas Gazette* features a cartoon with searchlights focused on a state map. The map displays neither topography nor political boundaries, but merely contains the words, etched in black from Oklahoma to the Mississippi: "Scopes Trial II. Notoriety." I spent most of yesterday—with varying degrees of pleasure, righteousness, discomfort, and disbelief—in the witness box, trying to convince Federal Judge William R. Overton that all the geological strata on earth did not form as the result of a single Noachian deluge. We are engaged in the first legal test upon the new wave of creationist bills that mandate equal time or "balanced treatment" for evolution and a thinly disguised version of the Book of Genesis read literally, but masquerading under the nonsense phrase "creation science." The judge, to say the least, seems receptive to my message and as bemused as I am by the fact that such a trial can be held just a few months before the hundredth anniversary of Darwin's death.

The trial of John Scopes in 1925 has cast such a long shadow into our own times that the proceedings in Little Rock inevitably invite comparison. I appreciate the historical continuity but am more impressed by the differences. I sit in a massive alabaster building, a combined courthouse and post office, a no-nonsense, no-frills edifice, surrounded by the traffic noises of downtown Little Rock. The Rhea County Courthouse of Dayton, Tennessee—the building that hosted Scopes, Darrow, and Bryan in 1925—is a gracious, shaded, and decorated Renaissance Revival structure that dominates the crossroads of its two-street town. The Scopes trial was directly initiated by Dayton's boosters to put their little town on the map; many, probably most, citizens of Arkansas are embarrassed by the anachronism on their doorstep. John Scopes was convicted for even mentioning that humans had descended from "a lower order of animals"; we have made some progress in half a century, and modern creationists clamor for the official recognition of their pseudoscience, not (at least yet) for the exclusion of our well-documented conclusions.

I decided to be a paleontologist when I was five, after an awe-struck encounter with *Tyrannosaurus* at the Museum of Natural History in New York. The phenomenology of big beasts might have been enough to sustain my interest, but I confirmed my career six years later when I read, far too early and with dim understanding, G. G. Simpson's *Meaning of Evolution* and discovered that a body of exciting ideas made sense of all those bodies of bone. Three years later, I therefore approached my first high school science course with keen anticipation. In a year of biology, I would surely learn all about evolution. Imagine my disappointment when the teacher granted Mr. Darwin and his entire legacy only an apologetic two days at the very end of a trying year. I always wondered why, but was too shy to ask. Then I just forgot my question and continued to study on my own.

Six months ago, in a secondhand bookstore, I found a copy of my old high school text, *Modern Biology*, by T. J. Moon, P. B. Mann, and J. H. Otto. We all appreciate how powerful an unexpected sight or odor can be in triggering a distant "remembrance of things past." I knew what I had the minute I saw the familiar red binding with its embossed microscope in silver and its frontispiece in garish color, showing a busy beaver at work. The book, previously the property of a certain "Lefty," was soon mine for ninety-five cents.

Now, more than half a life later (I studied high school biology in 1954), I finally understand why Mrs. Blenderman had neglected the subject that so passionately interested me. I had been a victim of Scopes's ghost (or rather, of his adversary, Bryan's). Most people view the Scopes trial as a victory for evolution, if only because Paul Muni and Spencer Tracy served Clarence Darrow so well in theatrical and film versions of *Inherit the Wind,* and because the trial triggered an outpouring of popular literature by aggrieved and outraged evolutionists. Scopes's conviction (later quashed on a technicality) had been a mere formality; the battle for evolution had been won in the court of public opinion. Would it were so. As several historians have shown, the Scopes trial was a rousing defeat. It abetted a growing fundamentalist movement and led directly to the dilution or elimination of evolution from all popular high school texts in the United States. No arm of the industry is as cowardly and conservative as the publishers of public school texts—markets of millions are not easily ignored. The situation did not change until 1957, a year too late for me, when the Russian Sputnik provoked a searching inquiry into the shameful state of science education in America's high schools.

Moon, Mann, and Otto commanded the lion's share of the market in the mid-1950s; readers of my generation will probably experience that exhilarating sense of *déjà vu* with me. Like many popular books, it was the altered descendant of several earlier editions. The first, *Biology for Beginners,* by Truman J. Moon, was published in 1921, before the Scopes trial. Its frontispiece substituted Mr. Darwin for the industrious beaver, and its text reflected a thorough immersion in evolution as the focal subject of the life sciences. Its preface proclaimed: "The course emphasizes the fact that biology is a unit science, based on the fundamental idea of evolution rather than a forced combination of portions of botany, zoology and hygiene." Its text contains several chapters on evolution and continually emphasizes Darwin's central contention that the *fact* of evolution is established beyond reasonable doubt, although scientists have much to learn about the *mechanism* of evolutionary change. Chapter 35, on "The Method of Evolution," begins: "Proof of the *fact* of similarity between the various forms of living things and of their very evident relationship, still leaves a more difficult question to be answered. *How* did this descent and modification take place, by what means has nature developed one form from another? [Moon's italics]"

I then examined my new purchase with a growing sense of amusement mixed with disgust. The index contained such important entries as "fly specks, disease germs in," but nothing about evolution. Indeed, the word evolution does not occur anywhere in the book. The subject is not, however, entirely absent. It receives a scant eighteen pages in a 662–page book, as chapter 58 of 60 (pp. 618–36). In this bowdlerized jiffy, it is called "The hypothesis of racial development." Moon, Mann, and Otto had gone the post-Scopes way of all profitable texts: eliminate and risk no offense. (Those who recall the reality of high school courses will also remember that many teachers never got to those last few chapters at all.)

This one pussyfooting chapter is as disgraceful in content as in brevity. Its opening two paragraphs are a giveaway and an intellectual sham compared with Moon's forthright words of 1921. The first paragraph provides a fine statement of historical continuity and change in the *physical* features of our planet:

> This is a changing world. It changes from day to day, year to year, and from age to age. Rivers deepen their gorges as they carry more land to the sea. Mountains rise, only to be leveled gradually by winds and rain. Continents rise and sink into the sea. Such are the gradual changes of the physical earth as days add into years and years combine to become ages.

Now what could be more natural and logical than to extend this same mode of reasoning and style of language to life? The paragraph seems to be set up for such a transition. But note how the tone of the second paragraph subtly shifts to avoid any commitment to historical continuity for organic change:

> During these ages, species of plants and animals have appeared, have flourished for a time, and then have perished as new species took their places. . . . When one race lost in the struggle for survival, another race appeared to take its place.

Four pages later, we finally get an inkling that genealogy may be behind organic transitions through time: "This geological story of the rocks, showing fossil gradations from simple to complex organisms, is what we should expect to find if there had been racial development throughout the past." Later on the page, Moon, Mann, and Otto ask the dreaded question and even venture the closest word they dare to "evolution": "Are these prehistoric creatures the ancestors of modern animals?" If you read carefully through all the qualifications, they answer their question with a guarded "yes"—but you have to read awfully hard.

Thus were millions of children deprived of their chance to study one of the most exciting and influential ideas in science, the central theme of all biology. A few hundred, myself included, possessed the internal motivation to transcend this mockery of education, but citing us seems as foolish and cruel as the old racist argument, "what about George Washington Carver or Willie Mays," used to refute the claim that poor achievement might be linked to economic disadvantage and social prejudice.

Now I can mouth all the grandiloquent arguments against such a dilution of education: we will train a generation unable to think for themselves, we will weaken the economic and social fabric of the nation if we raise a generation illiterate in science, and so on. I even believe all these arguments. But this is not what troubled me most as I read chapter 58 in Moon, Mann, and Otto. I wasn't even much angered, but merely amused, by the tortured pussyfooting and glaring omissions. Small items with big implications are my bread and butter. I do not react strongly to generalities. I can ignore a displeasing general tenor, but I cannot bear falsification and debasement of something small and noble. I was not really shaken until I read the last paragraph of chapter 58, but then an interior voice rose up and began to compose this essay. For to make a valid point in the context of their cowardice, Moon, Mann, and Otto had perverted (perhaps unknowingly) one of my favorite quotations. If cowardice can inspire such debasement, then it must be rooted out.

The last paragraph is titled: Science and Religion. I agree entirely with the first two sentences: "There is nothing in science which is opposed to a belief in God and religion. Those who think so are mistaken in their science or their theology or both." They then quote (with some minor errors, here corrected) a famous statement of T. H. Huxley, using it to argue that a man may be both a Darwinian and a devout Christian:

> Science seems to me to teach in the highest and strongest manner the great truth which is embodied in the Christian conception of entire surrender to the will of God. Sit down before fact as a little child, be prepared to give up every preconceived notion, follow humbly wherever and to whatever abysses nature leads, or you shall learn nothing. I have only begun to learn content

and peace of mind since I have resolved at all risks
to do this.

Now a man may be both an evolutionist and a devout Christian.
Millions successfully juxtapose these two independent viewpoints,
but Thomas Henry Huxley did not. This quote, in its proper context,
actually speaks of Huxley's courageous agnosticism. It also occurs in
what I regard as the most beautiful and moving letter ever written by
a scientist.

The tragic setting of this long letter explains why Huxley cited, only
in analogy as Moon, Mann, and Otto did not understand, "the
Christian conception of entire surrender to the will of God." Huxley's
young and favorite son had just died. His friend, the Reverend Charles
Kingsley (best remembered today as author of *The Water-Babies* and
Westward Ho!) had written a long and kind letter of condolence with
a good Anglican bottom line: see here Huxley, if you could only
abandon your blasted agnosticism and accept the Christian concept
of an immortal soul, you would be comforted.

Huxley responded in tones that recall the chief of police in Gilbert
and Sullivan's *Pirates of Penzance* who, when praised by General
Stanley's daughters for expected bravery in a coming battle that
would probably lead to his bloody death, remarked:

> Still, perhaps it would be wise
> Not to carp or criticise,
> For it's very evident
> These attentions are well meant.

Huxley thanks Kingsley for his sincerely proffered comfort, but then
explains in several pages of passionate prose why he cannot alter a
set of principles, established after so much thought and deliberation,
merely to assuage his current grief.

He has, he maintains, committed himself to science as the only
sure guide to truth about matters of fact. Since matters of God and
soul do not lie in this realm, he cannot know the answers to specific
claims and must remain agnostic. "I neither deny nor affirm the
immortality of man," he writes. "I see no reason for believing in it,
but, on the other hand, I have no means of disproving it." Thus, he
continues, "I cannot assert the certainty of immortality to placate my
loss." Uncomfortable convictions, if well founded, are those that
require the most assiduous affirmation, as he states just before the
passage quoted by Moon, Mann, and Otto: "My business is to teach
my aspirations to conform themselves to fact, not to try and make
facts harmonize with my aspirations."

Later, in the most moving statement of the letter, he speaks of the
larger comfort that a commitment to science has provided him—a
comfort more profound and lasting than the grief that his uncertainty
about immortality now inspires. Among three agencies that shaped
his deepest beliefs, he notes, "Science and her methods gave me a
resting-place independent of authority and tradition." (For his two

other agencies, Huxley cites "love" that "opened up to me a view of the sanctity of human nature," and his recognition that "a deep sense of religion was compatible with the entire absence of theology.") He then writes:

> If at this moment I am not a worn-out, debauched, useless carcass of a man, if it has been or will be my fate to advance the cause of science, if I feel that I have a shadow of a claim on the love of those about me, if in the supreme moment when I looked down into my boy's grave my sorrow was full of submission and without bitterness, it is because these agencies have worked upon me, and not because I have ever cared whether my poor personality shall remain distinct forever from the All from whence it came and whither it goes.
>
> And thus, my dear Kingsley, you will understand what my position is. I may be quite wrong, and in that case I know I shall have to pay the penalty for being wrong. But I can only say with Luther, "Gott helfe mir, ich kann nichts anders [God help me, I cannot do otherwise]."

Thus we understand what Huxley meant when he spoke of "the Christian conception of entire surrender to the will of God" in the passage cited by Moon, Mann, and Otto. It is obviously not, as they imply, his profession of Christian faith, but a burning analogy: as the Christian has made his commitment, so have I made mine to science. I cannot do otherwise, despite the immediate comfort that conventional Christianity would supply in my current distress.

Today I sat in the court of Little Rock, listening to the testimony of four splendid men and women who teach science in primary and secondary schools of Arkansas. Their testimony contained moments of humor, as when one teacher described an exercise he uses in the second grade. He stretches a string across the classroom to represent the age of the earth. He then asks students to stand in various positions marking such events as the origin of life, the extinction of dinosaurs, and the evolution of humans. What would you do, asked the assistant attorney general in cross-examination, to provide balanced treatment for the 10,000-year-old earth advocated by creation scientists. "I guess I'd have to get a short string," replied the teacher. The thought of twenty earnest second graders, all scrunched up along a millimeter of string, created a visual image that set the court rocking with laughter.

But the teachers' testimony also contained moments of inspiration. As I listened to their reasons for opposing "creation science," I thought of T. H. Huxley and the courage required by dedicated people who will not, to paraphrase Lillian Hellman, tailor their convictions to fit current fashions. As Huxley would not simplify and debase in order to find immediate comfort, these teachers told the court that mechanical compliance with the "balanced treatment" act, although easy enough to perform, would destroy their integrity as teachers and violate their responsibility to students.

One witness pointed to a passage in his chemistry text that attributed great age to fossil fuels. Since the Arkansas act specifically includes "a relatively recent age of the earth" among the definitions of creation science requiring "balanced treatment," this passage would have to be changed. The witness claimed that he did not know how to make such an alteration. Why not? retorted the assistant attorney general in his cross-examination. You only need to insert a simple sentence: "Some scientists, however, believe that fossil fuels are relatively young." Then, in the most impressive statement of the entire trial, the teacher responded. I could, he argued, insert such a sentence in mechanical compliance with the act. But I cannot, as a conscientious teacher, do so. For "balanced treatment" must mean "equal dignity" and I would therefore have to justify the insertion. And this I cannot do, for I have heard no valid arguments that would support such a position.

Another teacher spoke of similar dilemmas in providing balanced treatment in a conscientious rather than a mechanical way. What then, he was asked, would he do if the law were upheld. He looked up and said, in his calm and dignified voice: It would be my tendency not to comply. I am not a revolutionary or a martyr, but I have responsibilities to my students, and I cannot forgo them.

God bless the dedicated teachers of this world. We who work in unthreatened private colleges and universities often do not adequately appreciate the plight of our colleagues—or their courage in upholding what should be our common goals. What Moon, Mann, and Otto did to Huxley epitomizes the greatest danger of imposed antirationalism in classrooms—that one must simplify by distortion, and remove both depth and beauty, in order to comply.

In appreciation for the teachers of Arkansas, then, and for all of us, one more statement in conclusion from Huxley's letter to Kingsley:

> Had I lived a couple of centuries earlier I could have fancied a devil scoffing at me . . . and asking me what profit it was to have stripped myself of the hopes and consolations of the mass of mankind? To which my only reply was and is—Oh devil! truth is better than much profit. I have searched over the grounds of my belief, and if wife and child and name and fame were all to be lost to me one after the other as the penalty, still I will not lie.

Postscript

On January 5, 1982, Federal District Judge William R. Overton declared the Arkansas act unconstitutional because it forces biology teachers to purvey religion in science classrooms.

Suggestions for Discussion and Writing

1. Who "won" the Scopes trial? Examine a current high school biology textbook. Does the book support your conclusion?

2. The first edition of Moon's *Biology for Beginners* (1921) was radically changed after the Scopes trial (1925). How does Gould explain this change? To what degree should textbooks reflect religious beliefs and/or current fashions of thought? Write an essay defending your views.

3. Gould speaks here as a scientist. Does he also speak as a concerned citizen? What elements of tone and diction suggest a second role?

4. What does Gould mean when he says that "small items with big implications are my bread and butter"?

5. Gould tells the story of Huxley's exchange with his friend, the Rev. Charles Kingsley. What does this exchange tell us about Huxley? about Moon, Mann, and Otto? about science?

6. In speaking of the forces that shaped his deepest beliefs, Huxley says that "science and her methods gave me a resting-place independent of authority and tradition." In a brief paragraph explain what Huxley means here. In what ways does this statement reflect the progress of science itself?

7. Though Gould is a distinguished paleontologist at Harvard University, he refers to high school teachers of science such as those who testified in Arkansas as "colleagues." In what sense are they colleagues?

TUNE IN, TURN OFF, DROP OUT

John S. Rigden
(b. 1934)
Sheila Tobias
(b. 1935)

John Rigden received his Ph.D. in physics from Johns Hopkins University and has taught at Middlebury College and the University of Missouri, St. Louis. He is currently director of physics programs at the American Institute of Physics in New York. Rigden was editor of the *American Journal of Physics* from 1978 to 1988. He has contributed numerous articles to scientific journals and is the author of two books, *Physics and the Sound of Music* (1977) and *Rabi: Scientist and Citizen* (1987).

Educated at Radcliffe and Columbia universities, Sheila Tobias has worked as a journalist, teacher, administrator, and consultant. She is currently a partner in a Washington, D.C., consulting firm and co-director of the Institute for the Study of Anxiety in Learning at the Washington School of Psychiatry. A founding member of the National Organization for Women, Tobias has contributed more than one hundred articles on math anxiety and women's studies to popular and scholarly journals. Her published work also includes *Overcoming Math Anxiety* (1978) and, more recently, *They're Not Dumb, They're Different: The Stalking of the Second Tier,* a study of college science undertaken for the Research Corporation in Tucson, Arizona.

In the following article, published in 1991, Ridgen and Tobias describe their studies of introductory college science courses and argue that the loss of thousands of potential science majors to other disciplines every year can be reversed only by radical changes in both the structure and teaching of these courses.

Every year at a typical large state university as many as 3,000 students enroll in introductory chemistry courses. Crowding into lecture halls and sometimes even into adjoining rooms outfitted with closed-circuit television are premedical students, agriculture majors and budding engineers, all there to fulfill a requirement for their specialties. But elbow to elbow with them are students who are in it for the chemistry. Attracted to the subject in high school or simply curious, they enroll as a possible first step to a chemistry major.

On the first day of class there is excitement in the air. And why not? Here is a chance for profound insight into the workings of the everyday world, for a grand, synthetic story of burning and decay; breathing and photosynthesis; the complexities of the atmosphere, the oceans and the soil; and, of course, the properties of millions of everyday and exotic materials: fuels and flame retardants, foods and poisons, bleaches and dyes, perfumes and deodorants and ultimately the stuff of life. Certainly there is also trepidation in the hall, for by reputation the subject will be hard. But for many students the anticipated intellectual mastery and the control of powerful laboratory tools will be rewards enough for their efforts.

The scene now shifts forward in time. Three years have passed, and the students are still at the university, as seniors. But most of them—even the ones who are intelligent and highly motivated—have left the crowded chemistry courses for other fields. Chemistry is so populous at the introductory level that some instructors are responsible for sections of 250 students each. In contrast, advanced chemistry classes are made up of merely a handful of students. Fewer than one out of fifty in beginning chemistry complete the major.

A similar pattern is repeated in other introductory science courses at the college level. Every year nearly half a million students leave high school planning to concentrate in science or engineering in college. And every year only 200,000 students, or 40 percent of the science-oriented high school graduates, complete one of those majors. Although it is true that many high school students are not being attracted to science in college, perhaps more ominous is that the majority of those who reach college hoping to do science end up changing their minds.

Some observers think such numbers presage a shortfall of scientists. The proportion of science majors who go on to earn doctorates has traditionally been small. The annual crop of 200,000 graduates yields about 10,000 PhD's—too few in some views to sustain the technological base of the U.S. economy. Foreign graduate students are filling the places vacated by American students, but there is no guarantee they will stay in the United States instead of taking their skills back home.

Whether a shortfall of scientists will develop, though, depends on several elusive factors: the vagaries of the economy, the rate at which scientists retire or otherwise leave the profession and the future level of spending for military research and development, which consumes much scientific talent. What is beyond doubt is that the drain of students from science drags down the country's level of scientific literacy, however that rather slippery term may be defined. Insofar as students quit science because of poor grades or boredom, their exodus also risks creating a voting public that will be uncomfortable with science or even hostile to it. Concern about diminishing enrollment takes many forms, but at bottom the message is this: too few Americans are studying too little science.

One set of solutions, much discussed these days, would encourage more youngsters to enter the science pipeline. Better science teaching in elementary and secondary schools might produce more students able and willing to begin college science majors. But finding common solutions for the multitude of school programs around the country is a daunting challenge. And high schools, for all their failings, deliver more than twice as many science-oriented students to college as complete a science major. A more direct approach is to focus on introductory college science, where the hemorrhaging of would-be science students is most severe. Indeed, given the nature of the great majority of introductory science courses for undergraduates, there is no guarantee that a more powerful pump at one end of the pipeline would have a proportional effect on the trickle emerging at the other end.

It is usually assumed that students who leave the study of science in college have simply been weeded out because they are not intelligent in science. Certainly many who abandon science are better off in other disciplines. But what about those who start off with both a taste for science and the necessary aptitude but choose, after a semester or two, not to go on? College science programs should struggle to keep those able students as well as to make converts of the ones who enroll because of curiosity or the requirements of another major. Doubtless, precollege science education needs attention. So does the support of science graduates: it is critical that prospective students be able to look forward to employment and grants at the end of their formal scientific education. But the introductory college science course presents a clear and urgent target for reform.

What goes wrong in introductory science? How can one improve the chances of retaining able students who are not yet deeply committed to science? To answer these questions, one of us (Tobias) did a series of studies focusing on students' experiences in physics and chemistry courses. The studies sought testimony about the failings of the courses from learners themselves.

College students, concerned about grades and careers and being short on time for reflection, might not be ideal observers of their courses and classmates. Instead, surrogate learners—faculty and graduate students in fields other than science—were recruited and placed in college science courses. In preliminary studies, at Indiana University at Bloomington and the University of Chicago, nonscience faculty members observed course segments. In a later, more extensive study, supported by the Research Corporation in Tucson, Arizona, seven stand-ins, among them a professor of classics and graduate students in literature and philosophy, enrolled in basic physics and chemistry courses at the Universities of Arizona and of Nebraska at Lincoln.

The participants kept up with homework and took the quizzes and midterm examinations. Throughout each course they kept journals in which they recorded their observations about the lectures, the work and their fellow students. At the end of the study, instead of taking the final examination, they wrote reports reflecting on the course as a whole, the culture of the classroom and their own attitudes about studying science.

In many ways the surrogates were good representatives of the many potential scientists who slip through the sieve of introductory courses. All were confident in their abilities and eager for intellectual rewards. Most had strong grounding in science and mathematics from high school, and many had considered science before settling on other fields. All were eager to reacquaint themselves with science. Yet most of them came away with serious reservations about the atmosphere of the classes, the teaching methods and the course structure.

To judge by the comments in their journals and final reports, these learners would not have stayed with science even if they had not already been committed to other careers. Yet their difficulties represented not a failure of intellect (most of them did well on the tests) but a failure of fit. Science as it was presented in their courses did not yield the intellectual rewards they hoped for.

The classroom atmosphere, for one, tended to dampen any spirit of intellectual adventure. The rapid pace of the courses, the large class size and the machine-graded examinations fostered the erroneous impression that science is authoritarian. As one participant wrote, the effect is to discourage beginners from thinking they can "interact creatively with the material." Midway through his chemistry course the classics professor wrote:

> The instructor's approach, probably set by department policy, was to recapitulate the textbook and work sample problems. . . . It was difficult to sit there for an hour of this without participating. And participation was definitely not encouraged.

The result, witnessed by many of the observers, is that students become "incredibly passive" in science lectures.

Outside the lecture hall there was little community among the students, little discussion or collaboration. Grades were the major topic of conversation. Typically, students in introductory science courses are graded on a curve, which permits only a fixed proportion of the class to receive top grades. On the one hand, this grading scheme led to a sense of helplessness. One learner wrote, "The message . . . seems to be that no matter how hard you work—so long as everyone else works as hard or has more talent or experience— you *cannot* improve your grade." On the other hand, the limited number of high grades promotes intense competition, which the learners found destructive: "Suddenly your classmates are your enemies."

The lectures offered few intellectual rewards to compensate for these rigors. The surrogates reported that instructors were reluctant to present the intellectual or historical background of the material they taught. Students never got what one of them called the big picture. In physics courses the amazing idea that "sitting at rest on a front porch" can be equated with "flying through the troposphere at 600 miles an hour"—the basic concept of inertia, which eluded the best minds for more than 2,000 years—was routinely presented as a codified law, with little or no discussion.

"I found myself craving some theory," a graduate student in anthropology reported of introductory chemistry, "some discussion of how the laws of nature were developed, rather than just being presented with the finished product." The classicist studying chemistry experienced a similar frustration. After some weeks, he noted that the class had spent more time on Avogadro's number than on Avogadro's insight that equal volumes of different gases contain equal numbers of molecules. He wanted to know "more of the background of Dalton's laws in ancient atomic theory and of the work done on gas laws during the 18th century." Instead the professor kept "working problems hour after uncomfortable hour."

The relentless problem solving frustrated most of the participants. Many of them realized they were learning techniques that belong in any scientist's toolbox. But almost without exception they found basic physical science to be characterized by a "tyranny of technique." "Simply by intuition," wrote one learner, "I know physics, and more generally science, to involve creativity and finesse; but [this professor] makes it into a craft, like cooking, where if someone follows the recipe, he or she will do well."

Even when instructors tried to step outside this arid regimen, they often undermined their own efforts. Some of them, learners reported, did present and expand on the concepts underlying the problem-solving techniques. One course even took a historical approach to Newtonian mechanics, describing Newton's rivalry with Descartes and the theological background of his laws of motion. But because none of this material ever appeared in homework assignments or was tested in examinations, students ignored these excursions. The professor was disappointed, but one of the participants observed perceptively:

> The way an instructor operationalizes the goals for his course is not simply to speak them or put them in a handout, but to incorporate them into his exams. While [the professor] was talking concepts, his exams were testing numerical solutions. And he probably never realized what the students knew very well, namely that the "concepts" and the "history" didn't really count.

In addition to longing for intellectual context, the surrogate students complained of what one of them called the missing overview. After a group of nonscience professors sat in on a basic physics course on waves in elastic media, one of them wrote:

> It seemed to me during these lectures that I lacked any framework of prior knowledge, experience or intuition that could have helped me order the information. . . . I had no way of telling what was important and what was not. I had difficulty distinguishing between what I was supposed to be learning and what was being communicated merely for the purpose of illustration or analogy.

A graduate student in creative writing, taking part in a course on Newtonian mechanics, was even more explicit:

> I never really knew where we were heading or how much . . . we had already covered. Each topic the professor discusses feels like it's being pulled out of a hat. So

the general feeling I was left with was that physics was endless, that there would always be one more complex way of describing motion. . . . Why, I wanted to know, did we begin by studying only the idealized motion of particles in straight lines? What about the other kinds of motion?

The content of the course was presented piecemeal, class by class, according to a logic internal to the subject but never articulated by the instructor. A concept was developed one day because it would be needed two weeks later. The instructor knew this; the students, as our observers reported, did not. In a physics course, for example, the transition from Newtonian dynamics to the work–energy theorem is a natural one for the professor; for the students it is a trip from one conceptual galaxy to another, a trip devoid of motivation and understanding.

The surrogate students were mature, interested and capable—everything a science instructor could wish. Yet their experiences in science were uniformly negative. How could this happen in courses that should introduce students to the beauty and power of science?

In a mature science such as physics or chemistry the conversation between the scientist and nature is a grand dialogue, leading to surprises, new mysteries, insights and syntheses. The terms of the dialogue change continually, as discovery modifies theory and theory suggests new routes for investigation. Science thrives on this dynamism, and for scientists it is a source of exhilaration. Contrast it with the rendition of science presented to students in introductory courses. There science appears static and dull. Analytical techniques that equip scientists to probe the universe are treated as ends in themselves—a hallowed body of knowledge that must be absorbed.

To some extent, of course, such an approach is implied by the nature of science. The knowledge that defines the content of basic courses is often centuries old, far removed from the dynamism that disturbs the sleep of contemporary scientists. And beginning students are not ready to take part in the dialogue of science. The freshman in introductory English and the graduate student in a literature seminar each can interpret a sonnet; they just do so at different levels of sophistication. Science, in contrast, is regarded as a vertical subject: finger exercises must come before music. As a professor of chemistry put it, the material "is dull to learn, and it is dull to teach. Unfortunately, it is the basic nuts and bolts stuff that must be mastered before anything useful can be accomplished." How are students to master this material? In quantitative sciences such as physics and chemistry the answer is clear: solve problems—lots of problems.

Even when instructors realize how uninviting the courses can be, many of them view their students' discouragement as a necessary evil. The true converts to science, they believe, will not be deterred, and introductory science is no place for making new ones. Many instructors view it as a training ground for those with a long-standing commitment to science. One professor wrote, "I assume that students in [my course] are preprofessionals who have already decided on a career in science and are in class to learn problem-solving techniques that will be required of them in their careers."

Some studies suggest that most scientists in the current generation discovered their calling very early, well before any college science course could influence them. But that finding can just as well be interpreted as showing that the colleges are losing many, if not most, of the students who might be attracted to science if college courses were more appealing. Undoubtedly there is a core of committed young people who are unshaken by classroom competition, relentless problem solving and the neglect of intellectual context. To capture the others, we need something better. Introductory science could— and should—become the best advertisement for the discipline.

Science instructors should begin by rooting out their own prejudices: Students who leave science, even the ones who leave with poor records, are not necessarily poor academic material. Understanding is not a function of cognition alone—of the "higher-order thinking" instructors value—and passivity is not merely an expression of poor motivation. A desire to understand is fueled by confidence that one *can* understand; apathy, as Che Guevara said in another context, is the "revolt of the powerless."

There are obvious ways of giving students a sense of greater power over their subject. Classes should be smaller, less competitive and more reliant on discussion. Science departments should conduct exit interviews of students leaving the major—in effect transforming the studies discussed here into an ongoing project. Professors should consider adding lessons on intellectual history, and examinations should test the additional material.

But improving the classroom climate and tinkering with course content will not be enough. Introductory physics or chemistry will always be time-consuming and sometimes counterintuitive and frustrating—the toughest course of the year for many students. "To some extent," one auditor wrote, "science is hard simply because it is hard." But the testimony of surrogate learners suggests it becomes still harder when the subject is atomized, presented one law or technique at a time with no sense of narrative. Course structure too needs attention.

Students who see their subject assembled one concept at a time cannot know where each piece fits into the larger whole. Instructors must find ways of giving students an early glimpse of where the class is going and why. Basic science must become a rigorous adventure instead of a catechism.

Suggestions for Discussion and Writing

1. What is the effect of the second paragraph? For example, what does it suggest about chemistry as a subject? How does it suggest it?

2. Write an essay in which you discuss your own experience in a science course. To what degree did your expectations coincide with those expressed in the second paragraph? Why did the course meet or not meet your expectations?

3. Consider the studies carried out by Tobias. What criticisms might be made of her methods? Does she anticipate any of those criticisms?

4. The authors cite a range of criticisms made by the surrogate learners participating in their study. Which is the most telling? Why? Write an essay relating the criticisms to your own experience in a science course.

5. The authors assert that the way science is commonly taught fosters "the erroneous impression that science is authoritarian." What in the nature of science tends to encourage such a view?

6. Do you agree with the surrogate learners that particular scientific issues and problems should be placed in their broader theoretical and intellectual contexts? Why?

7. How would you respond to the professor who wrote, "I assume that students in [my course] are preprofessionals. . . ." How might Mermin (this chapter) respond? What view about the university and about education does this assumption imply?

HUMANITIES AND SCIENCE

Lewis Thomas
(b. 1913)

An eminent physician and distinguished scientist, Lewis Thomas is also a celebrated essayist noted both for his ability to unite the concerns of the scientist with those of the humanist and for the grace of his style.

Born in New York, Thomas was educated at Princeton University and Harvard Medical School. He has served as a professor of pediatric research at the University of Minnesota, as chairman of the departments of pathology and medicine and as dean of the School of Medicine at New York University, and as chairman of pathology and dean at Yale School of Medicine. He is currently President Emeritus of Memorial Sloan-Kettering Cancer Center. Thomas has contributed about 200 articles to medical and scientific journals. He is a member of the National Academy of Science's Institute of Medicine, the American Academy of Arts and Sciences, and the American Philosophical Society.

In 1971 Thomas began writing essays for the *New England Journal of Medicine*. These essays were immediately popular, and some were later collected and published as *Lives of a Cell: Notes of a Biology Watcher* (1974). Widely praised in the literary as well as the scientific community, *Lives* earned the National Book Award (1975). It was followed by *The Medusa and the Snail* (1979), *The Youngest Science* (1983), and *Late Night Thoughts on Listening to Mahler's Ninth Symphony* (1983).

Perhaps the most consistent theme in Thomas's essays is that of the interconnection and community of all living things. Other themes include the importance of basic research and the inevitable unpredictability of that research, whose constant element is surprise. Thomas writes about the complexities of modern biology and biochemistry with the detailed knowledge of the research scientist, but he does so with the imaginative insight of the creative writer. His work, as one critic has said, "has the texture of permanence." In the following essay, taken from *Late Night Thoughts*, Thomas discusses the dangers of teaching science as though its findings were cut-and-dried. By focusing on the mysteries, on the strangeness of nature, he suggests, science teachers might bring the fun back into science and show it "as the high adventure it really is."

L ord Kelvin was one of the great British physicists of the late nineteenth century, an extraordinarily influential figure in his time, and in some ways a paradigm of conventional, established scientific leadership. He did a lot of good and useful things, but once or twice he, like Homer, nodded. The instances are worth recalling today, for we have nodders among our scientific eminences still, from time to time, needing to have their elbows shaken.

On one occasion, Kelvin made a speech on the overarching importance of numbers. He maintained that no observation of nature was worth paying serious attention to unless it could be stated in precisely quantitative terms. The numbers were the final and only test, not only of truth but about meaning as well. He said, "When you can measure what you are speaking about, and express it in numbers, you know something about it. But when you cannot—your knowledge is of a meagre and unsatisfactory kind."

But, as at least one subsequent event showed, Kelvin may have had things exactly the wrong way round. The task of converting observations into numbers is the hardest of all, the last task rather than the first thing to be done, and it can be done only when you have learned, before hand, a great deal about the observations themselves. You can, to be sure, achieve a very deep understanding of nature by quantitative measurement, but you must know what you are talking about before you can begin applying the numbers for making predictions. In Kelvin's case, the problem at hand was the age of the earth and solar system. Using what was then known about the sources of energy and the loss of energy from the physics of that day, he calculated that neither the earth nor the sun were older than several hundred million years. This caused a considerable stir in biological and geological circles, especially among the evolutionists. Darwin himself was distressed by the numbers; the time was much too short for the theory of evolution. Kelvin's figures were described by Darwin as one of his "sorest troubles."

T. H. Huxley had long been aware of the risks involved in premature extrapolations from mathematical treatment of biological problems. He said, in an 1869 speech to the Geological Society concerning numbers, "This seems to be one of the many cases in which the admitted accuracy of mathematical processes is allowed to throw a wholly inadmissible appearance of authority over the results obtained by them. . . . As the grandest mill in the world will not extract wheat flour from peascods, so pages of formulas will not get a definite result out of loose data."

The trouble was that the world of physics had not moved fast enough to allow for Kelvin's assumptions. Nuclear fusion and fission had not yet been dreamed of, and the true age of the earth could not even be guessed from the data in hand. It was not yet the time for mathematics in this subject.

There have been other examples, since those days, of the folly of using numbers and calculations uncritically. Kelvin's own strong conviction that science could not be genuine science without measuring things was catching. People in other fields of endeavor, hankering to turn their disciplines into exact sciences, beset by what has since been called "physics envy," set about converting whatever they knew into numbers and thence into equations with predictive pretensions. We have it with us still, in economics, sociology, psychology, history, even, I fear, in English-literature criticism and linguistics, and it frequently works, when it works at all, with indifferent success. The risks of untoward social consequences in work of this kind are considerable. It is as important—and as hard—to learn *when* to use mathematics as *how* to use it, and this matter should remain high on the agenda of consideration for education in the social and behavioral sciences.

Of course, Kelvin's difficulty with the age of the earth was an exceptional, almost isolated instance of failure in quantitative measurement in nineteenth-century physics. The instruments devised for approaching nature by way of physics became increasingly precise and powerful, carrying the field through electromagnetic theory, triumph after triumph, and setting the stage for the great revolution of twentieth-century physics. There is no doubt about it: measurement works when the instruments work, and when you have a fairly clear idea of what it is that is being measured, and when you know what to do with the numbers when they tumble out. The system for gaining information and comprehension about nature works so well, indeed, that it carries another hazard: the risk of convincing yourself that you know everything.

Kelvin himself fell into this trap toward the end of the century. (I don't mean to keep picking on Kelvin, who was a very great scientist; it is just that he happened to say a couple of things I find useful for this discussion.) He stated, in a summary of the achievements of nineteenth-century physics, that it was an almost completed science; virtually everything that needed knowing about the material universe had been learned; there were still a few anomalies and inconsistencies in electromagnetic theory, a few loose ends to be tidied up, but this would be done within the next several years. Physics, in these terms, was not a field any longer likely to attract, as it previously had, the brightest and most imaginative young brains. The most interesting part of the work had already been done. Then, within the next decade, came radiation, Planck, the quantum, Einstein, Rutherford, Bohr, and all the rest—quantum mechanics—and the whole field turned over and became a brand-new sort of human endeavor, still now, in the view of many physicists, almost a full century later, a field only at its beginnings.

But even today, despite the amazements that are turning up in physics each year, despite the jumps taken from the smallest parts of nature—particle physics—to the largest of all—the cosmos itself—the impression of science that the public gains is rather like the impression left in the nineteenth-century public mind by Kelvin. Science, in this view, is first of all a matter of simply getting all the numbers together. The numbers are sitting out there in nature, waiting to be found, sorted and totted up. If only they had enough robots and enough computers, the scientists could go off to the beach and wait for their papers to be written for them. Second of all, what we know about nature today is pretty much the whole story: we are very nearly home and dry. From here on, it is largely a problem of tying up loose ends, tidying nature up, getting the files in order. The only real surprises for the future—and it is about those that the public is becoming more concerned and apprehensive—are the technological applications that the scientists may be cooking up from today's knowledge.

I suggest that the scientific community is to blame. If there are disagreements between the world of the humanities and the scientific enterprise as to the place and importance of science in a liberal-arts education, and the role of science in twentieth-century culture, I believe that the scientists are themselves responsible for a general misunderstanding of what they are really up to.

Over the past half century, we have been teaching the sciences as though they were the same academic collection of cut-and-dried subjects as always, and—here is what has really gone wrong—as though they would always be the same. The teaching of today's biology, for example, is pretty much the same kind of exercise as the teaching of Latin was when I was in high school long ago. First of all, the fundamentals, the underlying laws, the essential grammar, and then the reading of texts. Once mastered, that is that: Latin is Latin and forever will be Latin. And biology is precisely biology, a vast array of hard facts to be learned as fundamentals, followed by a reading of the texts.

Moreover, we have been teaching science as though its facts were somehow superior to the facts in all other scholarly disciplines, more fundamental, more solid, less subject to subjectivism, immutable. English literature is not just one way of thinking, it is all sorts of ways. Poetry is a moving target. The facts that underlie art, architecture, and music are not really hard facts, and you can change them any way you like by arguing about them, but science is treated as an altogether different kind of learning: an unambiguous, unalterable, and endlessly useful display of data needing only to be packaged and installed somewhere in one's temporal lobe in order to achieve a full understanding of the natural world.

And it is, of course, not like this at all. In real life, every field of science that I can think of is incomplete, and most of them—whatever the record of accomplishment over the past two hundred years—are still in the earliest stage of their starting point. In the fields I know best, among the life sciences, it is required that the most expert and sophisticated minds be capable of changing those minds, often with a great lurch, every few years. In some branches of biology the mind-changing is occurring with accelerating velocities. The next week's issue of any scientific journal can turn a whole field upside down, shaking out any number of immutable ideas and installing new bodies of dogma, and this is happening all the time. It is an almost everyday event in physics, in chemistry, in materials research, in neurobiology, in genetics, in immunology. The hard facts tend to soften overnight, melt away, and vanish under the pressure of new hard facts, and the interpretation of what appear to be the most solid aspects of nature are subject to change, now more than at any other time in history. The conclusions reached in science are always, when looked at closely, far more provisional and tentative than are most of the assumptions arrived at by our colleagues in the humanities.

The running battle now in progress between the sociobiologists and the antisociobiologists is a marvel for students to behold, close up. To observe, in open-mouthed astonishment, the polarized extremes, one group of highly intelligent, beautifully trained, knowledgeable, and imaginative scientists maintaining that all sorts of behavior, animal and human, are governed exclusively by genes, and another group of equally talented scientists saying precisely the opposite and asserting that all behavior is set and determined by the environment, or by culture, and both sides brawling in the pages of periodicals such as *The New York Review of Books,* is an educational experience that no college student should be allowed to miss. The essential lesson to be learned has nothing to do with the relative validity of the facts underlying the argument, it is the argument itself that is the education: we do not yet know enough to settle such questions.

It is true that at any given moment there is the appearance of satisfaction, even self-satisfaction, within every scientific discipline. On any Tuesday morning, if asked, a good working scientist will gladly tell you that the affairs of the field are nicely in order, that things are finally looking clear and making sense, and all is well. But come back again, on another Tuesday, and he may let you know that the roof has just fallen in on his life's work, that all the old ideas—last week's ideas in some cases—are no longer good ideas, that something strange has happened.

It is the very strangeness of nature that makes science engrossing. That ought to be at the center of science teaching. There are more than seven-times-seven types of ambiguity in science, awaiting analysis. The poetry of Wallace Stevens is crystal-clear alongside the genetic code.

I prefer to turn things around in order to make precisely the opposite case. Science, especially twentieth-century science, has provided us with a glimpse of something we never really knew before, the revelation of human ignorance. We have been used to the belief, down one century after another, that we more or less comprehend everything bar one or two mysteries like the mental processes of our gods. Every age, not just the eighteenth century, regarded itself as the Age of Reason, and we have never lacked for explanations of the world and its ways. Now, we are being brought up short, and this has been the work of science. We have a wilderness of mystery to make our way through the centuries ahead, and we will need science for this but not science alone. Science will, in its own time, produce the data and some of the meaning in the data, but never the full meaning. For getting a full grasp, for perceiving real significance when significance is at hand, we shall need minds at work from all sorts of brains outside the fields of science, most of all the brains of poets, of course, but also those of artists, musicians, philosophers, historians, writers in general.

It is primarily because of this need that I would press for changes in the way science is taught. There is a need to teach the young people who will be doing the science themselves, but this will always be a small minority among us. There is a deeper need to teach science to those who will be needed for thinking about it, and this means pretty nearly everyone else, in hopes that a few of these people—a much smaller minority than the scientific community and probably a lot harder to find—will, in the thinking, be able to imagine new levels of meaning that are likely to be lost on the rest of us.

In addition, it is time to develop a new group of professional thinkers, perhaps a somewhat larger group than the working scientists, who can create a discipline of scientific criticism. We have had good luck so far in the emergence of a few people ranking as philosophers of science and historians and journalists of science, and I hope more of these will be coming along, but we have not yet seen a Ruskin or a Leavis or an Edmund Wilson. Science needs critics of this sort, but the public at large needs them more urgently.

I suggest that the introductory courses in science, at all levels from grade school through college, be radically revised. Leave the fundamentals, the so-called basics, aside for a while, and concentrate the attention of all students on the things that are *not* known. You cannot possibly teach quantum mechanics without mathematics, to be sure, but you can describe the strangeness of the world opened up by quantum theory. Let it be known, early on, that there are deep mysteries, and profound paradoxes, revealed in their distant outlines, by the quantum. Let it be known that these can be approached more closely, and puzzled over, once the language of mathematics has been sufficiently mastered.

Teach at the outset, before any of the fundamentals, the still imponderable puzzles of cosmology. Let it be known, as clearly as possible, by the youngest minds, that there are some things going on in the universe that lie beyond comprehension, and make it plain how little is known.

Do not teach that biology is a useful and perhaps profitable science; that can come later. Teach instead that there are structures squirming inside all our cells, providing all the energy for living, that are essentially foreign creatures, brought in for symbiotic living a billion or so years ago, the lineal descendants of bacteria. Teach that we do no have the ghost of an idea how they got there, where they came from, or how they evolved to their present structure and function. The details of oxidative phosphorylation and photosynthesis can come later.

Teach ecology early on. Let it be understood that the earth's life is a system of interliving, interdependent creatures, and that we do not understand at all how it works. The earth's environment, from the range of atmospheric gases to the chemical constituents of the sea, has been held in an almost unbelievably improbable state of regulated balance since life began, and the regulation of stability and balance is accomplished solely by the life itself, like the internal environment of an immense organism, and we do not know how *that* one works, even less what it means. Teach that.

Go easy, I suggest, on the promises sometimes freely offered by science. Technology often relies and depends on science these days more than ever before, but technology is nothing like the first justification for doing research, nor is it necessarily an essential product to be expected from science. Public decisions about what to have in the way of technology are totally different problems from decisions about science, and the two enterprises should not be tangled together. The central task of science is to arrive, stage by stage, at a clearer comprehension of nature, but this does not mean, as it is sometimes claimed to mean, a search for mastery over nature. Science may provide us, one day, with a better understanding of ourselves, but never, I hope, with a set of technologies for doing something or other to improve ourselves. I am made nervous by assertions that human consciousness will someday be unraveled by research, laid out for close scrutiny like the workings of a computer, and then, *and then!* I hope with some fervor that we can learn a lot more than we now know about the human mind, and I see no reason why this strange puzzle should remain forever and entirely beyond us. But I would be deeply disturbed by any prospect that we might use the new knowledge in order to begin doing something about it, to improve it, say. This is a different matter from searching for information to use against schizophrenia or dementia, where we are badly in need of technologies, indeed likely one day to be sunk without them. But the ordinary, everyday, more or less normal human mind is too marvelous an instrument ever to be tampered with by anyone, science or no science.

The education of humanists cannot be regarded as complete, or even adequate, without exposure in some depth to where things stand in the various branches of science, and particularly, as I have said, in the areas of our ignorance. This does not mean that I know how to go about doing it, nor am I unaware of the difficulties involved. Physics professors, most of them, look with revulsion on assignments to teach their subject to poets. Biologists, caught up by the enchantment of their new power, armed with flawless instruments to tell the nucleotide sequences of the entire human genome, nearly matching the physicists in the precision of their measurements of living processes, will resist the prospect of broad survey courses; each biology professor will demand that any student in his path must master every fine detail within that professor's research program. The liberal-arts faculties, for their part, will continue to view the scientists with suspicion and apprehension. "What do the scientists want?" asked a Cambridge professor in Francis Cornford's wonderful *Microcosmographia Academica*. "Everything that's going," was the quick answer. That was back in 1912, and universities haven't much changed.

The worst thing that has happened to science education is that the great fun has gone out of it. A very large number of good students look at it as slogging work to be got through on the way to medical school. Others look closely at the premedical students themselves, embattled and bleeding for grades and class standing, and are turned off. Very few see science as the high adventure it really is, the wildest of all explorations ever undertaken by human beings, the chance to catch close views of things never seen before, the shrewdest maneuver for discovering how the world works. Instead, they become baffled early on, and they are misled into thinking that bafflement is simply the result of not having learned all the facts. They are not told, as they should be told, that everyone else—from the professor in his endowed chair down to the platoons of postdoctoral students in the laboratory all night—is baffled as well. Every important scientific advance that has come in looking like an answer has turned, sooner or later—usually sooner—into a question. And the game is just beginning.

An appreciation of what is happening in science today, and of how great a distance lies ahead for exploring, ought to be one of the rewards of a liberal-arts education. It ought to be a good in itself, not something to be acquired on the way to a professional career but part of the cast of thought needed for getting into the kind of century that is now just down the road. Part of the intellectual equipment of an educated person, however his or her time is to be spent, ought to be a feel for the queerness of nature, the inexplicable things.

And maybe, just maybe, a new set of courses dealing systematically with ignorance in science might take hold. The scientists might discover in it a new and subversive technique for catching the attention of students driven by curiosity, delighted and surprised to learn that science is exactly as Bush described it: an "endless frontier." The humanists, for their part, might take considerable satisfaction watching their scientific colleagues confess openly to not knowing everything about everything. And the poets, on whose shoulders the future rests, might, late nights, thinking things over, begin to see some meanings that elude the rest of us. It is worth a try.

Suggestions for Discussion and Writing

1. Consider the following sentence: "There is no doubt about it: measurement works when the instruments work, and when you have a fairly clear idea of what it is that is being measured, and when you know what to do with the numbers when they tumble out." Which adjective most accurately describes Thomas's style here: polemical, argumentative, declarative, conversational? Does this style characterize the essay as a whole?

2. What does the author mean when, speaking of the compulsion to quantify in fields outside science, he says that "the risks of untoward social consequences . . . are considerable"?

3. In a brief essay, discuss Thomas's critique of science education in light of your own experience in science classes.

4. What are some of the dangers of focusing science education on the "known"?

5. Do you agree with Thomas that introductory courses in science should focus on "the things that are *not* known"? What is

the value of such a focus? To what degree does Thomas's view of science and science education offer a solution to the educational dilemma posed by Rigden and Tobias (this chapter)?

6. Thomas calls for the development of "a new group of professional thinkers . . . who can create a discipline of scientific criticism." What would be the task of such critics? Why can't scientists themselves perform this task? Could feminist criticism be seen as a step in the right direction? (You might wish to consult the essays of Keller, Bleier, and Levin in Chapter 12.)

7. The limits of science—of its way of knowing and of what it can know—and its incompleteness are themes found in many essays in this anthology. In what ways do these themes justify Thomas's call for the bringing together of the sciences and humanities in the educational enterprise?

☐ COMMENCEMENT ADDRESS, ST. JOHN'S COLLEGE, SANTA FE, MAY 18, 1986

N. David Mermin
(b. 1935)

Born in New Haven, Connecticut, N. David Mermin earned his Ph.D. from Harvard University. Specializing in theoretical solid state and statistical physics, Mermin has been on the physics faculty at Cornell University since 1964 and, from 1984 to 1990, was director of the Laboratory for Atomic and Solid State Physics. He has received numerous fellowships and awards, including the 1989 Lilienfeld Prize of the American Physical Society.

Published widely in professional journals, Mermin has also written many books, the latest being *Boojums All the Way Through: Communicating Science in a Prosaic Age* (1990), from which the following selection is taken. In this commencement address Mermin suggests that the habits of mind fostered by a liberal education are precisely those likely to be needed by the physicist.

I have to say that the only other time I was asked to talk at a commencement was 1952, when I graduated from high school. So while I suppose I should have spent the last month thinking hard about the great challenges lying ahead for all of you, I was actually more preoccupied with the great challenge lying ahead for me. What can a middle-aged theoretical physicist have to say to the graduating class of this unique college?

The answer came to me a few weeks ago, when I read in a pamphlet about St. John's College that the principal goal of a liberal education is to acquire the skills of *rational thought, careful analysis, logical choice, imaginative experimentation,* and *clear communication.* Having always regarded these as the primary tools of the physicist, I realized that I could do no better than to call to your attention a few examples of the application of these skills in public affairs, in private life, and on the frontiers of science.

Let's begin with *clear communication* in public affairs. Several years ago I was half listening to an early speech by a new President who was acquiring a reputation as a clear communicator. Talking about a trillion dollar national debt, he was saying: "A trillion dollars is so much money that it's hard to grasp the idea, so I want to tell you how to make it a little more real."

Instantly, the President had my full attention. I spend a lot of time trying to get students to think meaningfully about quantitative information, and I hate the mindlessness with which people publicly discuss numerical facts without any attention to scale. Here, I thought, was a new moment in public discourse. This President—this Clear Communicator—was probably going to explain that there were a quarter of a billion people in the country, so a trillion dollars was $4000 per person, or $16,000 per family of four. He would then go on to compare this public debt with the personal debt of such a family—maybe $40,000 on a home mortgage and $8000 on an automobile, and he would then discuss whether this 1 to 3 ratio of public to personal debt was or was not reasonable. A new era of *rational thought* was about to dawn.

That's what I expected. What he actually said was something like this: "If you took a trillion dollars in one dollar bills and stacked them on top of each other, the pile would reach halfway to the moon."

I had two reactions to this, and I maintain that the liberally educated person should have both. First, and most importantly, in the matter of *clear communication,* disappointment and dismay at this triumphant substitution of one meaningless number for another. Second, an annoying but irresistible urge—the unbreakable habit of one trained in *careful analysis*—to check this particular piece of foolishness. Was the President right?

Well, a dollar is a pretty sturdy piece of paper. A book of well-made pages like that would probably be an inch thick if it had 400 pages. Don't forget that 400 pages are only 200 pieces of paper, so an inch is $200. A foot (10 inches) is $2000. A mile (5000 feet) is $10 million, a hundred miles is $1 billion, and a hundred thousand miles—halfway to the moon—is $1 trillion. Right on! God protect us from such misuses of the noble art of arithmetic, but if you've got to do it, at least do it right.

Life will continually present you with such technically correct but wacky and wildly wrongheaded appeals to the fruits of arithmetic. Watch out for them.

Equally abundant are similar invocations of science. Last March I was at a meeting of the American Physical Society, which, improbably, took place in Las Vegas—the real Las Vegas—among the slot machines and blackjack tables of a huge establishment called the MGM Grand Hotel. After two days in this genuine lunatic environment I couldn't stand it anymore. I got a rental car, and drove out to Hoover Dam, which I'd always wanted to see. The contrast was powerful and dramatic between the dignity of this immense and overwhelmingly purposeful piece of architecture, and the vast monuments to bad taste and pointless frenzied activity that I had just escaped from, but what particularly intrigued me was a great plaza on the Nevada side of the dam built to commemorate the formal dedication by President Roosevelt.

Set in gleaming brass in an enormous marble pavement flanked at either end by two fierce, lean, gigantic white angels, was—what do you think? Surely a map of the Colorado river and the surrounding lands that his wonderful structure would fertilize and protect? No—not at all. Imbedded in that vast stretch of marble were a great many circular brass disks. They represented the positions of the planets with respect to the fixed stars on that day, September 30, 1935, that President Roosevelt dedicated the dam.

The attention to detail was impressive—the disks came in half a dozen sizes, representing stars of different magnitudes. Most remarkably, embedded in the pavement, in brass letters almost an inch high, was a giant astronomy lesson. To read it, you had to walk back and forth along each line of text, squinting in the blinding sunlight. But if you worked hard, walking back and forth, you could learn about red giants, white dwarves, cepheid variables, red shifts, and the expanding universe.

What did any of this have to do with Hoover Dam? Absolutely nothing. It was an expression of exuberance: "We've conquered the Colorado river, and we've frozen the planets in place against the stars to help any visitors from outer space figure out when we did it. And please note that we know one hell of a lot about those stars."

Is Hoover Dam a contribution to science? Certainly not. It is a contribution to human welfare, a spectacular achievement of engineering, and a great work of art. Somehow that wasn't enough, and it had to be additionally recorded in brass and marble that the achievement resembled the discovery of the expanding universe.

The world will continually present you with opportunities like these, to misinterpret big numbers and confuse with science things that are not. Often critical questions of *logical choice* depend on making the right interpretation or avoiding the confusion.

Fifty years after the construction of the Hoover Dam, the great public works projects of our time are done not by the Army Corps of Engineers, but by the National Aeronautics and Space Administration.

A new space shuttle will cost a couple of billion dollars to build. How does one find the measure of such a sum? Not in a stack of ones stretching from Albuquerque to Los Alamos. Nor as the yearly income of 30,000 commencement speakers, nor even as a tenth of one percent of the national debt.

No. A couple of billion dollars is somewhat larger than the annual budget of the entire National Science Foundation, the nation's most important source for pure research in all the sciences. Why do we need another space shuttle? For the science. What science? Well, maybe it will be possible to make more perfect ball bearings in a weightless environment, or grow more perfect crystals, or improve the manufacture of pharmaceuticals. Ah, then it must be being done as part of the crash national program in crystal growing, pharmaceutical, and ball bearing betterment. No. It's being done for many complex reasons, but few of them have anything to do with science.

The space shuttle teaches us that *careful analysis* and *rational thought* have suffered a decline since 1935. In 1935 we needed a dam, built it, and then, in a ceremonial moment, tried to lend it an absurdly inappropriate cosmic significance. Today we build on that grand scale out of some inarticulated sense of cosmic significance, and then search around frantically for a purpose.

Watch out also for heroic efforts, launched on behalf of an articulated but manifestly preposterous goal. Recently, scientists have been called upon to render nuclear weapons "impotent and obsolete." This is a new level of confusion—the confusion of science with magic. The level of expenditure is also new: twenty-five billion dollars over five years just for research and development.

Scientists and engineers are almost unanimous in agreeing that the protection of people and cities that this program ostensibly aims at is impossible. Powerful demonstrations of its absurdity can be found in the pages of *Scientific American* or even the *New York Times*. Over half the faculty of the top twenty physics departments in the nation have signed a pledge not to participate in such folly. Even the organization established to carry out this parody of a research program acknowledges, when pressed, that the announced goal is impossible to achieve. Yet it looks as if spending at the rate of five billion dollars a year will be approved for a fantasy that will, inevitably, drain the resources for real scientific investigation, which pays some attention to where we are and where we can get to from there, as well as where we might like to be.

So much for rational thought in public affairs. President Delattre told me that a good commencement address should illustrate how intelligence and the liberal arts can affect a life, so I also tried to think on a very small scale, of characteristic incidents in my own life. I offer you two:

The first, I flatter myself, comes under the category of *imaginative experimentation*. I've lived for several years in England, a country where people drive on the wrong side of the road. I discovered that in England I could not correctly use the words right and left when I was in a car. Something deep within me knows ineradicably that "right" means "easy turn" and "left" means "hard turn"; and I invariably produced the wrong term when I tried to give directions.

More recently I was in Japan where they also drive on the wrong side, and I had to learn enough Japanese to give directions to cab drivers. Double trouble. Getting straight the difference between right and left is hard enough in a language where each is represented by an entirely meaningless sound. Now added to that difficulty was the further problem of interchanging them while driving along the wrong side of the road.

The solution came to me in a great flash, and the same sense of pride and joy that accompanies a discovery in physics: don't learn the terms as "left" and "right"—learn them as "easy turn" and "hard turn." *"Hidari e magatte kudasai"*—"Please make the easy turn." It worked perfectly, and I see no flaw in my solution, until the improbable day I find myself giving instructions in Japanese in a country where they drive on the right.

Here's a second example of how *careful analysis* and *imaginative experimentation* can be put to work in your own lives. Suppose you add up the results of many measurements. Each has a certain error. How big is the error in the total? Well, you might think if you were adding up N items, the error in the total would just be N times the error in each. But it's not that bad. Some of the measurements will be too big, some too little, and when you add them up the errors start to cancel each other. In fact it's a famous theorem (which is very easy to prove—and I hope you learned it in your four years here) that the error in the total is not bigger than the individual error N, the number of measurements, but only by the square root of N, a much smaller number. If you're adding 100 items, the error in the total will not be a hundred, but only ten times the individual error.

You can put this principle to good use relieving tedium at the supermarket and checking the accuracy of the clerk. As you put items or groups of small items on the counter it's very easy to keep a running total of the price in your head if you estimate each item only to the nearest dollar—hardly more difficult than just counting what you put down. The size of the typical error in each estimate is 25 cents. If you have 35 items, then the square root of 35 is about 6 and so the typical error in your total will be 6 × 25 cents or about a dollar and a half. With a little practice you can begin to develop a sense of whether you've been rounding up more than you've been rounding down, and make the occasional adjustment to improve your total. I'm at the point where I often get to within a dollar of the right answer. My children are enormously impressed (or embarrassed) when I announce the total ("looks like about $43") just before the clerk rings up $42.38.

What is the point of all these examples? What have they to do with the life of a scientist, or the attitudes of the liberally educated? They share a few principles of almost banal simplicity: one should take nothing for granted; one should try to understand everything; one should constantly look for new ways to deal with old ideas, new ways to apply knowledge. One should take delight in surprises—in turning things upside down. In discovering that one was entirely wrong about something obvious.

One of the classic examples of this in the 20th century is the theory of relativity. You remember Newton's wonderful statement at the beginning of the *Principia:* "Absolute, true, and mathematical time, of itself, and from its own nature, flows equably without relation to anything external. . . ." Lovely as this is, as a description of nature one might think it was trivially self-evident, or one might think it was devoid of content. Neither view is correct: as you know, it is simply wrong.

There is no absolute, true, and mathematical time. One man's now is another man's then is a third man's yet to be. Time is something we impose on nature, as we impose lines of latitude and longitude on the world. Minkowski's poem isn't as magnificent as Newton's, but it has the advantage of truth: "Henceforth space by itself, and time by itself, are doomed to fade away into mere shadows, and only a kind of union of the two will preserve an independent reality."

This is a good thing to know. If this astonishing discovery had not been made we would not today have anything remotely comparable to our present understanding of matter or the universe. But, just as important in making this discovery or learning about it, we discover something very important about ourselves: that everything, no matter how evident or obvious, should be doubted, questioned, viewed with suspicion; that unexamined truths are likely to be falsehoods; and that there is much to be gained from the discovery that one has been deeply, persistently, and utterly wrong.

Here is a final example from my own work as a physicist in the last year and a half. Matter likes to solidify into crystals. The characteristic feature of crystals is that their atoms are arranged in regular periodic patterns, that repeat themselves like the design on a tile floor. Such patterns are often quite symmetric: if you take a crystal and rotate it appropriately it ends up looking exactly the same as before. It's very easy to prove that not any rotation is consistent with the periodicity of the crystal. Crystals can be symmetric under rotations that are a half, a third, a quarter, or a sixth of a complete revolution, but nothing else. (This is another nice theorem—if I had two hours and a blackboard I could teach you a lot of nice things.) In particular they cannot be symmetric under five-fold rotations, that are one-fifth of a complete revolution.

This means that of the Platonic solids only the tetrahedron, octahedron, and cube can have the same rotational symmetries as a crystal. The icosahedron and dodecahedron have five-fold rotational symmetries, and these are impossible.

This has been known for as long as the atomic theory of matter has been accepted, and has been one of the pillars of crystallographic science. It therefore caused a general sensation, when about a year and a half ago an alloy was produced whose electron diffraction pattern had certain characteristic features that occur only in crystal-line matter, but with a rotational symmetry precisely that of the icosahedron (or dodecahedron). To get a sense of how revolutionary this is, you should know that Landau and Lifshitz, probably the most authoritative series of physics texts in the world, baldly states that icosahedral symmetry is "of no physical interest," since it does not occur in Nature as a symmetry of inorganic matter.

This is the context in which it is the most fun to do physics. Everything has to be reexamined. We thought we knew all the ways atoms might arrange themselves into chunks of matter, but now we've found stuff that has some properties we were sure only crystals could have, and another property we know no crystals can have. All the old ideas have to be viewed with suspicion—all the obvious old definitions have to be reexamined. Any idea is worth trying out, and most of them will probably have to be rejected. Papers are flying back and forth—new experiments are being done all over the world—so many conferences are being organized that if you went to half of them you wouldn't have any time to think about the problem at all. Priority disputes have erupted. The crystallographers think the phys-icists have gone crazy. The physicists deplore the limited imagination of the crystallographers. It's science at its raucous best.

This is not how you go about building Hoover Dam. This stuff was found by accident. We have no idea what it's good for or where it will lead us. The entire national effort in this field probably amounts to a few hundred thousand dollars—to be viewed not as a hundred-foot stack of ones, but as the cost of supporting a few dozen graduate students, since most of the experiments are easily done with existing equipment. These icosahedral quasicrystals are provid-ing us a most excellent occasion for exercising the skills of rational thought, careful analysis, logical choice, imaginative experimentation, and clear communication.

The best I can wish for you on this commencement day is that you too will continue to find many such occasions.

Suggestions for Discussion and Writing

1. Is Mermin's address appropriate to the occasion? What adjec-tive(s) most accurately describe it: for instance, traditional, irrever-ent, humorous, academic?

2. Why was the President's attempt to make a trillion dollars "more real" a "piece of foolishness"? What point about numbers is Mermin making here? What larger point about numbers does the essay make?

3. The author follows an account of his visit to the Hoover Dam with a discussion of the space shuttle program. How does he evaluate the two projects? In what way do they illustrate a de-

cline in "careful analysis" and "rational thought"? What broader point about science is he making here?

4. The author warns his audience to watch out for "heroic efforts launched on behalf of an articulated but manifestly preposterous goal." Is his warning justified? Write an essay in which you discuss some contemporary examples of such "heroic efforts."

5. Do you agree that Mermin's solution to the problem of giving directions while driving on the "wrong" side of the road is a good example of "imaginative experimentation"? What larger point about science is he making?

6. In what ways does Mermin's view of science coincide with that of Thomas in "Humanities and Science" (this chapter)?

7. What kind of teacher do you think Mermin is likely to be? Why? Is he the kind described by the surrogate learners in "Tune In, Turn Off, Drop Out" (this chapter)?

8. In your own words, describe Mermin's "wish" for his audience. Do you agree that his wish is "best" for them?